W9-BCI-463

  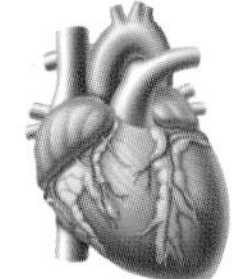 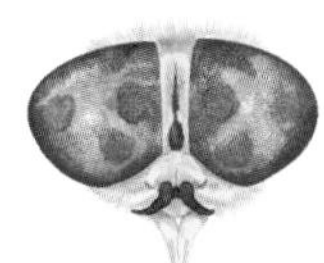

THE KINGFISHER A-Z ENCYCLOPEDIA

Editor: Ben Hoare
Art editor: Peter Clayman
Editorial director: Miranda Smith
Art director: Mike Davis
Editorial team: Catherine Brereton, Carron Brown, Sheila Clewley, Melissa Fairley, Russell McLean, Jennie Morris
Design team: Jo Brown, Jane Tassie
DTP manager: Nicky Studdart
Picture research: Jane Lambert, Cee Weston-Baker
Artwork archivists: Wendy Allison, Steve Robinson
Production: Jo Blackmore, Kelly Johnson
Contributors: Jacqui Bailey, Olly Denton, Clive Gifford, Marie Greenwood, Ann Kay, David Lambert, Keith Lye, Christopher Maynard, Isabelle Paton, Jill Thomas

KINGFISHER
a Houghton Mifflin Company imprint
215 Park Avenue South
New York, New York 10003
www.houghtonmifflinbooks.com

First published in 2002
10 9 8 7 6 5 4 3 2 1
ITR/0702/TPL/GRS/135MA

LIBRARY OF CONGRESS CATALOGING-IN-PUBLICATION DATA
has been applied for.

ISBN 0-7534-5569-2

Printed in Malaysia

THE KINGFISHER A-Z ENCYCLOPEDIA

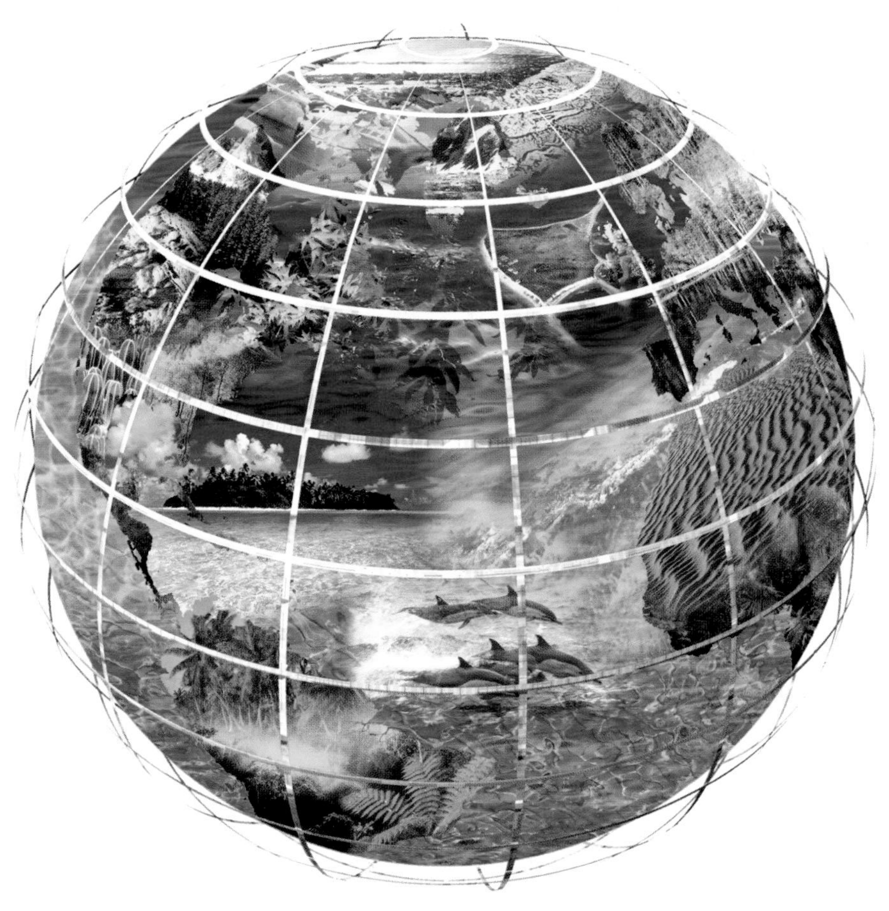

NEW YORK

Oceans
Plants
Prehistoric animals
Railroads
Rain forests
Roman Empire
Solar system
Space exploration
Sports
Vikings
Warfare
Weather
World War I
World War II
Special Features
Africa
Aircraft
Amphibians and Reptiles
Antarctic and Arctic
Architecture
Art

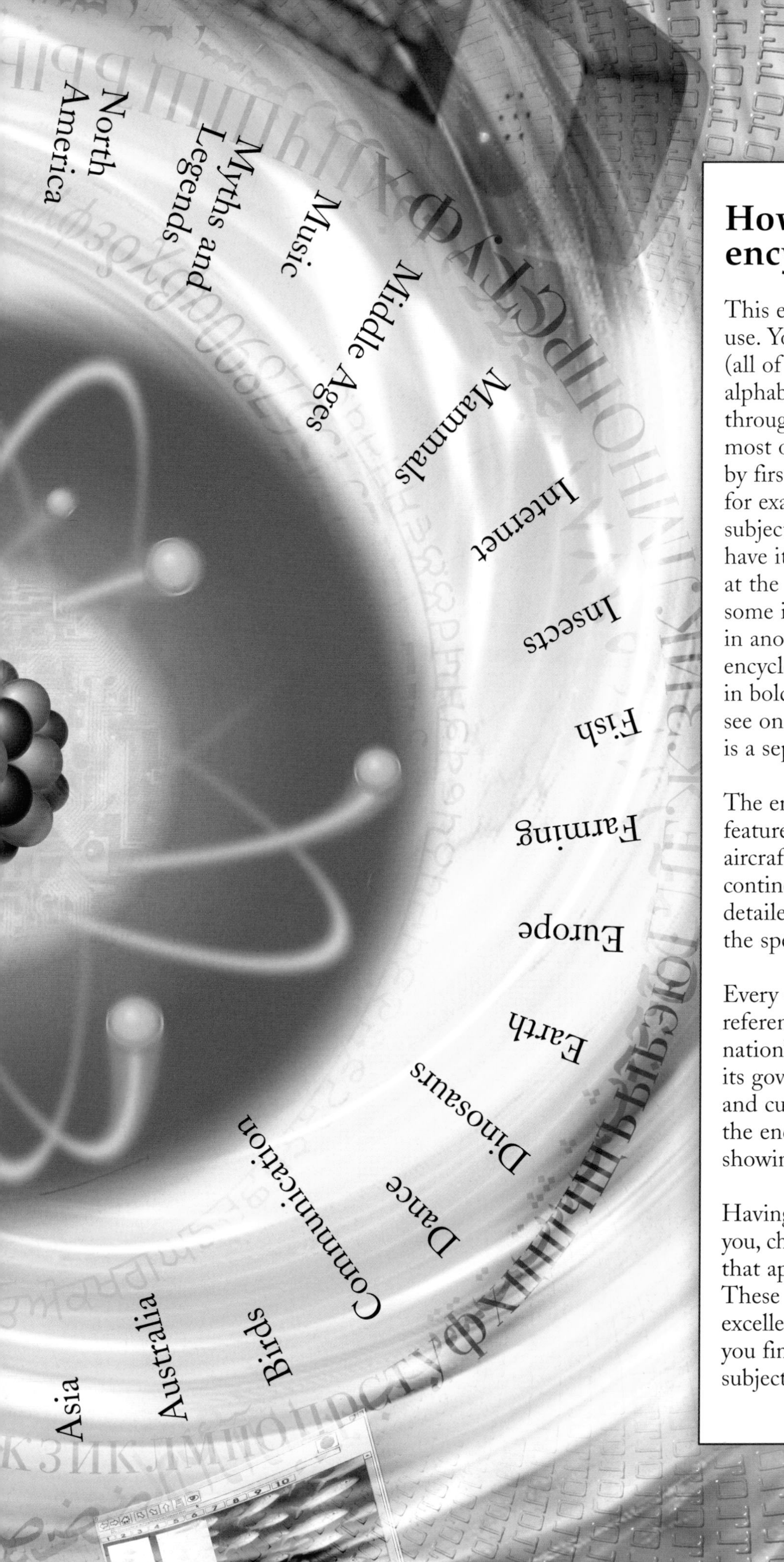

How to use this encyclopedia

This encyclopedia is fun and easy to use. You can either look up subjects (all of the entries are arranged in alphabetical order) or simply browse through the book. You should find most of the information you want by first looking up the main entry, for example, "bear" or "planet." If the subject you are looking for does not have its own entry, look in the index at the back. Usually there will be some information about your subject in another article. Throughout the encyclopedia you will find words in bold, like this: **laser**. When you see one, you will know that there is a separate entry on that subject.

The encyclopedia also includes special features on important topics such as aircraft, dinosaurs, and the world's continents. These are longer and more detailed than most entries. A list of the special features appears opposite.

Every entry on a country has a quick-reference panel that illustrates the nation's flag and provides details on its government, capital, area, language, and currency. On pages 382–383 of the encyclopedia there is a world map showing the countries of the world.

Having read the entries that interest you, check the guide to useful websites that appears on pages 384–385. These carefully selected websites are excellent research tools that will help you find more information on the subject that interests you.

Aardvark

The aardvark is a **mammal** that eats **termites**. When it has smashed open a termite nest with its powerful claws, it pokes its long, sticky tongue in and pulls it out covered with the insects. The aardvark lives in the open in central and southern Africa. It is a shy animal with large ears like a donkey and is an expert burrower. If caught away from its home, it can dig a hole to hide in at top speed. The word "aardvark" is Dutch for "earth pig."

Aardvarks use their keen sense of smell to track down termite nests then smash them open and lick up the tasty insects.

Abacus

The abacus is a simple counting machine first used in ancient **Greece** and the **Roman Empire**. It consists of rows of beads strung on wires. Beads on the first wire count as ones, those on the second wire count as tens, those on the third wire count as hundreds, and so on. People still use the abacus in parts of Asia and the Middle East.

The Romans sometimes used small stones as counters. They called these counters *calculi* and it is from this that we get our word "calculate."

Abbreviation

An abbreviation is a shortened form of a word or a group of words. Words and phrases are shortened to save space. Abbreviations are also useful because they are quicker to write, saving us time. Sometimes the first and last letters of a word are used, such as St. for "Saint" or Dr. for "Doctor." On other occasions, only the beginning of the word is used, as in Sept. for "September." A period is often placed after the abbreviation to show that it is a shortened form.

Robert Delaunay painted *Propeller* in Paris in 1923. Delaunay was one of the first European painters to make **abstract art**. He was more interested in patterns and colors than in showing what real things look like.

Aboriginal people

The term "aboriginal people" really means the first humans who lived in any country. The aboriginal people of **Australia** arrived there from Southeast Asia more than 40,000 years ago. They had no permanent homes but wandered across the land hunting or gathering their food. Their main weapons were the **boomerang** and the throwing spear.

At first the Europeans who settled in Australia about 200 years ago treated the aboriginal people very badly. However, the aboriginal people now have rights as Australian citizens, and the **government** has handed over some traditional areas claimed by them.

The **Aboriginal people** of Australia were the first humans to live there. They still make paintings on cave walls and on tree bark. Their subjects are often ancient myths that date back many thousands of years.

Abstract art

The main aim of abstract **art** is not to show what people, landscapes, or objects actually look like. In abstract art artists concentrate on the shapes, colors, and textures instead. However, they can still express all kinds of feelings and ideas in their work. Abstract art can be extremely bold and dramatic or more delicate and subtle. **Paintings**, drawings, and **sculptures** can all be abstract.

Throughout history many cultures have produced abstract art, including many African and **aboriginal peoples**. In Europe the first completely abstract art was created in Paris and Moscow in the early 1900s. In the 1950s the United States, especially New York, became a leading center of abstract art. Many modern artists have made abstract art, including Pablo **Picasso**, Jackson Pollock, and Mark Rothko.

Acceleration

When something increases speed, it accelerates. If you drop a ball from the top of a tall building, it reaches a speed of 32 ft. (9.8m) per second after one second. After two seconds it is moving at 64 ft. (19.6m) per second. Every second that it falls, it increases its speed by 32 ft. (9.8m) per second. The ball accelerates because it is being pulled down by the force of **gravity**.

Acid

An acid is a liquid chemical **compound** that is often poisonous. Some acids, such as sulfuric acid, nitric acid, and hydrochloric acid, are very powerful and can corrode, or eat away, even the strongest **metals**. Other acids are harmless. These include the citric acid that gives lemons and oranges their sharp taste and the acetic acid in vinegar. Lactic acid is produced when milk goes sour. All acids turn a special kind of paper called litmus red.

Some substances are the opposite of acids. They are called alkalis or bases and turn litmus paper blue. Caustic soda is a strong alkali, and alkalis are one of the main ingredients of **soap**.

Acid rain

All rain is very slightly **acid**. Theweak acid in rainwater can eat away the limestone in buildings and statues. Limestone is an alkali.

Rain can also react with the waste gases sent out by power plants, cars, and factories. When this happens, it falls as weak sulfuric acid and nitric acid and is called acid rain. After a time the acid rain slowly poisons lakes and streams, threatening the plants and wildlife that live there. For this reason people are trying to reduce the amount of waste gases that industrial nations release into the air.

Acoustics

Acoustics is the study of **sound** and how it travels. When an architect designs a concert hall or theater, they have to carefully consider the sound quality of the building. Will a full range of sound waves from speech and music reach every seat? Will there be disturbing echoes from the walls and ceiling?

Sound waves travel in straight lines, and they can be reflected or absorbed by the various surfaces they strike. By choosing different materials to cover each part of a wall or ceiling, architects can turn the sound waves in the best direction.

Acid rain is the result of pollution from factories mixing with water in the air. It kills wildlife and eats away at buildings.

Acids in laboratories carry warning labels (1). Acids in fruit taste sharp and are harmless (2). The acid in wasp stings (3) causes a painful reaction, while car batteries (4) contain strong sulfuric acid.

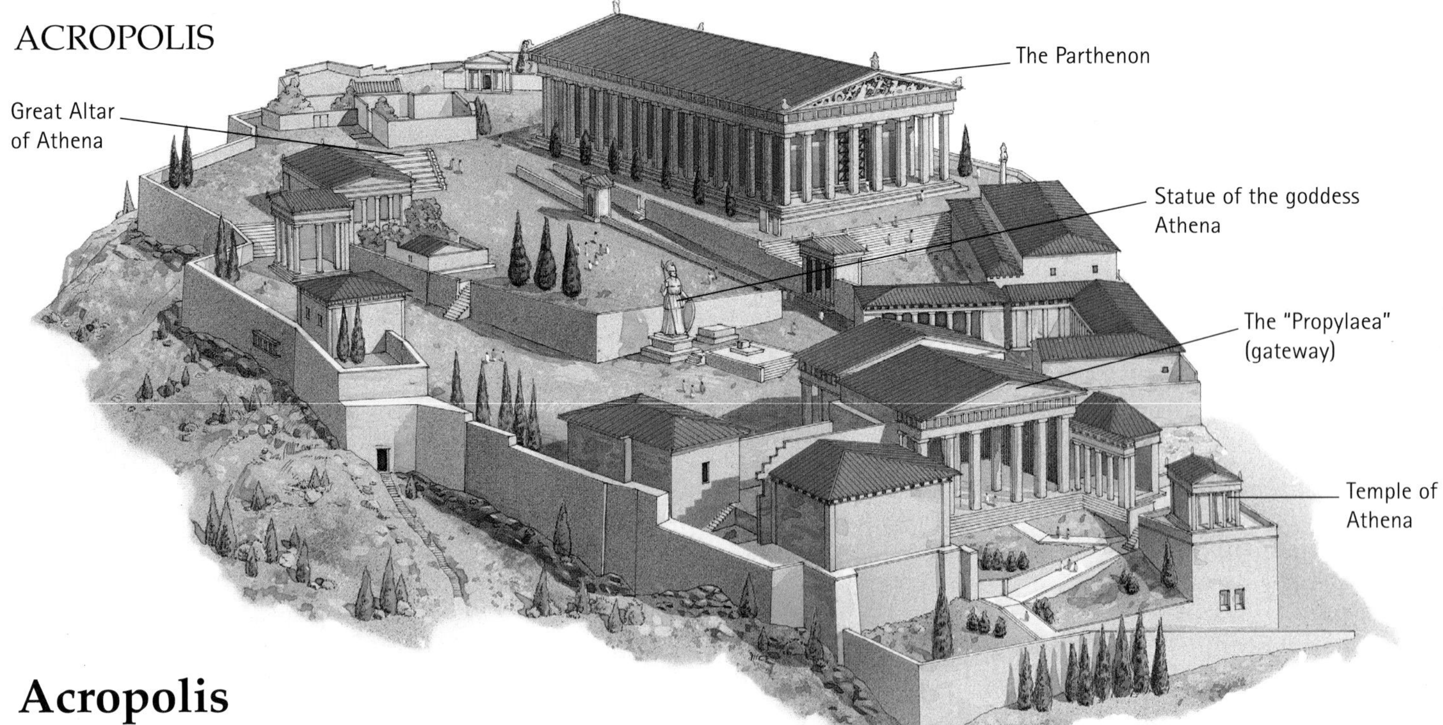

△ The **Acropolis** of Athens, pictured as it looked in about 400 B.C. At the top of the hill stood a temple called the Parthenon.

Acropolis

"Acropolis" is a Greek word for the high central part of many ancient Greek cities. The most famous surviving acropolis is in Athens, the capital of modern **Greece**. On top of it are the ruins of ancient temples built in the 400s B.C. when Athens was a rich and powerful city. The Parthenon, the largest and most important of these temples, was built to honor Athena, the patron goddess of Athens. It has many giant pillars of white **marble**.

In the early 1800s many of the Parthenon's marble sculptures were taken away by Lord Elgin, who was the British ambassador to Greece. They are now on display in the British Museum in London. However, many people think the sculptures should be returned to a museum in Athens.

Acting *see* Theater

Acupuncture

Acupuncture is a kind of medical treatment in which thin needles are used to puncture various parts of the body. Usually the needles are inserted only a short way into the patient. Acupuncture was first developed by the Chinese about 5,000 years ago, and it is still used today. In recent years acupuncture has become accepted in many countries as a branch of alternative **medicine**. It is often used in the treatment of such complaints as headaches, asthma, and arthritis.

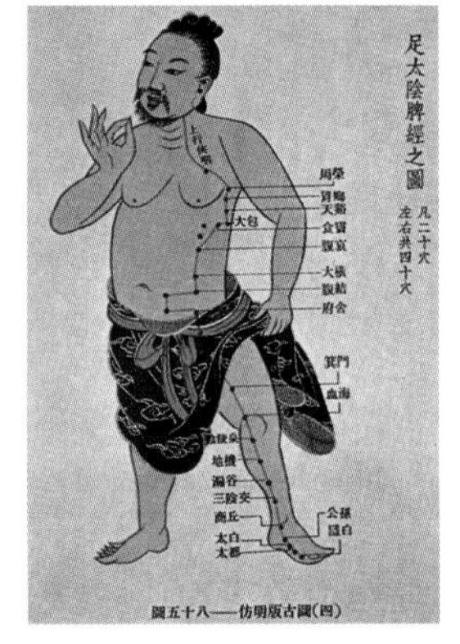

△ **Acupuncture** is a form of healing using needles. In Chinese medicine, the needles unblock the flow of *ch'i* (vital energy) to restore good health.

Adhesive

Adhesives are substances that are used to stick things together. There are many different kinds of adhesives. For centuries people have boiled animal **bones**, hides, and horns to produce an adhesive called glue. Plants that contain a lot of **starch**, such as potatoes and corn, can be made into a paste that is good for sticking paper. Today's artificial adhesives are better than natural ones because they are much stronger. Epoxy resins, for example, are very strong. For any adhesive to work well the surfaces to be stuck together must be clean. Adhesives have many uses, from envelopes and postage stamps to the construction of **aircraft** and race cars.

◁ An artificial **adhesive** holds together the plastic material used to make modern canoes.

Adjective

An adjective is any word that describes or modifies a **noun**. "A gray horse" is more exact than just "a horse." "A big, gray horse" is even more precise. The words big and gray are adjectives describing the noun horse.

Adjectives usually come before the noun, but they can also come after it: "The pie is delicious." The word delicious describes the pie. It is an adjective.

Adolescence

Adolescence is the time when a child is growing up to become an adult. The changes of adolescence usually begin to take place in girls 10 to 13 years old and in boys 11 to 14. The changes go on for several years, and the adolescent's body changes in many ways. A girl's hips become wider and her breasts start to develop. She has her first menstrual period. This is a sign that she can one day have babies. A boy's voice becomes deeper and his facial hair starts to grow. Both boys and girls develop hair in their pubic areas and under their arms.

During adolescence teenagers often feel awkward and have emotional upsets. However, these things soon pass and they become young men and women.

Advertising

Advertising is usually a way of telling people about things they can buy and persuading them to buy them. Ads appear in many different **media**, including **television**, **radio**, **newspapers**, posters, and leaflets. **Governments** use ads too. They tell us things like "Smoking is bad for your health."

Today advertising is a huge industry that employs millions of people, including writers, artists, photographers, actors, and salespeople. Many who work in advertising are employed by advertising agencies—firms that produce advertisements for clients who have goods or services to sell. Advertising agencies try to make the products and services they are selling appear as desirable and as good a value as possible. Many countries have **laws** that stop advertisers making false claims about their products.

Aerosol

An aerosol is something that sprays **paint**, **cosmetics**, or insecticides (chemicals that kill insect pests). It consists of a can containing a liquefied **gas** under high pressure. The can also contains the paint or other substance to be sprayed. When a button on the cap is pressed, a tiny nozzle opens and the gas forces out the can's contents in the form of a fine spray. Aerosols used to contain harmful chemicals called CFCs, but in most countries these have been replaced with less damaging substances.

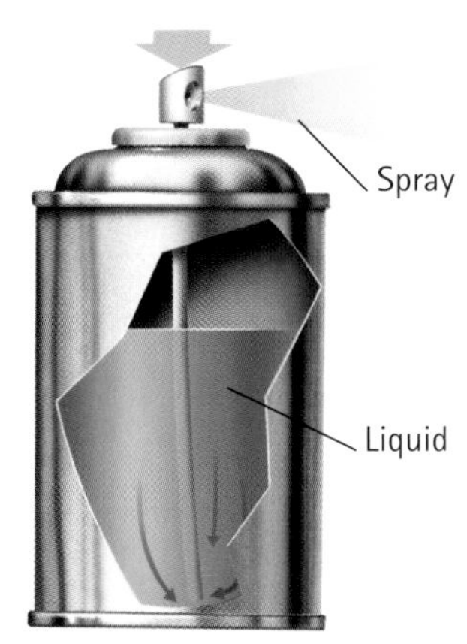

When you press down the button on an **aerosol** can, a gas under high pressure forces the liquid up a tube to the top and out as a very fine spray.

Aesop

Aesop (pronounced "ee sop") was an ancient Greek storyteller. His **fables**, or stories, are today known as *Aesop's Fables*. The characters in the stories are usually animals, but they behave like humans with the same virtues and weaknesses. Each story teaches its readers a moral and offers useful advice. Aesop's best known fables include *The Tortoise and the Hare*, *The Boy Who Cried Wolf*, and *The Wolf in Sheep's Clothing*.

According to legend, Aesop lived in about 620–560 B.C. However, it is likely that Aesop was an imaginary figure, and his fables were made up by other writers.

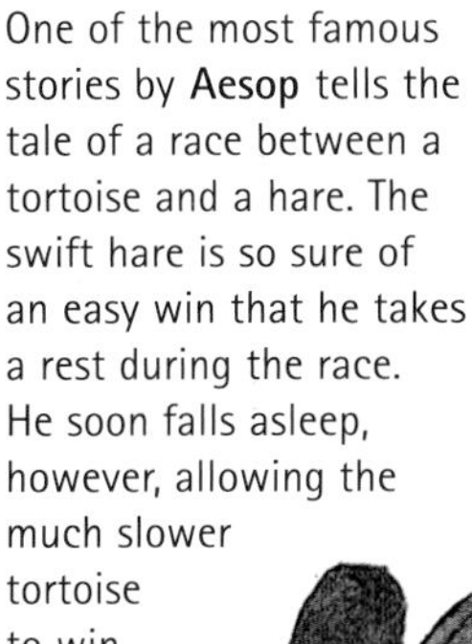

One of the most famous stories by **Aesop** tells the tale of a race between a tortoise and a hare. The swift hare is so sure of an easy win that he takes a rest during the race. He soon falls asleep, however, allowing the much slower tortoise to win.

AFRICA

Africa is the second largest continent. It stretches from the Mediterranean Sea in the north to the Cape of Good Hope at its tip in the south.

Lappet vultures eat the rotting flesh of dead animals.

WILD AFRICA

Large parts of Africa are still wilderness. The scorching Sahara Desert spreads over much of the northern part of the continent. This empty land of sand and gravel is one of the hottest places on the planet. Near the equator, which crosses the center of Africa, are huge rain forests packed with towering trees. The forests are always damp because they receive plenty of torrential rain.

More than one third of Africa is a high, flat plain, or plateau. Grassland called the savanna covers much of the plateau region. Great herds of grazing animals, including elephants, antelope, and zebras, roam the savanna. Other animals, such as lions, prey on the grazers.

MOUNTAINS, LAKES, AND RIVERS

A giant crack in the surface of the earth called the Great Rift Valley runs through East Africa. Along it are mountains, gorges, and deep lakes. The tallest peaks are in Ethiopia, Kenya, Uganda, and Tanzania. Africa's largest lake, Lake Victoria, fills a huge hollow in the middle of the Rift Valley. It is like an inland sea and is surrounded by fertile farmland.

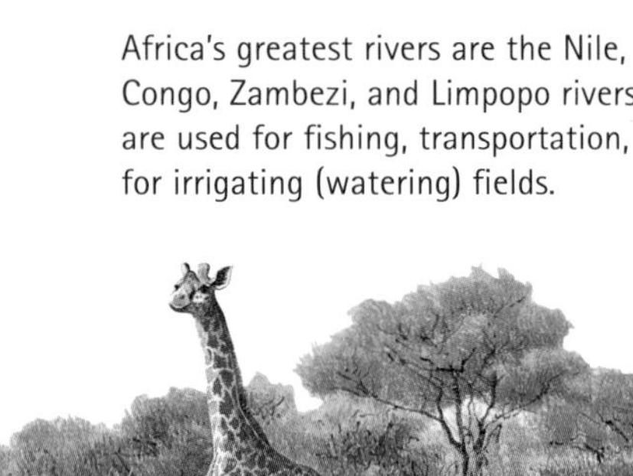

Africa's greatest rivers are the Nile, Niger, Congo, Zambezi, and Limpopo rivers. They are used for fishing, transportation, and for irrigating (watering) fields.

PEOPLE OF AFRICA

African people belong to several population groups with a variety of cultural backgrounds. In North Africa are Arabs and Berbers, most of whom are Muslims. Black peoples mostly live south of the Sahara Desert and make up three quarters of Africa's population.

There are 53 countries in Africa—more than any other continent. Between them African people speak over 2,000 different languages.

△ The Sahara Desert includes large areas of sand dunes, which are swept into shapes by the wind.

▽ Water holes are vital to the animals of Africa's hot, grassy plains—especially in the dry season.

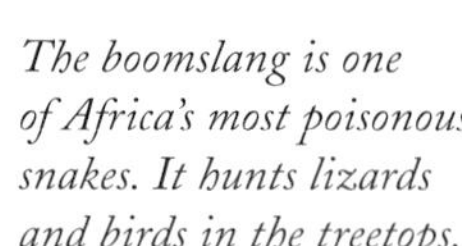

The boomslang is one of Africa's most poisonous snakes. It hunts lizards and birds in the treetops.

WAY OF LIFE

Many Africans farm the land, growing crops like cocoa, cotton, sugar, coffee, tea, bananas, and rubber. Africa produces three quarters of the world's palm oil, which is used to make soap and margarine. The continent has extremely valuable mineral resources too, including gold, diamonds, tin, and copper. There are rich oil supplies in parts of North and West Africa.

Most African people live in tribal villages, which usually have their own culture and way of life. However, Africa's factories and urban areas are growing fast. The biggest cities include Cairo and Alexandria in Egypt, Lagos in Nigeria, Kinshasa in the Democratic Republic of Congo, and Cape Town in South Africa.

Huge flocks of pink flamingos gather on the salt lakes of East African countries such as Kenya.

AFRICA FACT FILE
Area: 11,822,070 sq. mi.
Highest mountain: Mt. Kilimanjaro, Tanzania, 19,336 ft. (5,895m)
Lowest point: Lake Assal, Djibouti, 512 ft. (156m) below sea level
Largest lake: Lake Victoria, 26,863 sq. mi.
Longest river: Nile River, 4,135 mi.
Largest desert: Sahara Desert
Number of countries: 53
Largest country: Sudan
Smallest mainland country: Gambia
Smallest island nation: Seychelles
Largest city: Cairo, Egypt, 7 million
Total population: 780 million

EUROPEAN INFLUENCE

For centuries Europeans knew very little about Africa or its people. At the end of the 1400s the Portuguese found a sea route to India by sailing around the southern tip of Africa. Soon the African coastline was charted, although only a few traders and explorers trekked inland.

In the 1500s European sailors began to ship slaves from Africa. Up to 14 million slaves were taken to the Americas between 1500 and the 1800s. Usually traders bought these slaves from tribes on Africa's coasts.

◁ *The Masai women of East Africa wear bright cloth and beaded collars for special ceremonies.*

CONQUERING A CONTINENT

By the 1800s some European countries started to set up colonies in Africa. The continent was carved up between the English, French, Belgians, Germans, Portuguese, and Italians. The European powers brought new ways of life to Africa, but before long many Africans resented foreign rule.

WINNING INDEPENDENCE

During the 1950s and 1960s most colonies became independent African countries. Many were poor and some suffered bloody civil wars as rival groups fought for power. Today Africa faces many problems. However, its countries are developing their economies, and wealthier nations are giving them essential assistance.

Many African people are farmers. This Zambian woman is carrying corn husks.

SEE ALSO
Apartheid, Congo, Egypt, Ethiopia, Kenya, Nigeria, Nile River, Rain forest, Sahara Desert, Savanna, Slavery, South Africa

Afghanistan

AFGHANISTAN
Government: In transition
Capital: Kabul
Area: 249,700 sq. mi.
Population: 26 million
Languages: Pushtu; Dari
Currency: Afghani

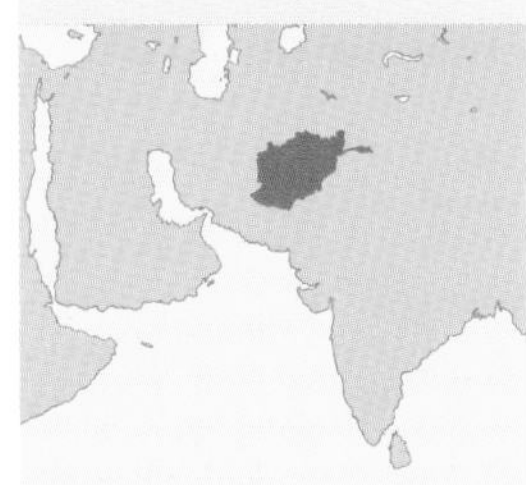

Afghanistan is a country in **Asia**. It is a mountainous land lying between the former **Soviet Union**, **Pakistan**, and **Iran**. The capital and largest city is Kabul. Nearly all the people, known as Afghans, are Muslims—followers of **Islam**. In 1979 Soviet troops invaded Afghanistan to support its **government**, which was friendly to the U.S.S.R. The Soviets withdrew in 1988, and a long **civil war** began. Eventually a Muslim group called the Taliban controlled more than 90 percent of the country.

Some of the Taliban leaders supported terrorist organizations (see **terrorism**) that attacked both New York and Washington on September 11, 2001. However, later that year the Taliban were defeated by a rebel force called the Northern Alliance. The rebels received military assistance from other countries, including the U.S. and U.K. Afghanistan now has a new government, but it remains politically unstable.

Africa *see* pages 10–11

Agriculture *see* Farming

AIDS

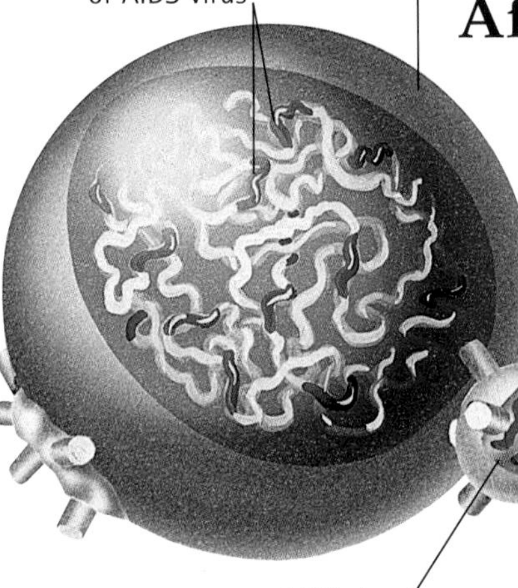

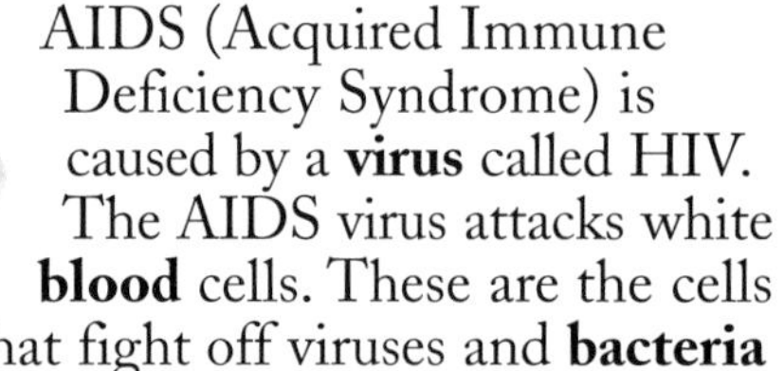

Once the **AIDS** virus has entered the bloodstream, it attaches itself to a white blood cell, multiplies and spreads through the body.

AIDS (Acquired Immune Deficiency Syndrome) is caused by a **virus** called HIV. The AIDS virus attacks white **blood** cells. These are the cells that fight off viruses and **bacteria** when they enter the body. When white blood cells are destroyed, the patient can become very ill with a **disease** that would not be serious to a healthy person. People with AIDS have no way of fighting disease and often die.

HIV is passed from person to person by intimate sexual contact, by exposure to blood infected with HIV, or by transmission to a baby in an infected mother's womb. People who have been infected with the HIVvirus may not become seriously ill until years later.

Currently there is no cure for AIDS. It is a serious world problem and kills millions of people every year.

Air

Air is all around us—it surrounds the **earth** in a layer we call the **atmosphere**. We need to breathe air in order to live. Air is colorless and has no smell. Yet it is really a mixture of different gases. We can feel air when the wind blows, and we know air has weight. The average roomful of air weighs more than 100 lbs (45kg)—about the weight of 20 bags of potatoes! Air also carries sound—without it we would not be able to hear because sounds cannot travel in a **vacuum**.

The chief gas in air is nitrogen, which makes up nearly four fifths of the air. About one fifth of the air is **oxygen**, the gas we need to keep us alive. Air also holds some water in very fine particles called vapor. When we talk about **humidity**, it is the amount of water in the air we are measuring.

The air that surrounds the earth gets thinner the higher up you go. Mountaineers carry their own air supply because the air at the top of high mountains is too thin to breathe

The wandering **albatross** has the longest wings of any bird—up to 11.5 ft. (3.5m.) It glides low over the ocean, skimming the waves.

properly. High-flying aircraft have to keep the air in their cabins at ground-level pressure so that passengers can breathe normally.

Warm air expands and becomes lighter. When the air around a heater becomes lighter, it rises. Cool air moves into its place. This, too, warms and rises, so the entire room is heated.

Aircraft *see* pages 14–15

Albania

Albania is a small, rugged country that lies between **Serbia** and **Greece** on the eastern shore of the Adriatic Sea. Most Albanians live in remote mountain villages. Albania was ruled by **Turkey** for over 400 years. After World War II it became a communist state (see **communism**), but by 1992 a multi-party system was in place. In 1997 the country was torn apart by an armed rebellion. Order was soon restored, but there have been several other civil disturbances since then.

ALBANIA
Government: Republic
Capital: Tirana
Area: 10,600 sq. mi.
Population: 3.5 million
Language: Albanian
Currency: Lek

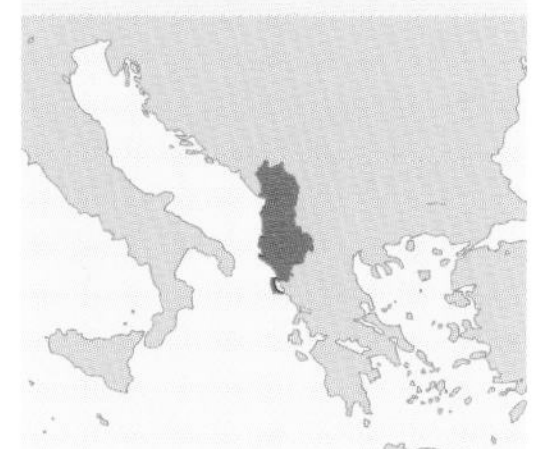

Albatross

The albatross is a large **bird** that spends most of its life in the air over the oceans. There are 14 different species of albatross. Most albatrosses live in regions south of the **equator**, where they soar gracefully over the waves. They come ashore only to breed or during fierce storms. Albatrosses often follow ships for days at a time, picking up scraps of food thrown overboard.

Albatrosses settle on the water to sleep and feed. They eat mainly **squid**, **jellyfish**, and **fish**. The giant birds drink so much seawater that they need special glands on their head to get rid of all the salt they take in. Every year thousands of albatrosses get tangled up in **fishing** nets and long fishing lines and die. They are becoming rare as a result.

Albino

Albino animals are born white with no coloring matter in their skin or hair. They have pink eyes. Albinos inherit their colorless condition from their ancestors (see **genetics**). An albino parent is still able to produce normal young, but these young may later produce albino offspring of their own.

Human albinos are very rare. In the U.S. and Europe less than five people per 100,000 are affected.

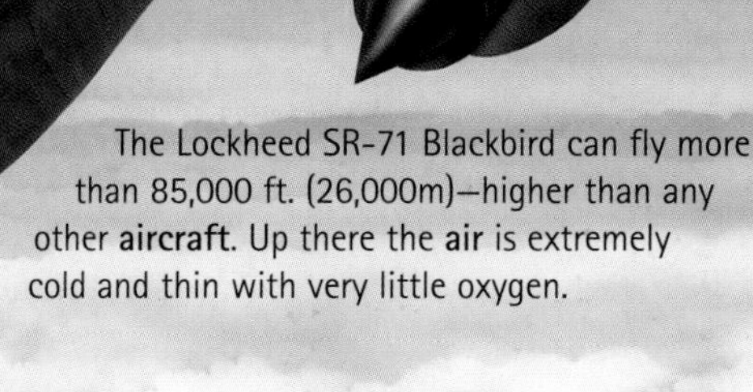

The Lockheed SR-71 Blackbird can fly more than 85,000 ft. (26,000m)—higher than any other **aircraft**. Up there the **air** is extremely cold and thin with very little oxygen.

AIRCRAFT

We live in a world where people take air travel for granted. But it was thousands of years before our dreams of flying like the birds became reality. The first successful powered flight did not take place until the early 1900s.

Drawing of a flying machine by Leonardo da Vinci

Montgolfier hot-air balloon

EARLY DAYS

Myths and legends are filled with extraordinary tales of people who could fly. Brave but foolhardy inventors leaped from high towers wearing wings, but all these attempts ended in failure. In the 1500s the artist and inventor Leonardo da Vinci drew plans for a helicopter, although such a machine could never have been built in his day.

The age of air travel began with the first balloon flight in 1783. Seventy years later airships, or blimps, took to the sky. These are large, steerable balloons with engines and propellers. At the same time inventors built the first gliders. Gliding proved that flight was possible by using winged airplanes that were heavier than air.

Biplanes have double wings

MILITARY AIRCRAFT

Aircraft were first used as fighting machines during World War I. By 1939 most large countries had an air force. Germany built up a strong air force called the Luftwaffe, which it used in surprise attacks at the start of World War II. The Germans knew that no land battle could be won without control of the skies above the battle area.

As World War II progressed long-range bombers played a larger part in the tactics of the British, U.S., German, and Japanese air forces. Since then, guided missiles have cut down the part played by bombers, but piloted planes are still needed as a defense against fast strike bombers. Modern fighter aircraft can fly close to the ground at very high speeds, slipping under the enemy's radar screen without being spotted.

CONQUEST OF THE AIR

The development of the gasoline engine in the 1880s made powered aircraft a possibility. On December 17, 1903 the Wright brothers climbed into their flimsy airplane, the *Flyer*, and made the first controlled flight with people on board. They flew only 118 ft. (36m). Since that historic flight, progress in aviation has been amazingly rapid. Early airplanes had piston engines that drove propellers, pulling the aircraft forward. Many small aircraft still use propellers, but most large planes have jet engines, which are far more powerful.

GIANT AIRLINERS

Thanks to jet airliners, traveling long distances is now cheap and easy. The Boeing 747 was the first of the big "jumbo jets." This highly successful airliner entered service in 1970, and carries up to 560 passengers. It has a wingspan of 197 ft. (60m), is 230 ft. (70m) long, and weighs nearly 320 tons. The 747 can fly at a speed of 564 mph (910km/h) for a distance of 4,960 mi. (8,000km).

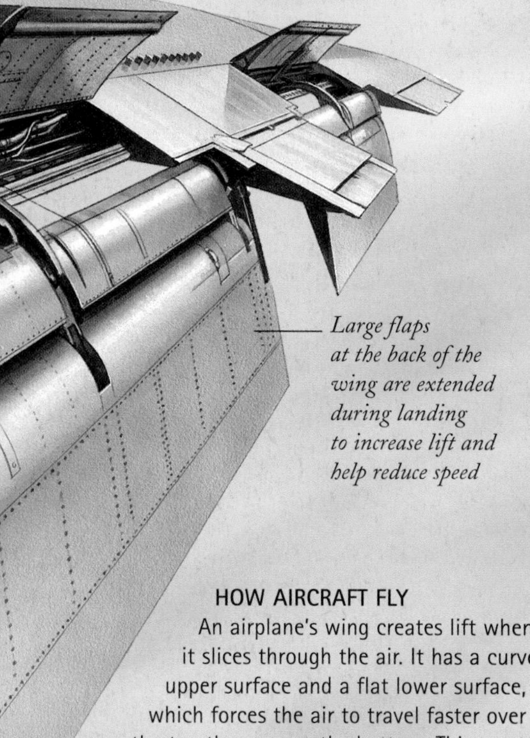

Large flaps at the back of the wing are extended during landing to increase lift and help reduce speed

HOW AIRCRAFT FLY

An airplane's wing creates lift when it slices through the air. It has a curved upper surface and a flat lower surface, which forces the air to travel faster over the top than across the bottom. This creates a sort of upward suction that makes the wing rise, taking the airplane up with it. A helicopter rotor blade has the same curved-and-flat shape, which is known as an airfoil.

Boeing 747-400

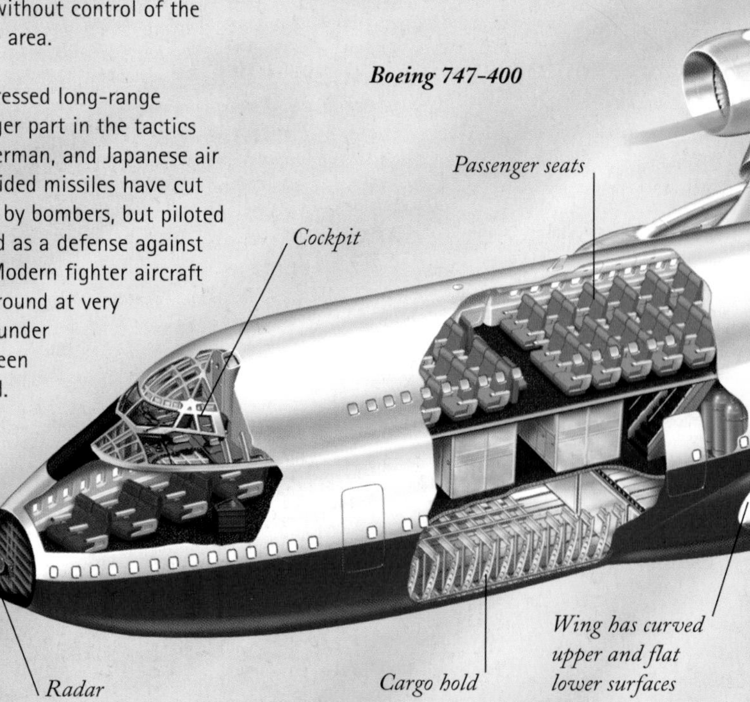

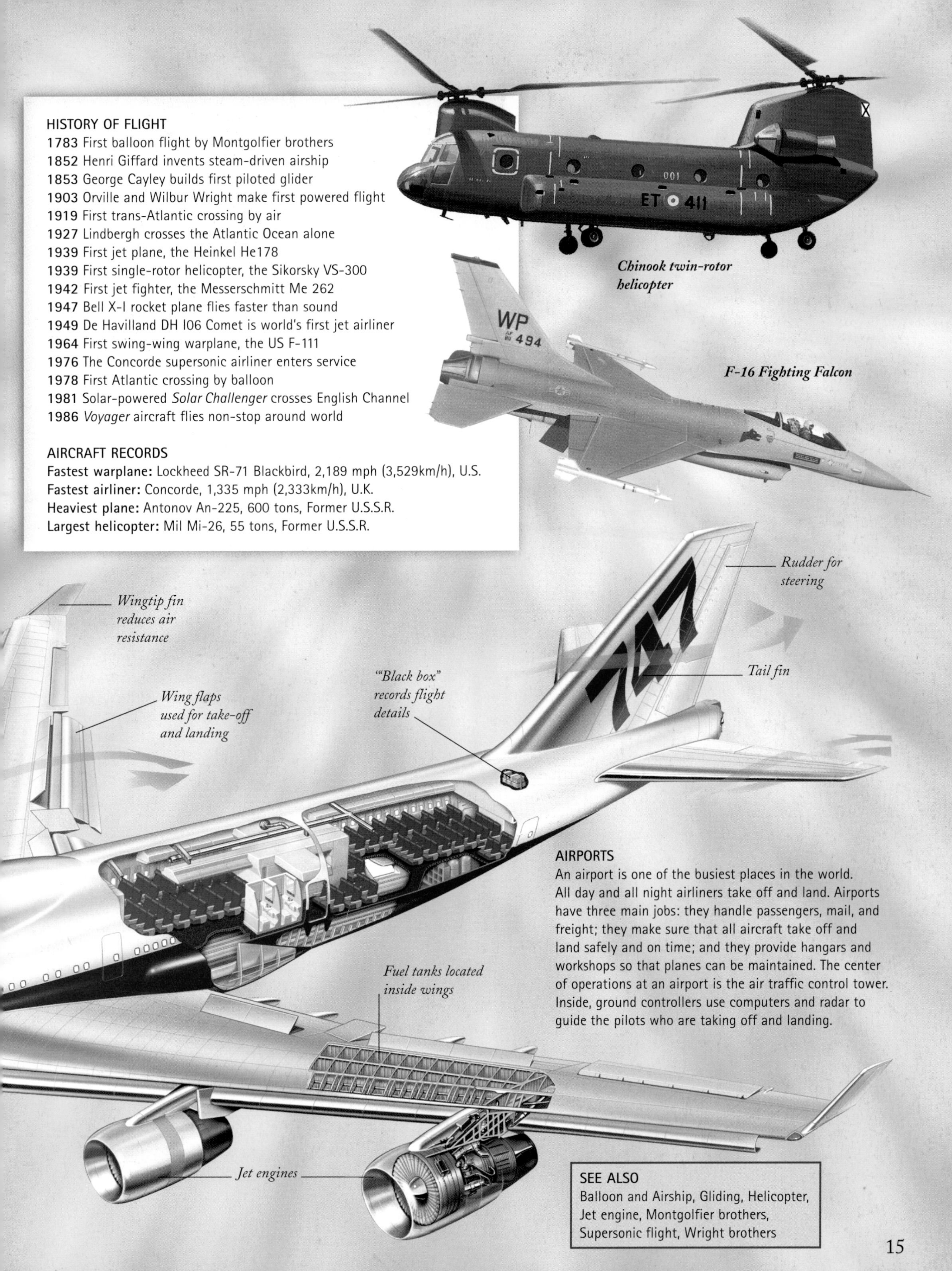

HISTORY OF FLIGHT

1783 First balloon flight by Montgolfier brothers
1852 Henri Giffard invents steam-driven airship
1853 George Cayley builds first piloted glider
1903 Orville and Wilbur Wright make first powered flight
1919 First trans-Atlantic crossing by air
1927 Lindbergh crosses the Atlantic Ocean alone
1939 First jet plane, the Heinkel He178
1939 First single-rotor helicopter, the Sikorsky VS-300
1942 First jet fighter, the Messerschmitt Me 262
1947 Bell X-l rocket plane flies faster than sound
1949 De Havilland DH l06 Comet is world's first jet airliner
1964 First swing-wing warplane, the US F-111
1976 The Concorde supersonic airliner enters service
1978 First Atlantic crossing by balloon
1981 Solar-powered *Solar Challenger* crosses English Channel
1986 *Voyager* aircraft flies non-stop around world

AIRCRAFT RECORDS

Fastest warplane: Lockheed SR-71 Blackbird, 2,189 mph (3,529km/h), U.S.
Fastest airliner: Concorde, 1,335 mph (2,333km/h), U.K.
Heaviest plane: Antonov An-225, 600 tons, Former U.S.S.R.
Largest helicopter: Mil Mi-26, 55 tons, Former U.S.S.R.

AIRPORTS

An airport is one of the busiest places in the world. All day and all night airliners take off and land. Airports have three main jobs: they handle passengers, mail, and freight; they make sure that all aircraft take off and land safely and on time; and they provide hangars and workshops so that planes can be maintained. The center of operations at an airport is the air traffic control tower. Inside, ground controllers use computers and radar to guide the pilots who are taking off and landing.

SEE ALSO
Balloon and Airship, Gliding, Helicopter, Jet engine, Montgolfier brothers, Supersonic flight, Wright brothers

The American **alligator** nests on sandy banks. Each female lays about 30 to 40 eggs and builds a mound of plants and soil to keep them warm. This female is taking her newly hatched babies down to the water.

Alchemy

The **chemistry** of the **Middle Ages** was called alchemy. It was a strange mixture of magic, science, and religion. The people who practiced alchemy dreamed of producing a magic substance that they called the "philosopher's stone." This substance would be able to change cheap metals, such as lead, into **gold**; it would also cure diseases and keep people young. Needless to say the alchemists never found the philosopher's stone, but in their search they learned a great deal about chemistry and invented apparatus that chemists still use today.

Alcohol

There are many different kinds of alcohol. The kind we know best is the alcohol in beer, wine, and hard alcohol, such as whisky. It can make people intoxicated, or drunk. Alcohol is formed by a process called **fermentation**. In fermentation **yeasts** act on the sugar in grain and fruit to produce alcohol. If strong alcohol is needed, the liquid has to be distilled.

Alcohols are used in the making of perfumes and drugs. They dissolve oils, fats, and plastics. The alcohol called glycol is used as an antifreeze in car radiators because, like all alcohols, it has a very low freezing point.

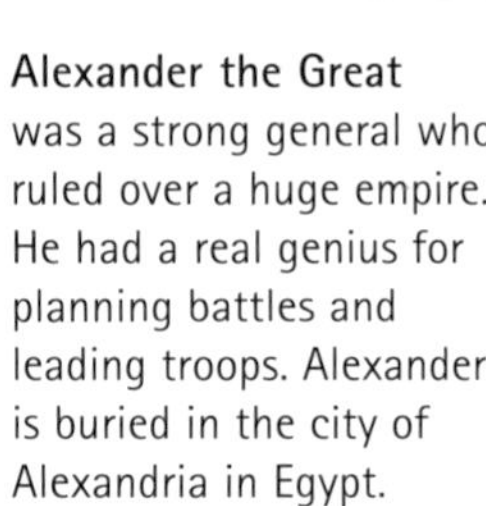

Alexander the Great was a strong general who ruled over a huge empire. He had a real genius for planning battles and leading troops. Alexander is buried in the city of Alexandria in Egypt.

Alexander the Great

Alexander the Great (356–323 B.C.) was a ruler of **Greece** and one of the most powerful generals in history. As a young man he was taught by **Aristotle**, the Greek philosopher.

Alexander became king in 336 B.C. He conquered the Greek city-states and then marched east to conquer Persia, which was at that time the world's greatest empire. By 327 B.C. Alexander's own empire stretched from Greece to India. When his armies reached India, they were worn out from marching and fighting. Alexander had to turn back. When he reached **Babylon,** he became sick and died. He was still only 33.

Algebra

Algebra is a branch of **mathematics** in which letters stand for numbers. It uses various signs to represent connections between the different letters. Algebraic equations are statements in which both sides of the equals sign (=) balance each other out; for example $x + 3 = 9$. Solving an equation means finding the number for "x" that makes the statement true (6).

Algeria

The large North African country of Algeria is bordered by six countries and the **Mediterranean Sea**. The enormous **Sahara Desert** covers most of Algeria, and only a few people, called Berbers, live there. Most Algerians live in a narrow strip along the **Mediterranean**. Algiers is the capital and largest city.

The French seized Algeria in 1830 and stayed there until the country won its independence in 1962 after a long and bitter war. However, many Muslims fiercely opposed the new Algerian **government** because they believed that it was introducing Western values.

Alligator and Crocodile

Alligators and crocodiles are large, powerful animals that belong to the same family of **reptiles**. There are two species of alligators: the American alligator of the southern U.S., and the smaller Chinese alligator that lives in the **Yangtze River**. There are 20 species of crocodiles, including the Nile crocodile of Africa, and the saltwater crocodile of Australia and southern Asia.

Alligators and crocodiles are aggressive predators that hunt fish, turtles, and large mammals. They have become less common because of hunting and damage to their wetland homes.

Alloy

An alloy is a mixture of two or more **metals**. The mixture is often more useful than each metal on its own. For example, a soft metal such as **copper** can be strengthened by adding **zinc** to form brass, or **tin** to form **bronze**. Pure **iron** is not very strong and rusts easily. It is mixed with chromium, nickel, and carbon to make stainless steel, the alloy from which silverware is made.

Alphabet

An alphabet is a collection of letters, or symbols, used to write down a **language**. The word alphabet comes from the names of the first two letters in the Greek alphabet: *alpha* and *beta*. The 26 letters in the English alphabet come from the **Roman** alphabet of 2,500 years ago. Other alphabets in common use today include the Greek, Arabic, Hebrew, and Russian, or Cyrillic, alphabets. Most contain symbols for vowels (soft sounds like "a" and "e") and consonants (hard sounds like "s" and "t"). But the Arabic and Hebrew alphabets have consonants only.

Alps

The Alps form the largest **mountain** range in **Europe**. They are centered in Switzerland, but stretch from the east of France and southern Germany all the way to the former Yugoslavia. Mont Blanc—15,766 ft. (4,807m) high—is the highest peak in the Alps. Thick forests cover the mountains' steep slopes, and there are many lakes in the valleys; the largest is Lake Geneva. The Alps attract many tourists, who go to climb, ski, and fish.

▷ The **Alps** are home to a wide variety of rare mountain wildlife.

The alpine chough is a species of crow that lives on the highest cliffs and slopes

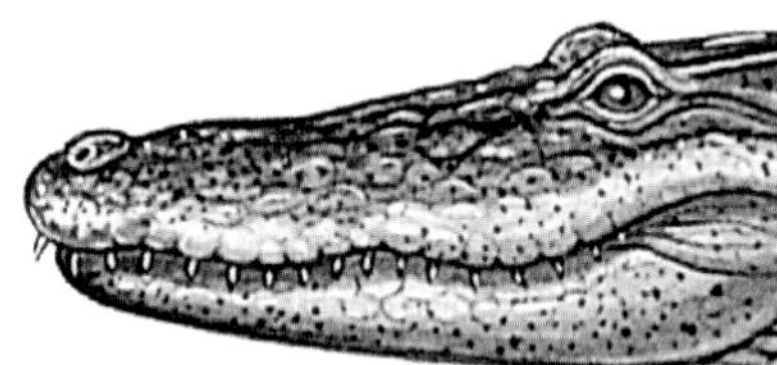

Alligators (top) look like **crocodiles** (bottom), except they have broader, flatter heads. Another difference is that when crocodiles close their jaws, a tooth sticks out on each side.

ALGERIA
Government: Republic
Capital: Algiers
Area: 918,500 sq. mi.
Population: 31 million
Language: Arabic
Currency: Dinar

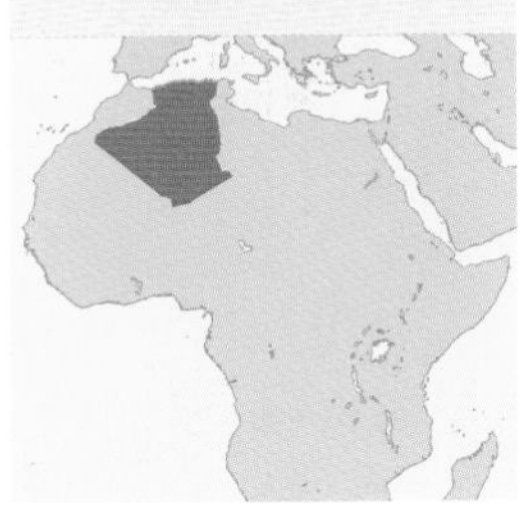

Aluminum

There is more aluminum in the earth's crust than any other **metal**. Most aluminum is produced from bauxite, which is a kind of ore (an ore is a rock or **mineral** containing metals). The bauxite is treated with chemicals and placed in a large electric furnace. An **electric current** is passed through and aluminum falls to the bottom of the furnace. It is silver in color.

Aluminum is light—it weighs only one third as much as steel. It is especially useful where lightness and strength are important, for example in **aircraft** and in **tennis** rackets. It is also a good conductor of heat and **electricity**, and for this reason it is used for electric power cables and to make tinfoil.

Aluminum is a very useful metal. Among many other things, it is used in tennis rackets, power lines, aircraft, and tinfoil.

There are 3,500 kinds of lizards. Lizards make up just over half of the world's reptiles

Amazon River

The Amazon is the mightiest river in **South America** and, at 4,000 mi. (6,440km), it is the second longest in the world after the **Nile River**. It flows from **Peru** through **Brazil** to the **Atlantic Ocean**. Almost all of the Amazon River basin is dense **rain forest**. In the 1540s a Spanish explorer saw female warriors on the Amazon's banks, so the river was named after the Amazons (female warriors) of Greek legends.

American Revolution *see* Revolutionary War, American

Amundsen, Roald

Roald Amundsen (1872–1928) was a Norwegian explorer. In 1910 he set out to be the first to reach the **North Pole**, but he was beaten by the American Robert Peary. Amundsen then went to the **South Pole**, which he reached on December 14, 1911, the first person ever to do so—a month before Captain **Scott**'s ill-fated expedition.

ANDORRA
Government: Co-principality
Capital: Andorra la Vella
Area: 174 sq. mi.
Population: 67,000
Language: Catalan
Currency: Euro

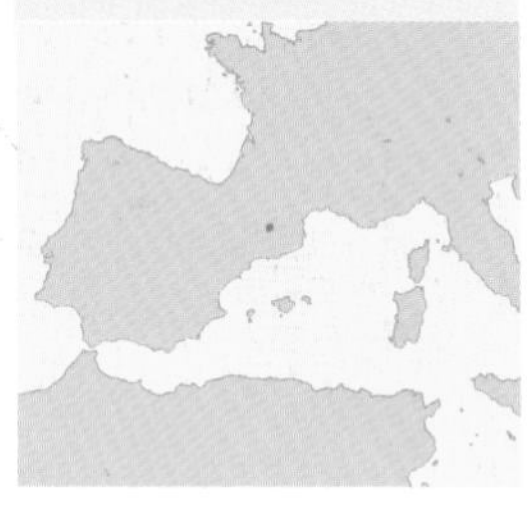

Andersen, Hans Christian

Hans Christian Andersen (1805–1875) was a Danish storyteller. His fairy tales, such as *The Little Mermaid*, *The Ugly Ducklings*, and *The Snow Queen*, are still popular all over the world.

Andes

The Andes **mountain** range is the longest in the world. It stretches for more than 4,340 mi. (7,000km) down the west side of **South America**, running the whole length of the continent. Several peaks are more than 19,680 ft. (6,000m) high, and Aconcagua, on the border between **Argentina** and **Chile**, is the highest mountain in the Americas at 22,830 ft. (6,960m). Many of the peaks are active volcanoes. The Andes are rich in minerals such as copper, silver, and gold.

Andorra

Andorra is a tiny, mountainous country on the border between **France** and **Spain**. From 1278 until 1993 it was ruled jointly by the president of France and the bishop of Urgel in Spain.

continued on page 20

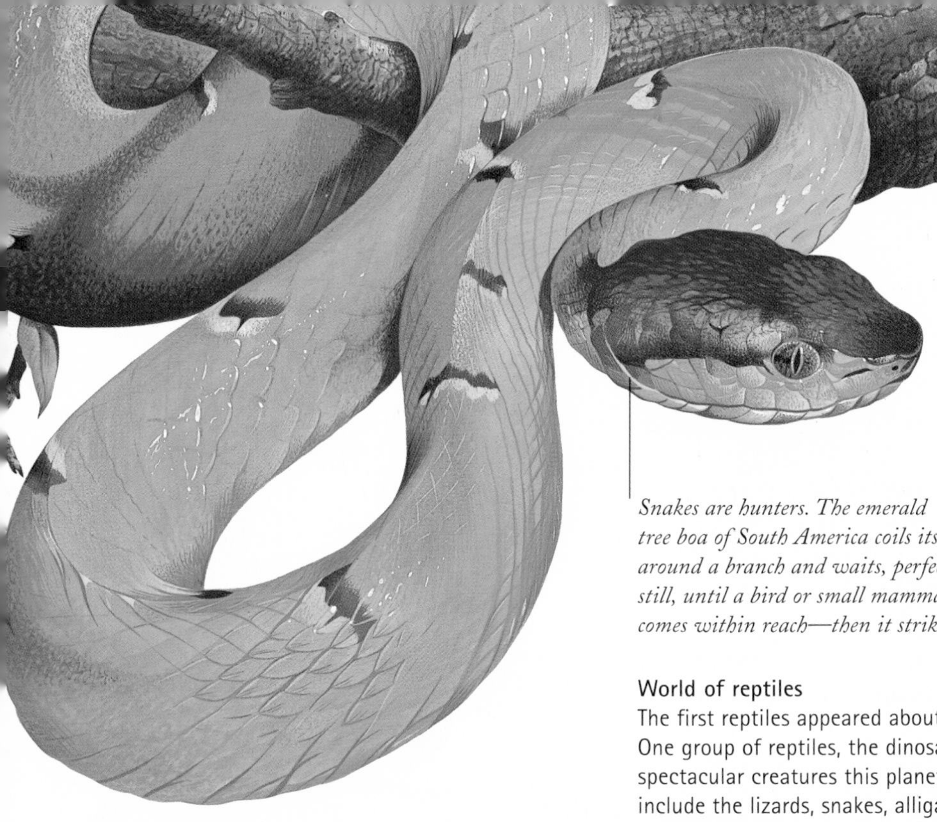

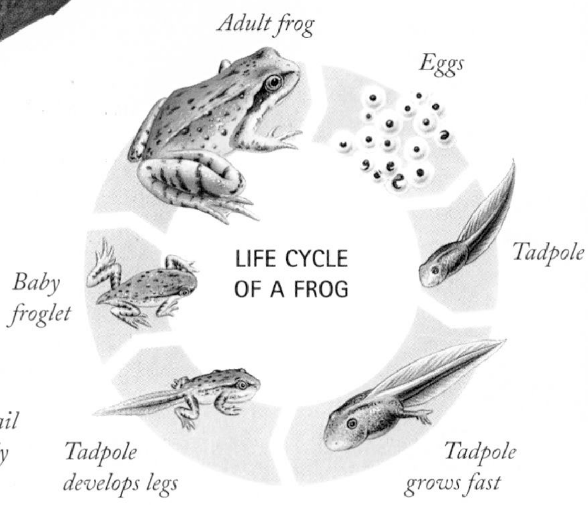

AMPHIBIANS and REPTILES

Amphibians and reptiles are two amazingly varied groups of animals. Amphibians have soft, moist skin, but reptiles are covered with tough scales.

World of amphibians

Amphibians include the frogs, toads, salamanders, and newts. They are able to live both in water and on land, but most of them start their lives in water. Common places to find amphibians are ponds, streams, ditches, marshes, and damp woodlands. Amphibians absorb water and oxygen from the air directly through their skin. For this reason they must keep their skin moist.

All amphibians are predators. They hunt a variety of insects and other small animals, usually by hiding and making a sudden lunge to snatch their victims.

◁ *The gliding frog of Malaysia has special webs on its feet that it uses as tiny wings. They allow the frog to glide between trees.*

Snakes are hunters. The emerald tree boa of South America coils its tail around a branch and waits, perfectly still, until a bird or small mammal comes within reach—then it strikes.

LIFE CYCLE OF A FROG

Adult frog
Eggs
Tadpole
Tadpole grows fast
Tadpole develops legs
Baby froglet

△ *Most amphibians lay their eggs in water in a jellylike layer that protects them. The babies are called larvae and the larvae of frogs and toads are known as tadpoles. The larvae can breathe underwater, just like fish. After two or three months they begin to turn into adults and are able to leave the water.*

World of reptiles

The first reptiles appeared about 360 million years ago. One group of reptiles, the dinosaurs, were the most spectacular creatures this planet has seen. Today reptiles include the lizards, snakes, alligators, crocodiles, turtles, and tortoises. Most reptiles live on land or in rivers and swamps, but some turtles and snakes live in the sea. Some snakes have poisonous bites with which they kill their prey. Turtles and tortoises have armored shells for protection.

When baby alligators and crocodiles hatch, they look like miniature versions of their parents.

Balancing act

Amphibians and reptiles are cold-blooded animals. This means that their body temperature goes up and down as the surrounding air or water gets warmer and cooler. When it gets too cold, they sunbathe to warm up. But if it gets too hot, they have to find shelter from the sun.

Most amphibians and reptiles live in warm parts of the world. Those that live in cooler regions spend the winter in a deep sleep called hibernation.

▷ *The Australian frilled lizard raises its collar and gapes its mouth to frighten off attackers.*

SEE ALSO
Alligator and Crocodile, Frog and Toad, Hibernation, Lizard, Salamander and Newt, Tortoise, Turtle and Terrapin

Predators are **animals** that catch and eat other animals, known as prey. The cheetah's main prey is **antelope**.

ANGOLA
Government: Republic
Capital: Luanda
Area: 480,800 sq. mi.
Population: 10 million
Language: Portuguese
Currency: Kwanza

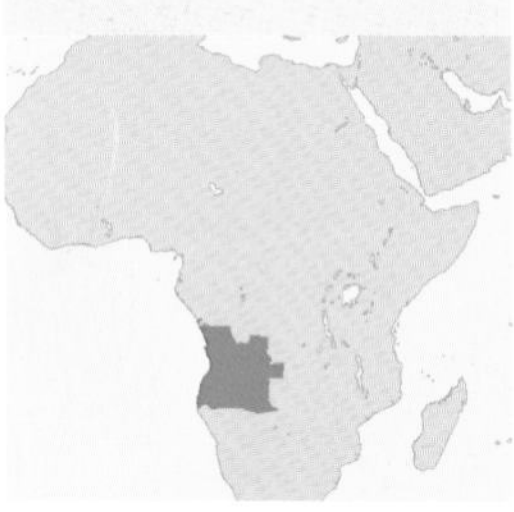

Since 1993, the people of Andorra have elected their own **government** officials. Andorra is surrounded by the **Pyrenees** mountains, and its main industry is tourism.

Angle

An angle is formed when two straight lines meet. The size of all angles is measured in degrees. A "right" angle forms the corner of a square and has 90 degrees. An acute angle is less than 90 degrees and an obtuse angle is between 90 and 180 degrees.

Anglo-Saxons

Anglo-Saxon is the name given to the group of Germanic tribes who settled in Great Britain during A.D. 400 through 500. These tribes were the Angles, Saxons, and Jutes. They gradually occupied all of England and drove the original Celtic people of Britain (see **Celts**) into Wales and Cornwall. By the 700s there were seven main Anglo-Saxon kingdoms: Wessex, Sussex, Kent, Essex, East Anglia, Mercia, and Northumbria. About half the words in the English language come from Anglo-Saxon.

◁ Life was hard for ordinary **Anglo-Saxons**. Most of them were farmers and lived in simple houses made of mud, thatch, and timber.

Angola

The Republic of Angola is a large country on the coast of the Atlantic Ocean in southwestern **Africa**. It has valuable reserves of **diamonds**.

Portugal claimed Angola in 1482. Native Angolans rebelled against the Portuguese in 1960 and fighting broke out. In 1975 Portugal granted the Angolans full independence. A violent struggle then began between rival Angolan factions, some of them aided by foreign troops. The war ended in 1991 when the **government** and the rebels agreed to a ceasefire. However, despite attempts to keep the peace, fighting continued into the 21st century.

Animals

An animal is any living thing that is not a **plant**. No one knows how many different kinds of animals there are on earth, and hundreds of new kinds are discovered every year. The biggest difference between animals and plants is in the way they get their food. Animals eat plants or other animals. Plants make their own food out of substances taken in through their roots or leaves. Animals, unlike plants, can also move around at some time in their lives.

Some animals, such as tiny amoebas, reproduce simply by splitting in two. In most other animals the female produces eggs that are then fertilized by the male.

Animals with backbones are called **vertebrates**. Vertebrates include **birds**, **mammals**, **fish**, **amphibians**, and **reptiles**. **Invertebrates** are animals without backbones. **Insects**, **jellyfish**, **mollusks**, **worms**, **spiders**, and **snails** are all examples of invertebrates. As invertebrates lack internal bones, some of them have a shell for protection.

Ant

Ants are "social" **insects**—they live together in colonies. Some colonies are in heaps of twigs, while others are inside chambers deep in the ground or hills of soil or sand. There are three types of ants: males, queens, which lay eggs, and workers, or females that neither mate nor lay eggs.

Army ants march across land in a great horde that may have as many as several million ants. They devour anything in their path—even cattle.

Antarctic *see* page 23

Anteater

The South American anteater is a curious **mammal** with a long, tapering snout. This snout is specifically shaped to extract ants, **termites**, and grubs out of their nests. The anteater catches the insects with its long, whiplike tongue.

There are four different kinds of anteaters. By far the largest is the giant anteater, which can measure over 6 ft. (2m) from the tip of its tail to its snout. Anteaters live in tropical forests, grassy plains, and swamps.

△ The giant **anteater** uses its long, tube-shaped snout and sticky tongue to catch ants and termites. It may eat up to 30,000 of the insects in a single day.

Antelope

Antelopes are grazing animals with **horns** and **hoofs**. They look a lot like **deer**, but are actually related to goats and cattle. Most antelopes live on the African plains, or **savannas**. They are fast runners and often live in large herds, fleeing suddenly at any hint of danger. Their main enemies are lions, cheetahs, and hyenas. Some of the best-known kinds of antelope are the impala, eland, waterbuck, wildebeest, gazelle, and the tiny dik-dik, which is hardly bigger than a rabbit.

Antibiotics

Antibiotics are substances, produced by living things, that are poisonous to harmful **bacteria**. Early in the 1900s scientists began to discover **drugs** that would kill bacteria but not harm the patient. The most important of these

▽ Leaf-cutter **ants** live in tropical forests in the Americas. Great trails of worker ants climb to the treetops where the ants cut pieces of leaves. They take the leaves back to the nest and dump them in piles. A fungus grows on the heaps of leaves, and the ants harvest it as food.

drugs was penicillin, a drug produced by a mold. Penicillin was a wonder drug that saved many lives. It was especially useful against pneumonia, a **disease** that inflames the **lungs**. Scientists have found many more useful antibiotics that can fight diseases such as tuberculosis, typhus, and whooping cough. But antibiotics do not work against **viruses**—the organisms that cause colds, flu, mumps, measles, **AIDS**, and other diseases.

Apartheid

The word apartheid was used by the white rulers of **South Africa** to describe their policy for keeping the white and nonwhite people of South Africa apart—apartheid means "apartness" in the Afrikaans language. In the late 1940s the white South African **government** began to pass a series of laws that made apartheid the official government policy.

Strict apartheid laws kept whites and nonwhites apart and ensured that whites had a much better way of life than the rest of the population. In 1991 the South African government overturned major apartheid laws.

In 1994 South Africa's first free elections led to the black African National Congress being the governing party, and **Nelson Mandela** was elected president.

Archaeologists clean finds by brushing away the soil

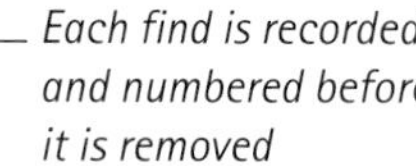

Each find is recorded and numbered before it is removed

Archaeology is the study of the remains of the past. In 1974 thousands of life-size clay soldiers were found near the tomb of an ancient Chinese emperor.

Ape

The apes are our closest animal relatives. We have the same kind of skeleton and blood and catch many similar diseases.

Apes have large brains, but the gorilla's brain is only half the size of a human's. Unlike **monkeys**, apes have no tails. There are four kinds of apes: the **gorilla** and **chimpanzee** are African; **orangutans** live in Borneo and Sumatra; and gibbons live throughout Southeast Asia. They are all forest animals.

Apes have extremely nimble hands and fingers for holding food and swinging from branches. They eat a wide variety of leaves, fruits, and nuts. Apes are becoming rare in many places because of hunting and because their forest homes are being cut down.

Apes, like these gorillas, are sociable animals that live in family groups. Each group has a large, strong male who rules over all the females, babies, and younger males.

Archaeology

Archaeology is the study of history through the things that people have made and built. They may include tools, coins, pottery, houses, temples, and graves. Even a garbage dump can help reveal how people lived.

At first archaeological sites were ransacked for their treasures. But by the early 1800s archaeologists had begun to uncover sites carefully, noting everything they found, and where they found it. Many exciting and important discoveries were made, including the remains of ancient Troy (1871), the early **Greek** civilization at Mycenae (1876), and the tomb of the pharaoh **Tutankhamen** in **Egypt** (1922).

continued on page 24

ARCTIC and ANTARCTIC

The Arctic and Antarctic lie at opposite ends of the earth. They are the coldest places on the planet, and life there is very hard.

Like many Arctic animals, the snowy owl is white to camouflage it against snow.

The polar bear hunts seals, fish, and small whales in the frozen seas of northern polar regions. Arctic foxes often follow behind, looking for scraps.

TO THE ENDS OF THE EARTH

The Arctic is the region within the Arctic Circle—an imaginary line drawn around the northern part of the globe. It is made up of the Arctic Ocean, the surrounding seas and islands, and the northern parts of Alaska, Canada, Greenland, Norway, Sweden, Finland, and Russia. At the center of the Arctic is the North Pole. There is no land at the North Pole, only a huge area of frozen sea.

The Antarctic region includes Antarctica, the world's fifth largest continent, which surrounds the South Pole. Nearly all of the Antarctic is covered by a thick ice cap, broken only by a few mountain ranges. This ice cap averages 8,200 ft. (2,500m) thick. Off the coast of Antarctica there are many islands, icebergs, and ice sheets.

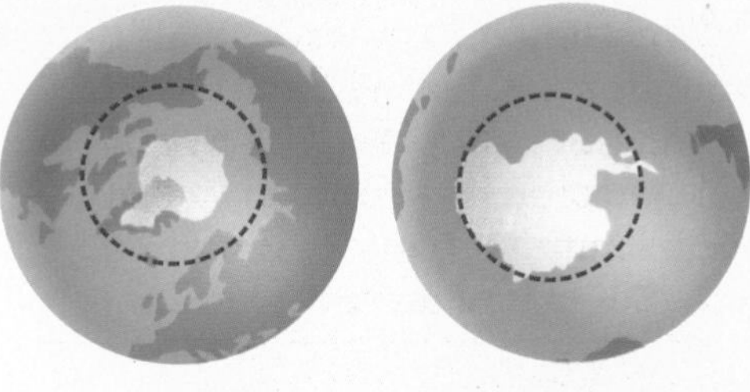

The Arctic and Antarctic circles are imaginary lines around the world. Most of the area inside the Arctic Circle is sea, but the Antarctic Circle is filled by an icy continent called Antarctica.

Many kinds of whales and dolphins swim to the Arctic and Antarctic to feed. Sperm whales dive deep in search of their favorite food—squid.

POLAR WILDLIFE

Despite the harsh conditions, many kinds of animals live in the Arctic and Antarctic. The Arctic's wildlife includes lemmings, reindeer, Arctic hares, and polar bears. Many Arctic animals spend the winter in burrows underground. Most of the birds migrate (fly south) to warmer areas for the winter and return in the spring to breed. Arctic seas are home to seals, walruses, and whales.

Very few animals can survive near the South Pole. However, the Antarctic's seas teem with fish and tiny, shrimplike animals called krill. They provide food for large numbers of squid, whales, penguins, and albatrosses.

ICE AND SNOW

The Arctic and Antarctic get some of the most extreme weather anywhere on earth. In the Arctic, temperatures rise above freezing (32°F/0°C) for only four months of the year. However, the Antarctic is even colder—the world's lowest-ever temperature, -130°F (-90°C), was recorded there. Fierce winds race across the open landscape, creating snowdrifts and raging snowstorms.

It is cold near the North and South poles because the sun never rises high in the sky. In the winter some days it does not rise at all. In midsummer the sun can be seen all day and night—it never gets dark.

POLAR PEOPLES

The Inuit of Canada and Greenland and the Lapps of Norway, Sweden, and Finland live in the Arcic. They hunt and fish for a living. The only people living in the Antarctic are scientists.

Emperor penguins breed in the Antarctic winter. To survive the bitter cold, they have thick layers of body fat and huddle together in groups.

Even today one of the fastest ways to travel in the Arctic is on sleds pulled by teams of huskies.

SEE ALSO
Albatross, Amundsen (Roald), Bear, Climate, Iceberg, North Pole, Penguin, Scott (Robert Falcon), Seal, South Pole, Whale

ARGENTINA
Government: Republic
Capital: Buenos Aires
Area: 1,055,400 sq. mi.
Population: 37 million
Language: Spanish
Currency: Peso

Today science helps the archaeologist in their work. Radiocarbon dating helps tell us when particular objects were made (see **carbon**). **Infrared** and **X-ray** photography can reveal designs under the rotted surface of a bronze bowl. Archaeology has even gone under the sea. With modern diving equipment, archaeologists can explore sunken wrecks and other long-lost remains of the past.

Archery

Archery is the use of the bow and arrow—once for hunting and warfare, now mostly for sport. No one knows when bows and arrows were first used, but prehistoric man certainly used them to shoot animals for food and to protect himself. Until the discovery of gunpowder the **army** with the best archers usually won the battle (see **war**). Modern bows are usually made of laminated wood or fiberglass.

▽ The **Armada** of 1588 was a huge fleet of Spanish fighting ships. It carried a force of 30,000 people, including priests, surgeons, lawyers, and administrators.

Architecture *see* **page 26**

Arctic *see* **page 23**

Argentina

Argentina is the second largest country in **South America**. Most of its people are farmers and ranchers, and much of Argentina's wealth comes from crops and livestock. It is one of the world's top producers of beef and wool.

The chief farming region in Argentina is the pampas, a Spanish word meaning "flat land." The pampas lies in the center of the country around its capital, Buenos Aires. Here huge farms raise millions of **cattle** and **sheep**. Northern Argentina is an area of tropical forests. In the far south, near the tip of South America, is Patagonia, a cold land of windswept plains and high, snowy mountains. The western part of the country rises steeply to the **Andes** mountains.

Argentina was ruled by **Spain** from 1535 until 1810. Today, most of the population is descended from Europeans, although there are still about 20,000 native Argentinians.

Aristotle

Aristotle (384–322 B.C.) was a Greek philosopher and a student of another famous Greek philosopher, **Plato**. At the age of 17, Aristotle went to Athens to become Plato's pupil. He worked there for 20 years and then became the tutor of **Alexander the Great**. Aristotle invented the method of thinking called logic. His writing covers many areas, including nature and politics.

Arkwright, Richard

Richard Arkwright (1732–1792) was an English inventor best known for his spinning frame, which made factory production of **cotton** cloth possible.

Arkwright patented his new spinning machine in 1769, after which he built his first spinning mill. He became the pioneer of the modern factory system. His success laid the framework for the **Industrial Revolution**.

Armada

Armada is a Spanish word for a great fleet of armed **ships**. The most famous armada was the fleet that tried to invade England in 1588. The 130 Spanish ships were large, clumsy, and heavily armed. The English ships were faster and easier to maneuver. The English sent fire ships toward the Spanish fleet, which retreated out to sea. Several Spanish ships were sunk in battle and the Armada was forced to flee around the northern tip of Britain, where many of its ships were wrecked in storms. Only 67 of the original 130 ships finally reached **Spain**.

Armadillo

Armadillos are strange **mammals** that live in Central and South America. Their backs are covered with an armor of bony plates. They have strong claws, which they use for digging burrows and tearing open termite nests to find food. There are 20 different kinds of armadillos.

Armadillos get their name from the armor plating on their backs. They roll into a tight ball when under threat of attack.

Armor

Armor is covering used to protect the body in battle. It was first worn at least 5,000 years ago and was originally made of tough **leather**. Then metal breastplates, helmets, and shields were made. But the rest of the body was still protected by leather or by chain mail, hundreds of small **iron** rings linked together to form a flexible metal coat.

In the **Middle Ages** knights rode into battle encased from head to toe in suits of plate armor that weighed up to 66 lbs (30kg). But as **guns** became more powerful and accurate, heavy armor was no longer of any use, and it gradually died out. Today lightweight metals and **plastics** are used in bulletproof vests worn by soldiers and **police**.

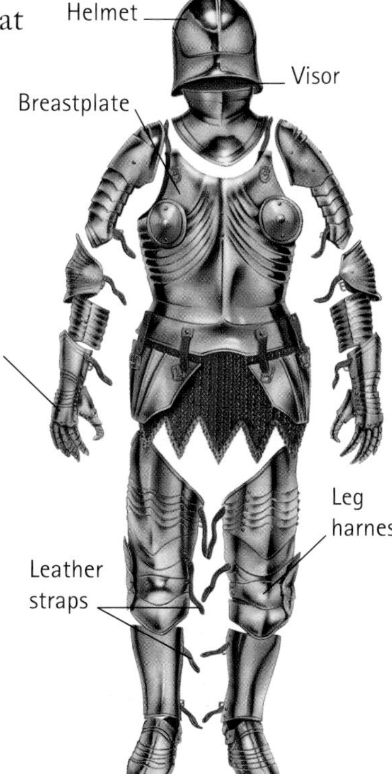

Suits of plate **armor** were made from silvery steel. They had so many pieces that knights took up to an hour to dress for battle. But although the armor looked difficult to move around in, it was actually very flexible.

Army

The first effective armies appeared in the Middle East more than 3,500 years ago. In the ancient world Egypt, Greece, and Rome all had large armies. Until modern times infantry (foot soldiers) made up the bulk of most armies, but today's troops do a variety of jobs.

Most armies now consist of combat troops, service troops, and staff officers. Combat troops include the infantry, armored troops that are equipped with tanks, artillery that operate the heavy **guns**, and paratroopers that parachute behind enemy lines.

Service troops provide the food, fuel, ammunition, and other supplies needed by the combat troops. They include medical personnel and engineers, who build bridges and prepare landing strips for **aircraft**. The staff is made up of headquarters officers who plan and direct the army operations.

Art *see* page 27

Artery

An artery is a **blood** vessel that carries blood from the **heart** to all parts of the body. **Veins** are different from arteries because they carry used blood back to the heart. Arteries have thick, elastic walls. The largest artery is the aorta, which is connected directly to the heart itself.

ARCHITECTURE

Architecture is the art of designing buildings and other structures. The main aims of architecture are to make sure that the constructions are strong, look good, and are suitable for their purpose.

△ *In 3000–2000 B.C., the Sumerians of ancient Iraq constructed tall pyramid-shaped temples called ziggurats.*

△ *The massive dome of Florence cathedral, built in the Renaissance, was admired across Europe.*

△ *India's Taj Mahal built in 1650, features domes and minarets (towers) typical of Islamic architecture.*

EARLY ARCHITECTURE

The earliest buildings were simple structures made of dried grass or mud that provided shelter from the sun, wind, and rain. More than 5,000 years ago the ancient civilizations of Mesopotamia (present-day Iraq) started building one-room houses out of sun-baked clay bricks. As workers became more skilled and their construction techniques advanced people began to create more elaborate buildings. In the period 2600–1000 B.C., the ancient Egyptians constructed huge pyramids as tombs for their dead kings. The largest of these pyramids used more than two million stone blocks.

GREEK AND ROMAN ARCHITECTURE

Western architecture as we know it today began to take shape in Greece around 600 B.C. Over the next 450 years Greek architects developed a classical style that featured beautiful pillars of stone or marble. Surviving examples of ancient Greek architecture include temples, such as the Parthenon in Athens, and outdoor theaters.

The Romans copied the Greek architectural style but also invented their own building techniques, such as curved arches and domed roofs. Arches can support a lot of weight, allowing architects to design larger, stronger buildings. Roman architects built a wide range of structures, mainly from 100 B.C. to A.D. 300, including public baths, palaces, bridges, and gigantic sports arenas.

CHANGING STYLES

During the Middle Ages, European architects developed new ways of building with stone. They built everything from fortified castles to churches.

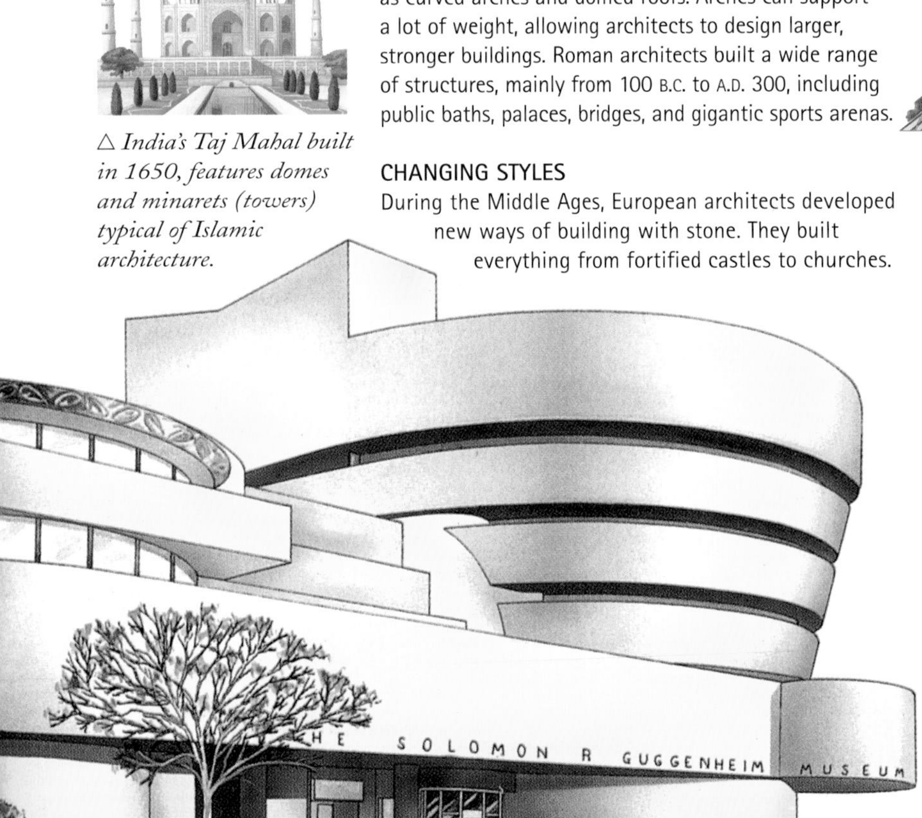

The Gothic style flourished from the mid-1100s to the 1400s. Many of the fine, old cathedrals of Europe were built in the Gothic style. They featured graceful, pointed arches, high ceilings, and stained-glass windows.

The Renaissance, which began in Italy in the late 1300s, triggered a new wave of architectural development. The direction of architecture also changed during this period. Instead of concentrating mainly on churches and other religious buildings, architects began to spend more time designing private houses and public buildings, such as government offices and town halls.

In the 1500s architects started to become famous for their work. Since then, the best architects have always been in high demand. They are able to adapt their styles to suit the needs of their clients.

▷ *In the 1980s, a glass pyramid was built in the courtyard of the Louvre Museum, Paris.*

MODERN ARCHITECTURE

In the modern age the main building materials are still bricks and stone, but architects now have many new materials to choose from for their designs. Concrete and steel, glass and plastic are shaping the new world in which we live. Many other inventions have also helped to revolutionize architecture, such as central heating, electric lighting, and air conditioning. When the elevator was invented in 1854, it allowed architects to design much taller buildings. The first steel-framed skyscrapers were erected in Chicago and New York in the late 1800s.

Today architects work together with engineers and surveyors. They use computers to calculate the different weights and forces within their planned building and alter the design if necessary. Some modern buildings have very dramatic or futuristic shapes that would have been impossible to build without recent technology.

◁ *New York's Guggenheim Museum was opened in 1960.*

SEE ALSO
Church, Dome, Egypt (Ancient), Greece (Ancient), House, Mosque, Parthenon, Pyramid, Skyscraper

ART

Art is any creative work used to portray images and to express feelings. People produce art in many ways and in many different forms, including painting, drawing, printing, sculpture, photography, and movies.

△ *Cave paintings made up to 30,000 years ago exist in places as far apart as Africa, China, and Europe. This cattle-herding scene was painted on rock in the central Sahara Desert.*

THE STORY OF ART

In the past art usually had a practical purpose. The earliest cave paintings, for example, probably had a religious or ritual meaning. In ancient Egypt, Greece, and Rome rulers and wealthy people used art to show off their importance and power. They owned decorated pottery, mosaics, and statues, which often depicted gods, goddesses, and mythical scenes.

In Europe during the Middle Ages, art was used to teach people about their religion and to help them pray. Today medieval paintings may look "flat" and unnatural. This is partly because artists did not know how to make their images appear three-dimensional. They first began to find out how to do this from the late 1300s onwards in Italy. The new, more realistic style spread across Europe during the 1400s and 1500s. This period—the Renaissance—was a time when artists tried out many new techniques.

In the 1600s artists started to illustrate nonreligious subjects, such as portraits of ordinary people, still lifes (collections of objects), and everyday scenes. They also signed their work so that people knew who they were. Medieval artists never signed their work.

◁ *Ancient Egyptian tombs were covered with wall paintings of gods, religious ceremonies, and hunting expeditions.*

△ *Japansese art includes dramatic natural scenes. This print,* The Great Wave, *was made by Hokusai in 1831–1833.*

The invention of photography in the mid-1800s had a big impact on art. Because photographs were so lifelike, many artists decided to create art that was less realistic instead. In France painters introduced a new, loose style called Impressionism, in which they used bold strokes of color to give the impression of changing lighting effects. Since then, art styles have continued to change. Some artists have made abstract art, which has no obvious subject and is more about their ideas and feelings. Artists now produce a wide variety of work in many different styles.

◁ *Sandro Botticelli, a leading artist of the Italian Renaissance, painted* Spring *in about 1478.*

△ *Henry Moore, a sculptor, used different materials to make sculptures with interesting shapes and textures.*

SEE ALSO
Abstract art, Impressionism, Michelangelo, Painting, Picasso, Renaissance, Sculpture, Van Gogh

ASIA

Asia is the largest continent. It covers one third of the earth's land area. More people live in Asia than in all the other continents put together.

The buildings of ancient Petra in Jordan were carved out of solid rock. This beautiful city was built in 400 BCE by the Nabateans, an Arab people.

LAND OF EXTREMES

Asia stretches from the Mediterranean Sea in the west to the Pacific Ocean in the east, and from the Arctic Circle in the north to sun-drenched, tropical islands in the south. Asia is so wide that the sun rises almost 11 hours earlier in Turkey than in Japan.

The far north of Asia is mainly an area of tundra—a treeless wilderness that is frozen for most of the year. Vast forests and grasslands lie to the south of the tundra. Much of western Asia is barren desert. Asia has many mountain chains, including the mighty Himalayas, which form a barrier across the heart of the continent. Farther south are fertile plains and lush rain forests.

△ *Many of the fastest growing cities are in Southeast Asia. They are leading centers of industry and commerce.*

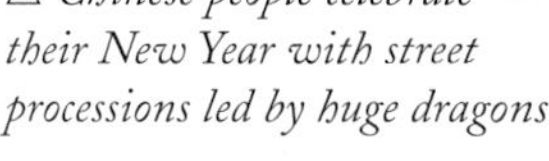

△ *Chinese people celebrate their New Year with street processions led by huge dragons.*

ANCIENT CIVILIZATIONS

Some of the world's earliest civilizations developed in Mesopotamia (modern Iraq), the Indus Valley (modern Pakistan), and China. These peoples built the first large cities and invented written languages, legal systems, and farming techniques. They also made many advances in architecture, mathematics, and science.

By the 1500s Asia included four of the most powerful states in the world—the Ottoman Empire of the Middle East, the Safavid Empire of Iran, the Mogul Empire of India and China's Ming Dynasty. Their wealth came from trade.

▽ *Major Japanese cities are connected by a high-speed train called the* Shinkansen, *which travels at up to 300 km/h.*

BIRTHPLACE OF RELIGION

Asia is the birthplace of all the world's major religions. India gave rise to both Hinduism, in about 2000 B.C., and Buddhism, 1,500 years later. Buddhism is now the main religion in large parts of East Asia, including Tibet, China, Japan, and Thailand. Israel was the home of Judaism and Christianity, which later spread to Europe and the rest of the world. Islam was founded in the Arabian Peninsula in the 600s, and is now practiced by Muslims around the globe. However, Sikhism has relatively recent origins. It was established in the Punjab region of northern India in the early 1500s.

THROUGH THE AGES

Europeans began to visit Asia in the 1400s, and trade quickly developed between the two continents. All kinds of goods were traded, such as spices, silk, ceramics, and jewels. Later, for several centuries, China and Japan closed their doors to Europe, halting trade and other contacts. During the 1800s, much of Asia was colonized by European powers, whose armed forces were stronger and better equipped. The colonists created large plantations for growing tea, coffee, rubber, and cotton.

After World War II (1939–1945), during which Japan occupied parts of East Asia, many of the colonies won their freedom. Several countries adopted the communist political system, among them the Soviet Union, China, and North Korea. With the breakup of the Soviet Union in 1991, eight new Asian states were created, including Kazakhstan and Tajikistan. Today there are 50 independent nations in Asia, from tiny states like Brunei and Bahrain, to powerful giants such as Russia and China.

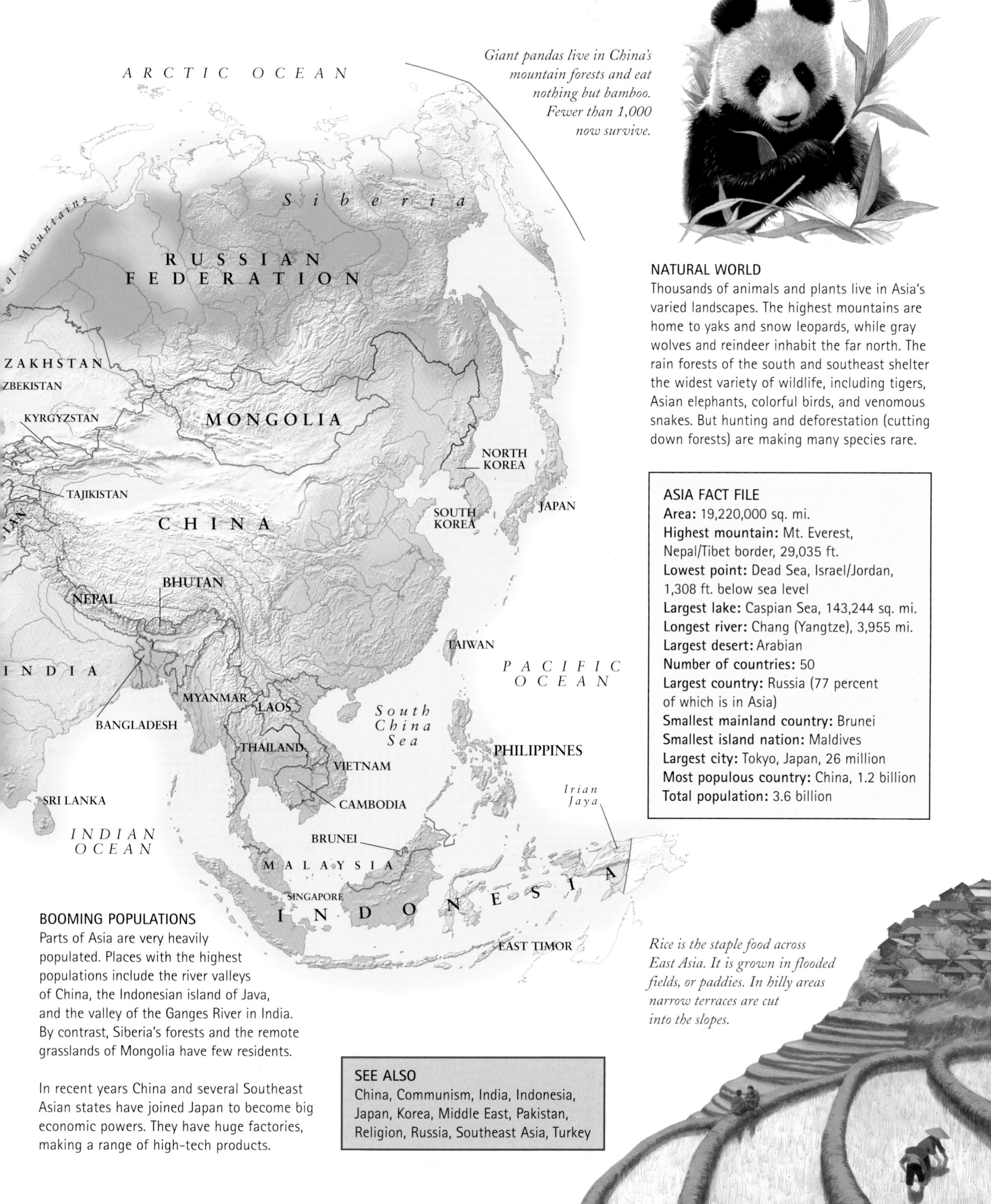

Giant pandas live in China's mountain forests and eat nothing but bamboo. Fewer than 1,000 now survive.

Rice is the staple food across East Asia. It is grown in flooded fields, or paddies. In hilly areas narrow terraces are cut into the slopes.

NATURAL WORLD

Thousands of animals and plants live in Asia's varied landscapes. The highest mountains are home to yaks and snow leopards, while gray wolves and reindeer inhabit the far north. The rain forests of the south and southeast shelter the widest variety of wildlife, including tigers, Asian elephants, colorful birds, and venomous snakes. But hunting and deforestation (cutting down forests) are making many species rare.

ASIA FACT FILE

Area: 19,220,000 sq. mi.
Highest mountain: Mt. Everest, Nepal/Tibet border, 29,035 ft.
Lowest point: Dead Sea, Israel/Jordan, 1,308 ft. below sea level
Largest lake: Caspian Sea, 143,244 sq. mi.
Longest river: Chang (Yangtze), 3,955 mi.
Largest desert: Arabian
Number of countries: 50
Largest country: Russia (77 percent of which is in Asia)
Smallest mainland country: Brunei
Smallest island nation: Maldives
Largest city: Tokyo, Japan, 26 million
Most populous country: China, 1.2 billion
Total population: 3.6 billion

BOOMING POPULATIONS

Parts of Asia are very heavily populated. Places with the highest populations include the river valleys of China, the Indonesian island of Java, and the valley of the Ganges River in India. By contrast, Siberia's forests and the remote grasslands of Mongolia have few residents.

In recent years China and several Southeast Asian states have joined Japan to become big economic powers. They have huge factories, making a range of high-tech products.

SEE ALSO

China, Communism, India, Indonesia, Japan, Korea, Middle East, Pakistan, Religion, Russia, Southeast Asia, Turkey

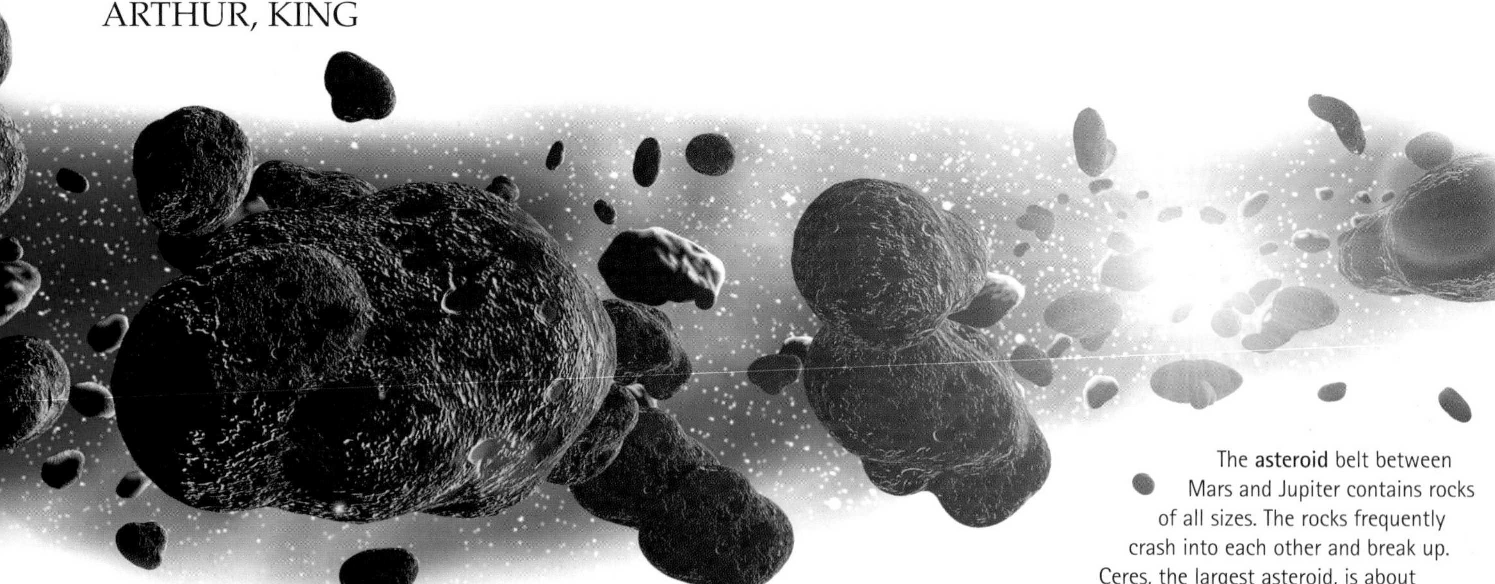

The **asteroid** belt between Mars and Jupiter contains rocks of all sizes. The rocks frequently crash into each other and break up. Ceres, the largest asteroid, is about 620 mi. (1,000km) across.

Arthur, King

King Arthur was a legendary British ruler of the 500s. His kingdom was supposed to have been in western **England**. Many stories grew up around King Arthur's court, and his Knights of the Round Table. The stories were first written down by Sir Thomas Malory in the 1400s.

Asia *see* pages 28–29

Asteroid

Asteroids are many thousands of rocks left over from the time when the **Sun** and **planets** were being formed. Most of them can be found in the wide gap between the orbits of **Mars** and **Jupiter**. Asteroid collisions formed the craters that can be seen on the **Moon** and **Mercury**. Occasionally asteroids still hit **Earth**. Telescopes now look out for rocks that pose a threat.

Astrology

Astrology is the art of foretelling the future by observing the movements of the **Sun**, **Moon**, **planets**, and **stars**. It is based on the zodiac, an imaginary circle in the sky in which the sun, moon, and planets move. Also in this circle are the 12 **constellations**, or groups of stars that look like different shapes. Each shape is a sign of the zodiac and occupies a month in the astrologer's calendar. The 12 signs of the zodiac are Capricorn, Aquarius, Pisces, Aries, Taurus, Gemini, Cancer, Leo, Virgo, Libra, Scorpio, and Sagittarius. Some people believe that persons born under each sign have special character traits.

The **Atlantic Ocean** is the world's second largest ocean. It covers 17 percent of the earth's surface area.

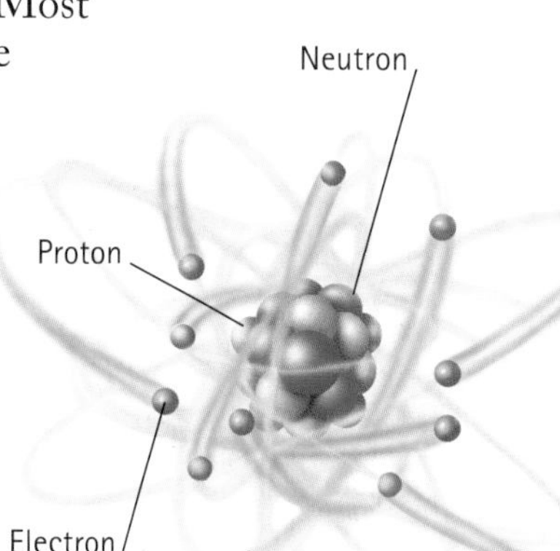

The nucleus of an **atom** consists of protons and neutrons. Electrons move in fixed orbits all around the nucleus.

Astronomy

Astronomy is the scientific study of objects in space and is the oldest science of all. Early observations of the night sky enabled people to divide the year into months, weeks, and days, based on the movements of the **Sun**, **Earth**, and **Moon**. The development of the **calendar** helped early astronomers to forecast the appearance of **comets** and the dates of **eclipses**. For many centuries people believed that the earth was the center of the universe. In the 1540s, Nicolaus **Copernicus** revived the idea that the sun was at the center of our **solar system**. In 1608, Hans Lippershey invented the **telescope**, an important, new tool for astronomers. Modern radio telescopes use giant dishes to collect radio waves sent out by objects in space, such as **pulsars** and **quasars**.

Atlantic Ocean

The Atlantic is the second largest **ocean** in the world, after the **Pacific**. It lies between Europe and Africa in the east and the Americas in the west. Its average depth is more than 5,904 ft. (1,800m). There are several strong currents in the Atlantic, including the **Gulf Stream**, which carries warm water toward the coasts of western Europe.

Atmosphere

The atmosphere is the blanket of **air** and moisture that surrounds our planet. It gives us **oxygen** to breathe, keeps the earth's temperature at just the right level, and shields us from most of the sun's harmful **ultraviolet** rays.

Most air is concentrated in the lowest layer of the atmosphere, which extends from sea level to about 11 mi. (18km) high. The final layer of the atmosphere, at 310 ft. (500km) high, is the start of outer space.

Atom

Everything is made of atoms. We cannot see atoms—they are far too small. Look at the period at the end of this sentence. It contains about 250 billion atoms! But even atoms are made up of smaller pieces.

The simplest atom is that of the light gas **hydrogen**. The center is a tiny body called a proton. Around it spins an even smaller electron. Other atoms are much more complicated than the hydrogen atom. The **carbon** atom, for example, has at its center six protons and six other things called neutrons. Around these spin six electrons. The largest normal atom is a **uranium** atom.

Atomic bomb *see* Nuclear energy

AUSTRIA
Government: Parliamentary Democracy
Capital: Vienna
Area: 31,900 sq. mi.
Population: 8 million
Language: German
Currency: Euro

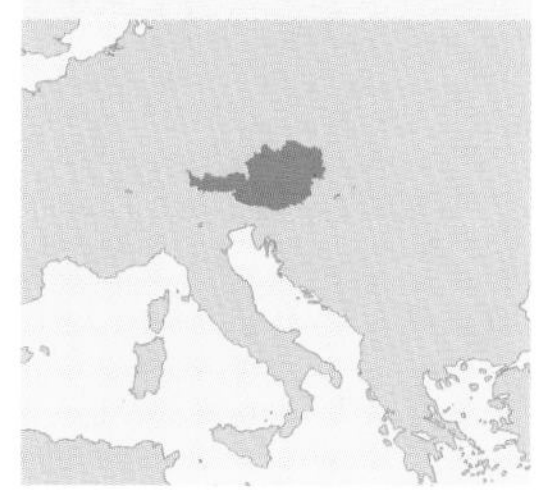

▽ The **Aztecs** worshiped the gods of war, rain, sun, and wind, and they carried out human sacrifices to win the gods' favor. Captives taken in battle were killed by priests, who cut out their still-beating hearts using ceremonial daggers made of stone.

Australia *see* page 32

Austria

Today, Austria is barely bigger than Maine. But once it was one of the largest and most powerful nations in **Europe**. For almost 700 years, from 1278 to 1918, Austria was ruled by a dynasty of kings and queens called the **Hapsburgs**. Their lands covered most of central Europe. The Austrian Empire collapsed after **World War I**. However, there are many relics of the mighty Hapsburg emperors. Vienna, Austria's capital city, is filled with beautiful churches, castles, statues, and parks.

Ayers Rock *see* Uluru

Aztecs

The Aztecs were a civilization that created a powerful empire in **Mexico** during the 1300s and 1400s. Aztec emperors used well-trained warriors to conquer nearby peoples. The Aztecs built large cities and erected stone **pyramids** with broad stairways leading to a temple at the top. The last Aztec ruler was Montezuma II. He was killed by Spanish troops led by Hernando **Cortes** in 1520.

AUSTRALIA

Australia is the world's smallest and driest continent. It is a huge island about three fourths the size of Europe.

Sydney is Australia's oldest and largest city. It is built around a large bay on the country's east coast. The dramatic shape of the Sydney Opera House has made it world-famous.

DESERTS AND PLAINS

Much of Australia is dry, flat desert. The rest of inland Australia is covered with areas of grass and scattered trees and bushes. These hot plains are some of the world's most remote and thinly populated areas. The Australians have a special name for them—the outback.

MOUNTAINS AND FORESTS

Australia has few mountain ranges. The main one is the Great Dividing Range, which runs down the east coast. It separates the vast inland deserts from a strip of fertile land by the sea. Forests of eucalyptus trees grow on the mountain slopes.

Lush rain forests flourish in the far northeast of the country, where the climate is much wetter. Tasmania is a large, mountainous island off the southeastern tip of Australia.

CORAL REEFS

One of Australia's most spectacular natural wonders is the Great Barrier Reef, which lies off the coast of Queensland. It stretches for over 1,240 mi. (2,000km), and is made up of more than 2,500 smaller reefs and coral islands.

▽ *The Great Barrier Reef is home to a tremendous variety of sea life.*

The didgeridoo is an aboriginal instrument that produces a deep, droning sound.

HISTORY

The first inhabitants of Australia were aboriginal peoples. They wandered across the country, hunting and gathering food. In the late 1700s settlers began to arrive from Great Britain, searching for a new way of life. Today, Australia retains strong links with Britain, and its head of state is still the British monarch. However, its government is completely independent. Most Australians live in large coastal cities, such as Sydney, Melbourne, and Perth.

PACIFIC POWER

Australia is one of the main economic powers in the Pacific. Ranchers raise huge herds of cattle and sheep on the inland plains where it is too dry for crops. Australia's sheep stations produce one third of the world's wool. Mining and wine making are also very important.

AUSTRALIA FACT FILE

Area: 2,937,800 sq. mi.
Highest mountain: Mt. Kosciuszko, 7,307 ft.
Largest lake: Eyre, 5,941 sq. mi.
Longest river: Murray, 1,605 sq. mi.
Number of states: 6 (Western Australia, South Australia, Queensland, New South Wales, Victoria, and Tasmania)
Number of territories: 2 (Northern Territory and Australian Capital Territory)
Government: Federal state system
Capital: Canberra
Largest city: Sydney, 3.7 million
Population: 19 million
Language: English
Currency: Australian dollar

SEE ALSO
Aboriginal people, Canberra, Desert, Emu, Great Barrier Reef, Marsupial, Sydney, Uluru

A WORLD APART

Australia became an island 65 million years ago. Since then, its plants and animals have gradually evolved (changed) into new and different forms. Many species are unique to Australia—they do not live anywhere else.

Australia's eucalyptus trees have fire-resistant bark and can grow in desert conditions. Typical Australian animals include koalas, kangaroos, and wombats, which are all marsupials. Unlike any other mammals, female marsupials have a special pouch on their belly in which they carry their young offspring.

▽ *Kangaroos have become so common that in many areas they are pests.*

Babbage, Charles

Charles Babbage (1792–1871) was a British inventor and mathematician who is often called the father of the computer. In 1833 he began working on an analytical engine, which was intended to perform any arithmetical calculation. Although Babbage's engine worked by using wheels and levers, it contained the key parts of a modern **computer**—including a memory. Numbers and instructions were to be fed in on punched cards. However, Babbage's invention was never finished.

△ Charles **Babbage** with his mechanical calculating machine, which he built in the 1830s but never completed. It is now in the Science Museum in, London, England.

Babylon

Babylon was one of the greatest cities of the ancient world. It lay on a fertile plain between the Tigris and Euphrates rivers in a region that is today called **Iraq**. Babylon rivaled even **Egypt** in its wealth and splendor.

The city of Babylon was founded in around 2300 B.C., and it continued to flourish for 2,000 years. It became a major center of trade and religion. The Babylonian people were also skilled in **mathematics** and **astronomy**. A strong Babylonian king, Nebuchadnezzar (ruled from 605–562 B.C.), built magnificent palaces and pyramid-shaped temples. He also built the Hanging Gardens of Babylon, one of the **Seven Wonders** of the ancient world. The Gardens were filled with plants and flowers, which cascaded down high stone terraces.

▽ **Babylon** was the capital of the Babylonian empire. Its main entrance, the impressive Ishtar Gate, was guarded by two large fortresses. Inside the city walls were temples, palaces, and the famous Hanging Gardens of Babylon.

Bach, Johann Sebastian

Johann Sebastian Bach (1685–1750) was one of the greatest composers of all time. He was born in Eisenach, **Germany**, into a musical family. From an early age Bach played the **violin** and the viola. At the age of 38, Bach moved to Leipzig, where he lived for the rest of his life. There he wrote some of his greatest pieces of **music**—mostly for choirs and for the **organ**.

When Bach died, his music was forgotten almost at once. Nearly one hundred years passed before people rediscovered his music and realized what a genius he had been.

Bach composed hundreds of pieces of music, but his most famous works are the Brandenburg Concertos, the "St. Matthew Passion," and the Mass in B Minor.

Bacteria

Bacteria are tiny living things that cannot be seen with the naked eye. They are some of the simplest kinds of life. Bacteria are more like **plants** than **animals**. They come in various shapes—some are rodlike, some spiraled, and others are round.

There are thousands of different kinds of bacteria. They are found in huge numbers almost everywhere you look. Many bacteria live in the **soil**. They help break down animal and vegetable matter and make the soil rich. Some bacteria even live inside our bodies. They help with the digestion of our food.

Bacteria multiply extremely fast. Some of them can divide in half every 20 minutes. From a single bacterium there can be millions of bacteria made in just a few hours.

Although most bacteria are harmless, some cause **diseases**. These kinds are known as germs. Pimples and boils are caused by bacteria. A few are deadly once they get inside the human body. We now have **antibiotics** (drugs) such as penicillin that destroy bacteria. But because bacteria multiply so quickly, they change into new kinds of bacteria that are not affected by the drugs. New drugs have to be made to kill the new bacteria.

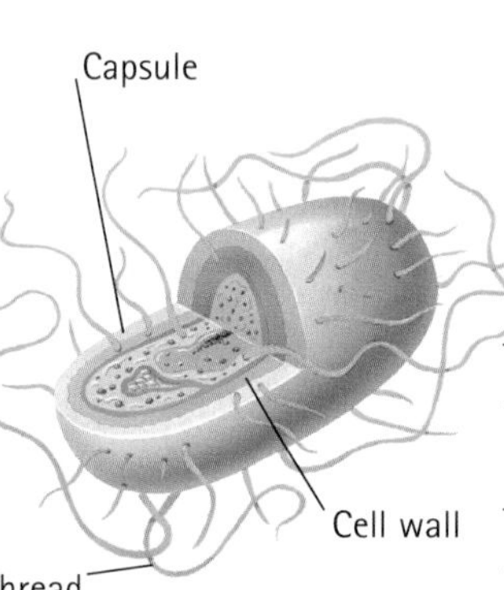

Bacteria are simple cells. They are surrounded by a cell wall and a protective outer capsule. Some are covered with threads that help them move or attach themselves to other cells.

Badger

Badgers are **mammals** that are related to ferrets, weasels, and **otters**. They have thickset bodies, long blunt claws for digging, and powerful jaws. There are several kinds of badgers, including the Old World badger, the American badger, and the honey badger, or ratel, of Africa and India.

People rarely see badgers during the day because they are nocturnal (active at night). After sunset they emerge from their underground dens to begin feeding. Badgers eat almost anything, from roots and fruits to worms, mice, and other small animals.

The **badger** of Europe and Asia has a striking pattern of stripes on its head.

Bahamas *see* Caribbean

Balboa, Vasco Núñez de

Vasco Núñez de Balboa (1475–1519) was a Spanish soldier and explorer who was the first European to set eyes on the **Pacific Ocean** in the New World. Balboa joined a Spanish expedition to **South America** in 1501, exploring the north coast of the continent. He later led an expedition across the narrow strip of land that is now known as the Isthmus of **Panama**. There, from a mountaintop, he looked down upon the Pacific Ocean.

Balkans

The Balkans are a group of countries in southeastern Europe. They include **Greece**, **Albania**, **Romania**, **Bulgaria**, **Bosnia-Herzegovina**, **Croatia**, **Serbia**, and the European part of **Turkey**. The Turks ruled much of this region from the 1300s to the 1800s. It was in the Balkans that Archduke Ferdinand of Austria was assassinated in 1914. This event triggered **World War I**.

German *Zeppelin* airship

Ballet

Ballet is a precise form of dance that is usually performed in a theater. A kind of ballet first appeared in **Italy** in the 1400s, but ballet as it is danced today began in **France**. Traditional, or classical, ballet follows strict rules. There are standard positions for the arms, legs, and hands and set movements that make the **dance** flow smoothly.

Classical ballet makes use of splendid costumes, elaborate scenery, and full **orchestras**. Many ballets tell a story, but the dancers do not speak any words. They **mime** (act out) the story using their bodies. *Giselle*, a tragic story of a young village girl who dies in love-stricken grief, was written by Adolphe Adam and first staged in 1841. The Russian composer **Tchaikovsky** wrote three long-time favorites: *Swan Lake* (1890), *Sleeping Beauty* (1890), and *The Nutcracker* (1892).

Modern ballets often look different from classical ones. They borrow dance steps from many different styles of dance. Sometimes instead of telling a story, they dwell on certain moods.

△ A modern **balloon** uses a gas burner to heat the air inside a lightweight bag. This takes the balloon up because hot air rises.

▽ Professional **ballet** dancers spend a long time practicing to improve their timing and balance.

Balloon and Airship

Balloons and airships, or blimps, use gases that are lighter than air to fly. Balloons can only drift in the wind, but airships can be flown and steered.

The first piloted balloon was launched in 1783. It was built by the French **Montgolfier brothers**. A fire was burned under the balloon to fill it up with hot air. Hot air rises, lifting the balloon. In the same year the first gas-filled balloon took to the skies. The gas used was **hydrogen**. To descend, the pilot opened a valve and let out some of the gas. Today balloons are used to study the **weather**, and hot-air ballooning is a popular sport.

Most airships are larger than balloons. The simplest kind looks like a cigar-shaped bag with a cabin and **engines** hanging under it. The first successful airship flew in 1852. By the early 1900s there was a number of airship passenger services. But a series of disasters brought the age of airships to an end. They were not safe enough for passenger use because they were filled with dangerous hydrogen gas. Modern airships are lifted with helium, a safer gas that does not catch on fire. They are used for advertising and for televising sports events.

Baltic States

The Baltic States are Estonia, Latvia, and Lithuania. They are situated north of **Poland** on the southern shore of the Baltic Sea. Formerly part of the Russian Empire, the Baltic States became independent countries in 1918. In 1940, during **World War II**, they were seized by the **Soviet Union** and became Soviet republics. German troops invaded and controlled the Baltic States until they were driven out by the Soviet Army at the end of the war.

In 1991, while the Soviet Union was in a state of political turmoil, Estonia, Latvia, and Lithuania declared their independence and became completely free from foreign control. They have kept their own literature, traditions, and languages, although most people can speak Russian.

Bandicoot

Bandicoots live in **Australia** and **New Guinea**. Like **kangaroos**, they belong to a large group of mammals called **marsupials**. Like all marsupials, female bandicoots have pouches of loose skin in which they carry their young. Bandicoots have grayish-brown fur and are similar in size and shape to rats, although some can be larger. They make their nests in underground burrows and feed on insects, worms, and roots.

Bangladesh

Bangladesh is an Asian country that came into being in 1971. Before then it was part of **Pakistan**. It is one of the world's most densely populated countries, and most of the people are very poor. In the rainy season branches of the **Ganges** and Brahmaputra rivers flood the flatland. A cyclone in 1991 killed 125,000 people.

After years of rule by the military Bangladesh adopted a parliamentary system in 1991, but there is still political turmoil. The largest cities in Bangladesh are Dhaka, the capital, and Chittagong, the main port. Rice, jute, tea, and sugercane are the main crops.

BANGLADESH
Government: Parliamentary Democracy
Capital: Dhaka
Area: 51,600 sq. mi.
Population: 131 million
Language: Bengali
Currency: Taka

Bank

Banks are companies that take people's **money** for safekeeping. When you first put money in the bank, you are opening an account. Every time you put more money in, you make a deposit. If you want to take money out, you make a withdrawal. Banks do not only hold money. They also make loans to people and businesses, and they provide other ways of making saving and spending easier.

Barbados *see* Caribbean

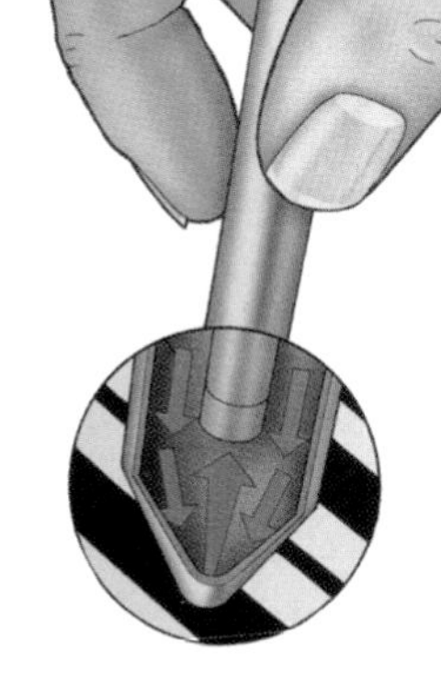

Bar codes are patterns of stripes that can be read by a laser scanner. Each stripe stands for a number.

Bar code

The pattern of black and white stripes printed onto many cartons and packages is called a bar code. The stripes make a number using a **binary system**, and each product that you buy has a different number. At the store's checkout a machine called a scanner reads the bar code using a **laser** light. The scanner turns the bar code into a signal that goes to the store's cash register. A **computer** inside the cash register searches its memory to find the price of each item and calculates the final cost. It also works out how many products have been sold and orders new supplies when necessary.

Barometer

High **air** pressure is a sign of good **weather**. Low air pressure is a sign of changing and bad weather. A barometer is an instrument used to measure such changes.

There are two kinds of barometers, the aneroid and the **mercury**. The aneroid is more widely used. Inside it is a flat metal box. The air inside the box is at a very low pressure. The metal walls of the box are so thin they will bend easily, but they do not collapse because a spring keeps them apart. As air pressure drops, the spring pushes the sides of the box apart. As it rises they are squeezed together. These movements are picked up by levers and gears that move a pointer around to show different measurements.

Basketball is played at a fast and furious pace on indoor courts. There are two teams of five players.

Baseball

Baseball is the national **sport** of the **United States**. No one knows exactly how it began, but it may have come from a similar English game called rounders. Baseball was probably first played in **New York**, where Alexander Cartwright founded the Knickerbocker Baseball Club in 1845.

Today baseball is played between two teams of nine people each. It is played on a field that has a square, known as the diamond, marked on it. The diamond has four bases 90 ft. (27.5m) apart. In the game each batter tries to advance around the bases safely and score a run. A team bats until three players are out.

The pitcher throws a ball to the batter, who stands in an area called the home plate. When the batter swings at a pitch and misses, or if they hit a foul ball, it is called a strike. Three strikes and the batter is out. A batter can also be caught out, or is out if a fielder picks up and throws the ball to a base before the batter reaches it.

Baseball is big business in the United States. It is also popular in Central and South America, Cuba, Japan, and the Philippines.

Basketball

Basketball is an American **sport** that has won popularity all over the world. It has been played at the **Olympics** since 1936. Professional basketball is played by two teams of five players. Each team tries to score points by shooting a ball into a net, or basket. The basket is 10 ft. (3m) from the floor and 18 in. (46cm) in diameter at the top. The ball can be advanced by bouncing it along the floor (dribbling) or by passing it to a teammate. A player cannot take more than one step while holding the ball. The opposing players try to block them without making contact. Successful shots are worth two or three points depending on how close to the basket the player is standing.

Bat

Bats are the only **mammals** that can truly be said to fly. Their wings do not have feathers but are made of a sheet of skin stretched between the long "finger" bones. In most bats the wings are also joined to the legs and tail.

There are nearly 1,000 different kinds of bats. Most of them live in the tropics and warm parts of the world. Where winters are cold, bats **hibernate**. Many bats eat ripe fruit, especially in tropical areas. Other bats feed on insects, which they catch in midair.

Most bats are nocturnal—they sleep in the day and fly at night. Scientists have shown in experiments that bats do not need good eyesight for flying. They find their way in the dark by using a **sonar** system. They make a series of high-pitched shrieks and use the echoes bouncing off objects to tell where they are.

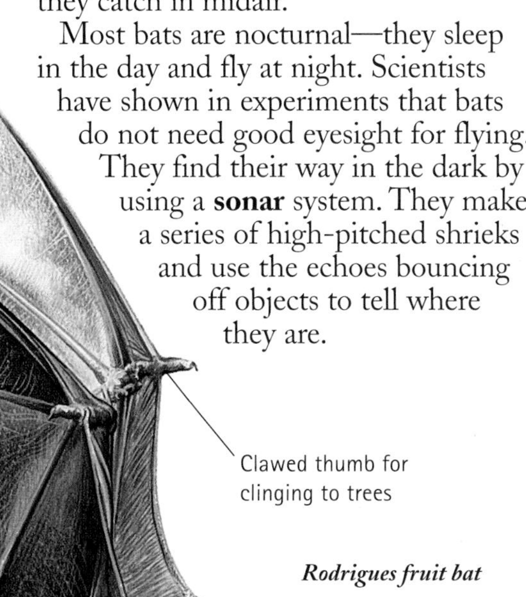

Rodrigues fruit bat

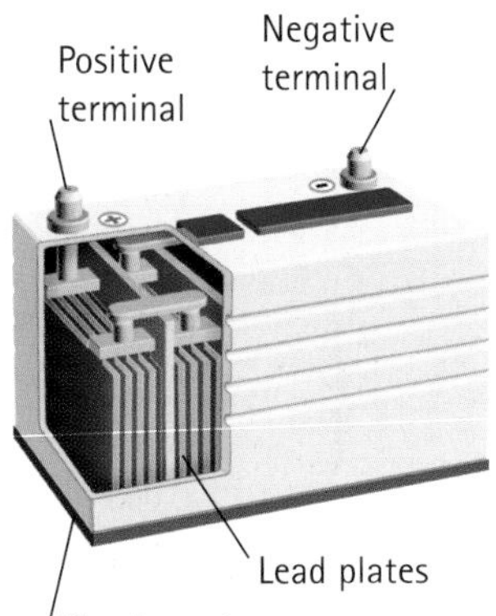

△ Most vehicles have a **battery** that powers their electrical systems. While a vehicle is running, its engine drives a generator that recharges the battery.

Battery

Batteries make **electricity** from chemicals stored inside them. Dry batteries such as those used in many radios, flashlights, and calculators make electricity for only a limited time. In dry batteries a pastelike chemical mixture is packed around a **carbon** rod. When the chemicals are used up, the battery cannot be recharged.

Car batteries can be recharged with electricity and used again and again. They contain pairs of **lead** and lead oxide plates covered in diluted sulfuric **acid**. As the battery is used the chemicals in the plates change until no more electricity is produced. But feeding an electric current into the battery changes the chemicals in the plates back to their original state. A current will then flow again.

The images on the **Bayeux Tapestry** were woven in eight colors of wool on small strips of linen, which were then sewn together to make one long strip.

Bayeux Tapestry

After **William the Conqueror** invaded England in 1066, one of his relatives had a **tapestry** embroidered to record the conquest. This masterpiece is called the Bayeux Tapestry. It is a piece of linen 230 ft. (70m) long on which there are 72 colorful scenes telling the story of William's victory. Latin words explain what is happening in the pictures. The tapestry is kept under glass in a museum in Bayeux, France.

Bear

Bears are found in most of the world except for Australia and Africa. They have short, powerful limbs and heavy, broad heads with strong jaws. They also have long claws for digging and tearing. Their eyesight is poor, but their sense of **smell** is excellent. Although bears usually move slowly and look clumsy, they can run extremely fast if they have to, and most bears can climb trees.

There are seven species of bears, which include several of the world's largest

Alaskan brown bear

Sun bear

Polar bear

European brown bear

◁ Despite their size, **bears** are usually shy. They attack only if disturbed or cornered.

carnivores. The largest bear of all is the Alaskan brown bear, or Kodiak, which can weigh over 1,650 lbs (750kg) It is actually the same species as the grizzly of western North America and the brown bear of Europe and Siberia. The polar bear lives in snowy **Arctic** regions, where its all-white coat provides it with perfect camouflage. All of the five remaining bears have black coats. They are the American black bear, the Asiatic black bear, the spectacled bear, the sloth bear, and the sun bear. Bears that inhabit cold areas **hibernate** for the winter.

Brown and black bears eat almost anything, including leaves, roots, fruits, honey, worms, fish, and small animals. Polar bears hunt small whales and seals. Sloth bears are more fussy—they only eat ants and **termites**.

Beaver

Beavers are large **rodents** more than 3 ft. (1m) long and weigh over 55 lbs (25kg). They live in woods by the side of lakes and rivers in many parts of North America and Europe. Beavers are good swimmers and can stay underwater for up to 15 minutes. They have a broad, flat tail covered in scaly skin. The tail is used for steering when they swim. Beavers eat leaves, twigs, and bark, mainly from alder and willow **trees**.

Beavers need pools in which to build their homes, and often block up, or dam, streams with mud and sticks to make one. They cut down trees with their sharp teeth and drag them to the pool to strengthen the dam.

Becket, Thomas à

Thomas à Becket (1118–1170) was an Archbishop of Canterbury who angered King Henry II of England by demanding special rights for the Church. He was exiled but returned later and once more angered the king.

After years of quarrels, Henry is said to have shouted, "Who will rid me of this turbulent priest?" Four knights mistakenly thought the king wanted Becket killed, and murdered him in Canterbury Cathedral in 1170.

△ **Thomas à Becket** was Archbishop of Canterbury during the 1100s. He was brutally murdered in his own cathedral for standing up against King Henry II. In 1173, three years after his death, Becket was made a saint.

Bee

There are many different kinds of bees, but the best known is the honeybee. Honeybees live in hives or colonies of about 50,000 worker bees. Each hive of honeybees is established by a large queen bee. She mates with stingless male bees called drones.

▽ **Beavers** dam streams with mud, sticks, and trees that they have cut down. When a pool has formed behind the dam, they build a safe island home, known as a lodge. The lodge has an underwater entrance.

Inside a honeybee hive there are hundreds of cells made of wax. The queen bee lays eggs in the cells. Larvae (grubs) hatch out of the eggs and are fed by the workers. Worker bees collect nectar and pollen from flowers and take it back to the hive to be made into honey for food.

Queen honeybee

There are several hundred drones in each hive, and their only purpose in life is to find a queen bee to mate with. After mating they die.

Worker bees are all female and do not breed. A worker bee's life is very short, usually about four weeks, so the queen has to lay many **eggs** to provide enough bees. From time to time a new queen hatches. One of the queens leaves the hive with a swarm of about half the workers to seek another home.

Beekeepers are people who look after hives of honeybees and collect the sweet honey that the bees produce. They feed the bees **sugar** syrup to replace the honey they remove.

There are other types of bees that do not live in large colonies. These are called solitary bees.

Beethoven, Ludwig van

Ludwig van Beethoven (1770–1827) was a German musician who composed many great pieces of **music** that have become famous all over the world. His compositions included concertos, symphonies, choral, and chamber music (see also **orchestra**). When he was young, Beethoven became well known as a brilliant pianist. He met **Mozart**, and he later studied under another famous composer, **Haydn**. Beethoven began to go deaf at the age of 32, but he continued to compose music even when he was totally deaf.

Beetle

Beetles are **insects**. More than 300,000 different kinds of beetles are known. Some beetles are as small as a pinhead. Others are very large. The African goliath beetle grows up to 4 in. (10cm) long and can weigh 3.5 oz. (100g).

Beetles start their lives as eggs that hatch into grubs, or larvae. The larvae then turn into chrysalises, or pupae, before the adult beetles emerge.

Many beetles and their larvae are destructive pests. Weevils, wireworms, and Colorado beetles do great damage to crops, and woodworms eat through timber. However, some beetles can be extremely useful. Ladybugs are small, colorful beetles that eat harmful insects such as aphids. Burying beetles and dung beetles are also useful—they clear away dead animals and dung, which the beetles later use for food.

Burying beetles bury the corpses of small birds and mammalsby digging soil from under them. Then the beetles lay their eggs on the buried animals for their grubs to feed on when they hatch.

Beijing (Peking)

Beijing, formerly called Peking, is the capital of **China**. In 1267 the Mongol

Beethoven was one of the greatest pianists of his time. He played to Mozart in 1787 when he was only 17.

conqueror Kublai Khan made it the capital of his empire. Modern Beijing is a major center of industry and learning. Its population is more than 11 million. In the center of the city are the palaces of the ancient Chinese emperors. Ordinary citizens were not allowed to step inside the palaces' high walls, which is why the imperial zone of Beijing became known as the Forbidden City.

Giraffe beetle

Beetles come in many shapes, but they all have six pairs of legs and a hard case covering their back.

Belgium

Belgium is a small country situated between **France**, **Germany,** and the **Netherlands**. Its capital is Brussels. Belgium's population consists of two main groups: the Germanic Flemings of the north, and the French-speaking Walloons of the south. Because of its central and strategic position, Belgium has been invaded and fought over throughout the course of European history. Today, the headquarters of the **European Union** (EU) and **NATO** are both in Brussels.

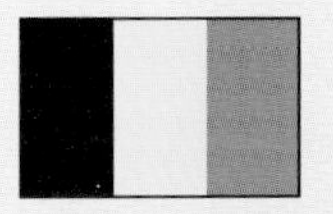

BELGIUM
Government: Constitutional monarchy
Capital: Brussels
Area: 11,700 sq. mi.
Population: 10 million
Languages: Flemish, French, and German
Currency: Euro

Bell, Alexander Graham

Alexander Graham Bell (1847–1922) was an American who invented the **telephone**. Through his work with devices to help the deaf, Bell became interested in sending voices over long distances. On March 10, 1876 his voice was transmitted by telephone for the first time.

Berlin

Berlin is the largest city in **Germany**, and has been the German capital since 1990. It is one of Europe's main cultural and economic centers.

Berlin was largely destroyed by heavy bombing during **World War II** (1939–1945), but at the end of the war rebuilding was rapid. In 1945, when Germany was split into two countries, East and West, Berlin was divided into four zones between the Americans, British, French, and Soviets.

In 1948 the Soviets quarreled with the other allies and blockaded Berlin by cutting its road and rail links with West Germany. But Great Britain and the U.S. flew in supplies to keep the city going. After a year the Soviets gave up and reopened the roads and railroads.

In 1961 the communist government of East Germany built the Berlin Wall to separate the eastern and western parts of the city (see **communism**). It was difficult for people to cross between the two halves of the divided city. In 1989, after massive public protests, the Berlin Wall was demolished.

Bernhardt, Sarah

Born in France, Sarah Bernhardt (1844–1923) became one of the most famous actresses of her time. Her excellent speaking voice won her the admiration of audiences everywhere she went. Her best known performance was in *Camille*, a play by French writer Alexandre Dumas (see **theater**).

Bible

The Bible is the sacred book of two religions: **Judaism** and **Christianity**. Jews and Christians consider the Bible to be the Word of God. Many of their religious beliefs, ceremonies, and holidays are based on the text of the Bible.

The Bible is in two parts. The first is called the Old Testament, which begins by describing God's

At the heart of **Beijing** are many palaces dating from the age of the emperors who ruled China for 2,000 years until 1911.

One story in the **Bible's** Old Testament tells how God spoke to Moses from a burning bush. God told Moses to lead the Jewish people out of Egypt and into Israel.

creation of the heavens and the earth. Then it records the history of the Jewish people and the teachings of their prophets before the birth of **Jesus**. The second part of the Bible, called the New Testament, records the life and sayings of Jesus and his disciples (personal followers).

For centuries all Bibles were handwritten. The first printed one was produced in the mid-1400s. The Bible has always been the best-selling book—more than 2.5 billion copies have been sold since 1816. It has been translated into over 1,500 languages.

Bicycle

The bicycle is a two-wheeled vehicle powered by its rider, who turns two pedals by foot. The earliest bicycles were invented in the 1700s. They were simply two **wheels** joined by a rod with a seat on top. Riders pushed them along the ground with their feet.

The first bicycles with pedals did not appear until 1865. These machines were known as "bone shakers" because the seats had no springs. The next major development was the penny farthing, which had an enormous front wheel and a tiny rear wheel. The modern style of bicycle appeared in the 1880s. It had a chain-driven rear wheel and air-filled tires, and this basic style has changed very little since then except for the addition of **gears**.

Penny farthing **bicycles** were heavy and clumsy. They had solid tires and a step at the back to help the rider climb on.

The modern racing **bicycle** is made from lightweight materials. It is streamlined in shape and has as many as 15 or 20 gears.

Binary system

The binary system is a number system that uses only two numerals – 0 and 1. Our everyday decimal system uses ten numerals – 0 to 9. In the decimal system you multiply a number by 10 by moving it one place to the left: 20, 200, and so on. In the binary system when you move a numeral one place to the left, you multiply its value by two. A 1 by itself is 1. Move it a place to the left and it becomes 1 times 2, or 2. It is written 10. Move it another place to the left and it becomes 1 times 2 times 2, or 4. It is written 100.

Electronic devices such as **computers** use the binary system to perform calculations and other operations.

Biochemistry

Biochemistry is the study of chemical reactions that take place inside the tiny **cells** that make up all living things. It is a huge subject. Biochemists find out about the **food** people have to eat to be healthy. They help farmers by finding out what foods are needed by plants and animals. They help fight **disease** by developing chemicals that kill harmful **bacteria**. Biochemists are also discovering more and more about the chemistry that makes us what we are (see **cloning** and **genetics**).

Biology

Biology is the study of living things and how they relate to each other. The part of biology that deals with **plants** is called **botany**. The study of **animals** is known as zoology. Biologists study everything from the tiniest amoeba, which consists of just one **cell**, to a mighty oak tree or a human being.

One of the earliest biologists was the ancient Greek thinker **Aristotle**, who was the first to dissect, or cut open, and classify animals. There was not much interest in biology for more than a thousand years until the **Renaissance**, when scholars such as Leonardo **da Vinci** tried to discover how living things grew and worked. In the 1600s William **Harvey** showed how **blood** travels around the body.

The invention of the **microscope** opened up whole new areas of study for biologists. They were able to learn more about the animal and plant cells that are the building blocks of life. The study of other microscopic organisms, such as **bacteria**, helped people like Louis **Pasteur** understand more about disease and how to prevent it.

In the 1800s the English naturalist Charles **Darwin** revolutionized biology with his theory of **evolution**. Today biology is divided into many separate sciences.

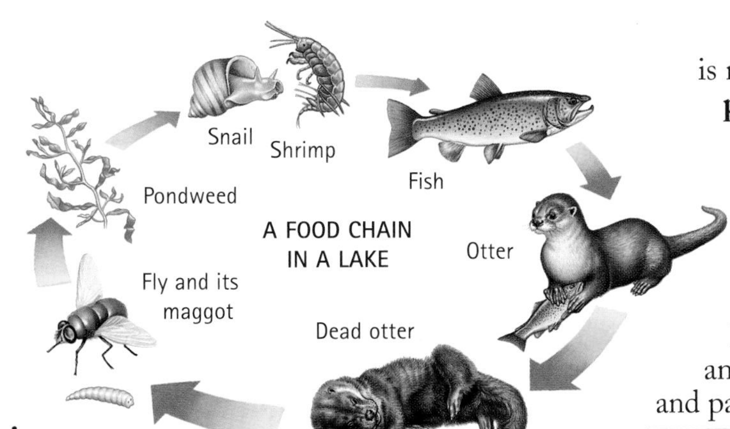

△ **Biology** is the study of living things. The complex links that connect plants and animals are known as food chains. For example, in the food chain above pondweed produces energy from the sun, soil, and water. It is eaten by snails and shrimp, which are in turn eaten by fish. An otter eats the fish. Fly maggots feed on the dead otter, and return nutrients from its body to the soil and water.

Birds *see* page 45

Birth control

Birth control is the means by which people can control the number of children they have. It is sometimes known as family planning. Birth control has been used since ancient times, but modern methods were not widespread until the 1800s and 1900s.

There are many methods of birth control. Some of them work by stopping the sperm of the male from fertilizing the egg, or ovum, of the female. This is known as contraception.

Some people are forbidden by their religion to practice certain kinds of birth control. However, birth control is now encouraged in many countries with large **populations**.

Bison *see* Cattle

Black Death

The Black Death was a terrible **disease** that was at its worst during the **Middle Ages**. During an outbreak in the 1300s, 25 million people died of the disease. About one third of all the people in Europe were killed by it. The Black Death is now called bubonic **plague**. It is carried by the **fleas** on **rats**. When a flea sucks the blood of a rat that has the disease and the flea later bites another rat or a person, the disease is passed on. It spreads very quickly and can lead to a slow and painful death.

Black hole

Stars are made up mostly of **hydrogen** gas. It is turning this hydrogen into helium that makes stars like our **sun** shine and give out heat. When a massive star uses up all its hydrogen fuel, it collapses. This collapse is called a supernova explosion. All that is left after such an explosion is a tiny star. The material in this star is so squashed together—so dense—that even **light** waves find it impossible to escape from them. Because light waves cannot get out, we call them black holes. Astronomers have never seen a black hole because they are invisible, but

▽ **Black holes** are shaped like funnels. Objects are pulled into the funnel, like water going down a drain. Once inside, the space debris cannot escape.

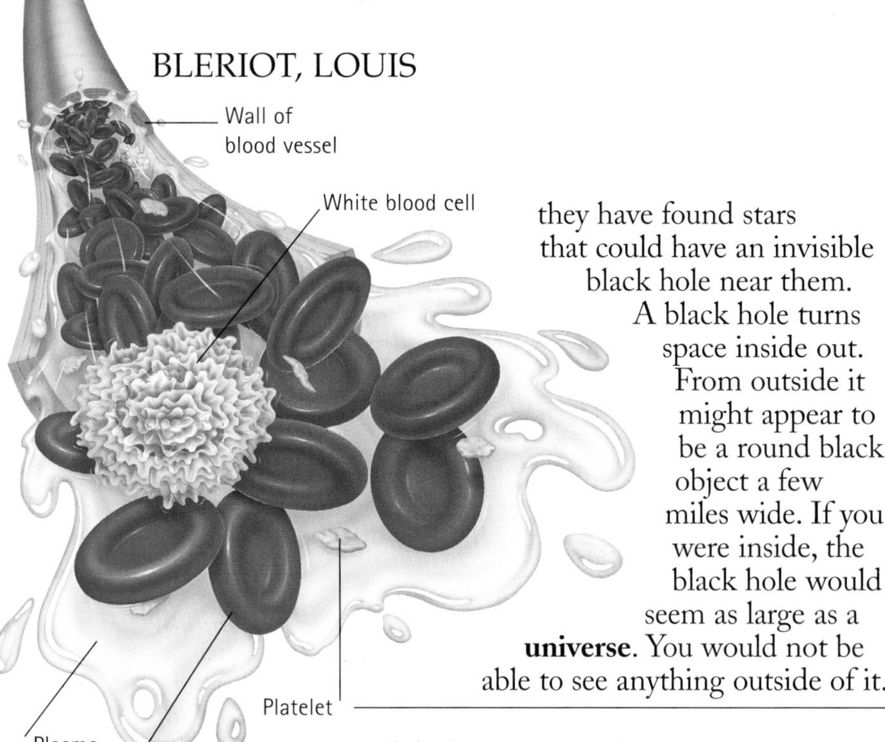

Blood travels around the body through a network of thousands of blood vessels. Each drop of blood contains 250 million red blood cells, 375,000 white blood cells and about 16 million platelets.

they have found stars that could have an invisible black hole near them. A black hole turns space inside out. From outside it might appear to be a round black object a few miles wide. If you were inside, the black hole would seem as large as a **universe**. You would not be able to see anything outside of it.

Blériot, Louis

Louis Blériot (1872–1936) was a famous French airman. He was a pioneer of aviation and designed and built a number of early airplanes. On July 25, 1909 Blériot took off from Calais in one of his own **aircraft**. Twenty-seven minutes later he touched down in Dover on the south coast of England, becoming the first man to fly the English Channel. Blériot went on to design other aircraft and became the owner of a large aircraft company.

Blood

Blood is the fluid that nourishes our bodies and removes waste products. The **heart** pumps blood around the body, through a complex system of blood vessels—**arteries**, **veins,** and capillaries. Blood takes in food from the digestive system and **oxygen** from the **lungs** and carries them to all of the **cells** in the body. Each cell takes exactly what it needs from the blood, and the blood carries away cell waste, including **water** and carbon dioxide. Blood also carries special body chemicals to where they are needed, kills germs and keeps the body at the right temperature.

Blood is made in the marrow of the **bones**. The adult human body contains about 13 pints (6*l*) of blood. This blood is made up of a pale liquid called plasma, and many millions of red blood cells, or corpuscles. Corpuscles are tiny red disks that give the blood its color.

The blood also contains smaller numbers of white blood cells, or white corpuscles. White corpuscles attack germs that enter the body by absorbing them. Often many white corpuscles are killed in the fight against disease or infection. Large numbers of dead white corpuscles collect as pus. Other blood particles, called platelets, help our blood clot when we bleed. This helps scratches and other wounds heal more quickly.

We can all be classified into blood groups A, B, AB, or O, according to the type of blood we have. Blood groups are important when patients are given blood transfusions. Transfusions are given to replace either diseased blood or blood that has been lost in an injury. The blood a person is given is generally the same blood type as their own.

Louis **Blériot** made his epic flight across the English Channel in an aeroplane that he had designed and built. In doing so, he won a prize of £1,000 offered by the *Daily Mail* newspaper.

Blues

The blues is a kind of **music** that developed among black musicians in the **United States**. Blues music was first played in the late 1800s, in the southern states near the mouth of the **Mississippi River**. It is an extremely varied type of music, and many blues musicians have created their own individual styles of playing.

The main instruments used in traditional, or country, blues are the classical guitar, **piano,** and harmonica. Other instruments used include **guitars** and **drums**. The words to the songs are frequently sad, and are often about loneliness or love problems.

The blues influenced a style of piano music called "boogie-woogie," which

continued on page 46

BIRDS

Birds come in all shapes and sizes and live all over the world. They are the only animals to have feathers.

The peregrine falcon is the fastest flying bird. It can accelerates to 198 mph (320km/h) when swooping to attack other birds.

The anhinga uses its spearlike bill to stab fish.

WORLD OF BIRDS

Birds are vertebrates (animals with backbones). There are nearly 9,000 different types of birds. They range in size from tiny hummingbirds that weigh less than .07 oz. (2g) to the colossal ostrich, which reaches over 332 lbs (150kg) and stands as high as an adult human.

Birds can live almost everywhere, including hot deserts, polar ice caps, and in the middle of cities. Some rain forests are home to more than 400 species (varieties) of birds.

Toucans have massive bills for splitting open tough fruit. Each kind of toucan has a different colored bill.

RAISING A FAMILY

All birds lay eggs. After laying her eggs the female sits on them to keep them warm. This is called incubation. Sometimes both parents take turns to incubate the eggs. Eggs need at least ten days to hatch, and those of some birds take as long as two months.

Most birds build a nest to protect their eggs and young. Common nesting sites are trees, bushes, and cliffs. Some birds, such as pheasants and ducks, lay their eggs on the ground.

▽ *Barn swallows build a cup-shaped nest from dried mud. Feeding hungry chicks is hard work.*

The meadowlark has a beautiful song. Male birds sing to attract a female partner and to warn rival males to stay off their patch.

PERFECTLY FORMED

The appearance of a bird tells us a lot about what it eats and where it lives. For example, eagles have hooked beaks for tearing meat, and woodpeckers have sharp, pointed bills for hammering tree trunks. Waterbirds like swans need waterproof plumage and webbed feet for swimming on lakes and ponds. Birds that spend a lot of time in the air, such as swallows, often have long wings and streamlined bodies to help them fly fast and smoothly.

THE POWER OF FLIGHT

Birds developed from scaly reptiles that lived during the age of the dinosaurs. Their scales changed over millions of years into feathers, and their front legs became wings. Birds have hollow bones making them light in the air and strong breast muscles for working their wings. Large birds, such as eagles and storks, can flap their wings slowly and float, or soar, on air currents. Small birds need to flap their wings fast to stay in the air.

Some birds can fly thousands of miles. Their long journeys are called migrations. Other birds, like penguins, cannot fly at all.

The cassowary is a giant, flightless bird found in the rain forests of New Guinea and Australia.

LIVING TOGETHER

When it is time to breed, most birds get into pairs. To attract a suitable mate, the males sing or show off their plumage. They may also perform special dances or make dramatic display flights. Some birds breed together in large groups, or colonies. Each colony is made up of lots of breeding pairs.

▷ *Gannets nest on the ledges of sea cliffs.*

SEE ALSO
Albatross, Cuckoo, Dodo, Duck, Egg, Falcon, Feather, Hummingbird, Migration, Nest, Ostrich, Owl, Penguin, Woodpecker

Blues music was a major influence on jazz musicians such as Duke Ellington (1899–1974). They liked its strong rhythms and its very varied style.

was popular in the 1930s. Blues music also contributed to the development of **jazz** and has been a big influence on many rock musicians.

Boat

see **Ships and Boats**

Boer War

The Boer War (1899–1902) was fought in **South Africa** between the Boers—settlers who originally came from The **Netherlands**—and the British. The slow and badly led British troops were no match for the fast and determined Boers in the early days of the war. However, in the end Great Britain's overwhelming strength won. There were about 450,000 soldiers in the British armies during the Boer War, and only about 60,000 Boers.

Bolivia

BOLIVIA
Government: Republic
Capital: La Paz
Area: 1,098,581 sq. km
Population: 8.1 million
Language: Spanish
Currency: Boliviano

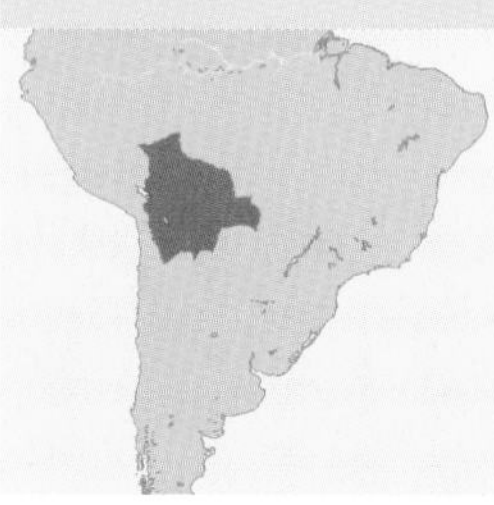

Bolivia is a landlocked country in central **South America**, west of **Brazil**. Most of Bolivia is an enormous plain, stretching from the Brazilian border to the eastern foothills of the **Andes** Mountains. High in the Andes lies the great Bolivian plateau, over 13,120 ft. (4,000m) high. Two thirds of Bolivia's people live here. The capital is La Paz, the highest capital in the world, and Lake Titicaca, at 12,503 ft. (3,812m) above sea level, is one of the highest lakes in the world.

Bolivia was ruled by **Spain** from 1532 until 1825. It gained independence with the help of Simón Bolívar, a Venezuelan general, after whom Bolivia is named. More than half the people are native Bolivians, one third are *mestizos* people who are part-European, part-Bolivian) and the rest are direct descendants of Europeans. Bolivia is the world's second largest producer of **tin**, and **mining** is the country's main industry.

Bone

Bones make up the hard framework that supports the flesh and organs of all **vertebrates** (animals with backbones). All bones are made up of the same thing, mostly calcium—an element found in limestone and chalk, and in certain foods, especially **milk** and **cheese**. Bones are hard on the outside but soft on the inside. Bone marrow, in the hollow center of the bone, is where new red **blood** cells are made.

The human **skeleton** has four kinds of bones: long bones, such as arm and leg bones; flat bones, such as the skull; short bones, including ankle and wrist bones; and irregular bones, such as those that make up the backbone. If bones are broken, they will join together again if they are rejoined or set properly. The **cells** in the broken ends of the bone produce a substance that helps the ends grow together again. A mended bone is as strong as it ever was. As people get older their bones become brittle and break more easily.

Book

Books are used for storing and passing on all kinds of knowledge, ideas, and stories. Some of the earliest books were made by the ancient Egyptians. These were written by hand on rolls of **paper** made from the papyrus plant.

By the time of the **Roman Empire** many books were handwritten on parchment or vellum. This material was made from animal **skin**. It was cut into sheets that were bound together to look much the same as a modern book. During the **Middle Ages**, monks made many beautiful books. These were carefully decorated, or illuminated, by hand with bright colors and sometimes gold and silver.

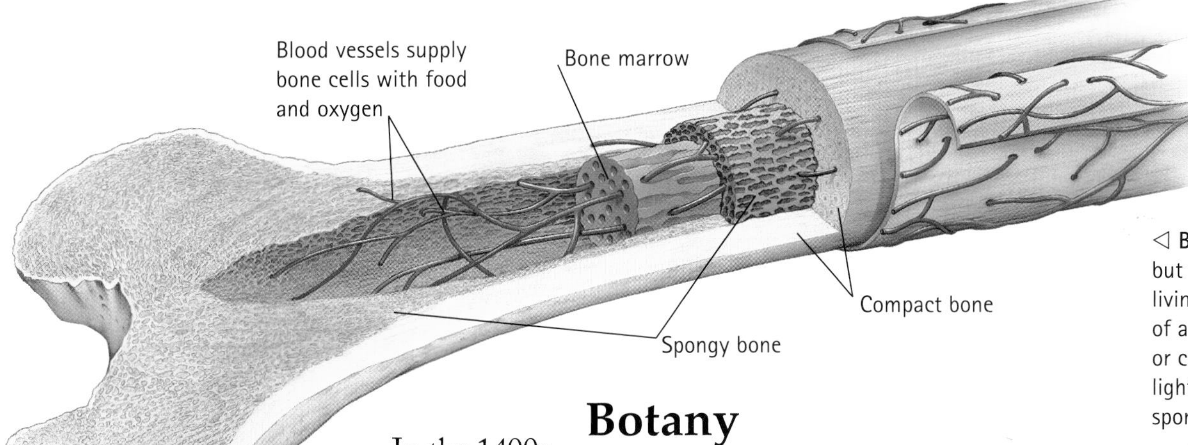

◁ **Bones** may look lifeless, but they are a mass of living cells. They are made of a very hard outer layer, or compact bone, and a lighter, inner layer, called spongy bone.

In the 1400s printing on paper was introduced to Europe. At first this was very slow because much of the work still had to be done by hand. Then Johannes **Gutenberg** invented a machine with movable type that could print books quickly. Today millions of books are produced every year in all the languages of the world.

Boomerang

The boomerang is a wooden throwing stick used mainly by the **aboriginal people** of Australia. There are two kinds. One is very heavy and is thrown straight at the target. The other is lighter. It is shaped in a special way so that when it is thrown skilfully, it is possible to make it return to the thrower.

Bosnia-Herzegovina

Bosnia-Herzegovina was formerly a republic of **Yugoslavia**, but it became independent in 1992. Its people are Croats, Muslims, and Serbs. Fighting broke out between the Bosnians and the Serbian-dominated Yugoslav army as the Serbs attempted to make Bosnia-Herzegovina part of Yugoslavia again. Muslims and Croats were forced out of parts of Bosnia conquered by the Serbs in a process called "ethnic cleansing."

The fighting in Bosnia-Herzegovina was some of the worst in Europe since **World War II**. A peace agreement was signed in 1995 with **NATO** troops remaining to enforce it.

Botany

Botany is the study of **plants** and how they grow. There are more than 400,000 different kinds of plants. They vary from tiny algae that can be seen only with a microscope, to massive redwood **trees** nearly 328 ft. (100m) high. Other types of plants include **grass**, **flowers**, **ferns**, **moss**, and fungi (see **fungus**).

Without plants there would be no animals because animals depend on plants for all of their food. There would be no **cattle** for us to eat if there was no grass for the cattle to eat. Animals also breathe the gas **oyxygen** that all plants release.

By studying the way in which the features of one generation of plants are passed on to the next generation, scientists are able to grow bigger and better crops. They can breed varieties that are better at fighting plant disease.

In 1753 the Swedish botanist Carl von Linné, who is usually known as Linnaeus, invented the first real system for naming plants. He gave every plant a name made up of two Latin words.

Botswana

Botswana is an African country that lies far from the sea. It is bordered by **Zimbabwe**, **South Africa**, and **Namibia**. In 1885 the country, then called Bechuanaland, came under British control. It gained independence in 1966. Botswana is a hot, dry country that includes the Kalahari Desert. Mining of **diamonds** and other minerals is the most valuable industry, but cattle raising and tourism are also important.

BOSNIA-HERZEGOVINA
Government: Republic
Capital: Sarajevo
Area: 19,700 sq mi.
Population: 3.9 million
Language: Serbo-Croatian
Currency: Marka

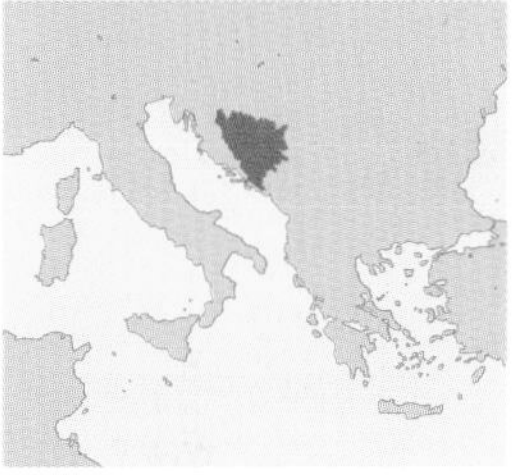

BOTSWANA
Government: Republic
Capital: Gaborone
Area: 225,700 sq mi.
Population: 1.6 million
Languages: Setswana and English
Currency: Pula

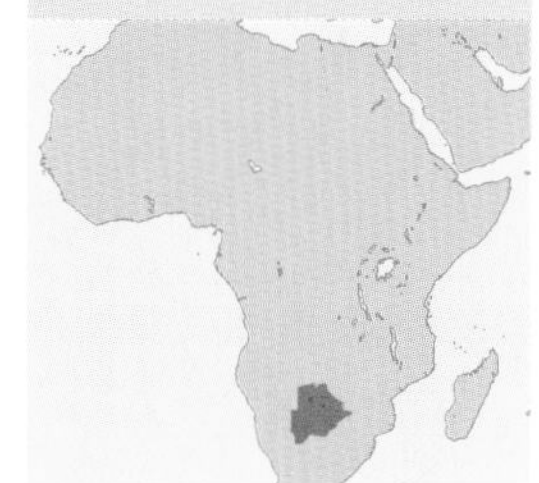

Boudicca

◁ **Boudicca** was a fierce Celtic queen who led her people into battle against the heavily armed Roman forces. Half of England joined Boudicca in the rebellion.

Boudicca, who is often called Boadicea, was the ruler of a British tribe in about the year A.D. 60. Her tribe, the Iceni, belonged to an ancient people known as the **Celts**.

The Roman rulers in Britain said that the Iceni lands should become part of the **Roman Empire**. Led by Queen Boudicca, the Iceni tribe at once rebelled. The strong Roman Army quickly crushed the rebellion, and Boudicca poisoned herself.

Boxing

People have fought with their fists since ancient times. But modern boxing started in 1867 when the Marquess of Queensberry drew up a set of rules. Boxers today are divided into weight categories, from light flyweights (below 106 lbs/48kg) to super heavyweights (any weight over 201+ lbs/91+ kg). Judges award points after each three-minute round for skill in attack and defense. Amateur contests usually consist of three rounds of three minutes each, with one-minute rests between rounds. Professional contests can be of any number of rounds up to 12 or 15.

Brain

The brain controls all of the other parts of the body. In some tiny **insects** it is no larger than a speck of dust. But **mammals** have large brains in relation to their size. Human beings have the largest brains of all. The brain controls involuntary (automatic) activities such as breathing and blood pressure. It also controls **muscles** and the organs of balance, feeling, and movement.

The human brain uses one fifth of all the energy produced in the body. It is largely made up of gray and white matter. Gray matter contains **nerve** cells, and white matter contains nerve fibers that carry messages from the nerve cells to the body. These nerve fibers leave the brain in large bundles and reach out to all parts of the body. Messages from the body are traveling back along the fibers to the brain all the time. Different parts of the brain control different parts of the body. For example, most thinking is done in the front part. Sight, on the other hand, is controlled from the back of the brain.

BRAZIL
Government: Republic
Capital: Brasília
Area: 3,261,200 sq. mi.
Population: 741 million
Language: Portuguese
Currency: Real

Brazil

Brazil is by far the largest country in **South America** and the fifth largest country in the world. Much of Brazil is low-lying and contains the huge basin of the **Amazon River** and the world's largest **rain forest**. Until recently only tribes of native people lived here. Over half of Brazil's people live in cities that include Rio de Janeiro, Sao Paulo, and Belo Horizonte. Brasília, a specially built modern city, has been the capital of Brazil since 1960.

Brazil was ruled by **Portugal** from the early 1500s until 1822, and most people still speak Portuguese. Many Brazilians work on farms. The country leads the world in producing **coffee**, and oil is becoming a more important product. Brazil also produces a lot of beef, cocoa, cotton, maize, sugar cane, and tobacco.

Bread

Bread is one of our oldest **foods**, dating back to at least 2000 B.C. It may be made from wheat, maize, oats, barley, or rye flour (see **cereal**). At first bread was flat, but the Egyptians added **yeast** to make the dough rise. Today most bread is baked with yeast.

▽ **Bronze** can be cast into shape by heating it until it melts and pouring it into a mold. This bronze shield is 2,000 years old.

Breathing

Breathing is something we rarely have to think about. As soon as a baby is born it starts to breathe, and we go on breathing all of our lives. It is the **oxygen** in the air that we need. Like all other animals we must have oxygen to stay alive. This oxygen is used with the food we eat to give us energy to move around and keep our bodies going.

We draw air into our **lungs**. From there it goes through tiny tubes that allow the oxygen to pass into the **blood** vessels. Oxygen goes around our bodies in the blood. We breathe out another kind of gas—carbon dioxide.

When you breathe in, your rib cage is pulled up and air is sucked into your lungs. These actions are reversed when you breathe out.

Bridge

Bridges are used to take roads, paths, and railroads over rivers, valleys, or other obstacles. The first bridges were probably fallen tree trunks placed across a river or small valley.

The **Romans** were among the first great bridge builders. Some of their stone bridges are still standing today. In the **Middle Ages** bridges in towns often had shops and houses built on top of them. Modern bridge building began with **iron** bridges in the 1700s. By the end of the 1800s steel was being used. Today there is a great variety of bridges. There are three main kinds of bridges. These are the beam, the arch, and the suspension bridge.

A modern beam bridge works in the same way as a simple tree trunk bridge. It is made of strong girders, or beams, that stretch from one bank to the other. Sometimes the middle of the bridge rests on pillars.

An arch bridge may have one arch or more. In the past arch bridges were usually built from stone, but today some are made of steel or **concrete**.

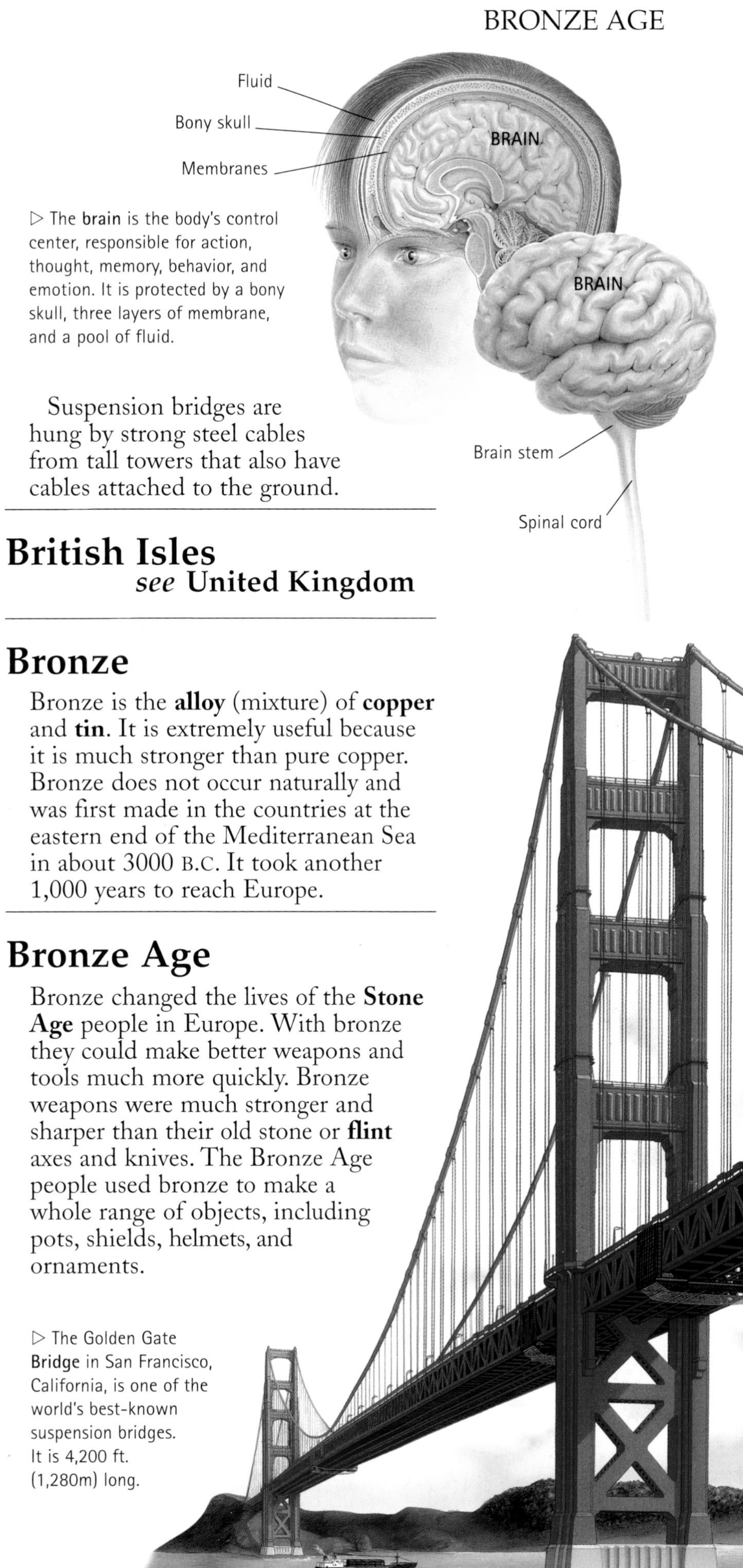

▷ The **brain** is the body's control center, responsible for action, thought, memory, behavior, and emotion. It is protected by a bony skull, three layers of membrane, and a pool of fluid.

Suspension bridges are hung by strong steel cables from tall towers that also have cables attached to the ground.

British Isles

see **United Kingdom**

Bronze

Bronze is the **alloy** (mixture) of **copper** and **tin**. It is extremely useful because it is much stronger than pure copper. Bronze does not occur naturally and was first made in the countries at the eastern end of the Mediterranean Sea in about 3000 B.C. It took another 1,000 years to reach Europe.

Bronze Age

Bronze changed the lives of the **Stone Age** people in Europe. With bronze they could make better weapons and tools much more quickly. Bronze weapons were much stronger and sharper than their old stone or **flint** axes and knives. The Bronze Age people used bronze to make a whole range of objects, including pots, shields, helmets, and ornaments.

▷ The Golden Gate **Bridge** in San Francisco, California, is one of the world's best-known suspension bridges. It is 4,200 ft. (1,280m) long.

As the Stone Age gave way to the Bronze Age, huts were replaced by towns, and people began to build palaces and temples. The Bronze Age lasted until about 800 B.C. At this time **iron** started to be used in Europe.

Buddha

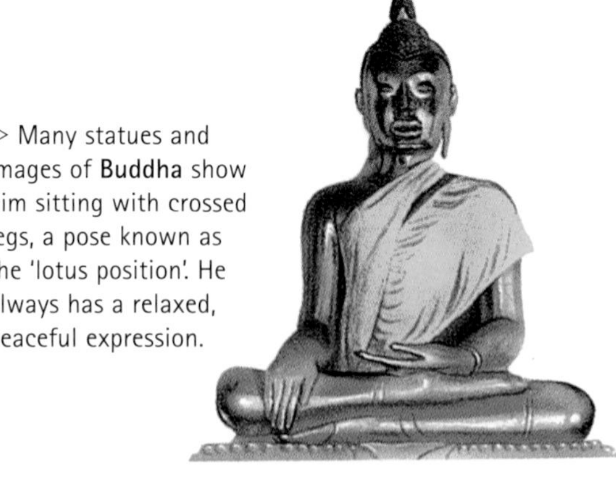

▷ Many statues and images of **Buddha** show him sitting with crossed legs, a pose known as the 'lotus position'. He always has a relaxed, peaceful expression.

The word Buddha means "enlightened one." This name is given to great teachers of the Buddhist religion. The first Buddha was Siddhartha Gautama, who was born in about 563 B.C. in northern **India**. For most of his life he traveled around India teaching people. Buddha taught his followers that the only way to true happiness was to be peaceful and kind to other people and animals and to avoid evil.

Buddhism

Buddhism is a **religion** that was first practiced in Asia about 2,500 years ago. Like the Hindus (see **Hinduism**), Buddhists believe that after they die they are born again as an animal or human being. This belief is known as reincarnation. Buddhists think that if they are very good, they will eventually end up in a heaven called Nirvana. Buddhists spend a long time meditating.

There are now 350 million Buddhists worldwide, but mainly in India, Tibet, China, Japan, and Southeast Asia.

Bulgaria

BULGARIA
Government: Republic
Capital: Sofia
Area: 42,600 sq. mi
Population: 7.7 million
Language: Bulgarian
Currency: Lev

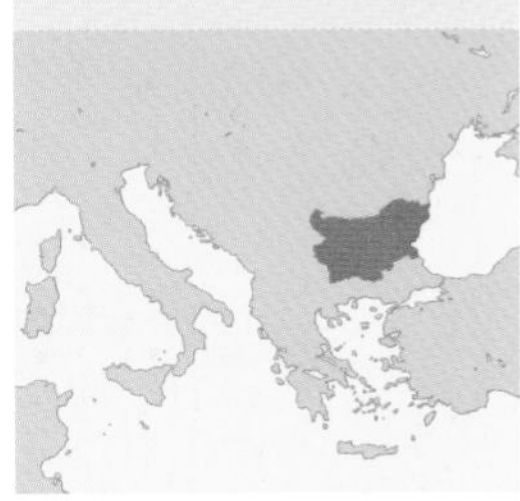

Bulgaria is a country in Eastern **Europe**. Like several of its neighbors, Bulgaria was governed by the Communist party during the second half of the 20th century. It became a fully democratic republic in 1990. In the north of Bulgaria are the Balkan Mountains. To the east is the **Black Sea**, where many people from Eastern Europe spend their holidays. Bulgaria has many factories, mines, and farms, but it is a relatively poor country compared with Western Europe.

Burma *see* Myanmar (Burma)

Butterfly

Butterflies are flying **insects**. They are related to **moths** and live in most parts of the world, even as far north as the Arctic Circle. All butterflies begin their lives as **caterpillars**, which hatch from eggs. When a caterpillar is fully grown, it changes into a chrysalis with a hard skin. Inside this the chrysalis changes into an adult butterfly. When it is ready, the butterfly breaks out and flies away to find a mate and lay eggs of its own.

Butterflies come in many colors, shapes, and sizes. The largest kind is Queen Alexandra's birdwing of New Guinea (below), which has a wingspan of 11 in. (28cm). At the other end of the scale the dwarf blue of South Africa measures just 5 in. (14mm) from wingtip to wingtip.

Byzantine Empire

The Byzantine Empire was founded by the Roman emperor Constantine I in A.D. 330. It was an eastern division of the **Roman Empire**. Constantine decided to move the empire's headquarters to the east. He built a new city as his capital, which he called **Constantinople** after himself. It is now Istanbul, and it is the capital of modern **Turkey**. In the 500s the Byzantine Empire ruled most of the lands around the Mediterranean Sea and Black Sea. The Byzantine Empire lasted until 1453, when Constantinople was captured by the Turks.

△ A group of **Caesar**'s enemies plotted to kill him. On March 15, 44 B.C. they stabbed him to death in the Roman Forum, the great meeting place in the center of Rome.

Caesar, Julius

Julius Caesar (about 102–44 B.C.) was a great leader of the **Roman Empire**. He is most famous for his part in turning the Roman Republic into an empire ruled by one person.

Caesar first became powerful when he commanded an army that conquered what is today France and Belgium. In 55 B.C. he crossed the English Channel and invaded Britain. He later rebelled against the Roman Senate (the main **government** of the entire Roman Empire) when he led his victorious armies into Italy. Caesar captured Rome without a struggle, and in 48 B.C. he defeated Pompey, his main rival for power. Caesar then became the sole ruler of the Roman Republic.

Caesar made many enemies who hated what he was doing to the Republic. A group of them murdered him in Rome.

Cactus

There are hundreds of different cacti, but they all have one thing in common. They are able to grow in very hot and dry **climates**. Cacti can do this because they store water in their fleshy stems. They are covered with prickly spines instead of leaves. The spines protect the plants' stores of water from raids by thirsty **desert** animals.

Cacti come in all shapes and sizes, from small pincushion-sized specimens to the giant saguaro cactus that may reach 50 ft. (15m) high.

▽ **Cacti** grow in dry places, especially deserts. They make ideal nesting sites for birds, including owls and woodpeckers. Cacti also provide food for a variety of small animals.

Calculator

About 5,000 years ago the **abacus** was invented. This was the first calculator. Then in 1642 the French scientist Blaise Pascal built the first machine for adding numbers. It worked by turning dials. After this mechanical adding machines were used for years in offices

The Aztecs of Central America made a **calendar** from a huge stone shaped like the sun. It had the face of the Aztec sun god in the center, and signs for the days around the edge.

and stores. They were useful but slow and could not do difficult calculations.

Everything changed in the 1970s when the **silicon chip** was invented. Now it was possible to make small, **electronic** calculators that can add, subtract, and divide as fast as we can press the keys. More advanced calculators can also do more difficult calculations needed in science.

Calendar

Every civilization has used some kind of calendar to keep track of days, weeks, months, and years. Calendars are used to plan the planting and harvesting of crops and also to mark special holidays and **festivals**. Western countries use the Gregorian calendar, which was first introduced by **Pope** Gregory XIII in 1582. It is based on the time it takes the **earth** to orbit (travel around) the **sun**—1 year, or 365 days. The Chinese calendar is based on the orbit of the **moon** around the earth.

Cambodia

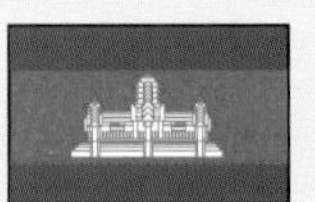

CAMBODIA
Government: Constitutional monarchy
Capital: Phnom Penh
Area: 68,100 sq. mi.
Population: 12.4 million
Language: Khmer
Currency: Riel

Cambodia is a flat, low-lying country in Southeast **Asia**. It changed its name to Kampuchea in 1976 and back to Cambodia in 1988. Most of Cambodia's people live in small villages and grow rice, vegetables, and fruit. The country was formerly part of the French colony of Indochina. It became independent in 1955. Since then, Cambodia has seen bitter **civil war** and **famine**, which killed more than 2.5 million people between 1976 and 1978. In 1993, after free elections, Cambodia became a constitutional **monarchy** again.

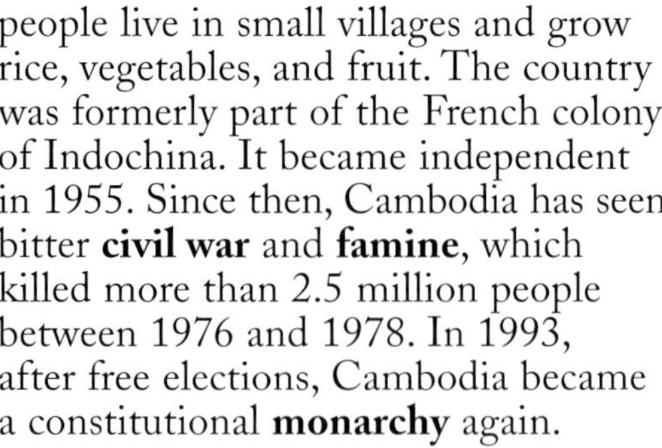

Camel

With its wide splayed feet, gangly legs, humped body, and long, thick neck, the camel has a unique appearance. It is one of the few **mammals** that can stand up to extreme heat and still do work carrying heavy loads.

Camels are ideally suited to making long journeys across **deserts**. Their padded feet grip well on loose, sandy ground. They are powerful and swift, and can go for days without eating or drinking, living off of the **fat** stored in their humps. Camels will eat almost anything, including the thorny shrubs and thistles found in deserts.

There are two kinds of camels, the single-humped camels of North Africa and the Middle East, and the Bactrian or two-humped camel of the Gobi Desert in **Mongolia**.

▽ **Camels** are vital beasts of burden in the desert regions of North Africa, the Middle East and Asia.

Camera

Modern cameras work the same way as those of 100 years ago. A shutter opens to let **light** from the scene being photographed pass through a glass **lens** and fall on the film. The amount of light that gets through can be varied by adjusting the size of the hole through which the light passes—the "aperture." The light forms an upside-down image of the scene on the film. The film is then developed with chemicals. The image on the developed film is printed onto a special type of paper. The result is a photograph (see also **photography**).

Today most cameras have many different parts to help us take photographs in all kinds of situations. The flash produces a strong burst of light to illuminate subjects in poor light or at night. Long telephoto lenses allow us to zoom in on things that are a long way away. There are even cameras that work underwater.

Taking pictures with early cameras was a slow process. The first real camera, invented by the Frenchman Louis Daguerre (1787–1851) in the 1830s, needed a very long exposure time. The subject had to sit motionless for as much as ten minutes, usually with his or her head in a clamp to keep it still. Modern cameras have fast shutter speeds of less than one thousandth of a second for taking photographs of very fast-moving objects.

Digital cameras do not use film—the image is converted into digital form and stored on disk. The number of separate photographs they can take depends on the size of their memory chip.

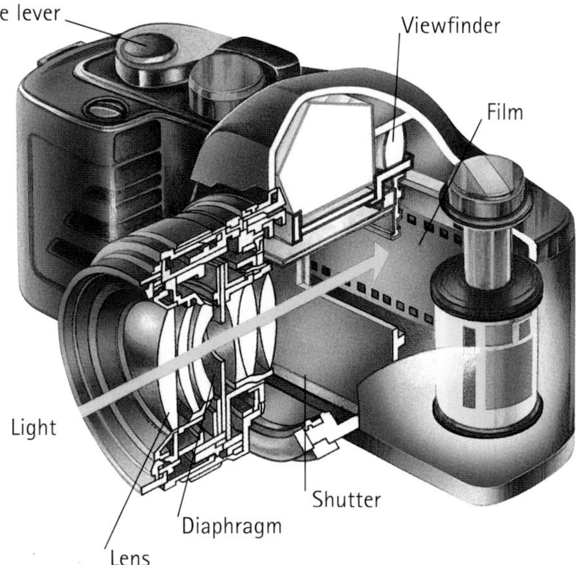

◁ When you take a photo, the **camera**'s shutter flicks open and shut again to let the right amount of light hit the film. The aperture controls the strength of the light that reaches the film.

Cameroon

Cameroon is a republic on the west coast of **Africa**. Most of the country's people live in scattered tribal villages and are farmers. Cocoa, coffee, cotton, **peanuts,** and bananas are the chief crops. Oil is also produced.

CAMEROON
Government: Republic
Capital: Yaoundé
Area: 181,000 sq. mi.
Population: 15.8 million
Languages: French, English, and various African languages
Currency: CFA Franc

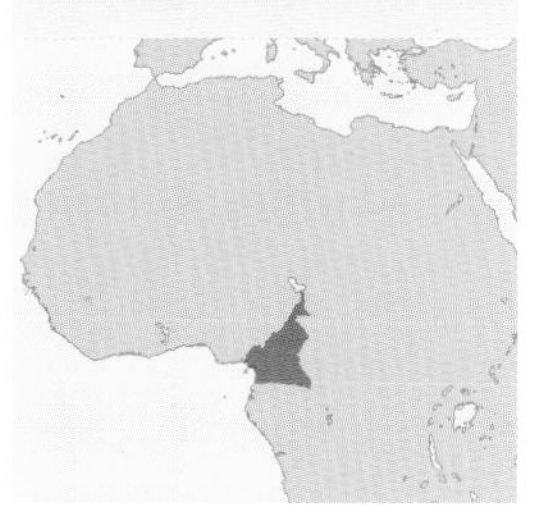

Canada

Canada is the second largest country in the world after **Russia**. In the Arctic, Canada reaches almost as far north as **Greenland**. To the south it extends to the same **latitude** as southern France. The distance from Canada's west coast, the Pacific Ocean, to its east coast, the Atlantic Ocean, is farther than from North America to Europe. But despite its size, two thirds of the population of Canada lives in a narrow belt of land no more than 124 mi. (200km) from its border with the **United States**.

In the east of Canada are the **Great Lakes** that lie on the border with the United States. These huge inland seas empty into the St. Lawrence River, which flows into the Atlantic Ocean. The two largest cities are Montreal and Toronto, however, the capital is **Ottawa**.

In the past, Britain and France each governed all or parts of Canada. Today about 24 percent of Canadians regard French as their mother tongue.

Canada's vast forests have made it the world's largest producer of pulpwood for making **paper**. The country also has enormous mineral reserves, especially of **oil** and **iron**, which have helped make Canada one of the ten leading industrial nations in the world.

CANADA
Government: Confederation
Capital: Ottawa
Area: 3,556,000 sq. mi.
Population: 31.6 million
Languages: English and French
Currency: Canadian dollar

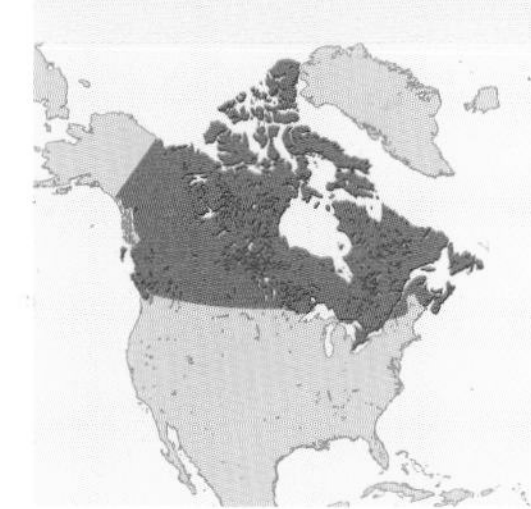

Canal

A canal is an artificial waterway built to carry water traffic. Until the 1500s canals could be built only across flat land. With the invention of canal locks, however, they could be built across high ground too. Canal locks use a system of locking gates and channels to change the water level. Before a boat or **ship** can enter a lock, the level of water inside the lock must be the same as that in the lower pool. Early canals could only be used by narrow, shallow-bottomed boats.

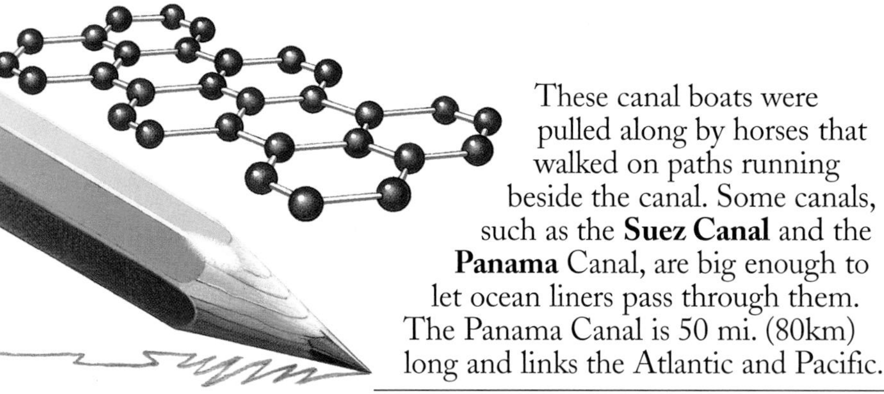

These canal boats were pulled along by horses that walked on paths running beside the canal. Some canals, such as the **Suez Canal** and the **Panama** Canal, are big enough to let ocean liners pass through them. The Panama Canal is 50 mi. (80km) long and links the Atlantic and Pacific.

△ Graphite is a pure form of **carbon**. Its atoms (top) are arranged in layers that slide over each other easily. For this reason graphite is one of the softest solids. The "lead" used in pencils (above) is actually a mixture of graphite and clay.

Canberra

Canberra is the capital of **Australia**. It is a small city in which the main activity is **government**. All the major departments of government have their headquarters here. Canberra has little industry. The city was founded in 1908 by an act of the Australian Parliament, and it expanded soon after the end of **World War I** in 1918.

△ The world's earliest **car** was a three-wheeled steam carriage invented by Nicholas Cugnot of France in 1769.

Cancer

Cancer is a **disease** that causes **cells** in the body to grow uncontrollably. These cancerous cells can mass together to form a swelling known as a tumor. A severe tumor is described as malignant because it may spread to other parts of the body; a benign tumor will not spread. Finding a cure for cancer is one of the greatest challenges facing modern **medicine**, and researchers all over the world are working hard at it.

Cancer is especially likely to affect older people. There are about 100 different kinds of cancer. Some of the most common include breast cancer, **lung** cancer, and skin cancer.

Car

Motorized vehicles were invented as long ago as the mid-1700s, but the first successful motor cars were not built until the 1880s. Since then, cars have made enormous changes to the world we live in. The cars themselves have changed too. Clumsy "horseless carriages" have become the fast, comfortable, and reliable cars of today.

Most cars have gasoline **engines**. Gasoline is burned inside the engine, generating enough power to turn the wheels of the car. Other cars run on diesel fuel instead of gasoline (see **diesel engine**). The driver makes the car accelerate (go faster) by pressing the accelerator pedal. This makes more

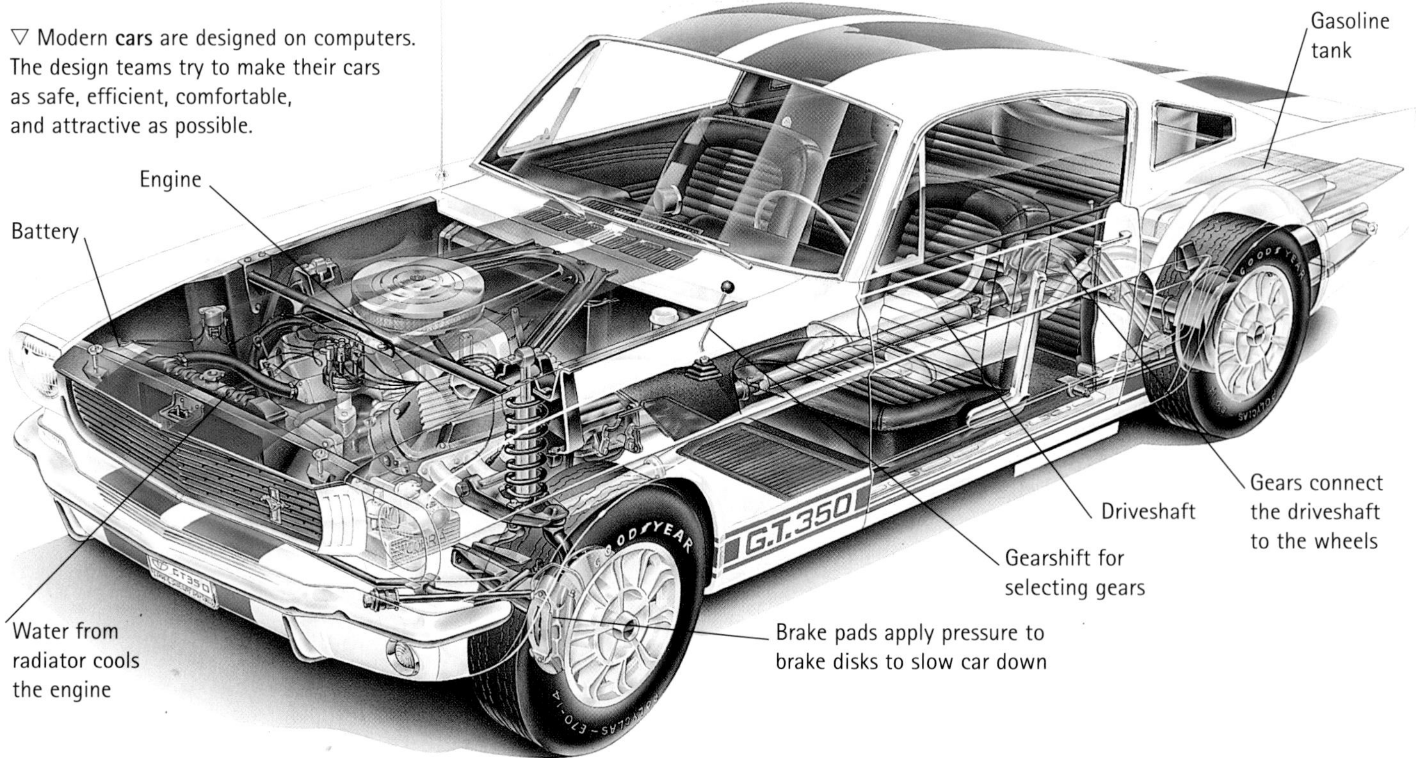

▽ Modern **cars** are designed on computers. The design teams try to make their cars as safe, efficient, comfortable, and attractive as possible.

gasoline or diesel fuel go into the engine.

Cars are pushed along by either their front or back wheels. As the engine's pistons go up and down they turn the driveshaft, which is linked to the wheels by **gears**. If a car has manual transmission, the driver uses a clutch pedal to change gears. If the car has an automatic transmission, a microcomputer controls what gear is being used based on the car's speed. The car needs plenty of power for starting or going up a steep hill. When drivers travel along a clear road at average speed, they use top gear. Most cars have four or five forward gears, plus reverse.

Carbon

Carbon is an important **element** that is found in every living thing—both plants and animals. Many of the things we use every day contain carbon, such as sugar and paper. Forms of carbon also exist as **coal**, **oil**, **diamonds,** and graphite.

Radiocarbon dating is a method of finding out the age of many objects that are less than 50,000 years old.It works by measuring the amount of radiocarbon in an object. All living things contain radiocarbon. When they die, the radiocarbon begins to decay.

Caribbean

The Caribbean is a region that lies to the east of **Central America**, between North America and South America. It includes dozens of islands, forming a chain about 1,980 mi. (3,200km) long. The largest Caribbean islands are **Cuba**, **Jamaica**, **Puerto Rico,** and Hispaniola (which is divided into two countries—**Haiti** and the **Dominican Republic**). Among the smallest islands are Barbados, **Grenada,** and the Virgin Islands.

Another name for the Caribbean islands is the West Indies. This is because when the explorer Christopher **Columbus** first saw them in 1492, he mistakenly thought that he was near India. Later many Europeans arrived to settle in the region. Today the people of the Caribbean reflect its mix of cultures. They speak Spanish, French, or English, often with local accents and variations.

Tourism is by far the largest industry in the Caribbean. Tourists flock to enjoy the beautiful sandy beaches and snorkel in warm waters. The main crops include sugarcane, bananas, and coffee.

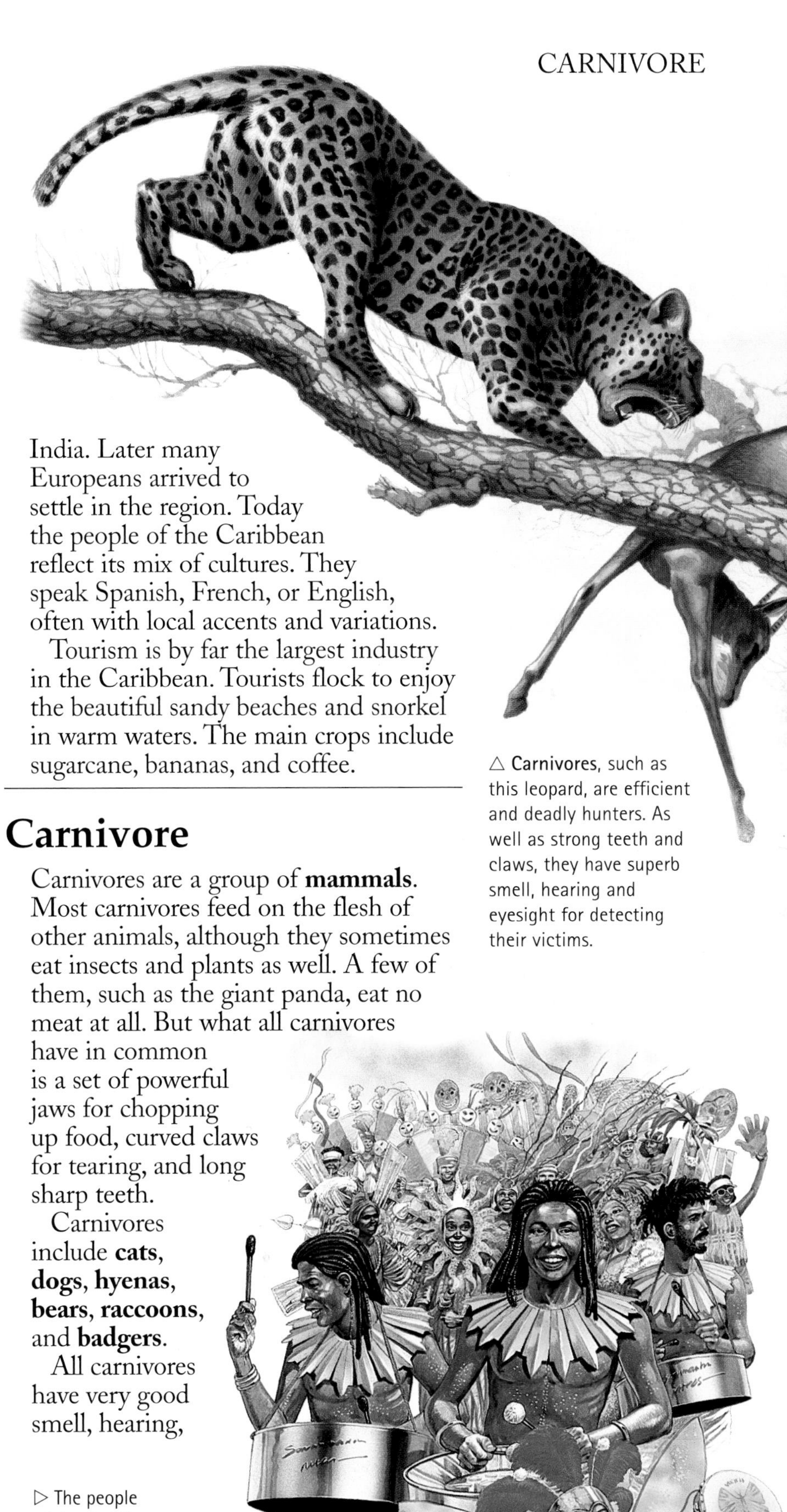

△ **Carnivores**, such as this leopard, are efficient and deadly hunters. As well as strong teeth and claws, they have superb smell, hearing and eyesight for detecting their victims.

Carnivore

Carnivores are a group of **mammals**. Most carnivores feed on the flesh of other animals, although they sometimes eat insects and plants as well. A few of them, such as the giant panda, eat no meat at all. But what all carnivores have in common is a set of powerful jaws for chopping up food, curved claws for tearing, and long sharp teeth.

Carnivores include **cats**, **dogs**, **hyenas**, **bears**, **raccoons**, and **badgers**.

All carnivores have very good smell, hearing,

▷ The people of the **Caribbean** stage a spring carnival every year. Many of them wear spectacular costumes. Empty oil drums are made into dish-shaped musical drums called steel drums.

Castles often had double walls for extra protection. They also had plenty of towers for shooting attackers from different directions at the same time.

and eyesight. They are also fast and skilled at hunting down their prey. Some carnivores, such as wolves and hyenas, hunt together in packs. **Lions** hunt in groups called prides. In this way they can kill animals much larger than themselves. Other carnivores, like the **leopard** and **tiger**, hunt alone.

Carroll, Lewis

Lewis Carroll (1832–1898) is the pseudonym of an English author named Charles Dodgson. Dodgson was a mathematics professor at Oxford University, but he is best known for his children's stories. The most famous is *Alice in Wonderland.* The story was written for the daughter of a fellow professor at the university.

△ The **cats** kept as pets all over the world were first domesticated (tamed) in Africa more than 4,000 years ago probably by the ancient Egyptians.

▽ The **caterpillar** of the monarch butterfly is highly poisonous. Its pattern of stripes warns hungry animals to leave it alone.

Cartoon

Most people think of short, funny **films** with amusing characters and talking creatures when they speak of cartoons. But the word cartoon was originally used by artists to describe the rough sketches they produced when planning a **painting** or a **tapestry**.

In the 1840s **newspapers** started to print drawings that made fun of politicians and other important people. These were also called cartoons. The traditional way of making cartoon movies is to join a lot of individual drawings. Each of the drawings is slightly different from the one before. When they are shown one after another at a very fast speed, it looks as if the scene is moving. To create a cartoon, the original sketch is drawn onto sheets of transparent film, called cels, then photographed onto film.

Since the 1980s, many cartoons have been made by a new technique called **computer** animation. The artists use computers to produce all of the images and can create exciting special effects.

Castle

Castles are fortified homes built by rulers and lords in the **Middle Ages**. Safe behind the thick stone walls of their castles, the owners and their supporters could fight off attacks by bandits and angry mobs of people, and they could sit out long sieges by invading armies. Some castles are still lived in, but many are now in ruins.

The first castles were constructed in about A.D. 950. They included a hill or mound surrounded by a ditch. From the late 1000s some larger castles had a stone tower called a keep. As castles developed they became larger and more comfortable. Instead of having all the living quarters crowded into the keep, small villages of huts sprang up inside the castle walls.

All kinds of tactics and siege machinery were needed in an attack on a heavily fortified medieval castle. Troops rushed the ramparts from giant siege towers wheeled up to the walls. Powerful catapults hurled stones against the walls or into the castle to create confusion. Archers kept up a steady hail of arrows to force the defenders back from the walls, while troops with scaling ladders swarmed up them.

Cat

Cats belong to the group of **mammals** called the feline family. Although cats range in size from domestic breeds to **lions** and **tigers**, they all have many things in common. Cats have short, rounded heads, long whiskers, sharp teeth, which serve as weapons for grabbing and biting their prey, and powerful claws. All cats, except the **cheetah,** can retract (pull back) their claws into a sheath of skin when they are not in use. Cats' long tails help them balance, jump, and climb.

There are about 38 kinds of cats. One of these—the domestic cat—has been bred into numerous different varieties. Wild cats are usually loners, but lions and cheetahs live in family groups.

Caterpillar

All **insects** have a life cycle with three main stages—first the egg, then the larva, and finally the adult. "Caterpillar" is simply another name for the larva of a **butterfly** or a **moth**.

Butterflies and moths usually lay their eggs on plants. After the eggs hatch small, soft, wormlike creatures—the caterpillars—emerge. Caterpillars spend their whole time feeding. Their only purpose in life is to eat, grow and prepare for the change into adults. For this reason they have powerful jaws for chewing up plants. Many feed on crops and can cause great damage.

As caterpillars grow they become too large for their skins. After a while the skin stretches and splits, and they emerge with a new one. This happens several times. The last skin is different from the others. It forms a hard layer, which makes it impossible for the caterpillar to move. In this state it is called a chrysalis. Inside the chrysalis the caterpillar changes into a butterfly. A moth caterpillar spins a cocoon around itself before turning into a chrysalis.

Cathedral

see **Church**

Cattle

Cattle are large, grass-eating animals. **Grass** is difficult to digest, and all cattle have four **stomachs** to make this easier. During **digestion**, the food is returned to the mouth to be chewed and swallowed again. When cattle do this, we say they are chewing their cud.

The best known kinds of cattle are cows, oxen, and water buffalo. They provide us with **milk**, meat, and hides for making **leather**. Buffalo are the largest cattle, with massive bodies covered in shaggy hair. Once huge herds of millions of buffalo roamed the plains of North America where they were hunted by the **native Americans**. But when European hunters arrived, they killed far too many buffalo, and now wild buffalo survive only in national parks.

△ **Cattle** are still used to plow fields and pull carts in many parts of the world.

Cave

A cave is an underground hollow or passage. The largest caves are formed when slightly **acid** water flows or seeps through limestone rock. The **water** gradually dissolves the rock, sometimes leaving behind a whole network of caves. After a cave has been formed water may go on dripping through the walls and ceiling. This often creates odd-shaped deposits of **minerals** called stalactites and stalagmites.

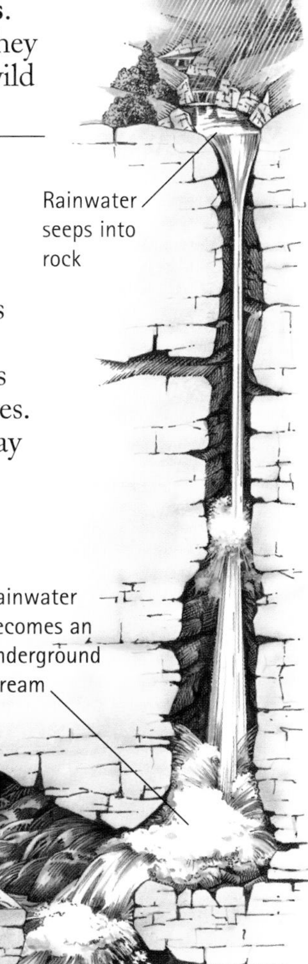

▽ A **cave** in limestone rock takes thousands of years to form. It may feature several vertical shafts, side passages, caverns, and underground lakes and streams.

Cave dweller

Caves are ideal places to shelter from the weather and from wild animals. They were among the first dwelling places used by **human beings**. The mouth of a cave is often dry, and it is possible to build a **fire** inside when the weather is cold. In hot weather caves give shelter from the sun. Also, with walls all around them, the cave people could fight off dangerous animals from the cave mouth.

The remains of ancient cave dwellers have been found in sites all around the world—China, southern Asia, Africa, and Europe (see **prehistoric people**). Bits and pieces of their tools and weapons have been dug up along with bones of the animals they hunted. On the walls of some caves paintings of animals have been found.

The Neanderthals were **cave dwellers** who lived in Europe and the Middle East until 35,000 years ago. At that time it was much colder than it is now, and caves provided vital shelter.

Cell

Cells are the smallest living parts of plants and animals. Single cells can only be seen under a **microscope**. Even a tiny bit of human **skin** contains millions of cells. Cells are usually round in shape. A few are spiraled and some, like **nerve** cells, have many treelike branches.

In 1665 the English scientist Robert Hooke examined a piece of cork under a microscope and saw that it was made up of tiny compartments. He named them cells, and this term has been used ever since.

Every living thing is made up of cells. They differ in shape, size, and function, but all have a control center called the nucleus. **Animal** cells have a thin cell wall, or membrane. **Plant** cells have a thicker cell wall containing cellulose, a stiffening substance. Plant cells also have chloroplasts, tiny structures that contain a green substance called chlorophyll. Plants use chlorophyll to make their own food in a process known as **photosynthesis**.

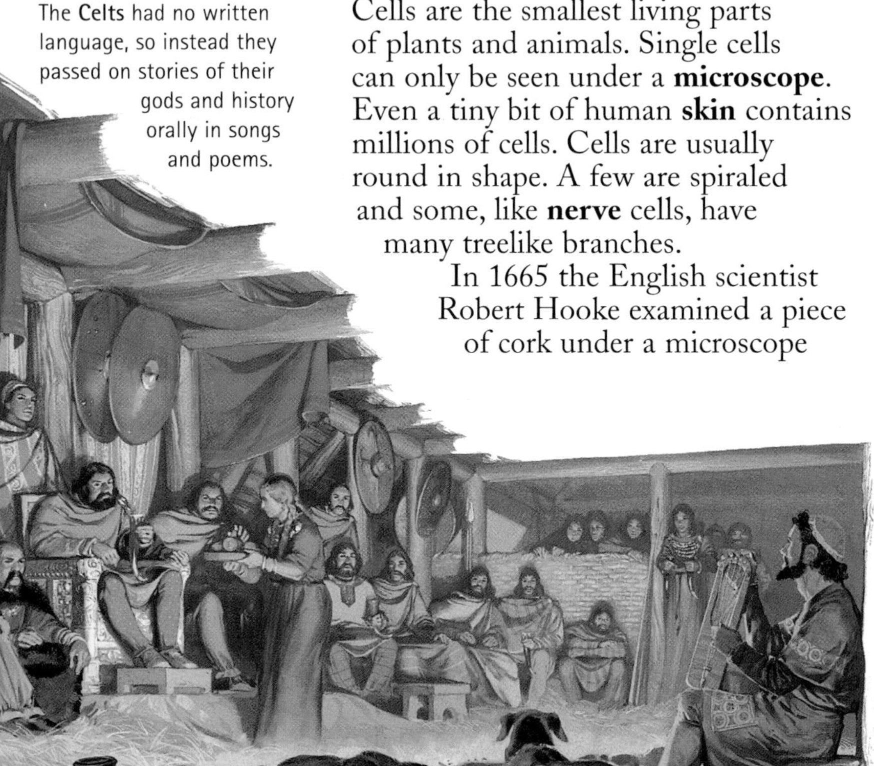

The **Celts** had no written language, so instead they passed on stories of their gods and history orally in songs and poems.

Celts

The Celts were an ancient people of northwestern Europe. At one time, over 2,000 years ago, they lived all over Britain, France, and parts of Spain and Germany. In about 400 B.C. they even crossed into Italy and attacked Rome.

Celtic people were tall and warlike. They lived in tribes made up of a chief, nobles, free men and women, and slaves. The tribes often fought each other. The Celts were highly skilled metalworkers and often decorated their weapons and armor with bright designs and exotic creatures. They were also gifted poets and musicians. The Celtic **religion** was known as Druidism, and their priests were called Druids.

When the armies of the **Roman Empire** spread out, many Celts fled to remote regions. In the lands that the Romans conquered, the Celtic way of life was soon lost. It was only in far-off corners of Europe that the Celtic language and customs survived.

Up until a few hundred years ago Celtic speech was very common in **Ireland**, **Wales**, Cornwall (a county in southwestern England), **Scotland,** and Brittany (a region of northwestern France). Today, although less common, Celtic speech can still be heard. Celtic languages include the Welsh language and Irish and Scottish Gaelic.

Census

Nearly all countries of the world regularly count the number of people living in them. This **population** count is called a census. Most countries take a census every ten years. A census can also provide useful facts about what jobs people do, how much money they earn, what kind of homes they live in, whether they are married or single, and how many children they have.

In ancient Rome census takers made lists of people and their property. They used these lists to make sure that each person paid the right amount of **tax**. When **William the Conqueror** invaded England in 1066, his officials made a count of all the country's land and property. This census was listed in the **Domesday Book**.

An animal cell

△ **Cells** are tiny building blocks that make up plants and animals. Within each cell are many even smaller structures, each of which does a different job. For example, some produce energy, while others fight off invading bacteria.

Centipede

Centipedes are long **invertebrates** (animals without backbones). Their bodies are made up of many parts, often up to 100 or more. Each body part has a pair of legs. The head has long antennae (feelers), powerful jaws, and two stinging claws that are able to inject poison into victims. All centipedes are active hunters. They feed mainly on worms, insects, and snails.

Centipedes are found in most parts of the world. The largest centipede is a 46-legged giant that lives in the **rain forests** of South America. It is about 10 in. (25cm) long and 1 in. (2.5cm) thick.

Centipedes look similar to another group of creatures known as millipedes. The main difference between them is that centipedes have two legs on each body segment, whereas millipedes have four.

▽ **Centipedes** are fierce hunters. Many can move fast to catch prey or scurry away from danger.

Central America

Central America is a strip of land between the **United States** and **Mexico** to the north, and South America to the south. It consists of the republics of Belize, **Guatemala**, **El Salvador**, **Honduras**, **Nicaragua**, **Costa Rica**, and **Panama**.

Lowland plains, thick forests and swamps lie along the coasts of Central America. In the center are high mountains.

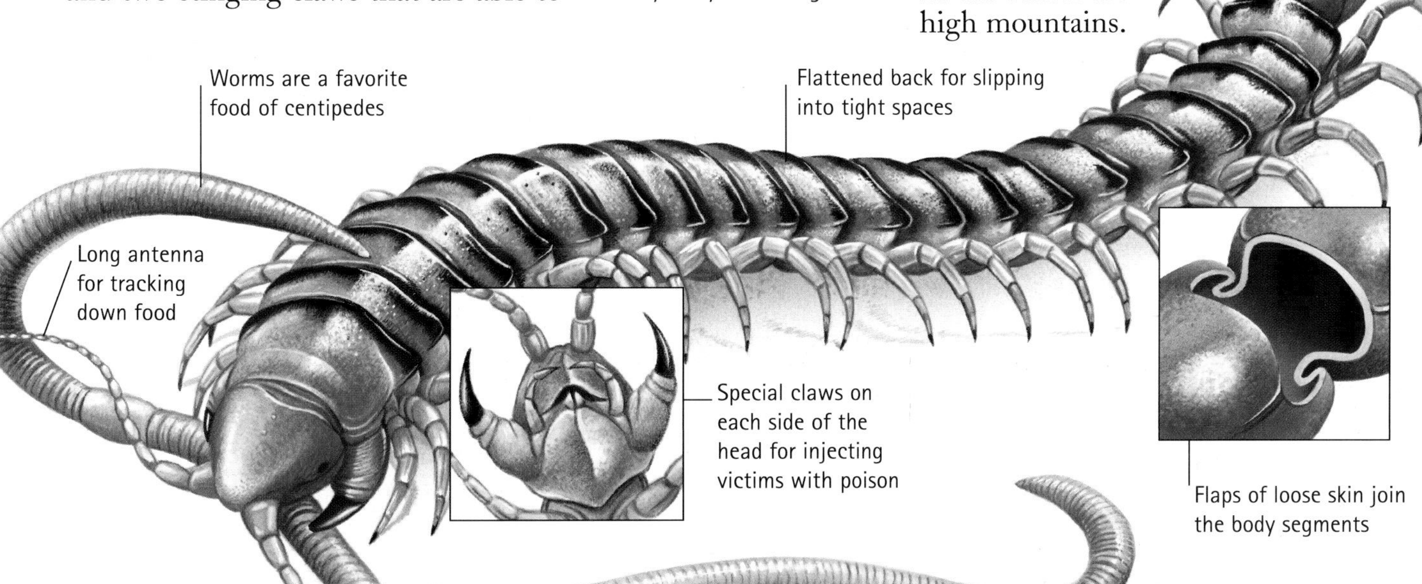

Central America is a hot area. Most of the large cities are in the cooler highlands.

Central America does not include Mexico. However, people often use a different term—Latin America—to describe all of the area from Mexico, south to Brazil and Argentina. This is because the people who live there mainly speak Spanish or Portuguese, which come from ancient Latin.

The people of Central America farm tropical crops such as sugarcane, coffee, cotton, and bananas. There is relatively little industry in the region.

In the 1500s Spanish soldiers and settlers arrived in Central America. Much of the land became Spanish colonies. Before then the region was home to various tribes, including the **Maya**. In 1838 Guatemala, Honduras, Costa Rica, Nicaragua, and El Salvador all gained independence from Spain. Panama separated from **Colombia** in 1903, but Belize remained a British colony until 1981.

△ **Central America** includes seven countries. Most people who live there speak Spanish and many are Roman Catholics.

△ A carving of a menorah, the special candlestick lit by Jewish families during the holiday of **Chanukah**.

Cereal

Cereals are the **seeds** of a group of plants that belong to the **grass** family. Throughout human history they have been the most important of all types of **food**. In prehistoric times cereals were collected from wild plants. Later, when they began to be grown on farms, cereals became the most important food of early civilizations.

Some cereals, such as **rice** and maize (corn), are eaten in their natural form. Rice is the main food crop for half the world's population. Other cereals, such as **wheat** and rye, are ground into flour before being baked or cooked. Pasta is made from a mixture of plain wheat, flour, and water. Cereals are also used to make alcoholic drinks like beer and whisky (see **alcohol**), and some are grown as animal feed.

△ **Cereals** are grasses that are grown for food. They include several of the world's major crops.

Chalk

Chalk is a pure white, soft, and crumbly form of limestone.

Land that is rich in chalk is found in southern England, France, and parts of North America.

Most chalk was formed between 135 and 65 million years ago. It is made up of the crushed **shells** of countless tiny sea creatures. When these creatures died, their empty shells built up in thick layers at the bottom of warm, shallow seas. As the shape of the surface of the **earth** changed these chalk layers were lifted up out of the seas to become dry land.

We usually think of chalk as a writing tool, but it is also used in many other ways. Mixed with other substances, chalk is used to make ink, **paints**, medicines, **rubber**, **paper,** and even toothpaste.

The famous white cliffs of Dover on England's south coast, are made of thick layers of chalk formed in the Cretaceous Period 100 million years ago.

Chameleon

Chameleons are a group of **lizards** found in Africa, Asia, and parts of southern Europe. They have narrow bodies with a crest along the back and helmeted or horned heads. The most unusual thing about chameleons is that they can change the color of their skin.

Most chameleons live in trees. They move very slowly and sit on branches for hours—still as statues—waiting until **insects** come close to them. The chameleons catch the helpless insects with their long, sticky tongues, which shoot out with such speed that the insects seem to vanish without a trace.

Chanukah

Chanukah (also written Hanukkah) is a Jewish holiday that lasts for eight days each December (see **Judaism**).

Jewish families light candles and exchange presents on each night of Chanukah to celebrate an ancient miracle. Long ago the Jewish people had just one day's supply of oil for their temple, but miraculously it lasted for eight days until they managed to get a new supply.

Chaplin, Charles

Charlie Chaplin (1889–1977) was one of the most famous comic **film** actors of all time. He is best known for his role as a gentle, well-meaning tramp who was always making mistakes and getting into trouble.

Chaplin was born in London, England, but he spent most of his working life in the United States. He started as an actor on stage, but he became famous for the parts he played in silent films in Hollywood. Chaplin also wrote, directed, and produced the movies that he made in later years.

△ Charlie **Chaplin** starred in dozens of silent movies. He was often called the world's funniest man.

Charity

A charity is an organization that exists to help people in need or to do work that is for the public good. Unlike a commercial business, its main aim is not to make money. Many charities rely on donations to keep going.

When times are hard, people have always given a helping hand to one another. This could be anything from a few coins to a free meal or a bed for the night. Many **religions** say that their followers should offer assistance to the poor or the sick.

The first charitable organizations probably appeared in the **Middle Ages**. They were able to help only small numbers of people. Modern charities do all kinds of work. For example, some help homeless people and others distribute food and supplies to people who are suffering from **famine** or natural disasters, such as **earthquakes**. Charities also raise money for **schools**, museums, and **hospitals**; they help protect the environment, and they fund important medical research.

△ **Charlemagne** ruled over much of western Europe in the early Middle Ages.

Charlemagne

Charlemagne (742–814) was a great military leader. In the 700s he founded an enormous empire that covered most of western **Europe**.

In the year 768 Charlemagne became the king of the Franks, a people who lived in the country we now call **France**. Through his skill in war, he took over northern Spain, Italy, and Germany. He fought for the Christian Church in Rome, and in return the **pope** crowned him Holy Roman Emperor on Christmas Day in the year 800.

Charlemagne's court was a great center of culture and learning. Artists and scholars traveled there from far and wide. When Charlemagne died, his sons fought among themselves. Eventually his empire was divided between his grandsons, Charles, Louis, and Lothar.

Charles I

Charles I (1600–1649) is known in history as the only English king to have caused his people to rebel and execute him. He came to the throne in 1625, but it was not long before he made enemies almost everywhere. Finally, in 1642, the country was split by **civil war**. The war lasted for several

◁ A **chameleon** can swivel each eye separately to help it look all around itself. It is also able to change color to match its surroundings. This helps the chameleon to hide from its enemies.

years and thousands of people died in the fighting. But Charles refused to give in.

One of the reasons that Charles was unpopular is that he married a Catholic. He also imposed high taxes to pay for wars that people did not want, as well as trying to limit the powers of the English **Parliament**. In 1649 Charles was put on trial. He was found guilty of treason, and the court sentenced him to death.

Charles I of England was put on trial in 1649. The charges against him were very serious. In the end the court found him guilty and he was beheaded.

Cheese

Most cheese is made from cows' **milk,** but it can be made from the milk of goats, sheep, buffalo, and even reindeer. To make cheese, the milk is turned sour so that it will curdle. The solid bits, called curds, are taken away from the liquid, or whey. They are then pressed into a firmer shape. Finally, the cheese is dried and left to ripen.

Chemistry

Chemistry is the study of materials—solids, liquids, and gases. A chemist finds out what things are made of and how they are joined together. If a piece of wood is burned in a **fire**, this is a chemical reaction. The wood turns to ash, and at the same time more heat and light are given off. It took chemists a long time to find out that burning is the joining together of the wood with the gas **oxygen** from the air. There are many kinds of chemical reactions.

The true science of chemistry as we know it began only in the 1600s. Chemists at this time began to find out how chemicals really work. Then they discovered the **elements**, from which all the millions of substances on earth are made. There are only about 100 elements, each of them made up of tiny **atoms**. The atoms of elements often join together to make different substances. The **salt** you put on your food consists of atoms of the elements sodium and chlorine.

CHILE
Government: Republic
Capital: Santiago
Area: 288,800 sq. mi.
Population: 15 million
Language: Spanish
Currency: Peso

Chess

Chess is a game that has been enjoyed for hundreds of years. It is played by two people on a board with 64 black and white squares. Each of the two players has 16 pieces, which they line up on either side of the board. Every piece can only be moved around the board in a special way. They are used to attack and retreat, to defend each other, and they can be captured and taken out of play. The most important piece for each player is the king. The game is won when one player manages to capture the other player's king.

Chile

Chile is a narrow country that stretches for 2,644 mi. (4,265km) down the western coast of **South America**. The area that people can inhabit is made even narrower by the **Andes** mountains, which lie along the country's eastern border. Chile has over one quarter of the world's **copper** resources. Its people speak Spanish and are mainly Roman Catholics. In 1973 a military government seized power, but in 1988 the Chilean people voted for an end to military rule.

Chimpanzee

Chimpanzees are the most human looking of all the **apes**. Fully grown, they are about 3–10 ft. (1–3m) tall and are able to walk upright, although they usually walk on all fours, using their hands to help push themselves along. Chimps are found in the tropical forests of West and central **Africa**. They live in family groups. Chimps take good care of their young and are playful and intelligent animals. Tame chimpanzees can learn to talk in sign language and perform simple tasks.

Chimpanzees are among the noisiest of all **mammals**. They scream and shriek, drum on trees, slap the ground, and keep up an almost constant hooting and muttering.

China

China is the third largest country in the world and the nation with the greatest **population**. There are more than one billion Chinese people—one fifth of the earth's total population. China has the oldest continuous civilization of any country.

Natural barriers, including deserts and the **Himalayas** mountain chain, cut China off from its neighbors on mainland **Asia**. In the east are great plains and rivers, including China's longest river, the Chang (**Yangtze River**), and the slightly shorter Huang Ho (Yellow River). It is here that most of the people live. Many Chinese people live in the cities and work in factories. But there are also millions of farmers living in the country.

For more than 3,000 years China was an empire. It was ruled by emperors who were members of royal families known as dynasties. The magnificent imperial palaces can still be seen in China's capital city, **Beijing**. In about 200 B.C. one emperor ordered the construction of the **Great Wall of China** to keep out invading armies from the north. It stretches for more than 1,488 mi. (2,400km) and is the longest fortification ever built.

Chinese inventions include **paper**, **printing**, ink, **silk**, porcelain, fireworks, and gunpowder—all discovered long before such things were known in Europe or elsewhere. Today more people speak Chinese than any other language. It is written in picture-signs. There are as many as 40,000 of these symbols, although only about 5,000 of them are in everyday use.

Since 1912 China has been a republic. A bitter **civil war** between Nationalists and Communists ended in 1949 with the victory of the Communists (see **communism**). **Mao Zedong** (also written Mao Tse-tung) was one of the most important communist leaders. He tried to make China into a superpower by speeding up the growth of its factories and farms. While Mao Zedong was in power, China became isolated from the rest of the world. Later leaders increased contacts with the West, but many people who opposed the regime were imprisoned. In 1997 Britain handed over its colony of **Hong Kong** to Chinese rule.

China's main language, Mandarin, is written in picture-signs, or characters. The symbols above read "Chinese People."

CHINA
Government: Communist party-led
Capital: Beijing
Area: 3,596,600 sq. mi.
Population: 1.3 billion
Languages: Mandarin Chinese
Currency: Yuan

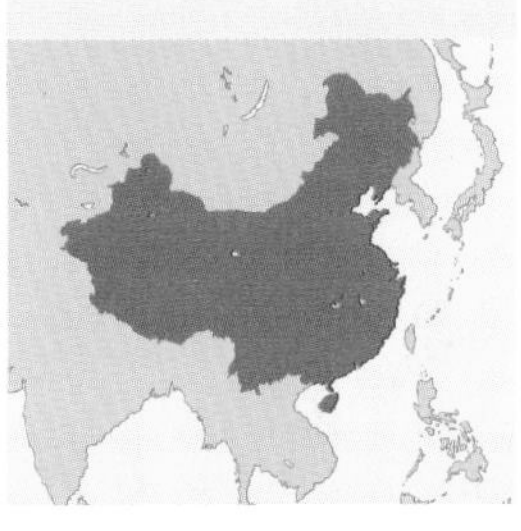

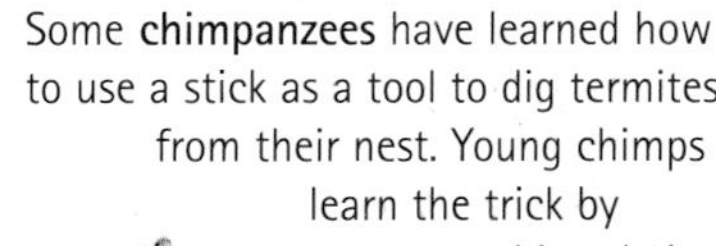

Some **chimpanzees** have learned how to use a stick as a tool to dig termites from their nest. Young chimps learn the trick by watching their older relatives.

△ **Chocolate** is made from cacao trees. First, the trees' huge pods are cut off with a large knife. The beans inside are then dried and roasted.

Chocolate

The chocolate we eat is made from the beans of the cacao **tree**. The beans grow inside pods, which hang from the trunk and branches of the tree. To make chocolate, the beans are first roasted and then ground up to and release an oily liquid called chocolate liquor. Other ingredients may then be added to the liquor. **Milk** chocolate, for example, has milk and **sugar** added to it.

Christianity

Christianity is one of the world's largest **religions**. About two billion people call themselves Christians. They follow the teachings of **Jesus** and believe that he is the son of God who came to earth in human form.

Christianity is 2,000 years old. In fact the main **calendar** used in many countries today is dated from the year in which it was thought that Jesus was born. Christians accept the **Bible** as their holy book and Sunday is their holy day, when they go to church, pray, and observe other religious traditions.

In some ways Christianity grew out of the religion of **Judaism**. But the teachings of Jesus upset the Jewish and Roman leaders of the time, and in the year 29 he was crucified (executed by being nailed to a cross).

After the death of Jesus his followers, or disciples, spread his teachings far and wide.

There are many different forms of Christianity. The Roman Catholic Church is the oldest and largest Christian church. The **pope** is its head. For hundreds of years popes have lived in **Vatican City** in Italy. The main church service of Catholics is called the Mass.

In Greece and Russia the Eastern Orthodox Church is the main form of Christianity. Protestants are Christians but do not belong to the Roman Catholic or Eastern Orthodox churches. They believe that the things written in the Bible are more important than what church leaders say.

Protestantism began in the 1500s, when a German named Martin **Luther** led a movement to change the Roman Catholic Church. This period is now called the **Reformation**. Luther's followers became known as Protestants because they protested against the teachings and policies of the Roman Catholic Church. Other groups wanted more changes to Luther's Christianity. These include Baptists, Quakers, and Mennonites—all groups that developed their own forms of worship.

▽ **Christianity** began in the area that is now Israel but has spread throughout the world. Saints (below) are holy people who have led a good life and have taken part in a miracle.

Christmas

This **festival**, celebrated by Christians on December 25, marks the birth of **Jesus**. It is not known if Jesus was actually born on this date. In fact the first mention of a festival of Christmas comes from a **Roman** calendar over 300 years after his death. Christmas customs vary from country to country, but people often exchange gifts, send greeting cards, and decorate their homes.

Church

Christian churches are as varied as the countries in which they are found. They come in all shapes and sizes—from tents and tiny wooden huts to towering stone cathedrals. But all churches are used for the same purposes. They serve as places of prayer, as venues for religious services, and as places that house all kinds of religious objects. In most churches the main entrance is at the west end and the altar is located at the east end.

Throughout the ages churches have been built in many different styles of **architecture**. In the 1000s and 1100s most churches were built in the Romanesque style. They had wide, rounded arches and low, round **domes**. In the **Middle Ages** in western Europe a style known as Gothic appeared. Gothic churches had pointed spires, soaring arches, stone carvings, and stained-glass windows. Building a cathedral, such as Chartres in France or Canterbury in England, was a huge task that took many years. Modern churches often have plainer interiors and use a variety of materials.

△ **Churches** are at the heart of many Christian communities. In the past they served as important meeting places and gave shelter and charity to people in need.

Chartres Cathedral, France (built from 1194 to 1260)

▽ Many **churches** have the same basic floor plan, whether they are small parish churches or huge city cathedrals.

Most churches, especially Catholic ones, are built in the shape of a cross. Worshipers sit in the center, in a section called the nave. They all face toward the altar and the place where the choir sings. On either side are the two wings, called transepts, which give the building its cross shape.

△ **Churchill** was Britain's most important leader during World War II.

Churchill, Winston

Sir Winston Churchill (1874–1965) was a British prime minister, war leader, and writer. Although he was a senior minister in **Parliament** before and during **World War I**, he was not very powerful. But in 1940, when **World War II** threatened Great Britain, the country chose him as its prime minister. As a wartime leader, Churchill showed great courage and determination. His rousing speeches helped the people of Great Britain fight against Germany and its allies. He told the people: "I have nothing to offer but blood, toil, tears, and sweat."

Cinema *see* Film

△ This government poster from the Spanish **Civil War** shows crimes supposedly carried out by the enemy.

Circus

The **Romans** first used the word "circus" to describe a large open-air space where exciting displays of horseback riding, chariot racing, acrobatics, and wrestling were held. The modern type of circus began in the 1700s, and circus acts today include jugglers, clowns, and acrobats. Some circuses include acts performed with trained animals such as elephants, bears, tigers, and lions.

Civil rights

People have always fought for the right to govern themselves. But this does not always mean that people have freedom in their own lives, and sometimes they have to fight for this freedom—for their civil rights. The most important of these rights are freedom to follow your own **religion**, freedom to say what you like in speech and in **newspapers**, equality in **law**, and the right to elect and dismiss a **government**.

In the United States civil rights were an important issue for African-Americans in the 1950s. Dr. Martin Luther King, Jr. led the movement for racial equality and civil rights in the U.S. (see **racism** and **King, Martin Luther**).

Civil war

Civil war happens when an entire country is divided into two or more groups that fight each other over their different political or religious beliefs. Sometimes friends and even families are forced to take opposite sides in the fighting. Major civil wars took place in **Great Britain** (1642–1649), the **United States** (1861–1865), **China** (1926–1935), and **Spain** (1936–1939).

Civil War

The Civil War took place in the **United States** from 1861–65. It was fought between Northern States (the Union), and the Southern States (the Confederacy). In 1861 Mississippi, Florida, Alabama, Georgia, and Louisiana joined South Carolina and tried to break away, or secede, from the U.S. and form their

▽ More than 600,000 soldiers died in the **American Civil War**. The Battle of Gettysburg, July 1-3, 1863, was the bloodiest battle ever fought on U.S. soil.

own country. The main argument was over **slavery**. People in the Northern States wanted to free the black slaves who still worked on the big farms, or plantations, in the Southern States. These quarrels finally led to civil war.

When war broke out, 11 states left the Union to join the Confederacy. At first the Confederates, under General Lee, won many battles, but they were defeated at the Battle of Gettysburg in July 1863. The Union army, under General Grant, began to win the war. In April 1865 the Confederate army surrendered to General Grant.

The North had stronger industries than the South, and—in the end—that decided the war. After the war many people in the South were bitter. The war had destroyed their prosperity. However, most people in the North felt it was more important that slavery be ended and the Union be preserved.

Civil War, English

In the British Isles the most recent civil war lasted from 1642–49. It was fought between King **Charles I** and the English **Parliament**. By this time it was established that, although the king ruled the country, he could **tax** the people only if Parliament agreed. Charles believed that God had given him the right to do this. In 1629 he got rid of Parliament and tried to rule without it.

Another important disagreement was about **religion**. Charles was married to a Catholic, but most English people at that time were Protestants. They were suspicious of Charles because several of England's enemies, including France and Spain, were Catholic countries.

In 1642 the king called his friends and supporters to arm themselves. They were called Royalists. Parliament had its own army. Its soldiers were known as Roundheads because many of them had short, closely shaved hair. The Roundheads had a great general named Oliver **Cromwell**. He was strict and trained his army carefully.

After numerous battles, sieges, and skirmishes the Royalist forces lost the war. Charles was captured and put on trial. In 1649 he was executed. For some years Parliament ruled without a king and with Cromwell as its leader.

Clay

Clay is **rock** that has been broken down by millions of years of weathering. It is made of tiny particles that make a thick, sticky paste. Clay particles are so small and closely packed together that a layer of them is waterproof. When a layer of clay lies underground, rain that seeps down into the soil cannot go through it. The water forms an underground pool, or reservoir. People can get the water out by digging wells.

Clay is easy to mold and can be baked hard in an oven, or kiln. It is used for making pots, tiles, and bricks.

Cleopatra

Cleopatra (69–30 B.C.) was a queen of **Egypt**. She married the Roman leader Julius **Caesar** and lived with him in Rome. After Caesar's death in 44 B.C. Cleopatra met Mark Antony, who jointly ruled the **Roman Empire** with Octavian. She soon fell in love

△ Martin Luther King, Jr. was a leader of the **civil rights** movement in the U.S. He demanded justice for African-Americans and led numerous protest marches and rallies.

△ Wet **clay** can be made into differently shaped pots using a potter's wheel.

▽ The **English Civil War** was decided at the Battle of Naseby on June 14, 1645. Parliament's soldiers, the Roundheads, won a great victory over Royalist forces.

Royalist soldier

Roundhead soldiers

Queen **Cleopatra** of Egypt is famous for causing a war by falling in love with the Roman leader Antony. Her fascinating life has inspired many writers, including Shakespeare.

with Antony, and Antony left his wife, Octavian's sister, to live with her. Octavian did not trust Cleopatra or Antony and started a war with them. He defeated them in a naval battle near Greece in 31 B.C.

Cleopatra and Antony fled to Egypt and decided to kill themselves. Antony stabbed himself and died in Cleopatra's arms. Cleopatra then died by allowing an asp (a poisonous snake) to bite her.

Climate

Climate is the usual **weather** of a place over a long period of time. The weather can change from day to day, but the climate stays the same.

The **sun** has the greatest influence on the climate. It heats the land, the seas, and the air. Countries near the **equator** get more of the sun's rays and usually have a hotter climate than places farther north or south. The sun's rays do not get to the **Arctic and Antarctic** easily. They have very cold climates.

When the sun heats the air it causes **winds** that can make the climate hotter or colder. The winds may also carry rain or dry air, which can make the climate wet or dry.

The earth can be roughly divided into several climate zones. Within each zone there are local variations. For example, high mountains may get different weather from lowland plains. Climates can also change over time. Many scientists think that the whole world is becoming warmer, a process called **global warming**.

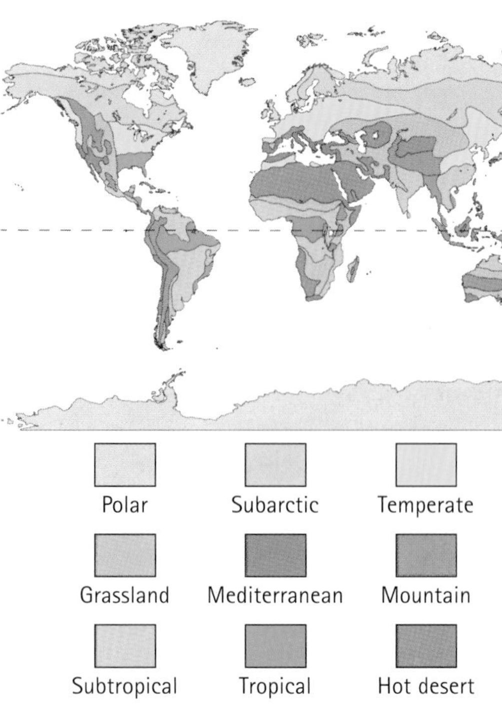

THE WORLD'S CLIMATE ZONES

One of the earliest kinds of **clock** was the sundial. As the sun moves across the sky the position of its shadow changes on a grid, indicating the time.

Clock

Long ago people measured **time** by putting a stick in the ground and watching its shadow move with the sun. Sundials work in the same way. However, sun clocks work only when the sun is shining. The first mechanical clocks were made in Europe in the 1200s, although the Chinese probably had simple clocks as early as the 600s. European clocks were first used in **churches** and **monasteries** to mark the time of services.

Early clocks were poor timekeepers and could lose or gain an hour a day. In 1581 the Italian astronomer **Galileo** discovered that the **pendulum** could be used to measure time. This helped people make much more accurate clocks. Further improvements were made, and ordinary clocks are now accurate to within a few minutes a year.

Today's scientists need very accurate clocks. They invented first the electric and then the quartz crystal clock. A quartz clock—the type used in most watches—tells the time by measuring the vibrations of a quartz crystal inside.

Cloning is a technique for making exact copies, or clones, of living things. In 1996 scientists cloned a sheep named Dolly. Her offspring was identical.

Cloning

Clones are organisms, or living things, that have exactly the same genetic material (see **genetics**). Many examples of clones exist in nature. The offspring of very basic organisms with a single cell, such as **bacteria** and **yeast**, are always clones. Some plants and simple animals, such as flatworms, produce clones through a process called asexual reproduction—that means, without joining a male and female cell together (see **reproduction**). Clones also occur in advanced animals and humans from time to time. Identical twins are clones of each other but are rare.

Recently scientists discovered how to clone living things in laboratories. They first used the technique to clone frogs in the 1960s. In Scotland, in 1996, a team of scientists cloned a sheep—the first **mammal** to be cloned. One day researchers may be able to clone a human, but many people think that would be dangerous and wrong.

The ability to clone animals and plants could be very useful in **farming** and **medicine**. However, cloning is extremely difficult and expensive at the moment.

Clothing *see* Fashion

△ **Coffee** comes from beans that are found inside the fruit of the coffee tree. These berries are bright red when ripe.

△ **Coins** were first made in ancient China. Virtually every country now makes them, and collecting coins can be a satisfying hobby.

Coal

Coal is a **fuel** that is found in layers, or seams, under the ground. It is known as a **fossil** fuel because it was made millions of years ago from deposits of dead plants. Coal is used for heating and in making **electricity** and chemicals.

Coffee

Coffee is a drink made from the beans of the coffee **tree**. The tree bears red berries that contain seeds or beans in yellow pulp, surrounded by a tough skin. The skin and pulp are removed, and the beans are dried and roasted until they are brown. Then they are ground to brew coffee for drinking.

Coin

The first **metal** coins were minted (made) in about 800 B.C. Before then all **trade** had been done by barter—by exchanging goods. For a long time coins were made of precious metals such as **gold** and **silver**. Then people realized that any metal would do as long as everybody agreed that each coin was a symbol for a certain value.

College *see* University and college

◁ **Coal** is mined in various ways according to how deep it is. When it reaches the surface, opencast and drift mines are used. Slope mines are used for slightly deeper layers of coal, and shaft mines extract coal from deep underground.

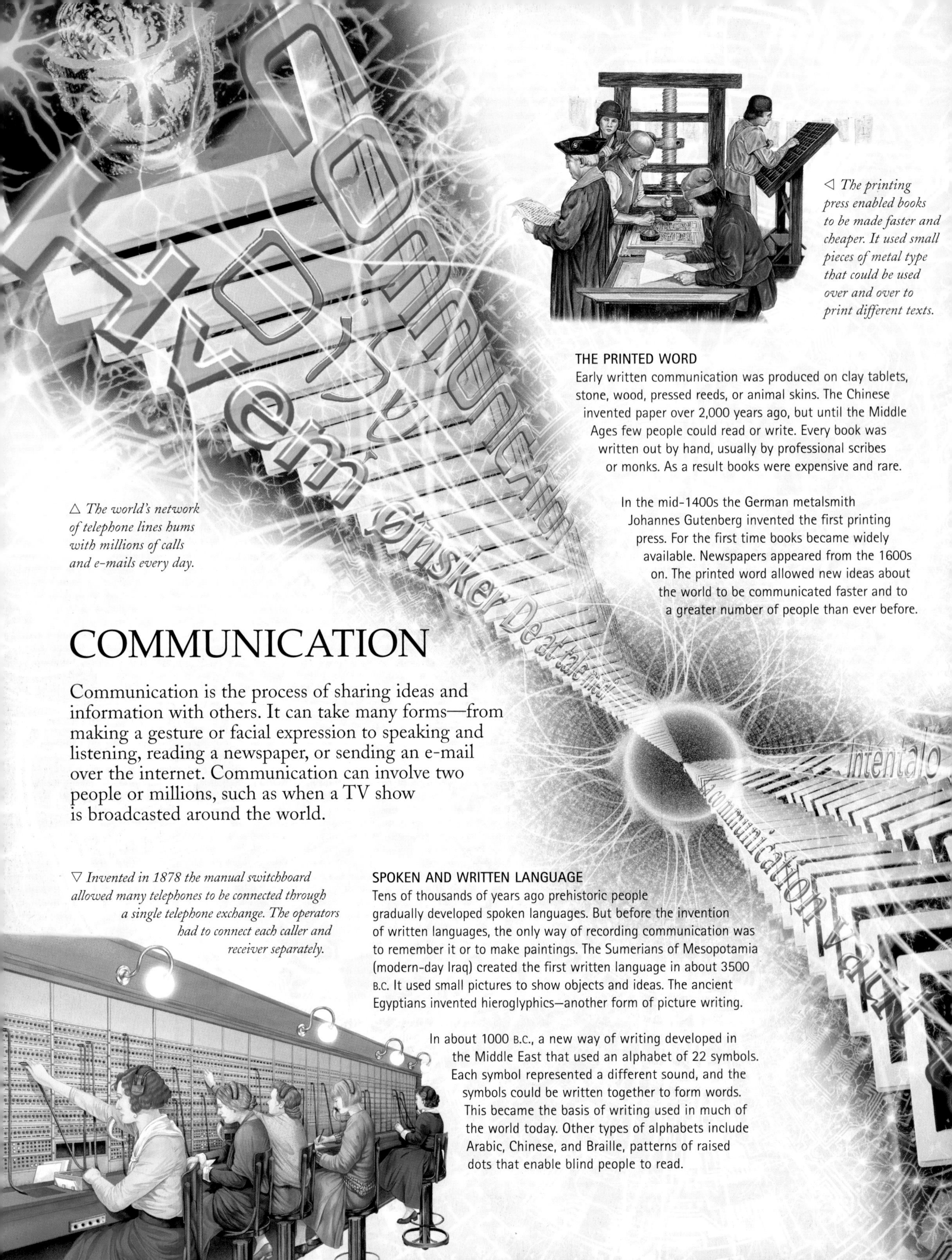

COMMUNICATION

Communication is the process of sharing ideas and information with others. It can take many forms—from making a gesture or facial expression to speaking and listening, reading a newspaper, or sending an e-mail over the internet. Communication can involve two people or millions, such as when a TV show is broadcasted around the world.

△ *The world's network of telephone lines hums with millions of calls and e-mails every day.*

◁ *The printing press enabled books to be made faster and cheaper. It used small pieces of metal type that could be used over and over to print different texts.*

▽ *Invented in 1878 the manual switchboard allowed many telephones to be connected through a single telephone exchange. The operators had to connect each caller and receiver separately.*

SPOKEN AND WRITTEN LANGUAGE

Tens of thousands of years ago prehistoric people gradually developed spoken languages. But before the invention of written languages, the only way of recording communication was to remember it or to make paintings. The Sumerians of Mesopotamia (modern-day Iraq) created the first written language in about 3500 B.C. It used small pictures to show objects and ideas. The ancient Egyptians invented hieroglyphics—another form of picture writing.

In about 1000 B.C., a new way of writing developed in the Middle East that used an alphabet of 22 symbols. Each symbol represented a different sound, and the symbols could be written together to form words. This became the basis of writing used in much of the world today. Other types of alphabets include Arabic, Chinese, and Braille, patterns of raised dots that enable blind people to read.

THE PRINTED WORD

Early written communication was produced on clay tablets, stone, wood, pressed reeds, or animal skins. The Chinese invented paper over 2,000 years ago, but until the Middle Ages few people could read or write. Every book was written out by hand, usually by professional scribes or monks. As a result books were expensive and rare.

In the mid-1400s the German metalsmith Johannes Gutenberg invented the first printing press. For the first time books became widely available. Newspapers appeared from the 1600s on. The printed word allowed new ideas about the world to be communicated faster and to a greater number of people than ever before.

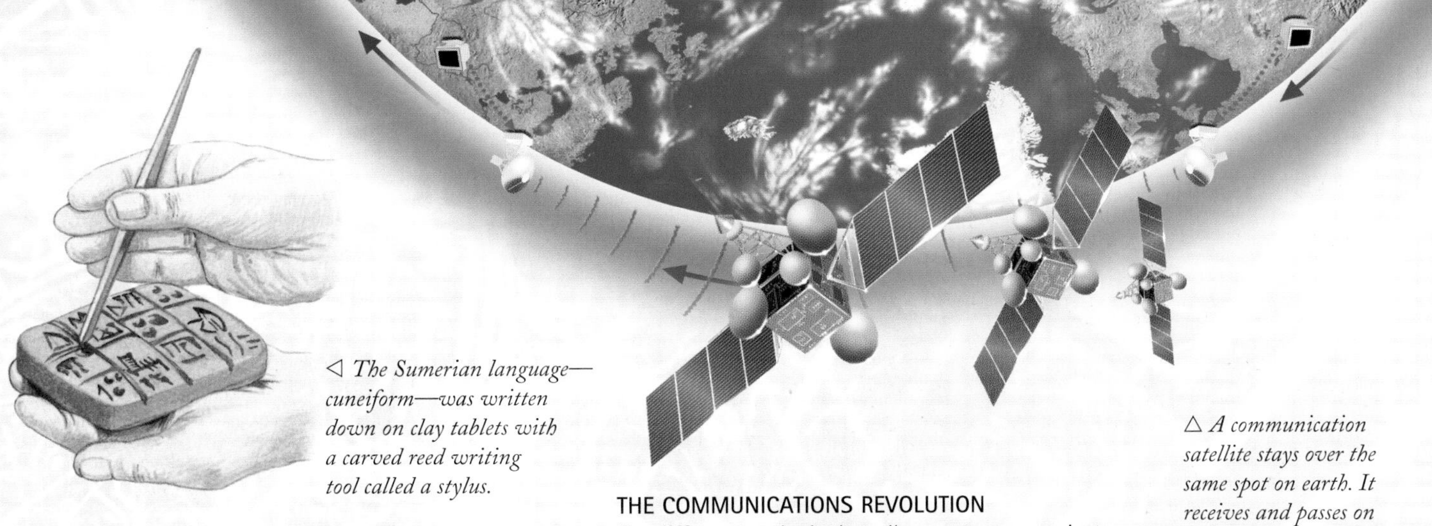

◁ *The Sumerian language—cuneiform—was written down on clay tablets with a carved reed writing tool called a stylus.*

△ *A communication satellite stays over the same spot on earth. It receives and passes on television and telephone signals from one point on the planet to another.*

TELECOMMUNICATION

Telecommunication is the ability to communicate over long distances. It was attempted in historic times using flags, drums, messengers, and smoke signals. During the 1800s communication systems using electrical signals carried down wires were invented. The first was the telegraph, which was developed in the 1830s and 1840s in the U.S.S.R., Great Britain, and the U.S. Before long thousands of miles of telegraph wires had been strung up.

In 1876 Scottish inventor Alexander Graham Bell found out how to send the human voice down telegraph cables, creating the telephone. The telephone developed rapidly. Within 21 years there were one million telephone lines in the world. Today the total is over one billion.

THE COMMUNICATIONS REVOLUTION

The different methods that allow us to communicate are called media. In the 1900s new communication technology provided people with many more types of media. Recorded sound, photography, and the movies all became available to millions of people. Italian Guglielmo Marconi created the first wireless telegraph, which transmitted messages using radio waves instead of wires. Broadcasting, where a message is sent from one source to many receivers, began with the first radio programs in the 1920s. Television followed in 1936.

Since 1962, satellites have relayed telephone calls and TV pictures across the globe. The arrival of personal computers in the 1970s vastly improved and sped up existing forms of communication. Computers also led to the birth of the World Wide Web and e-mail.

SEE ALSO
Books, Computers, Film, Hieroglyphics, Internet, Language, Newspapers, Photography, Printing, Radio, Recording, Satellite, Telephones

Colombia

Colombia is a country in northern **South America**. The **Andes** mountains cover about one third of its area. Most of the people live in the northwest, where the highlands are fertile. The Colombians won independence from **Spain** in 1819 under the leadership of Simón Bolívar. The country is a democratic republic but has many social problems, including a huge trade in illegal drugs. **Coffee** is Colombia's main commercial crop.

COLOMBIA
Government: Republic
Capital: Bogotá
Area: 400,600 sq. mi.
Population: 40 million
Language: Spanish
Currency: Peso

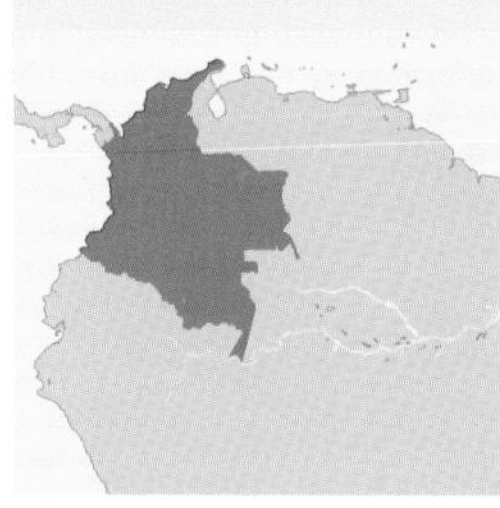

Color

The first person to find out about colored **light** was Isaac **Newton**. He shone sunlight through a piece of **glass** called a prism. The light that came out of the prism was broken up into all the colors of the **rainbow**—red, orange, yellow, green, blue, indigo, and violet. Newton had found out that "white" light is a mixture of several colors added together.

When sunlight falls on rain, we may see a rainbow. Rainbows are caused by the drops of **water** behaving like tiny prisms. They break up the sun's light into a spectrum of colors, which are always in the same order, from red to violet.

A red flower looks red to us because it absorbs (soaks up) all the other colors and reflects only red to our eyes. A green leaf absorbs all the colors of light except for green.

Colored light behaves differently from colored pigments (the substances that give inks and **paints** their color). All the colors in light combine to make white light, but mixing colored pigments results in black.

◁ **Color** is what we see when light from an object reaches our eyes. A tomato looks red to us because it reflects red light back into our eyes, but it takes in all of the other colors of light.

The **Colosseum** of Ancient Rome was completed in A.D. 80. It had four stories and a canvas roof that protected spectators from the sun and rain.

Colosseum

The Colosseum of Rome was a giant sports stadium built by the ancient Romans. It held more than 50,000 people and was the largest building of its kind in the **Roman Empire**. It still stands in the center of Rome but is mostly in ruins.

The floor, or arena, was used for **gladiator** combats, battles between men and animals, and fights between different kinds of animals. The floor could also be flooded so that mock sea battles could be fought on it.

Columbus, Christopher

Christopher Columbus (1451–1506) was a sailor and explorer. In 1492 he claimed several islands off the Americas for **Spain**. Although Columbus returned to the Americas three more times, he died believing that he had reached Asia.

Columbus—like many people of his time—knew that the earth was not flat but round. Sailors from Europe used to sail east to the "Indies" (Asia). They brought back rich cargoes of **gold** and **spices**. Columbus thought that if he sailed west instead, he could reach the Indies quicker. Ferdinand and Isabella, king and queen of Spain, gave him ships and money to make this voyage.

In 1492 Columbus sailed west with three ships. After three weeks, on October 12, they reached an island in the Americas. Columbus named it San Salvador—an island in the Bahamas.

Comet

Comets travel around the **solar system** in loops, or **orbits**. Sometimes they pass close to the sun. At other times they move far beyond the path of **Pluto**, the outermost **planet**. Their orbits may last from several years to many centuries.

Comets are clouds of frozen gas, ice, dust, and rock. The largest are only a few miles across, but their bright tails may be millions of miles long. One of the most famous comets is named after the English astronomer Edmond **Halley**.

△ As a **comet** travels toward the Sun the Sun's rays knock particles out of the comet and push them away to make a long tail. The tail is made of glowing gas and dust.

Commonwealth

A commonwealth is a group of countries or people who hold regular meetings and try to help each other. The Commonwealth of Nations is a commonwealth made up of many of the countries that were once ruled by Great Britain. Most of these countries now have their own **governments** and laws but some of them still have the queen or king of Great Britain as their **monarch**. The Commonwealth came into being at a meeting held in 1926. Its members include **Canada, Australia, New Zealand, India, Pakistan,** and many African, Pacific, and Caribbean countries.

Communication

see **pages 70–71**

Communism

Communism is a set of ideas about the way a country should be run. The main idea of communism is that people should share their wealth and property. Doing this makes people more equal because nobody is wealthy or poor.

In most communist countries the people own the factories and farms, but it is usually the **government** that runs them. The government controls almost everything, and personal freedoms are often restricted. There may be strict government control of the **media,**

▽ Christopher **Columbus** made four voyages across the Atlantic to the Americas. On his first trip, in 1492, he sailed with three ships, the *Santa María*, the *Pinta*, and the *Niña*.

An early European **compass**. The needle in a compass always points north and south because the earth itself is a giant magnet. The needle lines up parallel with the earth's magnetic field.

including newspapers, television, movies, and books. The purpose of all of these strict government controls is to organize the country for the benefit of everyone who lives there.

Many countries became communist during the course of the 1900s. They included the **Soviet Union**, **China**, **Cuba,** and North **Korea** and several countries in Eastern Europe. **Lenin** and **Stalin** of the Soviet Union and **Mao Zedong** of China were among the most important communist leaders of the last century.

Communism has not always been a successful form of government. Many of the people in communist countries have remained poor.

Compact disc
see **Recording**

Communism is a way of organizing a country so that everybody can share its wealth and property. At a meeting of the Chinese Communist Party in 1949 large posters of the party leaders form a backdrop while speeches are being made (below).

Company

A company is an organization that exists to make money—a profit—for the people who own it. It does this by selling goods or providing a useful service of some kind. Companies range in size from a single employee, or worker, to thousands of employees.

A company must keep records of the money and goods that come into and go out of the business. This is known as keeping accounts, or accounting. An accountant's job is to study whether the company is doing well or badly.

Some of the earliest companies formed in Europe in the **Middle Ages**. They bought and sold products such as wool, timber, and food (see **trade**). Today many companies are owned by shareholders. These are people who have bought a share of the company. Shares in companies are bought and sold at places called **stock exchanges**.

Compass

A compass is an instrument for finding the way. A magnetic compass always points to the earth's magnetic poles, which are close to the **North Pole** and the **South Pole**. It works by **magnetism**. It has a magnetic needle fixed to a pivot so that it is free to swing around. The needle always points north and south when it is at rest. With a compass showing where north and south are, it is easy to travel in a straight line in any direction you wish to go.

Compound

Compounds are chemicals that are made up of two or more **elements**. For example, **salt** is a compound made up of the elements sodium and chlorine. Compounds are formed when elements come together and make a new substance that is completely different from the elements. **Water** is a compound of the gas elements **hydrogen** and **oxygen**, and it is very different from either of them.

There are millions of compounds in the

world. They can be very simple, like water (with three **atoms** in each molecule), or complex like some plastics (with hundreds of atoms in their molecules).

Computer

Computers are playing an increasingly larger part in our lives. They have led to enormous advances in science and technology. For example, computers can guide airplanes and spacecraft, control life-saving medical equipment, and operate automatic cash machines that give us money in the street. This book was designed, edited, and produced using computers!

Computers can do all of these things because they are able to do millions of calculations each second. First the computer receives data, or information, put in by the user. Then it processes the data according to its program, and it produces a result.

All computers use a language called the **binary system**. There are only two numbers in the binary system: 1 and 0. Computers use this system because they have been designed to work with **electrical currents**. They can recognize the difference between a large current and a small current flow. If there is a large current, they register 1 and if there is a small current, they register 0. When we type on a computer keyboard, we are making a lot of electrical currents flow through tiny circuits in **silicon chips**. It is these tiny currents that give us the answers we need.

A computer has four basic parts. An input device, such as a keyboard, mouse, or joystick, is used to enter data into the computer. Then the computer's "brain"—the central processing unit or CPU—processes the data and performs the tasks it has been told to do. The resulting information is sent to the computer's output device, such as a screen or printer. And finally the computer's memory unit stores programs and data. These can also be stored on removable disks (see **recording**).

Computers can be linked to each other using a network of telephone lines and cables. The **internet** is a globe-spanning computer network, allowing messages and information to be sent across the world in seconds.

△ The Chinese thinker, **Confucius**, taught people to respect one another.

DEMOCRATIC REPUBLIC OF CONGO
Government: Republic
Capital: Kinshasa
Area: 875,500 sq. mi.
Population: 53.6 million
Languages: French
Currency: Congolese Franc

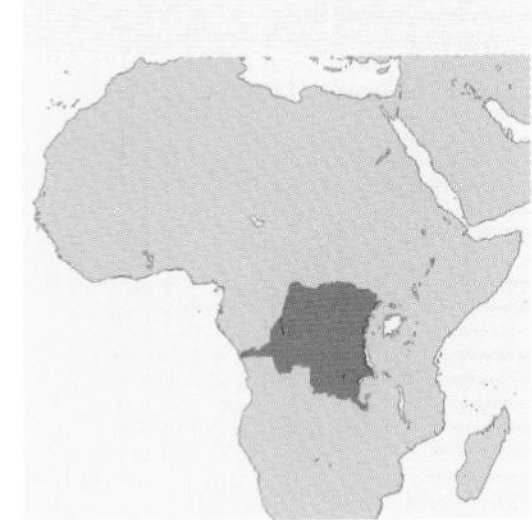

▽ **Computers** can be used to direct robots, such as this one that sprays paint on the bodies of new cars.

Concrete

Concrete is a mixture of cement, gravel, and **sand** combined with water. The pastelike concrete dries hard and is used to make buildings, **roads**, **bridges**, and **dams**. The cement that is the starting point for concrete is usually made from limestone and **clay**. These materials are crushed and mixed and then heated in an oven called a kiln. When cool, the mixture is ground into cement powder. Concrete is often strengthened by placing steel rods in it when it is soft.

Confucius

Confucius (551–479 B.C.) lived nearly 2,500 years ago in **China**. He was a famous philosopher (thinker) who taught people how to live and behave in a good way. The Chinese people have followed his teachings for centuries.

Congo (Zaire)

The Democratic Republic of Congo, which was known as Zaire between 1971 and 1997, is a huge country in **Africa**. It includes most of the Congo River basin. The Congo River is the second longest river in Africa—only the **Nile** River is longer. It is an important means of transportation for the peoples of central Africa. Thick forests and **savanna** (grassland with trees) cover much of Congo's land. The country is very rich in minerals, including **copper**, cobalt,

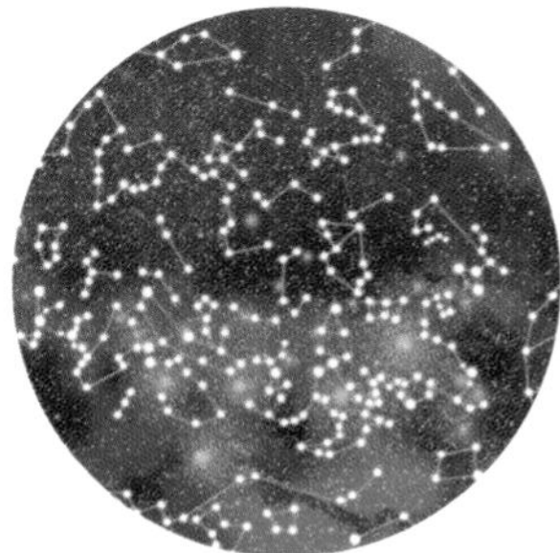

SOUTHERN HEMISPHERE

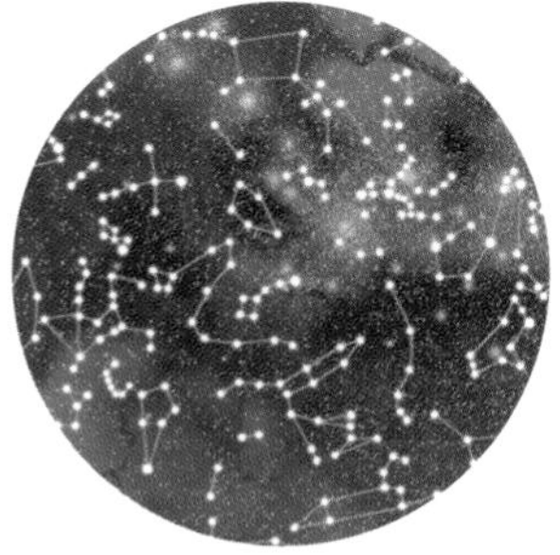

NORTHERN HEMISPHERE

Constellations are groups of stars that form patterns in the night sky. People who live north of the equator (in the Northern Hemisphere) see different stars from those who live south of the equator.

and **diamonds**, but most of its people live by farming.

The country was once ruled by **Belgium**, but it became independent in 1960. Since then, it has suffered from a long **civil war**. Across the Congo River lies the Democratic Republic of Congo's smaller neighbor, the Republic of Congo.

Conifer

Conifers are **trees** and shrubs that have cones instead of **flowers** for making seeds and pollen (the powdery grains that plants use to fertilize each other). Many conifers are found in cooler parts of the world. Vast forests of conifers cover much of **Canada** and **Russia**.

△ Conifers include firs, pines, spruces, larches, and cedars. Most of them have needlelike leaves that they do not lose in the winter.

Conservation

Humans use **plants, animals, soil, water,** and **minerals** for nearly everything that they make. Conservation means using these valuable resources wisely and protecting them for use in the future. It also means preserving areas of outstanding natural beauty.

Today the need to conserve wildlife and natural resources is a major world problem. It involves the study of **ecology**, the branch of **biology** that deals with the relationship between all living things and their surroundings. Conservationists are people who try to find a balance between the needs of human beings and care of the natural environment. Without care the world's fast-growing **population** will cause increasing damage to wild **habitats** such as forests, marshes, and seas.

There are many different aspects to conservation. It includes recycling (reusing) useful materials such as paper, plastic, glass, and metal. It also includes saving energy and reducing the amount of harmful **pollution** produced by factories and vehicles. Another concern of conservationists is to try to stop plants and animals from becoming extinct (vanishing forever). The best way of doing this is to create nature reserves that protect an entire habitat.

Constantinople

Constantinople is the old name for the city of Istanbul in **Turkey**. It lies between Asia and Europe and was the most important city in the western world for more than a thousand years.

Constantinople was named after the Roman emperor Constantine. In A.D. 330 he founded the city on the site of the ancient Greek town of Byzantium. He divided the **Roman Empire** into two to make it easier to rule. Constantinople was the capital of the eastern half—the **Byzantine Empire**.

After the last Roman emperor was overthrown in A.D. 476, Constantinople and the Byzantine Empire continued to be powerful. The city was a great center of **Christianity**, learning, and **trade** until it was invaded by the Ottoman Turks in 1453. It became a Muslim city and was renamed Istanbul.

▽ Continents lie on huge plates of rock, which move because they are floating on a layer of semiliquid rock called magma.

Constellation

Stars form patterns known as constellations in the night sky. In early times these were named after ancient gods, heroes, animals, and objects whose shapes people saw in the patterns. Examples include Orion the Hunter, Leo the Lion, Lyra the Lyre.

Astronomers have named a total of 88 constellations over the whole sky. Twelve of them form a wide track where the **sun** appears to travel in the course of the year and where the **planets** are usually found. These are the constellations of the Zodiac.

△ **Conservation** includes the battle to protect rare wildlife. In Africa wardens burn piles of confiscated elephant tusks to deter the illegal trade in ivory.

Continental shelf

Continents do not end where their coasts meet the sea. Their true edge lies far out under the sea. Each continent is ringed by a gently sloping shelf of land under the sea—he continental shelf. This shelf sometimes stretches for hundreds of miles from the shore. Beyond the continental shelf is the deep **ocean** floor.

Most sea life is found on the continental shelf. Sunlight shines through the water, helping plants, fish, and other animals grow.

△ **Constantinople** was attacked by the Ottoman Turks in 1453. They crushed the defenders, and turned the Christian city into a new Muslim capital.

Continent

A continent is a large area of land. There are seven continents—**Africa**, **Antarctica**, **Asia**, **Australia**, **Europe**, **North America**, and **South America**.

The continents are not attached to anything. They are made of **rock**, but heat from the center of the **earth** has made the surface rocks break into huge pieces called plates. These plates are floating on top of a layer of hot, molten (semiliquid) rock called magma. As the magma moves the plates slide on top of the magma, taking the continents with them. This movement is very slow. A continent moves only a few centimetres each century.

The shapes of North and South America, Europe, and Africa look like puzzle pieces that would fit together if they were pushed together. The continents look like this because they used to be one giant piece of land that later broke up. The name for this process is continental drift.

People who study **geology** have found evidence showing that South America once touched Africa. Geologists think that the movements of the continents pushed up some pieces of land to make mountain ranges such as the **Alps**, the **Andes**, and the **Himalayas**. The mountains are continually getting higher as the earth's plates push against each other.

Contraception
see **Birth control**

Cook, James

James Cook (1728–1779) was a British sea captain and explorer. His expeditions took him around the world and all over the **Pacific Ocean**. In 1770 Cook landed in Botany Bay, **Australia**, to claim the continent for Britain. **New Zealand** and many Pacific islands also became British colonies as a result of his trips.

Captain **Cook** was the first European explorer to visit the Antarctic and Hawaii. He also led voyages to the South Pacific and Australia.

Copernicus, Nicolaus

Nicolaus Copernicus (1473–1543) was a Polish scientist. He is sometimes called the father of modern **astronomy**. Copernicus showed that the **earth** is not the center of the **universe** as people used to believe. Instead, the earth and the **planets** revolve around the **sun**. Copernicus also showed that the earth itself moves around, or rotates, each day.

Copper

Copper is a reddish-brown **metal**. It was one of the first metals that people used. Copper is very soft when it is pure. But if it is mixed with other metals, it makes **alloys** such as brass and **bronze**, which are harder and better for making tools. Copper lets heat and **electricity** pass through it easily, so it is often used for pots, pans, and electric wires.

Coral

Corals are tiny animals that live in warm, shallow seas. They have soft bodies but build hard, chalky, "skeletons" around themselves for protection.

Most corals live in groups, or colonies. These can have many shapes, from lacy fans to stubby branches, usually in beautiful colors. Some colonies form thick underwater walls called reefs. Coral reefs support the richest variety of animals anywhere in the sea. The world's largest coral reef is the **Great Barrier Reef**, which lies just off the east coast of **Australia**.

◁ **Coral** reefs provide homes for many sea animals, which find shelter in crevices or burrow into the coral itself.

Cotton has green fruits called bolls. When they are ripe, they split open to reveal a fluffy mass of white fibers and seeds.

△ **Cowboys** are known as *gauchos* in South America. Many of them still lead a traditional way of life on the plains of Argentina.

Cortès, Hernando

Hernando Cortès (1485–1547) was a Spanish soldier and explorer who in 1519 landed on the coast of **Mexico**. With a force of only 600 soldiers and a handful of horses he conquered the great **Aztec** empire. His horses and guns helped convince the Aztecs he was a god. Cortès marched on their capital, Tenochtitlàn, captured the Aztec emperor, Montezuma, and by 1521 had taken control of Mexico.

Cosmetics

Cosmetics have been used since prehistoric times when **cave dwellers** decorated their dead with dyes and paints. Lipstick, eye shadow, nail paint, and hair dye were widely used by the ancient Egyptians. The Greeks and Romans bathed with scented oil and wore perfumes to make their bodies and clothes smell sweet. Most modern cosmetics are made from a base of **fats** and oils, to which a variety of natural and artificial substances is added.

Costa Rica

Costa Rica is a small Spanish-speaking country lying between **Nicaragua** and **Panama** in Central America. It was a

Spanish colony from 1530 to 1821 and became independent in 1848. Costa Rica is a largely agricultural country, the chief crops being coffee, bananas, sugarcane, and cocoa. **Rain forest** covers much of the rest of the land.

Cotton

Cotton grows in warm and tropical places all around the world. It is one of the most important plants grown by people. Its fibers are spun into yarn and then woven into cloth (see **weaving**). The seeds are used for oil and cattle food. Cotton oil is used to make soaps, paints, and cosmetics.

Cowboy

There are still many people in the western U.S. who ride **horses** and herd cows, but the great days of the cowboys lasted only 40 years, from the 1860s to 1900. At that time there were **prairie** grasslands stretching from Texas north to Canada. **Cattle** was grazed there and then driven in great herds by cowboys to the railroad stations.

The cowboys' life was simple and hard. They travelled light, and usually owned nothing more than their horse, saddle, bed-roll and clothes.

Crab

Crabs belong to a group of animals called **crustaceans** and are closely related to **lobsters**. Crabs have hard, thick **shells** that cover their flat bodies. They also have long, spidery legs for walking underwater, swimming, and burrowing. The first pair of legs have pincers, which are used for attacking and holding prey. Crabs have their eyes on the end of short stalks. These can be pulled into the shell for safety.

Most crabs live only in the sea, but there are some kinds that live in rivers or lakes and some tropical kinds that live on forested islands.

Cricket

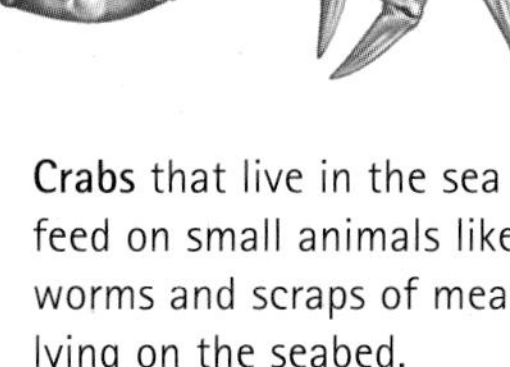

Crabs that live in the sea feed on small animals like worms and scraps of meat lying on the seabed.

Cricket is a **sport** that was probably invented in England in the 1300s. It is played with a bat and a ball by two teams of 11 players on an oval grass field. The teams take turns to bat and to field.

A member of the fielding side, the bowler, throws the ball to the batsman, who stands in front of three wooden stumps. The stumps have two small sticks resting on top of them, called bails, and the bowler tries to knock them off with the ball. If the bowler is successful, the batsman is out. The batsman is also out if a member of the fielding side catches a ball that they have just hit before it touches the ground.

The batsman scores runs, or points, by hitting the ball and by running the short distance to where the bowler was standing. There are two batsmen who run back and forth between the two wickets, or bases, swapping positions as they do so.

Cricket is played mainly in Britain and former British colonies, such as **India**, **Australia**, **Pakistan**, **Zimbabwe**, and several **Caribbean** nations.

COSTA RICA
Government: Republic
Capital: San José
Area: 19,500 sq. mi.
Population: 3.7 million
Language: Spanish
Currency: Colón

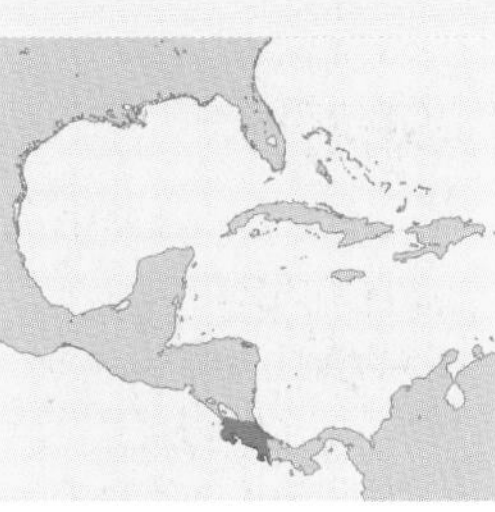

Croatia

Croatia is a small country in the **Mediterranean**. It was formerly a republic of **Yugoslavia**, but it declared its independence in 1991. This was followed by fighting between Croatia and the Yugoslav army. The army was dominated by another Yugoslav republic, **Serbia**.

Croatia has a long coastline with many islands. Steep mountains sweep down to the sea, separating the coast from fertile inland plains.

CROATIA
Government: Parliamentary Democracy
Capital: Zagreb
Area: 21,800 sq. mi.
Population: 4.3 million
Language: Serb-Croatian
Currency: Kuna

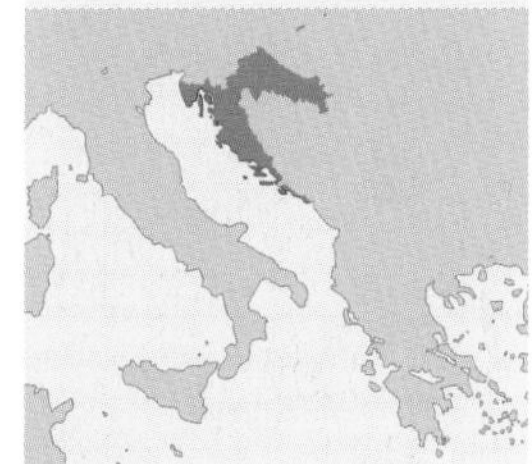

Crocodile

see **Alligator and crocodile**

The **Crusades** were a series of eight wars between Christian knights (left) and the Muslim Turks (right), called Saracens.

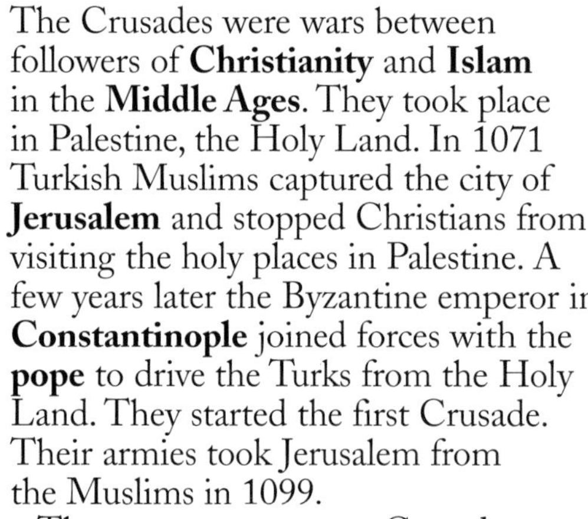

Cuba is one of the world's leading producers of cigars. They are rolled by hand from dried tobacco leaves.

CUBA
Government: Communist State
Capital: Havana
Area: 42,800 sq. mi.
Population: 11.2 million
Language: Spanish
Currency: Peso

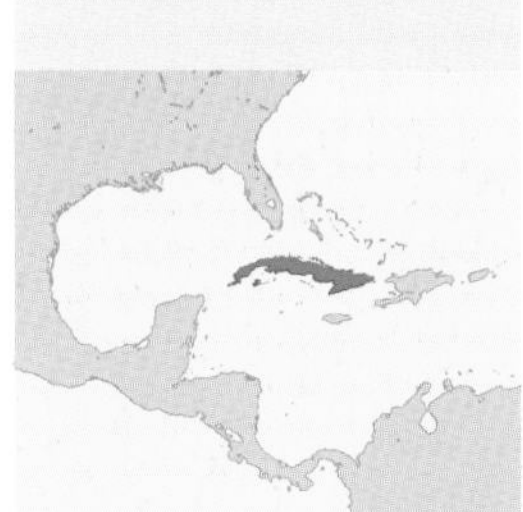

Cromwell, Oliver

Oliver Cromwell (1599–1658) was the only ruler of Britain never to have been a **monarch**. He came to power after the English **civil war** of the 1640s. Cromwell fought against **Charles I** with the army of the English **Parliament** and became its leader. After Charles I was executed, Cromwell became the head of the country, but he never declared himself king. In 1660, two years after Cromwell's death, Charles's son was restored to power as King Charles II.

Crusades

The Crusades were wars between followers of **Christianity** and **Islam** in the **Middle Ages**. They took place in Palestine, the Holy Land. In 1071 Turkish Muslims captured the city of **Jerusalem** and stopped Christians from visiting the holy places in Palestine. A few years later the Byzantine emperor in **Constantinople** joined forces with the **pope** to drive the Turks from the Holy Land. They started the first Crusade. Their armies took Jerusalem from the Muslims in 1099.

There were seven more Crusades after the first one. Many of them failed because the Crusaders quarreled with each other. The third Crusade, in 1187, was defeated by a great Muslim general called Saladin. The Muslims took back much of the Holy Land.

During the Crusades, Europeans learned more about the eastern parts of the world. When they returned to Europe, they brought new things such as spices, silk, and paper with them.

Crustacean

Crustaceans are a large group of about 10,000 **invertebrates** (animals without backbones). They include wood lice, barnacles, oysters, shrimp, **lobsters,** and **crabs**. Most of them live in the sea.

All crustaceans have numerous joints in their bodies and legs. They often have claws, or pincers, on their front legs. They use these for defense and to grab prey. Many crustaceans live inside **shells**, which keep their soft bodies safe.

Cuba

Cuba is an island in the **Caribbean**. It was ruled by **Spain** from the 1500s until 1898, when the **United States** took Cuba from Spain. In 1902 the island gained independence. Cuba became a communist country in 1959 under its leader Fidel Castro (see **communism**). Cuba has large farms, growing sugarcane and **tobacco**, but forest covers the center of the island.

Curie, Marie and Pierre

Marie Curie (1867–1934) and Pierre Curie (1859–1906) were scientists who worked together and then married each other. She was Polish, he was French. They studied **radioactivity** and discovered the element **radium**, for which they were given the **Nobel Prize** for physics in 1903.

Cyclone *see* Hurricane

Czech Republic

The Czech Republic is in Eastern Europe. It used to be part of the country known as Czechoslovakia, which split into two nations, the Czech Republic and **Slovakia**, in 1993. Much of the Czech Republic is covered by mountains. Prague, its capital, is one of the most historic cities in Europe.

In 1938 **Germany** took control of western Czechoslovakia. This ended with the defeat of Germany in **World War II**. Czechoslovakia was then ruled by a communist government, but in 1989 the government fell and was replaced by a more democratic government.

D

Dali, Salvador

Born in Spain in 1904, Salvador Dali was one of the most inventive artists of the 1900s. His **art** was often bizarre, and at first many people who saw his work found it shocking.

Dali's **paintings** are unsettling because they are full of weird objects and strange landscapes. They frequently feature illusions, or "tricks of the eye." Dali made many other things beside paintings, including **sculptures**, movies, furniture, and even pieces of **jewelry**.

Dali belonged to a group of artists and writers called the Surrealists, who claimed to produce their work without having to think about what they were doing. Dali used to say that he was just painting his **dreams**. He died in 1989.

△ Salvador **Dali** often made sculptures from unusual combinations of objects. He created his famous "lobster telephone" in 1936.

Dalai Lama

The Dalai Lama is the religious leader of **Tibet**, a disputed area that currently forms part of southwest **China**. Tibet has its own form of **Buddhism**. The teachers of Tibetan Buddhism, called lamas, live in monasteries and instruct people in the ways of the Buddhist **religion**. The most important lama is known as the Dalai Lama.

Followers of the Dalai Lama believe that he is the reincarnation of a godlike buddhist teacher who lived long ago. When a Dalai Lama dies, the other lamas search for a young boy they believe to be the next reincarnation to take his place.

▽ Many **dams** are curved so that the great weight of water behind them pushes against the sides of the valley instead of against the dam wall.

Dam

A dam is a barrier built across a **river** to control its flow. Modern dams are usually made of **concrete** and include some of the largest structures built by people. There are several reasons for building dams. The main one is to make a reservoir—an artificial **lake**.

continued on page 84

△ *Before a game the All Black rugby team of New Zealand performs a ritual dance, which helps build the players' team spirit.*

▽ *Traditional Indian dances have close links with the Hindu religion. The dancers enact tender love stories and tales of epic battles between gods and demons.*

DANCE

Dance is one of the oldest human arts. It is the rhythmic movement of the body, usually in time to music.

WHY PEOPLE DANCE

Humans seem to have a powerful urge to dance. This may be because moving the body in rhythm is a natural way of expressing our feelings. For example, children often jump up and down when they are excited and sway gently when they are happy and resting. Dance can tell a story and create an atmosphere. It is also lots of fun. Many people dance simply to enjoy themselves.

AN ANCIENT ART

Dance is almost as old as human civilization itself. Prehistoric cave paintings in Africa and southern Europe show people dancing. Dance later became part of religion. It was used to bring rain, make crops grow, and guarantee good hunting. Warriors performed war dances to make themselves feel brave before a battle. People also danced at ceremonies and feasts.

WORLD OF DANCE

Every country has its own dance traditions, which often evolved from the simple dances of ordinary people. Gradually set moves and steps were introduced. Some dances became very formal, with strict rules for the dancers. The first formal social dances were held in Japan 1,500 years ago.

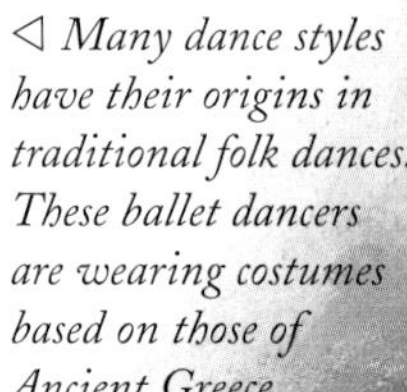

◁ *Many dance styles have their origins in traditional folk dances. These ballet dancers are wearing costumes based on those of Ancient Greece.*

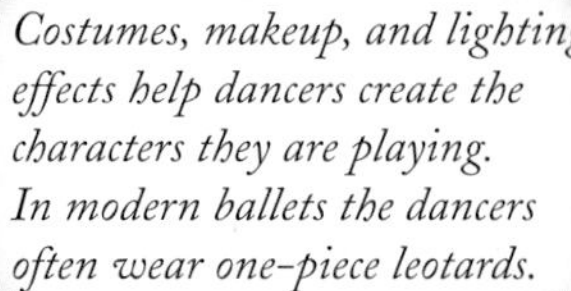

Costumes, makeup, and lighting effects help dancers create the characters they are playing. In modern ballets the dancers often wear one-piece leotards.

△ *Ballet dancers start classes at an early age. They learn the basic steps and how to move to music.*

◁ *Some ballet steps take a lot of practice to perfect. The grand jeté is a large leap in which the dancer stretches both legs out, like doing a split in midair.*

THE BEAUTY OF BALLET

Ballet emerged during the Renaissance (1400s) at the royal courts of Italy and France. It is like a language, but it uses music and dance instead of words. Ballet dancers mime (act out) the story using their whole bodies. They show feelings by exaggerating their movements.

A new ballet is the result of a partnership among many people. Choreographers have the idea for the ballet and arrange the dance movements. They work closely with the composer, who writes the music. Then there are the set, costume, and lighting designers.

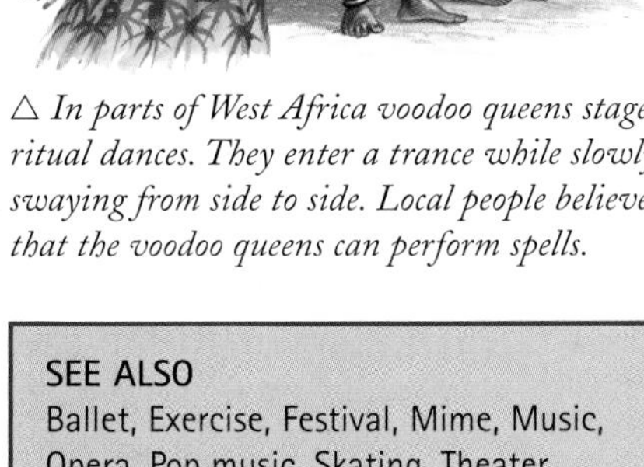

△ *In parts of West Africa voodoo queens stage ritual dances. They enter a trance while slowly swaying from side to side. Local people believe that the voodoo queens can perform spells.*

CHANGING STYLES

When the way people live changes, the way they dance often changes too. Many new dances have emerged over the last 200 years. In the 1800s the waltz swept across Europe and North America. It was a type of ballroom dance with swift, gliding turns. At first the waltz caused an uproar because the man and woman held each other so close. Tap dancing, a combination of African, Irish, and English traditions, developed among black Americans. Rock 'n' roll burst onto the scene in the 1940s and 1950s. It gave birth to disco, which is now danced all over the world.

CARNIVAL TIME

Dancing plays a major part in many festivals. In spring the people of Central and South America organize a five-day-long carnival in which people flood the streets in breathtaking costumes and dance to samba music. In China the Chinese New Year is celebrated with giant dragons that are "brought to life" by teams of dancers.

◁ *On the island of Java people perform a traditional horse dance. The dancers imagine they are possessed by the spirits of horses.*

SEE ALSO
Ballet, Exercise, Festival, Mime, Music, Opera, Pop music, Skating, Theater

continued from page 81

A reservoir stores **water** to be sent in pipes over long distances so that people can use it for drinking, washing, and cooking. Dams are also built to store water for **irrigation** (watering fields) in the dry season. In hot countries, people have been doing this for hundreds of years.

Whenever water is at a height from which it can fall, it can be made to do work. Dams are often built to harness this power. In the past small dams were built to force streams of water into narrow channels. The rushing streams turned waterwheels, which drove machinery. Today huge dams build up an enormous pressure of water that is released by opening gates. When the dam gates are open, water gushes down wide pipes and hits the blades of **turbines**, making them spin and turn **generators**. The generators produce **electricity** (see **hydroelectric power**).

△ Rock climbing is a very popular **danger sport**. It requires a combination of strength, agility, fitness, and good concentration.

Danger sports

A **sport** is a game or activity involving physical skills, usually in competition with other players or teams. "Danger sports" is a term for a range of sports in which there is an added element of risk, or "danger," to the participants. However, despite their name, danger sports are less perilous if people use the correct equipment and take the appropriate safety precautions.

Danger sports include hang **gliding**, snowboarding (see **skiing**), whitewater rafting (traveling down fast-flowing rivers in inflatable rafts), and spelunking (exploring underground **caves**). Rock climbing involves scaling cliffs using ropes and harnesses. Rock climbers often descend by rappeling—attached to a rope, they gradually "walk" down the rock face. **Skydiving** is a danger sport that began in the 1940s. Skydivers jump from a high-flying **aircraft** and fall through the air for several minutes before opening their parachutes.

Dark Ages

Early scholars gave the name "Dark Ages" to the period in **Europe** after the fall of the **Roman Empire** around A.D. 400. During the Dark Ages, which lasted for about 500 years, the Goths, Vandals, and **Huns** swept into Europe from the north and east. The invaders destroyed many of the fine buildings and works of **art** that had existed in Roman times. This is why the period was called the Dark Ages.

Toward the end of the Dark Ages the **Vikings** began to venture into **Norway**, **Denmark**, and **Sweden** in search of treasures and better farmland. They were settlers and traders as well as fierce warriors.

Despite the destruction that took place during the Dark Ages, civilization did not come to an end as historians once thought. Learning, art, crafts, and **trade** continued to flourish. For **Ireland** the period was a golden age. Some of Europe's first Christian churches were built there, and beautiful **Bibles**, like the *Book of Kells*, were made.

▽ During the **Dark Ages** raiders from Scandinavia threatened large parts of Europe. They attacked many towns, villages, and churches, forcing people to flee for their lives.

Darwin, Charles

Charles Darwin (1809–1882) was an English biologist and thinker. In 1859 he published his greatest book, *On the Origin of Species*. Darwin put forward the theory that all living things have evolved, or are descended, from earlier living things. They are alive because they have won the struggle to survive.

Darwin noticed that within every species of **animal**, **plant**, or **bacteria**, there are variations between different individuals. For example, they may be a different size, shape, or color, or they might behave in a different way. Darwin realized that some of these variations can increase the living thing's chance of survival. His ideas have become known as the theory of **evolution**.

When Darwin's book was published, it outraged many people. Christians objected because they thought it was against the teachings of the **Bible**. Today most people accept Darwin's theory, although some think that it conflicts with their religious beliefs.

Da Vinci, Leonardo

Leonardo da Vinci (1452–1519) was an Italian artist and inventor. He lived during the **Renaissance**. One of his most famous **paintings** is the *Mona Lisa* (painted about 1503), which hangs in the Louvre Museum in Paris, France. It is a portrait of a woman who is smiling mysteriously. Many people have wondered at what she was smiling.

As well as paintings, Da Vinci made thousands of detailed **drawings** of human bodies, plants, animals, rocks, and water. He was also interested in **architecture**, **music**, and **engineering** and worked as an engineer for members of the Italian nobility and for the French king. Among the many things Da Vinci designed are cranes, forts, **bridges**, and **canals**. The canals had locks so that boats could travel up and down sloping ground.

Da Vinci also drew ideas for things long before they had been invented and actually built. His drawings include a **helicopter** and a machine gun.

△ **Leonardo da Vinci** was a creative genius. This is an illustration of what his planned flying machine might have looked like.

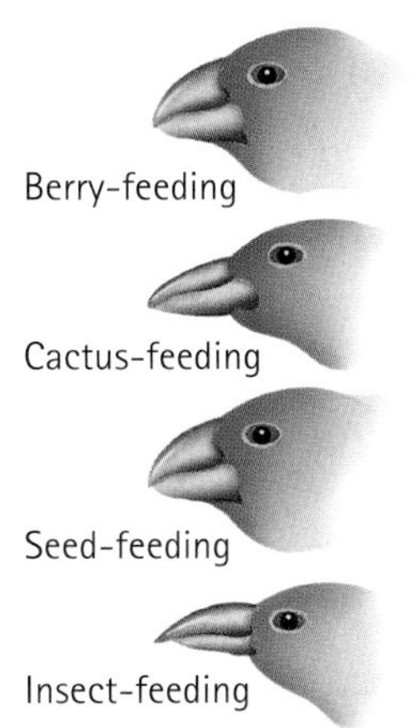

△ When **Darwin** visited the Galapagos Islands, in the Pacific, he noticed that the finches there had differently shaped beaks. He also noticed that each finch ate a different type of food. This gave him the idea that livings things can change, or evolve, to suit their surroundings.

Day and night

Earth spins as it moves around the **Sun**. The part facing the Sun is light, while the part facing away from the Sun is dark. The light part is day, and the dark part is night. Because Earth is spinning, day and night follow each other continuously.

Scientists describe a day as the time Earth takes to spin around once, or complete one turn. If you measure how long it takes between one sunrise or sunset and the next, you will find that it is almost exactly 24 hours.

Days vary in length between different points on Earth. This is because Earth's axis is tilted at an angle to its path around the Sun. As a result, some parts of the planet receive longer periods of daylight than others. In addition

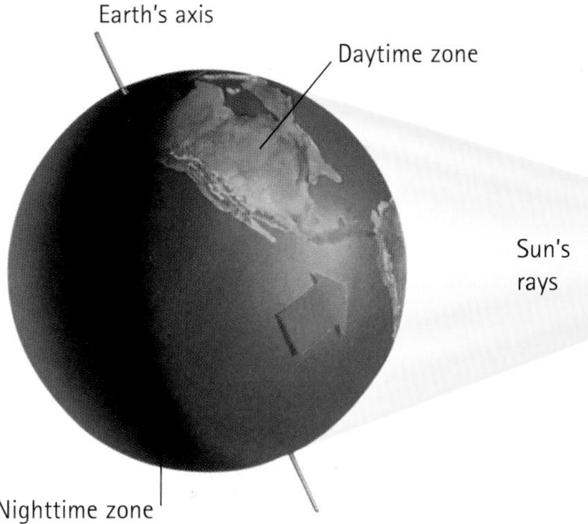

▷ **Day and night** happen because Earth spins on its axis as it circles the Sun. Only part of the globe faces the Sun at any one time. We say that this region is in daylight. The other side of the world is in darkness, or night. As Earth spins different parts of Earth fall into the zone of darkness.

most parts of Earth receive different amounts of daylight at different times of the year. These differences are a major feature of the **seasons**.

D-Day

D-Day—June 6, 1944—was one of the turning points of **World War II**. On this day a huge force of soldiers from the Allied countries landed on the coast of Normandy in northern **France**. At that time France was occupied by the armies of Hitler's **Germany**.

The D-Day invasion force was the largest the world had ever seen. It involved 132,500 troops—British, Americans, Canadians, and their allies—as well as 1,200 **ships**, 4,100 landing craft, and 10,000 **aircraft**. The supreme commander of the force was the U.S. general Dwight D. Eisenhower (1890–1969). The force set off before dawn from England's south coast. On the same day a Russian **army** attacked Germany from the east. After heavy fighting, in which many thousands of troops died, the Germans were forced to retreat. They finally surrendered to the Allies on May 7, 1945.

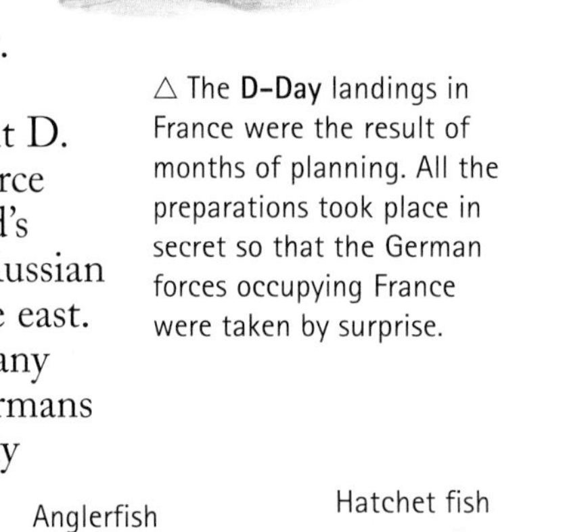

△ The **D-Day** landings in France were the result of months of planning. All the preparations took place in secret so that the German forces occupying France were taken by surprise.

Deep-sea fish

Most of the **animals** and **plants** that live in the world's seas and **oceans** stay in the top 656 ft. (200m). Below this conditions become less and less suitable for living things. At a depth of 3,280 ft. (1,000m) it is very cold and dark. No sunlight penetrates that deep. Plants cannot live at such depths because they need **light** to make their food through photosynthesis. But some animals can live at great depths. Their bodies are designed to withstand the enormous pressure deep down.

Most deep-sea animals are small, and they often have enormous jaws, **teeth**, and **eyes**. Many of the **fish** also possess light-producing organs. These "lights" help the fish communicate with other members of their species in the darkness. Some deep-sea fish use their lights as lures to attract prey. Other animals found in the deep sea are **jellyfish**, **crustaceans**, and **corals**.

Anglerfish

Hatchet fish

Lantern fish

Viper fish

△ **Deep-sea fish** look very different from fish that live in higher levels of the ocean. Many of them have huge eyes, jaws, and teeth.

Deer

Deer are **mammals** related to **cattle** and **antelopes**. They are different from their relatives because they have antlers rather than permanent **horns**. Male deer, or stags, shed their antlers and grow a new set every year. Female deer, or does, lack antlers. The exception is the caribou, in which both sexes have antlers and keep them throughout the year.

In early spring **blood** starts to flow into two hard lumps on the male deer's forehead. The blood carries a bony substance that makes the antlers grow rapidly. At first they are covered with a soft, hairy **skin** called velvet. In early summer the antlers are fully grown. The blood supply is then cut off, and the velvet dies. The male deer rubs off the velvet until his antlers are hard and shiny. Some antlers can be very large. Those of moose measure up to 6.56 ft. (2m) across.

Most species of deer live in the woods and **forests** of the Northern Hemisphere. But there are also species in **South America** and southern **Asia**. Although deer are wild animals, some of them can be tamed successfully. Reindeer can be trained to pull sleds, and their meat and hides are used by the Lapp people of Scandinavia. Deer are also farmed for their meat, which is called venison.

De Gaulle, Charles

Charles de Gaulle (1890–1970) was a French general and statesman. He fought in **World War I** and in 1916 was badly wounded. After the war he continued his **army** career. When **World War II** broke out in 1939, he was put in command of a tank division. After the Germans occupied **France** in 1940 De Gaulle escaped to **London**, England and formed the Free French Movement, which organized the resistance struggle against the German forces.

In 1944 De Gaulle returned from exile and became head of the French **government**. But two years later he resigned when the political parties could not agree. By 1958 France was in serious political trouble. The French settlers in **Algeria** and the French army were rebelling. De Gaulle was elected president of France in 1959 and finally resolved the Algerian problem. He was one of the most powerful European leaders and stayed in office until 1969.

△ In 508 B.C. **democracy** came to Athens. The people of the city met on Pnyx Hill to debate important issues.

△ **De Gaulle** led the "Free French" fighters who were struggling against the German forces during World War II. He was French president in 1945 and 1959–1969.

Delta

When a **river** flows across a flat plain into the sea, it moves very slowly. On its way it deposits **soil** and **sand** on the plain. In time this sediment builds up into mud banks. The river creates many small channels through the mud, which often change direction. This maze of mud banks and channels is called a delta because its shape often resembles the Greek letter "delta" (△).

The **Mississippi** delta stretches 198 mi. (320km) into the Gulf of **Mexico**. Another large delta is formed by the **Nile** in **Egypt**.

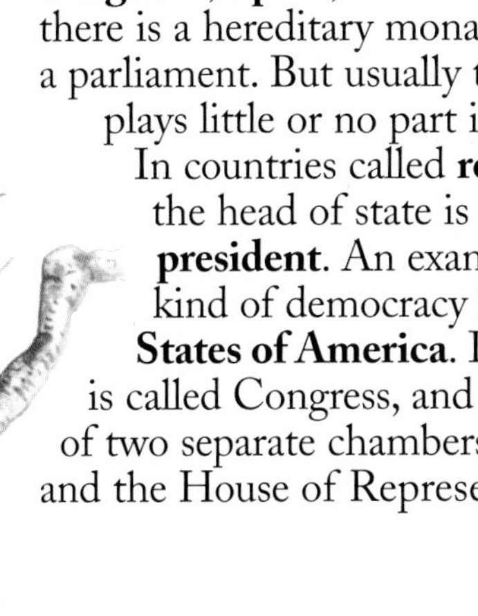

Male wapiti

▷ In the summer male deer rub their antlers against branches to remove the outer layer of dead skin.

Democracy

Democracy is a type of **government** in which the people take part in ruling the state. In most democracies people can elect their own government. The representatives of different political parties stand for **election**, and people vote for the candidates they prefer. Usually the candidates and parties with the most votes then form a government.

Elections are held regularly, which gives the people the chance to elect a new government. In a true democracy people can say, read, and believe what they like. They cannot be imprisoned without a fair trial.

There are many kinds of democracy. The most common form has an elected **parliament** made up of officials from the various political parties. Its leader is often known as the prime minister. In some countries, such as the **United Kingdom**, **Spain**, and the **Netherlands**, there is a hereditary monarchy as well as a parliament. But usually the **monarch** plays little or no part in politics.

In countries called **republics** the head of state is an elected **president**. An example of this kind of democracy is the **United States of America**. Its parliament is called Congress, and it is made up of two separate chambers—the Senate and the House of Representatives.

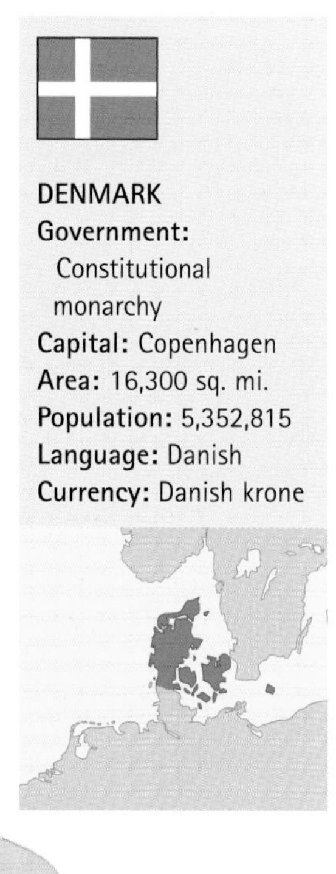

DENMARK
Government: Constitutional monarchy
Capital: Copenhagen
Area: 16,300 sq. mi.
Population: 5,352,815
Language: Danish
Currency: Danish krone

Denmark

Denmark is a small country in northern **Europe**. It forms part of Scandinavia, which also includes **Norway**, **Sweden**, **Finland**, and **Iceland**. Denmark consists of a peninsula called Jutland, which is surrounded by about 600 islands. To the west is the North Sea, to the east is the Baltic Sea, and to the south is **Germany**. Denmark is a flat country where the soil and **climate** are ideal for agriculture. Dairy and pig **farming** are especially important.

This is a scene from *David Copperfield* by Charles Dickens. Dickens' writing both entertained and informed his readers about social problems.

Descartes, René

René Descartes (1596–1650) was a French thinker who was interested in many different subjects, including **mathematics**, **physics**, **astronomy**, and **law**. He thought that all the **sciences** were connected, just like the links in a chain. Descartes devoted a lot of time to searching for a system that would link together all knowledge.

Descartes' revolutionary ideas influenced many other thinkers. He has often been called the "father of modern **philosophy**."

Desert

Not all deserts are hot and sandy. Some are cold, and others are rocky. But all deserts are very dry. Any area where less than 10 in. (25cm) of rain falls per year is a desert. Most of the world's large deserts are in the tropics.

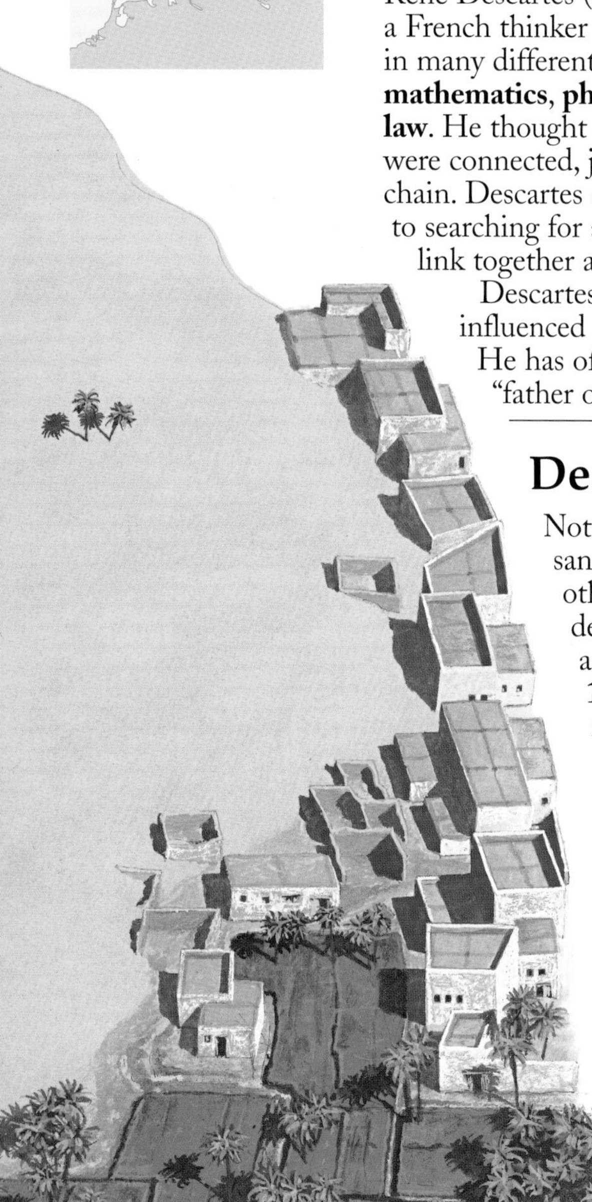

◁ **Deserts** are tough places for people as well as animals. Most people live in oases—pockets of fertile land where an underground spring rises to the surface.

This is because the air is too hot and dry for rain-bearing clouds to form. Other deserts exist because they are located far from the sea's moist **winds** or because they lie behind high **mountains** that block rain-bearing winds (see also **weather**).

There are three main types of deserts. The first is rocky, where any soil is blown away by the wind. The second has large areas of gravel. The third is made up of **sand** dunes and is burning hot by day and bitterly cold at night.

It is difficult for **plants** and **animals** to live in such conditions. Some plants, like **cactus**es, store moisture in their fleshy stems. Others have **seeds** that lie apparently lifeless in the ground for long periods. When a shower of rain falls, they burst into life and can **flower** and produce new seeds within weeks. Many desert animals seek shelter from the sun by day and come out only at night. Some never drink but get all the moisture they need from their food.

The world's largest desert is the **Sahara Desert** in **Africa**. The driest desert is the Atacama in **South America**, which lies to the west of the **Andes** mountains. Cold deserts include the icy continent Antarctica, a large part of the Arctic (see **Antarctic** and **Arctic**), and the Gobi Desert of central **Mongolia**. In total, deserts cover about one seventh of the land on **earth**.

Detergent

Strictly speaking, the word "detergent" means any substance that will clean things. **Soap** is a detergent. But today the word detergent usually means synthetic, or artificial, detergents such as most washing powders. Detergents are similar to soaps, but they can reach dirty areas better than soaps, and they do not leave a deposit, or scum, behind.

Developing world

The "developing world" is a term that describes the world's poorer countries, many of which are in **Asia**, **Africa**, and **South America**. These nations are still in the process of developing some of the features typical of wealthier states such as modern industries, **hospitals**, **schools**, **roads**, **railroads**, and other important public services.

Life is usually hard for the majority of people in developing countries. They often suffer from bad living conditions, especially in the towns and cities. Parts of the **population** do not have easy access to clean drinking **water**, doctors, and medicine, which leads to more frequent outbreaks of **diseases**.

Many countries in the developing world supply the rest of the world with **food**, **minerals**, **timber**, and **textiles**, as well as providing cheap labor. This pattern of wealth in one part of the world and poverty in another is very difficult to change. The wealthy countries do not want to give up the wealth and power they have been used to for so long. This means that many developing countries continue to get poorer, while the rich countries continue to get richer.

Diamond

Diamonds are made of pure **carbon**, the same **mineral** that is found in **coal**. They are usually colorless, although a few are blue, pink, or yellow.

Diamonds have many smooth, flat sides that meet in sharp edges. This type of substance is known as a **crystal**. Other crystals include snowflakes, **salt** crystals, and **sugar** crystals.

Diamonds are harder than anything else in the world. They are formed by great **heat** and pressure deep beneath the surface of **earth**. They have to be cut in a special way to catch the **light** and sparkle. After cutting they are polished. Diamonds are not only worn as **jewelry**—they are used in industry for drilling and cutting materials such as **glass** and **metal**.

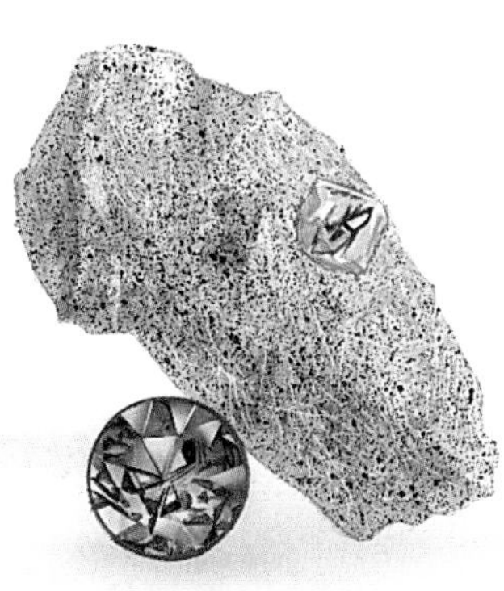

△ **Diamonds** occur naturally in rock. By the time a diamond has been removed from its lump of rock, cut into shape, and polished it has lost about 50 percent of its weight.

Dickens, Charles

Charles Dickens (1812–1870) was a famous English writer. His books give us a vivid picture of life in Victorian England in the mid-1800s (see also **Victoria, Queen**). Several of Dickens' novels are about children, especially poor children and orphans. He tried to improve the lives of the poor by making their suffering more widely known through his books. He also created some of the best-known characters in English literature. Some of his most important books are *Oliver Twist*, *David Copperfield*, *Great Expectations*, and *A Christmas Carol.*

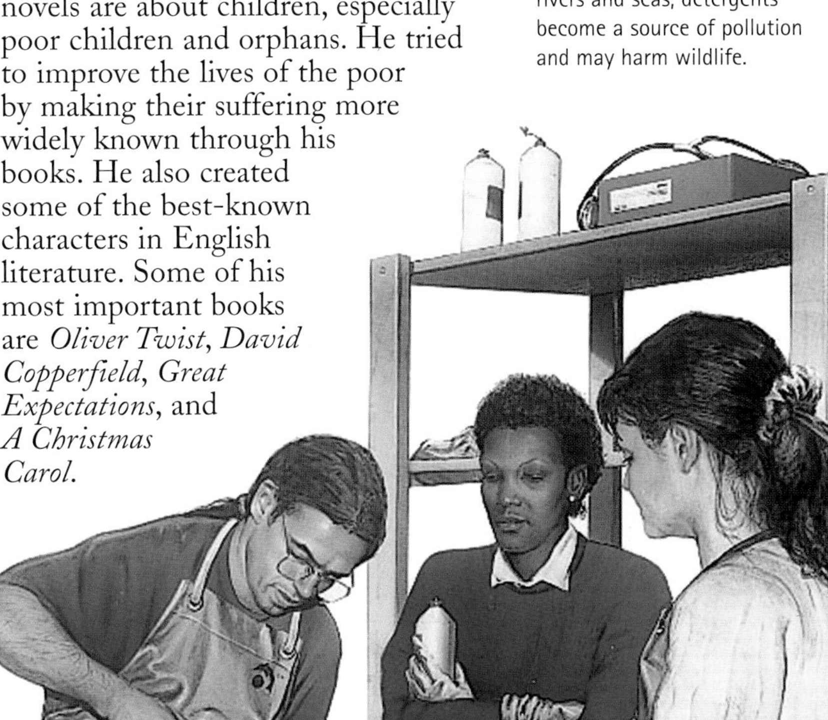

▽ **Detergents** can be used to clean the fur of animals that have been affected by oil spills. But if washed into rivers and seas, detergents become a source of pollution and may harm wildlife.

Dickinson, Emily

Emily Dickinson (1830–1886) was one of the U.S.'s greatest poets and is considered to be among the most important poets of the 1800s. Her poetry is recognized for its originality, variety, and beauty. She wrote about the difficulty of making sense of the world and of how quickly and strangely life passes. Dickinson was a very private person who refused to publish any of her poems during her lifetime. She lived all of her life at her parents' home in Amherst, Massachusetts.

Dictator

A dictator is the leader of a country who rules with absolute power and authority. In the **Roman Empire** a dictator was a magistrate who was given absolute power to deal with emergencies when decisions had to be made quickly. Today the term is used to describe a tyrant who uses force to take away people's rights and freedoms. Frequently those who try to oppose a dictator are imprisoned, killed, or forced to leave the country until the dictator is overthrown. A dictatorship is the opposite of a **democracy**, in which the people choose their own government in elections.

△ General Franco became a **dictator** in 1939 when he took control of Spain. During the Spanish Civil War (1936–1939), his rebel forces defeated Spanish government troops.

▽ **Diesel engines** are used on railroads throughout the world such as on this mountain railroad in the south of Mexico. In diesel trains a diesel motor produces the electricity that drives the train.

Some dictators of the 1900s include Adolf **Hitler** of **Germany** (1889–1945), Benito **Mussolini** of **Italy** (1883–1945), Francisco Franco of **Spain** (1892–1975), and Antonio Salazar of **Portugal** (1889–1970), all of whom believed in a political theory known as **fascism**. Many people now think that Josef **Stalin** (1879–1953), who led a cruel regime in the former **Soviet Union**, should also be called a dictator.

Dictionary

A dictionary is a **book** that tells us what words mean. The words are arranged in alphabetical order from "A" to "Z." Often the meanings, or definitions, include a brief history of the words and an explanation of how they are used and pronounced. One of the first large dictionaries of the English language was produced by the Englishman Dr. Samuel Johnson (1709–1784).

Diesel engine

Diesel engines are a type of **engine** in which **fuel** is burned inside the engine. They are named after the German inventor Rudolf Diesel (1858–1913), who built his first successful engine in 1897 to replace the **steam engine**. The fuel used in diesel engines is known as diesel. It is produced from **oil**, as is gasoline.

Diesel engines are cheaper to run than gas engines, but they are also heavier and more difficult to start. As a result, they were not widely used in **cars** until the 1970s. But their main use is still to drive large machines such as trains (see **railroad**), tractors, **ships**, buses, and trucks. A properly working diesel engine causes less **pollution** than a gas engine.

A diesel engine is similar to a gas engine, but instead of using a spark from a spark plug to ignite the fuel, the diesel engine uses **heat** that is made by a piston squeezing **air** inside a cylinder. If air is tightly compressed—pushed into a much smaller space than it filled before—it becomes very hot. This heat sets fire to the diesel fuel, which burns instantly, like a small explosion. The burning fuel produces hot gases, which push the piston down and thus drive the engine.

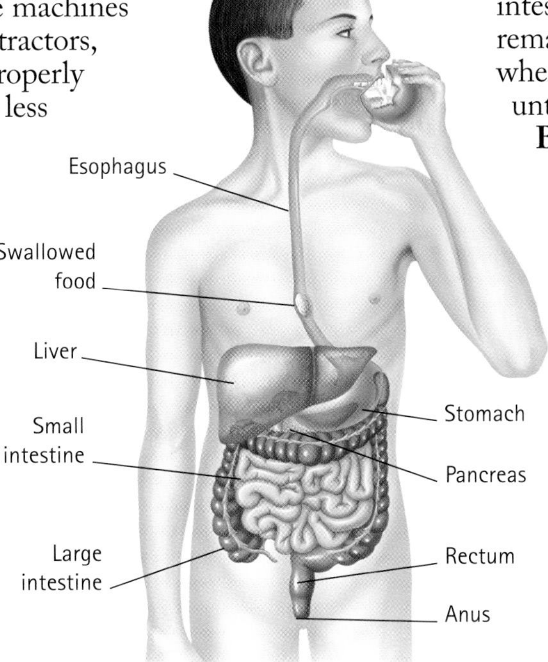
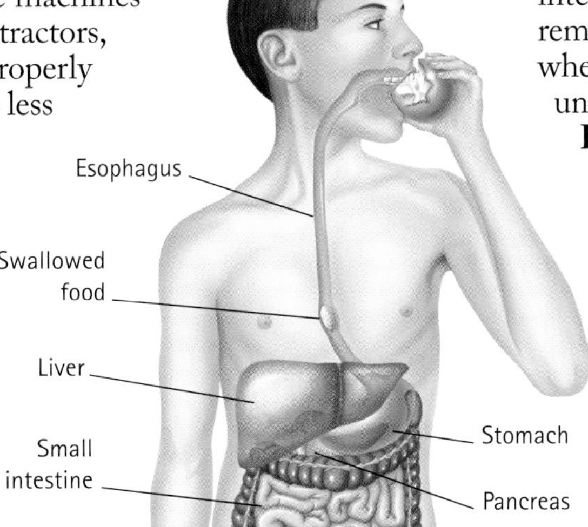

△ In humans **digestion** involves many different organs. Food passes from the mouth to the stomach and intestines. After all the useful substances have been removed, feces are excreted from the anus.

Digestion

Digestion is the way in which the **food** that **animals** eat is broken down into substances that can be used by the body. In humans this takes place in the digestive tract, or alimentary canal, a long tube that runs from the mouth to the anus. Digestion starts in the mouth, where the **teeth** and special chemicals in the saliva help break down the food. The food then passes down a tube called the esophagus. **Muscles** in the esophagus push and squeeze the food through to the **stomach**. There **acids** and more chemicals help to turn the food into a creamy **liquid**. A muscle at the lower end of the stomach opens from time to time to release food into the small intestine.

Inside the small intestine bile from the **liver** and juice from the pancreas help to further break down the food. Much of it passes through the thin walls of the intestine into the bloodstream. The remainder enters the large intestine, where liquids and salts are absorbed until only solid waste material is left. **Bacteria** living inside the large intestine digest any remaining food products. The final waste product is passed out of the body as feces.

Dinosaurs

see **pages 92–93**

Disease

Diseases make us ill. Some are caused by **bacteria**, or germs, that invade our bodies. Others are caused by **viruses** or **parasites**. Some diseases are passed down from parents to children in the genes with which they are born (see **genetics**).

The body resists diseases through its immune system. Special **cells**, such as white **blood** cells, fight the invading organisms. The body also produces antibodies to fight disease. Antibodies produced to "defeat" diseases such as measles or chicken pox stay in our systems and usually prevent us from having the same disease again—we become immune. Many **drugs** and **vaccines** have been developed to help us fight diseases, although some diseases have no known cure.

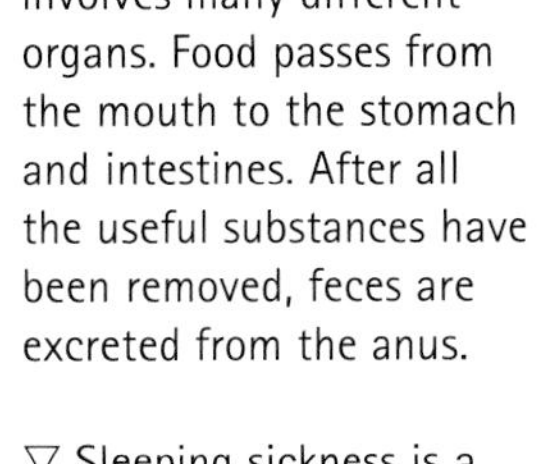
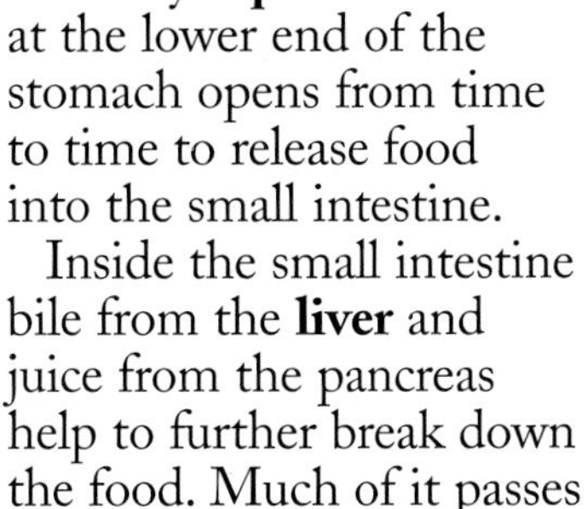

▽ Sleeping sickness is a common **disease** in parts of Africa. It is caused by a tiny parasite that is carried by the tsetse fly. When an infected fly bites someone, the parasites enter their bloodstream. There the parasites breed rapidly, causing fever, headaches, and sleepiness.

△ Apatosaurus, *also known as* Brontosaurus, *was a huge plant eater that could reach leaves growing in the treetops. It weighed up to 30 tons.*

DINOSAURS

Dinosaurs were a type of reptile that first appeared on earth about 230 million years ago. Some dinosaurs were only the size of a chicken, but others were the largest land animals that ever existed. The dinosaurs became extinct about 65 million years ago.

▽ *In the Late Triassic period, about 220 million years ago, a herd of* Coelophysis *is washed away in a flash flood. In 1947 scientists discovered their fossilized remains at Ghost Ranch in New Mexico.*

WORLD OF DINOSAURS

The word dinosaur means "terrible lizard," but this is misleading because the dinosaurs were not actually lizards. They belonged to a group of reptiles called the archosaurs, which also included primitive crocodiles and giant flying creatures called pterosaurs. The dinosaurs roamed the planet for over 160 million years. They lived during three different geological periods—the Triassic, Jurassic, and Cretaceous—which are often known collectively as the "Age of Reptiles."

MANY DIFFEFRENT KINDS

Scientists have so far identified more than 500 types of dinosaurs, but there are probably many more that remain undiscovered. The dinosaurs ranged in size from chicken-sized species, such as *Compsognathus*, to giants such as *Argentinosaurus*, which weighed up to 100 tons and was the largest land animal to ever walk earth. There were two main groups of dinosaur—the saurischians, which had hip bones arranged like a lizard's and the ornithischians, which had hip bones arranged like a bird's. Each species of dinosaur had a different diet and lifestyle. Some were vegetarian, while others were hunters or scavengers.

THE PLANT EATERS

Most dinosaurs were herbivores (plant eaters). The world's climate was much warmer during the Triassic, Jurassic, and Cretaceous periods than it is today, and the tropical conditions provided an abundant supply of vegetation to eat. The largest plant eaters, such as *Brachiosaurus* and *Diplodocus*, walked on all fours. Their long necks allowed them to reach the leaves and cones of tall trees. Smaller species walked on their back legs and grazed lower down.

THE MEAT EATERS

The meat-eating dinosaurs, or theropods, had razor-sharp claws on their feet for capturing prey and strong jaws full of teeth for tearing flesh. They walked upright, using their long, heavy tails for balance. The theropods hunted a wide range of dinosaurs and other animals and fed on carrion (dead remains), as well as fresh meat.

◁ *The swimming reptiles that lived in the sea and the flying reptiles, such as pterosaurs, were not dinosaurs. The dinosaurs lived only on land.*

◁ Deinonychus, *whose name means "terrible claw," was a fast-moving hunter with a 5-in. (12-cm) -long retractable claw on the inside of each back foot.*

WAY OF LIFE

Like all reptiles, dinosaurs laid eggs. Fossilized nests suggest that a female dinosaur would lay 10–40 eggs in a shallow hole on the ground. The baby dinosaurs hatched 3–4 weeks later and probably left the nest quickly to fend for themselves. It is likely that many plant-eating dinosaurs lived in herds to make it harder for the meat eaters to attack them. Some of the predators hunted in packs, like wolves, while others waited to ambush.

▷ *Plant-eating dinosaurs had several methods of defense, including swinging their tails at their attackers.*

▽ *The dinosaurs evolved into many different species. Most of the largest dinosaurs were plant eaters.*

OTHER REPTILES

Dinosaurs could neither swim nor fly, but many of the other reptiles alive at the same time could. Pterosaurs used their leathery wings to glide on rising air currents. The largest pterosaurs had a wingspan of up to 39–49 ft. (12–15m)—wider than a hang glider. Many reptiles lived in the sea, like the long-necked elasmosaurs. Almost all of these reptiles died out at the same time as the dinosaurs.

END OF THE DINOSAURS

No one knows for certain why the dinosaurs died out. The most popular theory suggests that earth was hit by a huge meteorite. This would have thrown up a cloud of dust that blotted out the sun for months or even years, killing many plants and animals. Some scientists believe that gradual climate change was to blame, perhaps caused by frequent volcanic eruptions over a period of 500,000 years. But although the dinosaurs became extinct, many other types of animals survived.

▽ Tyrannosaurus rex *lived in North America 95–65 million years ago. It had a massive head packed with 6-in. (15-cm) -long teeth. Instead of chasing its prey, it may have launched surprise attacks.*

DINOSAUR FACT FILE

Earliest: *Eoraptor*, which first appeared about 230 million years ago
Heaviest: *Argentinosaurus*, up to 80–100 tons
Tallest: *Sauroposeidon*, up to 59 ft.
Smallest: *Microraptor*, 15 in. long
Largest meat eater: *Gigantosaurus*, up to 43 ft. long and 8 tons in weight
Largest skull: *Triceratops*, up to 10 ft. long
Longest tail: *Diplodocus*, up to 43 ft.
Most teeth: *Edmontosaurus*, up to 1,200
Largest egg: *Hypselosaurus*, 12 in. long and 10 in. wide

SEE ALSO
Amphibians and Reptiles, Fossil, Meteorite, Prehistoric animals

Disney, Walt

Walt Disney (1901–1967) was an American filmmaker best known for his **cartoons** and movies for children. Disney characters, especially Mickey Mouse and Donald Duck, are famous all over the world. Walt Disney began his work in the 1920s. His cartoon artists, or animators, produced characters and settings that moved realistically. Full-length Disney cartoon features include *Snow White and the Seven Dwarfs*, *The Little Mermaid*, and *The Lion King*.

Distillation

When saltwater from the sea is boiled in a pan, it turns into steam. If the steam then hits a surface, such as a window, it cools and becomes a **liquid** again. But the boiled **water** has changed—it is now pure freshwater. The **salt** is left behind in the pan. This boiling and cooling of liquids to make them pure is called distillation.

Distillation is often used to separate different liquids mixed together. The mixture is heated, and the liquid that boils at the lowest temperature evaporates (turns to a **gas**) first and is separated from the other liquids. Then the liquid with the next lowest boiling point evaporates and so on. This process is called fractional distillation. It is used to separate the materials crude **oil** from oil wells. Distillation is also used to make alcoholic drinks such as whisky and gin (see **alcohol**).

△ During the festival of **Diwali**, Hindus decorate their homes and streets with lights. They also hold feasts and stage parades and firework displays.

Diwali

Diwali (also written Divali) is one of the most important **festivals** in **Hinduism**. It is held in October each year and celebrates Rama, the Hindu **goddess** of wealth and beauty.

△ The **dodo** died out because nonnative rats and pigs plundered all of its eggs and chicks.

Dodo

About 400 years ago a Dutch ship landed on Mauritius, a remote island in the **Indian Ocean**. The crew found flocks of turkey-sized **birds** that had useless wings and could not fly. In time people called the birds dodos, from the Portuguese word *doudo*, meaning "stupid person." But people introduced **rats** and **pigs** to the island, which began eating dodo eggs and chicks. By the 1690s the dodo had become extinct.

▽ **Dolphins**, such as these spotted dolphins, live in groups, or schools. They hunt as a team, working together to track down their main prey—fish.

Dog

Humans have been owning dogs for as long as 10,000 years. Dogs are often pets, but many do useful work such as herding sheep or guarding buildings. They can be trained to serve as guide dogs for blind people and to sniff out illegal **drugs** hidden inside bags or vehicles.

The first domesticated dog probably descended from a **wolf**. There are now more than 100 breeds of domestic dogs in many different colors, shapes, and sizes. Other kinds of wild dogs include **foxes**, coyotes, the **jackals** of Asia and Africa, and the Australian dingo.

Dogs are **carnivores,** and all belong to the same family. They have superb senses of **smell**, **hearing**, and **sight**.

△ Domestic **dogs** are bred for specific purposes. This greyhound has been bred for speed. It can reach 35 mph (57km/h).

Doll

Children all over the world play with dolls. Dolls may be made of **wood**, china, **plastic**, or many other substances. The very first doll may have been just a forked twig that resembled a human. Homemade dolls can cost nothing. Some old dolls may be very valuable.

Dolphin and Porpoise

Dolphins and porpoises belong to the same group of **mammals** as **whales**. Like all mammals, they breathe air, suckle their young on milk, and are warm-blooded. They have sharp **teeth**, and their heads end in beaklike snouts. Dolphins and porpoises are highly intelligent and communicate with each other using a sophisticated "language" of whistles and clicks. They use **sonar**—an underwater **radar** system—to navigate and to locate **fish** to eat. There are about 45 species of dolphins and porpoises in the world, of which the largest is the orca, or killer whale.

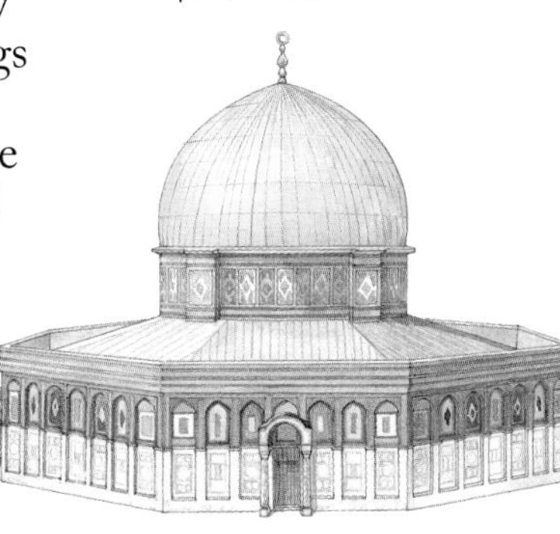

△ The **Dome** of the Rock, Jerusalem, was completed in A.D. 691. It is a Muslim shrine known as al Aqsa.

Dome

Domes are roofs shaped like overturned bowls. Some domes are made from bricks or stones. Other domes are made of **concrete**, steel, or **plastic**. Domed roofs cover many **mosques** and **churches**. Famous examples include the Dome of the Rock in **Jerusalem**, **Israel**; St. Sophia in Istanbul, **Turkey**; St. Peter's in **Rome**, **Italy**; and St. Paul's Cathedral in **London**, England. The world's largest dome—the Louisiana Superdome in New Orleans—has a span of 731 ft. (223m).

Domesday Book

Twenty years after the Norman invasion of 1066 **William the Conqueror** ordered that a great survey of property owners in England should be made. It became known as the Domesday Book. William wanted to find out how much land people owned so that he could be sure that he was getting all the **taxes** that were due to him. This survey, or **census**, was completed in 1086.

DOMINICAN REPUBLIC
Government: Republic
Capital: Santo Domingo
Area: 19,006 sq. mi.
Population: 8,442,533
Language: Spanish
Currency: Peso

Dominican Republic

The Dominican Republic occupies the larger part of the island of Hispaniola in the **Caribbean** Sea. The rest of the island is occupied by **Haiti**. It has large **forests**, and its main crop is **sugar**.

Donkeys can carry heavy loads for their size. They have large heads, long ears, and a short mane.

Donkey

Donkeys are small, sturdy relatives of **horses** and are descended from the wild asses of Africa. They are sure-footed and can carry large loads over rough ground. Donkeys are still used for work in southern **Europe**, North Africa, **Asia**, and **South America**.

Dragon *see* Myth and Legend

Drawing

Drawings are pictures or designs that are usually made with pencil, pen, **chalk**, or some similar material other than **paint**. Drawings are produced for all kinds of reasons and play an important role in **architecture**, **art**, **engineering**, and **fashion**. Some drawings are detailed. In others a powerful effect is produced by using few lines and little detail.

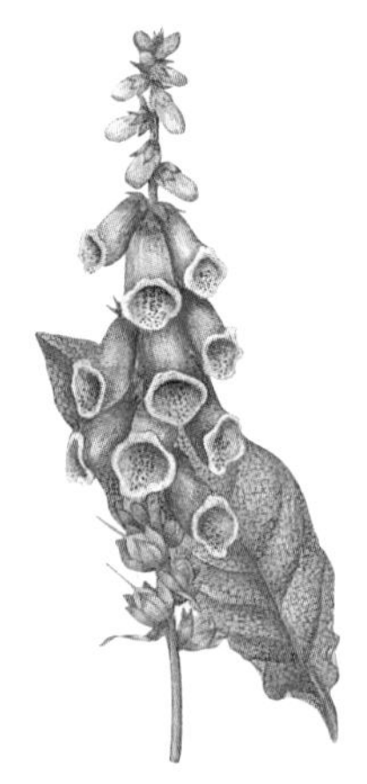

Many **drugs** are made from plants, animals, or minerals. For example, an extract from this foxglove is used to produce a drug that fights heart disease.

Dream

Dreams occur when our **brains** are active during **sleep**. Some dreams are of everyday occurrences. Others may be just a series of jumbled images. People often dream of falling, being chased, or of water. Frightening dreams are called nightmares. Upon waking, we may not remember what we have dreamed.

We do not know exactly why people dream. Dreams may be sparked by indigestion or a similar physical cause such as a cramped sleeping position. External noises may also cause dreams.

Drug

Drugs are chemicals that affect the way the body works. Doctors give drugs to patients to help them fight **diseases**. **Antibiotics** are a common type of drug that attack certain kinds of germs. These drugs help cure people suffering from pneumonia and other illnesses. Drugs such as aspirin and ibuprofen help relieve **pain**. The strongest painkillers are anesthetics. General anesthetics are used to send patients to sleep during operations (see **surgery**).

Some people need to take drugs containing **vitamins** or other essential substances. But people sometimes take drugs simply because they can give a pleasant feeling. These drugs include cocaine, cannabis, **alcohol**, and nicotine, which is found in **tobacco**. However, many of these drugs are addictive (habit-forming), and some can cause illness or even death.

Eider **ducks** live at sea. We use their soft feathers, or eiderdown, to fill comforters, pillows, and cushions.

Drum

Drums are important percussion instruments (**musical instruments** that are played by being struck). The **sound** is made by hitting a tightly stretched sheet of skin or plastic called a drumhead. A kettledrum has one drumhead stretched over the top of a metal basin. A bass drum or a side drum has two drumheads, one across each end of a large, open "can."

Duck

Ducks are web-footed water **birds** related to **swans** and **geese**. The two main groups of ducks are dabbling ducks, which feed at the surface of the water, and diving ducks, which dive underwater in their hunt for food. The mallard, one of the best-known dabbling ducks, lives on ponds, **lakes**, and **rivers** across the northern half of the world.

DVD *see* Recording

Dye

Dyes are substances used to color **textiles** and other materials. Some dyes are extracted from **plants**, but most modern dyes are made from chemicals. To dye an object, you dip it in water containing dissolved dye.

Eagle

Eagles are large **birds** of prey. They spend hours soaring high in the sky or perched on a rock or in a tree and use their sharp eyesight to scan their surroundings. When an eagle spots its prey, it swoops down from the air and pounces. It seizes its victim with sharp talons and tears off pieces of flesh with a strong, hooked beak.

There are more than 50 species of eagles in the world. They feed on a variety of prey, from small mammals to birds, fish, snakes, and lizards. Eagles are related to **hawks** and **falcons**.

△ The golden **eagle** preys on medium-sized animals such as rabbits.

Ear

Our ears equip us with the sense of **hearing** and allow us to keep our balance. Each ear has three main parts—the outer ear, middle ear, and inner ear. The outer ear is the part we can see and the tube that leads from it into the head. **Sounds** reach the outer ear as vibrations, or sound waves, in the air. The cuplike shape of the ear collects these sound waves and sends them into the tube, known as the ear canal.

Next the sound waves reach the middle ear. Here the waves make the eardrum—a thin "skin" across the entrance of the middle ear—move back and forth. The moving eardrum makes tiny **bones** inside the middle ear vibrate. These are called the hammer, anvil, and stirrup.

The vibrations travel on into the inner ear, where they make liquid move in the cochlea. This structure looks like a snail's shell. **Nerves** inside the cochlea turn vibrations into electrical messages that travel to the brain. The inner ear also has three hollow loops containing liquid. These loops send signals to the brain to help us keep our balance.

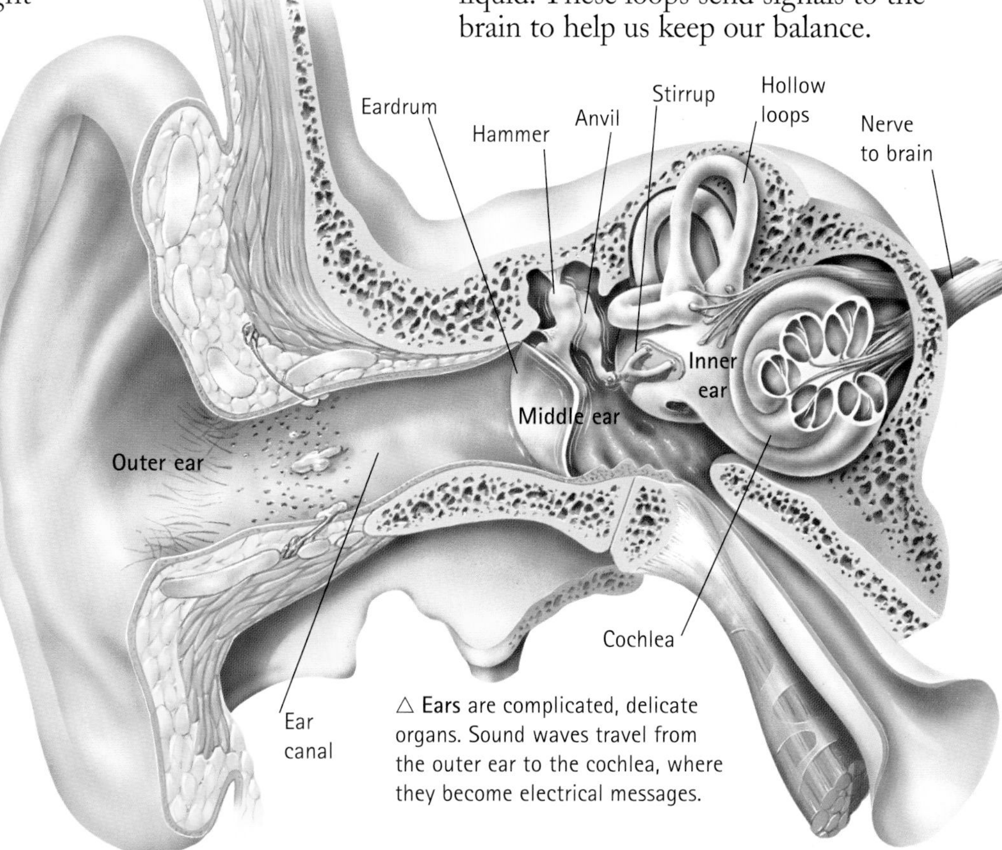

△ **Ears** are complicated, delicate organs. Sound waves travel from the outer ear to the cochlea, where they become electrical messages.

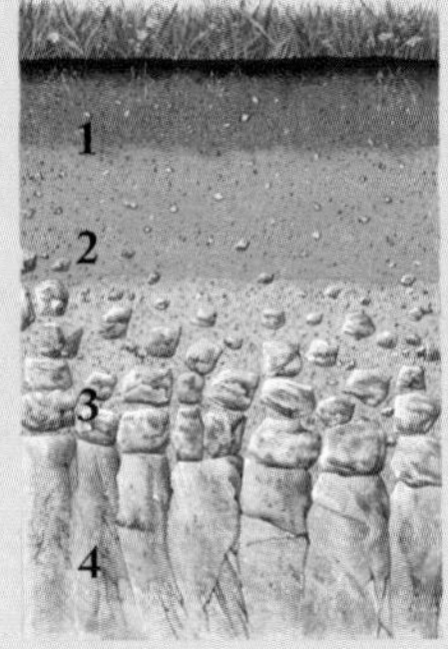

△ *The upper layer of land on Earth is made up of topsoil (1), subsoil (2), fragmented rock (3), and hard bedrock (4).*

EARTH

Our planet, Earth, is one of the nine planets that move around the sun. It is a giant ball of rock with a central core of intensely hot, dense metal. Unlike the other planets in the solar system, Earth is surrounded by a blanket of gases called the atmosphere, and much of its surface is covered in water. These are the conditions that allow Earth to support life.

▷ *Earth formed from a vast cloud of dust that surrounded the Sun. The dust clumped together and over millions of years became a rocky planet.*

TURNING EARTH

Earth is constantly moving around the Sun along an elliptical (oval-shaped) path called its orbit. It travels at an average speed of 18.6 mi. (30km) per second and takes 365.25 days—one year—to make a complete orbit. During this time Earth covers a total distance of 220 million mi. (958 million km). As well as orbiting the Sun, Earth rotates in a circle on its axis—an imaginary line joining the North and South poles. It does this once every 24 hours. As Earth spins one side faces the Sun and is in daylight, while the other side faces away and is in darkness, or night.

△ *This diagram uses different colors to represent the tectonic plates of Earth's crust. The arrows show the direction in which each plate is moving.*

VIOLENT EARTH

The surface of Earth is made up of about 20 tectonic plates, like jigsaw pieces. On top of them lie the continents. The plates are not attached to anything and move slowly, causing the continents to collide and tear apart. This movement is known as continental drift. When two plates collide, the land folds, and mountains are formed. When two plates move apart, molten magma rises up from beneath the surface to create new land or ocean floor. At certain points on Earth, neighboring plates rub together. This creates a massive buildup of pressure, which eventually escapes in the form of volcanic eruptions and earthquakes.

CHANGING SEASONS

Earth is tilted toward the Sun at an angle of 23.5°. As Earth moves along its orbit the parts that are tilted toward the Sun receive more light and warmth—they experience summer. As Earth travels farther along its orbit, these places tilt away from the Sun—they experience winter.

INSIDE EARTH

Earth's solid inner core is almost pure iron, while its outer core consists mainly of semiliquid iron and nickel. The outer core is slowly circulating all the time, and powerful electrical currents within it generate Earth's magnetic field. Surrounding the core is the mantle—a mixture of minerals and metals such as quartz, silicon, and aluminum. It is topped by a rocky crust.

◁ *Earth's rocks, sand, and soil are made up of minerals. Many minerals are formed deep underground from "lakes" of hot magma.*

Magma

Lighter minerals form at the top

Denser minerals form at the bottom

EARTH FACT FILE

Age: about 4,550 million years
Diameter: 7.883 mi. (from North Pole to South Pole through Earth's center)
Circumference: 24,847 mi. (around the middle of Earth at the equator)
Area of water: about 141 million sq. mi.—71 percent of Earth's surface
Area of land: about 577 million sq. mi.—29 percent of Earth's surface
Highest mountain: Mount Everest, Asia, 29,021 ft. above sea level
Greatest ocean depth: Mariana Trench, Pacific Ocean, 36,092 ft.
Hottest place: Al'Aziziyah, Libya, where 135.9°F was recorded in 1922
Coldest place: Vostok, Antarctica, where -128.6°F was recorded in 1983

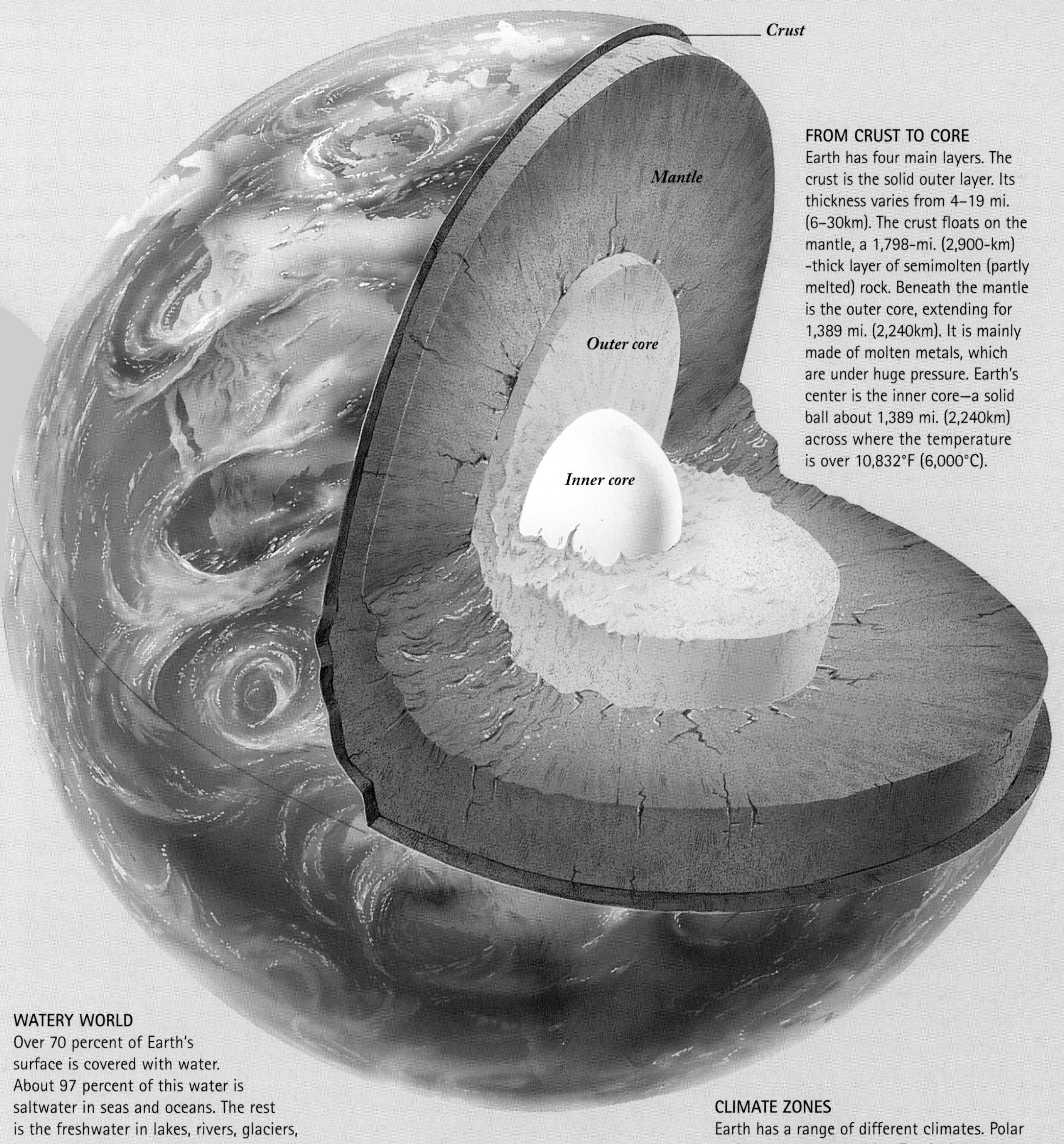

FROM CRUST TO CORE

Earth has four main layers. The crust is the solid outer layer. Its thickness varies from 4–19 mi. (6–30km). The crust floats on the mantle, a 1,798-mi. (2,900-km) -thick layer of semimolten (partly melted) rock. Beneath the mantle is the outer core, extending for 1,389 mi. (2,240km). It is mainly made of molten metals, which are under huge pressure. Earth's center is the inner core—a solid ball about 1,389 mi. (2,240km) across where the temperature is over 10,832°F (6,000°C).

WATERY WORLD

Over 70 percent of Earth's surface is covered with water. About 97 percent of this water is saltwater in seas and oceans. The rest is the freshwater in lakes, rivers, glaciers, ice sheets, and snow. Although we usually see only their surface, the oceans are vast and deep—the average depth of the oceans is 16,400 ft. (5,000m), and the deepest ocean trenches reach down 36,080 ft. (11,000m). The immense volume of water on Earth helps to regulate the planet's climate. It is continually recycled—it evaporates from the rivers, lakes, seas, and oceans to form water vapor, which forms clouds and falls as rain. Every living thing needs water to survive.

LIFE ON EARTH

Earth's distance from the Sun is ideal—not too hot like Venus, nor too cold like Mars. This allows it to support a tremendous variety of plant and animal life, from tiny bacteria to human beings. Life on earth began millions of years ago. Simple plants evolved, which began to release oxygen. Gradually enough oxygen built up to create the atmosphere. Animals rely on the atmosphere for the oxygen they breathe.

CLIMATE ZONES

Earth has a range of different climates. Polar regions are snowy and icy. Tropical areas, near the equator, are hot and wet. In between are the temperate regions, which have warm summers, cool winters, and moderate rainfall.

SEE ALSO

Atmosphere, Climate, Continent, Desert, Earthquake, Gravity, Mountain, Ocean, Orbit, Planet, Seasons, Solar system, Weather

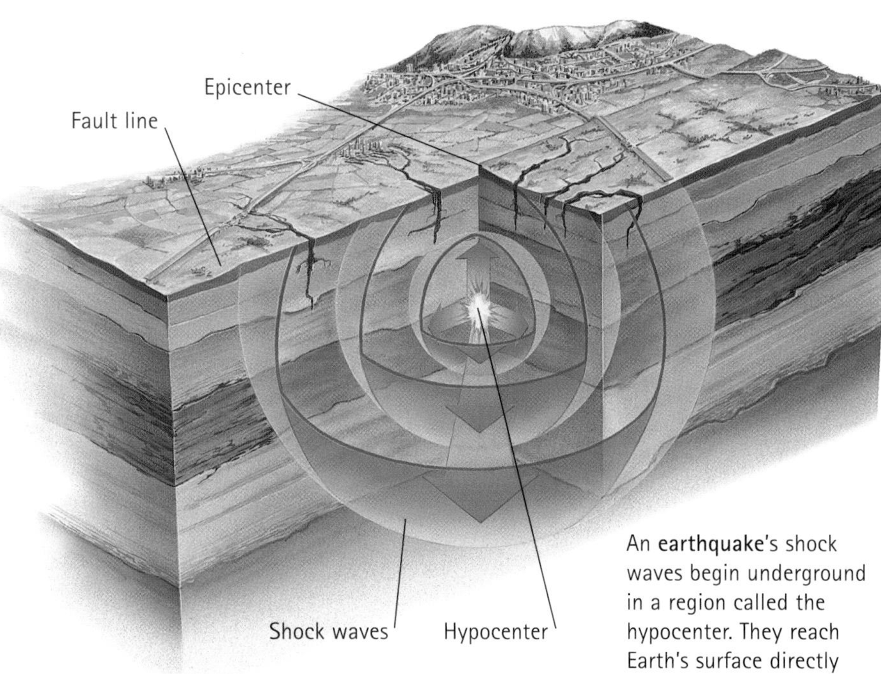

An **earthquake**'s shock waves begin underground in a region called the hypocenter. They reach Earth's surface directly above at the epicenter. From here they spread out in all directions.

Earthquake

An earthquake is when the surface of **Earth** shakes. It is caused by the sudden release of pressure through weak parts of Earth's crust called fault lines. About 500,000 earthquakes happen every year. Most are so weak that only special instruments called seismographs prove that they have taken place. A seismograph shows earth tremors as changes in a line traced on a turning drum. Tremors vibrate the weight that holds the tracer.

Tremors can happen when **volcanoes** erupt, when the roof of an underground **cave** falls in, or when there is a landslide. But the largest earthquakes occur when one huge piece of Earth's crust slips suddenly against another piece. This may take place deep underground, but the shock waves travel up through Earth's crust and make the surface shake. A seabed earthquake may trigger a tsunami—a massive ocean **wave** that quickly travels great distances.

Only one earthquake in 500 does any damage, but some earthquakes cause terrible destruction. In 1906 a powerful earthquake and the massive **fires** it caused destroyed most of **San Francisco**, California. When an earthquake shook the Kwanto Plain, Japan, in 1923, 570,000 buildings collapsed. One of the most devastating earthquakes of recent times hit the Chinese city of Tangshan in 1976. As many as 750,000 people are thought to have died.

At **Easter**, Christians give each other decorated eggs to symbolize the new life that returns to nature around this time.

Echoes are reflected sound waves. Sometimes if you face a cliff and shout, sound waves from your voice hit the rock and bounce back.

Earthworm *see* Worm

Easter

Easter is the most important religious **festival** in **Christianity**. On Easter Day, Christians remember the resurrection of **Jesus**. Easter falls on a different date each year, but it is always on a Sunday in April or late March.

Echo

An echo is a **sound** bounced back from a wall or some other hard object. Sound always travels at the same speed, so we can use echoes to find how far away objects are. A ship's **sonar** uses echoes to find the depth of the sea. Echoes also help **bats** fly in the dark. **Radar** is a device that uses the echoes from **radio** signals to track moving objects.

Eclipse

An eclipse happens when the shadow of one **planet** or **moon** falls on another. If the shadow hides all of the planet or moon, there is a total eclipse. If it hides only a part, there is a partial eclipse.

The only eclipses you can see easily without a **telescope** take place when the **Sun**, Moon, and **Earth** are in line. When Earth lies between the Sun and the Moon, Earth's shadow falls on the Moon. This is an eclipse of the Moon. When the Moon lies between Earth and the Sun, the Moon's shadow falls on a part of Earth. An eclipse of the Sun, or solar eclipse, can be seen from that region. About two or three of each kind of eclipse happen every year.

Ecology

Ecology is a branch of **biology**. It is the study of the relationship between living things and their surroundings or environment. Ecologists are scientists who study how living things and their surroundings affect each other.

Ecology shows us that most species of **plants** and **animals** can live only in a particular kind of environment such as a **lake**, **forest**, **desert**, or **mountain**. These places are called **habitats**.

Within each habitat lives a variety of plants, all of which are suited to the habitat's **soil**, **temperature**, sunshine, rainfall, and so on. The animals living in the habitat eat the plants or one another. The plants and animals are linked in what ecologists call a **food chain**. If some species die out and vanish from the food chain, those that eat them lose their food and may die too.

Habitats are always changing. Often these changes are good for some plants and animals but are bad for others. For example, if a pond dries up, its fish will die, but the dead fish will provide food for a heron. Human activities can also change habitats. For example, we may cut down a forest to make way for a new field. We change the natural landscape by **farming** the land and by building cities and roads. **Pollution** from our factories poisons the **water**, soil, and **air**. Ecologists study the ways in which we change the natural environment and can help us limit the damage we do. Taking steps to protect the natural world is called **conservation**.

Economics

Economics is the study of people's needs, such as food, clothing, goods, and housing and the ways in which people meet these needs. Economists study the ways in which a community's needs can be met. No country has enough resources to supply all the things that its people want. It has to decide the best way of using the resources that it has. Many economists believe that this is the most important decision nations must make.

There are several different economic systems, including **communism** and capitalism. In the capitalist economic system most of the land, resources, and industries are owned by private individuals and **companies** rather than by **governments**.

Ecuador

Ecuador is a country in northwestern **South America**, and it lies on the **equator**. Its name is Spanish for equator.

△ **Ecology** is the study of living things and where they live. Inside this huge greenhouse in the Sonoran Desert in southwest U.S. and northwest Mexico, ecologists have created replicas of seven major world habitats, including a rain forest and a 4.5-million-liter ocean.

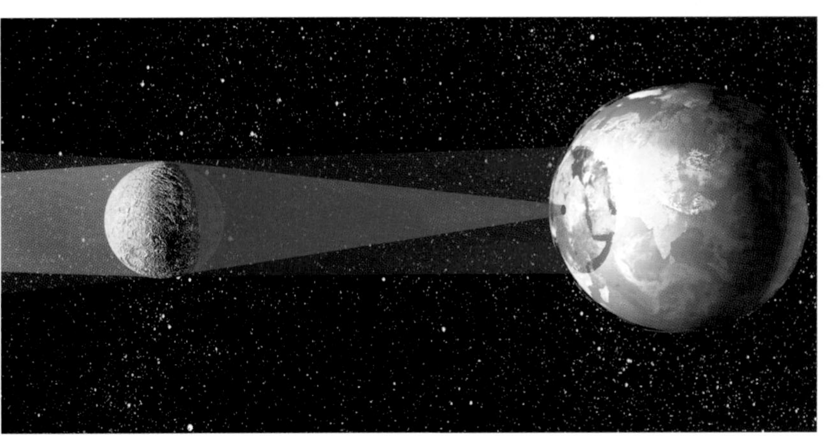

▽ During an **eclipse** of the Sun, or solar eclipse, day becomes night. When the Moon moves in between Earth and the Sun, it temporarily casts a shadow onto part of Earth.

ECUADOR
Government: Republic
Capital: Quito
Area: 106,800 sq. mi.
Population: 13,183,978
Language: Spanish
Currency: Sucre

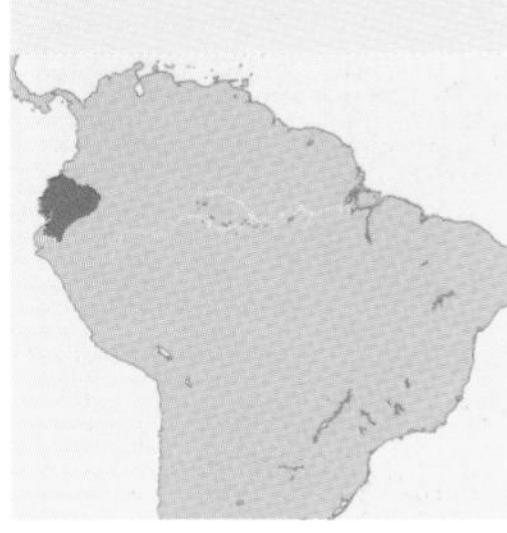

Most of eastern Ecuador is dominated by the **Andes** mountains. More than half of Ecuador's population lives in the high mountain valleys, where they keep herds of **sheep** and **llamas**. However, the country's chief products are **coffee**, bananas, **sugar**, and **oil**.

The Galapagos Islands lie 595 mi. (960km) off the Pacific coast of South America. They belong to Ecuador and have a unique range of wildlife. One of the first scientists to visit them was the English biologist **Charles Darwin**.

Edison, Thomas

Thomas Alva Edison (1847–1931) was an American inventor. He spent only three months at school when he was a child, but he went on to produce more than 100 **inventions**. The most famous are the electric light (see **electricity**) and the phonograph for **recording** and playing back **sounds**. Edison finished building his phonograph in 1877. It was a hand-operated device that played recordings made on tinfoil cylinders.

Eel

Eels are long, slim **fish** with tiny scales and fins like narrow ribbons. The two best-known species are the European and American freshwater eels, which have a remarkable life cycle. When it is time to breed, the adult eels leave their **rivers**, streams, and marshes and swim thousands of miles into the **Atlantic Ocean**. There they spawn (release their eggs and sperm). After spawning the adult eels die.

When they hatch, the tiny young eels are transparent and look nothing like their parents. These babies find their way back to their parents' original homes in North America and Europe. The young eels grow up in freshwater and stay there until they are ready for their long journey back across the Atlantic Ocean. The eels' long journeys are an example of **migration**.

Egg

An egg is a female **cell** that will grow into a new **plant** or **animal**. Most eggs only grow if they are joined with or fertilized by male cells. The male cells of animals are usually known as sperm (see **reproduction**). In most **mammals** the fertilized eggs grow inside the mother's body. However, all **birds** and most **fish**, **amphibians**, and **reptiles** lay eggs that contain enough food for the young to grow inside the egg.

Egypt

Modern Egypt dates from A.D. 642, when Egypt was conquered by Muslim soldiers from Arabia. Egypt has over 60 million people, more than any other nation in **Africa** apart from **Nigeria**. Its capital, Cairo, is the largest African city. Most Egyptians are Arabs, and **Islam** is the primary religion.

The **Nile River** flows through Egypt to the **Mediterranean Sea** on the country's north coast. Water from the river creates large areas of fertile farmland, where **cotton** and other crops are grown. In the east is the **Suez Canal**, which allows **ships** to sail from the Mediterranean to the **Red Sea**.

▽ The greatest pyramids of **ancient Egypt** were built on the banks of the Nile River in Giza, near the modern city of Cairo. This illustration shows a royal boat approaching the pyramid complex.

Egypt, ancient

Around 5,000 years ago the ancient Egyptians began building one of the world's first great civilizations. For the next 2,500 years ancient Egypt was one of the strongest and wealthiest states in the world.

The population of ancient Egypt was probably no more than six million. Scarcely any of the people lived in the hot sand-and-rock **deserts** that cover most of inland Egypt. Almost all of them settled near the banks of the mighty **Nile River**.

Each year the river overflowed and left rich mud on nearby land, creating ideal conditions for **farming** to flourish. Farmers learned to dig and **plow** their fields and could grow two crops per year in the warm, fertile **soil**. The farmers grew more than enough grain, fruit, and vegetables to feed themselves. The surplus food was used to feed the rest of Egypt's population—merchants, craftspeople, miners, priests, and noble families, as well as the **pharaohs** who ruled over the entire land.

Most ancient Egyptians were poor and lived in simple mud-brick huts with palm-leaf roofs. Wealthy Egyptians lived in large, well-furnished **houses** and could afford luxury foods such as meat and cakes. They wore fine clothes, **jewelry**, and even **cosmetics**.

The ancient Egyptians were highly skilled at **architecture** and **engineering** and built splendid cities, temples, and tombs. They constructed impressive **pyramids** as tombs for their dead pharaohs. Building a pyramid was an enormous task, which took thousands of workers and many years to complete. The workers cut huge stone blocks for the pyramid, ferried them down the Nile on rafts, and hauled them into place. Each block weighed up to 2.5 tons.

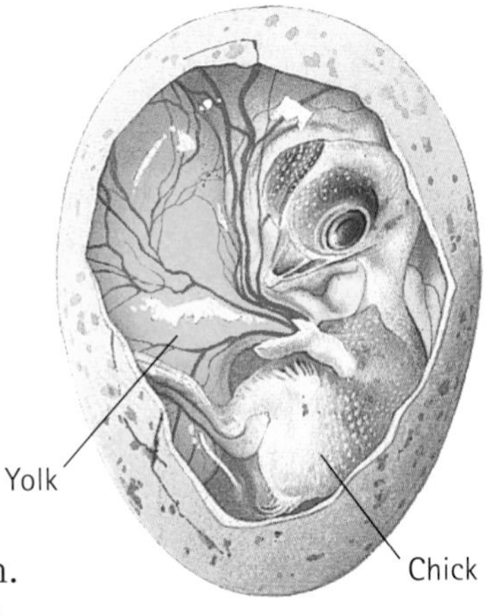

Inside a bird's **egg** the chick is fed from the yolk. When the chick hatches, its feathers and claws are fully formed.

EGYPT
Government: Republic
Capital: Cairo
Area: 383,900 sq. mi.
Population: 69,536,644
Language: Arabic
Currency: Egyptian pound

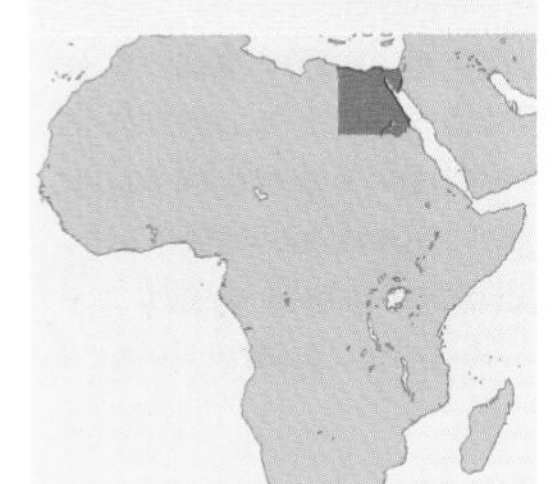

Inside each pyramid the ancient Egyptians would place the mummy (preserved body) of a pharaoh. They believed the dead went on living, so they placed food and furniture beside each mummy. Thieves later emptied many tombs. However, the boy pharaoh **Tutankhamen**'s tomb was discovered almost intact in 1922.

The dry Egyptian air has preserved many examples of **hieroglyphics**, a system of picture writing that was written on fragile **paper** made from the papyrus plant. Hieroglyphics and wall **paintings** tell us a great deal about how the ancient Egyptians lived. The **art** they made often depicted gods such as Ra, the sun god, or Osiris, the god of the dead (see **god and goddess**).

The ancient Egyptians also believed in the sphinx—a creature with the body of a lion and the head of a pharaoh. The most famous sphinx guards the huge pyramid of Khafre at Giza.

In time foreign armies equipped with **iron** weapons conquered the ancient Egyptians. Their land fell under foreign rule after 525 B.C. When the Egyptian queen **Cleopatra** died in 31 B.C., Egypt became part of the **Roman Empire**.

Eid

Eid is a religious **festival** of **Islam**. Muslims celebrate two Eids each year—Eid ul-Adha (Festival of Sacrifice) and Eid ul-Fitr (Festival of the Breaking of the Fast). Eid ul-Adha occurs at the end of the 12th month of the Islamic **calendar**. Animals, such as sheep or goats, are sacrificed in

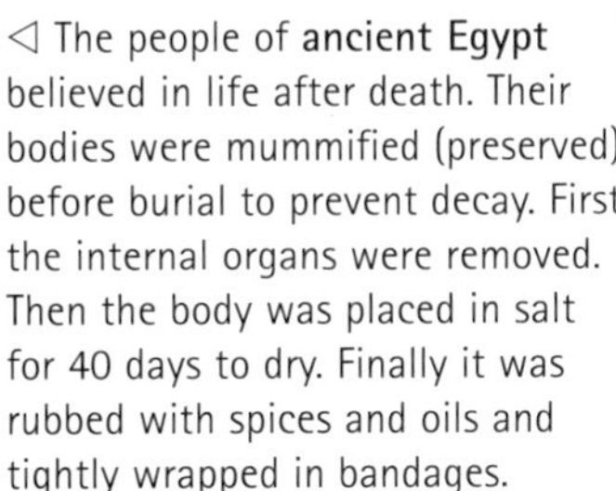

◁ The people of **ancient Egypt** believed in life after death. Their bodies were mummified (preserved) before burial to prevent decay. First the internal organs were removed. Then the body was placed in salt for 40 days to dry. Finally it was rubbed with spices and oils and tightly wrapped in bandages.

memory of the prophet Abraham, who was so faithful to God that he was prepared to sacrifice his own son.

Eid ul-Fitr is a joyful feast held at the end of **Ramadan**—the Islamic month of fasting. During Ramadan, Muslims fast (do not eat or drink) from sunrise until sunset every day.

Einstein, Albert

Albert Einstein (1879–1955) was an important scientist whose main area of research was **physics**. He was born in **Germany** but in the 1930s went to live in the **U.S.** His theory of relativity was a new way of looking at **time**, **space**, **matter**, and **energy**. Einstein proved that a small amount of matter could be transformed into a vast amount of energy. This made it possible for people to use **nuclear energy**.

Elasticity

When you pull a **rubber** band, it stretches. When you let go, it springs back to its original size. The rubber band is elastic—it has elasticity. If you drop a rubber ball, the part of the ball that hits the ground is flattened. Then the ball springs back into its original round shape. As this happens the ball pushes on the ground and jumps up—it bounces. The ball has elasticity.

Elasticity exists because the molecules that make up an elastic material try to stay at a certain distance from each other. If they are squeezed more tightly together, they immediately push apart. If they are pulled apart, they try to come together again. All solids and **liquids** have some elasticity.

Election

Most countries, local regions, and public organizations hold elections from time to time. Elections give people the chance to elect, or choose, a new **government**,

Albert **Einstein** helped to develop the first atomic bomb, but he became very concerned about the need to control nuclear weapons after World War II.

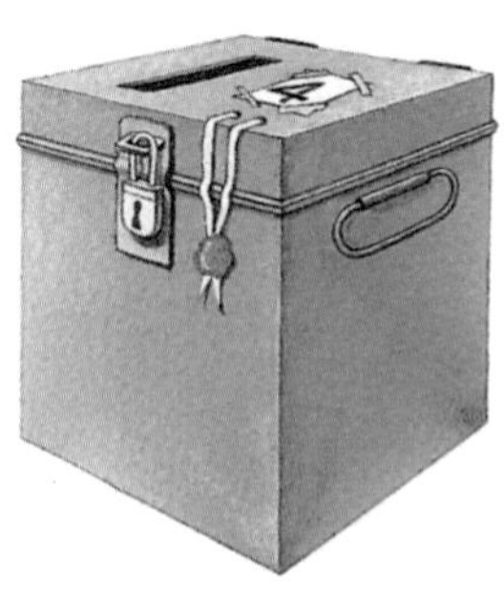

In some **elections** people vote by making a mark next to a candidate's name on a piece of paper. The papers, or votes, are inserted into a sealed box to be counted later.

Pole-vaulting relies on **elasticity**. When the pole hits the ground, it bends. Because the pole is highly elastic, it starts to straighten out, hurling the vaulter over the bar.

council, or leader. We do this by voting. Voting is essential to the political system called **democracy**.

In democratic countries voters go to a certain building on election, or polling, day. Each voter chooses their candidate in secret either in a polling booth or by checking the candidate's name on a piece of paper. Sometimes the rules of the election say that the voter has to choose several candidates for different offices.

Many elections are decided by a system in which the candidate with the most votes wins. But others are decided by another system called proportional representation. In this system the number of candidates elected from each party is calculated according to the percentage of the total vote that the party receives.

Only adults may vote in political elections. In many countries people earn this right when they reach 18.

Electricity

Electricity is an invisible form of **energy**. It is used to power electric trains, lightbulbs, **computers**, **radios**, **televisions**, and many other devices.

The electricity that we use flows through wires as an electric current. An electric current flows when tiny particles called electrons jump between the **atoms** that make up the **metal** in the wire. A current can flow only if a wire makes a complete loop called a circuit. If a gap is made in the circuit, the current stops flowing. Switches are devices that open and close gaps in circuits.

The unit of electric current is the amp—short for ampère. An average domestic lightbulb carries no more than one amp. A **lightning** flash can peak at about 20,000 amps. A nuclear **power plant** can deliver 10 million amps. Voltage is a unit of measurement that describes how powerfully a source of electricity, such as a **battery** or a **generator**, sends an electric current.

Batteries are a highly convenient source of electricity. The electric current they produce can be used to start **cars**, illuminate flashlight bulbs, and work radios. But most of the electricity we use is produced in power plants. Inside a power plant's generators coils of wire are made to rotate between powerful magnets (see **magnetism**). This makes an electric current flow through the coils of wire.

Electricity travels from the power plant through a network of overhead power lines and underground cables to wherever it is needed. This network is called the electricity grid. The current flowing through the power lines has a very high force, or voltage. Before it reaches homes and factories devices called transformers reduce the voltage of the current to a lower level that can be used safely.

In a house, an electric current flows out of the sockets in the walls and through any electrical equipment that is in use. Then it returns to the generator in the power plant through another set of wires. This completes the circuit.

The electricity used in houses is in the form of an alternating current—it flows in one direction and then in the opposite direction. Each movement back and forth happens about 50 times per second. This is so fast that we do not notice, for example, that lights flicker.

Nuclear power plant
Substation
Large factory
Underground transformer
Substation
Homes
Transformer

△ **Electricity** produced by the power plant travels along a network of high-voltage power lines. It passes through a series of transformers and substations, where the current is changed to the lower voltage used in homes and factories.

Electronics

Electronics is an important branch of **engineering** that involves the study of **electricity**. It deals with the way in which tiny particles called electrons flow through certain solid materials, **gases**, or a **vacuum**.

Modern electrical devices contain tiny electronic parts such as **silicon chips** and **transistors**. These parts, or components, are joined together by lines of metallic **paint** on circuit boards. Electronic engineers figure out which components need to be put together to make circuits that can perform specific tasks. These circuits are found in all kinds of devices, including **computers**, **television** sets, **radios**, pocket **calculators**, **telephones**, digital watches, and **radars**. Without electronics, **aircraft** could not fly and **space exploration** would be impossible.

▽ Electricity can be generated by turbines that harness the power of the wind. They are built in groups called wind farms, which are located in exposed places where it is always windy. There are plans to build many offshore wind farms like this one in the future.

Element

Everything that you see around you is made up of chemical ingredients called elements. In each element all the **atoms** are of the same type.

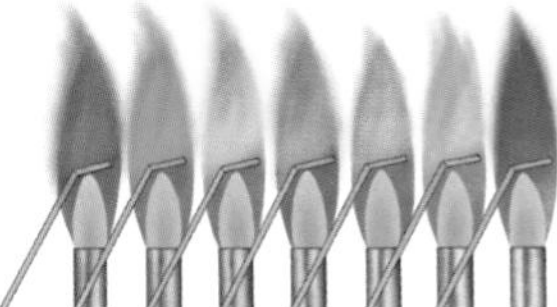

△ Every **element** behaves in a different way. For example, metals burn with different colored flames. The picture above shows (from left to right) the flames of calcium, copper, sodium, lithium, potassium, barium, and lead.

△ **Emus** live on Australia's grasslands. They gather in small flocks and move from place to place in search of seeds, berries, and fresh leaves to eat.

Different elements can be joined to make more complicated substances called **compounds**, but an element cannot be broken down into a simpler kind of substance.

Chemists have found more than 100 different elements, of which 92 occur naturally. Scientists have produced some of the other elements in laboratories. At ordinary room **temperatures** some elements are **gases**, some are **liquids**, and some are solids.

Elephant

Elephants are the largest living land **animals**. A large bull (male) elephant may stand twice as high as a human and weigh as much as seven family cars. Elephants have huge ears, long trunks, **ivory** tusks, and very thick **skin**. There are two species of elephants. The African elephant has larger ears and tusks than the Indian, or Asian, elephant. Most African elephants roam the grassy plains, or **savannas**, of East Africa, although they also live in forests. Indian elephants mainly live in thick **rain forests**.

Elephants are plant-eating **mammals**, or **herbivores**. They use their trunks to pull up grass and plants and to scoop food and water into their mouths.

◁ Hunters have killed thousands of African **elephants** for their ivory tusks. The species is now endangered.

Elizabeth I

Elizabeth I (1533–1603) was a famous English queen. She never married and ruled alone for 45 years. During the 1500s there was much religious conflict in **England**, **Scotland**, and the rest of **Europe**. A Protestant, Elizabeth tried to unite her country and end the wars of religion, but she had her Catholic rival, **Mary Queen of Scots**, put to death.

In 1588 Elizabeth's navy crushed the Spanish **Armada** and made England powerful at sea. England became a wealthier and more important country. Many writers, poets, and scholars lived in Elizabeth's reign, including the playwright **Shakespeare**. People often call her reign "the Elizabethan Age."

Elizabeth II

Elizabeth II (b. 1926) is queen of the **United Kingdom** of Great Britain and Northern Ireland and head of the British **Commonwealth**. Her husband is the Duke of Edinburgh. Her eldest son and heir to the throne is Charles, Prince of **Wales**. Elizabeth II's official residences are Buckingham Palace in London and Windsor Castle in Berkshire.

El Salvador

El Salvador is the smallest country in **Central America**, but it has more people per square mile than any other Central American country. Many of its people are farmers, and the most important crops are **coffee**, corn, and **sugar**. El Salvador has had several conflicts with its neighbor, **Honduras**, and suffered a 12-year **civil war**, which ended in 1992.

Emu

Only the **ostrich** is larger than this big Australian **bird**. An emu can run at up to 31 mph (50km/h) on its long, strong legs. It cannot fly because it is far too heavy, and its wings are small and weak.

Energy

Energy is the ability to do work. It exists in several forms, but there are two main kinds—potential energy and kinetic energy. Potential energy is the "energy of position," or stored energy. For example, the water stored behind a high **dam** has potential energy. Kinetic energy is the "energy of movement." When water from the dam moves through pipes and powers **turbines** to generate **electricity**, it has kinetic energy.

Other forms of energy are electrical, **heat**, chemical, **sound**, and **nuclear**. Energy can be changed from one form into another. For example, the chemical energy of gasoline is turned into kinetic energy as it works the moving parts of a car's **engine**, to electrical energy in the car's headlights, and to sound energy in the car's horn. At every stage some energy is turned into heat energy—this is why the car's engine becomes very hot. However, energy is never "lost" or destroyed.

The **sun** gives us most of the energy we use on **earth**. Energy from the sun is called solar energy.

Engine

Engines are **machines** that change potential (stored) energy into useful energy that does work. People have used simple engines, such as **windmills** and waterwheels, for many years.

▷ Elizabeth I of England wore elaborate costumes, makeup, wigs, and jewels. Her dramatic appearance impressed people, increasing her power and prestige.

The first **steam engines** were developed in the early 1700s. They provided power for factories and were later used to drive **ships**, trains, and **cars**. Today steam still drives some machines such as the steam turbines in nuclear **power plants**. However, steam engines have been largely replaced by **internal combustion engines**. These include gas engines and **diesel engines**. In an internal combustion engine, **fuel** burns inside the engine.

In a gas engine gasoline mixes with air inside a cylinder. A spark sets the mixture on fire, and it explodes. This happens over and over again. Hot gases from the explosions push a piston back and forth inside the cylinder. The piston drives the crankshaft around, which turns the vehicle's **wheels**. Most gas engines have up to eight cylinders.

The first **jet engine** was designed in 1930, and **rockets** followed not far behind. Jet engines are used in many **aircraft**. Rocket engines are used in **missiles** and **space exploration**.

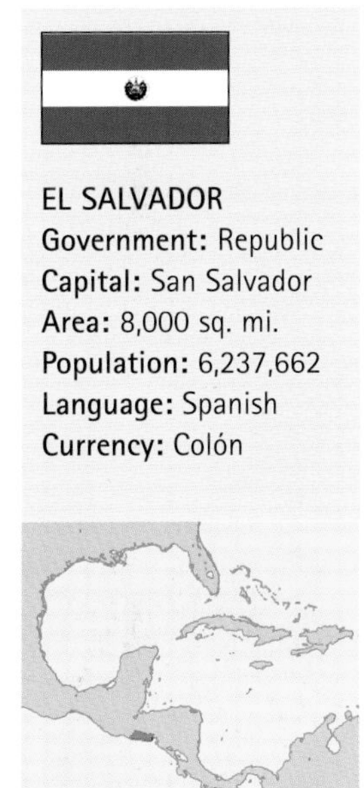

EL SALVADOR
Government: Republic
Capital: San Salvador
Area: 8,000 sq. mi.
Population: 6,237,662
Language: Spanish
Currency: Colón

▽ In a gas **engine** air and gasoline are mixed to produce explosions. The explosive force drives pistons, which turn the crankshaft. As the crankshaft rotates, it turns the vehicle's wheels.

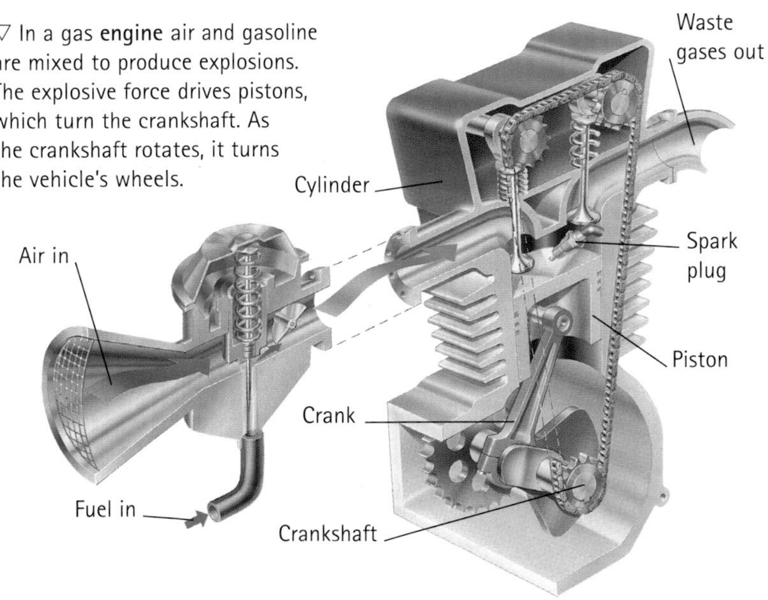

EUROPE

Europe is the second smallest continent. Its moderate climate, fertile land, and rich resources make it ideal for human habitation.

A FERTILE CONTINENT

Europe is a peninsula that lies to the west of the continent of Asia. It lies on the same tectonic plate (section of earth's surface) as western Asia. Europe has a long history of human settlement. This is mainly because more of its land is suitable for farming than on any other continent.

◁ *The Alps lie at the heart of Europe and are a major tourist destination.*

CHANGING LANDSCAPES

The north of Europe is covered with mountains and huge forests of conifer trees and lies partly in the Arctic Circle. It includes Scandinavia—Norway, Sweden, Denmark, and Finland—and part of western Russia.

A zone of flat lowland plains covers much of central Europe. It stretches from the United Kingdom east to the Ural Mountains of Russia. In this region lie many of Europe's great rivers such as the Rhine, Danube, and Volga. The warm summers, cool winters, and plentiful rainfall are ideal for growing wheat, barley, oats, potatoes, and vegetables.

◁ *Rotterdam, on the Netherlands' coast, is the busiest port in the world. It is used to export and import a huge range of products, from chemicals to steel, machinery, textiles, and grain.*

THE MEDITERRANEAN

The southern part of Europe is separated from the north by several mountain ranges. From west to east these are the Pyrenees, Alps, Carpathians, and Caucasus. The Mediterranean region includes Portugal, Spain, southern France, Italy, and Greece. It has a much warmer climate than the rest of Europe, with mild winters and hot, dry summers. The mixed landscape of rolling hills and plains is used to grow crops such as citrus fruit and olives.

EUROPE FACT FILE
Area: 4,108,494 sq. mi.
Highest mountain: Mount Elbrus, southwest Russia, 18,476 ft.
Largest lake: Ladoga, northwest Russia, 26,863 sq. mi.
Longest river: Volga, 2,189 mi.
Number of countries: 45
Largest country: Russia (23 percent of which is in Europe)
Smallest country: Vatican City
Largest city: London, U.K., 7.2 million
Largest population: Germany, 83 million
Total population: 727 million

SEE ALSO
Alps, Ancient Greece, European Union, Explorer, Farming, Renaissance, Roman Empire, Vikings, World War I, World War II

△ *The warm climate of the Mediterranean region is ideal for growing vines, which produce the grapes used in winemaking.*

△ *Europe has a large motor industry, with many highly automated vehicle-assembly plants.*

POWERFUL EMPIRES

Throughout history Europe has had a huge influence on world politics. The system of democracy—where the government is chosen by the people—was developed in ancient Greece about 2,500 years ago. Democracy is now the main political system across much of the world. Laws introduced by the Roman Empire, which controlled much of Europe until it was finally defeated in A.D. 476, still influence many legal systems today.

CONQUERING THE GLOBE

During the Middle Ages, European explorers began to explore unknown lands. England, Spain, France, and the Netherlands used their military strength to establish colonies abroad. The trade that flowed in and out of Europe from the colonies made these states extremely wealthy. In the 1800s Belgium and Germany also founded colonies. Most European colonies became independent states after World War II.

CULTURE AND RELIGION

Europe has been a leading center of learning since the days of ancient Greece. Impressive ancient Greek and Roman ruins are scattered across the south of the continent. During the Renaissance (1350–1500s) Europeans became interested in many new ideas about science, art, and literature. Europe is also an important center of Christianity. The headquarters of the Roman Catholic Church are in Vatican City in Rome, Italy, while the Orthodox Church flourishes in the east and southwest.

COMING TOGETHER

The map of Europe has often changed, mainly owing to wars between rival countries. Both world wars were begun and fought largely in Europe. After World War II Europe was divided between the noncommunist states of the West and the Russian-backed Communist states of the East. This period was called the "Cold War." In the late 1980s the Communist governments of Eastern Europe finally crumbled. Today 15 European states have formed the European Union. This organization attempts to improve the cooperation between its members.

△ *Fertile plains cover much of Eastern Europe. In some areas farmers still use teams of oxen to plow fields and pull carts.*

△ Many climbers tried to reach the summit of Mount **Everest** before two finally succeeded in 1953. They were New Zealander Edmund Hillary and a Sherpa tribesman from Nepal, Tenzing Norgay.

Engineering

Engineers do many different types of jobs. Metallurgical engineers separate **metals** from other substances to make them usable. Chemical engineers use chemicals to make such things as **soap**, **paint**, and **plastics**. Civil engineers plan and design structures such as **bridges**, **roads**, **railroads**, **tunnels**, and airports. Electrical engineers work with devices that use or produce **electricity**. Bioengineers use their skills for biological or medical purposes.

England

England is the largest country in the **United Kingdom** of Great Britain and **Northern Ireland**. It covers an area of 50,871 sq. mi. (130,439 sq km)—roughly three fifths of Great Britain's total area. England's neighbors are **Scotland** and **Wales**. Northern Ireland lies to the west, across the Irish Sea.

England is named after the Angles, a group of **Anglo-Saxons** who settled there about 1,500 years ago. Today, England is densely populated, with a population of nearly 50 million.

Equator

The equator is an imaginary line around the world, halfway between the **North Pole** and the **South Pole**. It divides earth into the Northern and Southern hemispheres.

Estonia *see* Baltic States

ETHIOPIA
Government: Republic
Capital: Addis Ababa
Area: 431,800 sq. mi.
Population: 65,891,874
Language: Amharic
Currency: Ethiopian birr

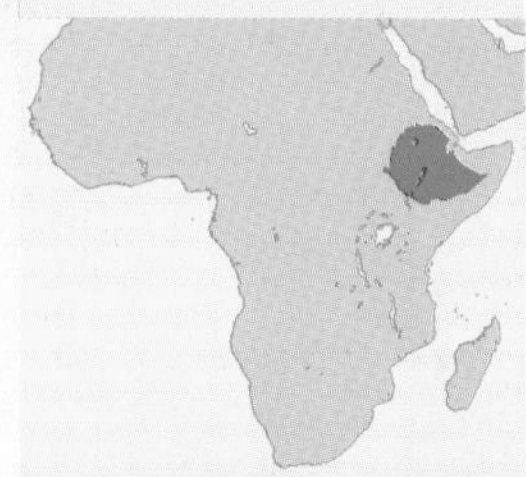

Ethiopia

Ethiopia is a huge country in the northeast of **Africa**. It was formerly called Abyssinia. Much of Ethiopia consists of rocky **mountains** and open areas of high ground called plateaus. Here farmers grow grain and **coffee**. For many years Ethiopia suffered from drought (a long period with no rain) and **civil war**. **Famine** was widespread. In the 1980s a worldwide campaign raised money to send food and medical supplies to the country.

European Union

The European Union (EU) is a group of nations that cooperate to make it easier for goods, **money**, and people to travel between the countries in the Union. Its 15 members are **Austria**, **Belgium**, **Denmark**, **Finland**, **France**, **Ireland**, **Italy**, the **United Kingdom**, **Greece**, **Luxembourg**, the **Netherlands**, **Portugal**, **Spain**, **Sweden**, and **Germany**. Several other European countries have applied to join them. The headquarters of the European Union are in Brussels, Belgium. In 2002, 12 members of the EU adopted a single unit of currency—the euro.

Everest, Mount

Mount Everest is the world's highest peak. It rises 29,021 ft. (8,848m) above sea level. The **mountain** stands in the **Himalayas** on the borders of **Nepal** and **Tibet**.

Evolution

The theory of evolution states that the **plants** and **animals** alive today are descended from other forms that lived long ago. This slow process of change has been going on for many millions of years—ever since life first appeared on **earth**—and it is still happening. Much of the evidence for evolution comes from **fossils**—remains of extinct plants and animals. Fossils give us an idea of what the ancestors of today's species looked like.

The theory of evolution says that plants and animals must adapt to their surroundings, or environment, if they are to survive. Those that adapt best are most likely to survive.

For example, in the past some **giraffes** may have had longer necks than others. The long-necked giraffes would have been able to feed on leaves that were too high for short-necked giraffes to reach. During food shortages the taller giraffes were more likely to survive than the shorter ones. In time all of the short-necked giraffes died out—leaving only giraffes with long necks.

Charles **Darwin** was one of the first to put forward the theory of **evolution**. He published his idea in 1859.

Exercise

Exercise usually means activities that strengthen the **muscles** and improve **health**. Many **sports** are good exercise, but it is better to gently exercise regularly than to do strenuous exercise only once in a while. Brisk walking is one of the best forms of exercise.

Explorer

Explorers are people who travel to find out about little-known places. There have been explorers ever since **Stone Age** people started to wander across continents. In the 1200s Marco **Polo** reached China from Europe, but the great age of exploration did not begin until the 1400s.

Famous western explorers include Vasco da **Gama**, Hernando **Cortés**, Christopher **Columbus**, Ferdinand **Magellan**, James **Cook**, David **Livingstone,** and Roald **Amundsen**.

Explosion

Explosions occur when people **heat** or strike certain solid or **liquid** substances. These suddenly turn into hot **gases**. The gases fill more space than the solids or liquids, so they rush out violently. High explosives, such as dynamite, explode faster and do more damage than low explosives such as gunpowder.

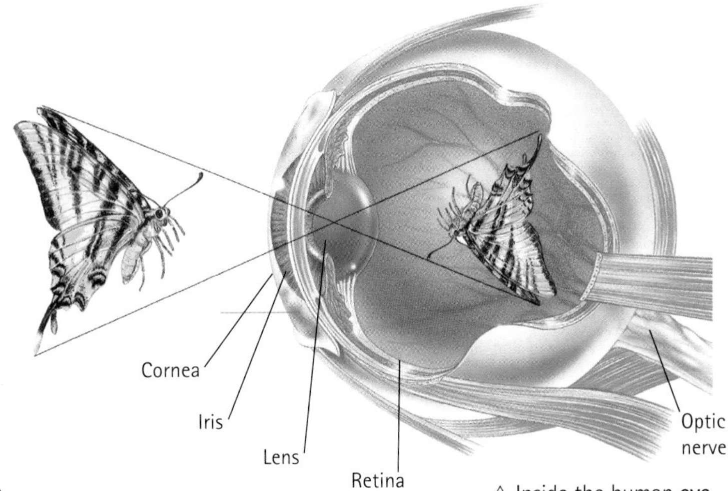

△ Inside the human **eye** the image on the retina is upside down. The brain turns it over so that we see things the right way.

Eye

Eyes are organs that provide **animals** with information about the appearance of objects. A human eye behaves much like a **camera**, by bending **light** rays to form images of objects.

Light rays enter the eye through a layer of transparent skin called the conjunctiva. The rays pass through a hard, transparent layer called the cornea. This bends the rays. The **lens** brings them into focus on the retina at the back of the eye. The focused image is "received" by light-sensitive **nerve** endings on the retina, which send the **brain** a message along the optic nerve. The iris—the eye's colored part—is a **muscle** that opens and closes to let more or less light through. This allows us to see in dim or bright light.

▽ **Explorers** have added greatly to our knowledge of the world. In 1947 the Norwegian Thor Heyerdahl used a log raft to sail from Peru, across the Pacific, to the Polynesian islands. This showed that it would have been possible for people to make a similar voyage thousands of years before.

"The Goose That Laid Golden Eggs" is a **fable** about greed. A farmer had a goose that laid eggs made of gold, which made him very rich. He greedily cut the goose open, hoping to find even more treasure, but there was none. Because the goose was dead, there were no more eggs.

Fable

Fables are stories that are usually told to teach lessons. Their main characters are usually animals that can speak and act like human beings. Some of the most famous fables include those of **Aesop**, an ancient Greek storyteller. Aesop's fables, such as "The Wolf in Sheep's Clothing" and "The Ant and the Grasshopper," are told to this day. Many modern writers have produced fables to comment on how they see the world. One of the best-known modern fables is *Animal Farm* (1945) by George Orwell (1903–1950).

The largest **falcon** in the world is the gyrfalcon, which lives in the Arctic regions of Europe, Russia, and North America. The gyrfalcon preys on other birds, and nests on cliff ledges.

Falcon

Falcons are fast-flying **birds** of prey. They are found all over the world and include species such as the peregrine falcon, the merlin, and several types of kestrels. Falcons have sharp talons for killing prey and strong, hooked beaks for tearing flesh. They swoop down on their victims from above, hitting them with their outstretched talons.

Falkland Islands

The Falklands are a group of cold, windswept **islands** that lie in the South **Atlantic Ocean** about 447 mi. (770km) east of the southern tip of **South America**. The islands are a British colony, and **sheep** farming is the main occupation. In 1982 **Argentina** invaded the Falklands, but the Argentine troops were defeated by British forces.

Famine

Sometimes a country does not have enough **food** to feed its **population**, and eventually some of the people may starve to death. This situation is known as famine. Many of the countries in the **developing world** suffer famines, often because there has not been enough rain to grow sufficient food. Nations that are unaffected by the famine send food supplies to help the starving people.

Faraday, Michael

Michael Faraday (1791–1867) was an English scientist who is best known for his experiments with **electricity**. He showed that an electric current could be made to flow along a **wire** when the wire was passed between the poles of a **magnet**. Today this is how most electricity is produced in large **generators**.

Farming *see* **page 114**

Fascism was perhaps at its strongest across Europe in the years before World War II, as can be seen by the size of this Nazi rally held in Germany in 1936.

Fascism

Fascism is a political belief. It takes its name from the Latin *fasces*—a bundle of rods with an axe that was the symbol of authority in ancient Rome. Fascism first appeared in **Italy** in 1919 when Benito **Mussolini** founded the Italian Fascist Party. In 1922 Mussolini seized power to become the **dictator** of Italy.

Fascist political ideas include the belief that the government of a country has to be all-powerful. Its citizens have to work hard and obey the government for the good of the nation. Fascists believe in strict discipline and training for all people, including children. Anybody who opposes a fascist government is made an outlaw. In Fascist Italy many people were jailed, exiled, or executed because they did not agree with the Fascists. All of the other political parties were made illegal.

Fascism became popular in many other countries between the two world wars, and fascist governments came to power in **Germany**, **Spain**, and **Portugal**. The supporters of Germany's Fascist party, the National Socialist Workers' Party, were known as Nazis. In 1933 Adolf **Hitler**, the Nazi leader, became German chancellor. Hitler's fascist policies led to the outbreak of **World War II**.

Fashion

Most people in the world wear some type of clothing. What they wear depends on the **climate** and how they live. Styles of clothing also change according to the latest fashions.

The earliest clothes were **animal** skins. In the ancient world people began wearing loose, draped tunics. By the **Middle Ages** the dress of poorer people was still simple, but the wealthy dressed in fine **silk** and damask (a luxurious, shiny fabric) from the East. During the **Renaissance** (1350–1500s) the new wealth and interest in art made rich, colorful fabrics popular. In the 1700s in **Europe** clothes became very elaborate to match the grand buildings of the period. People wore huge wigs and wide, stiffened skirts, which were often beautifully embroidered.

By the 1900s fashions had become more practical, especially for women. Today many people throughout the world dress in a similar way, wearing clothes such as jeans, T-shirts, and jackets. Clothes are often made from modern **textiles** that contain artificial fibers such as nylon and polyester.

How styles change from year to year is decided by fashion designers. Fashion is big business. Every season there are spectacular shows where models display the latest top designs.

△ Some clothing **fashions** are extremely elaborate. This is the costume worn by the actors of Japanese Kabuki theater, which combines a story with dances and songs.

△ In ancient Greece the **fashion** was to wear light, loose-fitting clothes made of wool or linen.

▽ Stiff ruffs made of starched linen and worn around the neck were the height of **fashion** in England during the 1500s.

Fat

Fat is an important **food** for both **animals** and **plants**. The tissue of these living things contains fat. Fat in a pure state may take the form of a **liquid**, such as

continued on page 115

FARMING

Farming is the business of growing crops and raising livestock on the land to produce food, drink, textiles, and other products.

△ *Irrigation was invented in the Middle East in around 4000 B.C. It is a system for watering fields to help crops grow.*

△ *Combines are machines that can cut and beat corn at high speeds.*

ORIGINS OF FARMING

Farming began about 13,000 years ago when Stone Age people started herding wild animals. By 7000 B.C. people had learned that scattered seed would grow, providing food for themselves and their animals. The first crops were probably wheat, barley, and millet, cultivated with sticks and hoes. In 3000 B.C. farmers in Mesopotamia (modern Iraq) invented the ox-drawn plow. The plow revolutionized agriculture because farmers could now turn over long lines of soil to make their crops grow better.

▽ *Milk is produced on dairy farms from cattle, although goats and sheep may also be kept for milk. On modern dairy farms cattle are milked by automatic milking machines.*

△ *Rice is the staple food of over half of the world's population. At first the rice plants are grown in dry fields, but then the crop is transplanted by hand to rice paddies (pools of shallow water).*

AGRICULTURAL REVOLUTIONS

Dramatic developments have taken place in farming over the last 500 years. Crop rotation began in the 1600s when it was realized that fodder crops, such as turnips, peas, and clover, put goodness back into the soil. Each year farmers alternated fodder crops with cereals such as wheat. Farmers also began feeding their livestock during the winter and developed larger, fatter breeds of cattle, sheep, and pigs. In the 1800s, as fields grew even larger, tractors started to replace horses and oxen. Combines were first introduced in the U.S. in the 1830s.

FARMING TODAY

Today most farms in developed countries are mechanized, with few people working on them. Poultry are often reared indoors in cages—this is known as battery farming. But while many countries produce an excess of food, poorer nations still suffer famines. Many new farming methods and crops have been brought to the developing world to try to solve the problem.

▷ *The traditional farming year begins in the late winter when the fields are plowed. The crops are sown in the spring and harvested at the end of the summer.*

ORGANIC FARMING

By the 1900s farmers were commonly using chemicals such as fertilizers and pest killers. These massively improved crop yields. But some farmers are returning to more "natural" organic farming methods because many people are concerned about the chemicals in their food.

SEE ALSO
Cattle, Cereal, Fertilizer, Food, Irrigation, Pig, Plow, Sheep, Vegetable, Windmill

continued from page 113

vegetable oil, or a solid, such as butter. Fat is a source of **energy**. A unit of fat contains twice as much energy as the same amount of **protein** or **starch**.

Fats play an important part in our diet. We get most vegetable fat from the **seeds** and **fruits** of plants, where it is stored. In animals and **human beings**, fat is stored in tiny "droplets" in a layer under the **skin** and in the **cells** of the body. Meat and dairy products, such as butter, **milk**, and **cheese**, are our main sources of animal fats. Animal fats are also important in the manufacture of **soaps**, **perfumes**, and polishes.

Fawkes, Guy

Guy Fawkes (1570–1606) was the most famous member of a group of plotters who attempted to kill King James I of England (1566–1625) by blowing up the English **Parliament** with gunpowder. They were protesting against laws that tried to control the rights of Catholics. The plot failed, and Fawkes was arrested on November 5, 1605 in the cellars of the House of Lords in London. Together with the other conspirators he was executed. Every November the defeat of the "Gunpowder Plot" is celebrated across Great Britain with **firework** displays.

Feather

The only **animals** to possess feathers are **birds**. Feathers protect birds, keep them warm, and give their bodies a smooth, streamlined shape. Feathers also form the broad surface area of the wings that allows birds to fly. Each feather is made of a central hollow tube, from which spring many branches and side branches. The side branches are "zipped" together by tiny hooks, or barbs, to form a flat surface.

Feathers are replaced one or two times per year. This process is called molting. Old feathers that are worn and broken fall out. New ones grow in their place.

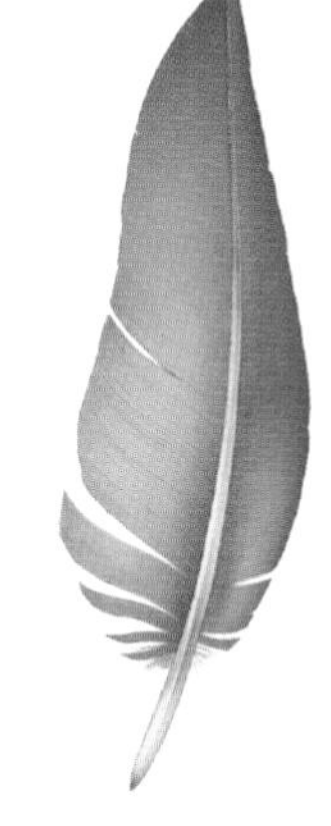

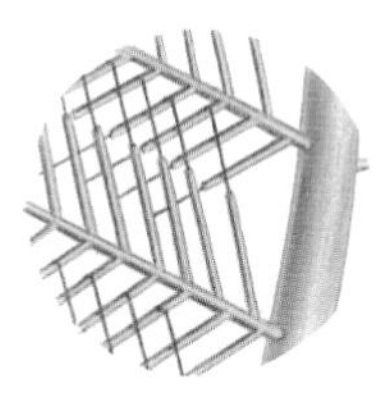

△ A close-up of part of a **feather** shows the interlaced network of tiny, hooked branches.

△ In **fencing** the fighters are protected from injury by wire-mesh masks, thick jackets, and a glove worn on the hand holding the foil—the weapon.

▽ This illustration shows Guy **Fawkes** and his fellow conspirators, who in 1605 plotted to blow up the English Parliament. Fawkes is the third from the right.

Fencing

Fencing can be described as the **sport** of "friendly dueling." Fencers each wear a special glove, padded jacket, and face mask. They fight with blunted swords. The winner is the one who scores the most points by touching his/her opponent with his/her sword. In the past fencing was a form of sword practice for real duels, but today it is a popular sport and an **Olympic Games** event.

Fermentation

With time, **milk** goes sour, **bread** dough rises, and grape juice turns into **wine**—all examples of fermentation.

Fermentation is caused by the action of microscopic **fungi** such as **bacteria**, **yeast**, and mold. These tiny living things break down substances into simpler forms. Fermentation has been used since the earliest times to make bread, beer, wine, and **cheese**. But it was not until the 1800s that French scientist Louis **Pasteur** found out how fermentation really works.

Fermi, Enrico

Enrico Fermi (1901–1954) was an Italian scientist. In 1938 his studies of the **atom** were rewarded with a **Nobel Prize**. In 1942, during **World War II**, Fermi built the first atomic reactor. He constructed it in an empty squash court under a football stadium, setting off the first artificial nuclear chain reaction.

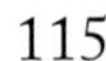

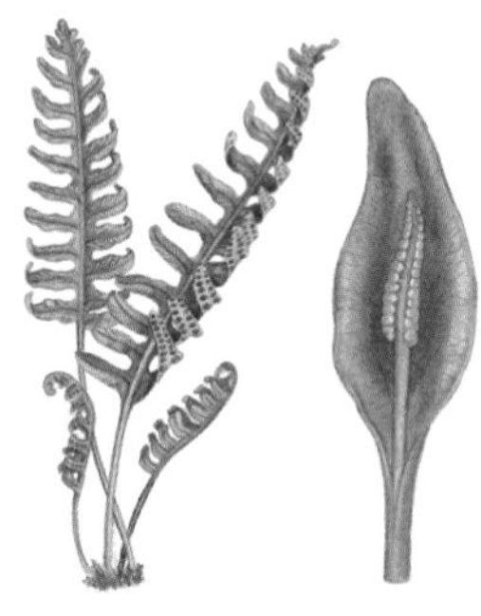

△ **Ferns** do not have seeds or flowers. Instead they produce spores—minute structures each consisting of a single cell—from which new ferns develop.

△ **Festivals** often play a big part in the life of local communities. This masked stilt dancer is performing at a village festival in Mali, North Africa.

FIJI
Government: Republic
Capital: Suva
Area: 7,000 sq. mi.
Population: 844,300
Languages: Fijian, English, Hindustani
Currency: Fiji dollar

Fern

The ferns were some of the earliest land **plants** on **earth**. Today their delicate, feathery leaves look the same as they did millions of years ago. There are about 10,000 different species of ferns. They are found all over the world, usually in damp, shady places such as under **trees**.

Fertilizer

Fertilizers are chemicals that are dug into the **soil** to nourish it. They help **plants** grow larger and healthier by giving them the chemical nutrients they need to grow. The most important fertilizers are calcium, phosphorus, potassium, and **sulfur**.

Festival

A festival is a period of celebration that may last for any length of time—from one day to several weeks. The word festival comes from the Latin *festa*, meaning feast. Festivals are often held for religious reasons. Important religious festivals include **Ramadan** and **Eid** (Islam), **Chanukah** and **Passover** (Judaism), **Christmas** and **Easter** (Christianity), and **Diwali** (Hinduism). Buddhist festivals are held to celebrate key events in the life of **Buddha** and to honor the Buddhist monks.

Fiber optics

An optical fiber is a flexible **glass** strand that is thinner than a human **hair**. Along this superfine fiber a beam of **light** can travel very easily. The light can then be used to carry **telephone** conversations and **television** pictures or to allow surgeons to see inside our bodies. The fibers are made of pure glass specifically designed to reflect the light in toward the center of the strand. Using **laser** light signals can be sent for more than 31 mi. (50km) before they have to be amplified, or increased in power. This means that optical fibers are far more efficient than the **copper** cables that were once used, as well as being much thinner and lighter.

Fiction

Fiction is literature that describes imaginary events and people. The main form of fiction is the novel—a written story. The opposite of fiction is nonfiction—any form of **writing** that has been produced to supply us with information or facts. Nonfiction includes textbooks and encyclopedias.

Novels developed from short stories written in **Italy** during the 1300s. Oneof the first famous novels was *Don Quixote* (1615) by the Spanish writer Miguel de Cervantes (1547–1616). Some of the first English novels with believable, or true-to-life, stories were written by Daniel Defoe (1660–1731). Defoe's best-known novel is *Robinson Crusoe* (1719), which tells the tale of a shipwrecked sailor.

There are many kinds of novels. For example, some are adventure tales, such as *Treasure Island* (1883) by Robert Louis **Stevenson**. There are horror stories such as *Frankenstein* (1818) by Mary Shelley (1797–1851), humorous novels like *The Adventures of Tom Sawyer* (1876) by Mark **Twain**, and satirical novels such as Jonathan **Swift**'s *Gulliver's Travels* (1726), in which Swift pokes fun at human society. All novels are meant to entertain us, but many of the best novels also offer different ways of looking at life. For example, Charles **Dickens** made his readers aware of how harsh life was for poor people in England during the mid-1800s.

Fiji

Fiji is a country made up of hundreds of **islands** in the **Pacific Ocean**. The largest island is Viti Levu. Fiji became a British territory in 1874 but gained its independence in 1970. In 1987 Fiji's army leaders seized power. Civilian rule was restored in 1990, but in 2000 the **government** was again overthrown. New **elections** were held in 2001.

Film

The art of making moving pictures began with a **machine** called the kinetoscope, which was invented by Thomas **Edison**, in 1891. Soon after two French brothers, Auguste Lumière (1862–1954) and Louis Lumière (1864–1948), built a similar device of their own—the *cinématographe*. This machine projected pictures from a piece of film onto a screen. The pictures were shown one after the other so quickly that the images appeared to move. In 1896 in **Paris** the Lumière brothers gave the world's first public film show. Before long many people in **North America** and **Europe** were making movies.

These early movies did not look much like the ones we are used to seeing today. They were in black and white, the movements were jerky, and there was no sound. At first movies were made to show news and real events, but by 1902 filmmakers began to make up their own stories, using actors to play the different parts. The first "talkie," as movies with sound became known, was *The Jazz Singer*, which opened in 1927.

As the movie industry grew enormous sums were spent on lavish productions. However, after **World War II** a more realistic type of movie became popular. In the 1950s the growing popularity of **television** led to a decline in filmmaking because people stayed at home to watch TV rather than go to the movies. But the movie industry began to recover in the 1970s, when modern blockbusters were born. These films were full of dramatic special effects.

Hollywood—a suburb of **Los Angeles**, California—has long been the filmmaking capital of the world. However, most countries have their own movie industries. One of the largest is in Mumbai (formerly Bombay), **India**.

▽ Making a **film** often involves a large team of people, including actors, camera operators, lighting designers, sound recordists, and technicians. The director controls what is seen on screen.

Fingerprint

Fingerprints are marks we leave behind whenever we touch something. You can see them by pressing your fingertips into an ink pad and then onto a sheet of white **paper**. Everybody has patterns of lines and swirls on their fingers, but each person's fingerprints are different. Because of this, **police** officers can use fingerprints to help identify criminals.

△ **Fingerprints** never change and are unique to each person. Detectives often check the scene of a crime for fingerprints, which they use to try to identify the criminals.

Finland

Finland is a country in northern **Europe** between **Sweden** and **Russia**. Northern Finland stretches north of the **Arctic** Circle. Thousands of **lakes** and **rivers** dot the Finnish landscape, forming a great inland waterway. About 75 percent of the land is covered by forests of **conifer** trees such as spruce, pine, and larch. Finland's main industries are logging and making wood products such as **paper**.

FINLAND
Government: Republic
Capital: Helsinki
Area: 117,800 sq. mi.
Population: 5,167,486
Language: Finnish
Currency: Euro

FISH

Fish were the first vertebrates (animals with backbones) to develop on earth, about 500 million years ago. They live in water and breathe oxygen through their gills.

△ *Angelfish live on coral reefs, which are home to a greater variety of fish than any other part of the ocean.*

△ *The bright colors of the lionfish are a warning to other animals that its spines are highly poisonous.*

△ *When a puffer is threatened, it rapidly gulps water to "inflate" its body to twice its normal size.*

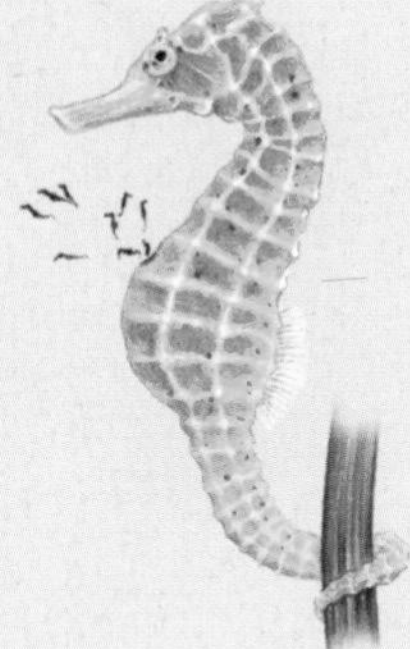

◁ *Sea horses have an unusual life cycle. The female lays her eggs in a pouch on the male's belly. When the eggs hatch, the male pushes the tiny babies out through the opening of his pouch.*

△ *The hammerhead shark has a long flap on either side of its head. Scientists think that these flaps may help the shark pinpoint its prey.*

WORLD OF FISH

There are 22,000 different species of fish, which are found in all kinds of water habitats throughout the world. About 60 percent of all fish species live in the saltwater of seas and oceans. The rest are freshwater fish, found in rivers, streams, lakes, and ponds.

Sea fish constantly lose water and have to drink a lot, whereas freshwater fish take in water through their skin.

TYPES OF FISH

Fish are divided into two main groups. Bony fish have bony skeletons and are covered with overlapping scales. There are about 20,000 species of bony fish, including salmon, sardines, and eels. Cartilaginous fish have skeletons of flexible cartilage, or gristle, and are covered with tiny, toothlike bumps that feel like rough sandpaper. There are more than 600 species of cartilaginous fish, including sharks and rays.

FOOD AND FEEDING

Most freshwater fish have a varied diet that may include water plants, snails, insects, larvae, worms, and other fish. Most of the fish that live in seas and oceans are meat eaters. They feed on a wide range of prey such as shrimp, squid, and other fish. However, some sea fish graze on algae or feed on plankton—tiny plants and animals floating in the water.

SHAPES AND SWIMMING

To help them move easily through the water, many fish have a streamlined shape and a tail shaped like a crescent or a fork. The fins of a fish have different uses. The tail fin pushes the fish forward, the pectoral and pelvic fins are for steering, and the anal and dorsal fins help the fish stay upright in the water.

Inside the body of a bony fish is a gas-filled bag called a swim bladder. This holds the fish up in the water and allows it to float, in a similar way to a life jacket. Sharks and other cartilaginous fish lack swim bladders and have to keep moving to avoid sinking to the seabed.

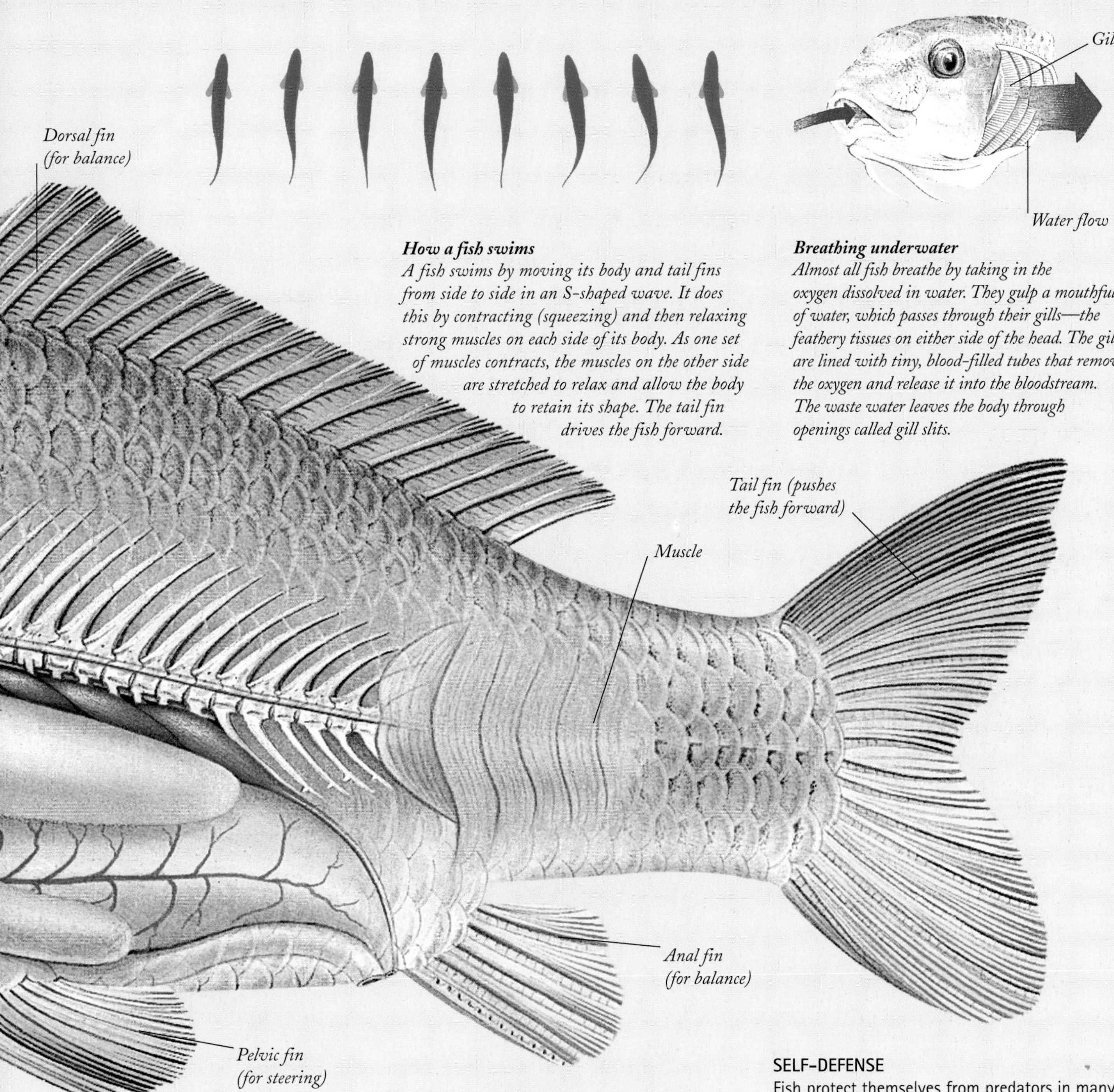

How a fish swims
A fish swims by moving its body and tail fins from side to side in an S-shaped wave. It does this by contracting (squeezing) and then relaxing strong muscles on each side of its body. As one set of muscles contracts, the muscles on the other side are stretched to relax and allow the body to retain its shape. The tail fin drives the fish forward.

Breathing underwater
Almost all fish breathe by taking in the oxygen dissolved in water. They gulp a mouthful of water, which passes through their gills—the feathery tissues on either side of the head. The gills are lined with tiny, blood-filled tubes that remove the oxygen and release it into the bloodstream. The waste water leaves the body through openings called gill slits.

SENSES
Most fish have good senses of sight and smell, and some species possess whiskerlike feelers, known as barbels, around their mouths. Fish also have a special structure called the lateral line—a row of tiny holes running along the side of the body. Tiny hairs in these holes pick up vibrations in the water, allowing the fish to detect a predator or food before it comes into view. In addition, sharks and some types of bony fish are able to sense the tiny electric currents given off by animals. This helps them find prey in dark or muddy water.

REPRODUCTION
Some species of sharks and rays give birth to live young, but most fish hatch from eggs. The female fish usually lays enormous numbers of eggs—hundreds or many thousands—which are then fertilized by the male. Eggs laid in rivers, lakes, and near the seashore sink to the bottom, where they may be hidden among plants. In the open ocean the eggs float in the water and are often eaten by fish and other marine animals. However, enough eggs are produced to guarantee that some will survive. Almost all newly hatched fish are independent right away, but some African cichlids shelter their young in their mouths.

SELF-DEFENSE
Fish protect themselves from predators in many ways. Some fish live in large schools (groups) because predators are often confused by the sheer number of bodies and find it harder to attack. Other fish use camouflage to hide. A few fish, such as stingrays and lionfish, have poisonous spines; flying fish can escape their enemies by shooting out of the water and gliding through the air on their winglike fins.

SEE ALSO
Deep-sea fish, Eel, Fishing, Goldfish, Lake, Migration, Ocean, Plankton, River, Salmon, Sea horse, Shark, Tropical fish, Tuna, Water

Fjord

The coasts of **Norway**, **Greenland**, and the South Island of **New Zealand** are broken up by a series of steep-sided valleys called fjords. These are where the sea has invaded the land. Narrow strips of water wind inland along the dramatic **mountain** gorges.

Fjords were formed when the great **glaciers** of the **ice ages** gouged out valleys as they flowed down to the sea. When the ice melted, the sea flooded the valleys. Fjords are very deep and so make perfect shelters for large **ships**.

Fire

The ability to make and use fire is one of the great advantages people have over **animals**. Early **human beings** were frightened by fire. However, in ancient times people discovered that two **flints** struck sharply together produced a spark. Later a flint was struck against a piece of **iron** to make a spark that could be used to light an easily burned material called tinder.

Once humans had learned to make and control fire, it became a necessary part of life. Fire provided illumination and warmth at night, cooked food, and scared away animals. However, even today fires that get out of control may cause terrible damage and suffering.

Fireworks

Fireworks are devices that produce spectacular displays of **lights**, **colors**, smoke, and noise. They were invented in **China** centuries ago but only became known in **Europe** in the 1300s.

Fireworks are often launched into the air by **rockets**. They explode because of gunpowder—a black powder produced from charcoal (charred wood), **sulfur**, and saltpeter (potassium nitrate). The brilliant colors of fireworks are created by different combinations of burning chemicals.

Fireworks were invented by the Chinese hundreds of years ago.

Gill net

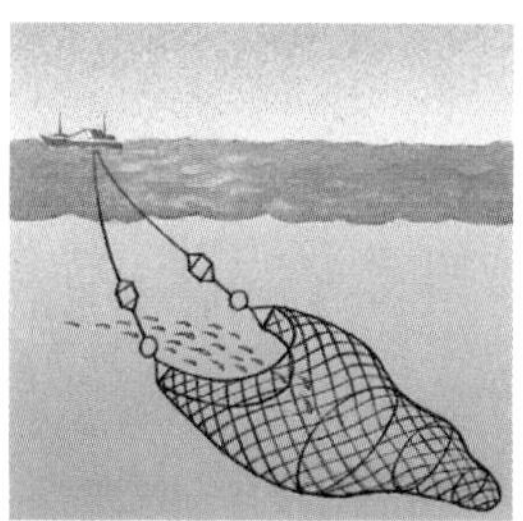

Trawl net

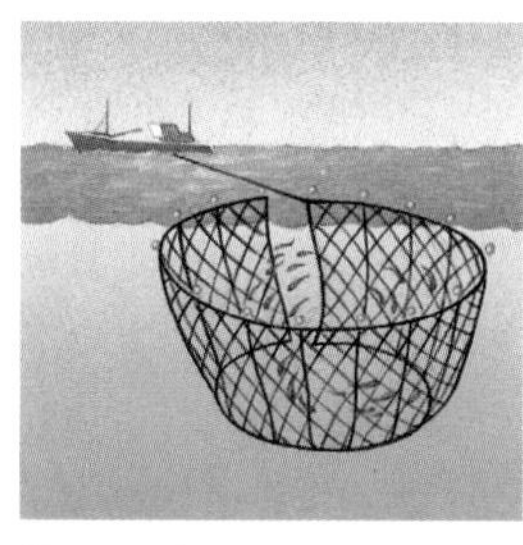

Purse seine net

The **fishing** industry uses three types of nets. Gill nets trap fish by their gills. Trawl nets have a funnel shape and are dragged along the seabed. Purse seine nets encircle fish and then are pulled shut.

Fir tree *see* Conifer

Fish *see* pages 118–119

Fishing

Fishing is one of the most important industries. Each year about 60 million tons of **fish** are caught in the **oceans**, **rivers**, and **lakes** of the world. Fish are a good source of **food** because they are rich in **protein**. They are also used as animal feed and **fertilizer**, and oil from fish is used to make **soap**.

Most fishing takes place at sea, and usually the catch is made far from the home port. The fish must be preserved, or they will go bad quickly. In the past fish were often dried, smoked, or salted because there were no **refrigerators**. Today fish are packed in ice or frozen. Some fishing fleets include very large factory **ships**. These take fresh fish straight from the other ships and can package the fish while still at sea.

The best places to fish are where the sloping seabed is no more than 590 ft. (180m) deep. These coastal waters lie above the **continental shelf** and are the feeding grounds of huge numbers of fish. However, improved fishing techniques and the growing number of fishing boats mean that too many fish are now being caught. The populations of many fish species have suffered large declines, depriving both humans and animals of a valuable food supply.

Fitzgerald, Ella

Ella Fitzgerald (1918–1997) was an American **jazz** singer whose many **recordings** are still played all over the world. She sang with many different jazz musicians during her long career. She became famous for the beautiful tone of her voice and for her ability to improvise—to change her songs and add new parts while on stage.

Flag

Flags are pieces of colored cloth, usually decorated with bold markings. They have special fastenings so that they can be flown from masts and poles. Flags are used by countries, **monarchs**, **armies**, and **ships** and by organizations such as political parties, **sports** teams, and the **scouting** movement.

Flags have been used as emblems since the time of the ancient Egyptians. Their flags were flown on long poles as battle standards, held by "standard-bearers." Flags showed which soldiers belonged to which ruler or general.

Today national flags are flown as a symbol of a country's **history**, its power, and its importance. Flags are also used for signaling. Since 1857 ships at sea have used an international code for flag signals. For example, a yellow flag means that a ship is in quarantine because of illness on board. Other well-known signals are a white flag—a sign of truce during war—and a flag raised only to half-mast—a sign that people are mourning someone's death.

Flame

When something is heated enough to make it burn, it will frequently burst into flames. These flames are **gases** that are given off during burning. Bright flames that give off plenty of **light**, such as those of candles, **wood**, or **coal**, have tiny **carbon** particles in them that glow brightly. Flames are not all equally hot. Wood fires burn at about 1,832°F (1,000°C); acetylene **welding** torches are about 5,432°F (3,000°C).

Flamingo

Flamingoes are large water **birds** that live on shallow **lakes** in the warmer parts of the world. The bright color of their **feathers** ranges from pale to deep pink. Flamingoes wade through the shallows on their stiltlike legs in search of tiny **plants** and **animals** to eat. When feeding, they tuck their heads under the water's surface and use their broad, hooked beaks like sieves to filter **food** from the water and mud.

Flamingoes nest together in huge gatherings called colonies. The largest colonies have thousands of birds.

A **flamingo**'s body is not much larger than that of a goose, but its long legs and neck can make it up to 5.9 ft. (1.8m) tall. The bright pink color of its plumage comes from its food and from minerals dissolved in the water.

Flea

Fleas are tiny, wingless **insects** less than .12 in. (3mm) long. They live on the bodies of **birds** and **mammals**, including **human beings**. Fleas are **parasites** and feed on their hosts by biting through the skin and sucking the **blood**. Fleas carry germs and other **bacteria** from one host to another. **Rat** fleas, for example, used to pass bubonic **plague** to people.

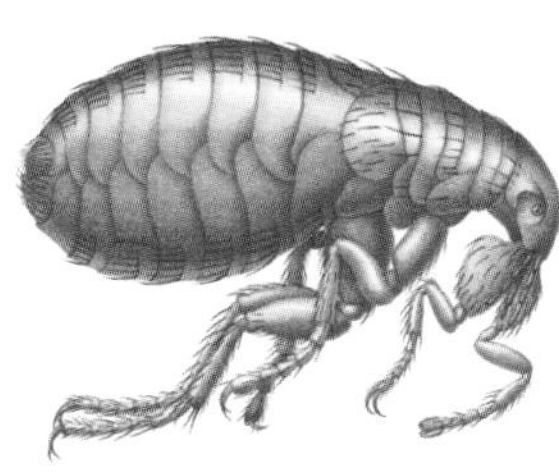

This greatly magnified image of a **flea**'s body shows the large abdomen where blood is stored.

Fleming, Alexander

Alexander Fleming (1881–1955) was a British doctor who discovered the **antibiotic** called penicillin. It is one of the most important **drugs** known. Penicillin fights infections caused by many kinds of **bacteria**. Although the drug fights the infection, it does not usually harm the body. Penicillin has saved millions of lives.

Fleming discovered penicillin by accident in 1928 when he noticed an unknown kind of mold (see **fungus**) growing in his laboratory. For his work Fleming was awarded the 1945 **Nobel Prize** for **medicine**.

Flint

Flint is a **mineral** that is a form of **quartz**. It is found in layers of **chalk** and limestone. A lump of flint is dull white on the outside and shiny gray to black on the inside. Flint is very hard, but it can be chipped into sharp-edged flakes. **Stone Age** people made tools and weapons out of flint. Because flint gives off a spark when struck against **iron**, it can be used for starting a **fire**.

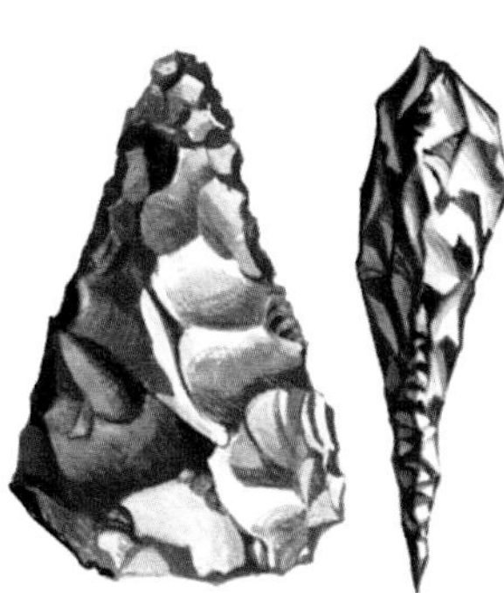

Pointed **flint** tools such as these were used by early cave-dwelling humans about 50,000 years ago.

Flood

There are two main kinds of floods—those caused by **rivers** overflowing their banks and **ocean** floods caused by high **tides** and strong **winds** blowing from the ocean toward the land. Rivers usually flood in the spring when rains add to the water produced by melting snow and ice. The water level in the rivers rises so much that they burst their banks.

Throughout **history** three great rivers have flooded regularly—the **Nile** in Egypt, the **Mississippi** in the U.S., and the Huang Ho (Yellow River) in China. Two huge **dams** were built across the Nile in Aswan to produce **hydroelectric power** for generating **electricity**. Before the Aswan dams controlled the waters of the Nile the annual floods created a zone of fertile land in the middle of a sandy **desert**.

The best-known flood story is from the book of Genesis in the **Bible**. The event on which this Old Testament story is based may have taken place in about 3000 B.C., when the Euphrates River flooded a vast area of southern Mesopotamia (present-day Iraq).

Flower

There are more than 250,000 different species of flowering **plants**, ranging from small, ground-hugging plants to spectacular **orchids**, spine-covered **cactuses**, and giant, long-lived **trees**. The flowers that these plants produce come in a dazzling array of **colors**, sizes, and shapes. Some flowers grow singly, while others grow in tight clusters. Many flowers have bright colors, a strong scent, and produce a sweet nectar, but some are drab and unscented by comparison.

Whatever they look like, flowers all play the same part in the life of the plant. Flowers help plants reproduce (see **reproduction**). Inside each flower there are male parts called stamens, which are made up of anthers and filaments, and female parts called pistils, which are made up of stigmas, styles, and ovaries. The stamens contain hundreds of powdery grains of pollen, which fertilize the pistils. Fertilization occurs when pollen grains are transferred from the stamens of one plant to the pistils of another plant of the same variety. Once this has happened, **fruit** begins to form and grow. The fruit contains the **seeds** that will eventually grow into a new generation of plants.

The flowers that we grow in our gardens and use to decorate our homes are all descended from wild flowers. But cultivated flowers, such as roses, lilies, and orchids, often look different from their wild relatives—over many years they have been bred specifically to improve their appearance and scent and to make them easier to grow.

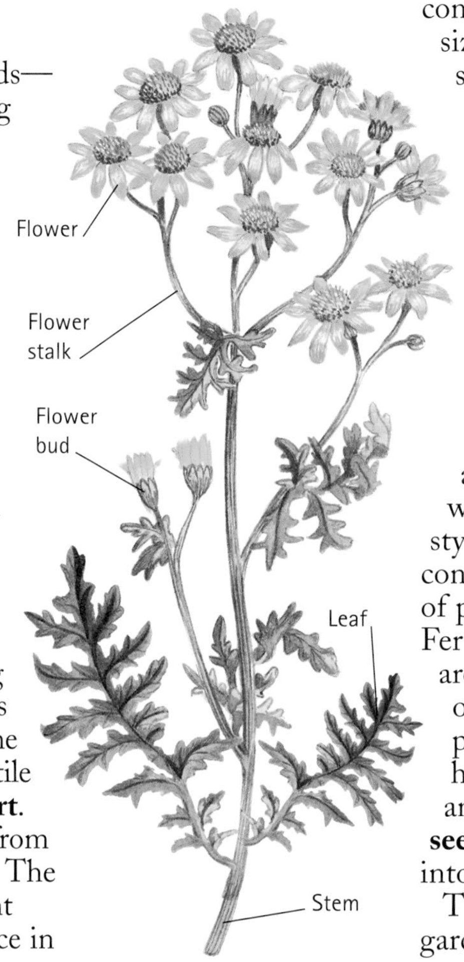

△ **Flowers** are the part of a flowering plant that are involved in reproduction. They make seeds that will form a new generation of the same type of plant.

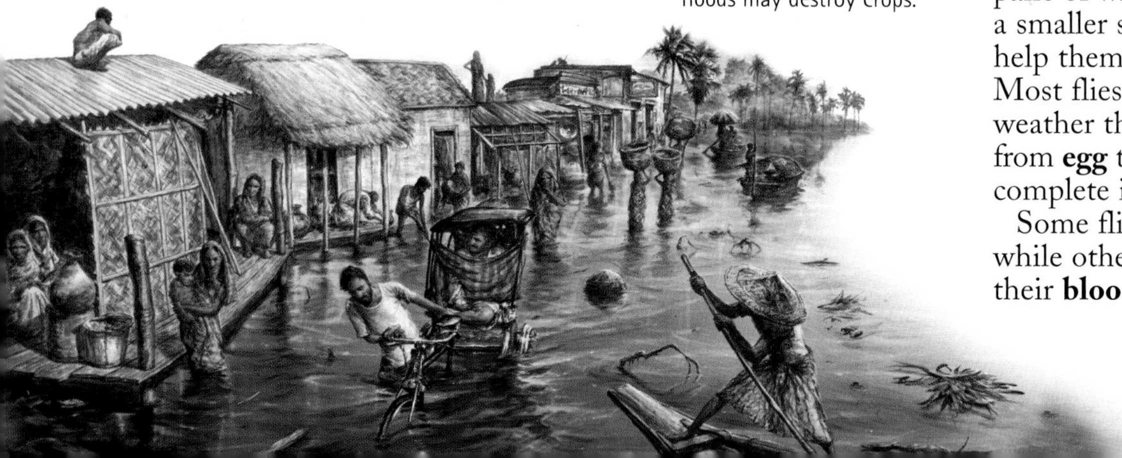

▽ Much of Bangladesh lies in a **flood** zone. The floods create fertile land where farmers can reap two or three harvests per year. But unexpected floods may destroy crops.

Fly

Flies are one of the largest groups of **insects** in the world. They have two pairs of wings—one pair for flying and a smaller set behind the main pair to help them maintain balance in the **air**. Most flies do not live long. In warm weather the life cycle of a housefly—from **egg** to maggot to adult—may be complete in just one week.

Some flies feed on decaying matter, while others bite **animals** to feed on their **blood**. Horseflies often attack

horses and **cattle** in large swarms. Blowflies lay their eggs in open wounds on the skin of animals. The maggots that hatch from the eggs eat into the animals' flesh and cause great harm. Houseflies lay their eggs in piles of rotting matter.

Some types of flies are dangerous to humans because they spread **diseases** such as cholera and dysentery. Tsetse flies, which live in the tropics, spread sleeping sickness, a serious disease that causes sleepiness and high fever. Even ordinary houseflies can pose a health risk to humans because they pick up harmful **bacteria** from manure and rotting food and carry them into our homes, where they leave the germs on our fresh food.

A **fly** has a pair of huge compound eyes. Each is made up of many thousands of microscopic six-sided lenses.

Food

Food is any substance that is a source of nutrition to a living thing. Without food, nothing can live. Humans need food for a variety of reasons. It gives us the **energy** to move and stay warm and keeps our bodies healthy. The three main kinds of human food are **proteins**, **fats**, and carbohydrates. We also need certain **minerals** and **vitamins**. A "balanced diet"—one that includes all of these things—is necessary for good **health**.

Today we eat a huge variety of different foods, which may be skillfully prepared, decorated, and cooked before being eaten. An increasing proportion of our food is prepared in factories. It may be bottled, canned, frozen, or dried before it is sold to us.

Food chain

When you eat **fish** from the sea, such as **tuna**, you are taking part in a food chain that began somewhere in the **ocean**. There tiny floating **plants** and **animals** called **plankton** were eaten by tiny fish. The tiny fish were eaten by larger fish, and these fish were then eaten by even larger fish such as the tuna.

Every living thing has its place in a food chain, and most belong to several different food chains. A food chain begins with green plants, which manufacture their own food from **water**, chemicals in the **soil** and **air**, and sunlight. This process is called **photosynthesis**. Unlike plants, animals cannot make their own food. Instead some of them eat plants, and the rest eat other animals. When animals or plants die, **bacteria** that live in the soil break down the animal or plant tissues. The chemicals that make up the animals or plants are released into the soil. These chemicals act as **fertilizers** to enrich the soil and help the green plants grow. And so the food chain begins all over again.

In this **food chain** grass makes its own food using energy from the sun. The grass is eaten by rabbits, which provide food for a red fox.

Ford, Henry

Henry Ford (1863–1947) was a pioneer **car** manufacturer in the U.S. In 1903 he founded the Ford Motor Company, which is today one of the world's largest **companies**. Henry Ford was the first person to use assembly lines on which the cars were put together from standard parts. Conveyor belts brought the parts to the workers, who each performed a particular task. By building his cars in this way, Ford was able to produce hundreds each day, and they were cheap enough for ordinary people to buy. Henry Ford's biggest success was the Model T, launched in 1908.

Henry **Ford**'s Model T was the first mass-produced car in the world. More than 15 million Model Ts were sold between 1908 and 1927.

Forest

A forest is a large area of land covered mainly with **trees** and other **plants**. It is one of the world's most important **habitats**, and forests occupy almost 30 percent of **earth**'s land area.

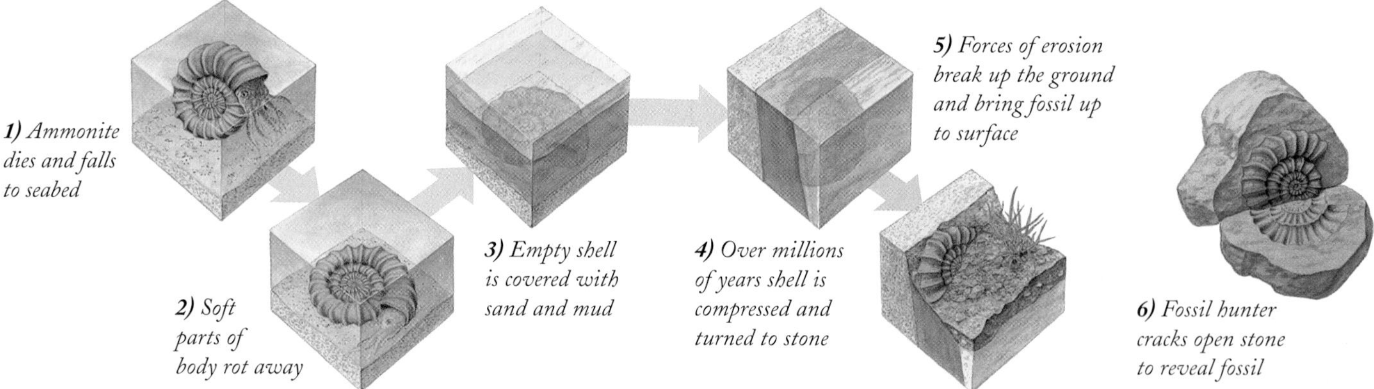

△ This diagram shows how the **fossil** of an ammonite—a type of mollusk that lived in the sea 150 million years ago—was formed.

▽ **Forests** once covered twice as much of earth's land as they do today. Huge areas of forests have been felled to provide timber or to make way for fields, roads, and towns. However, it is important to control the rate at which forests are cut down because they provide us with firewood, building materials, natural foods, and many other useful products.

There are three basic types of forests. Tropical **rain forests** are found near the **equator**, where the **climate** is hot and wet. In these conditions many kinds of trees and plants grow very quickly. Coniferous forests are found mainly in the cold, northern areas of **Canada**, **Europe**, and **Asia**. These forests are made up largely of **conifers**, such as spruce, fir, larch, or pine, which do not shed their leaves in the winter.

The third type of forest is known as a broad-leaved, or deciduous, forest. Broad-leaved trees drop their leaves in the winter and include species such as oak, beech, birch, and willow. Broad-leaved forests are found in the temperate regions of the world, which have mild winters, warm summers, and rain all year round. The **United States**, Europe, and the cooler parts of **Africa** all have large broad-leaved forests.

Forests grow in layers. At ground level **fungi**, **mosses**, **ferns**, and wild **flowers** grow in the forest **soil**. Then comes a layer of larger bushes and shrubs. Above this is a layer of smaller trees. Finally the tops of the tallest trees form a layer called the forest canopy.

Fossil

Fossils are the hardened remains or impressions of **animals** and **plants** that lived millions of years ago. A fossil may be a shell, **bone**, tooth, **leaf**, or **skeleton** or even sometimes an entire animal.

Most fossils have been found in areas that were once in or near the sea. When a plant or creature dies, its body sinks to the seabed. The soft parts rot away, but the hard skeleton becomes buried in the mud. Over millions of years more and more mud settles on top of the skeleton. Eventually these layers of mud harden into **rock**, and the skeleton becomes part of that rock. **Water** seeping through the rock slowly dissolves the original skeleton. It is replaced by stony **minerals** that form exactly the same shape—creating a fossil.

Fossils lie buried until movements in **earth**'s crust push up the seabed, and it becomes dry land. In time water, ice, and **wind** wear away the rock, and the fossil is exposed. The oldest known fossil is over three billion years old.

Fox

Foxes are **mammals** and belong to the same family as domestic **dogs**. They are active, fast-moving hunters that have superb senses of **smell**, **sight**, and **hearing** for catching their prey. The most common species is the red fox, which is found in **Europe**, North **Africa**, **North America**, and parts of **Asia**. It hunts small **birds**, **insects**, and **rodents** up to the size of **rabbits**. The red fox lives in holes in the ground called dens, which it either digs itself or takes over from rabbits or **badgers**. Recently more and more red foxes have been found in cities. They live under the floors of buildings or in any hidden place they can find and eat scraps from garbage cans. Other species of foxes include the gray fox of North America, and the bat-eared fox which lives in the open **desert** country of Africa.

The kit **fox** lives in North American deserts and spends the day in a deep burrow where the air is cool. It comes out at night to hunt for insects, rodents, and other small animals.

Fraction

If you cut a cake into equal parts, each part is a fraction of the whole cake. Each half can be written as a number—$\frac{1}{2}$. If the cake is cut into four, each quarter is written $\frac{1}{4}$. The number above the dividing line in a fraction is called the numerator. The number below is called the denominator.

France

France is the largest country in Western **Europe**. In ancient times France was inhabited by **Celts**, but Julius **Caesar** conquered it, and for 500 years it was part of the **Roman Empire**. The Franks, from whom the country got its present name, invaded in the A.D. 400s.

Throughout much of the **Middle Ages**, France was divided into many small parts, which often had their own rulers. However, the French kings gradually became more powerful and united the different territories into a single country. The city of **Paris**, on the Seine River in the northern half of France, became the country's capital.

France has a temperate **climate** and a diverse landscape. Farmland covers about half of the country, and much of the population is employed in **farming**, **fishing**, and forestry. France produces a large amount of grain, **vegetables**, and **fruits**, and it is famous for its **wines**.

For centuries the French and English were enemies and fought many wars. The rival nations were at war, almost without a break, from 1337 to 1453. This period is known as the **Hundred Years' War**. In 1789 France was shaken by a violent uprising called the **French Revolution**. During the Revolution, which lasted for several years, the French people overthrew their monarchy and turned France into a **republic**.

After the Revolution a general named **Napoléon** Bonaparte came to power in France and made himself emperor. He went to war and conquered most of Europe before he was finally defeated at the Battle of Waterloo in Belgium in 1815. Later, France became a republic again. During the two world wars France was a battleground for Allied armies and the invading German forces. It was one of the first members of the **European Union** and today is among Europe's wealthiest states.

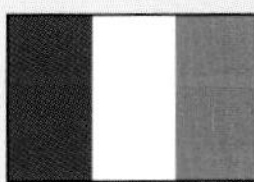

FRANCE
Government: Republic
Capital: Paris
Area: 210,400 sq. mi.
Population: 59,551,227
Language: French
Currency: Euro

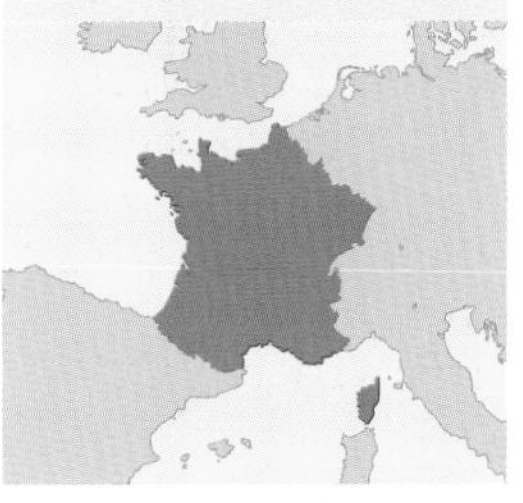

Francis of Assisi

Francis of Assisi (1182–1226) was named after the town in central **Italy** where he was born. After recovering from a severe illness at the age of 22 Francis decided to become a priest. He gathered around him a band of monks,

Francis of Assisi lived in poverty and devoted his life to the service of God. He was fond of birds and animals whom he called his brothers and sisters.

△ Anne **Frank**'s diary describes the hardships Jewish people faced in the 1930s under the German Nazis. The Nazis inflicted appalling suffering on Jewish people and forced each to wear a yellow star to show they were Jews.

▽ During the **French Revolution** the working-class people of Paris built barricades across the city's streets, from which to defy troops and police.

who became known as the Franciscans. The monks spent their lives preaching and caring for the poor and the sick. Francis himself spent his final years in private prayer, and in 1228, two years after his death, he was made a saint.

Frank, Anne

Anne Frank (1925–1945) was a young Jewish German girl who kept a secret diary while hiding from the German Nazis during **World War II**. In 1933 Anne's family fled from **Germany**, where the Nazis were persecuting **Jews** and other groups in society. The Frank family sought refuge in Amsterdam in the **Netherlands**. But in 1940 Germany invaded the Netherlands, and in 1942 the Franks decided to go into hiding. For 25 months the whole family lived inside a cramped attic above a shop.

Anne's diary is a powerful and moving account of the difficulties her family faced while in hiding. It records what it was like to be a Jew during World War II. In 1944 the Franks' attic was discovered. Anne, her sister, and her mother were taken away by the Nazis, and died in a concentration camp.

Franklin, Benjamin

Benjamin Franklin (1706–1790) was an American politician and scientist. He was born in Boston, Massachusetts, the youngest of 17 children. Franklin became a printer and then went on to publish a yearly almanac that made him his fortune. Later he became involved in America's **Revolutionary War**, which brought the U.S. freedom from British rule. Franklin was one of the politicians who signed America's Declaration of Independence, and he helped draw up the peace treaty at the end of the war.

Franklin's scientific inventions include bifocal spectacles and the **lightning** conductor—a rod that protects buildings from lightning. By flying a kite during a thunderstorm, Franklin proved that lightning was a form of **electricity**.

French Revolution

The French Revolution, which erupted on July 14, 1789, was one of the most important **revolutions** in history. It led to enormous changes in the political, religious, and cultural life of **France**, and its effects were felt in many other countries around the world as well.

In France during 1789 the king and nobles were seen as people who spent huge sums of money on luxuries. They built themselves lavish palaces and mansions, while many people starved in misery. Involvement in wars, such as the American **Revolutionary War**, had drained the Treasury, so the people had to pay even higher **taxes**. At the same time food prices doubled after the harvest had failed. More and more of the French people, including farmers, shopkeepers, townspeople, merchants, and even some nobles, wanted major changes to be made.

There was no **parliament** to stop the king from treating his subjects badly, and eventually in 1789 the French people's anger exploded into revolution. Food riots broke out, and mob violence spread. King **Louis XVI** tried to flee the country but was arrested and later beheaded. In the "Reign of Terror" that followed nearly 20,000 people were executed as enemies of the Revolution.

A new **government** was established in 1790 that tried to introduce the ideas of the Revolution. But the new leaders quarreled. In 1799 the government was overthrown by a French general named **Napoléon** Bonaparte.

Freud, Sigmund

Sigmund Freud (1856–1939) was an Austrian doctor who made a great contribution to our understanding of the human mind. Freud was awarded a degree in **medicine** in 1881 and began to study mental illness. He taught that the subconscious—the thoughts and memories we are not aware of—hold the key to a person's mental state. To open up the subconscious, Freud developed a system called psychoanalysis—a kind of medical examination of the mind.

Friction

When two things rub together, it causes friction. Friction makes it difficult to move something across a surface. Smooth objects cause much less friction than rough objects, so when things need to go fast, it helps to reduce friction. This is why the **wheels** of a train and the rails of the track are very smooth. When we want things to slow down, we add friction—for example, by applying the brakes in our **cars**.

If two things rub together at great speed, the friction produces **heat**. If you rub your hand fast against your leg, you can feel the heat generated by the friction. Without friction the world would be a strange place. We could not walk because our shoes would not grip the ground, and cars would stand still no matter how fast their wheels turned.

Frog and Toad

Frogs and toads are members of a large group of **amphibians**. This means that they can live both on land and in **water**. They breathe through their **skins**, as well as their **lungs**. Like all amphibians, frogs and toads have a complex life history. In the spring the adults lay mounds of jellylike **eggs**, or spawn, in a pond or some other damp place. The eggs hatch into larvae, known as tadpoles, which gradually develop legs and turn into miniature versions of their parents.

△ **Frogs and toads** are found all over the world. There are about 2,500 different species.

Fruit

Fruit is the ripe **seed** case of any flowering **plant**. The fruit protects the seeds as they develop and helps spread them when they are ripe. Some fruit scatters its seeds on the **wind**. Others are eaten by **birds** and **animals**, which then spread the seeds.

▽ **Fruit** spreads its seeds in many different ways. This squirting cucumber shoots out its seeds in a jet of liquid, which is produced by water pressure building up inside the fruit.

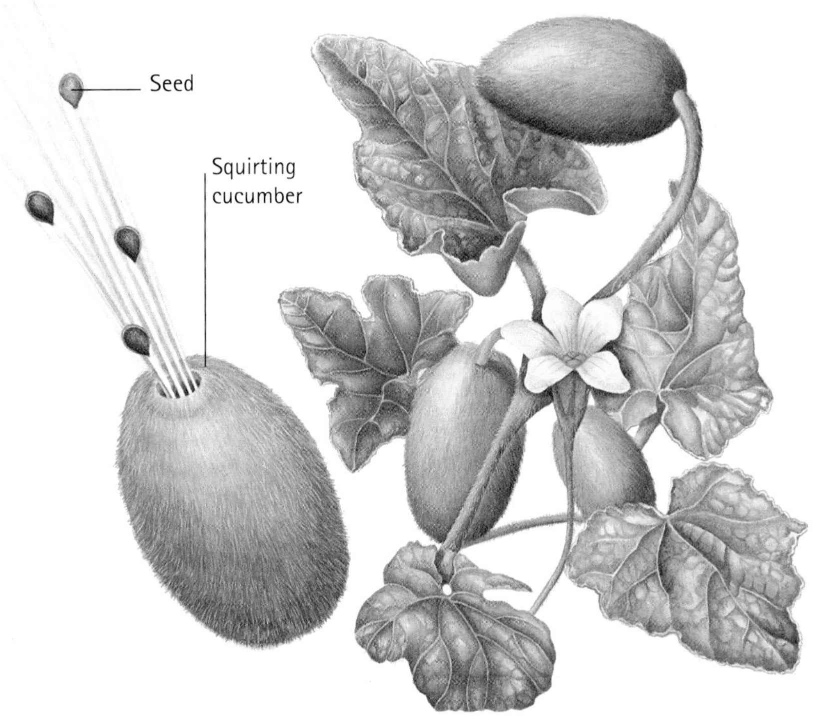

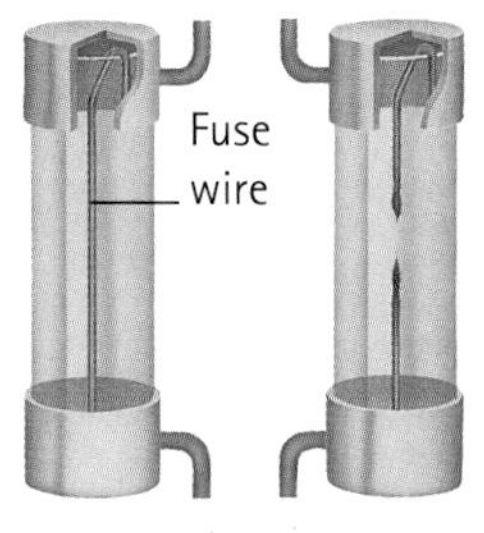

△ A **fuse** (left) is found in a fuse box. Too large a current will cause the wire inside the fuse to melt, thus breaking the circuit (right).

▽ A **fungus** is neither a plant nor an animal but belongs to a separate kingdom of living things—the fungi. There are more than 100,000 different species of fungi, including mushrooms, toadstools, molds, and yeasts. The toadstool shown below is called fly agaric.

To most of us "fruit" means juicy **foods** such as apples, pears, oranges, and bananas. These fruits are important in our diet. They give us **mineral** salts, **sugar**, and **vitamins**. The water, skins, and seeds of fruit help our **digestion**.

Fuel

Fuels are substances that give off **heat** when they burn. They provide us with the **energy** we use for cooking food, heating buildings, powering **aircraft**, **cars**, and **machines**, and producing **electricity**. The most important fuels are **oil**, **coal**, and **natural gas**, which are called **fossil** fuels because they were formed underground from the remains of prehistoric **plants** and **animals**.

Some fuels give off more heat than others. A pound of coal gives nearly three times as much heat as a pound of wood. Oil gives nearly four times as much and **hydrogen** gas about ten times as much. The radioactive element **uranium** can give over 500,000 times as much heat as hydrogen.

As earth's supplies of fossil fuels are used up we will have to make more use of **nuclear energy**, **solar energy**, and **wind** and **hydroelectric power**.

Fuel cell

A fuel cell is a special kind of electric **battery** that keeps on making **electricity** as long as **fuel** is fed into it. The main use for fuel cells is in **space exploration**. Fuel cells supplied the electricity in the various Apollo spacecraft that flew to the **Moon** in 1969–1972. These cells used **oxygen** and **hydrogen** as fuel, which combined to produce electricity and **water**. The water was not wasted—the Apollo astronauts drank it.

Fungus

A fungus is a simple, plantlike organism with no roots, stems, or leaves. Fungi also lack the chemical chlorophyll that allows green **plants** to make their food through the process of **photosynthesis**. Thus fungi have to find a ready-made supply of **food**. Some feed as **parasites** on living plants or **animals**. Others feed on animal and plant remains.

There are more than 50,000 species of fungi. Some have only a single **cell**, while other fungi are made up of chains of cells. These produce tiny, threadlike growths that spread through the substance on which the fungus feeds.

Many types of fungi grow a large fruiting body that sheds tiny particles called spores. New fungus plants grow from the spores. **Mushrooms** are the fruiting bodies of fungi that are hidden underground. The fungus family also includes molds. Uncovered food is a perfect place for molds to grow.

Fuse

A fuse is a safety device in an electric circuit. It contains fuse **wire**, which is made so that it will melt at a low **temperature**. If too much **electricity** flows through the circuit, the fuse "blows," or melts, breaking the circuit.

In this way an electric fuse stops the wire in the circuit from becoming too hot and possibly setting nearby objects on fire. Electric currents have to pass through fuse wire to get from the outside power line to the electric wiring in a house. Inside the house the fuse box holds the fuses.

Vostok I

Gagarin, Yuri

Yuri Gagarin (1934–1968) was the first human being to travel into space. The Soviet cosmonaut rocketed to space in *Vostok I* on April 12, 1961. He circled **Earth** once in 108 minutes and landed by parachute within 6 mi. (10km) of the planned spot. After his famous flight Gagarin continued to train as a cosmonaut, but he was killed in a plane crash in March 1968.

▽ The Milky Way **galaxy** belongs to the Local Group—a collection of about 30 galaxies.

Galaxy

Someone once called galaxies "star islands" in space. A galaxy is made up of a huge group of **stars**. Our **Sun** is just one star out of about 100 trillion stars that belong to the **Milky Way** galaxy. A beam of **light** would take about 100,000 years to shine from one side of the Milky Way to the other. Yet the Milky Way is only a medium-sized galaxy.

There may be as many as 10 trillion more galaxies beyond the Milky Way. The nearest large galaxy is called Andromeda. The light from this galaxy takes more than two million years to reach us.

Some galaxies have no particular shape. Others have spiral arms made up of many millions of stars, like the Milky Way and Andromeda galaxies. There are also galaxies that look like saucers or balls. From the side, a spiral galaxy looks like a flat disk with a swollen middle—the nucleus. From above it looks like a whirlpool of stars.

Astronomy has shown that **radio** waves are sent out from many galaxies. Strong radio waves also come from strange, starlike objects known as **quasars**, which are very powerful **energy** sources. Some people think that a quasar may be the beginning of a new galaxy. Scientists think that galaxies may form where **gravity** pulls huge clouds of **gas** together.

Galileo

Galileo Galilei (1564–1642) was an Italian math teacher and one of the first true scientists. One of his experiments showed that a **pendulum** takes the same time to make a long swing as it does to make a short one. He also learned that light objects fall as fast as heavy ones. He built a **telescope** and became the first person to use this tool for studying the **Moon** and **planets**. What Galileo saw made him believe **Copernicus**' idea that **Earth** was not the center of the **universe**. Later scientists, such as Isaac **Newton,** built on Galileo's theories.

△ With his telescope **Galileo** saw that the Moon was not smooth but was covered with craters.

Galleon

This kind of heavy, wooden sailing **ship** was used for carrying fighting men and cargo over **oceans** in the 1500s. A galleon was four times as long as it was wide. It had a special deck to carry cannons. There were square sails on its two front masts and three-cornered lateen sails on its one or two rear masts. Lateen sails helped galleons sail against the **wind**.

△ **Galleons** were faster and easier to manage than some other ships.

Gama, Vasco da

Vasco da Gama (c. 1469–1524), a Portuguese navigator, discovered how to sail from **Europe** to the **spice**-rich lands of **India** by way of southern **Africa**. He left Lisbon with four **ships** in July 1497 and reached Calicut, southern India, in May 1498. On the journey home 30 of the 90 crewmen died of scurvy (a **disease** caused by a lack of **vitamin** C), and only two of the four ships reached Lisbon.

Gambia, The

Gambia is mainland **Africa**'s smallest country. It is on the west coast and is about half the size of New Jersey. Most Gambians earn their living by **farming**, and peanuts are their main crop. Once a British colony, Gambia became an independent **republic** in 1965.

THE GAMBIA
Government: Republic
Capital: Banjul
Area: 3,900 sq. mi.
Population: 1,411,205
Languages: English, Mandinka, Wolof, Fula
Currency: Dalasi

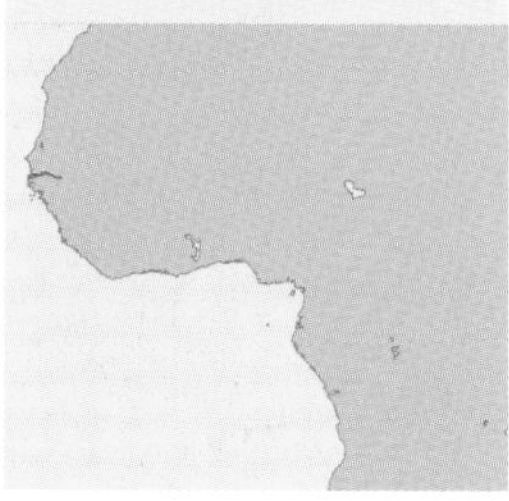

Gandhi, Indira

Indira Gandhi (1917–1984) was prime minister of **India** from 1966 until 1977 and from 1980 until her death. Her father, Jawaharlal Nehru (1889–1964), became India's first prime minister after independence. For years she helped her father and then went into politics herself. When in power, Indira Gandhi fought for economic progress, social reforms, and national unity. In 1984 she was killed by two Sikhs, members of a religious group (see **Sikhism**). Her son Rajiv succeeded her as prime minister but was assassinated in 1991.

Gandhi, Mohandas

Mohandas Karamchand Gandhi (1869–1948) is sometimes called the "father of modern India." This frail-looking Hindu lawyer helped free **India** from British rule by disobeying British laws peacefully. In 1920 he told Indians to spin cloth for their own clothes instead of buying it from Great Britain.

People admired Gandhi's beliefs, his kindness, and his simple way of life. He was called the Mahatma, meaning "Great Soul." In 1947 Great Britain gave India its independence. Soon after, one of his fellow Hindus shot Gandhi for preaching peace between Hindus (see **Hinduism**) and Muslims (see **Islam**).

Ganges River

The Ganges is the largest **river** in **India**. It flows for about 1,550 mi. (2,500km) and drains an area twice the size of Texas. The river rises in the **Himalayas** and flows southeast through India and **Bangladesh** to the Bay of Bengal. Rich farmlands and great cities line its banks. Hindus believe the river is sacred.

Garden

Gardens are pieces of land kept specifically for growing **flowers**, **fruits**, **vegetables**, or attractive shrubs and **trees**. There were gardens in Egypt 4,500 years ago. Later **Babylon** was famous for its hanging gardens. **Renaissance** Italy had gardens with fountains, pools, terraces, and steps.

In the 1700s European landscape gardeners placed natural-looking lawns and trees around large houses. In the 1800s gardens were laid out in cities for everyone. Today many houses have some type of a garden in their yard.

△ Wealthy Romans had grand villas in the country with **gardens** laid out in patterns. They also grew olives and kept sheep and goats for food and milk.

Garibaldi, Giuseppe

Giuseppe Garibaldi (1807–1882) was an Italian patriot who helped transform **Italy** from a collection of small states into a united and independent country. After two periods of exile in the **United States**, Garibaldi led his followers, the Redshirts, against the Austrians, who then controlled Italy. In 1860 he gained control of Sicily and southern Italy, and then he invaded the mainland and captured the important city of Naples. This victory helped make possible the uniting of Italy under King Victor Emmanuel (1820–1878).

△ Giuseppe **Garibaldi**, one of Italy's greatest heroes, fought against foreign rule in Italy during the 1800s.

Gas

Gases are substances with no shape or size. A gas takes up the size and shape of any container that holds it. This can happen because gases are made of **atoms** moving freely in space. When a gas becomes cold enough, it turns into a **liquid**. Liquids have a fixed size but no fixed shape. If that liquid becomes even colder, it turns into a solid. Solids have a fixed shape and size.

The gas we use to cook with and heat our homes is called **natural gas**. This gas is found underground in many parts of the world.

▽ Mohandas **Gandhi** led India to independence from Great Britain in 1947.

Polished emerald gem

Rough emerald gem

Emerald gem in rock

△ An emerald is a type of **gem**. Gems found in rocks look dull in their natural state. Experts cut them out of rock and shape and polish them.

Oil and natural gas collect in porous **rocks** (rocks that allow liquids to soak through). They are trapped between impervious rocks (rocks that will not allow liquids to pass through).

Gear

A gear is a **wheel**, or cog, with teeth along its rim. These teeth can fit into the teeth of other gears. **Metal** rods, or axles, are fitted into the center of each gear. If one axle is turned, the gear attached to it turns. This makes the second gear and its axle turn too.

Gears are used to increase or decrease the speed at which wheels turn. They are also used to increase or decrease the turning power of wheels.

Gear wheels turn at different speeds in proportion to the number of teeth they possess. If a small gear wheel fits into a large gear wheel with twice as many teeth, the big wheel will turn at only half the small wheel's speed but will have twice the turning power of the small wheel. When a **car** is in low gear, this is what happens. The car goes slowly, but it has plenty of power.

▽ Most cars have four or five forward **gears** and one reverse gear. A car's gearbox is the link between the engine and the car's wheels.

Gem

Some **rocks** contain hard crystals that can be cut to show clear, brilliant colors. These gems are frequently used in make **jewelry**. **Diamonds** are among the rarest, finest gems, but blue sapphires, green emeralds, and red rubies are also much sought after. Pearls are gems produced by **oysters**. Artificial gems are made from **glass** and **plastic**.

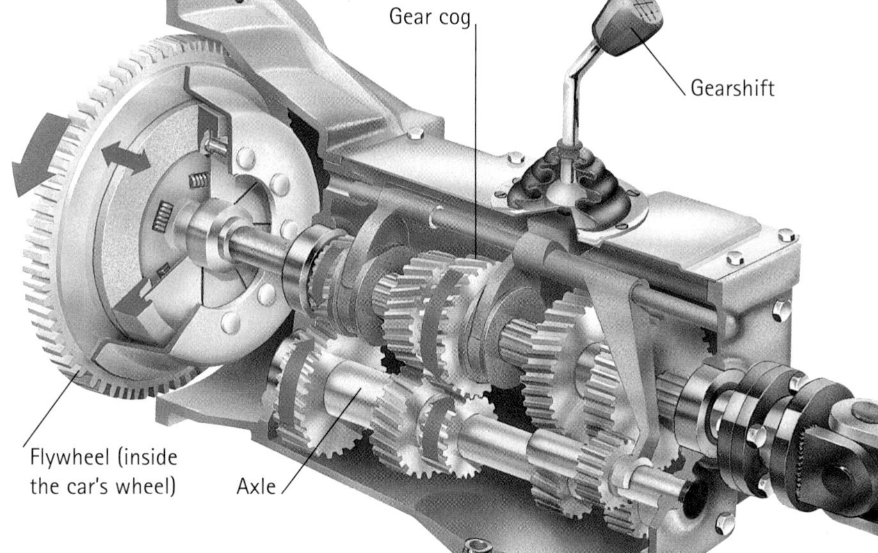

Generator

Generators produce electric currents. Huge generators in **power plants** provide **electricity** for homes and factories. The largest generators can light 20 million 100-watt electric lamps. But there are tiny generators too. A **bicycle** dynamo is a generator that you can hold in one hand.

If a loop of **wire** is turned between the ends of a horseshoe-shaped magnet (see **magnetism**), an electric current flows in the wire. Generators work like this. They change the **energy** of motion into electrical energy. The energy to work a generator's moving parts can come from **wind**, flowing **water**, or steam produced by **heat** from **fuels** such as **oil** or **coal**. Large generators have thousands of coils of wire that turn very quickly between powerful magnets.

Genetics

Each **animal** or **plant** passes on certain characteristics to its offspring. For example, we say that someone has their father's eyes or their mother's hair. The **science** of genetics explains why living things look and behave as they do.

Heredity works in an amazing way. Each individual produces sex **cells**. If a male and a female cell join, the female cell grows into an individual. Inside every cell there are tiny chromosomes, largely made of a chemical called DNA (deoxyribonucleic acid). Different parts of each chromosome, called genes, are arranged on the DNA. Genes carry coded messages that contain the information needed to make a new plant or animal look and behave as it does. They determine its sex and the characteristics it inherits from its parents.

Scientists are now able to isolate different genes within DNA. This means that they have the potential to modify or change DNA, for example, by taking out genes that cause hereditary **diseases**. However, many people worry that scientists may misuse genetic modification by creating individuals who look or act a specific way.

Genghis Khan

Genghis Khan (1167–1227) was a **Mongol** chief who cruelly attacked many Asian people and established a mighty empire. His real name was Temujin, meaning "ironsmith."

At only 13 years old he took his dead father's place as chief of a small Mongol tribe of **nomads**. He soon won power over nearby tribes as well. In 1206 he became known as Genghis Khan, meaning "very mighty king." Genghis Khan formed a huge army of tough, hard-riding nomads on the great grasslands of central **Asia**. Then he set off to conquer the lands around him. His troops pushed southeast to **Beijing** in **China** and south into **Tibet** and what are now **Pakistan** and **Afghanistan**. In the southwest they invaded Persia (modern-day **Iran**) and southern **Russia**.

After Genghis Khan died other Mongol rulers won more land and made the empire even larger.

△ Genghis Khan put together a huge organized army. Each man had five ponies, switching between them so that they would not get tired. When the Mongols besieged a city, most of the inhabitants were killed, and the surrounding land was destroyed.

Geography

Geography is the study of **earth**'s surface. Geographers examine everything on earth—the land, sea, **air**, **plants**, **animals**, and people. They explain where things are found, how they got there, and how they affect one another.

There are many different areas, or branches, of geography. Physical geography is the study of things such as **mountains**, valleys, **lakes**, and **rivers**. Meteorology is the study of **weather**. Economic geography deals with **farming**, **mining**, manufacturing, and **trade**. Human geography divides the peoples of the world into cultures.

Geology

Geology is the study of **earth** itself. Geologists are scientists who discover materials earth is made of, where

▽ Inside each cell are strands of DNA, which contain a sequence of genes (see **genetics**) that make up an individual's characteristics.

Cell

Genes are contained within the center, or nucleus, of a cell.

Chromosomes contain strands of DNA. There are 23 pairs of chromosomes in each human cell.

Genes are arranged on a corkscrew-shaped chemical called DNA, found within each chromosome.

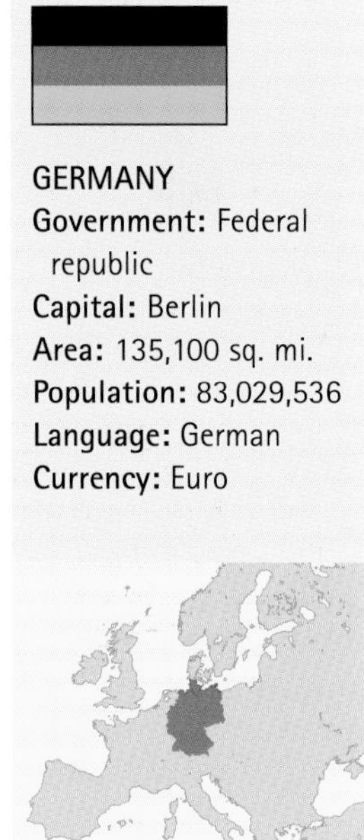

GERMANY
Government: Federal republic
Capital: Berlin
Area: 135,100 sq. mi.
Population: 83,029,536
Language: German
Currency: Euro

they are found, and how they got there. They also study the different chemicals in **rocks** and **minerals**. They try to find out how rocks are formed and how they are changed by movements beneath the surface of earth. **Volcanoes** and **earthquakes** give useful clues about movements deep underground.

Geologists study the history of earth. They have found rocks 3.8 billion years old and **fossils** showing that **evolution** began over 3.4 billion years ago. We now know that earth was formed nearly 4.6 billion years ago.

Geologists also help engineers (see **engineering**) choose where to build roads and tunnels. They help miners (see **mining**) find **coal**, **oil**, or natural **gas** underground. They were able to tell us what the **Moon** is made of by studying rocks brought back by astronauts.

▽ **Geology** helps us understand the structure of earth. To do this geologists study rocks, which also give clues to the history of earth.

Geometry

Geometry is a branch of **mathematics**. It can help establish the shape, size, and position of an object or how much a container holds. People draw lines and measure **angles** to help them solve geometric problems.

Germ *see* Bacteria, Virus

Germany

Until the late 1800s Germany was a country of separate states and cities, each with its own ruler. They were united by Otto von Bismarck (1815–1898), the prime minister of Prussia, one of the most powerful of these states. The united Germany became a great nation, but after **World War II** the area was divided into two countries—West Germany and East Germany. East Germany was a Communist country, closely allied to the **Soviet Union**. The two Germanys remained separate until 1990 when they were finally reunited under a federal **government**.

Germany lies in the middle of **Europe** and has the largest **population** of any Western European nation. Farms and cities stand on a low, flat plain to the north, while the south is a region of wooded **mountains**. In the far south the tall peaks of the **Alps** rise thousands of feet above sea level. Germany's major **rivers** are the Rhine, the Elbe, and the Oder. They flow north towards the North Sea and the Baltic Sea.

Before reunification West Germany was the richest nation in Europe. Its mines and factories produced more **coal**, steel, **cars**, and **television** sets than any other Western European nation. East Germany, less than half the size of West Germany, had mines and factories too, but much of its industry was old-fashioned and unproductive.

Once the rich West and the poorer East were united there were problems to be faced. In East Germany prices rose, and many people lost their jobs as inefficient businesses closed. **Taxes** were raised to pay for the costs of unification. However, Germany is still a very prosperous nation, and the German people are working together to overcome any remaining difficulties.

Geyser

Geysers are hot springs that shoot out steam and scalding **water**. Water fills a deep crack in the ground, usually near a **volcano**; hot rock heats the water deep underground, but the weight of the water above it stops the hot water from boiling until it becomes much hotter. Then it turns to steam, which forces the water up, emptying the crack. The next eruption happens when the crack is full again. There are many geysers in parts of **Iceland**, the **United States**, and **New Zealand**.

Ghana

Ghana is a nation in West **Africa**. The country is hot, with plenty of rain in the south where Ghana meets the **Atlantic Ocean**. The land here is low, with tropical **forests** and farms. The north is drier, with grasslands.

Most of Ghana's people are farmers, and they grow crops such as cocoa. Another occupation is mining **diamonds** and **gold**. **Lake** Volta provides **hydroelectric** power to make **electricity** for the whole of Ghana. This enormous artificial lake covers a greater area than any other artificial lake in the world.

GHANA
Government: Republic
Capital: Accra
Area: 88,700 sq. mi.
Population: 19,894,014
Languages: English, Akan, Moshi-Dagomba, Ewe, Ga
Currency: Cedi

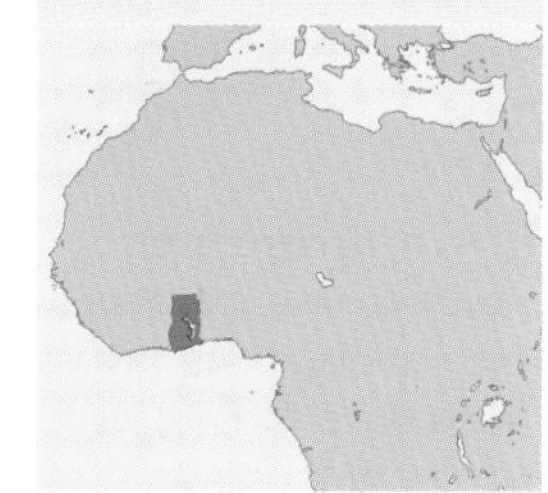

Gibraltar

This small British colony, won from **Spain** in 1704, is a rocky peninsula that juts out from the tip of southern Spain. Most of Gibraltar is a **mountain** called "the Rock." Gibraltar guards the western end of the **Mediterranean Sea**. It has an important port and British naval base.

△ The tallest **geyser** ever known was the Waimangu geyser in New Zealand. In 1904 it shot steam and water nearly 1,508 ft. (460m) into the sky.

△ An adult male **giraffe** may stand as tall as 16 ft. (5m). Giraffes have a number of different coat patterns, which vary from region to region.

Giraffe

Giraffes are the tallest **animals**. They have long legs and a long neck. Yet this neck only has seven **bones**, the same as any other **mammal**. Giraffes live in the hot grasslands of **Africa**.

A giraffe's long neck and legs enable it to eat the leaves from branches that are far above the reach of other browsing animals (see **evolution**).

Glacier

Glaciers are rivers of ice. Most form high up in **mountains** where snow falls and never melts. As snow piles up the lower layers are crushed and turn to ice. This ice begins to flow very slowly downhill through valleys. Most glaciers take one year to flow as far as you can walk in five minutes. The **rocks** they carry grind against the sides and floor of each valley until they make it deep and wide. Glaciers gradually melt when the **climate** warms up. During the **ice ages** glaciers spread worldwide. Many valleys in the **Alps** and **Rocky Mountains** once held glaciers.

△ Successful **gladiators** became famous in Rome. They were well fed and received medical care and could eventually earn their freedom.

Gladiator

Gladiators were men trained to fight to the death in shows to entertain crowds in ancient Rome (see **Roman Empire**). Many gladiators were criminals, prisoners of war, or slaves. Some fought with a sword and shield. Others had a three-pronged spear and a net. Most fights ended when one gladiator killed the other.

Gland

Glands are organs that produce substances needed by the body. There are two kinds—endocrine and exocrine glands. Endocrine glands send their substances, called **hormones**, directly into the bloodstream (see **blood**). One main endocrine gland is the thyroid. The hormone it produces controls the rate at which the body uses **energy**.

Exocrine glands release their substances through tubes either into the intestines or onto the **skin**. Sweat, tears, and saliva all come from the exocrine glands.

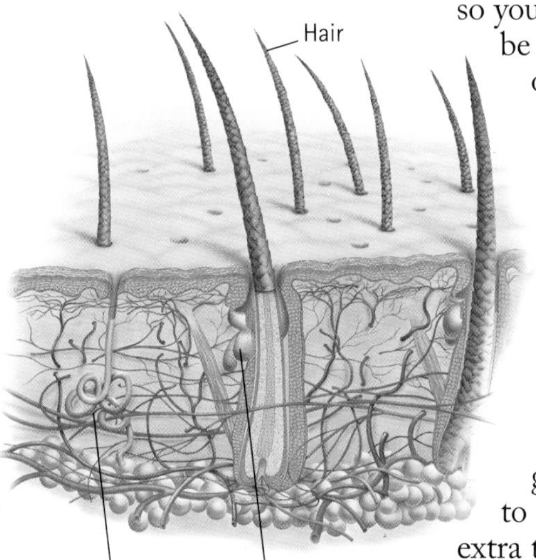

Hair

Oil gland

Sweat gland

△ Sweat **glands** deep in the skin produce watery sweat. Skin also contains oil glands that make oils to keep the skin soft.

The top of the valley is eroded into an armchair shape called a cirque.

The glacier picks up moraine, or rubble, which piles into ridges.

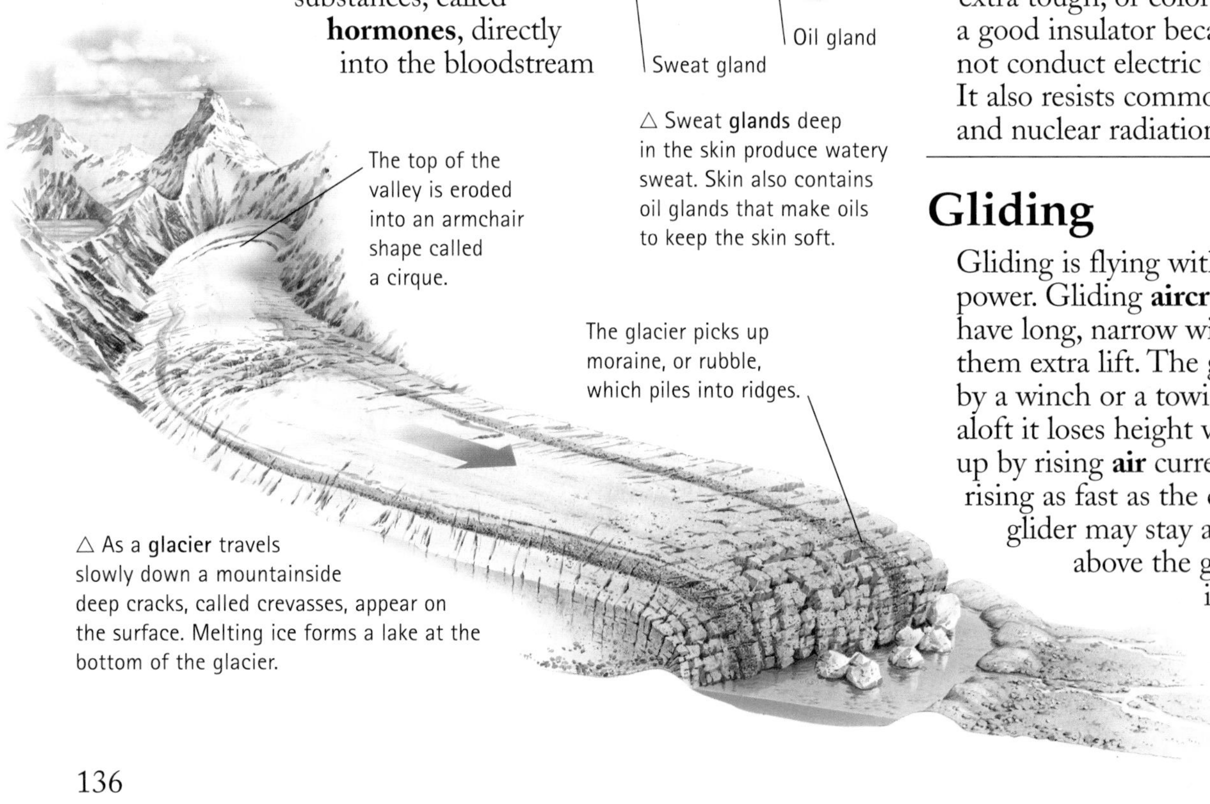

△ As a **glacier** travels slowly down a mountainside deep cracks, called crevasses, appear on the surface. Melting ice forms a lake at the bottom of the glacier.

Glass

Glass is one of the most useful materials. It is easy to shape and cheap to make. It is also transparent, so you can see through it. Glass can be made as flat sheets, thick castings, or delicate wafers. It can be made into curved **lenses** for **cameras**, **microscopes**, and other optical instruments. It can be blown into bottles or drawn out into tubes, **wires**, and very thin fibers.

Glass is made by mixing and heating **sand**, limestone, and soda ash. When these ingredients melt, they become glass. Ingredients can be added to make glass that is heatproof, extra tough, or colored. Glass is a good insulator because it does not conduct electric currents easily. It also resists common chemicals and nuclear radiation.

Gliding

Gliding is flying without using **engine** power. Gliding **aircraft** called sailplanes have long, narrow wings. This gives them extra lift. The glider is launched by a winch or a towing aircraft. Once aloft it loses height very gradually, kept up by rising **air** currents. If the air is rising as fast as the craft is falling, the glider may stay at the same level above the ground. If the air is rising at a faster rate, the aircraft can climb up.

In 1853 the first glider to carry a person flew across a valley in Yorkshire, England. Modern sailplanes can do much more than that. In 1986 one sailplane reached a height of 37,720 ft. (11,500m) over California.

Hang gliding is a sport in which the pilot is suspended from the glider by a harness and a trapezelike bar. The wing is light—usually 49–97 lbs (22–44kg) in weight—so that it can be carried and launched by one person. Takeoff is from a hill, cliff, or mountain steep enough to achieve flight. While in the air pilots use their body weight to control the glider.

Global warming

Global warming is the slow rise of **earth**'s **temperature**, which causes changes in **climate**.

Earth's **atmosphere** is made up of **gases**, such as carbon dioxide, that trap the heat **energy** from the **sun**. Without these gases the sun's **heat** would simply escape into space, and earth would be a lot colder. The gases are known as greenhouse gases because they keep heat in the atmosphere in a way similar to how heat builds up in a greenhouse.

However, the balance of these gases has been upset by human activity, for example burning **fossil** fuels such as **coal** and gasoline, and there is now far more carbon dioxide in the atmosphere. This traps in more of the sun's heat than earth needs. The resulting rise in temperatures may lead to higher sea levels and changes in rainfall patterns, which will have an impact on all living things.

Glue *see* Adhesive

Goat

Goats are taller, thinner, and more agile **animals** than their close relatives, **sheep**. Goats have hooves and hollow **horns**, and the male has a beard.

Wild goats, found in the **mountains** of central **Asia**, the **Middle East**, and **North America** live in herds and eat **grass** and leaves. Domestic goats are kept in many places. They provide **milk**, meat, and skins. Two kinds, Angora and Cashmere goats, are famous for their silky wool, which is woven (see **weaving**) into fine cloth.

God and Goddess

The words "god" and "goddess" are used to signify the person who created and controls the **universe**. People have always worshiped some kind of powerful god. The civilizations of ancient **Greece**, ancient Rome (see **Roman Empire**), and ancient **Egypt** believed in several gods, each of whom created one part of the world. The stories about these gods and goddesses are called **myths and legends**.

Most major world religions—**Judaism**, **Christianity**, **Hinduism**, and **Islam**—teach that there is one god who controls the universe. Worshipers of Islam, the Muslims, use the Arabic word "Allah" for God.

△ Hang **gliding** is a popular sport. The glider's design was the result of NASA research into spacecraft reentry as part of the U.S. space program.

▽ **Global warming** is a result of too much carbon dioxide in the atmosphere. The gas traps in the sun's heat and increases earth's temperature.

Jews, Sikhs, and Muslims forbid the creation of any idols (images of God). However, Hindus have many different images and names for God such as Vishnu and Kali.

△ The elephant-headed Hindu **god** Ganesh is the legendary scribe of the sacred Hindu text of the *Mahabharata*.

Gold

Gold is a soft, yellow **metal** that never **rusts**. Thin veins of gold were formed in **rocks** long ago by hot **gases** and **liquids** rising from deep within earth. Half of the world's gold is mined in South Africa. If washed out of the rocks, lumps of gold, called nuggets, may collect in the beds of streams and **rivers**.

Gold is beautiful and scarce, so it is valuable. Most of the world's gold is kept in brick-shaped bars, called ingots, in **banks**. **Jewelry** is made from gold mixed with other substances to make it harder.

△ The Romans worshiped many **gods**. Jupiter was king of the gods, while Diana was **goddess** of the moon and hunting.

Goldfish

Goldfish are a type of carp that are usually gold, gold and black, or gold and white in color. They are easy to keep as pets in tanks or ponds. Goldfish came originally from **China**. They can grow up to 12 in. (30cm) long and may live for over 20 years.

Golf

Golf is an ancient Scottish game that dates from well before the 1400s. Today golf is one of the most popular **sports** worldwide. The golfer's aim is to hit a small ball from the starting point, or tee, into a small hole in the fewest number of strokes. A complete game has 18 holes.

Goose

A goose is a large, powerful **bird** with a long neck, webbed feet, and a honking call. Geese live on both land and in water. The male goose is called a gander, and young geese are called goslings.

Gorbachev, Mikhail

Mikhail Gorbachev (b. 1931) became general secretary of the Soviet Communist Party and leader of the **Soviet Union** in March 1985. As leader he tried to reform the Soviet economy and promoted a more open society. He became the first **president** of the U.S.S.R. in 1989. Later he faced growing opposition to his policies and resigned at the end of 1991.

Gorilla

Gorillas are the largest of the **apes**—a large male may be as tall as a man. They live in family groups in the warm forests of central **Africa**, eating **fruit**, roots, tree bark, and leaves and making beds of twigs in the **trees**.

◁ In the late 1800s there were **gold** rushes in Canada, South Africa, New Zealand, the U.S., and Australia as people massed to seek their fortune.

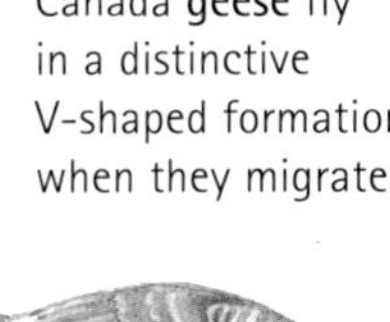

Canada **geese** fly in a distinctive V-shaped formation when they migrate.

Government

Every country needs a government to make **laws**, control **trade** and finance, and oversee relations with other countries. Most governments fall under one of two headings—totalitarian or democratic. **Democracy** is a system in which the people vote for their leaders and can remove them from power if they fail. Totalitarianism is a system in which one person or a group has complete control over the people and cannot be voted out of office. A **dictator**ship is when one person controls a country.

There are different kinds of democracies. The **United Kingdom** is a monarchy with a **monarch** as head of state. The country is, however, governed by **parliament**. The **United States** is a **republic** with a **president** as head of state. The U.S. government is divided into three branches—a law is introduced in Congress, the legislative branch; the executive branch carries out federal laws; the judicial branch interprets the nation's laws.

Grammar

Grammar is the study of the ways in which words are formed and arranged to make sentences. Words are classified as parts of **speech** according to what they do in a sentence. There are four kinds of words—**verbs** (action words), **nouns** and pronouns (naming words), **adjectives** (describing words for nouns or pronouns), and adverbs (describing words for verbs and adjectives).

To be a sentence there must be a subject (noun) and a verb. The order of words in a sentence is very important. "The dog bites the girl" means something different from "The girl bites the dog," but exactly the same words are used. It is usual in English for the subject of a sentence to come before the verb. Exceptions to this rule are called idioms—"There goes the boy."

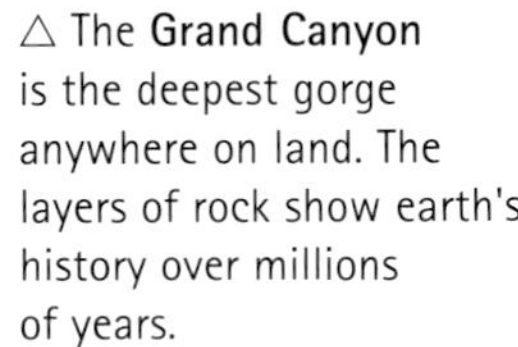

△ The **Grand Canyon** is the deepest gorge anywhere on land. The layers of rock show earth's history over millions of years.

Grand Canyon

The Colorado River carved this deep canyon in **earth**'s surface over millions of years. The canyon crosses northwest Arizona. The canyon is about 277 mi. (446km) long, up to 12 mi. (20km) across, and about 1 mi. (2km) deep.

Granite

Granite is a hard **rock** made largely of crystals of **quartz** and feldspar. Quartz is transparent, like **glass**. Feldspar is pink, white, or gray. Granite also has specks of dark **minerals** in it and is used in buildings and monuments.

Granite was once a mass of hot, melted rock underground. As the rock cooled it hardened. Then movements of **earth**'s crust forced it up to the surface.

△ **Grass** is home to many insects. It provides a good hiding-place from predators such as birds.

Grass

Grasses are flowering **plants** with long, thin leaves growing from hollow stems. Bamboo is as tall as a tree, but most grasses are short. **Herbivores,** such as **sheep** and **cattle,** eat grass. We eat the seeds of cultivated **cereal** grasses such as **wheat** and **rice**.

Grasshopper

These **insects** have feelers, wings, and long back legs. Grasshoppers eat leaves, and those called **locusts** damage crops. Many males "sing" by rubbing their back legs on their wings. A grasshopper can jump very far—20 times its own length!

Gravity

Gravity is the pull that tries to tug everything toward the middle of **Earth**. It is gravity that makes objects fall, stops us flying off into space, and keeps the **Moon** circling Earth. When we weigh something, we are measuring the force with which gravity pulls that object down. The more closely packed together the substances in an object are, the heavier it seems.

All **planets** and **stars** exert a pulling force called gravitation. The larger and denser a star or a planet is, and the nearer it is to other objects, the more strongly it pulls them toward it. The **Sun** is at a great distance from the planets, but it is so huge that its gravitation keeps the planets circling it.

GREECE
Government: Presidential parliamentary republic
Capital: Athens
Area: 50,400 sq. mi.
Population: 10,063,835
Language: Greek
Currency: Euro

▽ The **Great Wall of China** is made from soil and stone. Watchtowers were built every 656 ft. (200m) along it. Chinese sentries sent warning signals from the towers if anyone attacked the wall. The signal was smoke by day and a fire by night.

Great Barrier Reef

This is the longest **coral** reef in the world at about 1,240 mi. (2,000km) long. It stands in the sea off the northeast coast of **Australia**. Much of the reef's surface lies just underwater and is a danger to ships.

Most of the Great Barrier Reef is built by millions of tiny, soft-bodied creatures called coral polyps, related to the **sea anemone**, which live in colonies and build stony cases to protect themselves.

In the 1960s part of the reef was destroyed by crown of thorns starfish, which feed on the polyps. Today boats, **pollution** from oil spills and garbage, and people breaking up coral to sell to tourists are the main threats to the reef.

Great Lakes

This is the world's largest group of freshwater **lakes**. Lake Michigan lies in the **United States**. Lakes Superior, Erie, Huron, and Ontario are shared by the United States and **Canada**. The lakes were formed when a huge sheet of ice melted 18,000 years ago. **Rivers** and **canals** connect the lakes to each other and to the **Atlantic Ocean**.

Great Wall of China

Over 2,000 years ago the first emperor of China, Shih Huang Ti, built this wall to keep out China's enemies from the north. It is the longest wall in the world, stretching 1,488 mi. (2,400km) from western China to the Yellow Sea.

Greece

Greece is a country that lies in southeast **Europe**. Rocky **mountains** cover most of the land, and peninsulas poke out into the sea like giant fingers. Greece includes the island of Crete and many

Doric

Ionic

Corinthian

△ Originally there were two types of columns in **ancient Greece**—the Doric and Ionic. From the 400s B.C. the Corinthian style became popular.

△ The semicircular theater in Athens, **ancient Greece**, could hold over 10,000 people.

smaller islands in the Aegean and Ionian seas. Greek summers are hot and dry, while the winters are mild and wet. Many of the people work in the capital city, Athens. Greek farmers grow lemons, grapes, wheat, and olives.

Greece, ancient

The first great peoples in Greece were the Minoans and the Mycenaeans. The Minoans lived in Crete. They had rich cities and farms and led peaceful lives. The Mycenaeans lived on mainland Greece and were warriors and sailors. Both civilizations ended about 1200 B.C.

Around this time, new groups of people began to move to Greece from the north. Instead of making Greece one kingdom they built separate cities. They often fought with each other, but sometimes they joined together to fight enemies such as the Persians. Two of the strongest cities were Athens and Sparta. In the 400s B.C. Athens was ruled by a **democracy**.

The Greeks loved the **theater**, **art**, and **poetry**. They had many great thinkers, or **philosophers**, including **Aristotle**, **Plato**, and Socrates. Greek cities had many graceful buildings. They were decorated with beautiful **sculptures**. In 339 B.C. Greece was conquered by Philip of Macedonia, father of **Alexander the Great**.

Greenland

Greenland is the world's largest **island**, but it holds no more people than a large town. This is because Greenland has such a cold **climate**. Most of it lies in the **Arctic**. Thick ice covers seven eighths of the island. Bare **mountains** make up much of the rest. **Vikings** discovered it nearly 1,000 years ago. It lies northeast of **Canada**, but today it belongs to **Denmark**. Greenland has enjoyed home rule since 1979.

Most Greenlanders live in villages of wooden houses near the coast. Some are Danes; many are **Inuit**. Many Greenlanders work in the country's thriving **fishing** industry.

GREENLAND
Government: Part of Denmark but with home rule
Capital: Godthåb
Area: 840,000 sq. mi.
Population: 56,309
Languages: Inuit, Danish, and Greenlandic
Currency: Danish krone

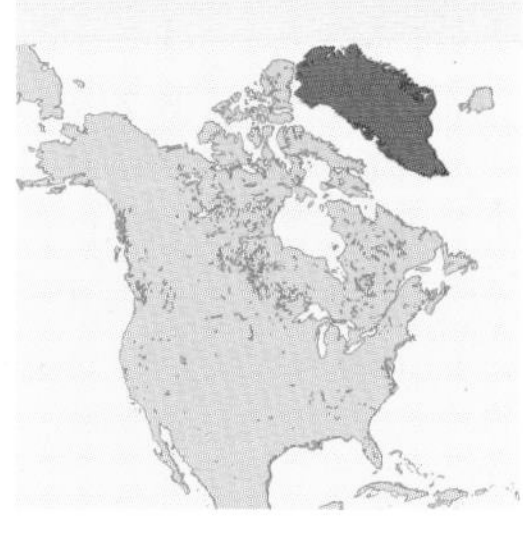

Guatemala

More people live in Guatemala than in any other **Central American** country. Nearly half of them are Indians, descendants of the **Maya**. Guatemala is a land of dense jungles, fiery **volcanoes**, dry **deserts**, and sparkling **lakes**. Most of the people earn their living by **farming**—**coffee**, **cotton**, and bananas are the main products. The country was conquered by the Spanish in 1524, declared its independence in 1821, and became a **republic** in 1839.

GUATEMALA
Government: Republic
Capital: Guatemala City
Area: 41,800 sq. mi.
Population: 12,974,361
Language: Spanish
Currency: Quetzal

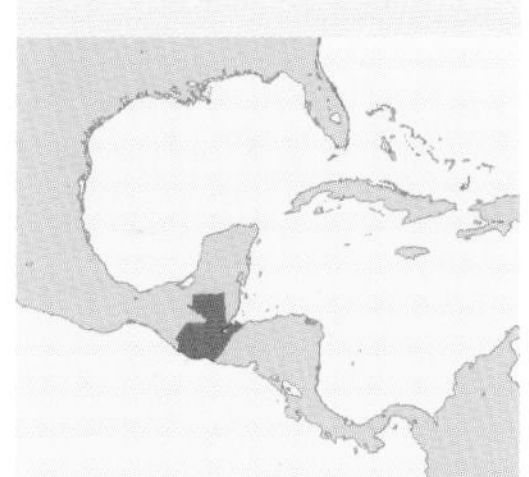

Guerrilla warfare

Guerrillas are "hit and run" fighters. Frequently they do not wear uniforms and live in places where they can easily hide such as **forests** or **mountains**. The word "guerrilla" is Spanish for "little war." Guerrilla tactics are usually used by small groups who are fighting against a larger, more organized force.

Guevara, Che

Che Guevara (1928–1967), born Ernesto Guevara de la Serna in **Argentina**, was a leading communist figure (see **communism**) in the Cuban Revolution (1956–1959). In the 1960s he held many government postions in Cuba under president Castro (b. 1926).

In 1966 Guevara led a guerrilla group in **Bolivia,** but in 1967 he was captured and shot by the Bolivian army.

Guinea

Guinea is a country on the west coast of **Africa**. It has a population of over seven million people. Some of the world's largest deposits of bauxite, from which **aluminum** is made, are in Guinea.

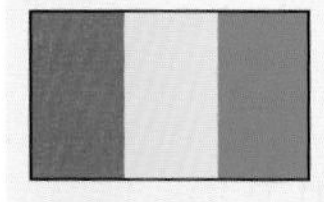

GUINEA
Government: Republic
Capital: Conakry
Area: 94,800 sq. mi.
Population: 7,613,870
Languages: French and tribal languages
Currency: Franc

Guitar

The guitar is a stringed **musical instrument**. It consists of a body with a flat back and a long "neck." The strings (made of nylon, **steel**, or catgut) and a series of **metal** pieces, called frets, run along the neck to the body. The player strums or plucks the strings with one hand and uses the other hand to press the strings against the frets. Different notes are made according to where the strings are pressed.

Most guitars have six strings. Acoustic guitars are wooden with a round hole in the front of the body to amplify the sound. Electric guitars are made of metal or **plastic** and lack the hole in the body, so they use a separate electric amplifier.

Guinea pig

The guinea pig, also called a cavy, is a **rodent** from **Peru**. Guinea pigs are up to 11 in. (29cm) long and are brown, gray, white, black, or a mixture. Some have long silky **hair** or hair that forms swirls called rosettes. They eat **grass** and hay. Many people keep guinea pigs as pets.

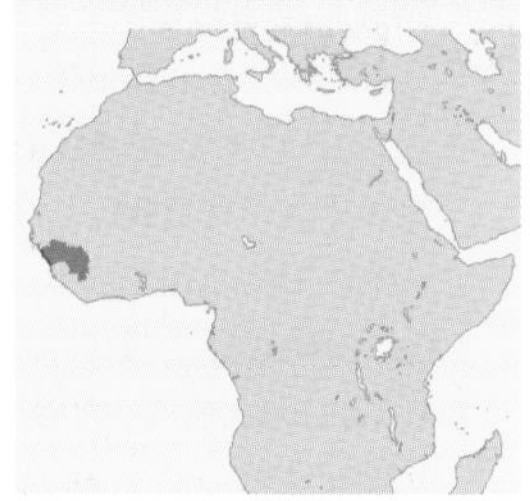

△ Large **guns** called cannons had wheeled bases to move them around. They fired large metal cannonballs.

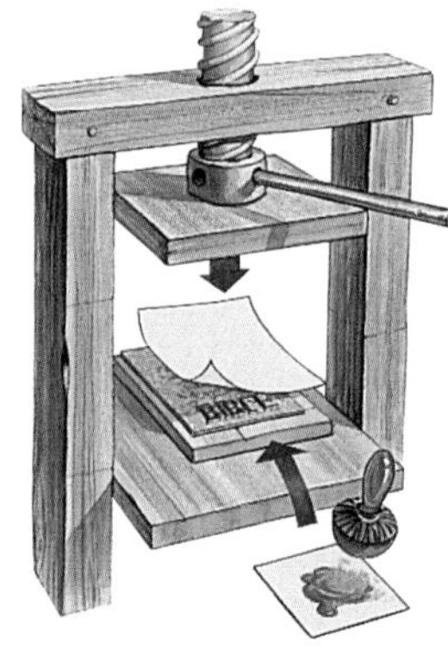

△ **Gutenberg**'s printing press was an important achievement, but he never made much money from it.

Gulf Stream

This **ocean** current is like a giant river flowing through the sea. It carries warm water from the Gulf of **Mexico** northward along the eastern coast of the **United States**. The Gulf Stream is up to 372 mi. (60km) wide and 1,968 mi. (600km) deep. One branch of the Gulf Stream crosses the **Atlantic Ocean** and brings warm water to northwestern **Europe**. If it were not for the Gulf Stream, the winters in northern Europe would be much more severe.

Gulf War

On August 2, 1990 Iraqi forces under President Saddam Hussein (b. 1937) invaded the small country of Kuwait. The **United Nations** imposed economic sanctions on **Iraq** and then voted to use force to restore Kuwait's independence. The Gulf War was fought from January 16 to the defeat of Iraq on February 28, 1991. The allied forces against Iraq included **France**, the **United States**, and the **United Kingdom**.

Gull

Few **birds** are more graceful than gulls, gliding and soaring over the sea. They have webbed feet and swim well, but most stay near land. They catch **fish** but also scavenge for **food** on the shore.

Gulls breed in noisy crowds called colonies. Many colonies live on islands, which helps keep their **eggs** safe from predators such as **rats** and **foxes**.

Gun

Guns are weapons that fire bullets or other **missiles** from a tube that is open at one end. Guns were probably invented in the 1200s. By the 1300s guns fired missiles that could pierce **armor** and break down **castle** walls. Large, long guns called cannons were first used in around 1350.

In the 1800s guns fired pointed shells that exploded when they hit. Soon shells could be fired farther and hit targets more often than before.

Troops first used handheld guns in the 1300s. Inventors developed pistols and revolvers for firing at nearby targets. Then muskets, rifles, and machine guns were developed to shoot distant targets.

Gutenberg, Johannes

Johannes Gutenberg (c. 1395–1468) was a German goldsmith who is sometimes called "the father of **printing**." In his day people slowly copied **books** by hand or printed them from wooden blocks where each letter was carved separately. Around 1440 Gutenberg learned to make **metal** letters called type. He placed them in rows to build pages. Each page was held together by a frame that he attached to a press. He then pressed the inky surface of his type onto sheets of **paper**. His movable type helped make copies of a book faster and cheaper than before.

Guyana

Guyana is a hot, rainy country on the northeast coast of **South America**. Most people live along the coast in a narrow strip of flat land about 12 mi. (20km) wide. Sugarcane and **rice** are grown here. Valuable **minerals**, including **gold** and **diamonds**, are found in the hilly region inland. Guyana produces bauxite to make **aluminum**.

Once a British colony, Guyana became independent in 1966 and became a **republic** in 1970.

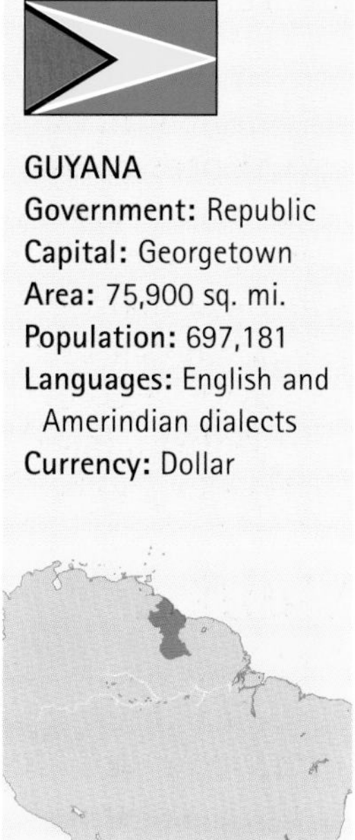

GUYANA
Government: Republic
Capital: Georgetown
Area: 75,900 sq. mi.
Population: 697,181
Languages: English and Amerindian dialects
Currency: Dollar

Gymnastics

Gymnastics are exercises that help keep the body in shape. The **Olympic Games** have separate gymnastic exercises for both men and women. Women perform difficult routines on a narrow, wooden balance beam. They swing back and forth between uneven bars. They leap over a vaulting horse and perform tumbling floor routines to **music**.

Men hang from a high bar and from rings, swinging up and down and back and forth. Using two parallel bars they swing, vault, and do handstands. They grip hoops that jut up from a pommel horse and swing their legs and body over it. They also leap over a vaulting horse.

Gypsy

Gypsies are a group of people found all over the world. Some speak a **language** called Romany. Some live in houses, and others constantly travel and live in caravans. Gypsies prefer to earn an independent living, for example by trading goods or selling arts and crafts.

The word "gypsy" comes from the word "Egyptian." It was once believed that gypsies came from **Egypt**, but they probably came from **India** in the 1400s.

Gyroscope

A gyroscope is a **wheel** that spins in a special frame. No matter how the frame tilts, the wheel's axle points in the same direction. Even **gravity** and **earth**'s **magnetism** do not affect the axle.

On a **ship** or **aircraft** a **compass** made from a gyroscope always points north. Gyroscopes can also keep an aircraft on course without the pilot steering.

▽ Modern competitive **gymnastics** developed from German and Swedish systems of exercise. Children and adults perform simpler exercises in gymnastics classes.

△ The astronomer Edmond **Halley**'s greatest achievement was to predict the appearance of a comet. This 1.2-mi. (2-km) -long ball of rock, dust, and ice was later named Halley's Comet.

H

Habitat

A habitat is the home of a particular species of **animal** or **plant**. It provides all the things that the species needs to survive such as **food**, **water**, and shelter. There are many thousands of different habitats across the world, including grasslands, swamps, **forests**, **deserts**, **rivers**, **lakes**, and **oceans**.

Biologists group similar types of habitats together in general categories known as biomes. For example, the North American prairie and the East African **savanna** are just two of the habitats that belong to the grassland biome. Within each habitat there are also many small, specialized living places known as microhabitats. For example, the microhabitats in a typical forest might include the topmost leaves of a tall **tree**, the bark on the tree trunk, a clump of flowers on the forest floor, and a rotting log underneath.

◁ In 1791 the Caribbean island of **Haiti** (then known as Santo Domingo) was shaken by a violent slaves' revolt. As many as 100,000 slaves rebeled against their owners, setting fire to the sugar and coffee plantations. France sent troops to the island, but after a bitter war Haiti eventually won its independence.

Hair

Hair grows like living threads on the **skin** of **mammals**. It is made from the same substances as **nails and claws**, **hooves**, **feathers**, and reptiles' scales. Hair helps keep the body warm and protects the skin. Each hair root is enclosed in its own case, or follicle, which has a **blood** supply, a tiny erector **muscle**, and a **gland**.

There are many types of hair. For example, **cats** have plenty of soft, thick fur, and **porcupines** are protected by sharp, stiff hairs called quills.

Haiti

Haiti is a small country in the western part of the island of Hispaniola in the **Caribbean** Sea. Much of the country is covered by rugged **mountains**, but there are fertile valleys and coastal plains where **coffee** and other crops are grown. Nine tenths of the people are descended from African slaves. In 1677 Haiti became a French colony. It gained its independence in 1804 following a rebellion.

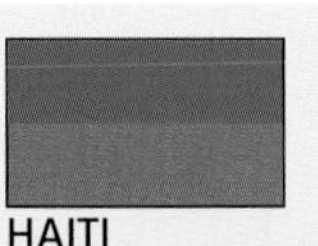

HAITI
Government: Republic
Capital: Port-au-Prince
Area: 10,600 sq. mi.
Population: 6,964,549
Languages: French and Creole
Currency: Gourde

Halley, Edmond

Edmond Halley (1657–1742) was an English astronomer who is best known for his study of **comets**. He noticed that the path followed by a comet that he had seen in 1682 was very much like those reported in 1607 and 1531. Halley decided that these sightings must all be of the same comet and predicted that it would return in 1758. On December 25, 1758 it did. Halley's Comet reappears regularly once every 76 years or so—it will next pass near **earth** in 2061.

Handel, George Frideric

George Frideric Handel (1685–1759) was a German-born British composer who is today known mainly for his oratorios—pieces of **music** written for large choirs. Handel's most popular work is the oratorio *Messiah* (1742). He also composed orchestral music, such as *Water Music* (1717) and *Royal Fireworks Music* (1749), for royal events and wrote a number of **operas**.

Hannibal

Hannibal (247–183 B.C.) was an emperor of the Carthaginian Empire, which in ancient times was one of the most powerful states in the **Mediterranean**. He fought several wars with the **Roman Empire** to keep control of the valuable trade routes that passed through Carthage, his empire's capital on the coast of North **Africa**.

Hannibal was a brilliant general, and his excellent military strategies allowed him to defeat armies much larger than his own. But although Hannibal won many important battles, in the end he was never able to conquer the Romans.

△ Despite its name, the black-tailed jackrabbit is in fact a type of **hare** that lives in North America's hot deserts. Its huge ears give off heat, which helps the animal stay cool.

▽ In 218 B.C. **Hannibal** led an army from Spain across the Alps to Italy. As well as 40,000 troops, he took 37 elephants, which he planned to use to frighten the enemy troops of the Roman Empire.

Hapsburgs

Many of **Europe**'s kings and emperors belonged to the Hapsburg royal family. Its name comes from a Swiss **castle** called Habichtsburg ("Hawk's Castle"), which was built in 1020 by a German bishop. The owners of the castle became the counts of Hapsburg.

In 1273 Count Rudolf of Hapsburg (1208–1291) was chosen to be the **Holy Roman Emperor**, and in 1276 Rudolf seized **Austria**. Later, Holy Roman Emperors were mostly Hapsburgs. Members of the Hapsburg family also married foreign princesses and thus increased their power by controlling the countries their wives inherited. By the 1500s the Hapsburgs ruled much of Europe from **Spain** in the east to **Hungary** in the west. However, they began losing power in the 1700s. **Napoléon** ended the Holy Roman Empire in 1806, and **World War I** finally smashed the Hapsburgs' huge Austro-Hungarian empire.

Hare

A hare is a type of **mammal** related to the **rabbit**. It has long ears, powerful, muscular legs, and a short tail. Unlike rabbits, which are naked and blind at birth, young hares are born with fur and eyes that can open. They are known as leverets. Hares may live in open fields and on plains, deserts, and high **mountains**. They do not dig their own burrows, and when resting they crouch in a hole in the ground. Hares can run extremely fast to escape their predators and may reach a speed of up to 43 mph (70km/h).

Harp

The harp is the oldest of all stringed instruments. Early harps were little more than bows with strings of different lengths stretched across them. Modern harps have a wooden frame with the strings attached between the hollow sounding board and the top of the instrument. There are seven foot pedals that can change the pitch of the strings. The harpist sits with the sounding board between his or her legs and plucks the strings using fingers and thumbs.

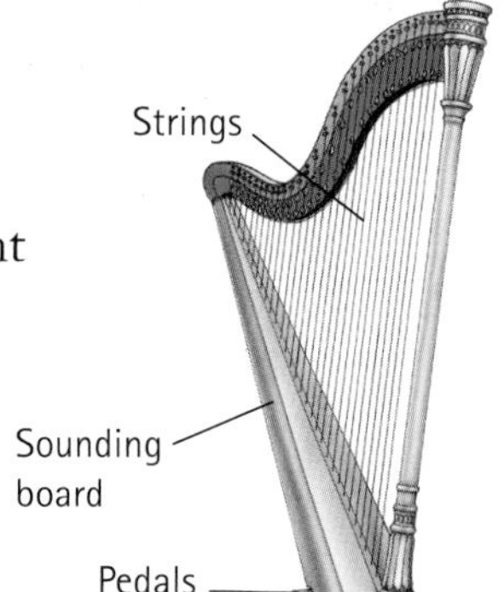

△ Concert **harps** produce a rich, powerful sound. The pedals are used to change the pitch of the strings.

Harvey, William

The English doctor William Harvey (1578–1657) was the first to show that **blood** flows around the body in an endless stream. Harvey proved that a beating **heart** squeezes blood through **arteries** and flaps in the heart and that the blood returns to the heart through **veins**. He calculated that the amount of blood pumped by a heart in one hour weighs three times more than an average adult.

Hawk

Hawks are **birds** of prey related to **falcons** and **eagles**. They have superb **sight** for spotting prey, hooked beaks and razor-sharp talons for catching and killing victims, and long tails for steering while in midair. Many species of hawks look like falcons, but they usually have broader wings with more rounded tips. Female hawks are always larger than males.

Hawks are found all over the world except on Pacific islands. The goshawk lives across the northern regions of **North America**, **Europe**, and **Asia** and is strong enough to kill prey as large as **ducks** and **rabbits**. Other types of hawks are sparrow hawks and buzzards.

Arteries (shown in red) carry blood without oxygen.

Veins (shown in blue) carry blood with oxygen.

△ William **Harvey's** experiments in the 1620s led him to discover how blood circulates in humans. He realized that the heart pumps blood through the arteries and around the body and that the blood returns to the heart through the veins.

Haydn, Franz Joseph

Franz Joseph Haydn (1732–1809) was an important Austrian composer who wrote 104 symphonies. Many of them used the **orchestra** in a powerful new way. He also wrote pieces for the **piano** and numerous string quartets (works for four stringed instruments). Later both **Mozart** and **Beethoven** were influenced by Haydn's **music**.

Health

Good health is one of the most important things in life. There are certain things we can do to stay healthy. We should eat a balanced diet that includes the right kinds of **food** and drink plenty of clean, fresh **water**. We should **exercise regularly**, strengthening our **muscles** and keeping us in shape. Exercise helps the **blood** circulate around our bodies, cleaning out waste and supplying plenty of **oxygen**. It is also important that we get enough **sleep**. The number of hours of sleep we need depends on our age. Young babies sleep for 20–22 hours each day, whereas older people often need only 6–7 hours.

Hearing

Hearing is the sense that allows people to pick up **sound**. The sense organ that makes this possible is the **ear**. Deaf people cannot hear—they either were born without the ability to hear or at some time their ears were damaged by an illness or in an accident.

All **vertebrates** (**animals** with backbones) have hearing organs, and some species can hear much better than people. **Cats** and **dogs**, for example, pick up more sounds than we can. **Bats** use their exceptional hearing to find their prey. They utter a series of high-pitched squeaks and listen for the **echoes** that bounce back off of flying **insects**.

Heart

The heart is a powerful, muscular **pump** that maintains a continual flow of **blood** around the body through **veins** and **arteries**. In a typical adult person the heart beats between 70 and 80 times per minute until death. It was the English doctor William **Harvey** (1578–1657) who discovered how the heart works.

A human heart is about the same size as a clenched fist. It is divided into two halves, each of which has a small upper chamber called the atrium and a larger lower chamber called the ventricle. The atria (plural of atrium) collect the blood flowing into the heart. The ventricles are strong **muscles** that pump blood into the arteries.

The right atrium receives **oxygen**-poor blood from all over the body through large veins called the superior (upper) vena cava and the inferior (lower) vena cava. This blood is pumped by the right ventricle through the pulmonary arteries to the **lungs**, where it absorbs oxygen. The left atrium receives the oxygen-rich blood from the lungs through the pulmonary veins. The left ventricle pumps this blood out to the body's **cells** along the large artery called the aorta.

Heat

Heat is a form of **energy** that we can feel but not see. When something burns, heat is produced. The **sun** gives out enormous amounts of heat, which is produced by **atoms** joining together, or "fusing," inside the sun. This same kind of energy can be released by a **hydrogen** bomb on **earth**.

Most of the heat we use comes from burning **fuels** such as **coal** or **natural gas**. Heat is also made by **friction**, or rubbing things together, and it is produced when **electricity** travels along a coil of **wire**. This is what makes the coils inside a toaster glow red.

We can measure how hot a thing is by finding its **temperature**. This is done with a **thermometer**. When a substance gets hot, the molecules, or tiny particles, of which it is made move around more quickly. Often the substance expands as this happens. **Metals** are the **elements** that expand the most when they are heated.

Heat energy moves around in three ways—by conduction, convection, and radiation. It travels from a region of higher temperature to a region of lower temperature. Conduction carries heat through solid objects, known as conductors. For example, if you dip a spoon into a hot drink, it soon starts to feel warm. Convection carries heat through **liquids** and **gases**. Radiation is a process that carries heat energy in straight lines through empty space. This is how heat from the sun reaches earth.

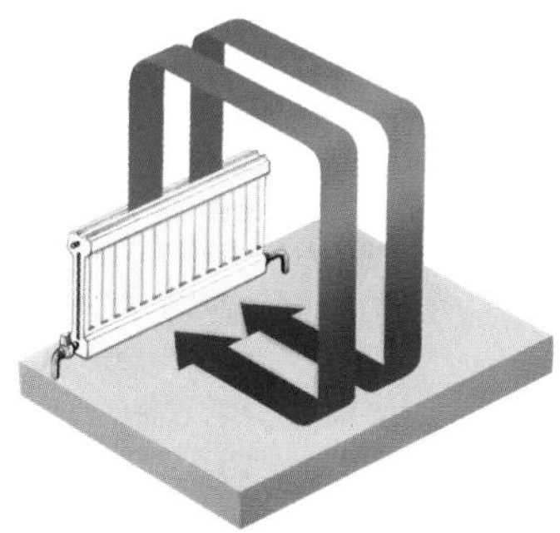

△ A radiator gives off, or radiates, **heat**. The heat travels through the air by the process of convection. As air above the radiator becomes warm it rises. Cooler air moves in to take its place, creating a convection current.

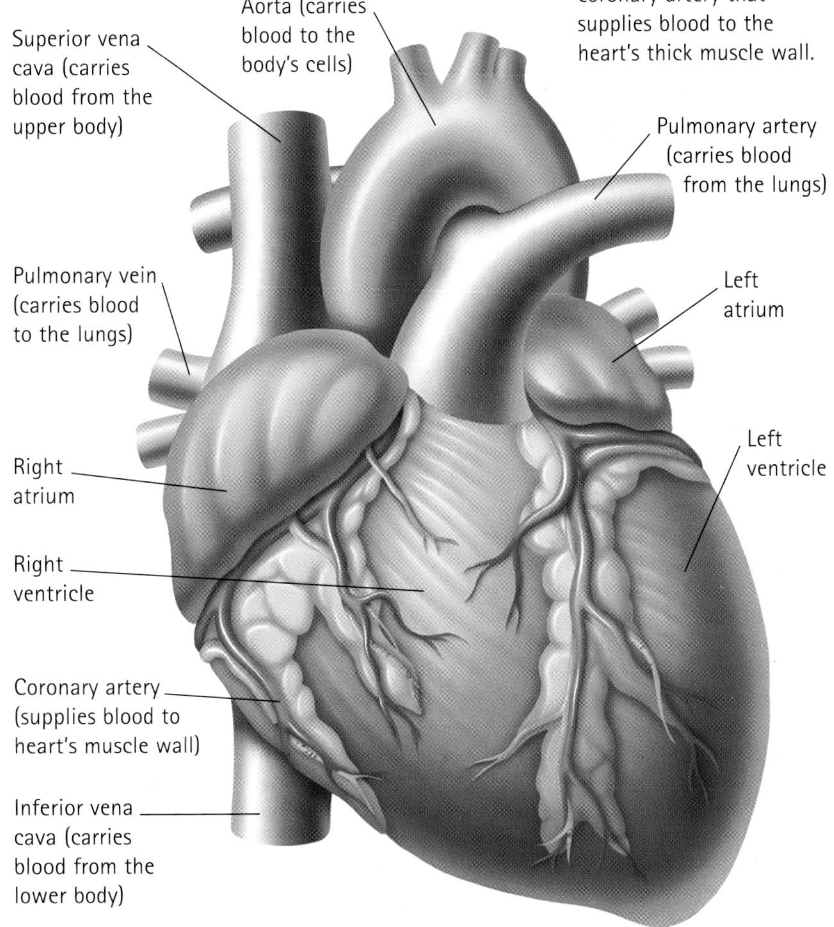

▽ This front view of the human **heart** illustrates the main blood vessels carrying blood to and from the heart and the coronary artery that supplies blood to the heart's thick muscle wall.

Hedgehog

The hedgehog is a **mammal** that has a covering of spines on its back for protection. The spines are modified **hairs**. When threatened, the hedgehog rolls up into a prickly ball.

There are several species of hedgehogs found in **Europe**, North **Africa**, and parts of **Asia**. The best-known species lives in forests, fields, and gardens across much of Europe. It emerges at night to hunt for **snails**, **slugs**, **worms**, and **insects**, which it tracks down with its excellent sense of **smell**. During the winter hedgehogs enter a form of deep sleep known as **hibernation**.

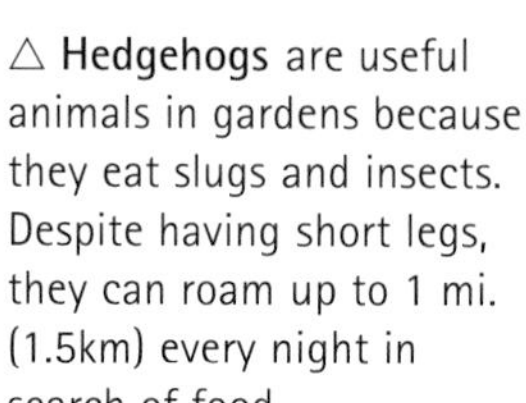

△ **Hedgehogs** are useful animals in gardens because they eat slugs and insects. Despite having short legs, they can roam up to 1 mi. (1.5km) every night in search of food.

Helen of Troy

In the legends of ancient **Greece**, Helen of Troy was the most beautiful woman in the world. She was the daughter of Zeus, the king of the **gods**, and Leda, a human. Helen married Menelaus, king of Sparta, but later ran away with Paris, prince of Troy. Menelaus followed with a large army and started the **Trojan War**. The story was told by the poet **Homer**.

▽ **Helicopters** play a major part in many search-and-rescue missions.They were used to rescue people who were stranded during the devastating floods that hit the African country of Mozambique in early 2000.

Helicopter

The helicopter is an extremely useful **aircraft** that was invented in the 1930s. It can take off and land vertically and therefore is able to work in areas too small for ordinary aircraft. In addition it can fly in almost any direction and hover in midair.

Helicopters do not have wings like a plane. Instead they have a moving wing called a rotor that acts as a wing and a propeller. The pilot controls the craft by changing the angle, or pitch, at which the blades of the rotor pass through the air. A smaller rotor on the tail keeps the helicopter from spinning around. Helicopters are used for a variety of purposes but are especially useful for rescue missions, aerial observation, and carrying troops to remote locations.

Henry V

Although Henry V (1387–1422) ruled as king of **England** for only nine years, he changed the course of English history during his short reign. By the time he died England had become the strongest kingdom in **Europe**.

In the period 1403–1408 the young Prince Henry led an army against the Welsh rebels. In 1413 he succeeded his father, Henry IV (1367–1413), and immediately began increasing the power of the English throne. Henry revived an earlier claim to the French throne and in 1415 invaded **France**. He was an excellent soldier and led his troops to a celebrated victory at the Battle of Agincourt. Henry's force included 900 foot soldiers and 3,000 archers. The French had at least three times as many heavily armed troops, but they were badly led and organized.

In 1417 Henry returned to France to try to conquer Normandy. But after a long military campaign Henry died near **Paris** in 1422 without achieving victory.

Henry VIII

Henry VIII (1491–1547) belonged to the Tudor dynasty and became king of **England** in 1509. His father was Henry VII (1457–1509), the first Tudor king. Henry was a popular but ruthless ruler and is remembered for his lavish court and efficient government.

Henry was married six times and broke away from the Roman Catholic Church when **Pope** Clement VII (1478–1534) refused to grant him permission to divorce his first wife, Catherine of Aragon (1485–1536). From 1536–1540 Henry closed 800 **monasteries**, removing 10,000 monks and nuns from their roles in the Church and selling or making gifts of their lands. He did this to break the power of the papacy in England and to raise money. He founded the Protestant Church of England and established himself as its head. Henry also fought several wars with **Scotland** and **France**.

△ **Henry VIII** abolished the authority of the pope in England and declared himself the head of the English Church.

Heraldry

In the **Middle Ages** a knight in full **armor** was hard to recognize because his face was hidden by his helmet. Thus knights began to use special designs worn on their surcoats and shields. These designs became coats of arms, family emblems that no one else could wear. Heralds were officials who kept records of coats of arms and awarded new ones. There are names for the different colors and patterns used in heraldry, and these shapes form the basis of the designs of many modern **flags**.

In 1415 **Henry V** led his troops to a great victory over a much larger French army at Agincourt in northern France.

△ **Herbs,** such as marjoram (above), can be used fresh from the garden, or they can be cut and dried for storage. Some herbs are also used to make herbal medicines, which can help treat a variety of illnesses.

Herb

Herbs are **plants** with soft, rather than woody, stems. Some herbs are added to **food** during cooking, while others are important for their healing qualities and are made into herbal **medicines**. Herbs used in cooking include mint, parsley, thyme, garlic, rosemary, basil, fennel, sage, and chives. Most can be grown easily anywhere, although they came originally from the warm, sunny lands of the **Mediterranean** region.

Herbivore

Herbivores are a group of **mammals** that feed mainly on **plants**. There are many kinds of herbivores, including **cattle**, **deer**, **elephants**, **goats**, **horses**, and **sheep**. Some herbivores eat only **grass**, while others feed on the leaves, **seeds,** and **fruit** of a variety of plants. Many herbivores have complex **digestion** systems that can extract the nutrients from the toughest plant matter.

Heredity *see* Genetics

Hibernation

When a **mammal**, an **amphibian**, or a **reptile** hibernates, it goes to **sleep** for the winter. It does this because **food** is scarce in the winter. Going to sleep during the cold **weather** saves the animal from starving to death.

Before hibernation **animals** eat as much food as they can find. The dormouse, for example, stuffs itself until it is plump and round. As fall approaches it makes a snug nest, curls into a ball, and falls into a deep sleep. In fact its **heart** beats so slowly that the dormouse looks dead. Its body uses hardly any **energy** while in hibernation in order to make its supply of **fat** last as long as possible. In the spring the thin and hungry dormouse wakes and emerges from its nest to look for food.

In cold **climates** many animals hibernate—but not all of them sleep right through the winter. For example, **squirrels** wake up on mild days and eat food they had hidden in the summer.

△ During **hibernation** the body temperature of a dormouse falls, and its heartbeat slows down. The dormouse will not wake up even if it is touched.

△ These picture signs are an example of Egyptian **hieroglyphics**—one of the world's oldest forms of writing. The symbols, or hieroglyphs, were carved on the walls of temples, tombs, and monuments and inscribed on a form of paper called papyrus.

◁ The **Himalayas** are the world's highest mountain range. The name literally means "home of the snows."

Hieroglyphics

Hieroglyphics are ancient **writing** systems. The modern Western **alphabet** has 26 letters. However, about 5,000 years ago the people of ancient **Egypt** used picture signs instead of letters. Later these signs developed into hieroglyphs—special marks that stood for things, people, and ideas.

Hieroglyphic writing was difficult to produce, and only a few people knew how to create it. When the ancient Egyptian civilization died out, the secret of reading hieroglyphs was lost—no one could understand the symbols carved on stones and written on papyrus scrolls. Then in 1799 a French explorer found the Rosetta Stone, which is now located in the British Museum in **London**. On the stone was something written in two known **languages** and also in hieroglyphs. By comparing the known languages with the hieroglyphs experts were at last able to translate the signs.

Several other ancient cultures also used hieroglyphic systems, including the Hittites, who lived in the region that is now **Turkey**, and the **Aztec** and **Maya** civilizations of **Central America**.

Himalayas

The Himalayas are a chain of high **mountains** that form a huge barrier across **Asia**, dividing **India** in the south from **Tibet** and **China** in the north. Many of Asia's largest **rivers** begin in the Himalayas and are fed by the melting snow and ice.

Until **aircraft** were invented hardly any outsiders ventured into the Himalayas. Even now there are few **roads** or **railroads** there. Often the only way to travel is on foot over steep mountain tracks. **Horses**, **yaks**, **goats**, and even **sheep** are used to carry heavy loads.

The highest mountain in the entire world lies in the Himalayas. This is Mount **Everest**, which is 29,021 ft. (8,848m) high.

Hinduism

Hinduism is one of the world's great **religions**. Most Hindus live in **Asia**, particularly in **India**. Their religion is thought to be 4,000 years old.

Hindus believe that God is present in all things. Only priests, known as Brahmins, can worship the supreme God. Ordinary people worship other **gods** such as Vishnu, god of life. Hindu gods all have different characters. Shiva has four arms and is often shown dancing. Kali is the wife of Shiva. Ganesh, Shiva's son, has the head of an **elephant**, and Hindus believe that praying to him will bring success.

The most important holy **books** of the Hindus are called the *Vedas*—the Books of Knowledge. The main manuscript is the *Rig Veda*, a collection of more than 1,000 hymns composed in Sanskrit, an ancient **language**. Hindus also believe that certain animals, such as the cobra and the cow, are sacred and must never be killed or eaten. Unlike many other faiths, Hinduism was not started by one teacher—its beliefs accumulated gradually over many centuries.

△ One of the chief gods in **Hinduism** is Shiva, who Hindus believe is both a creator and a destroyer. In this sculpture Shiva is depicted dancing in a halo of flames.

Hippopotamus

The name hippopotamus means "river horse," but in fact the hippo is related to the **pig**, not the **horse**. It is a huge, heavy **mammal** and lives in **Africa**. Of all the land animals, only the **elephant** is larger.

Hippos live near **rivers** and **lakes**. They spend most of their time in the water and are good swimmers. Their eyes are on the tops of their heads so they can stand underwater and peep out without being seen. Hippos can stay submerged for nearly ten minutes without coming up for breath.

Despite their fearsome-looking jaws, hippos only eat **plants**. They graze on water weeds and **grasses**, and at night they usually come ashore to feed.

▽ The **hippopotamus** rests in the water during the heat of the day and becomes active again in the evening.

History

History is the story of the past. People who study history are called historians. They often write about important events, such as **wars** and **revolutions**, and about rulers and **governments** because these affect nations. However, historians are also interested in the lives of ordinary people and in what they did and thought about.

Nowadays we think of history as being written down in history **books**. But in earlier times, before books and **printing**, history was passed on by word of mouth. People told stories about their rulers, wars, and adventures and also about their own families. It was in this way that the stories of ancient **Greece** were collected by the poet **Homer** to form the *Iliad* and the *Odyssey*. Some of these early stories were created in verse form and sung along to **music**. This made it easier for people to remember the stories correctly.

In ancient **Egypt** scholars recorded the reigns of the **pharaohs** and listed the victories they won in battle. These accounts were often written on stone tablets in the form of **hieroglyphics**. The scholars of the **Roman Empire** and ancient **China** were also very interested in history. It was these scholars who first took the writing of history seriously, describing how their civilizations rose to power.

△ The **history** of ancient civilizations frequently has to be pieced together from clues that have survived over the years. This huge stone head, one of eight carved over 3,000 years ago by the Olmecs of Mexico, may represent an important Olmec ruler.

In **Europe** during the **Middle Ages** many people could not read or write, and printing had not been invented. It was the priests and monks who preserved ancient books and kept the official records and documents. These records include the **Domesday Book** (1086), which tells us much of what we know about **England** at the time of **William the Conqueror**. It was not until the 1700s and 1800s that history became an important branch of study in the **universities** of Europe.

Historians get their information from hidden remains, such as things found buried in old graves, as well as from old books. The study of hidden remains is called **archaeology**. But history is not just concerned with the distant past. After all, history is our story—what is news today will be history tomorrow. So modern historians are also interested in **recording** the present. They talk to the elderly about their lives, and they keep records on **film** and videotape of the events of today. **Television** has become a very important source for historians.

◁ Events that change the course of **history** are called turning points. This photograph was taken at the Yalta Conference (1945), where Allied leaders met to discuss how to rebuild Europe after World War II. It shows (left to right) Winston Churchill of Great Britain, President Franklin D. Roosevelt of the U.S., and Joseph Stalin of the Soviet Union.

Hitler, Adolf

Adolf Hitler (1889 –1945) was the *Führer*, or leader, of **Germany** during **World War II**. An ex-soldier, born in **Austria**, Hitler became head of the Nazi Party, which took over Germany in 1933. At that time Germany was still weak after its defeat in **World War I**.

Under Hitler's leadership the Nazis promised to avenge this defeat and create a new German empire. In 1939 Hitler led Germany into World War II, conquering large parts of **Europe**—**Poland**, Austria, Czechoslovakia (see **Czech Republic** and **Slovakia**), the **Netherlands**, and much of **France**.

Hitler's policies were an extreme form of the political theory known as **fascism**. He held strongly racist views, and millions of Jews, gypsies, and others were killed in Nazi concentration camps. But by 1945 Germany had lost the war. Hitler killed himself in the ruins of **Berlin** to avoid being captured.

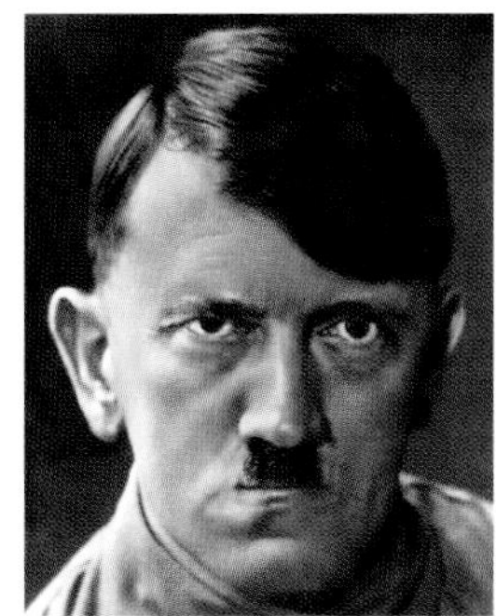

△ Adolf **Hitler** had a humble background but rose to become leader of the German Nazi Party. During political unrest in 1933 he was appointed chancellor of Germany.

HIV *see* AIDS

Hobby

Any activity that is enjoyed during your spare time is a hobby. It can be collecting things such as **stamps**, **coins**, or **rocks**. It can be a creative hobby such as **drawing**, **painting**, **photography**, or **weaving**. Or it can be an activity such as **chess**, **tennis**, **swimming**, or **sailing**. Part of the fun of any hobby is enjoying it with other people who share your interest.

△ Skateboarding is a **hobby** that has grown in popularity in recent years. Avid skateboarders learn how to perform special moves and tricks.

Holland *see* Netherlands

Holography

Holography is a way of making realistic, three-dimensional pictures called holograms. It is done by using **laser** light instead of a **camera**.

To make a hologram a laser beam is split into two. One beam hits the object and is reflected onto a photographic plate, and the other beam, angled by **mirrors**, strikes the plate directly. The photographic plate is developed, and a black-and-white pattern, the hologram, appears. When the hologram is lit up by a laser beam and viewed from the other side, it produces a three-dimensional image of the original object. The image seems real, with width, depth, and height, but it is not in the object's original **color**. Instead the hologram takes its color from the laser beam.

Holography was not developed until the 1960s, and scientists are still looking at practical uses for the technology. For example, holograms could prove to be useful in **medicine** as a way of probing the human body.

Holy Roman Empire

For over 700 years a large part of **Europe** was loosely united as the Holy Roman Empire. At different times the empire included **Italy**, **Germany**, and **Austria** and parts of the **Netherlands**, **France,** and **Switzerland**. The first emperor of the Romans was the French

▽ The emperors of the **Holy Roman Empire** had the right to be crowned by the pope in Rome.

king **Charlemagne**, who was crowned by **Pope** Leo III (d. 816) on December 25, 800. The word "holy" was not added to the emperor's title until later. After a while the popes began to have more trouble than help from the emperors, and there were many disputes between the empire and the Roman Catholic Church. By the end of the 1400s most of the emperors were from the **Hapsburg** royal family of Austria. As some German states grew larger and stronger in the 1500s the emperors began to lose power. By the 1800s the emperor was really only in control of Austria and **Hungary**.

△ Homer's *Odyssey* tells how Odysseus and his men encountered the Sirens, three female monsters whose beautiful voices lured sailors to their doom on the rocky coastline. Odysseus had himself tied to the mast of his ship, and his men plugged their ears so they would not be tempted.

Homer

Homer was a poet and storyteller in ancient **Greece**. He probably lived in around 700 B.C., but we know little else about him. All that is left are two great poems said to be created by Homer, the *Iliad* and the *Odyssey*. These poems tell us much of what we know about ancient Greek **history** and **myths**. The *Iliad* tells the story of the **Trojan War**, and the *Odyssey* recounts the adventures of Odysseus, a Greek hero.

Honduras

Honduras is a mountainous country in **Central America**. It has a long coastline with the **Caribbean** Sea and a shorter one with the **Pacific Ocean**. About one third of the land is covered with tropical **rain forest**s. Most of the population are farmers. They live mainly in small villages in the west of the country and near the large banana plantations on the northern coast.

In 1502 the explorer Christopher **Columbus** arrived in Honduras, and the country became a colony of **Spain**. Honduras declared its independence in 1821 and became a **republic** in 1838.

HONDURAS
Government: Republic
Capital: Tegucigalpa
Area: 43,100 sq. mi.
Population: 6,406,052
Language: Spanish
Currency: Lempira

Hong Kong

Hong Kong is a 408 sq. mi. (1,046 sq. km) area in southeastern **China**. Part of it is a small **island**, and the rest is a strip of land called the New Territories on the mainland. The **United Kingdom** governed Hong Kong from 1842 until 1997 when it was returned to China. Since then it has been a Special Administrative Region of China.

Hong Kong has a very large natural harbor surrounded by **mountains**—Hong Kong means "fragrant harbor." The capital is Victoria, and another busy city is Kowloon. Many of the people work in **trade**, **fishing**, and manufacturing. Tall apartment blocks have been built for housing, but there is still little room for the millions of people who crowd this small area.

Hoof

A hoof is the hard covering of **horn** that protects the feet of some **mammals**. **Animals** with hooves are divided into two main groups—those with an even number of toes and those with an odd

△ **Hong Kong** is one of Asia's leading centers of shipping, commerce, and manufacturing.

number of toes. The animals with an even number of toes include **deer**, **antelopes**, **cattle**, **goats**, **camels**, **pigs**, and **sheep**. All these species have either two or four toes. Animals with only one toe include **horses** and **zebras**. Domestic horses have their hooves cut and trimmed and wear iron horseshoes.

▽ Although a horse's **hoof** (below) is made of tough horn, it can still be worn down by walking on hard surfaces such as roads. This is why many horses wear horseshoes.

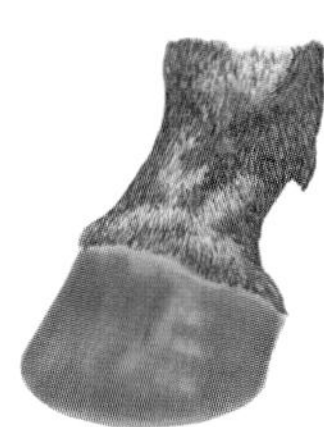

Hormone

Hormones are chemical messengers found in all **animals** and **plants**. In many animals hormones are produced in organs called **glands**, which are found in several parts of the body. From these glands the different hormones are carried in the **blood** to other parts of the body.

The pituitary gland, located in the center of our brain, produces several hormones. These "master" hormones control the hormone secretion of several other glands. The thyroid gland in the neck, for example, is stimulated by the pituitary gland to produce a hormone that controls how quickly **food** is used up by the body. Too little of this hormone makes people overweight. The hormone adrenalin is produced in the adrenal glands, just above the **kidneys**. It is controlled by **nerve** impulses and released when we are scared or excited. When adrenalin flows, the **heart** beats faster, blood pressure rises, and the body prepares itself for strenuous physical exertion.

Many hormones can now be made in laboratories. They are then used to help people suffering from **diseases** caused by the lack of certain hormones. **Insulin** is a hormone used to treat diabetes, a disease in which too much **sugar** stays in the blood.

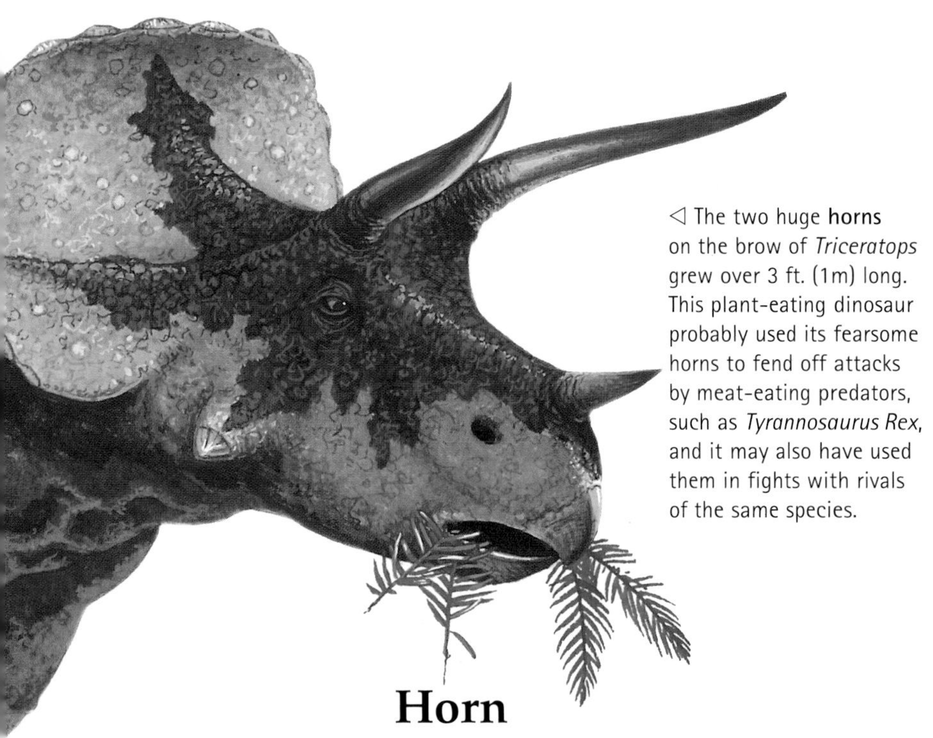

◁ The two huge **horns** on the brow of *Triceratops* grew over 3 ft. (1m) long. This plant-eating dinosaur probably used its fearsome horns to fend off attacks by meat-eating predators, such as *Tyrannosaurus Rex*, and it may also have used them in fights with rivals of the same species.

Horn

Horn is a form of hard **skin**. Human finger and toe**nails** are made of horn, as are the **feathers** and beaks of **birds** and the scales of **reptiles**. In addition, many animals grow horns—bony growths covered with a layer of horn and attached to the animal's skull. **Cattle**, **sheep**, **goats**, and most **antelopes** have curved horns. **Deer** horns are branched antlers made of bone covered with skin. Every year the antlers fall off, and a new set grows back in its place.

▽ **Horses** are built for speed, and even young foals are able to gallop. No one knows when horses were first tamed, but they were being used for riding and pulling carts in Egypt and central Asia around 5,000 years ago.

Horse

The horse was one of the first wild animals to be tamed. Today there are only a few wild horses left such as Przewalski's horse, which lives in the remote grasslands of **Mongolia** and northern **China**. Many so-called "wild" horses, such as the mustangs of **North America**, are actually descended from domestic horses that have run wild.

The horse is valued for its speed and strength. But the earliest kind of horse was a small, doglike creature with a way of life unlike that of modern horses. Called *Eohippus*, it lived millions of years ago. It had four toes on its front feet and three toes on its back feet, and it was small enough to hide from its enemies in the undergrowth.

Later horses began to live on the open plains. There was no undergrowth in which to hide, so they escaped from enemies by running away. Gradually their legs grew longer, and they lost all their toes except one. Finally after millions of years of **evolution** the modern horse appeared. It, too, has only one toe on each foot and actually runs on tiptoe. Its toe has become a **hoof**.

Horseback riding

People have been riding horses since around 3000 B.C. Horses remained the fastest form of transportation until the 1820s, when the first regular **railroads** were developed. Today farmers and ranchers still use horses to carry out their work in some parts of the world, but many people ride horses simply for pleasure. It takes a great deal of skill to ride a horse well.

One of the most important things a rider must learn is how to tell a horse what to do. There are two kinds of signals used for this. The first, called natural aids, are given by hand, leg, and voice commands. The second are artificial aids. These include using crops and spurs. Command signals must be given smoothly and correctly, otherwise the horse will become confused about what its rider wants it to do. People can test their horseback-riding skills by taking part in shows and events.

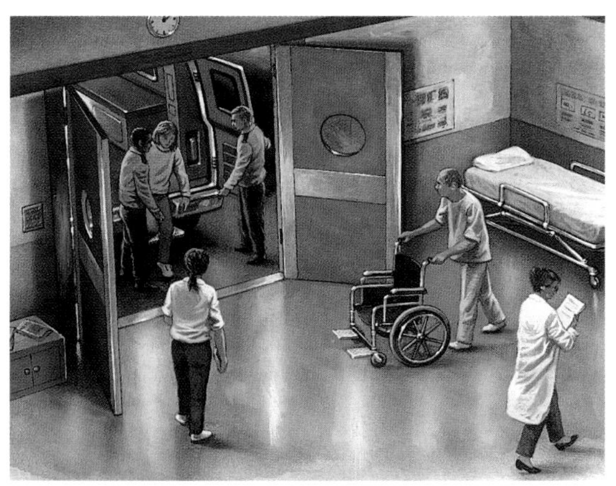

Many modern **hospitals** are huge organizations that employ hundreds of people doing all kinds of jobs. Running a large hospital is an extremely costly and complicated exercise.

Hospital

Hospitals are places where sick people, or patients, are cared for. Doctors and nurses take care of the patients and try to make them better.

There are two main types of hospitals. One, the general hospital, deals with everything from accidental injuries to infectious **diseases**. The other type of hospital specializes in certain conditions. For example, there are psychiatric hospitals for people who are mentally ill; maternity hospitals where women give birth; and geriatric hospitals for the elderly. In hospitals attached to medical schools student doctors gain experience through treating real patients.

In ancient times temples dedicated to the gods of healing used to have a hospital area. Sick people came there to pray and be treated. Later in the **Middle Ages** hospitals attached to **monasteries** were run by monks and nuns. But over the last 200 years nonreligious hospitals have become the most common. Some people have insurance that pays for their hospital care. Other people rely on the government to pay for their care. Health care is one of the main things on which **governments** spend the **money** that they have raised through **taxes**.

Hotel

Hotels are places where travelers or tourists can stay. Before 1800 there were no hotels as we now know them. Travelers spent the night at taverns or inns. Wherever people traveled there were inns that gave food and shelter to travelers and their horses. Today large hotels are like small towns and provide a wide range of facilities such as swimming pools, restaurants, and stores.

△ Some of the world's first **hotels** sprang up in the U.S., such as this one in San Francisco, California, which was built in around 1850.

House

The first houses were simple shelters made of mud, branches, leaves, or animal hides. Later, people learned how to make bricks by drying wet **clay** in the sun. For thousands of years brick, **wood**, and stone were the materials from which almost all houses were built.

Modern houses are built to keep out cold, drafts, and rain and to keep in warmth. Storm windows and insulation in the roof and walls help do this. Many homes have heating systems and, in hot **climates**, air-conditioning. In crowded cities homes are built on top of one another to form blocks of apartments.

▽ **House** design has gone through major changes, but there are still certain basic similarities between modern houses and the shelters of our earliest ancestors. For example, all houses must provide a way of cooking food, some form of heating, a water supply, and a method of dealing with waste.

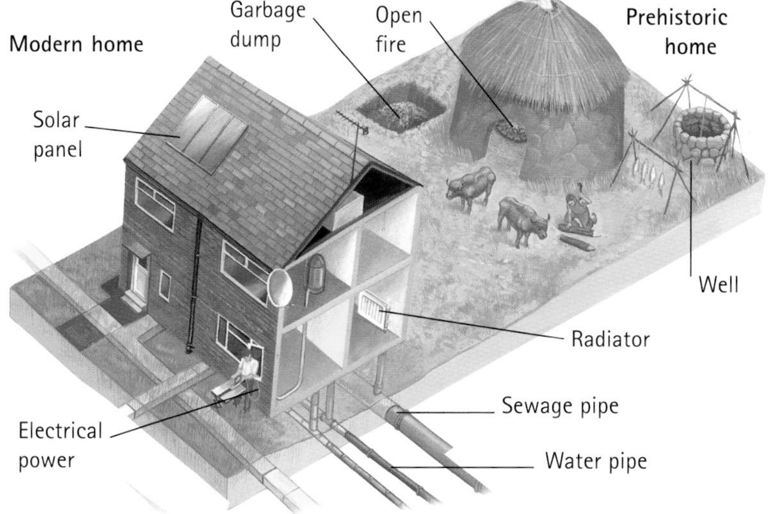

Hovercraft

Propeller

Fan

Flexible rubber skirt

△ A **hovercraft** has fans on each side that suck in air and push it underneath the craft to lift it up. Extra fans at the rear propel the vehicle forward.

A hovercraft is a type of vehicle that rides on a cushion of **air**. The air is blown down by fans and held in by a skirt or side wall around the craft. Hovercrafts work best over **water** but can also cross beaches and flat land. They are much faster than ordinary **ships**. Since they do not have to push against the water but can skim smoothly through the air, they can easily reach speeds of 74 mph (120km/h). Their advantage over **aircraft** is the size of the load they can carry. A large hovercraft can hold dozens of cars and up to 400 passengers.

Human beings

Human beings are **mammals**, and we are very similar to our closest relatives, the **apes**. We have the same kind of **blood**, **bones**, **muscles**, and organs. But the main difference between humans and any other **animal** is the size of our **brain**. The human brain is enormous compared to our body size. Humans use their brains to think, and when they have found a solution to a problem, they can talk about it with other humans. This is why humans are the most successful animal alive today. All people belong to the same species, which is classified as *Homo sapiens* ("thinking man").

△ The tiny ruby-throated **hummingbird** nests across the eastern U.S. and flies to Central America for the winter. This is a remarkable feat for such a small bird.

▽ **Human beings** are descended from apelike animals that lived in Africa about four million years ago. These creatures gradually evolved (changed) into modern humans.

15 million years ago — 4 million years ago — 2 million years ago — 1.5 million years ago — 130,000 years ago — 100,000 years ago

Human body

The human body is just like a **machine** with many parts. Each part has a special job, and all the parts work together to keep you alive and healthy. Like all machines your body needs fuel, which it gets in the form of **food**. The **oxygen** you breathe in from the **air** helps turn the food you eat into **energy**, which allows you to work, think, and grow.

Your body is made up of millions of tiny **cells**. A group of cells that work together is called tissue. For example, cells that allow you to lift things are called **muscle** tissue. Tissues that work together make up an organ. The **heart** is an organ that pumps **blood**. Other organs are the **brain**, **ears**, **eyes**, **liver**, **lungs**, **stomach**, and **skin**.

Organs that work together are called systems. You have a **digestion** system (the mouth, **stomach**, and intestines), a circulatory system (the heart, **arteries**, and **veins**), and a nervous system (the brain and **nerves**). The study of the human body is called anatomy.

Hummingbird

Hummingbirds are among the smallest **birds** in the world. They are only found in the Western Hemisphere. Nineteen varieties live in the U.S.

The tiniest of the 320 different species is the bee hummingbird of **Cuba**, which measures less than 2 in. (5cm) in length.

Hummingbirds can beat their wings up to 70 times per second. This is what causes their distinctive humming sound. It also allows hummingbirds to hover in midair and to fly backward and sideways like **helicopters**. In this way the birds dart from **flower** to flower and feed while flying. They drink the sweet nectar and eat tiny **insects** from deep within the cups of flowers.

Hundred Years' War

England and **France** were at war almost without a break from 1337 until 1453. This period is called the Hundred Years' War. The war was started by English King Edward III (1312–1377), who thought that he was the rightful heir to the French crown. Edward assembled an army, which landed in France in 1346. His foot soldiers and archers defeated the French at Crécy in 1346 and at Poitiers in 1356.

A treaty was signed in 1360, but the war started again in 1369. In the early 1400s **Henry V** of England decided to try again for the French crown. He invaded northern France in 1415, and at the Battle of Agincourt his bowmen mowed down the French cavalry. A new peace treaty was signed in 1422.

Henry married the daughter of the French king and was named heir to the French throne. But the two kings died, and war broke out again. This time the French were led by a young peasant girl, **Joan of Arc**. By 1453 the English had been driven from all of their lands in France except for the town of Calais.

Hungary

Hungary is a landlocked country in central **Europe**. The Danube River flows across the country on its way to the Black Sea, almost dividing it in two. **Ships** can sail upriver as far as Budapest, the capital and largest city. Hungary is low-lying and fairly flat. To the east it becomes a vast grassy plain where herds of **sheep**, **cattle**, and **horses** graze. **Farming** is important, but more of the people work in **mining** and manufacturing than on farms.

When the Austro-Hungarian empire collapsed after **World War I**, Hungary became an independent **republic**. In 1956 the Soviet Union imposed **communism** on Hungary but in 1989 a more democratic system was introduced.

HUNGARY
Government: Republic
Capital: Budapest
Area: 35,600 sq. mi.
Population: 10,106,017
Language: Hungarian
Currency: Forint

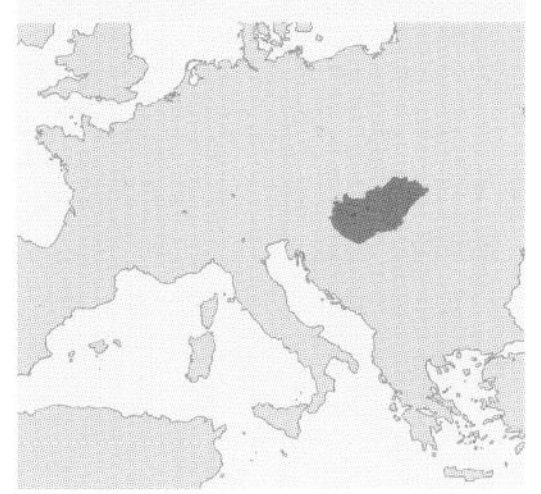

Huns

The Huns were a group of wandering warriors who swept into **Europe** in around 400 B.C. from the plains of central **Asia**. They conquered large parts of **Germany** and **France**. Their most famous general was Attila, who attacked **Rome** and nearly destroyed the **Roman Empire**. However, the Huns' power declined suddenly after Attila's death in 453 B.C.

Hunting

Hunting was the main way in which prehistoric humans survived, and in ancient times, in places such as **China** and **Egypt**, it became a popular sport for wealthy people. Nowadays hunting is an activity that is mainly carried out to provide a source of **food** or to control pests. Growing numbers of people around the world want to preserve wild animals, not kill them (see also **conservation**).

▽ **Hunting** was a very popular sport for wealthy people in ancient China. All kinds of game was caught, either shot with a bow and arrow or chased by hounds, cheetahs, and falcons.

Hurricane

A hurricane is a severe storm. To be called a hurricane a storm must have **wind** speeds of at least 74 mph (120km/h). Hurricanes form over **oceans** near the **equator** where the **air** is very moist. Hurricanes in the **Pacific Ocean** are known as typhoons, and those in the **Indian Ocean** are called cyclones.

During a hurricane winds whirl around in a great circle and may reach speeds of over 198 mph (320km/h). The largest hurricanes have measured 992 mi. (1,600km) across. At the center of the hurricane is a narrow column of air that spins very slowly. This is called the "eye" of the hurricane.

If a hurricane reaches the coast, it may cause immense damage to buildings and property. However, **satellite** pictures help scientists predict the route a hurricane will take, which usually gives people enough time to evacuate the area.

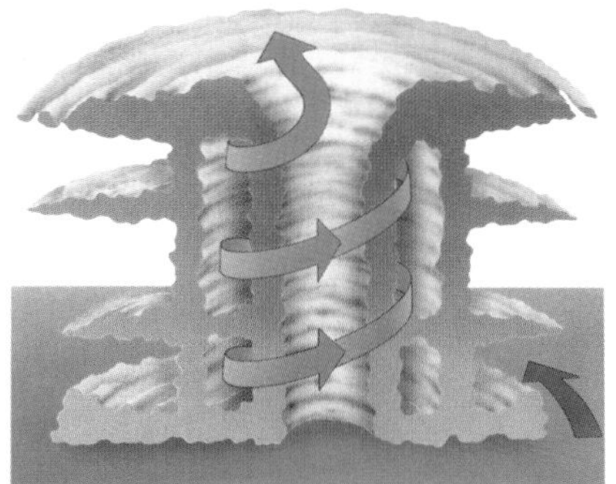

△ **Hurricane** winds spiral up at great speeds within a wall of storm clouds. They rotate around a narrow central column of slow-moving air.

Hydroelectric power

More than one fifth of the world's **electricity** is produced using the **energy** of fast-flowing **water**. This is called hydroelectric power. Most hydroelectric plants are found below artificial **dams**, but some are powered by natural **waterfalls**.

Water is heavy, and when it falls through large pipes from a high dam it can be made to turn the paddle-shaped blades of **turbines**. Shafts connected to the blades turn electric **generators** such as those in **coal**- or **oil**-fired **power plant**s.

△ **Hydrofoils** can travel faster than other boats because of their "wings" that lift them out of the water. They are mainly used for short-distance express passenger services.

Hydrofoil

Much of the **engine** power of a **ship** is used to overcome the drag of the **water** around the vessel's hull, or underside. A hydrofoil solves this with underwater "wings," called foils, which lift the craft right out of the water. The wings are attached to the hull of the hydrofoil at the bow (front) and the stern (back), and they lift the hull as the craft gathers speed. As the water's drag diminishes, the hydrofoil shoots ahead, traveling much faster than an ordinary boat can.

Hydrogen

Hydrogen is a **gas**. It is believed to be the most abundant **element** in the whole **universe** and is the single most important material from which **stars**, including our **sun**, are made.

Hydrogen is the lightest of all the elements—it is more than 14 times lighter than **air**. It is colorless and has neither **smell** nor **taste**. Hydrogen burns very easily. Huge volumes of hydrogen are always being burned in the sun. It is this fierce burning that gives us **light** and **heat** on **earth**.

Hydrogen is a very important part of the bodies of all **plants** and **animals**. It is also contained in fossil fuels—**coal**, **oil**, and **natural gas**. At one time hydrogen was used to fill airships (see **balloon and airship**), but because hydrogen catches on fire easily, it proved to be too dangerous for this purpose.

△ The spotted **hyena** lives in southern Africa. It has a loud cry that resembles human laughter.

Hyena

Hyenas are four species of meat-eating **mammals**. Although they have a similar shape to **dogs**, they are more closely related to the **cat** family. Hyenas often scavenge their meals from the kills of other animals, such as **lions**, **leopards**, and **cheetahs**, although they sometimes make kills of their own. They have very powerful **teeth** and jaws for crushing the **bones** and making the most of their source of leftover food.

Hyenas are found in parts of **Africa** and southern **Asia** and live in groups called packs. They feed at night and spend the day resting in holes or caves.

Ice ages

The ice ages were times when huge sheets of ice covered parts of **earth**. Each period lasted for thousands of years. In between were warmer periods. The last Ice Age ended about 20,000 years ago, but the ice might return.

During the ice ages the **weather** was very cold. Endless snow fell, and **glaciers** formed and spread. At times the glaciers covered much of **North America, Asia,** and **Europe** as far south as southern **England**. In some places the ice piled up more than 3,280 ft. (1,000m) high.

The sea level was lower during the ice ages than now. A land bridge formed between North America and Asia, and the first people to live in the Americas crossed this "bridge" from Asia.

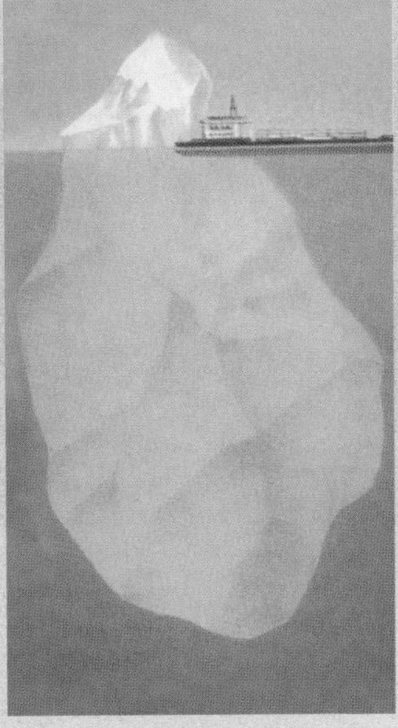

△ **Icebergs** pose a serious threat to shipping because they extend far below the waterline. Some icebergs reach as far as 3,116 ft. (950m) beneath the surface.

Iceberg

An iceberg is a chunk of a **glacier** or an ice shelf that has broken away and is floating in the **ocean**. The iceberg floats because when **water** freezes, it expands, so ice is less dense than water. Only part of the iceberg is visible—most of it is hidden under the water's surface. Icebergs are found in the freezing waters of the **Antarctic** and **Arctic**.

Icebergs can be very large—some weigh millions of tons and may be up to 93 mi. (150km) long. They provide an ideal resting place for **penguins** and **seals** but are dangerous to **ships**. Sometimes they float south from the Arctic into the **Atlantic Ocean**, and on the night of April 14–15, 1912 a liner called the *Titanic* hit an iceberg in the North Atlantic on her maiden voyage. The ship sank, and about 1,500 of the passengers and crew drowned.

Ice hockey

Ice hockey is a team **sport** played on an ice rink that is 197 ft. (60m) long and 85 ft. (26m) wide, with a goal at either end. The players, six per team, wear ice skates and hold a long-handled stick with a curved blade at the bottom. They use this to drive the puck, a rubber disk, around the rink. Both teams try to shoot the puck past the opposing team's defense and into their goal nets. Each game is divided into three 20-minute periods. Ice hockey is a fast-moving sport, and the players must wear padded clothing for protection.

▽ During the **ice ages** animals and early humans had to cope with bitterly cold conditions. Many of the mammals developed thick coats of shaggy fur to keep them warm.

Iceland

Iceland is a mountainous island that lies just south of the **Arctic** in the north **Atlantic Ocean** between **Norway** and **Greenland**. Warm waters from the **Gulf Stream** keep most of the country's harbors free of ice all year.

Iceland is a volcanic island with numerous **volcanoes** and hot springs. Water from some of the springs is used to heat homes. The northern part of the island is covered by **glaciers** and a wilderness of stone and lava (cooled volcanic matter).

Iceland was discovered by the **Vikings** in A.D. 874. Today most of the population live in the south and east where the land is lower. They live by **farming** and **fishing**. Iceland became an independent country in 1944 after breaking its ties with **Denmark**.

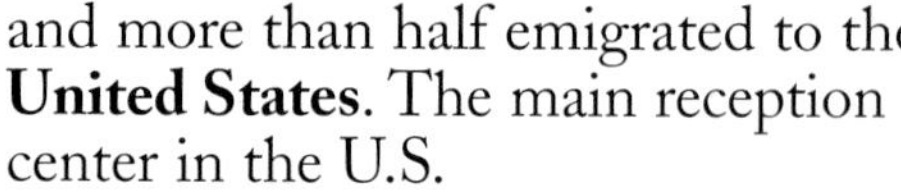

△ **Impressionism** was a style of art in which loose brushstrokes were used to give the impression of a scene. This painting of a field of poppies was made in 1873 by Claude Monet, one of the best-known impressionist painters.

ICELAND
Government: Republic
Capital: Reykjavik
Area: 38,700 sq. mi.
Population: 277,906
Language: Icelandic
Currency: Krona

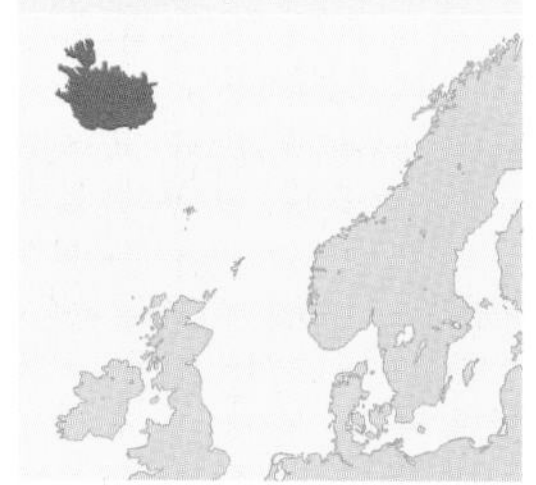

Immigration

Immigration is when people settle in a country in which they were not born. Throughout **history** millions of people have traveled to live in new lands. The act of leaving one's country in this way is called emigration.

People leave their native country, or emigrate, for many different reasons. Sometimes they are fleeing persecution, **war**, or natural disasters such as **famine** or outbreaks of **disease**. People who emigrate for these reasons are known as refugees. Sometimes people emigrate because they hope to improve their standard of living. Some of the heaviest immigration in history occurred during the early 1800s until the 1930s. About 60 million people moved to new countries. Most moved from **Europe**, and more than half emigrated to the **United States**. The main reception center in the U.S. at that time was Ellis Island, near **New York** City. The other countries that people emigrated to in this period included **Australia** and **South Africa**.

Immunity

Immunity is the name for the long-term protection against **diseases** that are acquired by **animals**, including **humans**. People develop immunity through their immune system. This constantly cleans the **blood** and body tissues and attacks invading germs (see **bacteria**). When the body detects the presence of germs, it immediately fights them. It produces antibodies—substances that attack certain disease-causing germs. These antibodies stay in the body to stop more of the same germs from invading again. For example, if you have had measles, you are unlikely to catch it again.

Vaccination is a process that allows us to acquire immunity to diseases that we have never caught previously.

The doctor or nurse puts a substance in our body that contains a tiny amount of a particular type of germ. This is often done by means of a shot. The quantity of germs we are given is far too small for us to become sick, but our bodies still produce antibodies to fight the germs. From then on our body is protected against these germs.

Impressionism

In the 1860s in **France** some artists began to paint in a new way. Instead of working indoors they started to paint outside in the open air. They painted scenes from nature and everyday life rather than grand historical scenes and tried to capture the ever-changing **light**.

In 1874 the group held an exhibition in **Paris**. Their **art** was laughed at, and one **newspaper** poked fun at a **painting** called *Impression: Sunrise* (1872) by Claude Monet (1840–1926). It called the group "Impressionists," and the name stuck. However, before long people began to appreciate the lively style of the Impressionists. In addition to Monet, the leading Impressionists were Edouard Manet (1832–1883), Camille Pissarro (1830–1903), Edgar Degas (1834–1917), Alfred Sisley (1839–1899), and Pierre Auguste Renoir (1841–1919).

Inca

The Inca were a people who ruled a great empire in **South America** from the 1200s until the 1500s. In the 1400s the empire grew until it stretched almost 1,984 mi. (3,200km) along the west coast of South America from present-day **Ecuador** to **Chile**. The center of the empire was in **Peru**.

The Incan king and his nobles ruled over the people in the empire. They laid down strict rules and told the farmers and craftsmen what to grow and make. The Inca built many **roads** through their lands.

In the 1500s Spanish soldiers led by Francisco Pizarro (c. 1478–1541) reached South America. They captured the Incan king Atahualpa (c. 1500–1533) and said they would free him in return for **gold**. The Inca brought treasures to free the king, but the Spanish still killed him. By 1569 the Spanish had conquered the whole empire.

India

India is a large country in southern **Asia**. It has a **population** of about one billion—only **China** has more people. To the north of India are the snowy peaks of the **Himalayas**. Many people live in the fertile northern plains, which are crossed by the great **Ganges** and Brahmaputra **rivers**. The south has high, flat land with **mountains** called the Ghats along the coast.

India is very hot and dry in the summer. Parts of the country are almost **desert**like. But **winds** called **monsoons** bring heavy rain to the northeast every year. The Shillong Plateau in eastern India is one of the wettest places in the world, with an average of 424 in. (1,087cm) of rain per year.

Most Indians are farmers who live in villages, growing **rice, wheat, tea, cotton**, and jute, a natural fiber used to make sacks and rope.

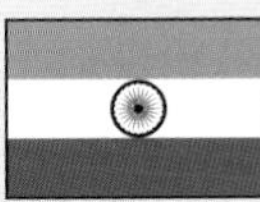

INDIA
Government: Federal republic
Capital: New Delhi
Area: 1,146,600 sq. mi.
Population: 1,029,991,145
Languages: Hindi, English, and others
Currency: Rupee

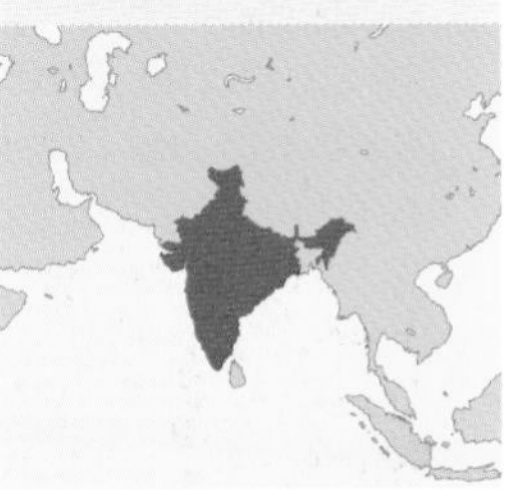

▽ The **Inca** were skilled engineers and constructed a network of roads that covered all of their empire. They even built highways in the Andes mountains.

India also has fast-growing industries. Its many bustling cities, such as Kolkata (Calcutta) and Mumbai (Bombay), are among the world's largest. Hindi and English are the two main **languages**, but there are many others. Most Indians practice **Hinduism**, but many follow **Islam**. There are also many other **religions** in India, including **Buddhism** and **Christianity**.

British trading companies began to visit India in the 1600s, and it became a British colony during the 1800s. In 1920 Mohandas **Gandhi** began a campaign against British rule, and in 1947 India won independence. The British **government** divided its former colony into two countries—India and **Pakistan**.

Indian Ocean

The Indian Ocean is the world's third largest **ocean**, with an area of 26,665 sq. mi. (73,500,000 sq km). It stretches from **Africa** in the west to **Indonesia** and **Australia** in the east. Two very large islands lie in the ocean—**Madagascar**, off southeastern Africa, and **Sri Lanka**, off the southern tip of **India**. Strong **winds** from the ocean, called **monsoons**, bring heavy rainfall to **Southeast Asia** each summer. The ocean's warm waters support large **coral** reefs.

Indonesia

INDONESIA
Government: Republic
Capital: Jakarta
Area: 704,400 sq. mi.
Population: 228,437,870
Language: Bahasa Indonesian and others
Currency: Rupiah

Indonesia is a country in **Southeast Asia**. It is a chain of over 3,000 **islands** around the **equator**. The islands stretch over a distance of 2,976 mi. (4,800km).

More than half of Indonesia's people live on Java, where the capital, Jakarta, is located. Most of the people are farmers, and major crops include **rice**, **tea**, **rubber**, and **tobacco**. Indonesia also produces **oil** and other resources as well as timber from its **forests**.

Parts of Indonesia became a colony of the **Netherlands** in the late 1700s, but the country gained independence in 1949. Indonesia formerly included East Timor, but in 1999 the people of East Timor voted to break away and form a new independent state.

Industrial Revolution

The Industrial Revolution is the name given to the great changes that took place in **Europe** in the 1700s and 1800s when people began to use **machines** to make goods in factories instead of by hand at home.

▽ The new factories of the **Industrial Revolution** were built near canals and railroads so that raw materials could be brought in and finished goods could be taken to markets easily. Factory owners built houses and schools for the workers, but many industrial areas turned into slums.

The new machines were run by **steam engines** and could produce things much faster than people could by hand. **Mining** and **metal**working became more important, and the first regular **railroads** were constructed. Many people moved from the country and began to work in factories in the fast-growing towns. Another reason why people moved to urban areas was the major changes taking place in **farming**. Improved methods of growing and harvesting crops meant that fewer workers were needed on the farms.

Inflation

Inflation is a word used to mean rapidly rising prices. Every time prices go up **money** is worth less because people need more money to buy the same things. As a result, people ask for higher wages. If wages rise, then the cost of making things in factories goes up. This often makes prices rise again. Because prices and wages affect each other like this inflation is hard to stop. There are many reasons why inflation starts. If inflation becomes high, money can become worthless.

Some countries have experienced hyperinflation, when prices increase by over 50 percent every month. This means an inflation rate of over 13,000 percent a year.

△ After World War I **inflation** in Germany was so high that it was called hyperinflation. The value of the German currency—the mark—was reduced to almost nothing. In late 1923 a loaf of bread cost 200 billion marks. Workers took their wages home in wheelbarrows, and children played with stacks of worthless notes.

Infrared rays

When you feel the **heat** from **fire** or the **sun**, you are feeling infrared rays. They are called infrared because they lie just beyond the red end of the **light spectrum**. This means that we cannot see infrared rays, although they behave in the same way as visible light rays. For example, they can be reflected.

Photographers use a special type of film that is sensitive to infrared rays to take pictures in total darkness (see also **photography**). Infrared-sensitive film can be used to take pictures in which hot and cold areas show up as different colors. White areas are the hottest, and blue are the coolest.

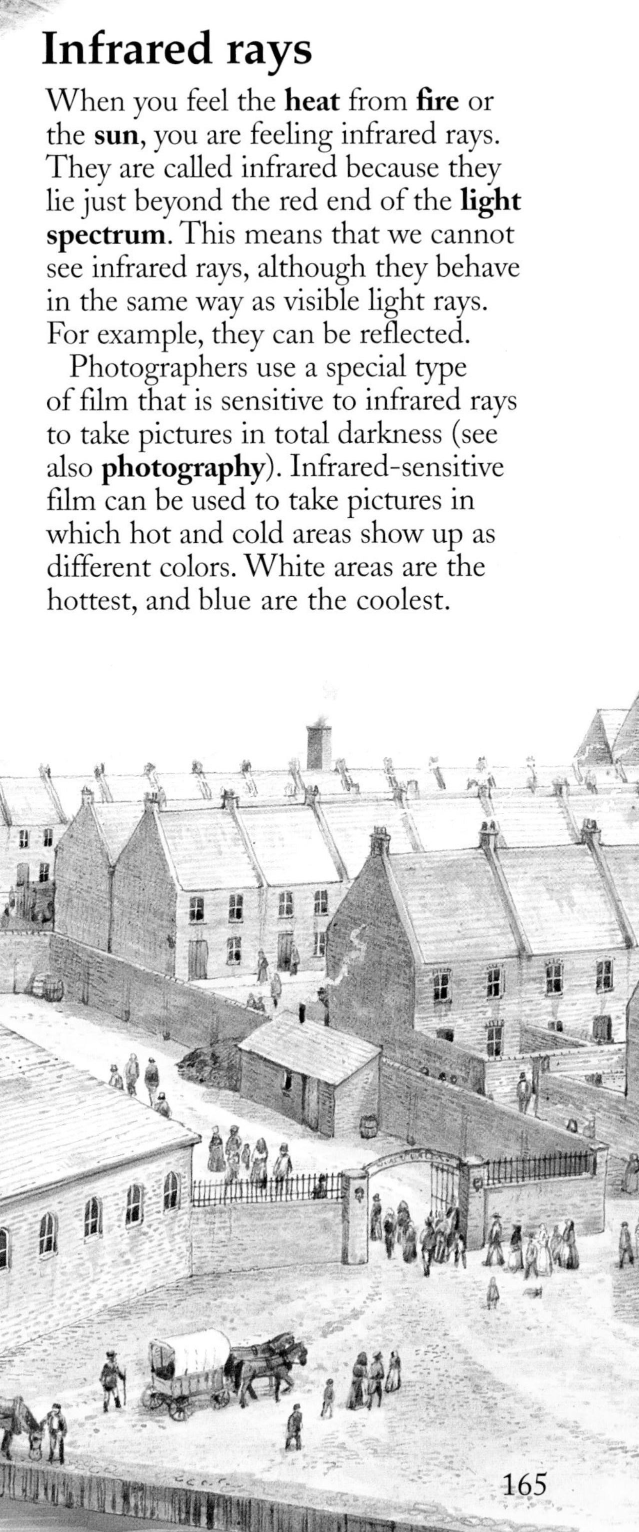

INSECTS

There are insects all over the world except in the sea. Their bodies are divided into three parts, and they have six jointed legs.

Male stag beetles have large jaws that are used in fights over females.

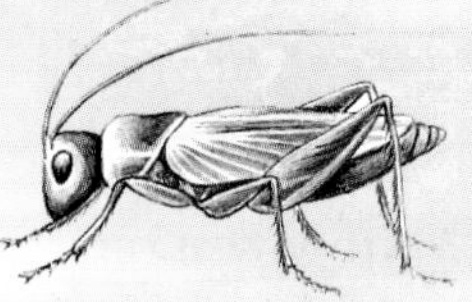

Crickets have long back legs for hopping and rub their wings together to chirp loudly to attract a mate.

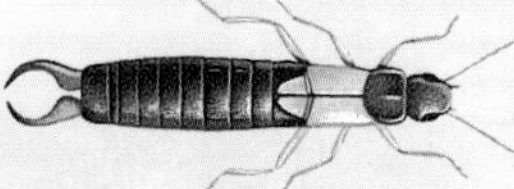

Earwigs are flat with pincers at the end of their tails and have wings that fold away.

Aphids have soft green or brown bodies and are less than 0.12 in. (3mm) in length.

▷ *Bumblebees are social insects that collect the pollen from flowers and store it in pollen sacks on their back legs. The pollen is used as food for the colony.*

Common wasp

Abdomen

An insect's legs are made up of small segments and flexible joints.

Thorax

Most winged insects have two pairs of wings.

Head

Antennae provide insects with a sense of smell.

Many insects have large compound eyes with hundreds of tiny lenses.

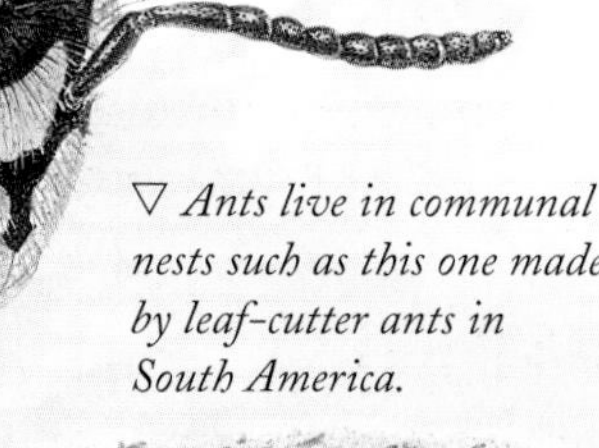

▽ *Ants live in communal nests such as this one made by leaf-cutter ants in South America.*

WORLD OF INSECTS

There are more than three million different kinds of insects, ranging from tiny fleas that can only be seen through a microscope, to 5-in. (13-cm) -long Goliath beetles. Insects are split into about 29 groups, including bees, flies, ants, grasshoppers, beetles, and butterflies.

All insects have three body parts—the head, the thorax, and the abdomen—and three pairs of legs, which are joined to the thorax. Most insects also have two pairs of wings. The body of every insect is covered with a tough body case called an exoskeleton.

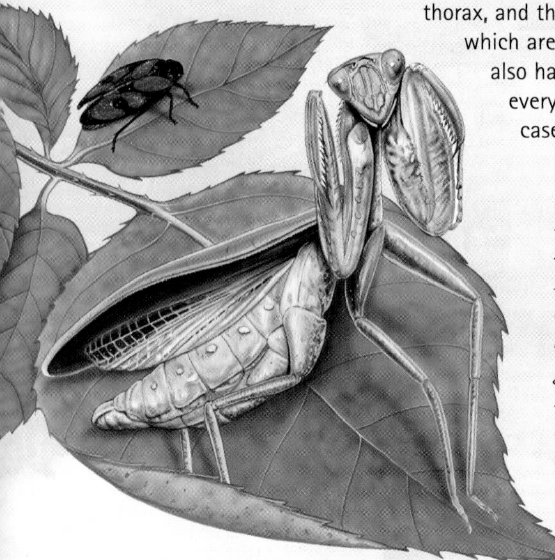

▽ *The praying mantis (below, right) is a fierce predator. It uses its huge front legs to grab prey such as beetles.*

▷ *An insect, such as this housefly, has four stages in its life cycle. It begins with an egg, which turns into a larva. The larva grows by shedding its skin and forms a chrysalis, or pupa. This finally splits open to reveal an adult.*

SOCIAL LIFE

Some insects, including ants, bees, and termites, live in large, highly organized colonies. Each insect within the community has a job to do such as hunting for food, caring for the larvae, or guarding the nest. There is a queen in every group, and only she can lay eggs.

HELPERS AND PESTS

Without bees and other flying insects flowering plants would not be pollinated, and fruit trees would not bear fruit. Bees also give us honey. Scavenging insects, such as dung beetles, are useful because they feed on animal dung and help keep soil fertile. However, some insects are pests that cause damage to crops, while others carry diseases.

SEE ALSO
Ant, Bee, Beetle, Butterfly, Caterpillar, Flea, Fly, Grasshopper, Invertebrate, Locust, Mosquito, Moth, Parasite, Termite, Wasp

Instinct

People have to learn to read and write, but a newborn baby will grasp tightly enough with its hands to support its own weight. This kind of behavior is called an instinct. Parents pass on instincts to their offspring through heredity (see **genetics**).

Animals do many things by instinct. For example, **birds** build their **nests** this way. Some animals, such as **insects**, do almost everything by instinct. They have established ways of finding food, defending themselves against predators, or escaping. **Bees** and **wasps**, for example, sting as an instinctive reaction to danger. Species that act only by instinct are said to lack **intelligence**, and they cannot easily change their behavior.

Insulin

Insulin is a **hormone** that controls the body's use of **sugar**. It is produced in the pancreas **gland**. When not enough insulin is produced, the body cannot use or store sugar properly, resulting in a condition known as diabetes. Many people with diabetes have to give themselves daily shots of insulin.

Insurance

Insurance is a way of safeguarding against loss, damage, or injury. A person with an insurance policy pays a certain amount of **money** to an insurance **company** every year. If they lose or damage something they have insured, the company gives them money to replace it or to pay for its repair. It is possible to insure all kinds of property, including **houses** and other buildings. People often take out health insurance policies to pay for medical treatment should they become sick.

Internet *see* **pages 168–169**

Intelligence

When a person uses experience and knowledge to solve a new kind of problem, they are showing intelligence. Intelligence depends on being able to learn. Creatures that act only by **instinct** lack intelligence. **Human beings**, **apes**, **dolphins**, and **whales** are the most intelligent **animals**.

△ A herring gull chick's natural **instinct** is to peck the red spot on its parent's beak. This encourages the parent to cough up food from its throat pouch for the chick to eat.

Inuit

The Inuit people live in the cold **Arctic** lands of **Greenland**, **North America**, and northeast **Asia**. At one time the Inuit lived in tents in the summer and built snow homes called igloos for the winter. They hunted in boats made of animal skin and canoes called kayaks and caught **fish** with harpoons. **Dogs** pulled their sleds. However, many Inuit no longer lead this kind of life.

Invention

An invention is the creation of something completely new. Many important inventions have come from

continued on page 170

▽ The **Inuit** hunters of Canada were probably the inventors of the igloo. It was built from blocks of frozen snow cut with an ivory-bladed snow knife. The gaps between the blocks were filled with loose snow.

INTERNET

The Internet is a globe-spanning computer network that gives people rapid access to information, knowledge, entertainment, and opinions from around the world.

△ *The Internet is a little like a library with a huge number of books—finding the web page you want can sometimes seem daunting. Search engines greatly speed up the process of locating web pages.*

LINKING COMPUTERS TOGETHER

A computer network is two or more computers linked in some way so that they can send and receive data (information) from each other. The world's largest computer network is the Internet, or "Net." Millions of computers can join the Internet using standard software. Internet users are able to share and exchange a variety of information, including images, sounds, and text messages.

EARLY DAYS

The Internet began in the U.S. in the late 1960s as a military communications system called ARPANet. This was a network of defense computers designed so that it could survive and continue working even if parts of the system were destroyed during a war. ARPANet gradually developed into the Internet, first as a way for scientists and academics to share information, and then by the early 1990s for the general public as well.

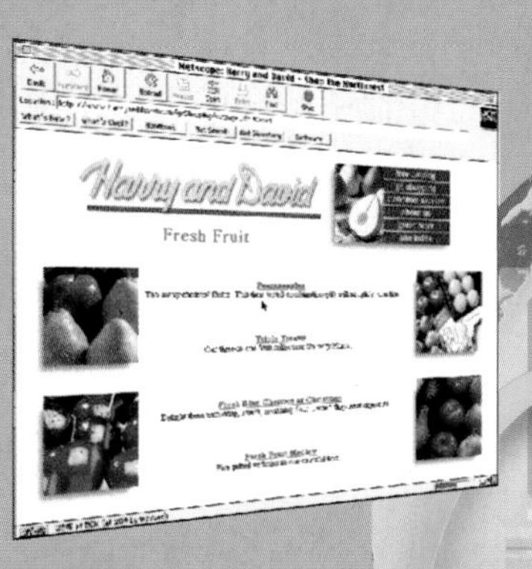

▽ *Many goods and services can be chosen, ordered, and paid for over the Internet.*

▽ *Today there are websites in many different languages, created by people and organizations all over the world.*

▽ *People can use the Internet to view live video clips such as these images from a recent NASA space mission.*

GETTING CONNECTED

Some computers have a permanent connection keeping the machines linked to the Internet all the time. However, most personal computers, or PCs, are not permanently linked. They need a device called a modem for this, and use a company called an Internet Service Provider (ISP) to gain access to the internet via a telephone line. The modem converts computer data into a signal that can be sent down a phone line. When receiving information from the Internet, the modem performs the opposite operation—it converts the phone signal into data that the computer can understand.

△ *Using E-mail, people can send messages to each other in minutes. Over nine billion E-mails are sent every day.*

△ *The Internet provides information on plays, movies, concerts, exhibitions, and many other forms of entertainment.*

THE INTERNET EXPLOSION

Connecting to the Internet is known as going online, and any computer connected to the Internet is called a host. The numbers of people using the Internet have risen sharply. In early 1981 there were just 213 hosts. By 1991 there were 376,000, and in 2001 the figure rose to over 130 million. People without access to the Internet at home, school, or work may rent a computer at a cybercafé for a small fee.

THE WORLD WIDE WEB

The World Wide Web allows people to surf the Net quickly and efficiently. It is a huge, linked collection of websites, which consist of separate web pages. Each web page is a document that has its own address known as a URL. By clicking on "hot spots" on the screen users can jump to different web pages.

SEE ALSO
Communication, Computer, Media, Telecommunication, Telephone

USES OF THE NET

A huge range of activities is carried out on the Internet, from education to online games that can link dozens of players. E-commerce occurs when companies do business over the Internet. Thousands of companies have websites that allow customers to view and order products online using a credit card. The ability of the World Wide Web to handle images and sound files has not just made websites more appealing to view. Museums can now show their exhibits on the Internet, while many radio stations release their programs in the form of sound files that people can download from the Internet.

△ *The Internet is often referred to as the "Information Superhighway" because it carries large amounts of computer data. It is also called cyberspace, a word first used in 1984 in William Gibson's science-fiction novel* Neuromancer.

HISTORY OF THE INTERNET

1965 Three computers are linked over a phone line in the U.S. to form an early computer network
1969 ARPANet created by U.S. military
1971 First E-mail sent
1974 Telenet, the first commercial version of ARPANet, starts running
1977 First modem for personal computers invented
1984 Domain name system, which gives computers a unique location ending in .com, .org, etc., is introduced
1991 World Wide Web invented
1994 Internet shops and banks set up
1998 First E-auctions on the Internet
2000 World Wide Web is estimated to contain over one billion web pages

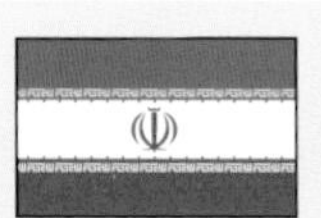

IRAN
Government: Islamic republic
Capital: Tehran
Area: 630,900 sq. mi.
Population: 66,128,965
Languages: Farsi (Persian) and others
Currency: Rial

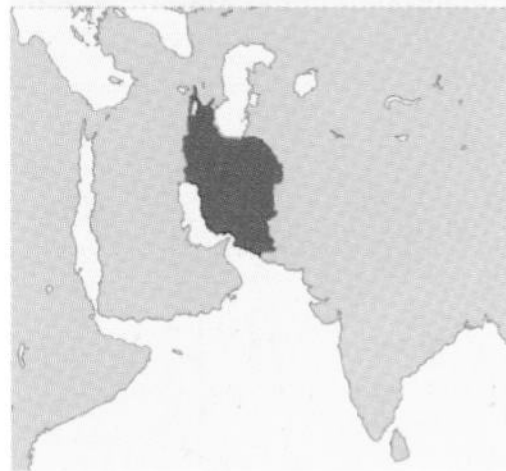

IRAQ
Government: One-party republic
Capital: Baghdad
Area: 167,400 sq. mi.
Population: 23,331,985
Language: Arabic
Currency: Dinar

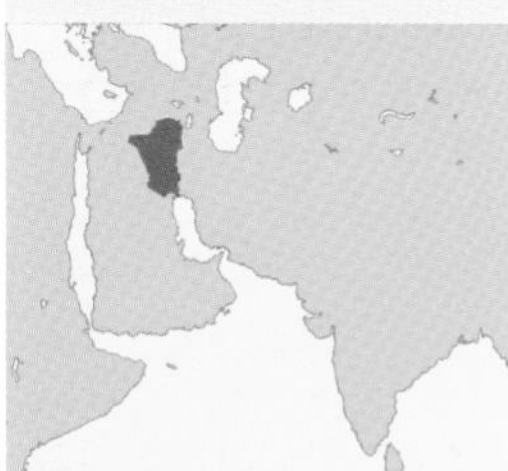

▷ **Iran** has many examples of traditional Islamic architecture. The Madrasa-i Chahar Bagh was built in the city of Isfahan in the 1700s as a college for religious studies. It features the tall minarets, or towers, found on every mosque.

continued from page 167

the work of one person, while others have been created by teams of people. It is not known who developed many of the earliest inventions such as the **wheel**, **plow**, **pottery**, loom, and **metal** tools.

Throughout **history** civilization has been driven forward by inventions. Each invention has been based on those that came before it and has made further progress possible. Some important inventions of the last 600 years include the **printing press** (c. 1440), **telescope** (1608), **steam engine** (1765), **camera** (1816), **telephone** (1876), **radio** (1895), **aircraft** (1903), **television** (1925), **laser** (1960), and **silicon chip** (1961).

Invertebrate

Invertebrates are **animals** that have no spine, or backbone. There are more than one million different species of invertebrates, with many more waiting to be discovered. They include all of the **insects**, **spiders**, **scorpions**, **worms**, **mollusks**, **crustaceans**, **starfish**, **jellyfish**, and many others.

Iran

Iran is a country in the **Middle East**. It lies between the Caspian Sea in the north and the Persian Gulf in the south. **Deserts**, snowy **mountains**, and green valleys cover most of the land. Most of the country experiences hot, dry summers and cold winters.

The old name for Iran is Persia, and the Iranian **language** is Persian. The main **religion** is **Islam**. Many Iranians are **nomads** who travel with flocks of **sheep** or **goats**. Iranian women weave beautiful rugs from **wool** or **silk**, which are famous for their detailed patterns and rich colors. Iran's most important product is **oil**.

Iran has a long **history**. In about 550 B.C. the Persian leader Cyrus and his army established an empire that stretched from **Greece** and **Egypt** to **India**. The Persian empire was then the largest in the world. **Alexander the Great** conquered Persia around 330 B.C. Later the country was ruled by Arabs and **Mongols**. During the 1900s Iran was ruled by emperors, or shahs. In 1979 the **government** of Iran changed, and the shah left the country. Religious leaders now rule this Islamic **republic**. From 1980 to 1988 Iran fought a long and bitter war with **Iraq**.

Iraq

Iraq is a country in the **Middle East**. Much of it is a dry, sandy, and stony plain that is cool in the winter and very hot in the summer. The Tigris and Euphrates **rivers** flow through the plain to the Persian Gulf. Their water allows the farmers to grow **rice**, **cotton**, **wheat**, and dates. Iraq is also one of the largest **oil** producers in the world. Pipelines carry the oil from the north of the country across the **desert** to ports in **Syria** and the **Lebanon**.

Many Iraqis are **nomads** who live in the desert and tend flocks of **sheep** and **goats**. But four million people work in Baghdad, the capital city. Some of the world's first cities, such as Ur, were built near Iraq's big rivers. Later the powerful Babylonian empire built the famous city of **Babylon** there.

Today, Iraq is a **republic** with Saddam Hussein (b. 1937) as its **dictator**. It was involved in a war with **Iran** from 1980–1988. In 1990 an Iraqi army invaded Kuwait, but it was forced to leave after the **Gulf War** in 1991.

Ireland

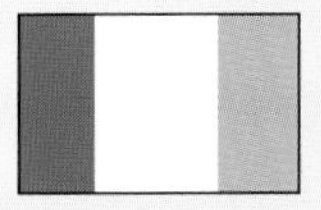

IRELAND
Government: Republic
Capital: Dublin
Area: 26,600 sq. mi.
Population: 3,840,838
Languages: English and Irish (Gaelic)
Currency: Euro

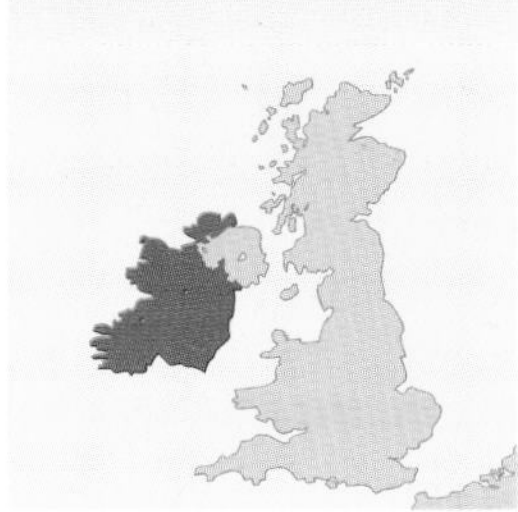

Ireland is the second largest **island** of the **British Isles**. It is a land of green fields, rolling hills, clear **lakes** (known as loughs), and winding **rivers**. The Shannon, which flows through Ireland's flat central plain, is the longest river in the British Isles. Low **mountain** ranges line the coasts.

The Irish **climate** is mild and moist, and a lush carpet of green **grass** covers much of the land, giving the country the nickname the "Emerald Isle." Much of the country's economy is based on **farming** and **fishing**.

England gained control of Ireland in the 1500s, after which Protestants from England and **Scotland** settled there. When Ireland became self-governing in 1921, the six Protestant-dominated northern counties stayed part of the **United Kingdom** and became known as **Northern Ireland**. In the Republic of Ireland most of the people are Roman Catholics. The division of the island causes continuing tensions.

Iron and steel

Iron is the cheapest and most useful of all **metals**. It is often mixed with **carbon** and other ingredients to create steel, which is a strong building material.

Iron is one of the most plentiful metals in **earth**'s crust, where it occurs in the form of a rocky material called iron ore. Before it can be used the iron ore has to be melted down, or smelted, in a blast furnace. The iron is then made into cast iron, wrought iron, or steel. Cast iron is hard but not as strong as steel. Red-hot molten cast iron is poured into molds to make such things as **engine** blocks. Wrought iron is softer than cast iron and is used for chains and gates. Steel is extremely hard and strong. Sometimes other metals, such as tungsten and chromium, are added to steel to produce steel **alloys**. These are used to make many different things from nails to **bridges**, buildings, and other objects that carry heavy loads.

▽ **Iron** is extracted from its ore in a blast furnace. Most of the iron is then processed again to make steel or steel alloys.

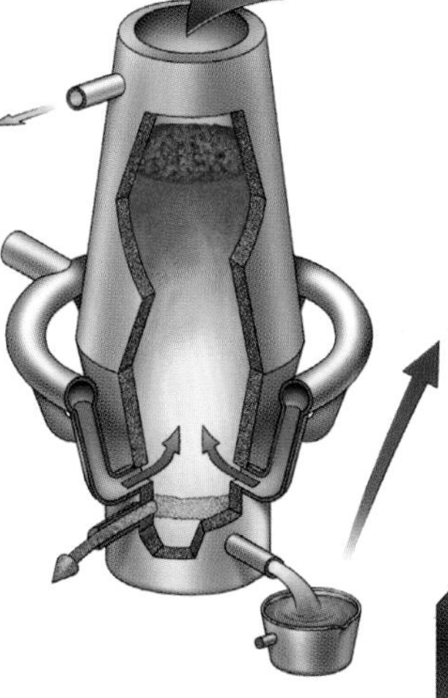

1) Iron ore, limestone, and coke (a form of carbon) are put into the furnace. These raw materials react with each other to produce poor-quality pig iron.

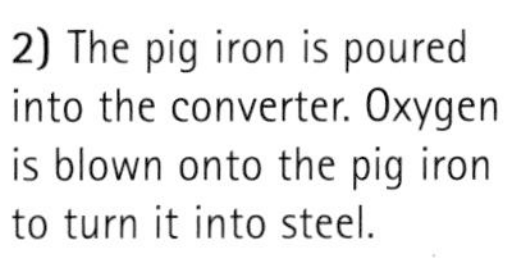

2) The pig iron is poured into the converter. Oxygen is blown onto the pig iron to turn it into steel.

3) The molten steel can be cast into different shapes while still liquid.

Irrigation

Farmers and gardeners who water **plants** are irrigating them. Irrigation makes it possible to grow crops and **flowers** in dry **soil**, even in a **desert**. Farmers in **China**, **Egypt**, and **Iraq** have been irrigating large areas of land for thousands of years.

Many countries store **water** in **lakes** made by building **dams** across **rivers**. **Canals** take water from the lakes to farms—one irrigation canal in **Russia** is 527 mi. (850km) long. Ditches or pipes carry water from each canal to the fields. In each field the water flows between the rows of plants, sometimes spurting up from holes in the pipes and sprinkling the plants like a rain shower.

△ The symbols of **Islam** are the crescent and star.

ITALY
Government: Republic
Capital: Rome
Area: 113,400 sq. mi.
Population: 57,679,825
Languages: Italian, German, French, Slovene
Currency: Euro

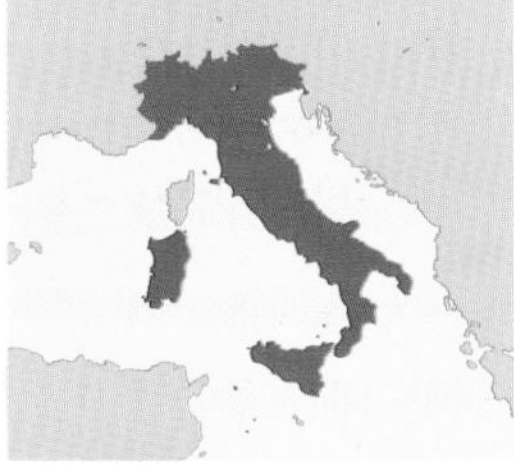

ISRAEL
Government: Republic
Capital: Jerusalem
Area: 7,800 sq. mi.
Population: 5,938,093
Languages: Hebrew, Arabic, English
Currency: New shekel

Islam

Islam is the second largest **religion** after **Christianity** with more than one billion followers known as Muslims. Many Muslims live in the **Middle East**, southern **Asia**, and **Africa**. Islam was begun by the prophet **Muhammad**, an Arab born in about A.D. 570 in the city of **Mecca** (in modern **Saudi Arabia**).

Muslims believe in one all-powerful **god** called Allah. The word "Islam" means "submission" in Arabic, and Muslims try to submit to Allah's will and live their lives according to his word. They pray five times per day, give gifts to the poor each year, and fast from dawn until dusk during the holy month of **Ramadan**. Muslims also try to obey the rules for living set out in the **Koran**, the Islamic holy **book**. If possible, Muslims must also make a pilgrimage to Mecca at least once during their lifetimes. There are two main Islamic **festivals—Eid** ul-Adha (Festival of Sacrifice) and Eid ul-Fitr (Festival of the Breaking of the Fast). Islam has no organized church and no priests. Instead there are holy men and teachers. The Muslim place of worship is called a **mosque**, and the holy day is Friday.

Island

An island is a piece of land surrounded by **water**. Some islands are chunks of land that became separated from **continents**. Other islands are **volcanoes** that have risen up above sea level.

Israel

Israel is a small country on the eastern shore of the **Mediterranean Sea**. The state of Israel was created in 1948 as a homeland for Jewish people from around the world (see also **Judaism**). More than half of the land is **desert** or dry, rocky **mountains**, but there are also fertile plains where farmers grow oranges, **cotton**, grain, and **vegetables**. The capital of Israel is **Jerusalem**, which is regarded as a holy place by Jews, Christians, and Muslims.

The Israelis have fought several wars against their Arab neighbors. In 1994 a treaty was signed between Israel and the **Palestine** Liberation Organization (PLO), which granted limited self-rule to two mainly Arab regions within Israel—the West Bank and Gaza Strip. However, the bitter conflict between the Jews and Palestinians continues.

Italy

Italy is a country in southern **Europe**. It sticks out into the **Mediterranean Sea** and includes the **islands** of Sicily and Sardinia. Much of Italy is covered with hills and **mountains**. The snowy peaks of the **Alps** cross northern Italy, while the Apennines run like a backbone down the middle of the country. The farmers grow large quantities of grapes, lemons, pears, olives, oranges, and **wheat**. Northern Italy is mainly industrial, making **cars** and **machines**.

The **Roman Empire** was founded in Italy, and the Roman Catholic Church established its headquarters at the **Vatican** in **Rome**. From the 1300s to the early 1500s Italy was the center of the **Renaissance**.

Ivan the Terrible

Ivan IV (1530 –1584), was the first czar, or emperor, of **Russia**. He is known as "Ivan the Terrible" because he was a cruel ruler who killed his own son, but he also seized Russia's neighbors to make it a stronger nation. During his reign **Moscow** became Russia's capital.

Ivory

Ivory is a hard, creamy-white substance that forms long **teeth**, or tusks, in the **elephant**, **hippopotamus**, and **walrus**. Elephants have long been hunted for their ivory but are now protected.

Jackal

The jackal is a member of the **dog** family. There are three species, which are found in eastern **Europe**, the **Middle East**, southern **Asia**, and North **Africa**. Like most wild dogs they are both hunters and scavengers and use their superb senses of **hearing** and **smell** to track down food after dark. They hunt a wide range of small animals. By day jackals hide in thick undergrowth.

Jaguar

One of the big **cats**, the jaguar lives in the **rain forests**, grasslands, and swamps of the northern half of **South America** and in parts of **Central America**. It is the largest species of American cat and can weigh up to 332 lbs (150kg). The jaguar's coat is rich yellow with black spots and resembles that of the **leopard** of **Africa** and **Asia**. However, unlike the leopard, many of the jaguar's spots are in the center of rings of dark fur.

Jaguars are good tree climbers, and unusually for a cat, they are also excellent swimmers. They hunt mainly at night for **rodents**, peccaries (a type of wild **pig**), **deer**, and other **mammals**. They also eat **turtles**, **frogs**, and **fish**.

△ The **jaguar** often lives near water and is an expert at fishing. It waits on the bank and flips fish out of the water with a paw.

◁ The golden **jackal** is known as "the howler" by Arabs because of its loud yapping and cries, which are usually heard at night.

JAMAICA
Government: Parliamentary monarchy
Capital: Kingston
Area: 4,200 sq. mi.
Population: 2,665,636
Languages: English, Creole
Currency: Jamaican dollar

Jamaica

Jamaica is a tropical **island** in the **Caribbean** Sea. Its name means "island of springs"—there are many streams flowing from springs on the sides of the country's forested **mountains**.

More than two-and-a-half million people live in Jamaica, most of whom have African ancestry. Many people work on farms that grow bananas, oranges, coconuts, **coffee**, and **sugar**cane. Jamaica also has large mines to extract bauxite—the ore from which **aluminum** is produced. Its capital, Kingston, is an important port.

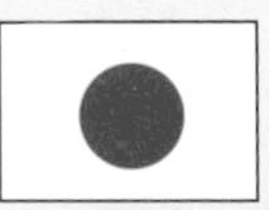

JAPAN
Government: Parliamentary democracy
Capital: Tokyo
Area: 152,200 sq. mi.
Population: 126,771,662
Language: Japanese
Currency: Yen

Japan

Japan is a long string of islands in the **Pacific Ocean** off the mainland coast of eastern **Asia**. Its largest island is Honshu, followed by Hokkaido to the north and Kyushu and Shikoku to the south. **Mountains** cover much of Japan. The highest is a snow-capped **volcano** called Fujiyama, or Mount Fuji, which last erupted in 1707. There are also large **forests** and many **waterfalls** and **rivers**. Northern Japan has cool summers and cold winters, while the southern islands have a much warmer **climate**.

Japan is a crowded country with more than 126 million people. To feed this population Japanese farmers grow huge amounts of **rice**, and the country has one of the world's largest **fishing** fleets. However, Japan still has to import large quantities of **food**.

Japan does not have many **minerals**, so it has to buy most of the minerals it needs from other countries. But because of its advanced technology and efficient factories, it is a great industrial power. Japan is one of the world's top producers of **cars**, **ships**, and **electronic** equipment such as **radios** and **television** sets.

During the 1800s Japan became one of the world's most powerful nations.It fought against the Allied powers in **World War II**, but in 1945 the **U.S.** dropped atomic bombs on the cities of Hiroshima and Nagasaki, which forced Japan to surrender. After the war Japan became a fully democratic country (see **democracy**), and the once all-powerful emperor became the head of state with only ceremonial duties.

Jazz musicians frequently start by playing a tune or rhythm and develop it by making it up as they go.

Jazz

Jazz is a kind of **music** that began in the **U.S.** in the late 1800s. The players use unexpected rhythms and often improvise—they make up the notes and melodies on the spur of the moment. However, the improvisations must complement the music made by the rest of the band. The main instruments used in jazz are the saxophone, trumpet, **piano**, **guitar**, and **drums** (see also **musical instruments**). The development of jazz has been influenced by various other styles of music, especially **blues**.

Jefferson, Thomas

Thomas Jefferson (1743 –1826) was the third **president** of the **United States** and one of the most important founders of the country. He was a champion of **democracy** and liberty and was the main author of the Declaration of Independence (1776), which forms the foundation of the U.S. **government** to this day. This document has had an immense influence all over the world. Its most important parts state that "all men are created equal" and have the right to "life, liberty, and the pursuit of happiness."

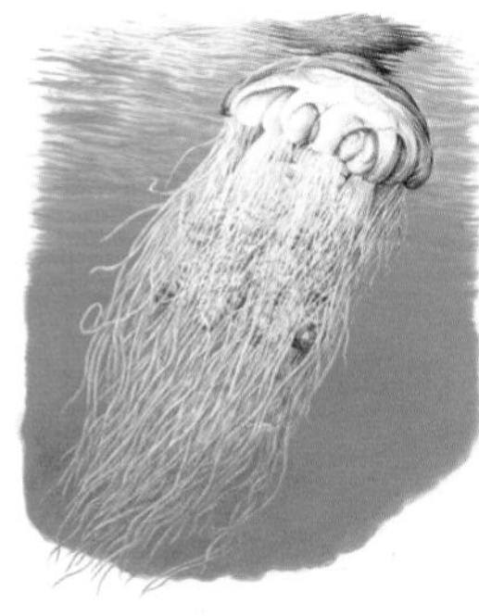

Jellyfish tentacles are covered with powerful stinging cells that paralyze passing animals and pull the victims up to the jellyfish's waiting mouth.

Jellyfish

A jellyfish is a kind of **invertebrate** (**animal** without a backbone) that lives in the **ocean**. It has a soft body and is armed with stinging tentacles, which it uses to catch and kill prey. It eats mainly small **fish**, shrimp, floating **plankton**, and other jellyfish.

Jerusalem

Jerusalem is the capital of **Israel** and is located high up in the hills. It is a holy city for **Judaism**, **Christianity**, and **Islam**. Huge walls surround the city's

▽ **Jerusalem**'s center is a centuries' old maze of streets and closely packed buildings. There are numerous holy sites, including synagogues, mosques, and churches.

oldest part. In 1948 Jerusalem was divided between Israel and **Jordan**, but Israel captured the entire city during a war in 1967. Since then the tensions between Jerusalem's Jewish and Muslim residents have frequently erupted into violence. There have been several attempts at drawing up a peace settlement, but there has been no success.

Jesus Christ

Jesus Christ was a religious leader on whose life and teachings **Christianity** was founded. Most Christians believe that he is the son of God and that he was sent to earth to save humanity. The life of Jesus is described in the New Testament of the **Bible**.

Jesus was born in Bethlehem (in present-day **Israel**) around 4–1 B.C. His date of birth is not certain but has long been celebrated on December 25—**Christmas** Day. His mother was Mary. When Jesus grew up, he traveled throughout the Holy Land, teaching and healing sick people. The Bible tells how Jesus performed miracles to show people the love of God.

Jesus had twelve followers, known as apostles, who were chosen to spread his teachings throughout the world. However, he also had enemies. In the end one of the apostles, Judas Iscariot, betrayed Jesus to his opponents in the **Roman Empire**. The Romans crucified Jesus on a cross, but the New Testament says that he was resurrected (came to life again) and rose to heaven. Jesus' followers were convinced he was the Messiah (king of the Jews), and they began to convert people to Christianity.

△ **A jet engine** has rotating blades at the front, which suck in air. The air is compressed, or squashed, and ignited with aviation fuel. This creates hot gases, which are forced out of the rear of the engine, pushing the aircraft forward.

▽ **Joan of Arc** was burned at the stake by her English enemies, who claimed she was a witch.

Jet engine

A swimmer travels forward by pushing **water** back, and a jet **engine** works in a similar way. It drives an **aircraft** forward by pushing **gases** back. **Air** is sucked into the front of the jet engine and is blown into the combustion chamber. There the air is ignited using aviation **fuel**—kerosene or paraffin. The burning fuel produces extremely hot gases, which shoot out of the back of the engine as exhaust fumes. **Rockets** work in a similar way but do not need a supply of air.

Jews *see* Judaism

Jewelry

Ornaments worn to decorate the body are called jewelry. The most common types are earrings, necklaces, brooches, bracelets, and rings. Jewelry has been found that dates from earliest human history. In addition to its use as personal decoration, jewelry has been worn as a symbol of wealth and status and for religious reasons. Expensive jewelry is often made of **gold** or **silver** and set with **diamonds** or other **gems**.

Joan of Arc

Joan of Arc (1412–1431) was born into an ordinary peasant family in **France** but led an **army** against the English during the **Hundred Years' War**. When she was still only 17 years old, Joan claimed that God told her to rid France of its English invaders. She left the farm where she worked and persuaded France's king,

Charles VII (1697–1745), to let her lead his army. Joan won five battles but was captured by the English and burned as a witch. However, she had managed to save France. In 1920 the **pope** made her a saint.

Johnson, Samuel

Samuel Johnson (1709–1784) was an English writer. He was famous for his witty remarks and for the sharpness of his opinions on people, politics, and literature. As well as writing novels, Johnson compiled one of the first English **dictionaries**.

Jordan

Jordan is a small country in the **Middle East** in the northwest corner of the Arabian Peninsula. Most of the country lies on a plateau 3,280 ft. (1,000m) above sea level. The Jordan **River** and Dead Sea lie to the west of the plateau.

In 1967 **Israel** captured Jordanian land west of the Jordan River. This area is known as the West Bank. In 1988 Jordan renounced its claims to the West Bank and passed responsibility for the area to the **Palestine** Liberation Organization (PLO).

JORDAN
Government: Constitutional monarchy
Capital: Amman
Area: 35,300 sq. mi.
Population: 5,153,378
Language: Arabic
Currency: Jordanian dinar

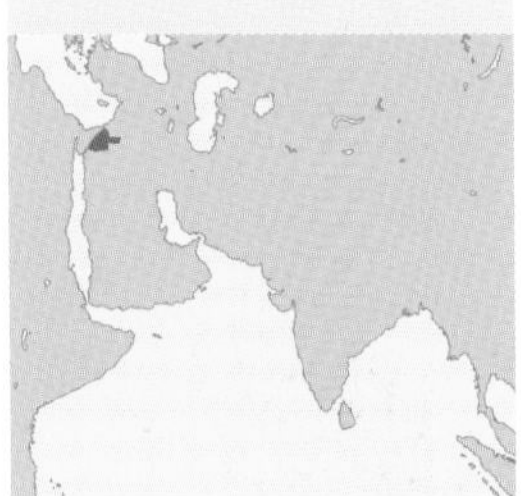

Judaism

Judaism is the **religion** of the Jewish people. It teaches that there is one true God, who revealed himself to the Jews and has given the human race rules by which to live. The Jewish holy **book** is the Hebrew **Bible**. This consists of the first five books of Moses (the Torah), historical accounts of the tribes of **Israel**, and books written by kings and prophets (messengers). Christians include all of this material in their Bible, calling it the Old Testament. Jews try to live their lives according to the Bible's Ten Commandments. They believe that God gave the Commandments to Moses on top of Mount Sinai after Moses led their ancestors out of **Egypt**, where they had been slaves. This flight from Egypt is known as the Exodus and is commemorated in one of Judaism's most important **festivals—Passover**. Other Jewish festivals include **Yom Kippur**, when sins are confessed and forgiveness is asked for, and **Chanukah**.

Today, Jews live throughout the world but regard Israel as their spiritual and historical home. Jews pray in buildings called **synagogues**, and their teachers are known as rabbis. The Jewish holy day is the Sabbath, which lasts from sunset on Friday to sunset on Saturday.

△ One of **Judaism**'s most sacred sites is the Western Wall, also called the Wailing Wall, in Jerusalem, which is all that remains of King David's Temple.

Jupiter

Jupiter is the largest of the **planets** in our **solar system**. It is twice the size of all the other planets put together. Jupiter's force of **gravity** is extremely powerful—anyone on Jupiter would weigh twice as much as on **earth**. Astronomers think that most of Jupiter is made up of hot **liquid hydrogen**. The planet appears to have light and dark belts around it, and it is circled by 28 moons. Jupiter spins so fast that a **day and night** last less than ten "Earth hours." But a **year** on Jupiter is 12 times longer than an "Earth year" because it is farther from the **Sun**.

JUPITER FACTS
Average distance from Sun: 482 million mi.
Nearest distance from Earth: 391 million mi.
Average temperature: -232°C
Diameter across the equator: 88,536 mi.
Atmosphere: Hydrogen, helium
Number of moons: 28
Length of day: 9 hours and 50 minutes
Length of year: 11.9 Earth years

△ **Kangaroos** are the largest type of marsupial. This picture shows a family group of eastern gray kangaroos, which live in eastern Australia and grow up to 7.9 ft. (2.4m) long, including the tail.

Kangaroo

Kangaroos are **marsupials** that live in **Australia**. Most of them live on grassy plains and in dry, open country known as the "bush." Kangaroos feed on **grass** and other **plants**. They move in groups, springing along on their large, powerful back legs. Their long tails help them keep their balance.

There are many species of kangaroos. Red and gray kangaroos are the largest. When it stands on tiptoe, a fully grown red kangaroo may be taller than an adult human. Gray kangaroos can run up to 34 mph (55km/h). Smaller members of the kangaroo family are called **wallabies**.

Kazakhstan

Kazakhstan is a large country that was a **republic** of the former **Soviet Union** until 1991. It stretches from the Caspian Sea in the west to **China** in the east. Much of country is steppe (a type of grassland) or **desert**. There are rich deposits of **metals** and **minerals** such as **copper**, **iron**, **coal**, and **oil**. For centuries the people of Kazakhstan lived as **nomads**, herding livestock from place to place. This lifestyle changed after **Russia** conquered the country in 1800, advancing **farming** and industries.

KAZAKHSTAN
Government: Republic
Capital: Astana
Area: 1,047,900 sq. mi.
Population: 16,731,303
Languages: Kazakh, Russian
Currency: Tenge

KENYA
Government: Republic
Capital: Nairobi
Area: 219,500 sq. mi.
Population: 30,765,916
Languages: Swahili, English, and others
Currency: Shilling

Kennedy, John Fitzgerald

John F. Kennedy (1917–1963) was the 35th **president** of the **U.S.** After serving with the U.S. Navy in **World War II** Kennedy entered politics and was elected to the House of Representatives. He became president in 1960 at 43 years old—the youngest person ever to win this office.

The Kennedy era was a time of great optimism and prosperity in the United States. To many people, Kennedy was a symbol of this strength. The **Soviet Union** was a major rival of the U.S. in this period known as the "Cold War." Kennedy forced the Soviet Union to halt its efforts to base **nuclear** missiles in **Cuba**, and relations between the two superpowers gradually improved. In 1963 Kennedy was assassinated in Dallas, Texas, by Lee Harvey Oswald (1939–1963).

Kenya

Kenya is a country in east **Africa.** Its southwest border touches the shores of **Lake** Victoria, and the **Indian Ocean** lies to the southeast. The **equator** runs across the middle of the country. Much of the land is covered by **mountains** and flat-topped hills. The rest is mainly **savanna**—a type of open grassland with scattered acacia **trees**. The savanna is home to herds of grazing **mammals**,

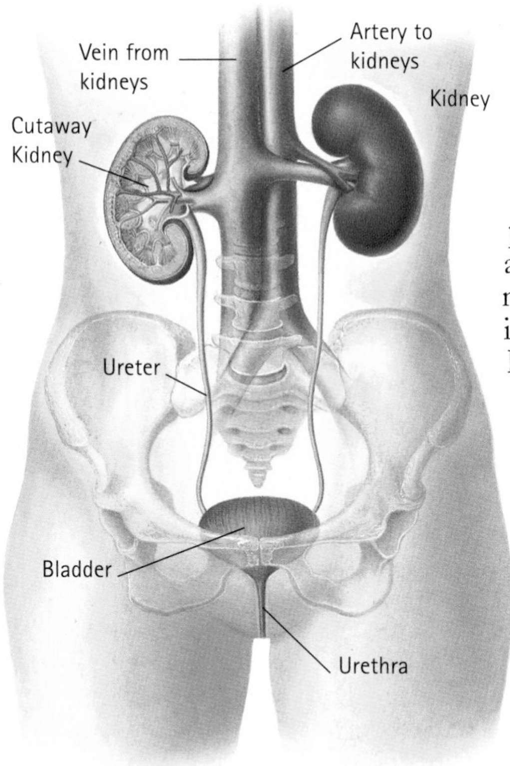

including **antelopes**, **zebras** and **elephants**, as well as **carnivores** such as **lions**, **leopards**, and **hyenas**. There are several huge national parks where animals are protected, attracting many tourists. Tourism is a major portion of Kenya's economy.

Kenya was a British colony from 1895 until 1963 when it became an independent state. However, it remains a member of the British **Commonwealth**. Some Kenyans, such as the Masai, herd **cattle**. Others grow crops such as corn, **tea**, and **coffee**, much of which are sold abroad.

△ The **kidneys** are part of a system for cleaning the blood of impurities and excess liquid. These substances drains through the ureter into the bladder and leavethe body through the urethra as urine.

▽ **Kiwis** are nocturnal, flightless birds unique to New Zealand's forests.

Kidney

All **vertebrates** (**animals** with a backbone) have two kidneys. These are bean-shaped, reddish-brown organs. Human kidneys are about the size of a person's fist and lie on each side of the backbone at about waist level.

Kidneys clean the **blood**. They do this by filtering out waste matter and straining any **water** that the body does not need. Blood pumped from the **heart** flows into each kidney through an **artery**. Inside the kidneys the waste matter and surplus water are removed from the blood and mixed to make urine. The urine drips slowly into the bladder. The filtered blood flows out of the kidney through a **vein**.

King, Martin Luther, Jr.

Martin Luther King Jr. (1929–1968) was an American **civil rights** leader who peacefully worked for racial justice. He was born in Atlanta, Georgia, and became a Baptist minister like his father. It was in Montgomery, Alabama, where he was a pastor, that he began his civil rights crusade.

In 1956 King organized a boycott of buses in Montgomery as a protest against the unfair treatment of black passengers. During the next ten years he led many peaceful demonstrations and meetings all over the **U.S.** Success came when Congress passed civil rights laws in 1964 and 1965.

King was awarded the **Nobel Prize** for peace in 1964 for his campaigns of nonviolence. However, in 1968 at 39 years old he was assassinated in Memphis, Tennessee.

Martin Luther King's speeches were an inspiration to many people and still have great influence to this day. One of his most famous speeches was in 1963 when he spoke to a crowd of 200,000 people who had come to **Washington, D.C.** to march for civil rights for all people. In his speech he said: "I have a dream that one day this nation will rise up and live out the true meaning of its creed: 'We hold these truths to be self-evident, that all men are created equal'."

Kiwi

This strange **bird** from **New Zealand** gets its name from the shrill cries made by the male. The kiwi is a stocky, brown bird as large as a chicken. It has tiny wings but cannot fly and instead runs on its short, strong legs. Its **feathers** are shaggy and look very much like the **hair** of **mammals**.

Kiwis are shy birds that live in **forests**. By day they sleep in burrows. At night they emerge to hunt for **worms** and grubs.

Kiwis have very poor **sight** and use their superb sense of **smell** to locate food. Unusually for birds, their nostrils are located at the tip of their long, thin beaks. The females lay very large **eggs**, which are incubated by the males.

Knight

In the **Middle Ages** a knight was a soldier on horseback who fought for his ruler. In peacetime he served his master in his household. Although, in theory, anyone could become a knight, **horses** and **armor** were so expensive that few people could afford them, and knighthood became an honor usually reserved for the wealthy. Boys trained for knighthood from the age of about seven.

Knights lost their usefulness in **war** when the introduction of **guns** changed fighting methods. The British **monarch** still makes people knights as a reward for special service to the country, but these knighthoods are purely honorary.

Knot

A knot is a way of fastening rope, cord, or thread. Knots are especially important for sailors and **mountain** climbers, although most people need to tie a knot at some time in their lives.

Knots are used to make a noose, tie up a bundle, or join the ends of small cords. There are also bends and hitches. A bend is used to tie the ends of rope together, and a hitch is used to attach a rope to a ring or post. Common knots include the reef knot, bowline, clove hitch, half hitch, and sheet bend. Rope ends can also be joined by weaving them together. This is called a splice.

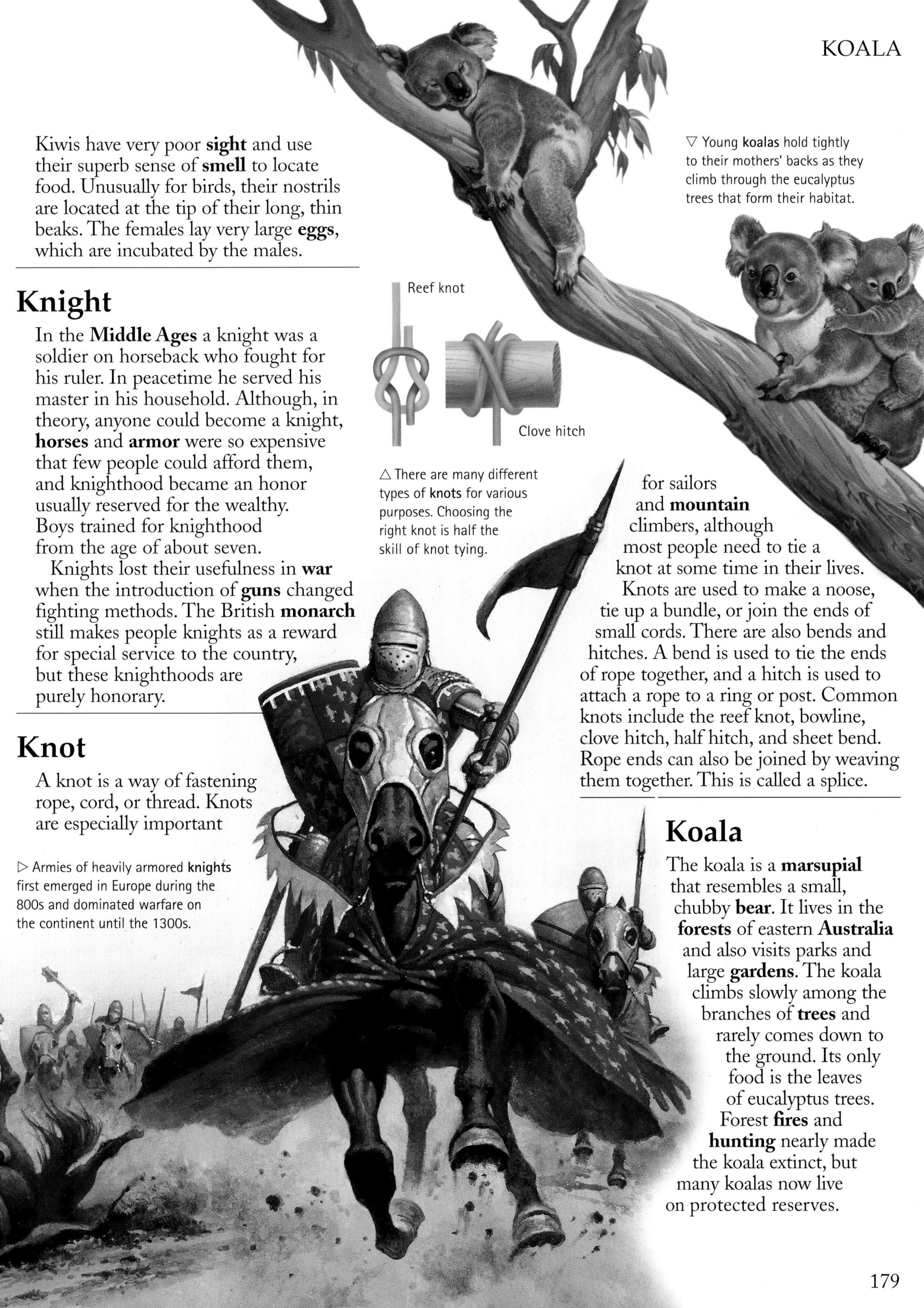

▽ Young **koalas** hold tightly to their mothers' backs as they climb through the eucalyptus trees that form their habitat.

△ There are many different types of **knots** for various purposes. Choosing the right knot is half the skill of knot tying.

▷ Armies of heavily armored **knights** first emerged in Europe during the 800s and dominated warfare on the continent until the 1300s.

Koala

The koala is a **marsupial** that resembles a small, chubby **bear**. It lives in the **forests** of eastern **Australia** and also visits parks and large **gardens**. The koala climbs slowly among the branches of **trees** and rarely comes down to the ground. Its only food is the leaves of eucalyptus trees. Forest **fires** and **hunting** nearly made the koala extinct, but many koalas now live on protected reserves.

◁ Muslims believe that the **Koran**'s sacred text was revealed to the prophet Muhammad by the angel Gabriel.

Koran

The Koran is the holy **book** of **Islam**. Its name means "a recitation." It contains 114 chapters of Arabic verse and says that there is one God whose prophets (messengers) included Abraham, **Jesus Christ**, and **Muhammad**. The book teaches Muslims to be humble, generous, and fair. It is said that the Koran was revealed to Muhammad by the angel Gabriel. The way it is written has influenced Arabic literature.

Korea, North

North Korea forms the northern half of the Korean peninsula in **Asia**, which juts out from **China** into the Sea of **Japan**. It was created in 1948 when the Korean peninsula was divided into two separate states—North Korea and **South Korea**. North Korea has many **mountains**, and **forests** cover large areas. **Farming** is the main occupation, and the main crops are **rice** and **silk**. Heavy industry, such as steelmaking (see **iron** and **steel**), is also important.

North Korea adopted **communism**, and from 1950 to 1953 it fought a war with South Korea. During the war it was helped by two other Communist powers in Asia—**China** and the **Soviet Union**. South Korea was supported by forces from the **United Nations** (mainly the **U.S.**). After the war North and South Korea remained hostile, but in the late 1990s relations between them gradually began to improve. There is now an uneasy peace in the region.

NORTH KOREA
Government: Communist state
Capital: Pyongyang
Area: 46,400 sq. mi.
Population: 21,968,228
Language: Korean
Currency: North Korean Won

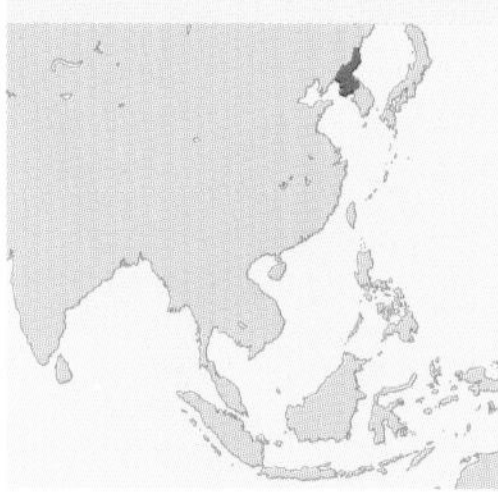

Korea, South

South Korea was created in 1948 as a result of the division of the Korean peninsula into two independent nations. It is smaller than **North Korea**, but its **population** is twice as large, and its industries are more developed. It manufactures **cars**, **ships**, **textiles**, steel (see **iron** and **steel**), and a wide range of **electronic** products. The capital, Seoul, is one of the world's largest cities with more than 10.5 million people.

SOUTH KOREA
Government: Republic
Capital: Seoul
Area: 37,900 sq. mi.
Population: 47,904,370
Language: Korean
Currency: South Korean Won

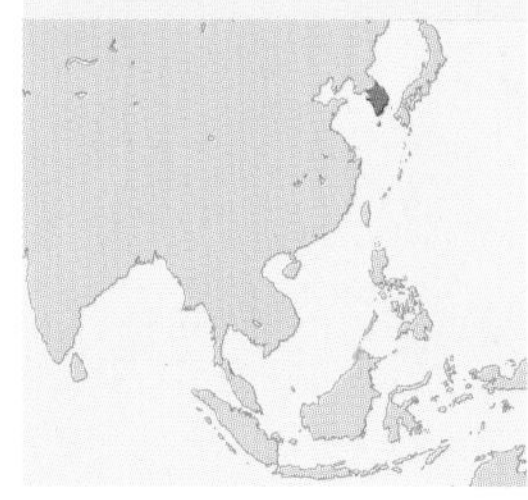

Kremlin

The Kremlin is the oldest part of **Moscow** in **Russia**. Some of its buildings date from the 1100s. For most of its history the Kremlin has been the seat of the Russian **government**, and it used to be the residence of Russia's czars, or emperors.

Kublai Khan

The grandson of the warlord **Genghis Khan**, Kublai Khan (1215–1294) was leader of the **Mongol** empire when it reached the peak of its power in **Asia**. Kublai became Great Khan in 1259. He conquered **China** and set up his capital at Cambulac (modern **Beijing**). It was the first time China had been completely overcome by outside forces. Kublai Khan also forced neighboring countries in **Southeast Asia** to accept him as their ruler.

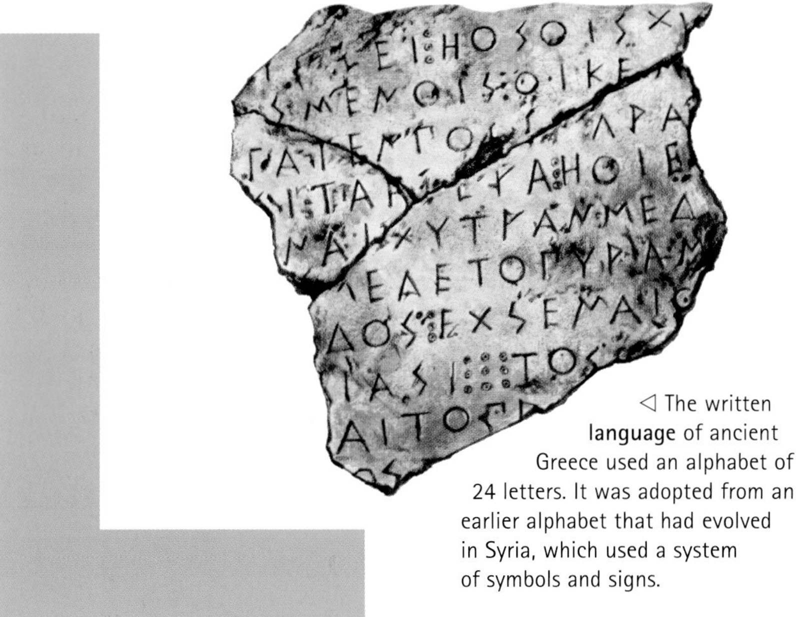

◁ The written **language** of ancient Greece used an alphabet of 24 letters. It was adopted from an earlier alphabet that had evolved in Syria, which used a system of symbols and signs.

Lake

A lake is an area of **water** that fills a hollow in the surface of **earth**. The world's largest lake is the salty Caspian Sea, which lies between **Europe** and **Asia** east of the Caucasus **Mountains**. The largest freshwater lake is Lake Superior, one of the **Great Lakes**.

Many lakes were formed during the **ice ages**. They began in valleys carved by **glaciers**. When the glaciers melted, they left behind mud and stones that formed natural **dams**. The meltwater from the glaciers piled up behind the dams to form lakes.

Lakes provide an important **habitat** for many types of **plants** and **animals** and are used by people as a source of water for **fishing** and transportation.

Language

Language is the way in which **human beings** communicate with each other. It includes **speech**, **writing**, and sign language. Many other **animals** have ways of communicating, including special body movements and **sounds**. But speaking is something that only humans can do. Spoken language came first, and later people invented a way of writing it down. Today there are 4,000–5,000 languages in the world. Some of the most widely spoken are Mandarin Chinese, English, Hindi, Arabic, Spanish, and French.

LAOS
Government: Communist
Capital: Vientiane
Area: 89,000 sq. mi.
Population: 5,635,967
Language: Lao
Currency: Kip

Laos

Laos is a country in **Southeast Asia**. Its capital and largest city is Vientiane on the Mekong **River**. It has a tropical **climate**, and most of the land is covered

▽ Many **lakes** are fed by rivers and streams, which often form marshy deltas where they enter the lakes. Other rivers drain water out of the lake and over time may form a valley or gorge.

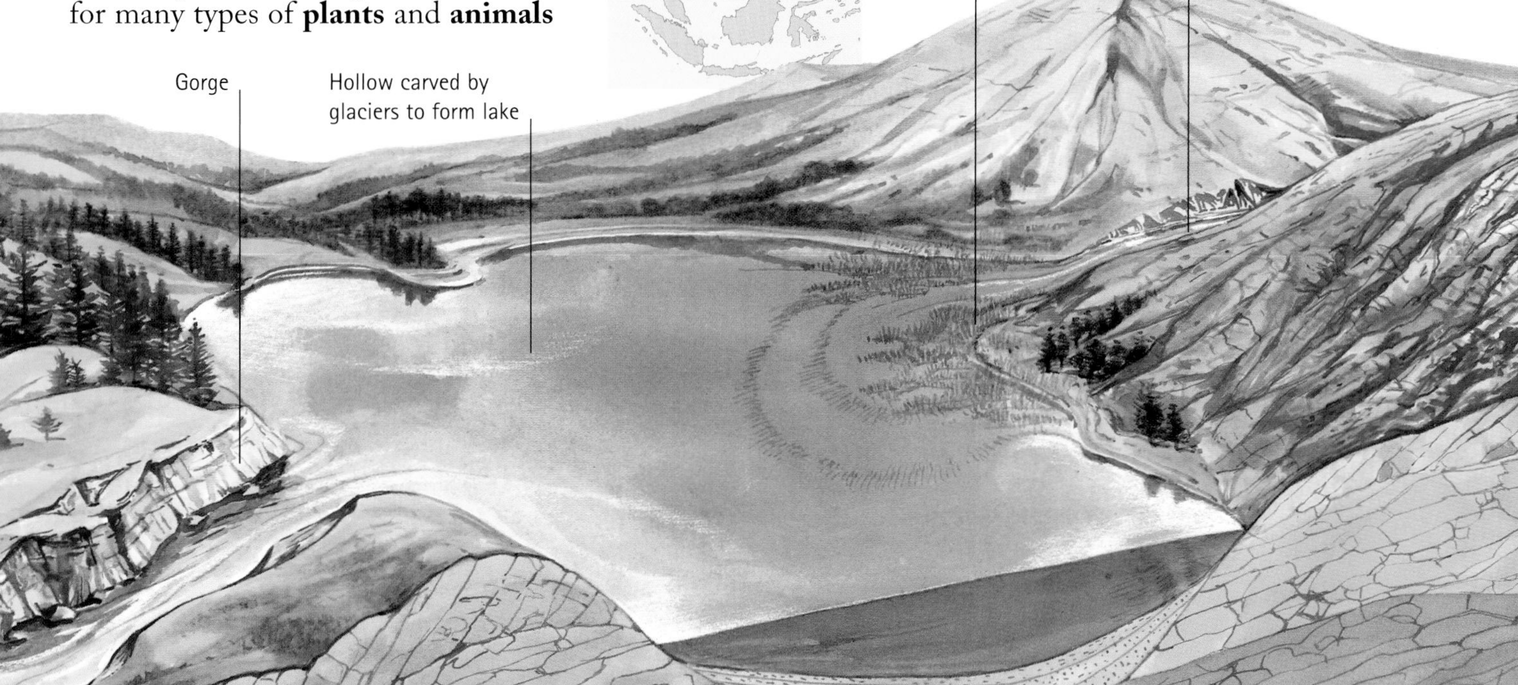

with **forests** and **mountains**. Almost all of the **population** earn their living by **farming**. **Rice** is the main crop. Laos came under the control of **France** in 1893 but won independence in 1949.

Lapland

Lapland is a region in the **Arctic** in the far north of **Sweden**, **Norway**, **Finland**, and **Russia**. The land is windswept **tundra** or **forests** of **conifers** and birch **trees**. Lapland is named for the people who live there, the Lapps, who are mainly **nomads**. They travel with herds of reindeer, sleep in tents, and eat reindeer meat. Other Lapps are fishers or farmers and live in villages. The Lapps' traditional clothing is made from reindeer hides and **wool**. They speak a **language** that is similar to Finnish.

Laser

A laser is a device that concentrates **light** to produce a narrow, powerful beam. Many lasers have a ruby crystal or **gas** inside them. Bright light, **radio** waves, or **electricity** are fed into the laser. This makes the **atoms** of the crystal or gas jump around very fast. The atoms give off strong light.

The light of lasers can be used for many things. Doctors use small laser beams to burn away tumors and tiny areas of **disease** in the body. Laser beams are also used to make precision cuts in **surgery**, repair damaged **eyes**, and correct near- or farsightedness (see **lens**). Dentists can use lasers to drill holes in **teeth**. Lasers are used in factories to cut **metal** and join tiny metal parts. Some lasers are strong enough to cut through materials as hard as **diamonds**.

Another use for lasers is to measure distance. The laser beam is aimed at objects far away, and the distance is measured by counting the **time** it takes for the light to travel there and back. Laser beams can also carry radio and **television** signals. A single laser beam can send many **telephone** calls and television programs without mixing them up (see **fiber optics**).

Artificial ruby rod
Mirror
Coiled fluorescent light
Mirror
Laser beam

△ Inside this **laser**a bright **light** is aimed at a ruby crystal. This energizes the ruby's atoms, and it flashes a light. Mirrors concentrate the laser beam.

△ Lines of **latitude and longitude** are drawn in a grid over **earth**'s surface and allow us to locate places quickly.

△ People accused of breaking the **law** may have to go to court, where lawyers argue their cases. The lawyers present evidence and question witnesses. A jury decides whether the accused is guilty or innocent.

Latitude and Longitude

Lines of latitude and longitude are imaginary lines drawn on **maps**, atlases, and globes. They form an interlocking network that allows us to pinpoint places with great accuracy. Every place on **earth** has a different position of latitude and longitude.

Lines, or parallels, of latitude show how far north or south of the **equator** a place is. They are measured in degrees (written as °). The equator lies at 0° latitude. The **North Pole** has a latitude of 90°N (north), and that of the **South Pole** is 90°S (south). Lines, or meridians, of longitude show how far east or west a place is. Greenwich in **London**, England, lies at 0° longitude. A place halfway around the world from London is at 180° longitude.

Latvia *see* Baltic States

Law

Laws are the official rules that people live by. They control many of the things that people do and help them live together in peace. In a **democracy** laws are proposed by the **government**, passed by an elected body, such as a **parliament**, and enforced by the **police** and courts.

The first written laws were enacted in **Babylon** 4,000 years ago. The ancient Jews based their laws on the Ten Commandments given to Moses by God as related in the **Bible** (see **Judaism**).

The Romans (see **Roman Empire**) developed many new types of laws such as family law, property law, and criminal law, some of which are still in use around the world.

Someone who is accused of breaking the law may be summoned to court and is known as the defendant. In court two teams of lawyers present each side of the case. The prosecution tries to prove that the defendant is guilty, and the defense attempts to show that he or she is innocent. Then it is up to the jury—a randomly selected group of members of the public—to decide. The judge determines the punishment.

Lead

Lead is a heavy, blue-gray **metal** that does not **rust**. It is used for many things, but its greatest single use is in **batteries** for **cars**. Lead shields protect workers from dangerous radiation in the **X-ray** departments of **hospitals** and in **nuclear** power plants (see also **radioactivity**). Lead is mixed with **tin** to make solder, which is used for joining pieces of metal. Many items are now made without lead because lead can be poisonous to humans. It interferes with the production of red **blood** cells and may damage organs such as the **brain**, **kidneys**, and **liver**.

△ **Lead** was formerly used in cosmetics before it was known that the metal is toxic to humans.

Leaf

A leaf is the **food** factory of a green **plant**. To make food the leaf needs **light** from the **sun**, carbon dioxide from the **air**, and **water**. Air enters the leaf through tiny holes called stomata. Water is drawn from the ground by the plant's roots. It flows up the stem and into the leaf through tiny tubes called veins. Inside the leaf is a green substance called chlorophyll. The chlorophyll uses light, carbon dioxide, and water to make **sugar**. This process is called photosynthesis. The sugar then passes through tubes to the other parts of the plant. The by-product of photosynthesis is **oxygen**, most of which passes into the air.

In the fall broad-leaved, or deciduous, **trees** shed their leaves. The water supply to the leaves is shut off, which destroys their green **color** and gives the leaves yellow, orange, and red tints. **Conifers** are trees with needle-shaped leaves that are not lost in the winter.

▽ A **leaf** is designed to catch as much sunlight and lose as little water as possible. It is held out to the light by stiff veins, and its upper surface has transparent cells that allow light to reach the internal structures where food is made. The leaf's waterproof outer layer stops the leaf from drying out.

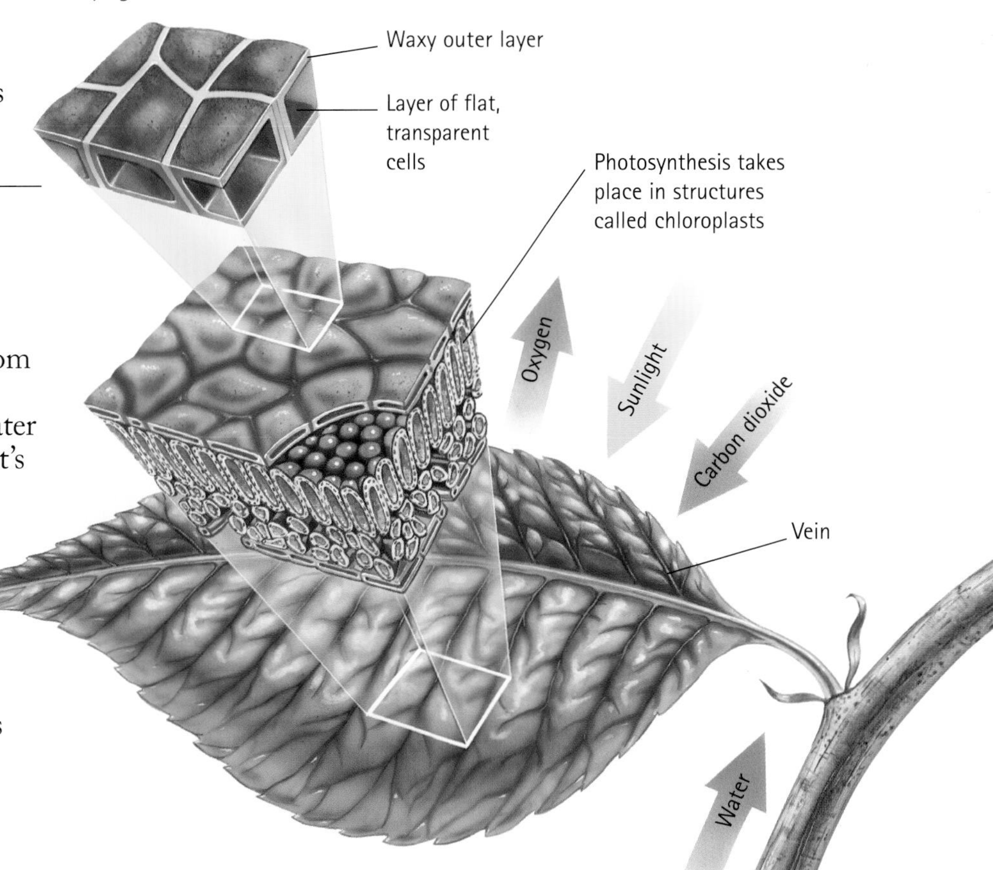

Leakey family

The Leakey family discovered **fossils** in East **Africa** that traced the **evolution** of modern **human beings** from early apelike ancestors. Born in **Kenya**, Louis Leakey (1903–1972) unearthed the fossil remains of a primitive human species in a gorge in **Tanzania**, which he suggested was our true ancestor. In 1978 Louis' wife, Mary Leakey (1913–1996), found human footprints that were made 3.5 million years ago. The Leakeys' son, Richard (b. 1944), discovered many more early human remains in Africa during the 1970s.

Leather

Leather is made from the **skin**, or hide, of **animals**. Most leather comes from **mammals** such as **cattle**. First the skins are cured by being soaked in salt**water**. Then the remaining **hair** and meat is taken off. Next the skins are treated with a chemical called tannin, which comes from **tree** bark. This process is called tanning, and it makes the skins strong and waterproof. Finally the leather is oiled to soften it and then dyed different **colors**. It is now ready to be cut, shaped, and stitched or glued into the final product.

Lebanon

LEBANON
Government: Republic
Capital: Beirut
Area: 3,900 sq. mi.
Population: 3,627,774
Language: Arabic
Currency: Lebanese pound

Lebanon is a country in the **Middle East** that borders the **Mediterranean Sea**. It lies between **Syria** and **Israel**. Lebanon's coast is flat, but inland there are dry, rocky **mountains**.

Lebanon has been a trading center for centuries. Ancient Lebanon was part of the Phoenician empire. The Phoenicians were great traders all over the Mediterranean. Later, Lebanon became part of the **Byzantine Empire**, ruled from **Constantinople**. It was famous for the fine cedar**wood** from its **forests**.

Since 1975 Lebanon has experienced instability caused by rivalries between **religions** and political groups. The country was torn apart by a **civil war** in 1975–1976, and there were further outbreaks of fighting in the late 1970s and throughout the 1980s. Lebanon has also suffered as a result of the ongoing conflict between **Israel** and Palestinians who are based in southern Lebanon (see also **Palestine**).

Legend

see **Myths and Legends**

Lenin, Vladimir Ilyich

△ **Lenin**'s revolutionary ideas led to the defeat of Russia's old regime ruled by emperors, or czars, and to the birth of Communist rule in Russia.

Vladimir Ilyich Lenin (1870–1924) helped to make **Russia** the world's first Communist country. Like the German Karl **Marx**, Lenin believed in a political system known as **communism**. He wanted every country to be run by the workers and no longer split into wealthy and poor sections of society.

For many years Lenin lived outside Russia and wrote **books** and articles for Communist **newspapers**. In 1917 he returned to Russia and became the leader of the Bolsheviks, a Communist group that overthrew the **government**. This event is called the **Russian Revolution**. Lenin played a major part in Russia's Communist government until his death in 1924.

Lens

Lenses make objects look larger or smaller. Artificial lenses are usually made of **glass** or **plastic**, but the lenses inside of your **eyes** are made of **protein**.

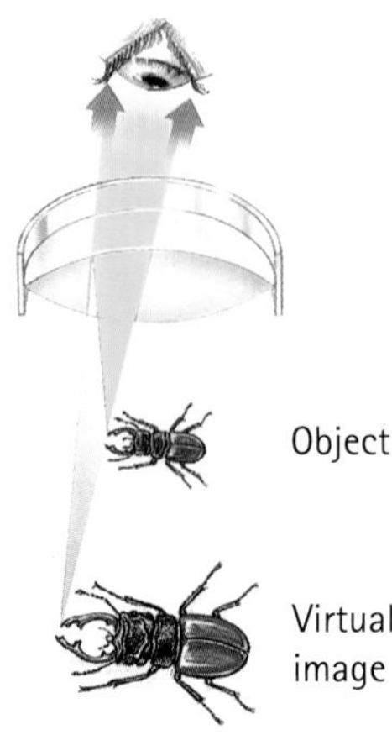

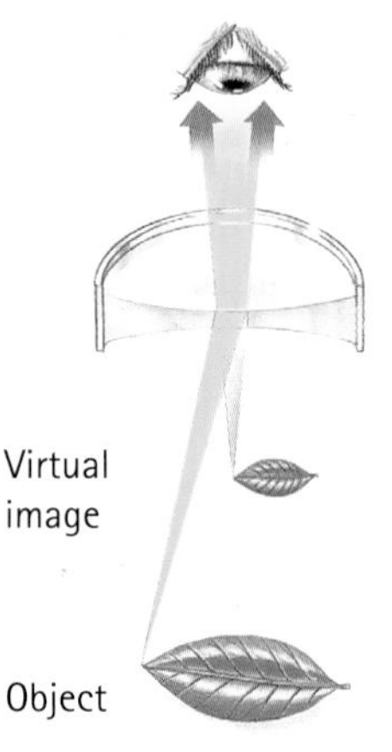

◁ **Lenses** come in two main forms: convex and concave. Light rays passing through a convex lens bend out, making the virtual image appear larger than it really is. The virtual image is what we see. A concave lens bends the rays in, and the image looks smaller.

△ The **leopard** often drags its kill, such as this antelope, up into trees. There the big cat can devour its prey at leisure, and other predators are unable to feed on the carcass.

A lens has smooth sides, which are often curved. There are two types of simple lenses. A lens where the middle is thicker than the edges is called a convex lens and magnifies objects. A lens in which the edges are thicker than the middle is called a concave lens and reduces the size of objects. Many types of devices use convex lenses, including **microscopes**, binoculars, **telescopes**, periscopes, and **cameras**. The human eyeball acts like a large convex lens and focuses **light** rays onto the back of our eyes. However, some people's eyes cannot focus well, and they may be unable to see clearly. Their vision can usually be corrected with eyeglasses and, in some cases, through **surgery**. Nearsighted people have difficulty seeing distant objects and wear glasses that have concave lenses. Farsighted people cannot focus on nearby objects and wear glasses with convex lenses.

Leopard

Leopards are big **cats** that live in much of **Africa** and in parts of southern **Asia**. They are also found in **Southeast Asia** and the **Middle East** but have become rare there. Leopards inhabit a range of **habitats**, including open grasslands, **forests**, **mountains**, and even the edges of **deserts**. Most leopards have spotted coats similar to those of the **jaguar**, but some, called panthers, are almost entirely black. Leopards are powerful and agile hunters. They catch and eat a wide range of **animals**, including **mammals**, **reptiles**, and **fish**.

Library

A library is a place where **books** and documents are stored so that people can refer to them. Some libraries also store other things such as old manuscripts, **maps**, **drawings**, and **recordings**. One of the world's largest libraries is the Library of Congress in **Washington, D.C.**, which has over 80 million different items in its huge collection.

LIBYA
Government: Islamic Arabic Socialist
Capital: Tripoli
Area: 678,600 sq. mi.
Population: 5,240,599
Language: Arabic
Currency: Libyan dinar

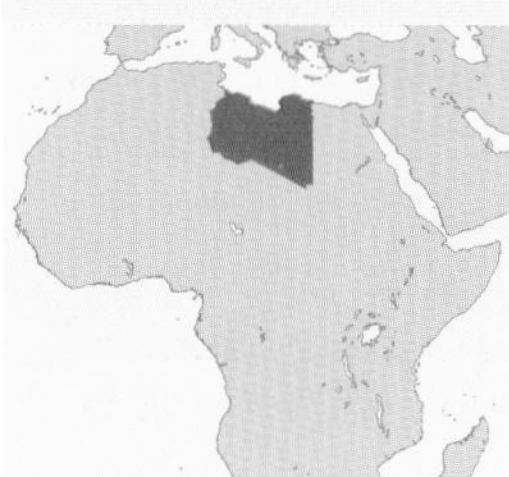

Libya

Libya is a large country in North **Africa**. It has a small **population** for its size because most of the country lies in the barren **Sahara Desert**. Most Libyans are Arabs, and **farming** is the chief occupation. Libya also has rich supplies of **oil**. The country became part of the Turkish Ottoman Empire in the 1500s (see **Turkey**) and was a colony of **Italy** from 1912 until the end of **World War II**. In 1952 Libya became an independent monarchy as the United Kingdom of Libya.

In 1969 **army** officers overthrew the king and took control, and Colonel Mu'ammar Muhammad al-Gadhafi (b. 1942) became head of the country's **government**. Since then al-Gadhafi has led a revolution in Libyan life. He has often argued that Arab countries should unite and promote the **religion** of **Islam**. However, under al-Gadhafi Libya has funded **terrorism** and revolutionary groups in other parts of the world. In 1992 the **United Nations** imposed economic sanctions on Libya, which remain in force today.

Lichens

Lichens are simple living things that are made up of fungi (see **fungus**) and algae living together. They lack roots, **leaves**, and **flowers**. Some lichens grow as crusty patches on **rocks**, **trees**, and walls. They grow very slowly—a patch no larger than your hand may be hundreds of years old. Other lichens grow as small, shrubby clumps close to the ground. Lichens can live in places that are too dry, cold, or hot for green **plants**.

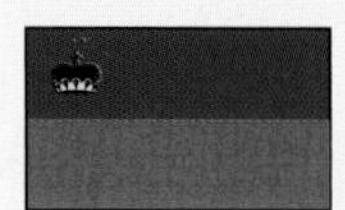

LIECHTENSTEIN
Government: Constitutional monarchy
Capital: Vaduz
Area: 60 sq. mi.
Population: 32,528
Language: German
Currency: Swiss franc

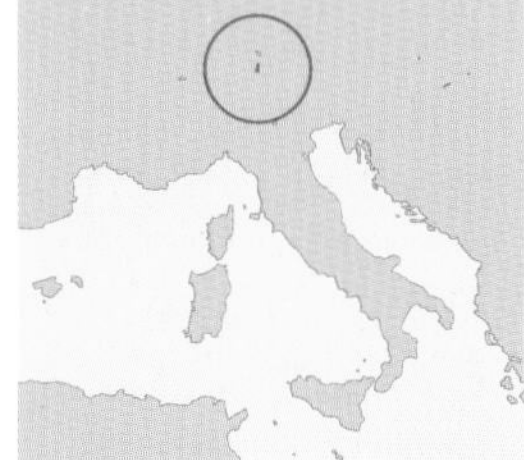

Liechtenstein

Liechtenstein is one of the smallest countries in the world. It lies between **Switzerland** and **Austria** in the **Alps**. Many international **companies** have their headquarters in Liechtenstein because businesses pay less **tax** there than elsewhere. Tourism also brings **money** into the country.

Light

Light is a form of **energy** that we can see. Some things, such as **stars**, electric lightbulbs (see **electricity**), and certain types of chemicals, produce light. However, most things do not produce light and are visible only because they reflect it. For example, we can see the **Moon** and **planets** in the sky only because they reflect light from the **Sun**.

Sunlight is normally the brightest light visible to humans. Bright sunlight seems white but is made up of the **colors** of the **rainbow** (see **spectrum**). The English scientist Isaac **Newton** first showed this by making a sunbeam shine through a prism—a 3-D triangle made of **glass**. Seven colors of light emerged from the prism—red, orange, yellow, green, blue, indigo, and violet.

A prism splits light into separate beams, each with its own wavelength. This is easy to understand if you think of light traveling in waves. The distance between the tops of the waves is the wavelength, and we see each wavelength as a different color. Long waves are red, short waves are violet, and the wavelengths in between appear as the other colors in the rainbow.

Light travels at more than 186,000 mi. (300,000km) per second. Even so, it takes eight minutes for the light from the Sun to reach **Earth**, a distance of about 93 million mi. (150 million km). A light-**year** is the total distance a beam of light travels in one year. Astronomers (see **astronomy**) use light-years to measure how far away stars are. Some stars are millions of light-years' distance from Earth.

△ Female **lions**, or lionesses, are lighter and faster than the males and hunt for all the lions in their pride. They usually hunt together, which means that they can tackle larger prey than if they hunted alone. Lions feed mainly on **zebras**, gazelles, and antelope.

Lightning

Lightning is a naturally occurring form of **electricity**. It is a sudden, massive flow of electric currents between two clouds or between a cloud and the ground (see **weather**). Lightning is caused by the movement through the **atmosphere** of **atoms** with positive and negative charges. A huge surge of charged atoms causes a flash and a bang—thunder (see **thunderstorm**).

There are three types of lightning. Streak lightning flashes in a single line from cloud to earth. Forked lightning happens when the lightning divides to find the quickest way to **earth**. Sheet lightning happens inside a cloud.

Lincoln, Abraham

Abraham Lincoln (1809–1865) was the **president** of the **United States** from 1861 to 1865. He had little formal schooling but studied **law** on his own. In 1854 a law was passed allowing people in the U.S.'s new western territories to own slaves (see **slavery**). Lincoln joined the antislavery Republican Party in 1856 and was elected president in 1860. He started a second term of office in 1865 just as he was trying to unite the nation at the end of the **Civil War**. But on April 14, 1865, on a visit to Ford's Theater in **Washington, D.C.**, he was assassinated by John Wilkes Booth (1838–1865), an actor who supported the defeated South.

Lindbergh, Charles

Charles Augustus Lindbergh (1902–1974) was an American pilot who became the first man to fly solo across the **Atlantic Ocean**. He took off from **New York** City on May 20, 1927 and landed the next day in **Paris, France**. His 3,472-mi. (5,600-km) flight had taken 33½ hours. Lindbergh's voyage made him an international hero. Later he helped to plan air tours to **South America** and over the Atlantic.

▷ **Lindbergh**'s historic flight across the Atlantic in 1927 inspired many other pioneering pilots. He made the trip in a single-engine aircraft named the *Spirit of St. Louis* in recognition of the financial support given by nine St. Louis businessmen.

Lion

Lions are big **cats** with plain, sandy coats. They live in the southern and eastern regions of **Africa** and in a tiny part of western **India**. An adult male lion weighs about 400 lbs (180kg) and has a long, shaggy mane. The female is smaller and has no mane. Lions usually live in groups called prides. A typical pride has one adult male, several adult females, and all of their cubs. Each pride defends its own hunting territory.

Liquid

A liquid is a substance that is able to flow and change its shape. If a liquid is poured into a container, it takes the shape of the container, but its **volume** remains the same. As a liquid becomes hotter the **atoms** inside it move faster. They begin to leave the liquid, and a **gas** is formed. When the liquid reaches a certain **temperature**, called the boiling point, all of it turns into gas.

When a liquid cools, its atoms slow down. At the freezing point they settle into fixed positions, and the liquid becomes a solid.

Different liquids have different freezing and boiling points. **Water**, **milk**, **mercury**, and **oil** are all liquid at ordinary room temperatures.

Lister, Joseph

Joseph Lister (1827–1912) was an English surgeon who pioneered a way of stopping patients from dying of infections after operations. He used antiseptics to kill **germs** on surgeons' hands and instruments (see **surgery**).

Literature

see **Fiction, Poetry**

Lithuania

see **Baltic States**

△ This cutaway of the **liver** shows the mass of blood vessels inside the organ. The liver performs over 500 different functions that control the chemical makeup of our blood.

△ **Llamas** are hardy animals and are well adapted to the harsh conditions of the Andes mountains.

Liver

The liver is a flat, triangular organ tucked under the ribs on the right side of the body. It makes the digestive juices that burn up the **fat** that you eat and manufactures the **proteins** contained in **blood**. It also gets rid of any poisonous substances in the blood, such as **alcohol**, or modifies them so that they are harmless. Another function of the liver is to store essential **minerals** and **vitamins**.

Livingstone, David

David Livingstone (1813–1873) was a Scottish doctor and missionary who explored southern and central **Africa**. He traveled there to help stop traders from selling Africans into **slavery** and to spread **Christianity**. Livingstone made three long journeys between 1841 and 1873. He discovered the Victoria Falls and searched for the source of the **Nile River**. In 1869, after no one had heard from him for several years, the *New York Times* sent a journalist, Henry Stanley (1841–1904), to find him. After a long search Stanley met Livingstone in 1871 near Lake Tanganyika in **Congo**.

Lizard

Lizards are **reptiles** with dry, scaly skin. Most species have four legs, but some have none and resemble **snakes**. A few lizards are born live like **mammals**, but most hatch from **eggs**.

▽ Some **lizards**, such as this thorny devil, have evolved spikes and spines to protect them from predators. The thorny devil lives in Australian deserts and feeds mainly on ants.

There are about 3,500 species of lizards, most of which are found in hot countries. Lizards that live in cooler regions often spend the winter in a form of **hibernation**. The main prey of lizards is **insects**, but the world's largest lizard, the 8-ft. (2.5-m) -long Komodo dragon, may attack and kill **mammals** as large as wild **pigs** and **deer**.

Llama

The llama belongs to the **camel** family but has no hump. It stands about 5 ft. (1.5m) high at the shoulder and has long, thick **hair** to keep it warm on the cold slopes of the **Andes** mountains in **South America**, where it lives. All llamas are descended from a wild species that was tamed by the **Inca** at least 4,500 years ago. Today, South American people still use llamas to carry heavy loads, and they make clothes and ropes from llama **wool**. Llamas are also farmed for their wool in many other parts of the world.

Lobster

The lobster is a **crustacean** related to shrimp and **crabs**. Its body has a hard shell (see **shellfish**). It has four pairs of legs and a pair of huge claws for grabbing **food**. When a lobster feels threatened, it tucks its tail under its body. This drives **water** forward, which pushes the lobster backward to escape.

△ By day **lobsters** hide among rocks or in holes dug into the seabed. They emerge at night to hunt prey, such as shrimp and small fish, and to scavenge for dead animals.

Lock and Key

There are two main types of locks. In the simplest when the key is turned, a piece of **metal**, called a bolt, moves out and fits into a slot. The key has a few notches that are made to fit exactly in similar notches in the lock. The second type is the Yale lock, invented in 1860. In a Yale lock the key turns a cylinder when several small metal pins in the lock are pushed to the right height by the notches on the key. Because there are many possible combinations for the heights of the pins, a Yale lock offers more security than simpler locks.

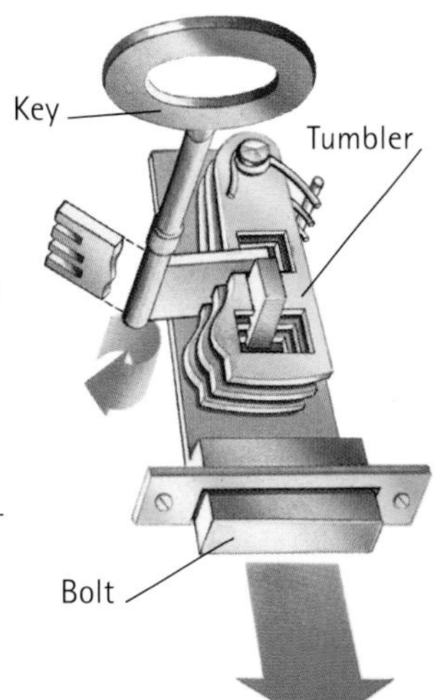

△ A **lock** contains a bolt that slides into a **metal** panel in the door frame when the correct key is inserted. In the lock shown above notches in the key fit into metal plates, called tumblers, to move the bolt.

Locust

The locust is a type of **grasshopper** that lives in **Africa**, southern **Asia**, and **Australia** and that sometimes breeds in enormous numbers. A large swarm may contain thousands of locusts. A swarm may travel far across both land and sea to find new feeding places, and when it lands, the locusts often eat all of the **plants** there. Swarms of locusts can destroy crops over huge areas.

London

London is the capital of the **United Kingdom**. It is the largest city in **Europe** with a **population** of 7.2 million people. It lies on the Thames River, which flows east to the North Sea.

London began as a Roman settlement called Londinium. In the **Middle Ages** it became the main home of the English kings and the location of the country's **parliament**. London also grew into an important port and trading center. During the 1600s the city's crowded buildings allowed the **plague** to spread quickly, and the Great Fire of 1666 destroyed much of the city center. Parts of London were heavily bombed in **World War II**.

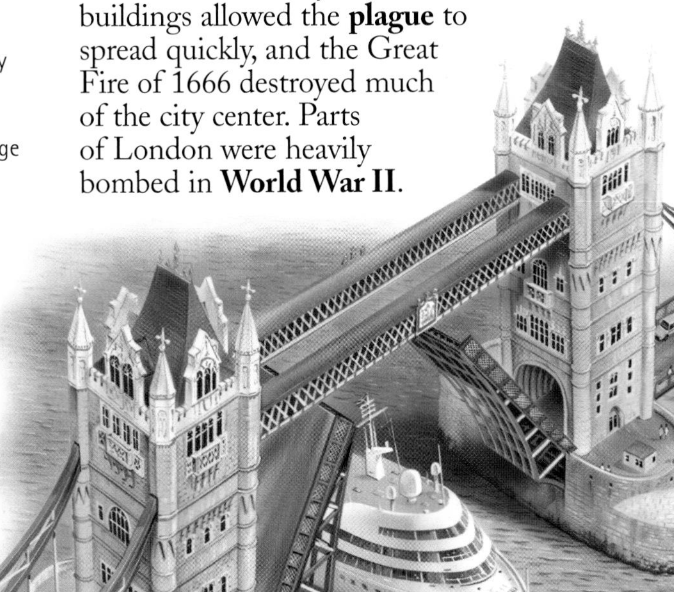

▷ **London** stands on the Thames, and its most famous river crossing is Tower Bridge, which was completed in 1894. The central section of this bridge opens to let large ships pass through.

△ Louis XIV of France was called the "Sun King" because of the splendor of his court and his royal palace at Versailles.

△ The French king **Louis XVI** proved to be a weak and unpopular ruler and was executed during the French Revolution.

LUXEMBOURG
Government: Constitutional monarchy
Capital: Luxembourg
Area: 1,000 sq. mi.
Population: 442,972
Languages: French, German, Luxembourgian
Currency: Euro

Today, London is one of the world's major financial centers, with many **banks**, **insurance** companies, and a busy **stock exchange**. Thousands of tourists visit London to see buildings such as Buckingham Palace, the Tower of London, and the Houses of Parliament.

Longitude

see **Latitude and Longitude**

Los Angeles

Los Angeles (L.A.) is the second largest city in the **United States** after **New York** City. It is surrounded by huge suburbs, and more than 13 million people live in the wider Los Angeles area. L.A. is in California with the **Pacific Ocean** to the west and the San Gabriel Mountains to the east. L.A. has a large port and business district. Many tourists flock to Hollywood, a hilly suburb where many movies are made.

Loudspeaker

A loudspeaker turns electric signals into **sound** waves. The most common type of loudspeaker has a **plastic** cone fixed to a **wire** coil. Inside the coil is a magnet (see also **magnetism**). Electric signals flow through the coil, making it move back and forth, which makes the cone vibrate. **Air** around the cone also starts to vibrate, and these air vibrations reach our **ears** as sounds.

Louis XIV

Louis XIV (1638–1715) ruled **France** for 72 years. He came to the throne when he was only four years old, although a chief minister, Cardinal Mazarin (1602–1661), governed in his name until 1661. Louis was determined to strengthen the power of the French monarchy and claimed to rule by absolute power. He once boasted to his courtiers: "I am the state."

Louis built a huge palace at **Versailles**, which was like a small town. He forced the nobles to live there and to serve him personally to prevent rebellions.

Louis XVI

Louis XVI (1754–1793) of **France** was criticized by his people for being more interested in hunting and entertaining than in important state affairs. His unpopularity ensured that his attempts to reform **government** finances were doomed. In July 1789 the **French Revolution** erupted, and in 1791 Louis tried to flee the country with his queen, **Marie Antoinette**. They were captured and guillotined in 1793.

Lungs

Lungs are the organs used in **breathing**. They are two large, spongelike masses in the chest that absorb **oxygen** from the **air** and remove waste and **carbon** dioxide from the **blood**. Air flows to the lungs down the windpipe, or trachea. Inside the lungs are thousands of tiny tubes called bronchioles, which end in cups known as air sacks, or alveoli. This is where the lungs give oxygen to the blood and take away carbon dioxide.

Luther, Martin

Martin Luther (1483–1546) was a German priest whose quarrels with the Roman Catholic Church started the Protestant **Reformation**. He objected to the way priests forgave people's sins in return for **money**. He also believed that God's teachings lay in the **Bible**, and this was more important to him than what the **popes** and bishops said.

Luxembourg

Luxembourg is one of the smallest countries in **Europe**. The **European Union** has offices in the capital, which is also called Luxembourg.

△ **Madagascar** is home to a variety of plants and animals found nowhere else on earth such as these ring-tailed lemurs (above). These mammals live in troops of up to 20 animals and eat fruits and leaves.

Machine

A machine is any device that makes work easier by allowing us to use force to complete a task. The machine is stronger than a person trying to carry out the task on their own because it exerts a greater force. When a force is used to move something, we say that work is done.

All of the machines we see working around us are related to one of six simple machines: the lever, **screw**, **pulley**, inclined, or sloping, plane, wedge, and **wheel** and axle.

There are many types of levers. The simplest is a long pole pivoted or balanced on a log and used to lift a heavy **rock**. The screw can pull things together or push them apart—with a screw jack someone can lift a **car** that weighs much more than they do.

A simple pulley is used in the winding mechanism that raises **water** from a well. The inclined plane makes it easier to raise heavy loads to higher levels—it takes less work to pull a load up a slope than to lift it vertically. The wedge helps us split things—chisels, knives, nails, and axes are all types of wedges.

Probably the most useful of all simple machines is the wheel and axle—used not only for moving loads but also as a component of all types of other machines such as **clocks**.

△ The pulley is a simple **machine** that helps us lift heavy objects. It changes the direction of a force. By pulling down on the rope a person can raise a large load. If several pulley wheels are joined together (see above), this increases the size of the load that can be lifted with the same effort.

MADAGASCAR
Government: Republic
Capital: Antananarivo
Area: 224,300 sq. mi.
Population: 15,982,563
Languages: Malagasy and French
Currency: Malagasy franc

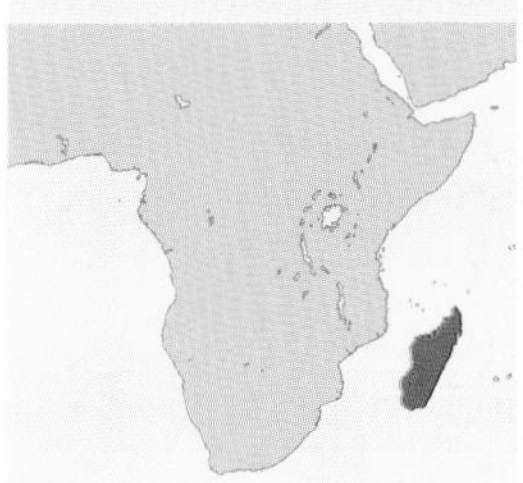

Madagascar

Madagascar is the fourth largest **island** in the world. It is in the **Indian Ocean** about 250 mi. (400km) off the east coast of **Africa**. Madagascar has fertile coastal plains, thick **forests**, a rugged central plateau, and a warm, tropical **climate**. Large areas of land have been stripped bare of natural vegetation to supply timber for export and to create new farmland. The main crops are **coffee**, **rice**, **sugar**cane, and vanilla. A unique range of wildlife lives on Madagascar, including **parrots** and **lemurs**.

Between the 800s and 1300s Arabs set up colonies in Madagascar. In the 1800s the island came under French control, but it won independence in 1960.

Madrid

Madrid is the capital of **Spain**. It was chosen by King Philip II (1527–1598) as the capital because it is in the middle of the country. Madrid is the seat of the country's **parliament**. It has many elegant buildings, including the Prado, which has one of the finest collections of **paintings** in the world.

Magellan, Ferdinand

Ferdinand Magellan (1480–1521) was a Portuguese sailor and **explorer**. He set out to find a new sea route to **Asia**, heading west and rounding the southern tip of **South America**.

In September 1519 Magellan sailed west from Seville, **Spain**, around Cape Horn (in the south of present-day **Argentina**), and into the **Pacific Ocean**. His expedition consisted of 270 sailors of several nationalities traveling on five **ships**. Magellan was killed in 1521 during a confrontation between his crew and the residents of Cebu, an **island** in the **Philippines**. But one of his ships returned safely to Spain in September 1522, having completed the first-ever around-the-world voyage. This epic journey provided the first positive proof that **earth** is round. Although Magellan did not live to complete the voyage, the expedition could not have succeeded without his brave leadership.

Magic

Many early peoples used magic. It was their way of attempting to control what happened around them. They chanted magic words, enacted special **dances**, and produced magical **paintings**.

△ Many **magic** tricks appear to be impossible but work because the audience is taken in by the magician's cleverly planned actions and words. Some tricks rely on secret devices that are prepared in advance.

▽ **Magellan** was killed when local villagers in the Philippines attacked his expedition after a dispute.

Throughout **history** people have believed that certain things (such as talismans or charms) or people (such as **witches** and sorcerers) have magical powers. Magic is often closely linked with **religion**. But most people today think of magic as the conjuring tricks performed by magicians.

Magna Carta

The Magna Carta is a signed agreement, or charter, that was drawn up in **England** in the time of King John (1167–1216). Not even the great barons, or nobles, of the time could argue with the king.

King John improved methods of record keeping and strengthened the **law** courts but was an unpopular ruler. He was forced to rule harshly and to demand extra **taxes** from the people in order to pay for the war with **France**, which he had inherited from the reign of his elder brother, King Richard (1157–1199). In 1215 the English barons met and demanded that John sign the Magna Carta, or "great charter." This document marked the beginning of a new system of **government** in which the king had to rule according to the law.

Magnetism

Magnetism is a type of force belonging to magnets, which attract **metals**, particularly **iron** and **steel**. **Earth** is a huge natural magnet.

Invisible lines of magnetic force spread out around the **planet**, joining the North and South magnetic poles. We call this Earth's magnetic field.

The needle in a **compass** is a magnet. It always turns to face magnetic north. In ancient times people noticed that lodestone, a type of iron ore, suspended from a string would always swing to point in the same direction. Lodestone, also called magnetite, is a natural magnet.

An electromagnet is made by coiling **wire** around a metal core and passing **electricity** through the coil. As soon as the current is broken, the magnetic field ceases to exist. Electromagnets can be altered in strength and made more powerful than ordinary magnets. They are able to produce magnetic fields strong enough to drive **generators** and electric **motors**.

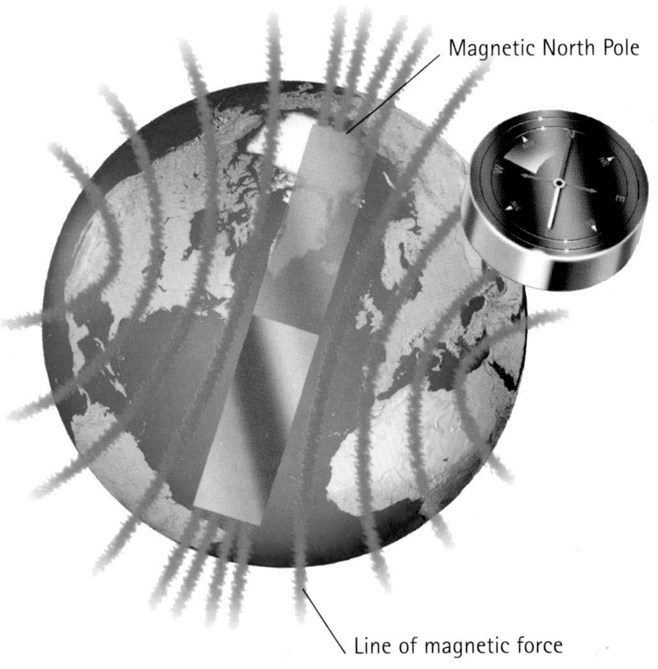

◁ Earth is itself a massive **magnet** with magnetic poles in the far north and south. These act like the ends of a magnet and make compass needles point north. Lines of magnetic force reach all around the planet, creating Earth's magnetic field.

Malaria

Malaria is a common and deadly tropical **disease**. It is caused by a tiny **parasite**, which is carried by the female Anopheles **mosquito**. When an infected mosquito bites someone, parasites pass into that person's bloodstream. Inside the **blood** the parasites multiply, causing a serious sickness that is often fatal.

Drugs are used to treat malaria, but they are not always effective because over time new strains of malarial parasites evolve that are not affected by the drugs. Scientists try to destroy the mosquitoes and the swamps in which they breed. However, so far it has proved impossible to exterminate the **insects** completely.

Malaysia

Malaysia is a country in **Southeast Asia**. It consists of two parts—Peninsular Malaysia and East Malaysia, or Sabah, which is part of the **island** of Borneo. These two regions lie 400 mi. (650km) apart and are separated by the South China Sea. Malaysia's **climate** is hot, humid, and rainy, and the country has large areas of **rain forests**.

Malaysia is a fast-growing nation. Its capital, Kuala Lumpur, is a large, modern city with many **skyscrapers**. The country exports **rubber**, **tin**, and timber, but some people are worried that its logging industry is cutting down too many **forests**. Malaysia developed modern industries in the late 1900s, and manufactured goods are now the most valuable exports.

Malaysia is a member of the **Commonwealth**. It is ruled by a sultan, who is the head of state, and a prime minister, who heads the **government**.

MALAYSIA
Government: Constitutional monarchy
Capital: Kuala Lumpur
Area: 126,700 sq. mi.
Population: 22,229,040
Languages: Malay, English, and Chinese
Currency: Ringgit

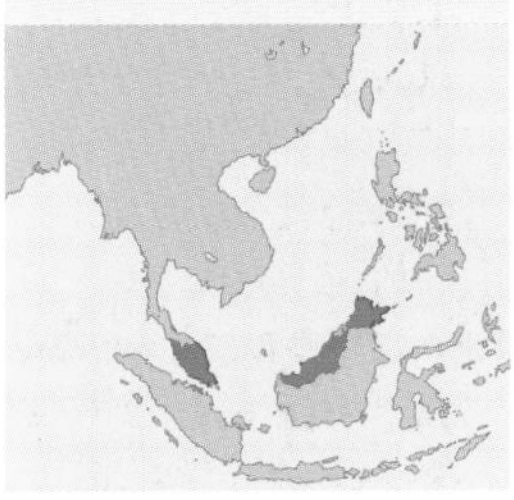

Maldives

The Republic of Maldives is a long chain of **islands** southwest of **India** in the **Indian Ocean**. Although there are about 2,000 islands, the country's total area is small. Most of the people make their living by **fishing**. Scientists think that some islands in the Maldives will vanish in the future because of rising sea levels caused by **global warming**.

MALDIVES
Government: Republic
Capital: Male
Area: 100 sq. mi.
Population: 310,764
Language: Divehi
Currency: Rufiyaa

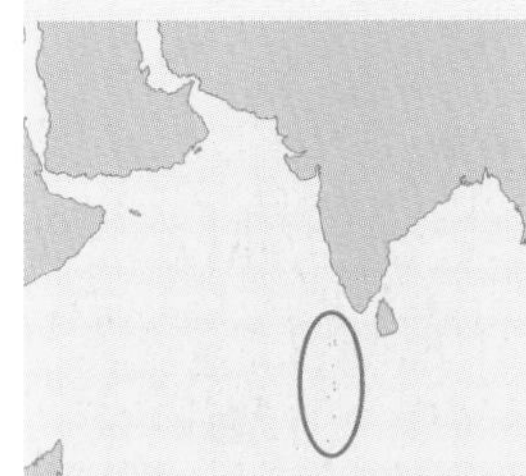

Malta

Malta is an island in the **Mediterranean Sea**. Since ancient times it has been a vital naval base because it guards **trade** routes to the East. For centuries Malta was ruled by the Knights of St. John, but in 1813 it became a British colony. During **World War II**, Malta survived heavy bombing raids. Since 1962 it has been self-governing, and it is now a parliamentary **democracy**. The capital, Valletta, has an old harbor surrounded by fine buildings.

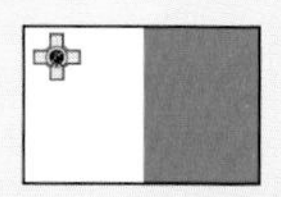

MALTA
Government: Parliamentary democracy
Capital: Valletta
Area: 620 sq. mi.
Population: 394,583
Languages: Maltese, English
Currency: Maltese lira

Mammals *see* pages 196–197

Mammoth

During the **ice ages** wooly mammoths roamed the plains of **North America** and **Europe**. They looked like shaggy-haired **elephants** with long, curling tusks. But they lived in a much colder **climate** than the elephants of today.

Mammoths lived together in herds and ate **grass** and other **plants**. Their enemies included **wolves** and fierce saber-toothed cats (see **prehistoric animals**), and **cave dwellers** hunted mammoths for food. Sometimes a group of hunters drove a mammoth into a pit, where it was killed with spears.

The frozen bodies of mammoths have been found by scientists in the icy **tundra** of **Siberia**. Mammoth remains have also been found in tar pits in California. The last mammoths died about 30,000 years ago.

Mandela, Nelson

Nelson Mandela (b. 1918) was one of the most important political leaders in **Africa** during the 1900s. The son of a tribal chief, he was born in the Transkei territory of **South Africa** and became a lawyer. After **World War II** the white South African **government** introduced the policy of **apartheid**—separate settlements for white and nonwhite people. Mandela helped form the African National Congress (ANC) in 1944, which began a campaign of nonviolent opposition to the government. In 1962 Mandela was arrested and put in prison. People all over the world demanded his release, and he was eventually freed in 1990.

In 1991 President de Klerk (b. 1936) took measures to end apartheid. Fully democratic **elections** were held in 1994, and Mandela was elected **president**. He was South Africa's first black head of state. Mandela retired in 1999 and was succeeded by Thabo Mbeki (b. 1942).

△ After 28 years as a political prisoner Nelson **Mandela** became an emblem of black peoples' struggle for equality in South Africa.

Maori

The Maori are the native people of **New Zealand**. It is thought that they came in canoes from islands in the **Pacific Ocean** to New Zealand in the 1300s. The Maori were fierce warriors who fought with clubs made of **bone** or greenstone (a type of jade). They waged a long, hard struggle against the Europeans who began to settle in New Zealand in the mid-1800s. This conflict did not end until 1865, and there were further outbreaks of fighting for years afterward. Today the Maori play an important part in the life of New Zealand, with their **population** growing at a faster rate than that of non-Maori.

Maori people are skilled at **weaving**, **dancing**, and carving **wood**. Maori carving is full of decoration. Every part of the surface of their work is covered with curves, scrolls, and spirals. Tattooing is also a key Maori **art**.

Mao Tse-tung

Mao Tse-tung (1893–1976) was a great Chinese leader. He was the son of a farmer and trained to be a teacher. In 1921 Mao helped form the Chinese Communist Party (see **communism**) and fought against the Chinese Nationalists under Chiang Kai-shek

△ **Mao Tse-tung** was chairman of the Chinese Communist Party for 27 years.

(1887–1975). In 1934 Mao led 90,000 Communists on a 368-day march through **China** to escape Nationalist forces. This feat was called the "Long March." In 1949 when Mao and the Communist armies had defeated the Nationalists, Mao became head of the Chinese **government**.

Mao wanted China to become as strong and wealthy as the **U.S.** and brought about radical changes in culture and **economics**. His strict policies meant that all aspects of life came under state control. However, many of Mao's plans for his country did not work. He resigned from his job as head of government in 1959 but continued as chairman of the Chinese Communist Party. Mao had many arguments with the Communists of the **Soviet Union**. He also wrote several **books** about **guerrilla warfare**.

After Mao's death in 1976 China's new leaders criticized his rule and increased contacts with the West.

△ The **Marathon** of the Sands is a grueling race in the Sahara Desert that covers about 143 mi. (230km) in six days—farther than five normal marathons.

Map

We need maps to help us find our way around and to discover details of the world's **geography**. There are many types of maps. Political maps show country boundaries and the positions of important towns, **roads**, and **railroads**. Physical maps show natural features such as **mountains**, **rivers**, and **lakes**. **Weather** maps show **temperatures** and **air** conditions.

Maps are drawn to different scales. The scale of some maps is so large that you might be able to find your **house** on one. The scale of other maps is so small that it is possible to squeeze the whole world onto a page of an atlas.

At first a lot of guesswork went into mapmaking. Today aerial **photography** is used to make extremely accurate maps. The pictures are taken from an **aircraft** flying at a constant height. Each photograph overlaps the next slightly so that no detail is lost. **Satellites** are used to produce weather maps.

Charts are maps of the sea. They tell sailors about lighthouses, **rocks**, channels, and the depth of **water** in various places. Detailed maps of the seabed can be produced using **sonar**.

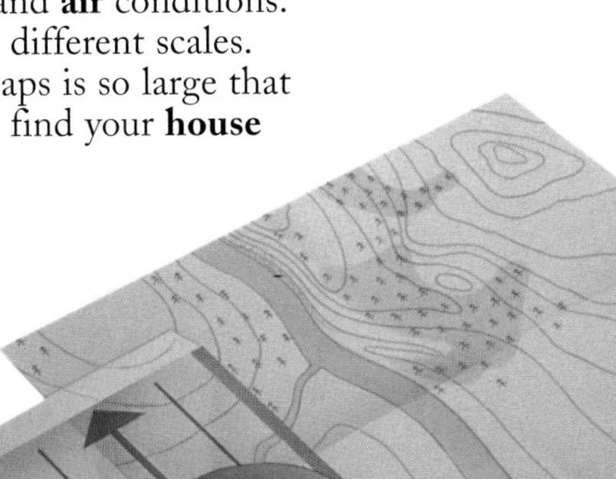

▷ Using a **map** and compass it is possible to locate your exact position. Maps often have contour lines to show features such as hills and valleys. Each contour line joins different points at the same height.

△ Guglielmo **Marconi** with his wireless telegraph, which could send radio signals across the world.

Marathon

The marathon is a long-distance race of 26 mi. (42.19km) that has been run in the **Olympic Games** since 1896. Its name commemorates a famous run by the Greek soldier Pheidippides, who ran from the town of Marathon to **Athens** in 490 B.C. to bring news of a Greek victory over the Persians.

Marble

Marble is a **rock** that is formed when limestone is squeezed and made very hot inside **earth**. Pure marble is white, but most of the rock has other substances in it that give it many colors. Marble has long been used in **architecture** and **sculpture**. It is easy to shape and can be polished until it is beautifully smooth.

Marconi, Guglielmo

Guglielmo Marconi (1874–1937) was a famous physicist who discovered how to transmit **radio** waves. Marconi built a **machine**, the telegraph, for sending radio signals, and in 1901 he sent the first message across the **Atlantic Ocean** (see also **communication**).

MAMMALS

There are a greater variety of mammals than any other animal group. They are found all over the world, and they live on land, in water, and underground.

△ *The slender loris is active only at night. Its huge, saucerlike eyes help it find insects and other prey in the darkness.*

WORLD OF MAMMALS

Mammals are warm-blooded animals, which means they can stay active and keep their bodies warm in cold weather. Most of them are covered with fur. Even sea mammals, such as dolphins and whales, have a thin layer of hair on their bodies. Unlike other animal babies, young mammals feed on milk from their mother's body. Mammals are named after the mammary glands (breasts) that produce this milk.

TYPES OF MAMMALS

The first mammals evolved from reptiles about 230 million years ago. They were small and ate insects. When the dinosaurs died out, many other types of mammals began to evolve. Today there are 4,200 species of mammals, divided into three groups. These groups are placental mammals (which give birth to fully developed young), marsupials (mammals whose young develop in pouches), and egg-laying mammals.

▷ *Mammals, such as this two-humped, or Bactrian, camel, suckle their babies with milk. The milk contains everything that the young need to develop and grow.*

△ *Lynxes are large cats with tufted ears. The fur of the North American lynx is covered with spots, but the larger Siberian lynx has a plain coat.*

△ *Echidnas are unusual mammals that lay eggs. They feed on insects and have spines for protection.*

PLACENTAL MAMMALS

Placental mammals are the largest group of mammals. They include a tremendous variety of species such as rodents, elephants, seals, and human beings. Placental mammals develop inside the mother's body and obtain food and oxygen through the placenta (the part of the womb that connects mother and baby). Some species can run just minutes after birth, but others rely on their parent or parents for months.

MARSUPIALS

Marsupials are mammals that nurse their babies in pouches on the female's body until the young are big enough to fend for themselves. Most marsupials, such as kangaroos, and koalas, live in Australia and New Guinea. Other species, including opossums, live in North America.

THE RIGHT TEETH

Mammals eat a wide range of foods and have teeth to suit their diets. Carnivores, such as cats and dogs, have sharp teeth for seizing prey and tearing flesh. Herbivores, such as horses and cattle, have broad, grinding teeth for eating plants.

◁ *The Mongolian gerbil lives in the deserts of central Asia and feeds on plant shoots and seeds.*

EGG-LAYING MAMMALS

The duck-billed platypus and the echidna are Australian mammals that lay eggs. They are the most primitive mammals alive today and have beaklike mouths with no teeth. The milk that the females produce does not come from teats but oozes from a slit in the skin on the belly.

RODENTS

Almost half of all mammals are rodents, including mice, rats, voles, squirrels, beavers, and porcupines. Rodents have sharp incisors (front teeth) for gnawing through food and burrowing. Many species dig underground tunnels in which to live. Most rodents live for only one or two years, but they breed rapidly.

SEE ALSO
Blood, Bone, Carnivore, Evolution, Food, Hair, Herbivore, Hibernation, Marsupial, Rodent, Prehistoric animals, Reproduction

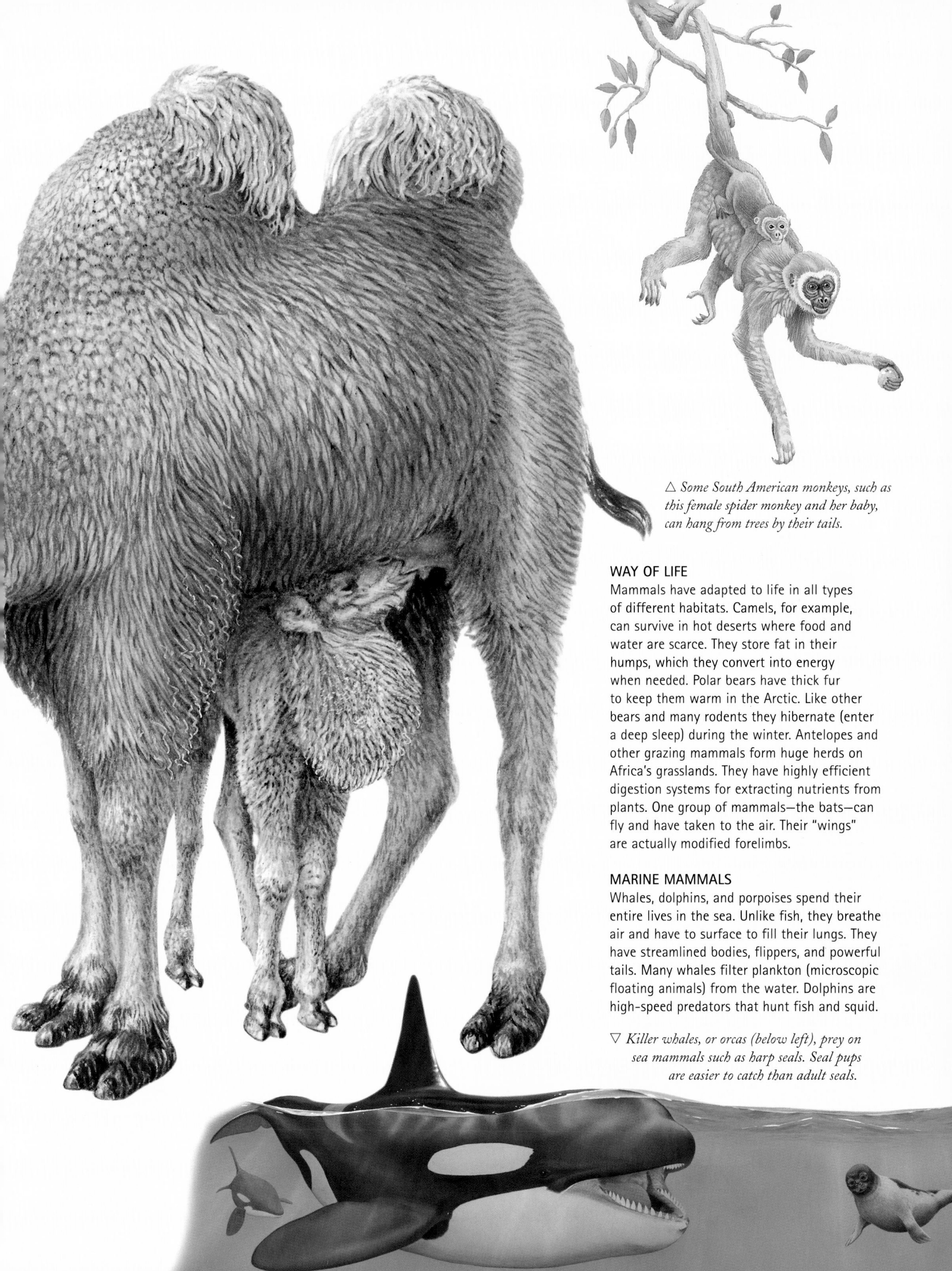

△ *Some South American monkeys, such as this female spider monkey and her baby, can hang from trees by their tails.*

WAY OF LIFE

Mammals have adapted to life in all types of different habitats. Camels, for example, can survive in hot deserts where food and water are scarce. They store fat in their humps, which they convert into energy when needed. Polar bears have thick fur to keep them warm in the Arctic. Like other bears and many rodents they hibernate (enter a deep sleep) during the winter. Antelopes and other grazing mammals form huge herds on Africa's grasslands. They have highly efficient digestion systems for extracting nutrients from plants. One group of mammals—the bats—can fly and have taken to the air. Their "wings" are actually modified forelimbs.

MARINE MAMMALS

Whales, dolphins, and porpoises spend their entire lives in the sea. Unlike fish, they breathe air and have to surface to fill their lungs. They have streamlined bodies, flippers, and powerful tails. Many whales filter plankton (microscopic floating animals) from the water. Dolphins are high-speed predators that hunt fish and squid.

▽ *Killer whales, or orcas (below left), prey on sea mammals such as harp seals. Seal pups are easier to catch than adult seals.*

Margarine

Margarine is a **food** like butter and is made from vegetable **fats** and **oils**. **Vitamins** are usually added to make it almost as nutritious as butter. Margarine was first produced in 1867 by the French chemist Hippolyte Mège-Mouriés (1817–1880). He won a prize offered by the French **government** for finding a cheap substitute for butter. Many people now eat margarine and similar spreads because they are low in unhealthy saturated fats.

Marie Antoinette

Marie Antoinette (1755–1793) was the Austrian-born wife of **Louis XVI** of **France**. A beautiful and vivacious young woman, she spent **money** lavishly. She spent most of her time inside the royal palace at **Versailles**, near **Paris**, and became a symbol to the poor people of France of all they hated about the royal court. When the **French Revolution** broke out in 1789, the king and queen were taken to Paris by force. They escaped but were swiftly recaptured and sentenced to death by guillotine in 1793.

△ The French queen **Marie Antoinette** showed great courage at her trial but was condemned to death in October 1793. She was executed by guillotine.

Mars

The **planet** Mars is about half the size of **Earth** and takes about two years to travel around the **Sun**. It has huge **volcanoes** and deep gorges, far larger than those on Earth. Most of Mars is covered with loose **rocks** scattered over a dusty, red surface, which is why Mars is called the "red planet." It has a north pole and a south pole, both covered with thick snow or frost. The planet's thin atmosphere is made up almost entirely of carbon dioxide, and strong winds whip up dust storms.

Seen through a **telescope**, the red surface of Mars is crisscrossed by thin, gray lines. Some early astronomers (see **astronomy**) thought that these lines were **canals** that had been dug by intelligent beings to irrigate the **soil**. But space probes sent to Mars in 1965, 1969, and 1976 (see **space exploration**) found no trace of the canals. The American *Viking* spacecraft landed on the planet itself and took samples of its soil but was unable to find any evidence of life.

Mars has two tiny moons—Phobos and Deimos. Phobos, the larger of the two, is only about 15 mi. (24km) across. Both of the moons are probably **asteroids** that were dragged toward Mars and began to **orbit** the planet.

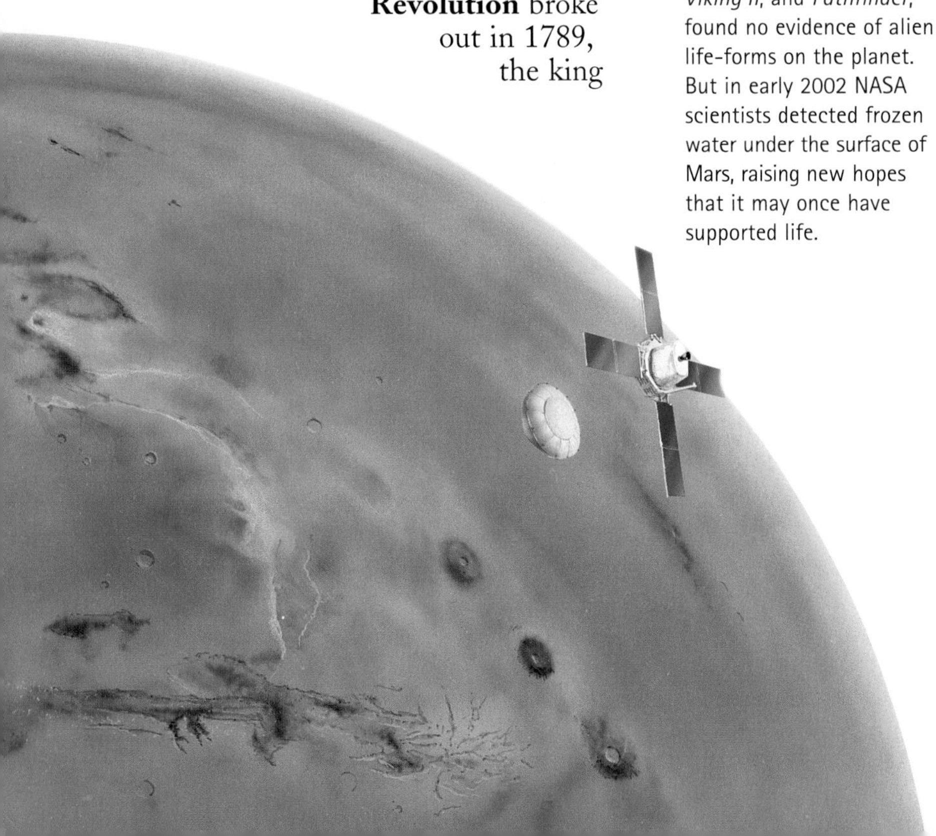

▽ Several space probes to **Mars**, including *Viking I*, *Viking II*, and *Pathfinder*, found no evidence of alien life-forms on the planet. But in early 2002 NASA scientists detected frozen water under the surface of Mars, raising new hopes that it may once have supported life.

MARS FACTS
Average distance from Sun: 141 million mi.
Closest distance to Earth: 48 million mi.
Average temperature: –22°F
Diameter across the equator: 4,212 mi.
Atmosphere: Carbon dioxide
Number of moons: 2
Length of day: 24 hours and 37 minutes
Length of year: 687 Earth days

Marsupial

Marsupials are a group of **mammals** that carry their young inside pouches. They include **kangaroos**, **wallabies**, **bandicoots**, **opossums**, and **koalas**. Most marsupials live in **Australia** or **New Guinea**, but there are also a few species in **North America** and **South America**.

A newly born marsupial is extremely small and is blind, deaf, and naked. It crawls into its mother's pouch and stays there, feeding on her **milk** until it can take care of itself. There are about 250 species of marsupials, most of which live in **forests** or grasslands. Many marsupials are nocturnal.

△ The common wombat is a heavily built **marsupial** with powerful front feet for digging its extensive burrows. A young wombat stays with its mother for at least one year.

Martial arts

The martial arts are various forms of combat that come from east **Asia**. They include judo, karate, and aikido, all from **Japan**, and kung fu from **China**. Judo, meaning "the gentle way," is the most popular martial art. It developed from jujitsu, at one time a violent way of fighting that could maim or kill. Today judo is a safe **sport** practiced by men, women, and children. It has been an **Olympic** sport since 1964 and is used in many parts of the world for self-defense. A trained judo student can quickly unbalance an opponent and throw them to the floor.

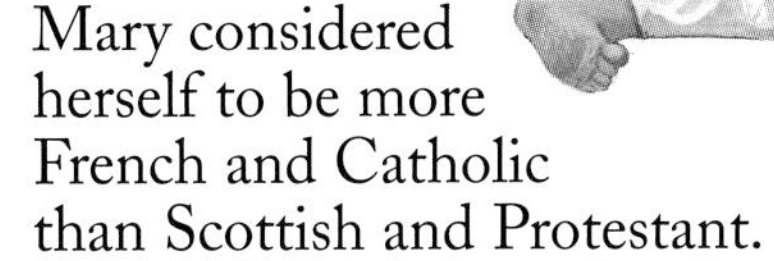

▽ Tae kwon do is a **martial art** based on Korean kick fighting. This black-belt student is demonstrating the power of a flying kick by breaking a piece of wood.

Marx, Karl

Karl Marx (1818–1883) was a political thinker and writer whose ideas brought about enormous social and political changes. Marx was born in **Germany**, and his ideas were the starting point of **communism**. He believed that people who own property, the capitalist class, exploit those who work for them in order to become wealthier. Marx also thought that the workers would one day rise up against the capitalists and take control. Marx wrote several **books**, the most famous of which is *Das Kapital*, which took 30 years to write and was still incomplete when he died in 1883.

Marx often collaborated with another German thinker, Friedrich Engels (1820–1895). The two men's writings later inspired several Communist **revolutions**, notably the **Russian Revolution** of 1917.

Mary, Queen of Scots

Mary, Queen of Scots (1542–1587) was **Scotland**'s last Roman Catholic **monarch**. The daughter of James V of Scotland (1512–1542), Mary was educated in **France** and did not return to Scotland until she was 19. By that time Mary considered herself to be more French and Catholic than Scottish and Protestant.

Mary was the second in line to the English throne after her Protestant cousin **Elizabeth I**. In 1567 Mary was forced to give up the Scottish throne, and later she was imprisoned for 20 years in **England** for plotting against Elizabeth. She was executed on Elizabeth's orders in 1587.

Mathematics

We use simple mathematics every day. For example, we add up the **coins** in our pockets to find out how much **money** we have, or we look at a **clock** and figure out how much **time** we have left before going somewhere. In business, people are constantly using some type of mathematics, often, with the help of **calculators** and **computers**. The branch of mathematics that deals with numbers is called arithmetic. **Algebra** uses symbols, such as "x" and "y," instead of numbers. **Geometry** deals with lines, **angles**, and shapes such as triangles and squares.

Matter

Everything you can see and touch is matter—and so are some things you cannot. Matter is anything that has **volume**, meaning it takes up space. Scientists say that matter has mass—the amount of matter in something. The mass of an item always remains the same. The pull of **gravity** gives you weight, but your weight can change. If you go to the **Moon** you will weigh only one sixth as much as you do on **Earth**, but your mass will still be the same.

Matter can be grouped into three main forms—solid, **liquid**, and **gas**. This **book** is solid, the **water** that comes from a faucet is liquid, and the **air** that we breathe is made of gases. The solid, liquid, and gas forms are called the three states of matter.

Almost all matter can exist in all three forms. If air is made cold enough it becomes a liquid. A gas can be turned into a solid by cooling it.

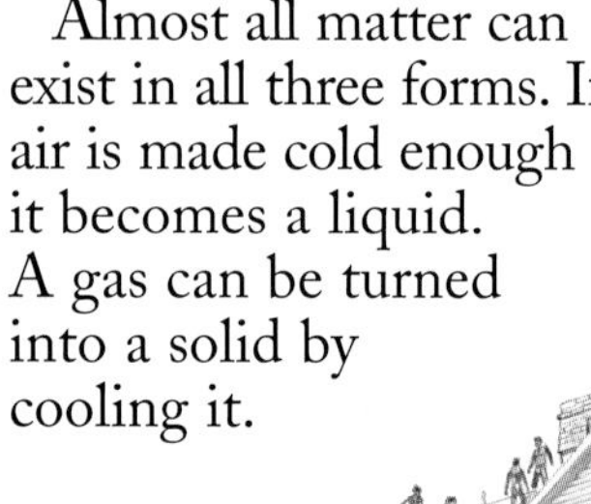

Solids, such as **iron,** can be turned into liquids by heating them. In the **Sun** iron exists as a gas because it is so hot.

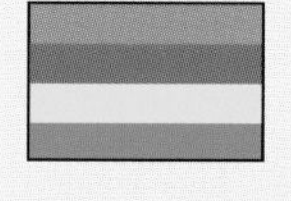

MAURITIUS
Government: Republic
Capital: Port Louis
Area: 700 sq. mi.
Population: 1,189,825
Languages: English, French, and others
Currency: Mauritian Rupee

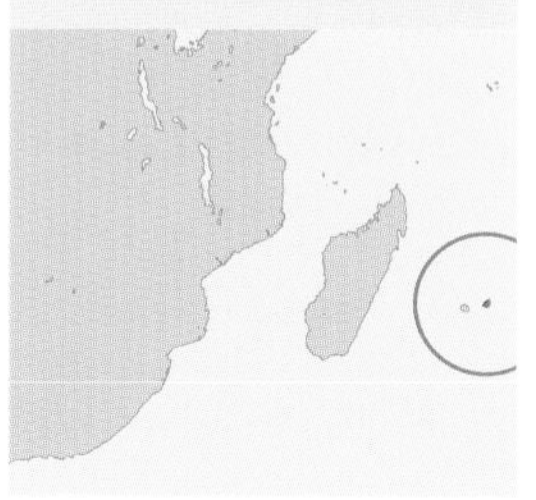

Mauritius

Mauritius is a small **island** nation in the **Indian Ocean**. Most of the island is surrounded by **coral** reefs. The island is thought to be the peak of an ancient **volcano** and has many volcanic hills.

Mauritius is one of the most densely populated places in the world. There are about 195 people for every square mile of the island. The chief crops are **sugar**cane and **tea**, and **fishing** is important in coastal regions. Tourism is a fast-growing industry.

Maya

The Maya first lived in **Central America** in the 400s. They grew corn, sweet potatoes, and **vegetables** and became wealthy through **trade** with neighboring peoples. Later the Maya built stone cities with richly decorated palaces, temples, and **pyramids**. Today many of these great buildings are still standing, hidden in the **rain forest**. The Maya were also skilled in **astronomy** and **mathematics**, and they developed an advanced **writing** system that was a form of **hieroglyphics**.

The Maya did not use **metals** until very late in their **history**. They built with stone tools and had no knowledge of the **wheel**. Their lives were controlled by **religion**. They worshiped many **gods**, including a **sun** god, rain gods, **soil** gods, and a **moon** goddess who protected women.

▽ The **Maya** built huge pyramids and palaces using only stone hand tools. The Castillo pyramid in Chichén Itzá was 98 ft. (30m) high, and its base measured 66 sq. ft. (55 sq m). Four staircases led up to a temple at the top.

Measure
see **Weights and Measures**

Mecca

The city of Mecca in western **Saudi Arabia** is the birthplace of the prophet **Muhammad**, who founded the **religion** of **Islam**. It is the holiest place in the world for Muslims. In the center of Mecca is the Great **Mosque**, and in the mosque's courtyard is the *Kaaba*, which houses the sacred Black Stone. Muslims believe that the stone was given to Abraham by the angel Gabriel. It is kissed by **pilgrims** to Mecca.

Media

The media is the means through which news and views are publicized. It includes newspapers, magazines, television, radio, and the **Internet.** The media offers a window on the world, bringing events from other countries close to home. Media can be aimed at providing information or entertainment, or it may be advertising something.

News put out through the media can affect public opinion. This means that today's media **companies** are extremely influential and powerful. Sometimes **governments** try to censor, or control, the output of the media. However, the freedom of the media to print or broadcast what it likes—as long as it is true—is an important civil right. In many countries there are **laws** that protect the media's independence.

△ Today's **media** can keep us informed of events as they happen. Satellite trucks allow TV crews in a war zone or at the scene of a disaster to broadcast their reports almost instantly. Reporters use cellular phones and laptop computers to E-mail stories to their newspapers.

△ Two million Muslims make the pilgrimage to **Mecca** each year. They perform rituals such as walking around the holy shrine, or *Kaaba*, a black structure containing a stone that dates from ancient times.

Medicine

Medicine is the **science** of healing. It includes the prevention, diagnosis, and treatment of all types of **diseases** and sickness. Early doctors relied on **magic**, prayers, and charms. **Acupuncture** is an ancient form of medical treatment that was developed in **China** 5,000 years ago. In ancient **Greece** doctors examined patients and prescribed herbal remedies. But medicine could not progress in a scientific way until the 1700s when doctors began to learn how the **human body** works.

Medicine has advanced faster during the last 200 years than in the whole of human **history**. The development of anesthetics (pain-killing **drugs**) in the 1800s allowed enormous progress to be made in **surgery**. Scientists have discovered all kinds of other important drugs, such as **antibiotics**, and certain diseases, including tuberculosis and smallpox, have been almost wiped out. Doctors can now transplant organs such as the **heart** and the **kidneys**. Modern **hospitals** are full of advanced equipment such as **X-ray** machines, **ultrasound** scanners, and life-support **machines**.

△ The **Mediterranean Sea**'s attractive coastline and pleasant climate make it a major tourist destination.

Mediterranean Sea

The Mediterranean Sea is surrounded by three **continents—Europe**, **Africa**, and **Asia**. It is joined to the Black Sea by a narrow strait, or passage, and flows out into the **Atlantic Ocean** through the Strait of **Gibraltar**. The **Suez Canal**, opened in 1869, cuts across **Egypt** and allows large **ships** to sail from the Mediterranean into the **Red Sea**.

Melbourne

Melbourne is the second largest city in **Australia** and the capital of the state of Victoria. It has a **population** of almost three million people. The city lies at the mouth of the Yarra **River** on Port Phillip Bay. Melbourne was the capital of Australia from 1901 to 1927 until it was changed to **Canberra**.

Mendel, Gregor

Born in **Austria**, Gregor Mendel (1822–1884) was a monk who became famous for establishing the basic laws of heredity. Heredity is the passing on of characteristics, such as **eye** color and **skin** color, from parents to their children (see **genetics**).

Mendel grew up on a farm, where he became interested in **botany**—the branch of **biology** that deals with **plants**. When Mendel entered a **monastery**, he began to grow peas. He noticed that when he planted the **seeds** of tall pea plants, only tall pea plants grew. Then he tried crossing tall pea plants with short pea plants by taking pollen from one and putting it in the other. He found that again he had only tall plants. But when he crossed these new mixed tall plants with each other, three fourths of the new plants were tall, and one fourth was short. Mendel had found out that characteristics, such as height, are controlled by genes passed on from each parent. Mendel also showed that some genes—for example, the gene that produces tallness in pea plants—are stronger than others.

△ A **mercury** barometer helps forecast the weather by measuring air pressure. It contains a glass tube full of mercury, which rises or falls when the air pressure changes. This makes a pointer move over a scale.

Mercury (metal)

Mercury is the only **metal** that is a **liquid** at ordinary **temperatures**. When mercury is poured onto a table, it forms small, beadlike drops. This is because of the attraction between mercury's molecules. Mercury is used in **thermometers** and **barometers**.

Mercury (planet)

The **planet** Mercury is one of the smallest in our **solar system** and is the closest to the **Sun**. A day on Mercury lasts 59 of our days. During the long daylight hours it is so hot that even **lead** would melt. During the equally long night the **temperature** drops to as low as (–274°F) –170°C. Little was known about Mercury's surface until the space probe *Mariner 10* flew past the planet in 1973, 1974, and 1975. It showed that Mercury has a thin atmosphere and big craters like those on our **Moon**.

△ **Mercury** has a dry, airless surface pockmarked with craters, and there is also evidence of ancient lava flows. During the day the planet is baked by heat and radiation from the nearby Sun. Its dense core is made of iron and nickel.

MERCURY FACTS

Average distance from Sun: 39 million mi.
Closest distance to Earth: 28 million mi.
Average temperature: 284°F
Diameter across the equator: 3,024 mi.
Atmosphere: Almost none
Number of moons: 0
Length of day: 59 Earth days
Length of year: 88 Earth days

△ As a **meteor** enters Earth's atmosphere friction heats it and makes it glow. Meteors may be chips off comets, the Moon, or Mars, but most are asteroid debris.

Metal

About two thirds of the **elements** on **Earth** are metals. The most important metals are **iron** (used for making steel), **copper**, and **aluminum**.

People have used metals since early times. Iron, copper, and **tin** were the first metals to be used. They were made into tools and weapons. **Gold** and **silver** were also discovered at a very early stage and used for **jewelry**.

Most metals are solid unless they are heated, and many are shiny. They all let **heat** and **electricity** pass through them. Copper and silver are the best heat conductors. Some metals are soft and are easy to pound into shapes or pull into thin **wires**. Other metals are brittle—they break easily—and a few are so hard that they are difficult to work with.

Metals can be mixed to form **alloys**, which have different properties to the metals from which they are made. For example, **bronze** is an alloy made from tin and copper and is stronger than either of them.

Earth has a huge supply of some metals, such as iron and aluminum, while others, such as gold and platinum, are rare. Metals may be found pure or mixed with other elements in **minerals**. Many metals are found as ores, which are **compounds** of metal and **oxygen**.

Meteor

A meteor is a lump of **metal** or stone that travels through space at a great speed. Millions of small meteors fall to **Earth** every day, but most burn up in the **atmosphere**. The burning meteors are called shooting stars and are visible on clear nights. Large meteors that reach Earth's surface are known as meteorites. The violent impact may create a large hole, or crater.

MEXICO
Government: Federal republic
Capital: Mexico City
Area: 741,600 sq. mi.
Population: 101,879,171
Language: Spanish
Currency: New peso

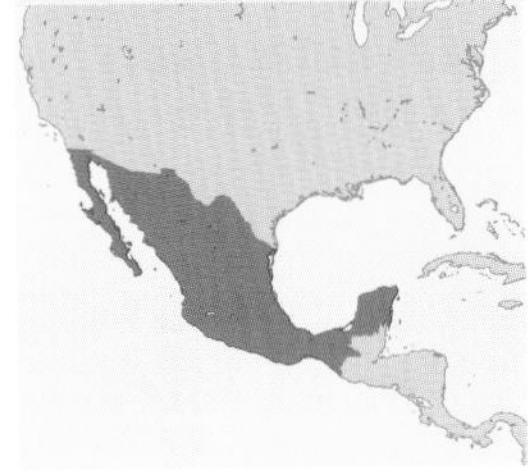

Mexico

Mexico is a country in **North America**. It lies between the **U.S.** in the north and **Central America** in the south. Much of the country is hilly with fertile uplands. The highest **mountains** reach over 18,696 ft. (5,700m). In the southeast the low Yucatán Peninsula sticks out far into the Gulf of Mexico, the western part of the **Caribbean** Sea. Seven tenths of Mexico has little rainfall, but lush **rain forests** grow in the south.

The first people in Mexico were Indians, including the **Aztecs**. Spanish settlers arrived in Mexico in 1519, and the country was under **Spain**'s control until 1821 when it won independence. Today many Mexicans are mestizos of mixed European and North American origin.

▷ Much of the fruits and vegetables that **Mexico** produces is sold at its colorful street markets, but the country also exports large quantities of food. Important crops for export include coffee, cotton, corn, and bananas.

△ **Michelangelo** worked on this statue of Moses from around 1513 to 1516. His statues were often larger than life and are famous for their accurate carving.

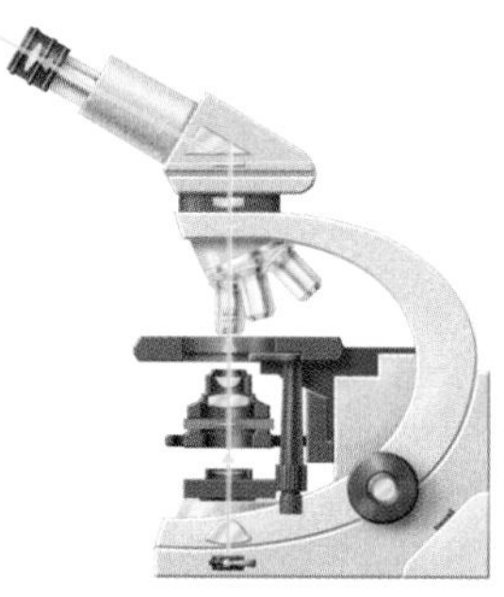

△ In an optical **microscope** the image can be seen by looking down through the eyepiece, which contains a series of magnifying lenses.

▽ The **Middle East** produces much of the world's oil, which is drilled from underground rocks that lie beneath the desert.

Most white people are descendants of the Spanish settlers. Many Mexicans are farmers or work in the country's **oil**, **natural gas**, **iron and steel**, and chemical industries. However, widespread poverty has led to a steady stream of people trying to enter the U.S. illegally in search of jobs (see **immigration**).

Michelangelo

Michelangelo di Lodovico Buonarroti (1475–1564) was a painter and sculptor who lived in **Italy** at the time of the **Renaissance**. He is famous for the large-scale **paintings** he made of religious and historical subjects and for his lifelike **marble** statues. He also made a large number of beautiful **drawings**.

Michelangelo's patrons included the **pope**, nobles, and wealthy townspeople. He spent four-and-a-half years painting huge pictures in the Sistine Chapel in **Vatican City** for Pope Julius II (1443–1513). This massive undertaking was finally completed in 1511. One of Michelangelo's best-known statues is David (1504), which stands 13 ft. (4m) high. Michelangelo was also the chief architect of St. Peter's, a spectacular **church** that towers over the Vatican.

Microphone

A microphone picks up **sound** waves and turns them into electric signals. These can be made into a **recording** or sent out as **radio** waves. They can also be fed through an amplifier and loudspeakers, which make the sound louder. A **telephone**'s mouthpiece has a microphone in it that changes **voices** into electric signals (see **communication**).

Microscope

A microscope is an instrument used for looking at tiny objects. It magnifies things, or makes them appear larger. Objects that are invisible to the naked **eye** are called microscopic. Many microscopic **plants** and **animals**, including **bacteria**, can be seen if you look at them through a microscope.

Microscopes work by using **lenses**. The simplest microscope is a magnifying glass, which has only one **lens**. The lenses in many microscopes work by bending **light** rays. Small microscopes can magnify about 100 times, but big microscopes used by scientists may magnify up to 2,000 times. The electron microscope is much more powerful—it can magnify up to two million times. Instead of bending light rays it bends beams of electrons (see **atoms**).

Middle Ages

see **pages 206–207**

Middle East

The Middle East is a group of countries in southwest **Asia** lying between **Africa** and **Europe**. Much of the region is **desert**, with rugged **mountain** ranges in eastern **Turkey**, **Afghanistan**, and **Iran**. Most people live along the coasts, in inland valleys, or around an **oasis**. The main **rivers**, the Euphrates and Tigris, rise in Turkey and flow through **Syria** and **Iraq** to the Persian Gulf. They are used to irrigate the farmland that lies on their banks (see **irrigation**).

In parts of the Middle East nomadic tribes herd **goats** and **sheep** (see **nomad**). The region's chief resource is

oil. **Saudi Arabia** has about one fourth of the world's known oil resources, and other leading oil producers include Iraq, Iran, Kuwait, Qatar, **Oman**, and the **United Arab Emirates**.

Many of the people in the Middle East are Arabs and follow the **religion** of **Islam**. During the second half of the 1900s there were several wars between Arab countries and the mainly Jewish state of **Israel**.

Migration

Migration is the regular movement of **animals** between one place and another. Some animals migrate every year, but others migrate only twice in their lifetimes. These journeys are made to reach new feeding or breeding areas and are usually linked to the **seasons**.

Animals migrate by **instinct**. They do not have to plan their journeys and are believed to use a range of methods to find their way. Some follow natural features such as **mountains**, **rivers**, and coastlines, while others use their sense of **smell**. **Birds** may be guided by the **Sun**, the **stars**, or by sensing **Earth**'s powerful magnetic field (see **magnetism**).

Birds are the greatest migrators of all animals. Every fall swallows and martins leave **Europe** and fly south to spend the winter in **Africa**. **North America**'s swallows and martins fly south to **South America**. These trips may be 6,200 mi. (10,000km) long. In the spring the birds fly north again to breed.

But birds are not the only animals that migrate long distances. **Butterflies**, **turtles**, **fish**, **whales**, and many grazing **mammals** migrate too. Whales and fish make long journeys through the **ocean** to find food and breed. The **eels** of Europe's rivers and marshes swim many miles across the **Atlantic Ocean** to breed. After mating the adults die. The eels that hatch take years to swim back to Europe. Herds of reindeer migrate from the **tundra** in the **Arctic** to spend the winter in **forests** farther south.

Milk

Milk is a **food** on which all baby **mammals** live. It comes from the mammary **glands**, or breasts, of the baby's mother. The baby sucks the milk from its mother's nipples, or teats.

Milk contains all of the things that a baby needs. At first the milk is pale and watery, but later it is much richer and creamier. It is full of **fat**, **sugar**, **starch**, **protein**, **vitamins**, and essential **minerals**. It also protects the baby from **diseases** and infections.

People also use milk from animals such as **cattle**, **sheep**, **goats**, and even **camels** and reindeer. The milk is consumed as a drink and is used to make foods such as cream, butter, yogurt, **cheese**, and ice cream.

△ The monarch butterfly's **migration** from North America to Mexico covers more than 1,860 mi. (3,000km). The butterfly gathers in huge swarms at its winter home and makes the return trip in the following spring.

Milky Way

When you look at the sky on a clear, moonless night, you can see a pale cloud of **light**. If you look at it through binoculars or a **telescope**, you will see that the cloud is really millions of **stars**. All of these stars and most of the other stars we see are part of our **galaxy**, which is called the Milky Way. Astronomers (see **astronomy**) think that the Milky Way has about 100 billion stars,

continued on page 208

▽ This view shows what the **Milky Way** might look like from several hundred light-years above our galaxy. It has a structure of spiral arms and a densely packed central bulge of older stars.

MIDDLE AGES

△ *Stained-glass windows were a type of painting that reached its greatest height in churches in France in the 1100s. The windows told stories about everyone and everything from Biblical events to the kings and queens of the day.*

In European history the Middle Ages stretched from the fall of the Roman Empire in around A.D. 470 to the dawn of the Renaissance at the beginning of the 1400s. It was a 1,000-year period of turbulence and strife.

Following the Roman Empire's collapse much of Western Europe was overtaken by barbarians. Their influence began to spread south until it reached almost to the Mediterranean.

CHRISTIANITY UNDER THREAT

In southeast Europe, Islam had begun to reach many countries from its base in the Middle East. By c. A.D. 750 Arabs controlled much of northern Africa and eastern Asia and had become powerful rivals to the Byzantine empire. They tried to capture the Byzantine capital, Constantinople, in 674-678 but failed. If the Byzantine empire and Christianity wished to survive the onslaught from barbarians in the north and Arabs in the south, a new rule would have to be established.

▽ *Most large European towns held a market once or twice a week, and the main square would be filled with traders selling their wares.*

△ *In Europe most people worked the land for a living, paying their dues to their feudal lord or to the Church. They would sow seeds by hand and use horses to pull the plows.*

THE EMPEROR CHARLEMAGNE

In an attempt to consolidate power and bring peace to Europe the pope crowned the king of the Franks, Charlemagne (747–814), Christian emperor in A.D. 800. Charlemagne's strong 14-year reign was a brief, settled period of enlightenment, but it ended with his death. The power structure of this relationship between emperors and popes became a dominant feature of the Middle Ages.

△ *In the Middle Ages women were considered inferior to men. A wealthy woman would be educated because she needed to run the household.*

EUROPE AT WAR

After the death of Charlemagne the Vikings began a series of raids and conquests that lasted almost 200 years. Their influence was felt from present-day Russia in the east to Ireland in the west. Viking raids on northern Europe ended with their leader's defeat by King Harold of England in the 1000s.

By this time the march of Islam seemed unstoppable and had become a major threat to European Christianity. Much of Spain and southern Italy had been conquered by the North African Arabs or Moors. In 1095 the pope urged all Christians to drive back the Arabs and recover the holy Christian sites in Palestine. This call resulted in the Crusades, which cost the lives of thousands of Arabs and Europeans and lasted for almost 200 years.

After the threats from the Vikings and Islam had passed, the European nations started to fight each other in an attempt to gain power and wealth. The Hundred Years' War (1337–1453) was fought by the kings of France and England over the sovereignty of France.

A decisive battle was won by the English king Henry V at Agincourt in France in 1415, but a century later England had lost all of its French possessions. The Hapsburg royal family in Austria and the Hohenzollerns of Germany fought long wars to conquer new lands for their respective peoples.

A FEUDAL SOCIETY

Life in Europe in the Middle Ages was very harsh for the poorest peasants. For most of the time Europe was divided into kingdoms, dukedoms, and other states. Agriculture was the source of wealth for the majority, and the richest landowners were mainly monarchs and the Church. In this feudal society the peasants were allowed to live on the land and to farm it as long as they surrendered most of their crops to their lord, who paid the king. Peasants also paid large taxes to the Church in the form of tithes. Many also worked in the houses of the wealthy as servants.

In contrast to the hand-to-mouth existence of the poor the rich lived a comfortable and even luxurious life. The rich lords and their families often held lavish feasts and banquets to celebrate special occasions. These were formal meals that lasted for hours and included many dishes of spiced meats as well as drinks of mead (a kind of beer) and wine.

NATURAL DISASTERS

Plagues and pestilence were common throughout Europe and spared neither rich nor poor. The Black Death (a form of bubonic plague) swept through Europe from Asia in 1347 and wiped out 25 million people, almost one third of the population of Europe.

TRADE AND PROSPERITY

During the latter half of the Middle Ages the growth in technology and industries allowed merchants and craftspeople to form trade guilds. These were powerful organizations that imposed regulations and rules and tried to control prices across Europe as a whole. They also encouraged the spread of skills throughout the region, and this promoted trade between countries. The guilds also helped raise the living and working conditions of the lowest classes.

When the Middle Ages finally came to an end in the 1400s with the beginning of the Renaissance, the Christian society of Europe began a period of stability and expansion through art, learning, trade, and exploration.

▷ *Sieges on castles were a common feature of the wars that took place during this period. Foot soldiers stood little chance against the sword of a fully armed knight.*

SEE ALSO
Armor, Black Death, Castle, Charlemagne, Christianity, Crusades, Dark Ages, Henry V, History, Islam, Knight, Renaissance, Trade

continued from page 205

including the **Sun**. The Milky Way stretches for 100,000 light-years. A light-year is the distance light travels in one **year** at a speed of 186,000 mi. (300,000km) per second. Our own **solar system** is 30,000 light-years from the center of the Milky Way.

Mime

Mime is the art of acting in silence. A mime artist does not speak. Instead their movements tell the story. The face, hands, and body are used to show how the artist feels. Mime artists are like dancers. They have to control every movement with great care so that the audience can follow the story.

In ancient **Greece** and the **Roman Empire** mime included some speaking, but most of the story was told with gestures. The actors wore masks. Gradually mime came to be face, hand, and body interpretations only, and the speaking parts were lost. Mime is used a lot in **dance**, especially in **ballet**.

Mineral

The **rocks**, **sand**, and **soil** of earth are made up of materials called minerals. There are over 3,000 types of minerals, but only 30 of them make up the majority of the **planet**'s rocks.

Some minerals, such as **gold** and platinum, are made up of only one **element**. Others, such as **quartz** and **salt**, consist of two or more elements. Some minerals are **metals** such as **copper** and **silver**. Other minerals, like **sulfur**, are nonmetallic.

Pure minerals are made up of **atoms** arranged in regular patterns, known as crystals. Minerals form crystals when they cool from hot **gases** and **liquids** deep inside earth. Crystals can grow very large if they cool slowly. Whether they are large or small, crystals of the same mineral usually have the same shape. Minerals that can be cut to a beautiful shape and polished are called gemstones. **Gems** include rubies, **diamonds**, and sapphires.

Azurite

Malachite

Realgar

Galena

△ Many of the **minerals** found on earth form three-dimensional shapes called crystals. Each mineral has differently shaped crystals.

Mining

Mining is the process of taking **minerals** out of the ground. It is one of the most important industries. When minerals lie in one place in large quantities, they are known as ores. People mine minerals such as **gold**, **silver**, **tin**, **coal**, and **salt**. They also mine stone for building.

Mines can be quarries (open pits) or underground **tunnels**. **Quarrying** is used to extract ores that lie close to the surface of the **soil**. First the soil is removed, and then giant excavators scoop up the **rock** that contains the minerals. Today's underground mines can reach as deep as 1.86 mi. (3km) below the surface. Problems with drainage and ventilation have been solved using **machines**, which pump out **water** and circulate fresh **air**. Another form of mining is dredging, in which minerals are scooped up from the beds of **rivers** and **lakes**.

◁ **Mining** is hard and dangerous work. Deep mines have always suffered from cave-ins, flooding, and poisonous gases. In the future some mining may be carried out by robots.

Mirror

A mirror is made from a sheet of **glass** that has a very thin layer of **silver** or **aluminum** sprayed on the back. This is then painted to protect the **metal** surface from scratches. Mirrors were first made in this way in the 1500s in **Venice**. Before that date mirrors were usually made of solid pieces of highly polished metal.

Light is reflected from a smooth surface, and the reflection, called an image, is what we see when we look into a mirror. However, the image is reversed. If you raise your left hand, the image raises its right hand.

A plane mirror has a flat surface. A convex mirror curves out like the back of a spoon. A concave mirror curves in like a hollow bowl.

Missile

A missile is a weapon powered by a **rocket** engine and armed with an explosive warhead. A guided missile is led to its target by **radio** or **radar** commands or by a device inside the missile. One type of guided missile is the ballistic missile. A ballistic missile follows a path that is partly outside of earth's **atmosphere**. It is guided as it flies up into the air, but when its rocket **engine** burns out, it returns to **earth** on an unguided path.

The only defense against a ballistic missile is to fire another missile at it before it hits its target. Such defensive missiles are called anti-ballistic missiles. However, some missiles are armed with warheads that split up into several separate warheads as they descend. This makes defense much more difficult.

Mississippi River

The Mississippi River is the longest **river** in the **United States**. It starts in Minnesota in the north and flows 2,343 mi. (3,779km) south to the Gulf of **Mexico**. It has over 250 tributaries—smaller rivers that flow into it. This huge network of rivers is extremely important for shipping and industries.

The waters of the Mississippi carry a huge amount of mud. As a result, its **delta**, the coastal zone where most of the mud is dumped, is growing out to sea at a rate of 0.62 mi. (1km) every 10 years.

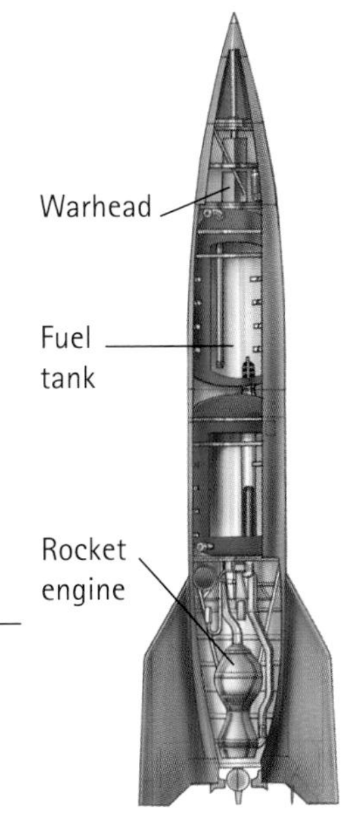

△ **Missiles** are very effective weapons and have changed the way wars are fought. Most of a missile is taken up with fuel tanks for its rocket engine.

△ **Moles** have supersoft fur that lies flat in any direction. This helps them squeeze down tunnels.

▽ A tremendous variety of **mollusks** live in the sea, including 1) whelks, 2) limpets, 3) cuttlefish, 4) cockles, and 5) mussels.

Modem *see* Internet

Mole

Moles are small burrowing **mammals** found all over the world. They spend most of their lives underground. Moles have narrow snouts and huge, clawed feet for tunneling quickly through the **soil**. They are almost blind, but they have excellent **hearing** and very sensitive noses for finding **food** by **smell**. Moles feed on **worms** and **insect** grubs. They store some of their food to eat in the future and have separate chambers for sleeping and raising their young.

Mollusk

Mollusks are one of the largest groups of **invertebrates** (**animals** without backbones). There are about 70,000 different species, including **snails** and **slugs**, **octopuses**, cuttlefish, **squid**, mussels, whelks, cockles, scallops, and limpets. After **insects** mollusks are the most numerous of all animals. Mollusks live in many **habitats**, but most are found in the sea.

All mollusks have soft bodies and no **bones**. For this reason many mollusks grow shells to protect themselves. As a mollusk grows its shell grows with it. The shell is made of the **mineral** calcium carbonate, which is produced from the **food** the mollusk eats.

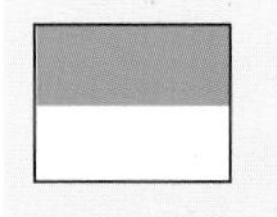

MONACO
Government: Constitutional monarchy
Capital: Monaco-ville
Area: 0.75 sq. mi.
Population: 31,842
Language: French
Currency: Euro

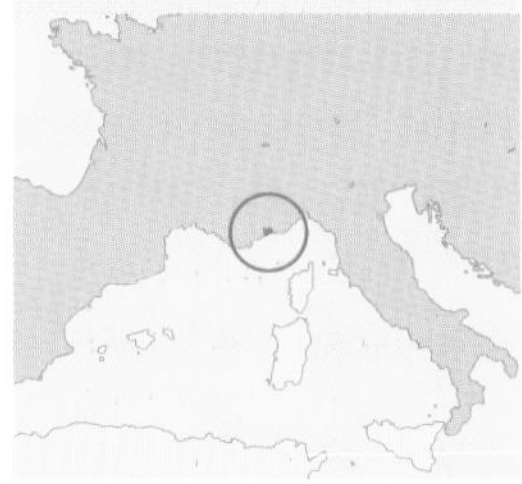

Monaco

The tiny country of Monaco lies on the French coast of the **Mediterranean Sea**. It is called a principality because it is ruled by a prince. Since the 1200s all of Monaco's rulers have come from the Grimaldi family.

Monaco's main industry is tourism. With a population of 32,000 in an area of 0.75 sq. mi. (1.9 sq km), Monaco has a greater **population** density than any other country in the world—42,458 people per square mile. More than half of the people of Monaco are French.

Monarch

A monarch is a person who inherits a country's throne and is the head of state for life. In the past the monarch was elected, but monarchs are usually the eldest child of the existing monarch. A family of monarchs is called a dynasty. There have been several royal families in the **British Isles**, including the House of Tudor, which ruled **England** from 1485 until 1603. One of Europe's most powerful royal families was the **Hapsburgs**, to which many of the continent's emperors and kings belonged.

Monarchs around the world have had many different titles such as king, queen, emperor, sultan, and shah. Many monarchs have ruled with absolute power, and sometimes it was believed that the monarch was responsible only to God. This system of **government** is the opposite of **democracy**, in which the people choose their government and officials in regular **elections**. But throughout **history** there have also been other forms of monarchies. In a constitutional monarchy, for example, the monarch's duties are ceremonial, and the real power lies with politicians.

▽ A **monastery** in Europe during the Middle Ages was like a small town. The most important building was the church, but there were also dormitories for the monks, a hospital for caring for the sick, and gardens. Cloisters were half-covered courtyards where monks could go for quiet prayer.

Monastery

A monastery is a place where monks live in a separate community. The monks lead a religious life and obey strict rules. Monks are always male, but there are also nuns who live in all-female religious communities in convents. Monasteries are especially important in **Buddhism** and **Christianity**.

Christian monasteries began in **Egypt** in about A.D. 300. The monks worked as farmers, laborers, and teachers and helped the poor. One of the most famous early Christian monks was St. Benedict (c. A.D. 480–547), who founded the Benedictine order in **Italy**. He divided the day into periods of prayer, religious study, and work. Another important Italian monk was Francis of Assisi (1182–1226), who founded the Franciscan order.

Life in a Buddhist monastery revolves around meditation, the study of religious texts, and taking part in ceremonies. In parts of **Asia**, such as **Thailand** and **Myanmar** (Burma), boys as young as eight are sent to monasteries to train to become Buddhist monks. One famous Buddhist monastery is the Potala, which stands on a rocky outcrop near Lhasa, the capital of **Tibet**. It was the home of the **Dalai Lama**.

Money

We use money every day to pay for things we buy. We pay with either **coins** or **paper** bills. This type of money is known as cash. There is also another type of money that includes checks and credit cards.

Almost anything can be used as money. In the past people used shells, beads, cocoa beans, **salt**, grain, and even **cattle**. **Metal** coins were first used in **China** as long ago as 800 B.C. They were also used in ancient **Greece** and the **Middle East**. At that time coins were valuable because they were made of either **gold** or **silver**. Later people began to use coins made of cheaper metals. The metal itself had no value, but the coins were still worth the amount stamped on them. Paper money was invented in China in about A.D. 600. Today a country's money is backed by its **government** and **banks**.

Mongolia

Mongolia is a **republic** in the heart of **Asia** between **Russia** and **China**. It is a high, flat country. Much of the land is **desert** or grassy plateaus with high **mountain** ranges in the west. The Gobi Desert covers a large area in the south.

Mongolia is a thinly populated country, and its people are descended from the **Mongols**. Until recently a Communist state (see **communism**), Mongolia now has a multiparty system.

MONGOLIA
Government: Republic
Capital: Ulan Bator
Area: 603,500 sq. mi.
Population: 2,654,999
Language: Khalka Mongol
Currency: Tugrik

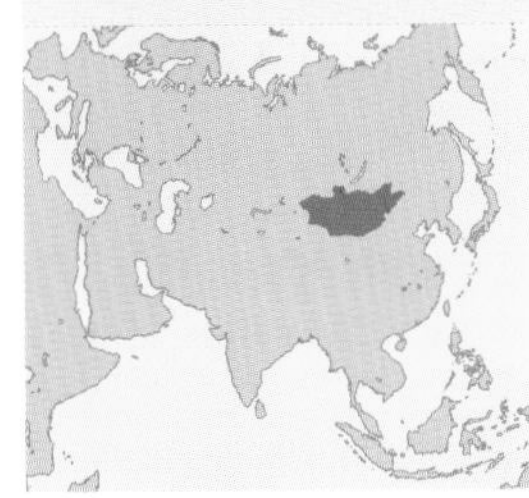

Mongols

The Mongols were **nomads** who lived on the great plains of central **Asia**. They herded huge flocks of **sheep**, **goats**, **cattle**, and **horses**, which they grazed on the vast grasslands of the region. They lived in tents called yurts, which were made of light **wood** and **animal** hides.

The Mongols were superb horsemen and highly trained warriors. In the 1200s they formed a mighty **army** led by **Genghis Khan**. Swift-riding hordes of Mongols swept through **China**, **India**, Persia (present-day **Iran**), and as far west as **Hungary**. Under Genghis Khan, and later his grandson **Kublai Khan**, the Mongols conquered half the known world, but they were unable to hold their empire together. Within 100 years the Mongol empire had been taken over by the Chinese.

Mongoose

The mongoose is a small **mammal** that lives in **Africa** and southern **Asia**. It is a relative of weasels and ermines. It has a long body, a bushy tail, and short legs. The mongoose lives in a burrow and feeds on small **birds** and **rodents** such as **rats** and **snakes**.

▽ The banded **mongoose** is famed for its ability to attack and kill venomous snakes such as this cobra. It relies on speed to grab the snake before it bites.

Monkey

Monkeys are **mammals** that belong to the primates—the same group of **animals** as **apes** and **human beings**. Most monkeys have long tails and thick fur all over their bodies. They are usually smaller than apes. Monkeys' hands and feet are used for grasping food, branches

▷ Red howler **monkeys** roar from the treetops at dawn to lay claim to their territory. They live in large family groups in the forests of Central and South America.

and other objects and are very similar in design to those of humans. Many monkeys use their long tails like an extra arm or leg when swinging through the **trees**.

Monkeys live in family groups called troops and spend much of their time playing, fighting, and grooming each other. Each troop of monkeys has its own territory where it lives and feeds.

There are about 200 different species of monkeys. Most live in the tropics, especially in **forests** in **Central America**, **South America**, **Africa**, and **Asia**. Many monkey species are becoming rare, due to **habitat** destruction and **hunting**.

Monsoon

Monsoons are **winds** that blow from land to sea during the winter and from sea to land during the summer. They occur mainly in southern **Asia**. Summer monsoons carry moisture from the sea, and rain falls over the land. Summer monsoons bring the rainy season. In **India** 68 in. (1,700mm) of rain falls from June to September, and only 4 in. (100mm) falls in all the rest of the year.

△ The **Moon**'s surface is pitted with craters, almost all of which were made by meteorites crashing into it.

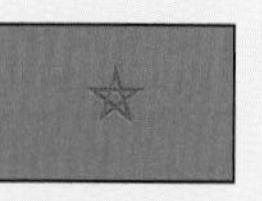

MOROCCO
Government: Constitutional monarchy
Capital: Rabat
Area: 172,100 sq. mi.
Population: 30,645,305
Language: Arabic
Currency: Moroccan Dirham

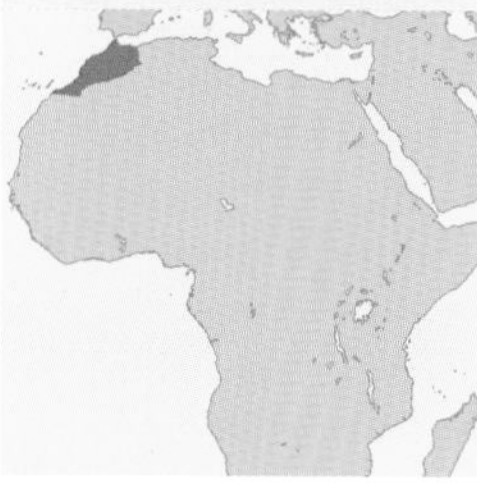

◁ **Monsoon** winds bring torrential rain that causes serious floods in southern Asia, especially in India and Bangladesh.

Moon

A moon is a natural **satellite** that travels around, or **orbits**, a **planet**. **Earth** has only one moon, but other planets in our **solar system** may have many. **Jupiter**, for example, has 28.

Earth's moon is our closest neighbor in space. It loops around Earth, never coming closer than 220,968 mi. (356,400km). It travels at about 2,269 mph (3,660 km/h) and takes $27\frac{1}{3}$ days to complete the circuit. The Moon was probably formed at the same time as Earth, but the **rocks** on its surface are older than those on Earth because the Moon has not changed in four billion years.

The Moon is a dry, lifeless world with no **air** or **water**. **Gravity** on the Moon is just one sixth of the gravity on Earth, yet the Moon's gravitational pull affects us every day. It is the Moon's pull that causes the **ocean tides** to rise and fall.

Mormonism

Mormonism is a **religion** founded by the American Joseph Smith (1805–1844) in 1830. Its name comes from the *Book of Mormon*, which Mormons believe is a sacred **history** of ancient North American peoples. Mormonism began in **New York**, but the Mormons were persecuted for their beliefs and driven out. They finally settled in Salt Lake City, Utah.

Morocco

Morocco is a country in northwest **Africa**. It has two coastlines. To the west is the **Atlantic Ocean**, and to the north is the **Mediterranean Sea**.

Most people in Morocco are farmers. They grow **wheat**, corn, **fruit**, and olives, and some keep **sheep**, **goats**, and **cattle**. Most are Muslims, followers of **Islam**. The largest city is Casablanca.

Morse code

Morse code is a simple way of sending messages. It is an **alphabet** of dots and dashes, and each letter has its own dot and dash pattern. The code was created by Samuel Morse (1791–1872), an American artist and inventor, to send messages along a telegraph **wire**. The telegraph operator presses a key at one end to send a signal along the wire to a sounder at the other end. A short signal is a dot, and a long signal is a dash. The first official telegraph message was sent in 1844.

Today, Morse code is used regularly only by **ships** and amateur **radio** operators. However, it is also used by people in emergencies when radio signals are too weak for other systems to work.

△ The first messages in **Morse code** were sent in the mid-1800s using a telegraph machine.

Mosaic

A mosaic is a picture made from small pieces of colored stone or **glass** set into plaster or cement. The pieces are arranged to make a design or a portrait or to show a scene. Mosaic making is an ancient **art**. The Sumerians of Mesopotamia (present-day **Iraq**) made mosaics almost 5,000 years ago.

Mosaics are a very practical way of decorating floors and walls because they can be washed without being ruined. In the **Roman Empire** villas and palaces had dazzling mosaics showing scenes of everyday life. Mosaics were also used to make pictures of saints, angels, and **Jesus Christ** in **churches** all over **Greece**, **Italy**, and **Turkey**.

△ This **mosaic** is of the Emperor Justinian, who ruled the Byzantine Empire during the A.D. 500s.

Moscow

Moscow is the capital of **Russia**. It is also the largest city in the country with a **population** of more than eight million people. Moscow lies on a plain across the Moskva **River**. It is Russia's main industrial and business center—everything is made in Moscow from **cars** to **clothing**. It is also the political and cultural center of the country.

Moscow was first made the capital of Muscovy in 1547 during the reign of **Ivan the Terrible**, the first czar (emperor) of Russia. The city developed around the **Kremlin**, an ancient fort from which the Muscovy princes used to defend their country. Moscow remained the capital of the czars until 1712 when Peter the Great (1672–1725) moved the capital to St. Petersburg. However, Moscow remained important even after it was largely burned down during **Napoleon's** occupation of 1812.

After the **Russian Revolution** of 1917 Moscow became the seat of the **Soviet Union**'s government. In 1992 it became the capital of Russia once again.

▷ **Moscow**'s Red Square is dominated by the onion-shaped domes of St. Basil's Cathedral and the fortress walls of the Kremlin.

Mosque

A mosque is a building used for worship by Muslims. It may also serve as a tomb or as a place where Muslims receive religious instruction (see **Islam**). Most mosques have up to six towers, called minarets, from which official criers, known as muezzins, call people to pray. There is also usually

△ The world's largest **mosque** stands beside the sea in Casablanca, Morocco. It can hold 100,000 worshippers, and a laser beam on top of its 577-ft. (176-m) - high minaret can be seen 31 mi. (50km) away.

a courtyard containing a fountain or well. This is where Muslims wash before they begin to pray, as specified by the holy **book** of Islam—the **Koran**. Inside the mosque there is an arch, called the mihrab, which is set in the wall closest to the holy city of **Mecca**. Muslims face this arch when they pray.

Mosquito

A mosquito is a small **insect** that looks like a **fly**. It has a slender, tube-shaped body, three pairs of long legs, and two narrow wings. Female mosquitoes bite and suck **blood**. They have sharp tubes, called stylets, with which they pierce tiny blood vessels in their victims. The male mosquitoes drink the juices of **plants**. Some types of mosquitos spread **diseases** such as **malaria**.

△ When a female **mosquito** bites, she injects a special substance into her victim that makes the blood flow more easily. This is why mosquito bites itch.

Moss

Moss is a type of **plant** that grows in low, closely packed clusters. It has slender stems covered with tiny leaves. Instead of roots that reach into the **soil** mosses have a mass of fine hairs that soak up moisture and **food**.

Moth

Moths are flying **insects** that resemble **butterflies**. However, there are several differences. Moths have plumper bodies than butterflies.

△ Some **moths**, such as this garden tiger, are just as colorful as butterflies. Strong coloration is often a warning sign to potential predators that the moth tastes bad or is poisonous.

Their antennae are like tiny combs or have feathery hairs on them, while butterfly antennae end in tiny knobs. Many moths fly in the evening and at night, while butterflies are active only in the daytime.

Motor, electric

An electric motor is a **machine** that changes electrical **energy** into mechanical energy. There are electric motors all around us. They drive things such as **refrigerators**, **vacuum** cleaners, electric **clocks**, hair dryers, washing machines, and some trains (see **railroad**).

A simple motor is made up of a coil of **wire** held between the poles of a magnet (see **magnetism**). When an electric current flows through the coil, the coil becomes a magnet with a north pole and a south pole. Since "like" poles repel and "unlike" poles attract the coil swings around between the poles of the magnet until its north pole is facing the south pole of the magnet and vice versa The direction of the current in the coil is then reversed so that the coil's poles are also reversed. The coil then has to swing around again to line up its poles with those of the magnet. The electric motor keeps on turning because it continues getting a series of magnetic pushes.

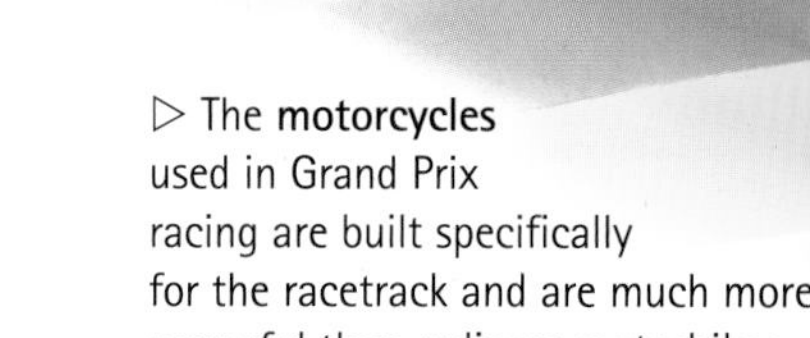

▷ The **motorcycles** used in Grand Prix racing are built specifically for the racetrack and are much more powerful than ordinary motorbikes.

Motorcycle

The first motorcycle was built in 1885 by the German engineer Gottlieb Daimler (1834–1900). He attached one of his gasoline **engines** to a wooden **bicycle** frame. Today's motorcycles are more complicated **machines**.

A motorcycle's engine is similar to that of a **car** but is smaller. It is either a two-stroke or a four-stroke engine, and it may have from one to four cylinders. The engine can be cooled by either **air** or **water**. It is started with an ignition button on the handlebars. This turns the engine and starts it firing.

Mountain

A large part of **earth**'s surface is covered by mountains. The greatest mountain ranges include the **Alps** of **Europe**, the **Rocky Mountains** of **North America**, the **Andes** of **South America**, and the **Himalayas** of **Asia**. There are also mountains under the **oceans**. The peaks of these submerged mountains may rise up above the sea's surface as **islands**.

Mountains are formed by movements in earth's crust. Some mountains are formed when two great landmasses move toward each other and push up the land in between. The Alps were formed in this way. Other mountains are heaps of ash and lava that poured out when a **volcano** erupted.

Mountains are constantly being worn away by a process known as erosion. The hardest **rock** is worn away by rain, **wind**, **sun**, and frost. **Rivers** and **glaciers** cut deep valleys into mountainsides.

▷ In **mountain** areas different plants grow at different altitudes. This is because the weather conditions change the higher you go.

Mouse

A mouse is a **rodent** like its relative the **rat**. There are many species of mice, which live in a wide range of **habitats**. Mice breed very quickly. A female can have 40 babies per year, and the young can themselves breed at 12 weeks old.

Mozambique

Mozambique is a **republic** in southeast **Africa**. It was ruled by **Portugal** but became independent in 1975. **Farming** is the most important industry in this hot, tropical country. Mozambique's ports of Maputo and Beira are used for importing and exporting goods to the inland regions of Africa. In the 1980s **famine** and **civil war** caused widespread hardship in Mozambique, and in 2000 **floods** devastated huge areas.

MOZAMBIQUE
Government: Republic
Capital: Maputo
Area: 302,400 sq. mi.
Population: 19,371,057
Language: Portuguese
Currency: Metical

Mozart, Wolfgang Amadeus

Frequently described as one of the greatest composers, Wolfgang Amadeus Mozart (1756–1791) began writing **music** at the age of five. He was born in **Austria**, and by the time he was seven years old he was performing concerts all over **Europe**. Mozart wrote over 600 pieces of music, including many beautiful **operas** and symphonies. But he earned little **money** from his hard work. He died at just 35.

Muhammad

The Prophet Muhammad (A.D. 570–632) was the founder and leader of the **religion** of **Islam**. He was born in **Mecca** in what is now **Saudi Arabia**. Muhammad believed that God had asked him to preach to his people at the age of 40. He taught that there

continued on page 217

△ The harvest **mouse** lives in fields and shrubs and weaves a domed nest the size of a tennis ball.

MUSIC

Music is an art form that consists of organized sounds played in time. It is perfomed on special occasions or simply for enjoyment.

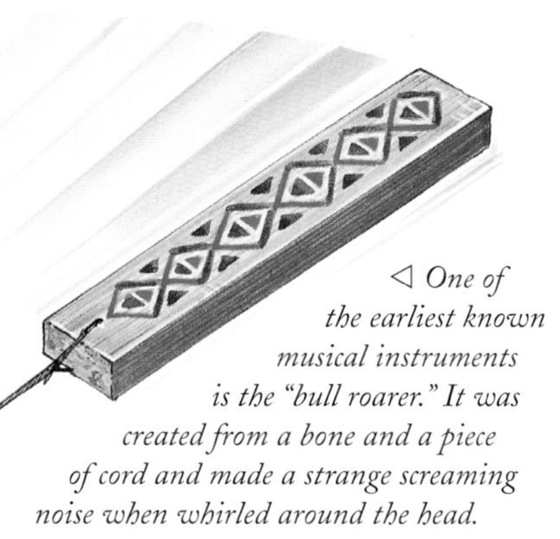

◁ *One of the earliest known musical instruments is the "bull roarer." It was created from a bone and a piece of cord and made a strange screaming noise when whirled around the head.*

MUSIC FOR ALL

The word "music" comes from the muses, or goddesses, of ancient Greece, who were said to inspire songs and dance. Music is often called a universal language because it is an art form that everyone in the world can understand. Even without musical training anyone can share the feelings and emotions that are conveyed by musical notes or songs.

△ *A gamelan is a type of orchestra from Indonesia. It includes up to 40 drums, gongs, xylophones, and chimes, which are played together to make a magical tinkling sound.*

MUSIC WITH A PURPOSE

Although the precise origins of music are unknown it seems likely that the earliest music was connected with religion, magical practices, and dance. Simple musical instruments that are thousands of years old have been found in some Stone Age sites. African tribal music is one of the oldest surviving musical forms. It is always accompanied by the rhythm of drums.

MUSIC AS ART

With the growth of civilizations people turned music into art. For example, the ancient *ragas* of India were tunes with beautiful rhythms. In the tomb paintings of the ancient Egyptian pharaohs musicians play versions of the lyre, the harp, and different forms of pipes.

THE CLASSICAL ERA

Musical notation—the way in which music is written down—was probably invented by Italian monks in the 800s. It meant that the same piece of music could be taken to different places and played by many musicians. In the Middle Ages most Western music was centerd around the church, but during the Renaissance there was a big increase in nonreligious music. The first orchestras appeared in the 1600s and featured new instruments such as violins, violas, and cellos. Gradually more instruments were invented, and orchestras grew in size.

MODERN MUSIC

Since the late 1800s many different types of music have developed, including blues, jazz, pop music, reggae, and R 'n' B (rhythm and blues). The invention of the radio and record player allowed new musical styles to spread and meant that people could listen to music in the comfort of their homes. People could buy and play their favorite pieces of music again and again. There are now many methods of recording music, including onto vinyl records, tapes or cassettes, CDs, DVDs, and digital sound files.

△ *The Etruscans, who lived in Italy before the Romans, made rich and varied music with instruments such as lyres and double flutes.*

△ *During the 1700s and 1800s music enjoyed a golden age in Europe. This picture shows the child prodigy Wolfgang Amadeus Mozart playing the piano while on a concert tour of Europe.*

MUSICAL THEORY

As painters and sculptors use lines, colors, and shapes, so musicians use the properties of sound. They use notes of different pitch (highness or lowness) and combine them with the beat of a rhythm to make a melody or tune. They sometimes add harmony, which is when two or more notes of different pitches are played together. Tone or timbre—the quality of sound produced by different instruments or voices—is another aspect of music.

In recent years computers have revolutionized the production of music. They allow musicians to make music that is without human flaws of rhythm and timing. Many genres have come out of computer music, including dance music, where repetitive beats are combined with influences from every other conceivable form of music.

▽ *The "classic" rock or pop band has keyboards, electric guitars (left), bass guitars, and drums (below).*

SEE ALSO
Ballet, Blues, Computer, Dance, Drum, Harp, Jazz, Mozart (Wolfgang Amadeus), Opera, Orchestra, Organ, Piano, Pop music, Recording, Sound, Violin

continued from page 215

was only one God called Allah. In 622 Muhammad was forced out of Mecca, and this is the year from which the Muslim **calendar** dates. After his death his teachings spread rapidly.

Muscle

Muscles are the things that make the parts of our bodies move. There are two different types of muscles. Some work when your **brain** tells them to. When you pick up a chair, your brain sends signals to muscles in your arms, in your torso, and in your legs. All of these muscles work together, and you are able to pick up the chair. The second type of muscle works even when you **sleep**. Your **stomach** muscles continue churning **food**, and your **heart** muscles continue pumping **blood**.

Muscles can only pull, not push, so they often work in opposing pairs. One contracts (tightens) as the other relaxes (stretches).

Mushroom and Toadstool

Mushrooms and toadstools are both forms of fungi (see **fungus**). They grow in damp places in forests and fields. Some taste delicious, but others are poisonous and may cause death if eaten. Mushrooms and toadstools lack the chlorophyll that allows **plants** to make their own **food** using the **Sun**'s **energy**. Instead they feed on decayed matter in the **soil** or are **parasites** that feed off plants.

Most of a mushroom or toadstool consists of a mass of threadlike fibers hidden underground. The part we can see is a soft, fruiting body that scatters millions of tiny particles, called spores, from which new fungi grow.

Music *see* page 216

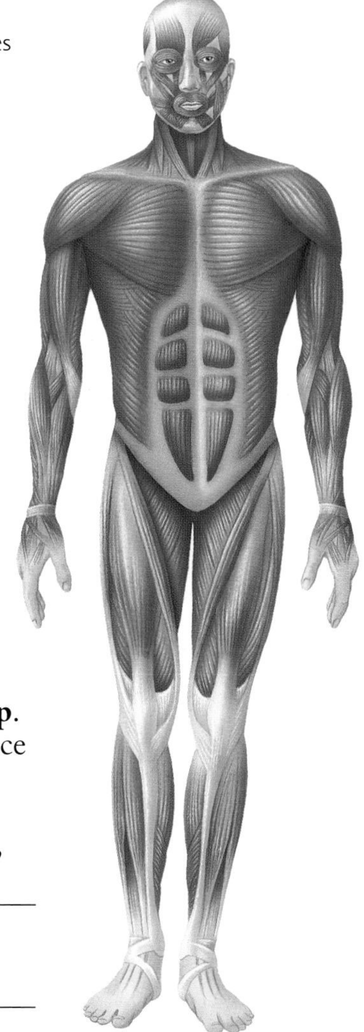

▷ There are 640 **muscles** in the human body, each of which moves a particular part of the body.

Musical instrument

There are four main types of musical instruments. Woodwind instruments produce a musical note by vibrating **air** inside a tube. They include the clarinet, oboe, bassoon, flute, piccolo, and recorder. In brass instruments, such as the trumpet, tuba, and trombone, the vibration of the player's lips makes the air in the instrument vibrate. String instruments work in one of two ways. The strings of the instrument are either made to vibrate by a bow, as in the **violin**, cello, and double bass, or the strings are plucked, as in the **guitar** and **harp**. In percussion instruments a tight piece of **skin** or a piece of **wood** or **metal** is struck to make a note. Percussion instruments include **drums**, cymbals, tambourines, and the **xylophone**.

Muslims *see* Islam

Mussolini, Benito

Mussolini (1883–1945) was the leader of **Italy's** Fascists (see **fascism**). In 1922 he persuaded the king of Italy to make him prime minister. Soon afterward he made himself **dictator**. He wanted military glory and led Italy into **World War II**. His armies were defeated, and he was shot by his own people.

Myanmar

Myanmar is a country in **Southeast Asia**. It was known as Burma until 1989. Most of its people are farmers and follow the **religion** of **Buddhism**. During the 1900s Myanmar suffered civil unrest, and it has had a military **government** since 1958.

MYANMAR
Government: Military
Capital: Yangon
Area: 262,000 sq. mi.
Population: 41,734,853
Language: Burmese
Currency: Kyat

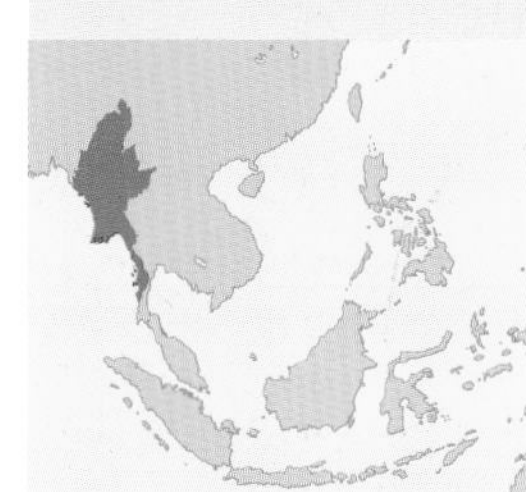

MYTHS and LEGENDS

Myths and legends are stories about heroes and religious beliefs. Most of these tales date from ancient times, and many are still told today.

△ *According to Greek mythology, the hero Perseus killed the monster Medusa by cutting off her head. The sight of her head, which had snakes for hair, turned people to stone. Here, in a fit of rage, Perseus holds it up to King Polydectes and his courtiers.*

ANCIENT ORIGINS

Every society has its own myths and legends, some of which are hundreds or even thousands of years old. Myths and legends first appeared before writing was developed and were passed down through generations by word of mouth. Later people began to write the stories down, and artists illustrated them.

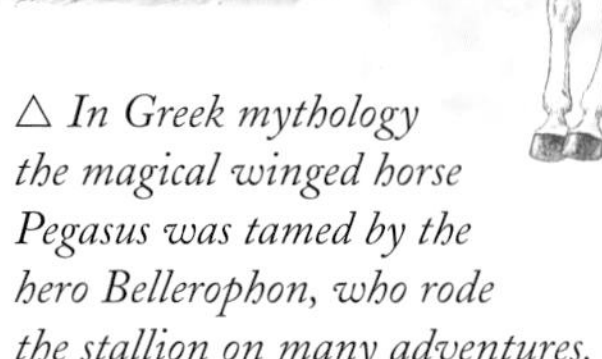

△ *In Greek mythology the magical winged horse Pegasus was tamed by the hero Bellerophon, who rode the stallion on many adventures.*

MYTH OR LEGEND?

In ancient times people knew little about nature or science, and they told myths to explain the world and their place in it. Myths developed around things such as the rising and setting of the sun, the seasonal flooding of a river, or a sudden storm. The collected myths of a civilization are known as its mythology. By studying mythology we can learn a lot about early people's way of life.

Unlike myths, which early people regarded as true or sacred, legends are folktales that may be based on fact. Legends often concern the exploits of heroes, gods, and creatures such as giants, dragons, mermaids, and witches. Although stories about legendary characters, such as Robin Hood and King Arthur, are probably made up, there may have been historical figures who inspired them.

△ *The ancient Egyptians believed in many gods and goddesses. Some were represented with the heads of animals that they considered to be sacred.*

GODS, GODDESSES, AND SPIRITS

In ancient times nature was vital to people's survival. If the crops failed or hunting was unsuccessful, there would be nothing to eat. These things were so important that humans came to believe that they were the work of powerful beings. People started to worship gods and spirits to make sure that they were helped. For example, if the sun god was happy, the sun would shine at the right times. But if he was angry, the sun could scorch earth or disappear forever, leaving the world in cold and darkness.

The ancient Greeks thought that the sun was the god Apollo driving a flaming chariot across the sky. For ancient Egyptians the sun was the god Ra sailing through the heavens. The Japanese, Aztecs, and Native Americans also had sun gods.

△ *The Zuni, a Native American tribe, believe that the first people came from inside earth and were trained by the medicine man Yanauluha to farm the land.*

GREEK AND ROMAN MYTHOLOGY

The people of ancient Greece developed a complex belief system of gods and spirits, which was later adopted by the Romans. The Greeks and Romans told long stories and epic poems about these supernatural beings as a form of entertainment. For example, in the 700s the Greek poet Homer wrote poems such as the *Iliad* and *Odyssey*.

Zeus (called Jupiter by the Romans) was the most important Greek god. King of the gods, he ruled over them and hurled thunderbolts when he was angry. Other deities (gods and goddesses) included Hades (Pluto), god of the underworld, and Athena (Minerva), goddess of wisdom.

△ *Garuda is a half-man, half-eagle creature that appears in Hindu mythology. He is said to be the sun in the form of a bird. In this picture Garuda is carrying the god Vishnu and his wife, Lakshmi.*

ABORIGINAL MYTHS

"Dreamings" are stories told by the Aborigines of Australia to explain how the world was made. They tell how, in a period called the "Dreamtime," spirits walked earth and created living things, including people. The spirits taught human beings how to survive and then returned to sleep in earth. The routes that the spirits made are called "songlines" and defined the land's features.

SEE ALSO
Aboriginal people, Arthur (King), Aztecs, Egypt (ancient), God and Goddess, Greece (ancient), Homer, Native Americans, Religion, Roman Empire, Vikings, Witch

△ *Legends were at the heart of Norse culture. Sigurd is a legendary Norse warrior who killed the dragon Fafnir and captured his treasure. But the gold carried a curse, and in the end Sigurd himself was killed.*

SCANDINAVIAN LEGENDS

The Norse (who were known as Vikings from the 800s to the 1100s) and other northern European peoples believed in many gods and warrior heroes. The most powerful Norse god was Odin—god of the sky, war, law, and poetry. Odin ruled the other gods and was married to the goddess Frigga. He rode an eight-legged horse called Sleipnir. Other Norse gods include Odin's son, Thor, god of thunder, and Loki, a trickster god. Giants, dwarves, and dragons also featured in many Norse legends.

▽ *The Norse believed that giants posed a constant threat to gods and humans alike. Here, Surt leads the fire giants of Muspell against the gods in what would be the last battle—and the end of the world.*

△ Claws are made of the same material as **nails**. Prehistoric animals, such as the dinosaur *Deinonychus*, had large, sharp claws to slash and kill prey.

Nail and Claw

Nails and claws are made of hard **skin**, like animals' **horns**, and grow at the ends of toes and fingers. When they are broad and flat, they are called nails, but if they are sharp and pointed, they are claws. Human nails are of little use. But most **birds**, **mammals**, and **reptiles** use their claws to attack and to defend themselves from predators.

A close look at an animal's claws will tell you a lot about its way of life. **Cats** and birds of prey have very sharp claws. They are hooked for holding onto and tearing prey. **Anteaters** have long, strong, curved claws for tearing apart **termites'** nests.

The claws of birds, reptiles, and mammals are vital to their survival. The claws of all members of the cat family can be retracted (pulled back) into the paws.

Namibia

Namibia is in southwest **Africa**. Most of the country is located on the plateau of Table Mountain, more than 3,280 ft. (1,000m) above sea level. The east of the country forms part of the Kalahari **Desert**. As a result, there is not much good farmland. The main industry is **mining**. Much of the land of the native San people—who have been living in the deserts of Namibia and **Botswana** for over 30,000 years—has been encroached on by international mining corporations.

In 1915 the country became a South African territory under the League of Nations. In 1946 the **United Nations** said that **South Africa** had no rights to Namibia, but South Africa disputed this. In 1989 it was finally agreed that South Africa would hand over power to the black majority. After a long armed struggle against South African control independence was achieved in 1990.

NAMIBIA
Government: Republic
Capital: Windhoek
Area: 317,500 sq. mi.
Population: 1,797,677
Languages: Afrikaans, English, and others
Currency: Namibian dollar

Nanak, Guru

Guru Nanak (1469–1539) founded the Sikh religion (see **Sikhism**) in the 1400s in the area of present-day **Pakistan** and northwest **India** known as Punjab.

Guru (meaning spiritual guide or teacher) Nanak was concerned by the tensions between Hindus (see **Hinduism**) and Muslims (see **Islam**). He gathered together a small group of like-minded followers to search for an understanding of God (see **god and goddess**) uncluttered by ritual. He based his religion on a simple desire to get close to God and do God's will.

Sikhs believe in one god called Satguru, which means "true teacher," who created the world. Satguru's will is made known through wise teachers—10 human gurus (Nanak and his nine successors)—and from the book *Adi Granth* ("first book"). Guru Nanak chose his successor, Guru Angad.

The first Sikh *gurdwara* (temple) was built in Kartarpur (present-day Pakistan), where Guru Nanak ended his days after being a wandering preacher.

As a mark of equality Sikhs often eat communally in a shared *langar* (dining room) attached to the gurdwara. The gurdwara is also a community center.

Napoléon Bonaparte

Napoléon Bonaparte (1769–1821) attended the best military school in **Paris**, **France**, and by 1792 he was a captain of artillery. Three years later he saved France by crushing a royalist rebellion in Paris. Soon he was head of the French **army** and won victories in **Italy**, **Belgium**, and **Austria**. In 1804 he crowned himself emperor of France in the presence of the **pope**.

Napoléon was a small man. His soldiers adored him and called him "the little corporal." With political skills equal to his skills as a general, Napoléon reorganized the **government** of France and drew up a new French code of **law**. Many of his laws are still in force today.

Napoléon set out to conquer the whole of **Europe**, but he could not defeat Great Britain at sea. Frustrated by this failure, he tried to stop all countries from trading with Great Britain, but **Russia** would not cooperate. In retaliation Napoléon led a great army into Russia in the winter of 1812. This campaign ended in disaster because his troops were defeated by the bitter **weather**. He met his final defeat at the Battle of Waterloo in 1815 where he was beaten by the British under the Duke of Wellington (1769–1852) and the Prussians under Gebbard von Blücher (1742–1819). He was imprisoned by the British on the lonely **Atlantic** island of St. Helena, where he died in 1821.

△ The Iroquois were a group of **Native American** tribes who existed mainly through hunting. They lived in village communities in the **forest** areas of what is now **New York**.

▽ **Napoléon** earned his reputation at the Battle of Marengo in **Italy** in 1800. He led a brilliant counterattack that crushed the Austrian army. He was finally defeated at Waterloo in 1815.

Native Americans

The original inhabitants of **North America** are called Native Americans. They formed hundreds of groups such as the Cherokee in the Appalachian **Mountains** and the Sioux on the Great Plains. From the early 1600s Europeans began to settle in their lands. As the Europeans spread out over the continent during the next 250 years many Native Americans died because of warfare and exposure to new **diseases**. The remainder were forced to live in reservations—pockets of land put aside for them by the Europeans.

NATO (North Atlantic Treaty Organization)

NATO is a defensive alliance that was set up after **World War II**. In 1949, 12 countries signed a treaty in which they agreed that an attack on one member would be considered an attack on all. The 12 countries were **Belgium**, **Canada**, **Denmark**, **France**, **Iceland**, **Italy**, **Luxembourg**, the **Netherlands**, **Norway**, **Portugal**, the **United Kingdom**, and the **United States**. **Greece** and **Turkey** joined in 1951, West **Germany** in 1954, **Spain** in 1982, and the **Czech Republic**, **Hungary**, and **Poland** in 1999. In 1990 the united Germany replaced West Germany in NATO.

The purpose of the alliance is to unify and strengthen the military defenses of the nations of Western **Europe**. Each member nation contributes soldiers and supplies to NATO forces. The members of NATO also cooperate on political and **economic** issues.

In the 1960s some NATO members felt that the United States had too much power within the alliance. France withdrew her NATO forces in 1966 but remained a member. With the collapse of many of the Communist **governments** (see **communism**) of Eastern Europe in 1990, NATO had to examine its role for the future. In 1991 NATO forces were restructured as the Cold War came to an end. A possible new role for NATO could be as a peacekeeper in troubled parts of the world using smaller forces.

Natural gas

Natural gas is a type of **gas** that occurs naturally underground and does not have to be manufactured. It is usually found in **oil** fields but is sometimes found on its own. When there is only a little natural gas in an oil field, it is burned off. If there is a lot, it is piped away and used for heating and to produce **electricity**.

Natural gas is found in large quantities in **Russia**, Texas, Louisiana, and in the North Sea oil fields. Half of the world's supply of natural gas is used by the **United States**.

▽ Pipelines take the **oil** and **natural gas** from oil rigs to land. An oil rig is a platform fixed to the seabed that drills into the rocks below and pumps up the oil and natural gas from these rocks.

▽ Modern **navigation** uses **satellite** technology to beam **radio** signals from place to place. The instruments are very accurate and allow **ships**, **aircraft**, and spacecraft to know their precise positions.

Navigation

Navigation means finding your way around, usually in a **ship** or an **aircraft**. For hundreds of years navigators at sea used the changing positions of the **sun** and **stars** to work out the **latitude**. Knowing the difference between the **time** on the ship and the time set at 0° **longitude** in Greenwich, **England**, helped them figure out their positions more precisely.

Today many navigational instruments are **electronic** and are very accurate. **Radio** beacons and **satellites** send out signals from which a ship can find its position. Then the navigator uses a **compass** to keep the ship on the right course. **Computers** help ships, aircraft, and **spacecraft** navigate so that their position is known precisely.

A sextant can be used to figure out a ship's position by measuring the angle between a star or the sun and the horizon. Once the angle has been measured, the star's position at that particular time can be looked up in a very accurate table. This allows the position of the ship to be calculated. By taking a series of sextant readings the ship can be kept on the right course.

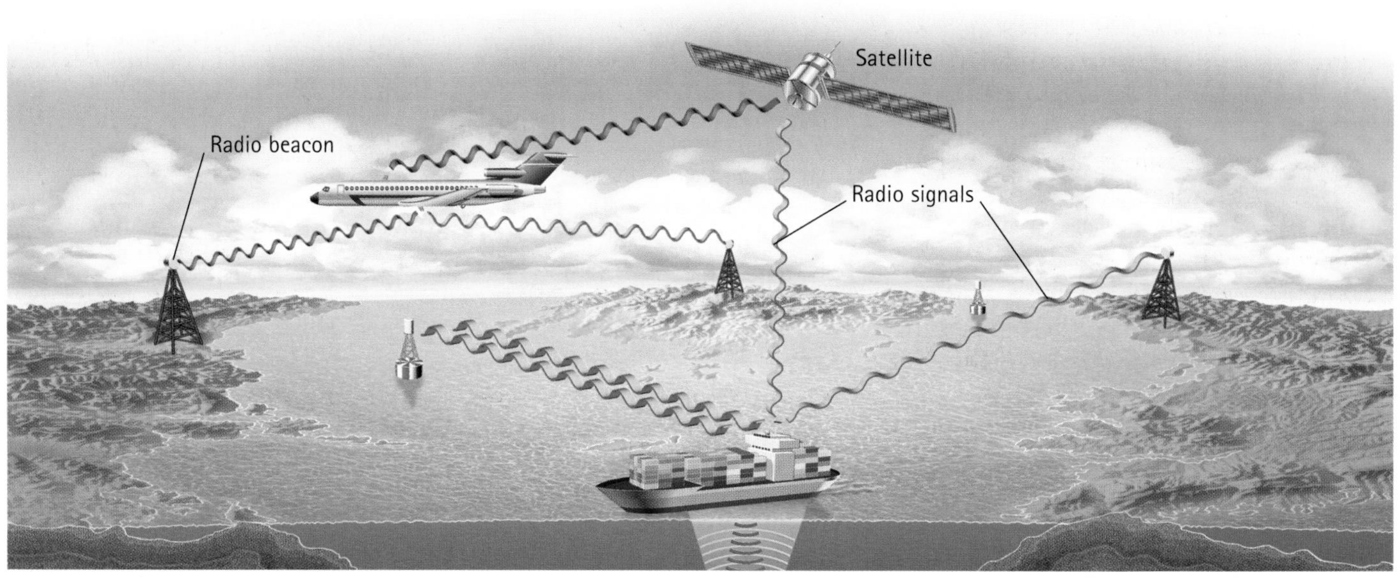

Neanderthal
see **Cave dweller**

Nepal

Nepal lies between **India** and **Tibet**. The north of the country is in the Himalaya **mountains** (13,776 ft./4,200m above sea level). Most of the people live in the fertile central valley and keep **sheep**, **goats**, and **yaks**. The capital, Kathmandu, lies at 4,395 ft. (1,340m) above sea level.

Tourism is a main source of income for Nepal. Visitors travel there from all over the world to climb the world's highest mountain, **Mount Everest** (29,021 ft./8,848m).

In 2001 the crown prince of Nepal assassinated his father, mother, and other members of his family. The royal family's authority has been damaged as a result.

NEPAL
Government: Constitutional monarchy
Capital: Kathmandu
Area: 52,800 sq. mi.
Population: 25,284,463
Language: Nepali
Currency: Nepalese rupee

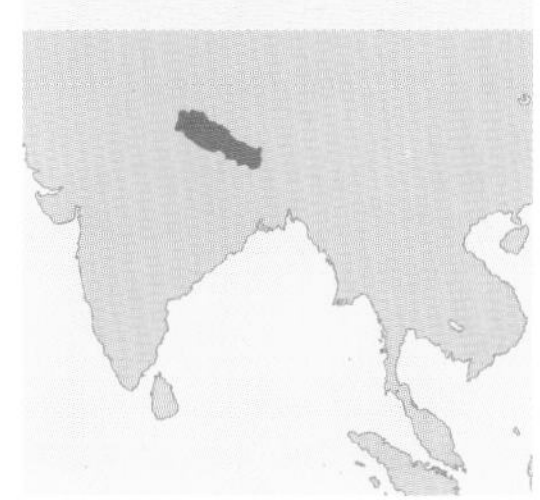

Neptune

The **planet** Neptune is named after the **Roman** god of **water** and the sea. It is a large planet far out in the **solar system** about 2.8 billion mi. (4.5 billion km) from the **Sun**. Only **Pluto** is farther away. It takes Neptune 164.8 years to circle the Sun. **Earth** takes 365 days.

Being so far from the Sun, Neptune is a very cold place. Scientists think its **atmosphere** is like **Jupiter**'s, which is mostly made up of the gas **hydrogen**. Neptune has eight **moons**, and there is a system of thin rings around the planet.

Early astronomers (see **astronomy**) were unable to see Neptune, but they knew it had to be there. They could tell there was something affecting the **orbit** of the nearby planet, **Uranus**.

In 1845 two astronomers, Englishman John Adams (1819–1892) and Frenchman Urbain Leverrier (1811–1877), used **mathematics** to figure out where Neptune should be. The following year astronomers used this information and spotted the planet.

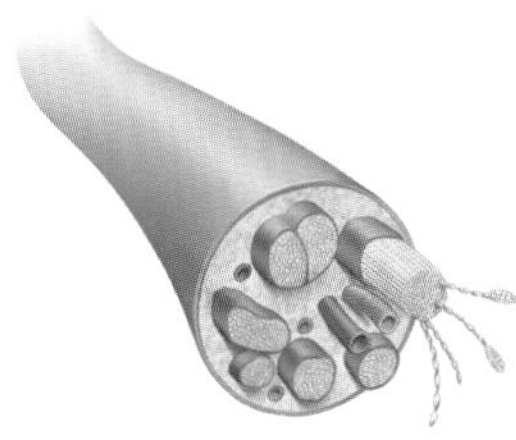

△ **Nerves** are bundles of fibers that contain cells called neurons. They carry impulses from parts of the body to the brain.

▽ If we could observe **Neptune** from its largest moon, Triton, it would look like this. The light from the Sun would be no brighter than that of a star.

Nerves

Nerves are tiny fibers made up of **cells** called neurons. They form a complex network all through the body—the nervous system. When a part of the body touches something, nerves send a message, or impulse, through the spinal column to the **brain**. If we feel **pain**, a message is sent back to tell the **muscles** to move away from whatever is causing the pain. Nerves also carry the **senses** of **sight**, **hearing**, and **taste**. The sense organs have special nerve endings that respond to **heat**, **light**, cold, and other stimuli. The **eye**, for example, contains the large optic nerve, which responds to light stimuli and transmits messages from the eye to the brain. The brain makes sense of the messages transmitted.

Nerve cells are covered with a layer of **fat** called a myelin sheath. Without this layer nerve cells cannot transmit their messages properly. Sufferers of the **disease** multiple sclerosis (MS) lose the use of their muscles as the disease destroys these fatty layers.

NEPTUNE FACTS
Average distance from Sun: 2.8 billion mi.
Closest distance to Earth: 3.6 billion mi.
Average temperature: -346°C
Diameter across the equator: 30,000 mi.
Atmosphere: 85% hydrogen, 13% helium, and 2% methane
Number of moons: 8
Length of day: 18 hours
Length of year: 164.8 Earth years

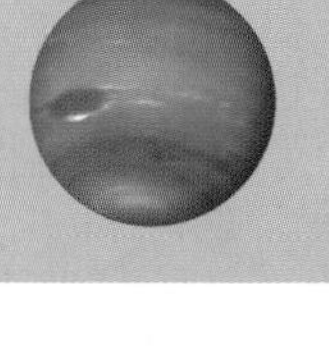

Nest

A nest is a home built by an **animal** or **bird** where its young are born and nurtured. Birds build nests when they are ready to lay **eggs**. With some birds the female builds the nest, but with others the male will help. Some nests are very complicated and may be lined with **wool**, **hair**, or **feathers**. Others have a more simple design or are very messy.

Coots live on open stretches of **water** but build their nests on piles of stones or sticks raised above the water.

The South American oven bird builds a nest shaped like an old-fashioned oven from mud and pieces of **grass**.

A few mammals, such as mice (see **mouse**) and **squirrels**, make nests for their young, but these are not as intricate as birds' nests.

Some **insects** make the most elaborate nests of all. These are not at all like birds' nests. They are often built for a whole group, or colony, of insects. There will be one queen, who lays eggs, and hundreds or even thousands of workers to take care of them. Most **bees** and wasps make this type of nest. Some wasps build their nests out of paper. **Termites** make huge mud nests. The complex pattern of cells in the hornet's papery nest makes a safe home for the young.

△ The male weaverbird hangs from a branch and weaves long strips of grass to make his **nest**. This is also how he attracts a mate. If the nest is appealing enough, a female will line it with feathers.

Netherlands

The Netherlands is one of three nations—including **Belgium** and **Luxembourg**—known as the Low Countries because they do not rise high above sea level. More than one third of the Netherlands is below sea level because much of the farmland has been reclaimed from the sea and marshes. The sea often floods the flat land near the coast, so sea walls have been built for protection against storms (see **weather**).

Living so close to the sea, the people of the Netherlands (who are known as the Dutch) have a long and successful history of seafaring, **trade**, and **exploration**. Rotterdam is the busiest port in **Europe**.

The country has one of the highest **population** densities in Europe with 1,221 people per square mile. Most live in the Randstad—a group of major cities that includes Rotterdam, Amsterdam, and the Hague. The Randstad lies in the provinces of North and South Holland. The Netherlands itself is often known as Holland.

The Netherlands is a prosperous country and was one of the first members of the European Community. It has a queen but is governed by a democratic parliament (see **democracy**).

NETHERLANDS
Government: Parliamentary democracy under constitutional monarch
Capital: Amsterdam
Area: 13,100 sq. mi.
Population: 15,981,472
Language: Dutch
Currency: Euro

New Guinea

New Guinea is one of the world's largest **islands**. It lies to the north of **Australia** in the **Pacific Ocean**. It is inhabited by people whose ancestors traveled to the islands from **Southeast Asia** around 40,000 years ago. They developed a way of life that depended on raising pigs and growing yams. This is still the basis of **farming** today.

The island is divided into two parts. The west is called West Papua (formerly Irian Jaya) and belongs to Indonesia. The east is called **Papua New Guinea**. About four million people live there. It used to belong to Australia but became independent in 1975. The capital is Port Moresby. Most of the people live in the central highlands. Over the centuries isolated villages in the **mountains** have developed their own **languages**—resulting in Papua New Guinea having more than 800 languages. As a result, many people in the Pacific Islands speak pidgin, a shared language used for trading. New Guinea's main exports are **tea**, cocoa, copra (coconut), **copper**, and **gold**.

Tourism brings foreign income to the Pacific Islands and gives the islanders a reason to preserve traditions of **dance**, **music**, and cooking.

Newspaper

Newspapers are just what their name says they are—papers that print news. They first appeared in the 1400s just after **printing** was invented. Printers produced pamphlets telling people what was happening in the country and what people thought about it.

The format of today's newspapers first appeared in the 1700s. Nowadays there are newspapers in almost every country in the world in many different **languages**. Some are printed every day, while others are printed every week.

One of the oldest newspapers is *The Times*, which is printed in **London, England**. It began in 1785 as the *Universal Daily Register*. It changed its name to *The Times* in 1788. Other famous newspapers are the *New York Times* and the *Washington Post* in the **United States**, *Pravda* in **Russia**, and *Le Monde* in **France**.

Newt
see **Salamander and Newt**

Newton, Isaac

Sir Isaac Newton (1642–1727) was an English mathematician (see **mathematics**) and scientist who made some of the world's greatest scientific discoveries (see **science**). He left Cambridge **University** in 1665 when the **plague** shut down the entire university. In the 18 months before the university reopened Newton did much of his most important work.

Newton's experiments showed that white **light** is a mixture of all of the **colors** of the **rainbow** (the spectrum). By studying the **spectrum** of light from a **star** or other glowing object, scientists can now find out what that object is made of. Newton's studies of light led him to build the first reflecting **telescope**.

Newton also discovered **gravity**. He realized that the same type of force that makes apples fall from **trees** also gives objects **weight** and keeps the **planets** in **orbit** around the **Sun**.

Newton determined the laws of motion that are still used in **physics** today. His discoveries made many later **inventions** possible.

△ **New York City** is well known for its towering skyscrapers, world-famous department stores, and cultural attractions from the Metropolitan Opera to off-Broadway productions.

New York City

New York City is the largest city in the **United States**. More than 14 million people live in the city and its suburbs.

The city stands mainly on three **islands** that lie at the mouth of the Hudson River. The **island** of Manhattan is the heart of New York City, and many of its most famous sights, such as the Empire State Building, are found there.

Ships from every continent dock at New York City's port, which is the world's largest. New York City is also one of the world's great business centers and is famous for having the biggest collection of skyscrapers in the world.

New York City probably has the most mixed population of any city in the world. Its black community is the largest in the United States. The world's largest Jewish (see **Judaism**) population lives in the New York area. The city also has a Little Italy and a Chinatown.

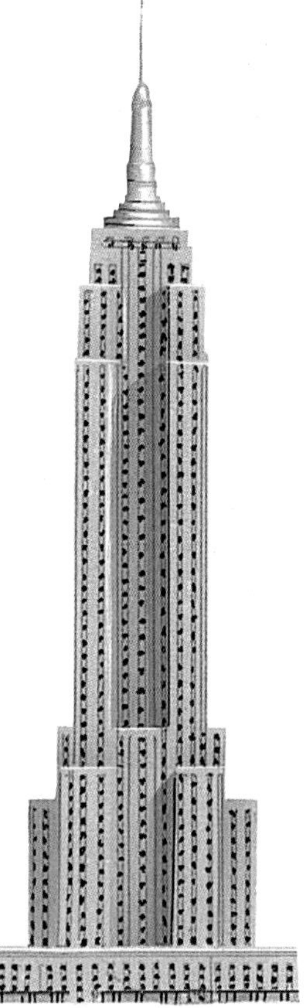

△ **New York City** is home to some of the tallest buildings in the world, including the Empire State Building, which is 1,250 ft. (381m) tall.

NEW ZEALAND
Government: Parliamentary democracy
Capital: Wellington
Area: 103,600 sq. mi.
Population: 3,864,129
Languages: English, Maori
Currency: New Zealand dollar

NICARAGUA
Government: Republic
Capital: Managua
Area: 46,400 sq. mi.
Population: 4,918,393
Language: Spanish
Currency: Cordoba

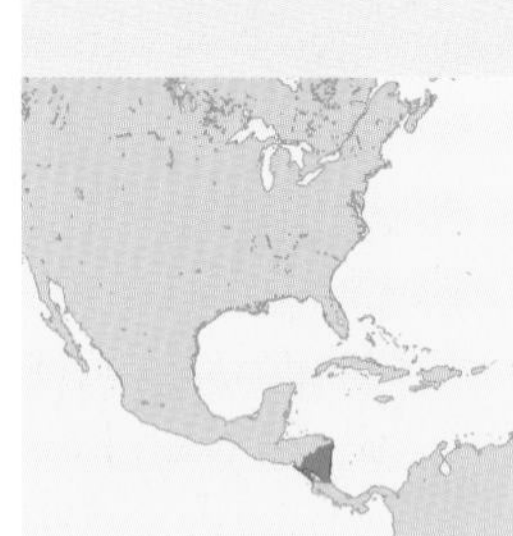

New Zealand

New Zealand is a remote **island** nation in the **Pacific Ocean** 992 mi. (1,600km) southeast of **Australia.** It is actually two **islands**. North Island is famous for its hot springs and **volcanoes**. South Island has a range of **mountains** called the Southern Alps and many **lakes**.

Both islands have plains and valleys. The mild climate helps farmers grow grains, **vegetables**, and apples. They also raise **sheep** and **cattle**. New Zealand is the world's third largest producer of sheep and **wool**. The estimated number of sheep is about 45 million.

There are nearly four million New Zealanders. About 85 percent of the people live in cities or towns. Auckland is the largest city, but the capital is Wellington. Both cities are located on North Island.

New Zealand is a member of the **Commonwealth**. Many of its people are descended from British settlers. Others are **Maoris**, descended from Pacific Islanders who lived in New Zealand before the British settlers arrived after 1769. By the end of the 1800s most Maori had been decimated by **warfare** and **disease**. However, their numbers are growing again, and now pure-blood Maori and the decendants of mixed marriages make up 14 percent of the **population**. The New Zealand **government** has also returned land to the Maori, and Maori is now an official **language** taught in schools.

▷ The **Niagara Falls** is one of the most spectacular sights in North America. It is made up of two huge **waterfalls**, the Horseshoe Falls in **Canada** and the American Falls in the **United States**.

Niagara Falls

The Niagara Falls are **waterfalls** on the Niagara **River** in **North America**. **Water** from most of the **Great Lakes** flows through this river. Each minute about 450,000 tons of water plunge about 164 ft. (50m) over the falls.

The falls stand on the border between **Canada** and the **United States**. Most of the water plunges down the Horseshoe Falls in Canada. The rest plunges down the American Falls in the United States.

People can gaze down on the falls from observation towers or take boats that sail close to the wild waters.

The sheer size of Niagara Falls has challenged people's courage and ingenuity for many years. Charles Blondin (1824–1897) walked across the top of the falls on a tightrope on June 30, 1859.

As the water plunges over the edge of Niagara Falls it slowly erodes (wears away) the **rock**. In this way the position of the falls is gradually changing. The falls are about 7 mi. (11km) farther north than they were when the water first flowed over them thousands of years ago. In another several thousand years Niagara Falls as we know it will have disappeared.

Nicaragua

Nicaragua is a country that stretches across **Central America** from the **Pacific Ocean** to the **Caribbean** Sea. Most of the people live on the western coast, where the land is flat and good for **farming**. A line of high **mountains** runs down the middle of Nicaragua. Farming is the main industry, and **cotton**, **coffee**, **fruit**, and **sugar** are the main products. But the country suffers from **economic** problems, partly caused by natural disasters. In 1998 **Hurricane** Mitch destroyed much of Nicaragua, **Honduras**, and **Guatemala**. Around 10,000 people were killed. The mountains are also frequently shaken by **earthquakes**.

Politics also plays a part in the country's economic instability. Corrupt regimes protecting the advantages of the wealthy few have faced armed rebellion from **Communist** groups in Central America.

Nigeria

This nation in western **Africa** is named after the Niger River that flows through it to the **Atlantic Ocean**. The **Sahara Desert** stretches across the country.

Nomadic people (see **nomad**), such as the Tuareg, live by herding—they travel with their **camels** and **goats** in search of pastures. Other peoples settle by oases (see **oasis**) and grow dates and grains. Life is difficult because the Sahel—an area of semi**desert**—is steadily becoming drier.

Niger also has one of the fastest growing **populations** in the world. Almost half of its people are under 15.

In 1995 international sanctions were declared against Nigeria, and the country was suspended from the **Commonwealth**. But membership was restored in 1999 when democratic **elections** (see **democracy**) were held.

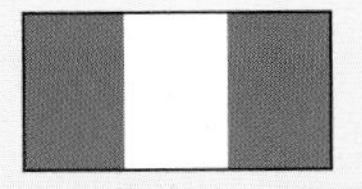

NIGERIA
Government: Republic
Capital: Abuja
Area: 351,200 sq. mi.
Population: 126,635,626
Languages: English, Hausa, Yoruba, Ibo
Currency: Naira

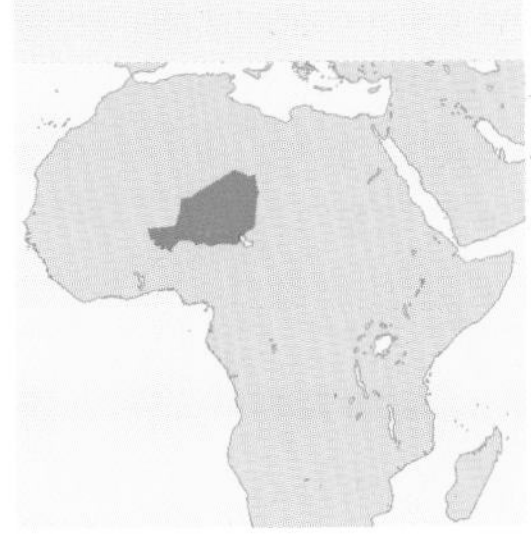

△ Florence **Nightingale** worked to improve the awful conditions of wounded soldiers in hospitals during the Crimean War.

Nightingale, Florence

Florence Nightingale (1820–1910) was one of the pioneers of modern **nursing**. She came from a wealthy family and could have had an easy life, but instead she chose to work caring for the sick. Florence Nightingale trained as a nurse and then founded a training **hospital** in **London, England**.

In 1854 she took 38 nurses to **Turkey** to care for British soldiers who had been wounded in the Crimean War (see **warfare**). Her hospital was a dirty barracks that lacked **food**, **medicine**, and beds. She cleaned it up, found supplies, and gave the wounded every care she could. Her work saved hundreds of lives.

Florence Nightingale was called "the lady of the lamp" by the soldiers.

Nile River

The Nile River in **Africa** is generally thought to be the longest **river** on **earth**—an astonishing 4,135 mi. (6,670km)—although some people believe that the **Amazon** is longer. The Nile rises in Burundi in central Africa and flows north through **Egypt** into the **Mediterranean Sea**.

The Nile is very important to farmers, who rely on it to irrigate their crops (see **irrigation**). Huge underground pipes carry **water** from the river underneath the **desert** to cities.

▷ The banks of the **Nile** in **Egypt** have fertile land that is good for farming.The **ancient Egyptians** used the Nile for irrigating crops and transportation.

Nobel Prize

These monetary prizes are given each year to people who have helped humankind in different ways. Three prizes are for **inventions** or discoveries in **physics, chemistry**, and physiology and **medicine**. The fourth is for literature. The fifth prize is for work to bring or keep peace between peoples, and the sixth is for **economics**. **Money** for the prizes was left by Swedish chemist Alfred Nobel (1833–1896), who invented the **explosive** dynamite.

When Alfred Nobel died in 1896, he left $9 million to set up the prizes that now bear his name. The interest that this money earns each year is used for the prizes.

△ The Tuareg people of the Sahara Desert, Africa, are **nomads**. They live by trading camels and goats and sleep in tents made of animal skins.

Nomad

People without a settled home are nomads. Many nomads live in lands that are too dry to farm. These people keep herds of **animals** and travel to find fresh pastures for them. They live in portable homes such as tents. Many nomads still live in or near the large **deserts** of **Africa** and **Asia**.

Northern Ireland

Northern Ireland consists of six counties in the northeast corner of the **island** of **Ireland**. It is part of the **United Kingdom** of Great Britain and Northern Ireland. Northern Ireland was separated from the rest of Ireland in 1921 when the Republic of Ireland (Eire) won independence from the U.K. Political problems in Northern Ireland date back to the 1600s when many English and Scottish Protestants settled there. From the 1960s protests by the minority Catholics (outnumbered by Protestants in Northern Ireland) against unfair treatment led to civil disorder. Bombings and other terrorist acts (see **terrorism**) have led to great losses of life, although the British and Irish **governments** are trying to settle Northern Ireland's future peacefully.

△ On the north coast of **Northern Ireland** lies the Giant's Causeway. This natural staircase into the sea was made when volcanic rock cooled and shrank to form thousands of six-sided columns.

North Pole

The North Pole is the furthest northern place on **earth**. Its **latitude** is 90° north. It is the northern end of earth's axis—this is an imaginary line around which earth spins like a wheel spinning around its axle.

The North Pole lies in the center of the **Arctic Ocean**. Here the surface of the sea is always frozen. The **sun** does not rise in the winter or set in the summer for many weeks. The first person to claim to have reached the North Pole was American **explorer** Robert E. Peary (1856–1920). He and his team arrived in 1909 using sleds pulled by **dogs**.

The first **ship** to reach the North Pole was the U.S. nuclear **submarine** *Nautilus*. It traveled under the ice-covered pole on August 3, 1958.

Northwest Passage

This was a longed-for sea route from **Europe** to **Asia** through the frozen waters of the **Arctic Ocean** north of **Canada**. **Explorers** took almost 400 years to find it. Ice continually hindered **ships** trying to sail through the passage.

It was Norwegian Roald **Amundsen** (1872–1928) whose ship first sailed through the Northwest Passage in 1906. In 1969 an **oil** tanker broke a path through the ice, but the ice is so thick that ships cannot regularly use this route.

Norway

Norway is **Europe**'s sixth largest country. This long, northern kingdom is wide in the south but narrow in the center and north. **Mountains** with **forests**, bare **rocks,** and snow cover much of Norway. Steep inlets, called **fjords**, pierce its rocky coast.

Summers in Norway are cool, and the winters are long. It is very cold in the **Arctic** north, but the rainy west coast is kept mild by the **Gulf Stream**.

NORWAY
Government: Hereditary constitutional monarchy
Capital: Oslo
Area: 118,700 sq. mi.
Population: 4,503,440
Language: Norwegian
Currency: Norwegian krona

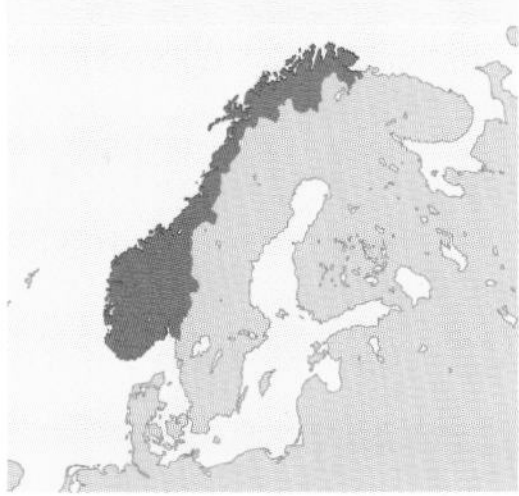

Noun

A noun is a word used as the name of something—a person (Mary), an animal (lion), a thing (book), a place (New York), or a quality (kindness).

The subject of a sentence—what a sentence is about—is always a noun or a pronoun. A pronoun is a word that is used in place of a noun. The most common pronouns are I, we, you, he, she, it, and they.

Nuclear energy

The tiny nucleus at the center of an **atom** contains the most powerful force ever discovered. This force gives us **nuclear energy**—sometimes called atomic energy. The heaviest **element** with the largest atom is **uranium**. The nuclear **fuel** used in nuclear **power plants** is a rare form of the metal called uranium-235.

Nuclear energy can be controlled to provide us with power. In a nuclear power plant control rods are lowered into a reactor to keep the reaction stable. But the uranium still gets very hot, so a coolant—a **liquid** or a **gas**—moves through the reactor. When the hot coolant leaves the reactor, it goes to a boiler to make steam. It is this steam that powers **generators** to make **electricity** for our homes and factories.

▽ British navigator John Franklin (1786–1847) set off to find the **Northwest Passage** in 1845. His ships froze into the ice, and Franklin and his men eventually all died.

NORTH AMERICA

North America is the third largest continent after Asia and Africa. It stretches from the Arctic Ocean in the north to the tropics of Panama in the south. North America includes the countries of the Caribbean and Central America, the United States of America, Mexico, and Canada.

NORTH AMERICA FACT FILE
Area: 9 million sq. mi.
Highest mountain: Mt. McKinley, Alaska, 20,316 ft.
Lowest point: Death Valley, California, 282 ft. below sea level
Largest lake: Lake Superior, 32,019 sq. mi.
Longest river: Mississippi, 2,343 mi.
Largest desert: Great Basin, 191,880 sq. mi.
Number of countries: 23
Largest country: Canada
Smallest country: Grenada
Largest city: Mexico City, 27.8 million
Total population: 477.3 million

△ *Cowboys herd cattle on ranches in Texas.*

LANDSCAPE

North America is a continent of great variety. Its climate ranges from bitter cold tundra in the north to hot, dry deserts and tropical rain forests in the south. The Rockies in the west and the Appalachians in the east form two of the continent's mountain ranges. In the center of the continent lie great plains where two of North America's largest rivers, the Missouri and the Mississippi, flow. In Alaska and northern Canada few, if any, trees grow in the harsh climate. There are huge evergreen forests elsewhere in Canada and in the northern United States, which provide North America with much of its timber. Natural wonders include Niagara Falls and the Grand Canyon.

PEOPLES OF NORTH AMERICA

North America is a melting pot of people and cultures. It was home to native populations, such as the Inuit in northern Canada and the Native American peoples all over the continent, for thousands of years before the first explorers arrived in the 1400s. Immigrants from Europe seeking a new life for their families followed in the footsteps of the explorers. Much of the Native Americans' land was taken by European settlers, and the native population suffered greatly through warfare and exposure to new diseases. Today the continent is largely populated by descendants of the immigrants.

△ *The New York Stock Exchange on Wall Street is a leading international stock market and the financial center of North America.*

From the 1600s huge plantations were developed by the European settlers. They needed plenty of labor to grow tobacco and cotton, so they shipped slaves across the Atlantic Ocean from Africa. Over 300 years more than a million slaves were transported. The issue of slavery was fiercely debated by the northern and southern states and caused a civil war that tore North America apart from 1861–1865. Slavery was abolished after the war, but many African-Americans still lived in poverty and did not have equal rights. In the 1960s civil rights campaigners protested against discrimination and did much to increase racial equality. African-Americans make up 12 percent of today's North American population.

Most of the continent's population live in eastern North America, and Mexico City is the continent's largest city. English and Spanish are the main languages, and French is spoken in parts of Canada.

INDUSTRY

Half of the world's manufactured goods are produced in North America, which is mainly owing to the huge natural resources of the continent such as lumber. Americans have also been involved in most of the technological advances of the past few decades, developing industries, such as computing, that have confirmed the continent's position at the forefront of world industrial production. The industries are found mainly in Canada and the United States, which are extremely wealthy and powerful countries as a result. In comparison most of the countries of Central America and the Caribbean are extremely poor. Many of these smaller countries in North America do not share the same natural resources as the United States and Canada, and their basic economies are weaker as a result.

▽ *Lynx live in the Canadian tundra where they hunt birds and small mammals.*

SEE ALSO
Canada, Caribbean, Central America, Civil War, Grand Canyon, Immigration, Inuit, Mexico, Native Americans, Niagara Falls, Revolutionary War, Slavery, Tobacco, Tundra, United States of America

ARCTIC OCEAN
Chukchi Sea
Bering Strait
Greenland Sea
Beaufort Sea
ALASKA
Baffin Bay
Davis Strait
Gulf of Alaska
Great Bear Lake
Cape Farewell
ROCKY MOUNTAINS
Coast Mountains
Great Slave Lake
Labrador Sea
CANADA
Hudson Bay
Lake Athabasca
Labrador
Reindeer Lake
Laurentian Highlands
PACIFIC OCEAN
Lake Winnipegosis
Lake Winnipeg
Lake Manitoba
WASHINGTON
MONTANA
NORTH DAKOTA
MINNESOTA
Lake Superior
MAINE
Ottawa
OREGON
IDAHO
SOUTH DAKOTA
WISCONSIN
Lake Huron
VERMONT
NEW HAMPSHIRE
Lake Ontario
WYOMING
Lake Michigan
Great Lakes
MASS.
Coast
Great Salt Lake
Great Plains
UNITED STATES OF AMERICA
MICHIGAN
NEW YORK
RHODE ISLAND
CONNECTICUT
Great Basin
IOWA
Lake Erie
PENNSYLVANIA
NEBRASKA
NEW JERSEY
CALIFORNIA
NEVADA
UTAH
INDIANA
OHIO
DELAWARE
ATLANTIC OCEAN
ILLINOIS
WEST VIRGINIA
Washington, D.C.
Range
COLORADO
KANSAS
MISSOURI
VIRGINIA
MARYLAND
Colorado Plateau
KENTUCKY
Appalachians
NORTH CAROLINA
ARIZONA
NEW MEXICO
OKLAHOMA
TENNESSEE
ARKANSAS
SOUTH CAROLINA
Baja California
ALABAMA
GEORGIA
TEXAS
MISSISSIPPI
LOUISIANA
FLORIDA
Gulf of California
Sierra Madre
Gulf of Mexico
Nassau
BAHAMAS
Havana
MEXICO
CUBA
DOMINICAN REPUBLIC
HAITI
Port-au-Prince
Santo Domingo
ST. KITTS AND NEVIS
ANTIGUA AND BARBUDA
DOMINICA
Mexico City
Yucatán Peninsula
Kingston
JAMAICA
ST. LUCIA
BARBADOS
ST. VINCENT AND THE GRENADINES
GRENADA
TRINIDAD AND TOBAGO
Belmopan
BELIZE
Caribbean Sea
ARUBA
NETHERLAND ANTILLES
GUATEMALA
HONDURAS
Guatemala City
Tegucigalpa
San Salvador
NICARAGUA
Managua
Lake Nicaragua
San Jose
COSTA RICA
Panama City
PANAMA

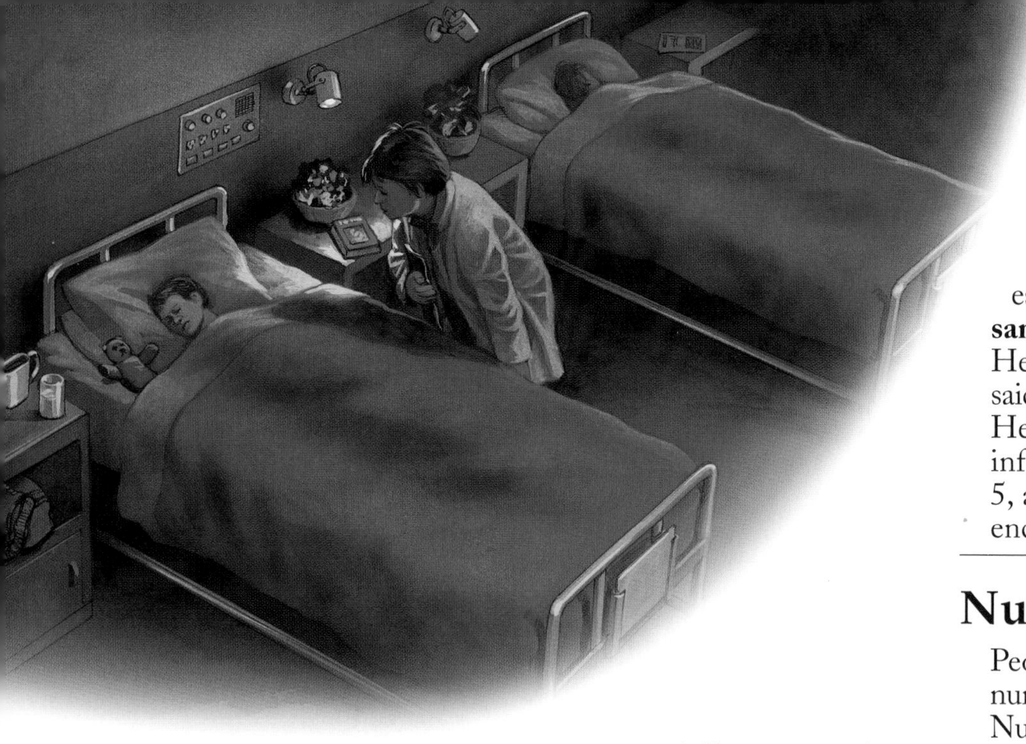

△ Many **nurses** work in hospitals in shifts. Some care for patients during the day, and others watch over them at night. Nurses also visit people in their homes and work in community centers and doctors' offices.

Number

In the **Stone Age** people wrote a number, such as 20 or 30, by making 20 or 30 separate marks. In many ancient **caves** the marks that these early peoples made can still be seen.

As time progressed people invented special signs or groups of signs to represent different numbers. These signs are called numerals. For centuries many people used Roman numerals, but these are rather clumsy. For example, the Roman numerals for 38 are XXXVIII.

The modern system is simpler and uses Arabic numerals that were first used in **India**. The most important numeral in today's system is the 0, which was invented in the the A.D. 300s by the **Maya**. If we write 207, we mean *two* hundreds, *no* tens, and *seven* ones. Without the 0 we would not be able to write 207.

The earliest known written numbers were those used by the Babylonians around 5,000 years ago. All the great civilizations have had their own ways of **writing** and using numbers.

There are many very large numbers such as the **population** of the world, the number of blades of **grass** in a garden, and the number of leaves on a **tree**. The famous Greek scientist Archimedes (287–212 B.C.) estimated the number of grains of **sand** it would take to fill the **universe**. He did not know the number, but he said it was finite—an exact number. He also knew that some numbers are infinite. If we go on counting 1, 2, 3, 4, 5, and so on, we will never come to the end. This set of numbers is infinite.

Nursing

People who are very sick or old require nursing in their homes or in **hospitals**. Nursing can mean feeding, washing, and giving treatment ordered by a doctor. It is hard work and requires special skills. Men and women train for several years before becoming nurses. Modern nursing owes much to the example set by Florence **Nightingale**.

The word "nursing" comes from the Latin word *nutricia*, meaning nourishing. Records from ancient **Egypt** and **Greece** mention various nursing practices, including administering herbal remedies. The Roman armies employed male nurses to care for the wounded (see **Roman Empire**).

▽ A well-balanced diet contains all of the **nutrients** a person needs to stay healthy. A wide variety of food and liquids needs to be eaten and drunk regularly to ensure enough nutrients are taken in.

Nutrition

Nutrition is the process by which we take in and use **food**. **Human beings** need food to keep our bodies running smoothly and to provide **energy**. Malnutrition is a weakening of the body and can be caused by eating food that lacks enough of the nutrients that keep the body strong and healthy.

Nutrients can be divided into six groups—**proteins**, carbohydrates, **fats**, **vitamins**, **minerals**, and **water**. No one nutrient is more important than another. Each has its own job to do. A well-balanced diet contains all of the nutrients.

Octopus

There are about 50 species of octopuses. They are soft-bodied **mollusks** that live in the sea. Octopus means "eight feet," but the eight tentacles of an octopus are usually called arms. The largest octopus has arms about 30 ft. (9m) across, but most octopuses are no larger than a person's fist. Unlike most mollusks, octopuses do not have a shell. Instead they have a tough **skin** that protects the organs in their bodies.

The octopus hides in underwater **caves** or crevices or creeps along the seabed searching for **food**. Its two large **eyes** look out for enemies. If danger threatens, the octopus may confuse an enemy by squirting an inky **liquid**. The ink hangs in the **water** like a cloud. The octopus can also propel itself forward fast by squirting water backward from a tube in its body.

The octopus is the most intelligent of the **invertebrates** (animals without backbones). It can be trained to find its way through a maze and is able to solve simple problems; for example it can remove the lid from a sealed jar containing food.

In many countries, particularly those bordering the **Mediterranean**, octopuses are a favorite food.

△ Suckers on the tentacles of an **octopus** are used to grip crabs, shellfish, or other prey. The tentacles pull the victim toward the octopus' mouth, which is hard and pointed like a bird's beak.

Oasis

An oasis is a fertile place in a **desert** where **plants** are able to grow (see plant). It may be simply a small clump of **palm** trees or a much larger irrigated area (see **irrigation**). Oases are found where there is **water**. This can come from **rivers**, wells, or underground springs that reach the surface at that point. These sources of water may be fed by rain that falls on nearby **mountains** and seeps through **rocks** beneath the surface of the desert. People can make oases by drilling wells and digging irrigation ditches.

▽ An **oasis** may be only a spring and a small group of palms. However, some oases are much larger. A variety of plants and animals makes their home in these oases, and some support large towns.

OCEANS

Oceans cover almost three fourths of the surface of earth. If you put all of the world's water in 100 giant tanks, 97 of them would be full of water from the oceans.

▽ 1) *An atoll begins as a coral reef around a volcanic island.* 2) *As the islands sinks the reef grows upward.* 3) *Eventually the island disappears, and all that remains is the atoll surrounding a lagoon.*

OCEANS OF THE WORLD

There are four oceans. The largest and deepest is the Pacific Ocean. The second largest is the Atlantic, which is only half the size of the Pacific. The Indian Ocean is smaller but deeper than the Atlantic Ocean. The Arctic Ocean is the smallest and shallowest ocean of all.

The oceans are never still. Winds crinkle their surface into waves. The Gulf Stream and other currents (some warm, others cold) flow like rivers through the oceans, and every day the ocean surface falls and rises with the tides. In the winter polar seawater freezes over, and icebergs from polar seas may drift hundreds of miles through the oceans.

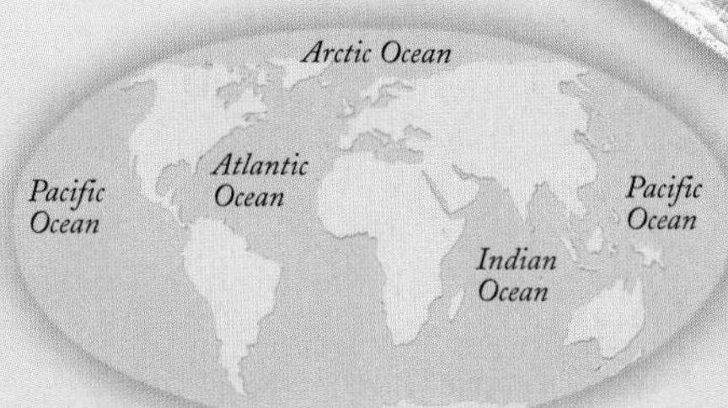

△ *The saltwater oceans and seas of the world cover nearly 71 percent of earth's surface.*

PLATE MOVEMENTS

Earth's crust is made up of a small number of large plates of solid rock. These float on the moving molten rock underneath and also move in relation to one another. New crust is formed at the edge of the plates. The plate movements mean that the ocean floor is always changing shape. It is constantly being created and destroyed by the movements.

WATER CYCLES

The oceans are always losing water as water vapor, which is drawn up into the air by the sun's heat, but most is returned as rain. Rainwater running off the land carries salt and other minerals to the oceans. If a square tank one mile long and one mile high was filled with seawater, it would hold 2.5 million tons of magnesium. In fact the oceans supply most of the magnesium used in the manufacture of items such as aircraft components, fireworks, flares, and batteries.

Continental shelf covered with salt and minerals washed off the land

Seamounts—underwater volcanoes

Continental slope

Spreading ridge with central valley flanked by steep mountains

Abyssal plain

Abyssal hills forming ridges

OCEAN FACT FILE

ARCTIC OCEAN
Surface area: 5,596,500 sq. mi.
Average depth: 3,247 ft.
Greatest depth: 15,088 ft.

INDIAN OCEAN
Surface area: 28,665,000 sq. mi.
Average depth: 12,759 ft.
Greatest depth: 24,436 ft.

ATLANTIC OCEAN
Surface area: 41,000,000 sq. mi.
Average depth: 5,904 ft.
Greatest depth: 29,992 ft.

PACIFIC OCEAN
Surface area: 64,834,000 sq. mi.
Average depth: 14,038 ft.
Greatest depth: 36,152 ft.

THE OCEAN FLOOR

The shape of the ocean floor is very similar to the shape of land. There are mountains and valleys, ridges and volcanoes, and plains and hills. A typical ocean floor has a continental shelf and slope leading down onto an abyssal plain, with abyssal hills rising to an abyssal ridge containing a rift valley. Beyond these may be a deep ocean trench.

MARINE LIFE

Oceans are home to countless living things. Most of the life is found within a layer of water about 328 ft. (100m) deep where the sunlight penetrates. The minerals in seawater help nourish tiny plants drifting on the surface. The plants are food for tiny animals, some of them one-celled. These tiny animals (zooplankton) and plants (phytoplankton) are collectively known as plankton and are the basis for the entire ocean food chain. All sea creatures depend either on plankton itself or on animals that feed on plankton for their food. For example, zooplankton feeds on phytoplankton, but both are eaten by small fish. These in turn are eaten by larger predators, who probably are eaten by one of the top predators such as a shark.

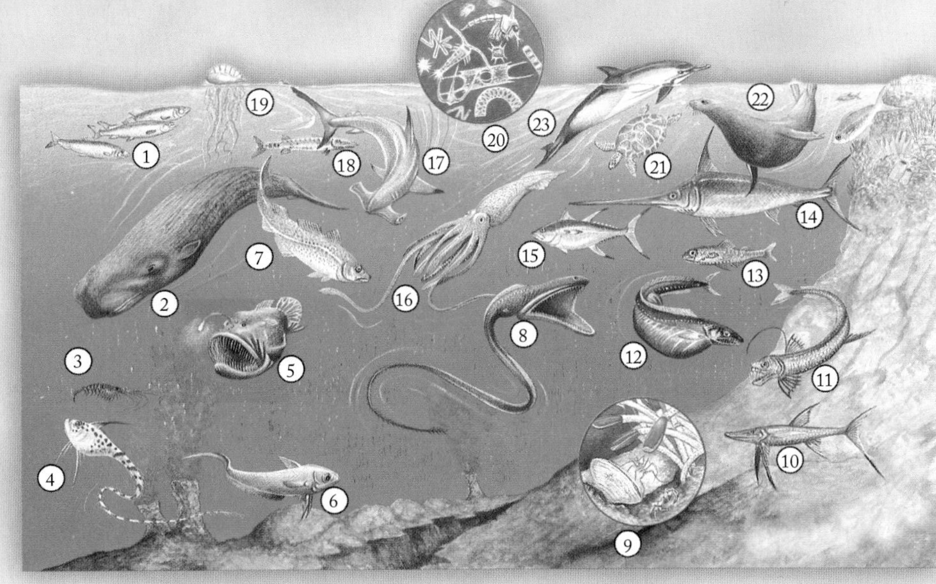

△ *There is an enormous variety of species living in our oceans—some very strange—each occupying its own space at particular levels.*

1. Herring 2. Sperm whale 3. Shrimp 4. Cattail 5. Anglerfish 6. Grenadier 7. Cod 8. Gulper eel 9. Sea spider, tube worms, clam, white ghost crab 10. Tripod fish 11. Viper fish 12. Swallower 13. Lantern fish 14. Swordfish 15. Yellowfin tuna 16. Giant squid 17. Hammerhead 18. Barracuda 19. Portuguese man-of-war 20. Plankton 21. Green turtle 22. Sea lion 23. Common dolphin

EXPLORING THE DEPTHS

The exploration of the deepest levels, more than 32,800 ft. (10,000m) down, was first carried out using special underwater vehicles called bathyscaphes. Today mini-submarines are still used to explore the seas, studying marine life, shipwrecks, such as the *Titanic*, and the geology of the ocean floor.

The deepest marine trench in the world is the Mariana Trench off the island of Guam in the Pacific Ocean. This trench marks the point where the fast-moving Pacific plate meets the slower-moving Philippine plate. Its deepest place, Challenger Point, was measured accurately in 1984 by a Japanese survey vessel using a multibeam echo sounder to make an echo map of the ocean floor. It found that the trench plunges deeper into earth (35,831 ft./10,924m) than Mount Everest, the tallest mountain, rises above sea level (29,041 ft./8,854m).

SEE ALSO

Antarctic and Arctic, Atlantic Ocean, Earth, Echo, Indian Ocean, Minerals, Mountain, Pacific Ocean, Salt, Water

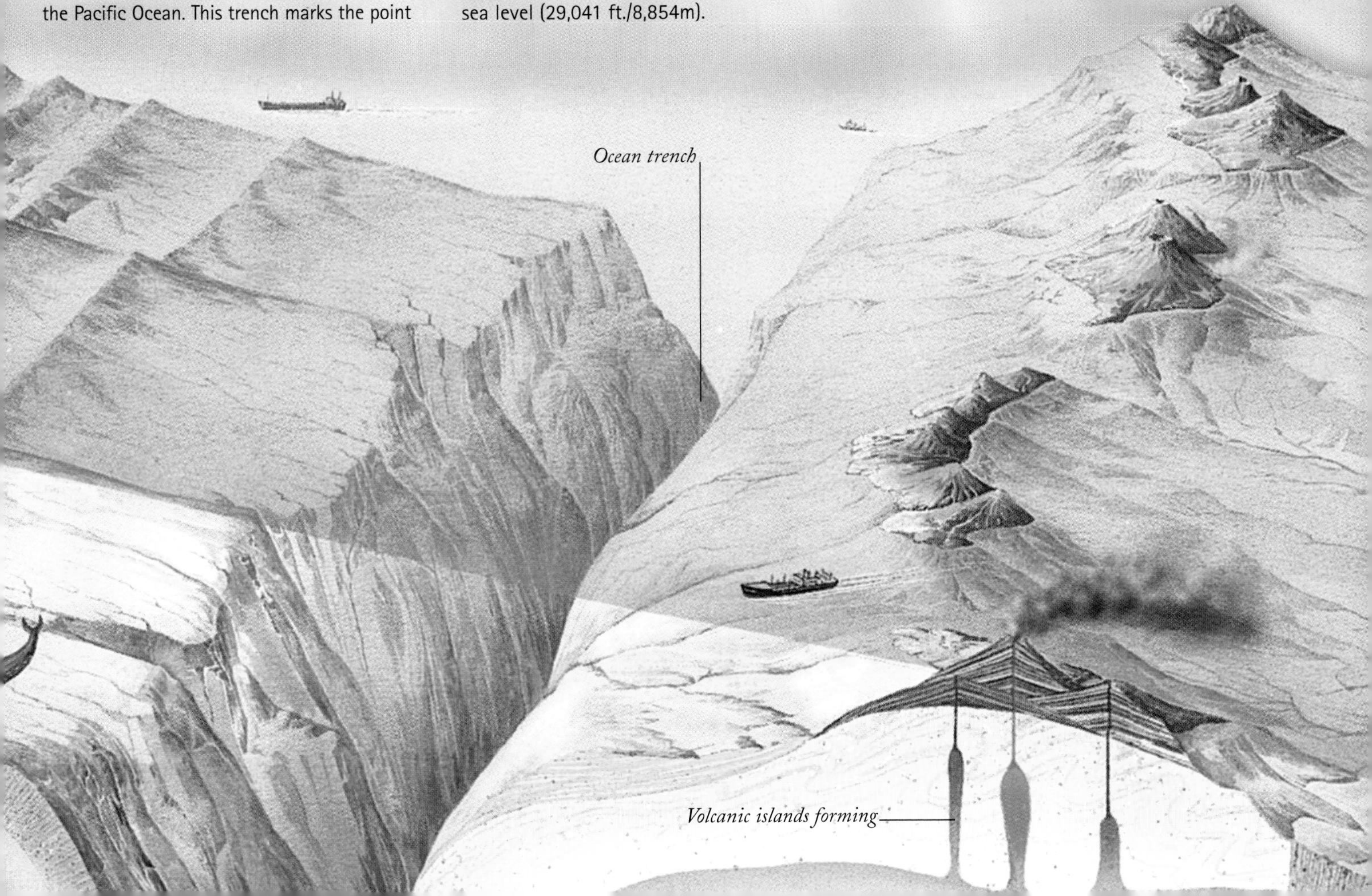

Ocean trench

Volcanic islands forming

△ **Oil** travels south from Alaska to ports through the Trans-Alaska pipeline. This pipeline was built on supports above the ground to prevent it from thawing the permafrost.

△ Sunflower seeds are rich in an **oil** that is used to make margarine and is a good substitute for olive oil in salads and cooking or for herb oils for skin treatments.

Oil

Oils are **fats** and other greasy substances that do not dissolve in **water**. Oil is also a mineral that was formed millions of years ago from dead **plants** and **animals**. The oil is trapped under **rocks** deep in the ground, and engineers drill holes through the rocks' surface to reach it.

Oil deposits are found on land and also offshore in the **ocean** bed. The world's largest known oil deposits lie in the **Middle East** in the countries of **Saudi Arabia, Iran, Iraq**, and Kuwait. The biggest part of an oil-drilling platform is the derrick—the tall **metal** tower that houses the drilling equipment. The drill bit, at the end of the drill pipe, cuts through rock with sharp metal teeth. By examining the fragments of rock cut by the drill scientists can tell when they are close to an oil deposit. The oil gushes out or can be pumped up (see **pump**) to the surface.

Oil refineries separate the oil into many different chemicals. As well as producing gasoline and paraffin, oil by-products can be used to make artificial **fertilizer**, many types of **medicine, plastics, perfumes, soaps, detergent**, paint, and even **animal** feed.

We may need to find new ways to make these products because the world's supplies of oil are running out. Today scientists are working on new ways of extracting oil from shale, a kind of rock, and from tar sands.

Olympic Games

This competition is the world's oldest sports event. The first Olympics took place in Olympia, **Greece**, in 776 B.C. The Greek Games ended in A.D. 394. The modern Olympic Games began in 1896.

The modern international Olympics are held every four years, each time in a different country. Athletes from different nations compete in races, jumping, **gymnastics**, soccer, yachting, and

▷ The Olympic Games have witnessed the triumph of many international athletes over the years. These are some of the winners between 1896–1996.

Thomas Burke, U.S., 100m · Canadian hockey team · Attilio Pavesi, Italy, cycling · Dawn Fraser, Australia, swimming · Joe Frazier, U.S., boxing · Nadia Comaneci, Romania, gymnastics · Steffi Graf, Germany, tennis · Jan Zelezny, Czech Republic, javelin

many more contests (see **sports**). More than 6,000 people from more than 100 countries take part. The winners are awarded medals but no prize **money**.

The opening ceremony of each Olympic Games features the lighting of the Olympic flame with a torch. Brought all the way from Greece, the torch is carried by athletes and sportspeople of all nationalities.

Today separate winter and summer Olympics take place every two years in alternating years for each.

Oman

Oman is a country in southeast Arabia on the Persian Gulf. On the fertile coastal plain, **fruits** (particularly dates) and **vegetables** are grown. **Oil** is the main source of income. Many of Oman's people are **nomads**.

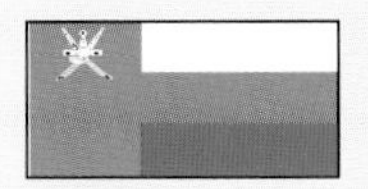

OMAN
Government: Absolute monarchy
Capital: Muscat
Area: 81,900 sq. mi.
Population: 2,622,198
Language: Arabic
Currency: Omani Rial

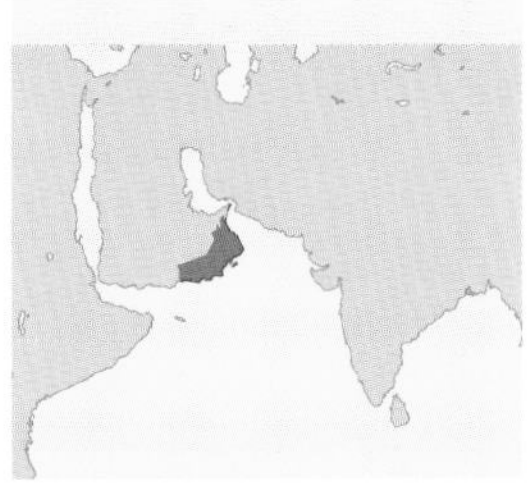

Opera

An opera is a play with **music**. The actors are performers who sing all or most of their words. An **orchestra** in an orchestra pit below the level of the stage accompanies the singers.

The first opera was performed in **Italy** nearly 400 years ago. Famous composers of opera include **Mozart**, Verdi, Puccini, and **Wagner**. Some shorter, less serious operas are called operettas. Operettas of the 1800s gave rise to the tuneful musical comedies of the 1900s.

△ **Opera** is a popular form of entertainment. Wagner even designed an opera house in Bayreuth in 1876 so that he could put on a complete performance of his *Ring* cycle.

Opinion poll

Politicians and manufacturers want to know what people think of their party's policy or the goods they make. In these circumstances they can employ a research firm to conduct an opinion poll—to ask questions and analyze the answers. It would be impossible to ask questions of everyone everywhere, so a carefully selected group of people, called a sample, is chosen to represent a larger group. The sample may be only one percent of the larger group, but it must contain the same type of people. For example, if 20 percent of the larger group is under 18 years of age, then 20 percent of the sample group must also be under 18.

The questions may be asked by a trained interviewer, or they may be printed on a questionnaire. The answers are then analyzed, and the results show the opinions of the larger group.

Some people say that opinion polls can be unfair. In **election** polls, for example, many people want to be on the winning side and therefore may switch their votes during the campaign to the candidate whom the polls show to be ahead. Careful studies have, however, failed to show that this "bandwagon effect" exists.

Opossum

Opossums are **marsupials** that live in North and **South America**. Some look like **rats**, and others look like **mice**. The Virginia **opossum** is as large as a **cat** and is **North America**'s only marsupial. It feeds at night and climbs **trees**, clinging to them with its tail. Opossums have superb eyesight and hearing and eat anything they can find, alive or dead. If danger threatens, the Virginia opossum lies still and pretends to be dead. If someone pretends to be hurt, we say he or she is "playing possum." A female Virginia opossum has up to 30 babies at a time, each no larger than a honeybee, but only a small number survives. Like all marsupials, opossums give birth to their babies when they are still in a very immature state, so the young rely on their parents to stay alive.

△ When an **opossum** baby reaches about three months old, it can ride around on its mother's back.

Orangutan

This large, red-haired **ape** lives on the **islands** of Borneo and Sumatra in **Southeast Asia**. Its name comes from the Malay "man of the woods." The male is as heavy as a human but not as tall. Orangutans use their long arms to swing through the branches of trees as they hunt for **fruit** and leaves to eat. Each night they make **nests** high up in the **trees**. A leafy roof helps keep out rain.

Orangutans live alone or in small family groups. People are their main enemies. Hunters catch the young illegally to sell to **zoos**, so orangutans are in danger of becoming extinct.

△ The **orangutan** is the second largest ape after the gorilla, and a fully grown male can weigh up to 200 lbs (90kg). Its arms are longer than its legs, and it has a high forehead. The male orangutan grows a moustache and beard, but the rest of his face is hairless.

Orbit

An orbit is the curved path of something that spins around another object in space. Artificial **satellites** and the **Moon** travel around **Earth** in orbits. Each **planet**, including Earth, has its own orbit around the **Sun**.

Every orbit is a loop rather than a circle. An orbiting object tries to move in a straight line but is pulled by **gravity** toward the object that it orbits. People used to think that planets moved in circular orbits, but actually the shape is more like an oval, or ellipse.

Orchestra

An orchestra is a large group of musicians who play together. The word orchestra originally meant "dancing place." In ancient Greek **theaters**, dancers (see **dance**) and musicians performed on a space between the audience and the stage. When **opera** was invented in **Italy**, the theater owners arranged their musicians in the same way. Gradually people began to use the word "orchestra" to describe the group of musicians and not the place where they performed.

The modern orchestra owes much to the composer **Haydn**. He arranged its musical instruments into four main groups: strings, woodwind, brass, and percussion. Most orchestras have a conductor. Soloists rehearse with an orchestra, and the conductor has the job of coordinating all the musicians, who may number over 100.

Orchid

There are more than 15,000 types of these rare and beautiful flowering **plants**, which live in **rain forests**. Many grow on **trees**. Their roots draw nourishment from the damp **air**. Usually each type of orchid is fertilized by one type

◁ Many bees in the rain forest feed on the nectar and pollen from **orchid** flowers. They help pollinate the orchids by carrying the pollen from plant to plant.

of **insect**. But some can be pollinated by **snails** or **hummingbirds**.

The common spotted orchid grows in damp or dry, grassy places and in open forests. Its **habitats** are being threatened by modern **farming** methods.

Organ

Pipe organs are **musical instruments** with many pipes of different heights and widths. The largest organ has more than 30,000 pipes. Each pipe makes a special **sound** as **air** flows through it. An organist plays an organ by pressing keys arranged in rows called manuals. Each manual controls a different set of pipes. Levers or knobs, called stops, allow the organist to combine different groups of pipes. **Electronic** organs sound similar but have no pipes.

△ Some more powerful church **organs** have one or more keyboards and several banks of pipes. They are often highly decorated.

Ore *see* Mineral

Ostrich

The ostrich is the largest living **bird**. An ostrich may weigh twice as much as a human and stand more than 6.5 ft. (2m) high. Ostriches cannot fly. If an enemy attacks, they run away, but they can kick hard enough to rip open a **lion**.

Ostriches live in **Africa**. They roam in large herds, led by a male. The females lay large, white **eggs** in **nests** dug in the **sand**. Ostriches can live for 50 years or more.

In addition to laying the largest egg, the ostrich has broken records for the number of eggs it lays—up to 15 at one time.

△ The **ostrich** is the only bird with two-toed feet. Although it cannot fly, it can run up to 43 mph (70 km/h) on its strong legs.

Ottawa

Ottawa is the capital of **Canada** and its third largest city with a **population** of about one million. It is in the province of Ontario in southeast Canada, and the Ottawa and Rideau **rivers** flow through the city.

Ottawa's best-known site is the Parliament buildings, which stand on a hill above the Ottawa River. They include the tall Peace Tower with its 53 bells. Ottawa also has several universities and museums.

Early British settlers began building Ottawa in 1826 and named it after the nearby Outawouais **Native Americans**. More than one citizen in three is French-speaking.

Otter

Otters are large relatives of weasels. They have long, slender bodies and short legs. An otter hunts in **water** for **fish** and **frogs**. Thick fur keeps its body dry, and it swims quickly by moving its tail and body like an **eel**, using its webbed hind feet as paddles.

By night otters hunt up and down **rivers** or roam overland to find new fishing grounds.

They love to play by sliding down banks of snow or mud. The number of otters in the wild is decreasing steadily, and they are now rare. This could be because of **pollution**, but no one is sure.

▷ **Otters** move very slowly on their webbed feet on land but are fast enough to catch animals such as rabbits. They are superb hunters in water, catching mainly fish and frogs.

Owl

These **birds** of prey hunt mainly at night. They have soft **feathers** that make no **sound** as they fly, and their large, staring **eyes** help them see in the dimmest **light**. Owls also have excellent **hearing**—some can catch mice in the pitch-black night simply by listening to the **sounds** they make. An owl can also turn its head around 180 degrees to look backward.

When an owl eats a **mouse** or small bird, it swallows it whole with **bones** and fur or **feathers**. Later the owl spits out the remains in a pellet.

There are more than 130 species of owls. Some of the largest and smallest owls live in **North America**. The great gray owl of the north is as long as a human's arm. The elf owl of the south is the smallest in the world—smaller than a sparrow. It has a short tail and tiny feet and is small enough to nest in holes made by woodpeckers. In the **desert** it is often found nesting in saguaro **cactuses**.

Barn owls are one of the world's most widespread species, but they are much less common today than they once were. This may be because there are fewer deserted buildings and hollow **trees** in which to lay their **eggs**. They do not build **nests** and feed mainly on small **rodents**.

The long-eared owl's tufted "ears" are really feathers. But they help in the recognition of this bird, which is found in most of **Europe**, northern **Asia**, and North America.

▽ Most **owls** hunt at night, swooping down silently on rabbits, mice, and other prey. Their fringed wing feathers can beat the air without making a sound.

Oxygen

△ A wax candle has a wick that is burned to provide light. **Oxygen** is needed to keep the flame burning.

Oxygen is a **gas**. It is colorless and odorless and one of the most abundant **elements** on **earth**. It makes up one part in every five of **air**. Oxygen is found in **water** and many different **rocks**. Most of the **weight** of water and half that of rocks comes from the oxygen in them.

Fire needs oxygen to burn. Almost all living things need oxygen for **breathing** and to give them the **energy** to stay alive. **Animals** need extra oxygen to move around. **Plants** give off oxygen into the air.

Oyster

△ People harvest tons of **oysters** each year for food. Pearl oysters are also farmed for their pearls, which are used in jewelry.

An oyster is a **mollusk** with a soft body protected by a broad, hinged shell. This shell is rough on the outside. The inside of a pearl oyster's shell is smooth, shiny mother-of-pearl. Pearl oysters make pearls.

An oyster makes a pearl when there is a foreign object, such as a grain of **sand**, inside its shell. To stop the irritation caused by the sand the oyster deposits a substance, called nacre, around it, which gradually builds up to form a pearl.

Several types of oysters are eaten as a **food**. They are farmed in shallow coastal **water**. Oysters cling to empty shells, **rocks**, or wooden posts on the seabed. When they have grown large enough, they are harvested.

Ozone layer

see **Global warming**

▷ When this girl touches the spines on a cactus, it causes her **pain**. Special nerves in her finger send a warning signal to her central nervous system. A message is sent back to the nerves that control the muscles of her arm, making her jerk her hand away.

Pacific Ocean

The Pacific Ocean is the largest and deepest of all the **oceans**. Its waters cover more than one third of the world's surface. All the **continents** on **earth** would fit inside the Pacific Ocean with room to spare. Its deepest part is deep enough to drown the world's highest **mountain**, Mount **Everest**.

The Pacific Ocean lies west of the Americas and east of **Australia** and **Asia**. It stretches from the **Arctic** to the **Antarctic**. There are thousands of tiny **islands** in the Pacific. Most were formed when **volcanoes** erupted from the seabed. Sometimes **earthquakes** shake the seabed and send out huge tidal waves.

△ The **Pacific Ocean** is the largest ocean on earth. Its average depth is 14,100 ft. (4,300m), but the deepest part is the Challenger Deep in the Mariana Trench, which is 35,801 ft. (10,915m) deep.

Pain

Pain is an unpleasant feeling. It is a warning that something is wrong somewhere in your body. You feel pain if something burns or presses hard on the ends of certain **nerves**. Those parts of the body with the most nerve endings, such as your hands, feel pain most easily. The nerves carry the pain signals to the central nervous system.

Sometimes pain is useful because it teaches you to avoid what caused it. For example, if you prick yourself with a pin, you learn not to do it again, and toothaches tell you it is time to go to the dentist. Chemists have invented painkillers to deaden pain caused by **disease** and injury.

Paint

Paint is used to decorate a surface and protect it from rotting. When paint is spread over a solid surface such as plaster, **wood**, or **paper**, it forms a thin coat. The paint then dries by evaporation. Oil-based paints are colored powder in **oil** or resin. Latex paints are powder and drops of oil or resin in **water**. Traditionally paints and **dyes** were produced from natural substances such as soil, fruit, or flowers. Today most are mass-produced.

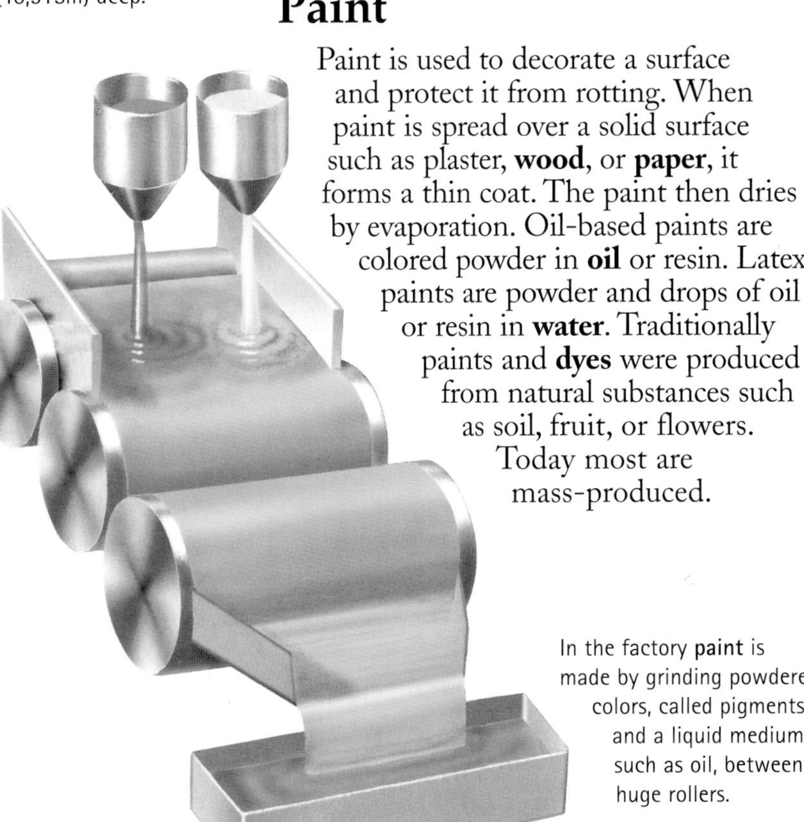

In the factory **paint** is made by grinding powdered colors, called pigments, and a liquid medium, such as oil, between huge rollers.

PAKISTAN
Government: Parliamentary democracy
Capital: Islamabad
Area: 300,300 sq. mi.
Population: 144,616,639
Languages: Urdu, English, and others
Currency: Rupee

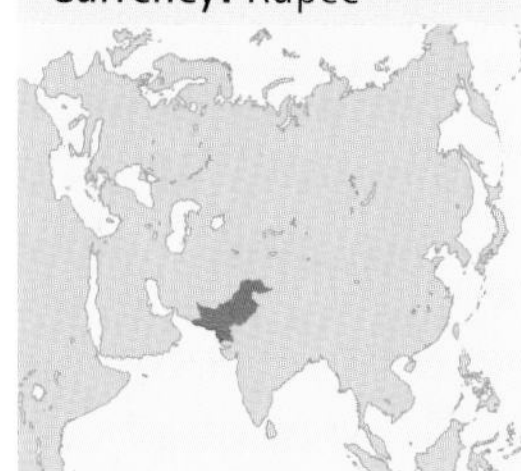

Painting can be a long, hard task, but rewarding for both the painter and the generations who follow. In 1508, the Italian Renaissance artist Michelangelo was asked by Pope Julius II to paint the ceiling and altar wall of the Sistine Chapel in the Vatican in Rome. It took him many years to complete his work.

Painting

Painting is a form of **art** in which people use colored **paint** to make pictures on canvas, plaster, **wood**, or **paper**. Today many people paint for their own pleasure, but in the past this was not always the case.

Stone Age hunters probably used painting as **magic**. They drew wounded wild beasts on their **cave** walls, maybe thinking that such pictures would help them kill real animals on the next hunt.

In the **Middle Ages** most artists worked for the church, and their paintings usually showed scenes from the **Bible**. Such paintings helped people who could not read to understand the stories in the Bible.

By the 1400s Europe's rich princes and merchants were paying artists to paint pictures to decorate their homes. The pictures might be family portraits, still-life scenes of flowers and fruit, and landscapes showing cities and country estates.

In the 1800s many artists began trying out new ideas. For example, some tried to give a feeling of **light** and shade in a landscape. Others used bright, flat **colors** to bring out the patterns in still lifes and landscapes. In the 1900s Pablo **Picasso** and other artists began to experiment with abstract paintings. These concentrate on the basic shapes, colors, and patterns of the things painted.

▽ **Pakistan**'s Punjab area is where archaeologists excavated the prehistoric city of Harappa (recreated here) in 1826. This early river settlement grew into one of the largest cities of its time—almost one sq. mi. in area. It was occupied c. 2300–1750 B.C.

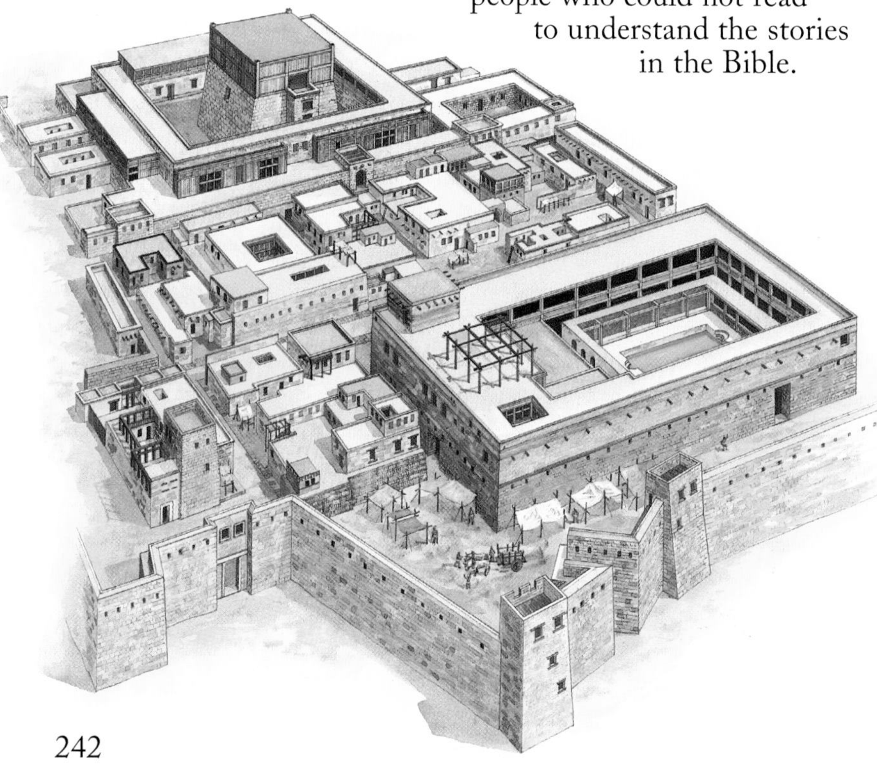

Pakistan

Pakistan lies between **India** and **Iran**. There are more than 140 million people living in Pakistan. Most of them follow the religion of **Islam**.

Much of Pakistan is hot and dry, but crops, such as **wheat** and **cotton**, grow with the help of **water** from the Indus River. The Indus flows from the **Himalayas** to the Arabian Sea. Until 1947 Pakistan was part of India, ruled at that time by the British. It then broke away to become an independent Muslim **republic**. In 1971 East Pakistan became **Bangladesh**. The military seized control in 1999 under General Pervez Musharraf, who intends to restore civilian rule.

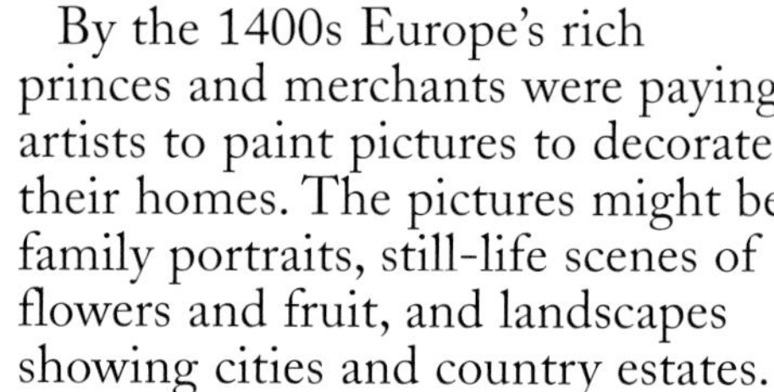

The giant **panda** feeds mainly on bamboo shoots (as here), grasses, and flowers such as irises and crocuses.

The red **panda** is a tree-dwelling mammal that is closely related to the giant panda.

Palestine

Palestine is a land on the eastern shore of the **Mediterranean Sea**. Historic Palestine covers an area of only 10,530 sq. mi. (27,000 sq km), about one third the size of Maine. People lived in Palestine at least 200,000 years ago during the Old **Stone Age**. Most of the stories in the **Bible** took place there, and Palestine gets its name from the Philistines who once lived in one area. By 1800 B.C. the Hebrews had made Palestine their home.

Later the Hebrews ruled Palestine as two nations called **Israel** and Judah. Today most of what was called Palestine lies in the nation of Israel. The rest is part of **Jordan**, **Lebanon**, and **Syria**. In the 1990s attempts were made to create a Palestinian state in territories occupied by Israel. But conflict between Palestinians and Israelis has continued into the 21st century.

Palm

The most familiar palm **tree** has leaves that sprout straight out of the top of its trunk. But there are more than 1,000 types of palms, and not all are trees. Some are shrubs, and some are vines. Most grow in warm **climates**.

Palms are useful **plants**. People make mats and baskets from their leaves and eat its **fruit** such as coconuts.

Panama

Panama is a country about the size of South Carolina. It occupies the narrow neck of land that joins **Central America** and **South America**. Panama has a damp, tropical **climate** in which **rice**, **sugar**, bananas, and pineapples are grown.

The Panama Canal cuts the country in half, and **ships** use the **canal** as a shortcut between the **Atlantic Ocean** and **Pacific Ocean**. Much of Panama's wealth comes from this **trade**, and Panama City is an international finance center because of it. Many ships are registered in Panama.

Sets of locks on the canal raise and lower ships as they cross the hilly countryside. In 1903 Panama granted the occupation and control of the canal to the **United States**. A new treaty in 1978 provided for Panama's gradual takeover of the canal. The takeover was completed on December 31, 1999.

PANAMA
Government: Democracy
Capital: Panama City
Area: 29,300 sq. mi.
Population: 2,845,647
Languages: Spanish and English
Currency: Balboa

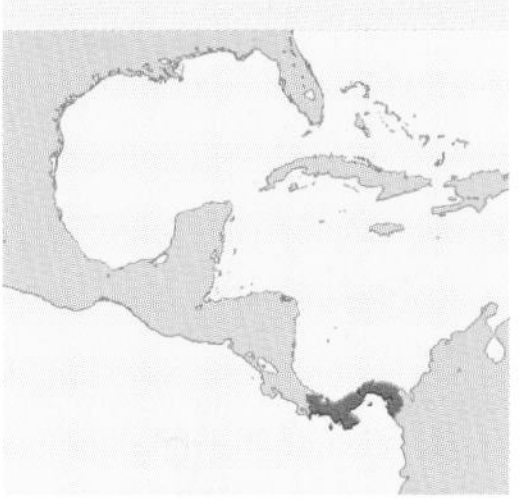

Panda

There are two kinds of pandas. Both live in the forests of eastern **Asia**. The giant panda looks like a black-and-white **bear**. It lives in bamboo **forests** in **China**. The red panda is not much larger than a **cat**. It has a bushy tail and reddish fur. It is nocturnal—it sleeps during the day and looks for food at night. Both kinds of pandas eat mainly **plants**. Their nearest relatives are the **raccoons** of **North America** and **South America**.

△ The coconut **palm** can grow as high as 98 ft. (30m). Its fruit, which is covered with hairs, contains a hollow space filled with coconut "milk." The white meat or kernel within the coconut is not only good to eat but can be used in making soap, wax, and oil.

Paper

Paper gets its name from papyrus. The papyrus plant grows in swamps in **Egypt**, and the ancient Egyptians made a kind of paper from it. However, the Chinese invented paper as we know it today. About 1,900 years ago they learned to separate the fibers from mulberry bark. They soaked these and then dried them, making a flat, dry sheet on which they could write. Paper is still made of plant fibers. Some of the best paper is made from **cotton**. Newspaper is made from **wood**.

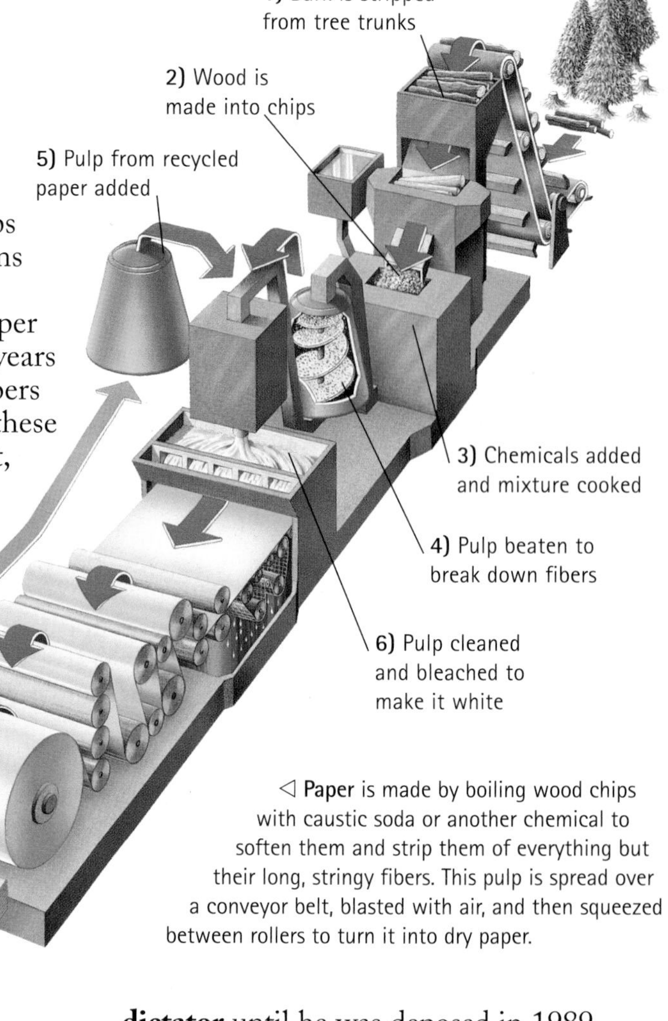

◁ **Paper** is made by boiling wood chips with caustic soda or another chemical to soften them and strip them of everything but their long, stringy fibers. This pulp is spread over a conveyor belt, blasted with air, and then squeezed between rollers to turn it into dry paper.

PAPUA NEW GUINEA
Government: Parliamentary democracy
Capital: Port Moresby
Area: 174,200 sq. mi.
Population: 5,049,055
Languages: English, Motu, and others
Currency: Kina

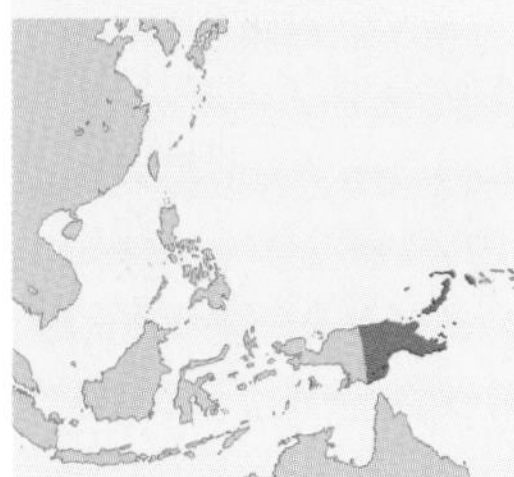

Papua New Guinea

Papua New Guinea is a country that occupies the eastern half of the island of **New Guinea**, north of **Australia**. The western half of the island, Irian Jaya, is Indonesian. Papua New Guinea gained its independence from Australia in 1975 and is a member of the **Commonwealth**. It is a hot, wet country, and the chief crops are **coffee**, coconuts, and cocoa.

PARAGUAY
Government: Constitutional republic
Capital: Asunción
Area: 153,200 sq. mi.
Population: 5,734,139
Languages: Spanish, Guarani
Currency: Guarani

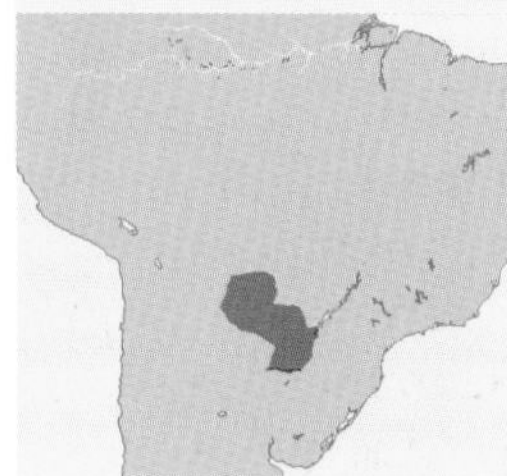

Paraguay

Paraguay is a landlocked country in **South America**. It is divided in half by the Paraguay River, and much of the **population** is in the east. Most Paraguayans are mestizos, people of mixed Indian and Spanish descent. They farm soybeans, **cotton**, sugarcane, **tobacco**, **rice**, and **fruits**. Many of the people living in Paraguay are farmers, and they produce barely enough to feed themselves.

General Alfredo Stroessner became president in 1954 and ruled as a **dictator** until he was deposed in 1989. Democracy was restored, and three **elections** were held in the 1990s.

Parasite

Parasites are living things that live and feed on and in creatures larger than themselves (called hosts). Animal parasites include **fleas**, lice, ticks, and mites. Different kinds live on different **birds** and **mammals**. Most suck **blood**, and some spread **germs** that cause **diseases**. Certain kinds of **worms**, including the tapeworm, get inside the body of the host and live in their intestines or burrow deep into their **muscles**.

Aphids and some other creatures live as parasites on **plants**. Plant parasites include many kinds of **fungi** that cause diseases in plants or animals. Mistletoe is a parasite. It feeds off the trees on which it grows.

△ **Parasites** like aphids suck the sap of plants, such as roses, and can spread disease.

△ **Paris** is dominated by the Eiffel Tower, designed by Gustave Eiffel (1832–1923) and erected for the Paris Exhibition of 1889. It was the tallest building in the world until 1930.

Paris

Paris is the capital of **France** and the country's largest city. More than nine million people live in Paris and its suburbs. The Seine River divides the city into the Left and Right banks.

From the top of the Eiffel Tower you can see parks and **gardens**, fine squares, and tree-lined avenues. Other famous landmarks are the cathedral of Notre Dame, the basilica of the Sacré Coeur, the Arc de Triomphe (built by **Napoléon**), and the Louvre Palace, now a museum and art gallery.

Paris is known for its **fashion**, perfume, and **jewelry**. Another key industry is the manufacture of **cars**.

Parliament

A parliament is the highest meeting of people held to make a nation's **laws**. The word "parliament" comes from the French word *parler*, meaning "to talk." One of the first parliaments was the Althing in **Iceland**, founded more than 1,000 years ago.

Parliaments exist in many countries around the world. In the **United Kingdom** the Houses of Parliament, in London, are the seat of the British Parliament, started in 1265. It grew gradually out of a meeting of nobles who advised the king. By the 1700s Parliament had become more powerful than the king. Congress, which meets in the Capitol Building in **Washington D.C.**, is the equivalent in the **United States**.

◁ The **Parthenon** in Athens was built with the best white marble to please the gods for whom it was erected. The huge stone blocks were carried to the site on ox-drawn carts and hauled up to the builders on ropes and pulleys.

The scarlet macaw is the world's largest **parrot**. It lives in the treetops of the jungles of Central and South America and feeds on fruit.

Parrot

These tropical **birds** have brightly colored **feathers**. They use their strong, curved beaks as "hands" to help them climb from branch to branch. Their beaks can also crack open nuts and bite off chunks of **fruit**.

There are hundreds of different kinds of parrots. Cockatoos, macaws, and lovebirds all belong to the parrot family. Budgerigars and other parrots can learn to "talk" by imitating **speech**, and one African gray parrot was taught to speak over 900 words.

Parthenon

The Parthenon is one of the world's most famous buildings. The ruins of this great white **marble** temple stand on the **Acropolis**, a hill that overlooks the Greek capital, Athens.

The Athenians built the Parthenon between 447 and 433 B.C. in honor of Athena Parthenos, their patron and the **goddess** of war. They used the finest materials and the best craftsmen to please her. Rows of columns like huge tree trunks held up the sloping roof. Elegant statues, tall columns, and painted friezes decorated the outside. Inside the rooms were filled with treasures, dominated by a huge **gold** and **ivory** statue of Athena made by the sculptor Phidias.

In 1687 the Parthenon was damaged by a shell during the Turkish-Venetian war, and more recently it has suffered from air **pollution**, but its ruins still dominate the city of Athens.

Passover

This Jewish **festival** celebrates the Israelites' escape from **slavery** in **Egypt**. The **Bible** tells how God punished the Egyptians ten times before they freed the Israelites. The tenth time, an angel killed the eldest child in each Egyptian family but passed over the Israelites' homes without harming them. The Passover feast, or Seder, is led by the head of the family on the first two nights of the eight days of Passover.

Weight

Pendulum swinging

◁ The swing of the **pendulum** makes the weight in a grandfather clock fall evenly. As the weight falls tiny toothed gearwheels turn and move the hands around the clock face.

Pasteur, Louis

The French scientist Louis Pasteur (1822–1895) proved that **bacteria** and other **germs** cause **diseases**. Pasteur injected weakened germs into animals and people to stop them from catching the diseases those germs usually caused. He also invented pasteurization, a way of heating **milk** and cooling it quickly to stop it from going bad. In addition, he discovered how **yeast** cells turn **sugar** into **alcohol**.

△ Louis **Pasteur** developed vaccines against cholera, rabies, anthrax, and other deadly diseases.

Peacock

Peacocks are male peafowl. Peafowl are large **birds** that live in **Asia**. Peacocks attract their mates by spreading out their long, blue-green **feathers**, which grow just above the tail. Big spots on the feathers look like rows of eyes. As the peacock struts before the female it looks extremely proud, hence the term "as a peacock."

◁ Only the **peacock** has the spectacular tail with its "eyes." The peahen is much less colorful and has a short tail.

Pendulum

This is a hanging weight that is free to swing back and forth. When the weight is pulled to one side and then released, **gravity** sets it swinging back and forth in a curved path called an arc. Each swing takes the same amount of **time** no matter whether the swing is big or small. This makes pendulums useful for keeping time in **clocks**. After a while a pendulum will stop moving. But a pendulum clock keeps its pendulum swinging with a mechanical device called an escape wheel. This is what makes the "tick tock" sound.

Emperor

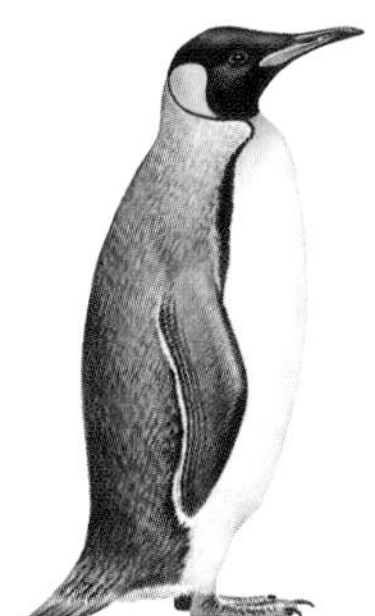
King

Chinstrap

Rockhopper

Gentoo

◁ There are 17 types of **penguins**, and many of them live in huge groups called colonies. All five types shown here live in Antarctica. Tough feathers and a thick layer of fat keep penguins warm in the icy conditions of the frozen continent.

Penguin

Penguins are **birds** that can swim. They cannot fly because their wings are shaped like flippers. Penguins use their wings to "row" themselves through the sea. They swim and dive very well.

All penguins come from the southern part of the world. Emperor penguins live in **Antarctica**. In the winter the female lays one **egg** on the ice. Her mate rolls the egg onto his feet and keeps it warm for two months until it hatches.

Pepys, Samuel

Samuel Pepys (1633–1703) was an English **government** official who became Secretary of the Admiralty and doubled the size of **England**'s navy, making it very strong. He also wrote a famous diary describing life in **London** under Charles II (1630–1685). Pepys wrote about the fire that burned down much of London in 1666. He recorded gossip about the king, described family quarrels, and told of visits to the theater.

Perfume

Perfumes produce a pleasant **smell**, and people use them on their bodies. Factories add perfumes to products such as **soap** and **detergent**. Natural perfumes are **oils** squeezed from **flowers**, leaves, or stems and mixed with substances like musk. Factories make synthetic perfumes from substances including coal tar.

Eva **Perón** was dearly loved by the people of Argentina—so much so that she became the subject of the musical *Evita*, which has been turned into a movie.

PERU
Government: Republic
Capital: Lima
Area: 493,600 sq. mi.
Population: 27,483,864
Languages: Spanish, Quechua, Aymara
Currency: New Sol

Perón, Eva

Eva Perón (1919–1952), also known as Evita, was born in **Argentina** and was an actress before her marriage in 1945. Her husband, Juan Perón (1895–1974), was a soldier and later became president of Argentina. Evita became a powerful political figure.

Peru

Peru is the third largest nation in **South America.** You could fit **France**, the **United Kingdom**, **Germany**, and **Italy** inside it with room to spare.

Peru shares borders with five other countries, and its western coast is washed by the **Pacific Ocean**. The sharp, snowy peaks of the high **Andes mountains** cross Peru from north to south like a giant backbone. Between the mountains and the **ocean** lies a thin strip of **desert**. East of the mountains, hot, steamy forests stretch for vast distances around the **Amazon River**.

People have been building towns in Peru for several thousand years. The most famous people were the **Incas**, who established an empire in the mountains. In the 1530s the Spaniards seized Peru. Since the 1820s Peru has been an independent nation.

Today, Peruvians grow sugarcane and **coffee**. **Sheep** and **llamas** are kept to produce wool and meat. Peruvian mines are worked for **copper**, **iron**, and **silver** for export, and the fishing grounds usually hold plenty of **fish**.

When the **pharaoh** sat on the throne holding the symbols of authority (the crook and the flail) the Egyptians believed that the spirit of the god Horus entered him, and he spoke to them as a god on earth.

Pharaoh

The word "pharaoh" is used to mean "king" when describing the kings of **ancient Egypt**. (The ancient Egyptians gave their kings other titles as well.) The word "pharaoh" comes from the Egyptian word *peraa*, which means "great house" and was the royal palace where the pharaoh lived. When he died, he was preserved in a **pyramid**.

Egyptians believed that pharaohs were descended from Ra, the sun **god**. The pharaoh took care of all the needs of his people, and he was king of a united Upper and Lower Egypt. The pharaoh owned all the land, and Egypt's nobles, priests, and soldiers were supposed to obey him. In reality the priests and nobles ran the country.

PHILIPPINES
Government: Republic
Capital: Manila
Area: 115,00 sq. mi.
Population: 82,841,518
Languages: Pilipino and English
Currency: Peso

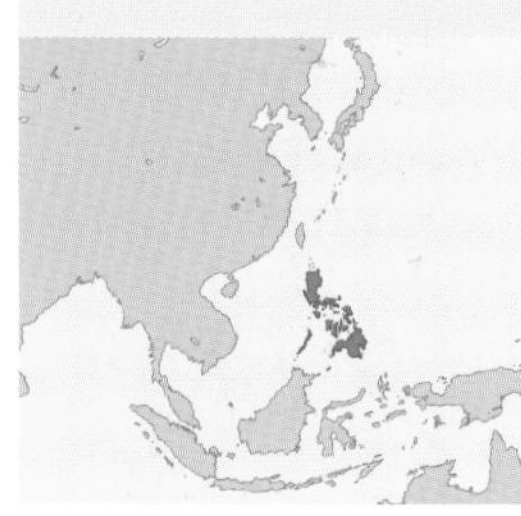

Philippines

The Philippines is a large group of **islands** in **Asia**. The largest islands are Luzon and Mindanao. Manila, the chief port and largest city, is the capital. Most of the people live in small villages and make their living from **farming**. They grow sugarcane, **fruits**, **rice**, coconuts, and **vegetables**.

Spanish **explorers** named the islands after King Philip II of **Spain**. In 1898 after the Spanish–American War the islands were turned over to the **United States**. They became independent in 1946, but the Philippines still has close links with the United States.

Ferdinand Marcos (1917–1989) was elected president in 1965 and restricted the activities of his opponents. In 1986 he fled the country. The subsequent **governments** faced economic problems and widespread poverty.

Philosophy

The word "philosophy" comes from the Greek *philosophia,* meaning "love of wisdom." Philosophers are thinkers who search for truth and knowledge about the **universe**. They do this by reflecting, reasoning, and arguing, and they ask questions such as: How much can we really know about anything? If we argue that something is what we say it is, how can we be sure that our ideas are truly correct? When we say that God exists, what do we mean by "God," and what do we mean by "exists"? The first great philosophers were Greeks and included Socrates, **Plato**, and **Aristotle**.

Photocopier

A photocopier is a **machine** that can copy a page of a **book** or a letter in only a few seconds. When you press the button on a photocopier, a bright **light** illuminates the page. A **lens** inside the machine shines an image of the page onto a smooth metal drum that is electrified (see **electricity**). When the image shines on it, the light in the bright parts destroys the electric charge, while the dark parts of the drum are still electrified.

A black powder is then dusted over the drum. This clings only to the parts of the surface of the drum that are electrified. When a sheet of **paper** is pressed against the drum, the powder comes off onto the paper, and this produces a copy of the page. This process is called xerography.

Photography

The word "photography" comes from the Greek words *photos* for "drawing" and *graphien* for "light" and means "drawing with light." When you take a photograph, rays of **light** produce a picture on the film in the **camera**.

First you look through a viewfinder at the subject you want to photograph. Then you press a button that opens a shutter to let light from the subject enter the camera. The light passes through a **lens** that produces an image of your subject on film in the camera. But the image shows up only when the film is developed (treated with chemicals). A developed film is called a negative. This shows black objects as white and white objects as black. From negatives you can print positives, which are the final photos, either as paper prints or slides.

Photosynthesis *see* Plant

Physics

Physics is a **science**, and physicists are interested in **matter**—in solids, **liquids**, and **gases**—and in the tiny **atoms** that make up all matter. They are also interested in different forms of **energy**—electrical, light, sound, mechanical, chemical, and nuclear. Some of the major fields of study in physics include mechanics (forces and motion; solids, liquids, and gases); optics (**light**); acoustics (**sound**); **electricity** and **magnetism**; atomic, molecular, and nuclear physics; and cryogenics (the study of extremely low **temperatures** and their effects, including superconductivity).

Physicists conduct experiments to make discoveries. They carefully record the results of their experiments so that other people can test them for themselves. Physics covers a very large field, and no single physicist today understands all the different aspects of the subject. For example, nuclear physicists who study the tiny atom in detail may know little about outer space and the movements of **planets**, **stars**, and **galaxies** because these are studied by astrophysicists. However, one subject all physicists must understand is **mathematics**.

Two of the greatest physicists who ever lived were Isaac **Newton** and Albert **Einstein**.

△ The first **photographs** were very different from today's snapshots. They were made by exposing large metal plates covered in tarlike chemicals to light. Photos, such as the one above, could take several minutes, and the subjects had to stay very still.

Piano

Piano is short for the Italian word pianoforte, meaning "soft" and "loud." The piano was invented by Bartolomeo Cristofori in 1709. The name refers to the piano's great range when compared with the harpsichord, which was in use before the piano was invented. The earliest instruments had strings that extended horizontally away from the keyboard like the modern grand piano (below). The upright piano, with vertical strings, was not developed until the 1800s.

A modern standard piano has 88 keys. It also has two pedals that can be used to soften or sustain (prolong) the notes.

▽ **Pianos**, like this grand piano, are played by pressing the keys. The lever movement of the key is transmitted to a felt-covered hammer that strikes the piano string. A damper stops the note from sounding after the key is released.

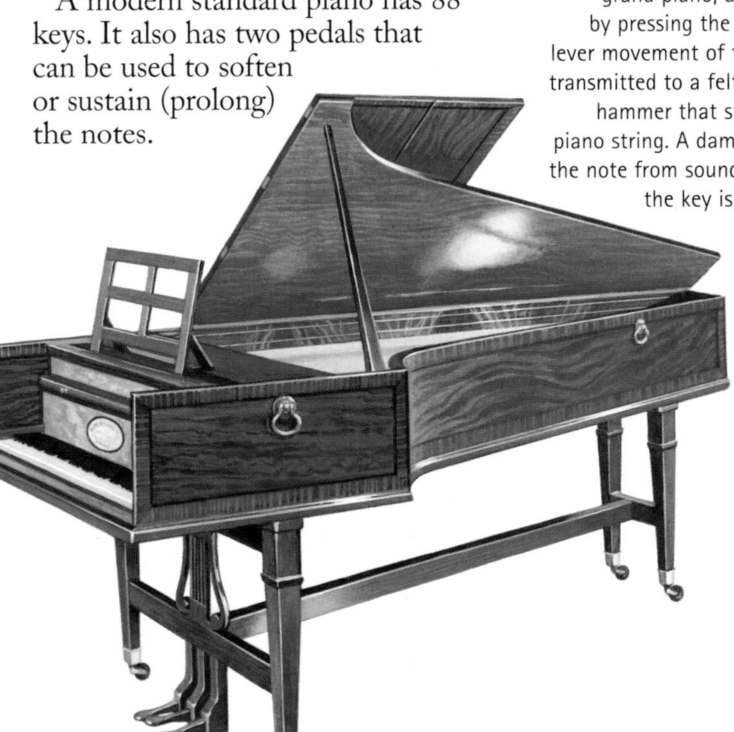

△ Pablo **Picasso** was a very influential artist whose work dominated art in the early 1900s.

Picasso, Pablo

Pablo Picasso (1881–1973) was the most famous artist of the 1900s. He was born in **Spain** but lived mostly in **France**. It is said Picasso could draw before he even learned to talk. At the age of 14 he spent one day completing an **art** school test that most people needed a month to take, and by 16 he had passed all the tests that Spain's art schools could offer. He disliked **paintings** that looked like **photographs** and admired the curving shapes of African **sculpture**. His style developed over the years until he began painting people as simple shapes—as cubes—and he became the most influential painter of the Cubist art movement. He also produced sculpture and **pottery**.

Pig

△ There are many different breeds of **pigs**. The ones shown are: 1) Gloucester Old Spot, 2) Poland, 3) China, and 4) Tamworth.

These farmyard **animals** have a long, heavy body, short legs ending in hooved toes, a long snout, and a short, curly tail. Males are called boars. Females are called sows. The heaviest boars can weigh over one ton.

Domestic pigs are descended from the wild boar of Asian and European **forests**. They provide us with bacon, ham, pork, and lard. Different parts of a pig's body are used to make brushes, **glue**, **leather**, and **soap**. The wild boar is a tough, fierce animal unlike most of its domestic relatives.

Pigeon and Dove

▽ **Pigeons** have a plump body, rounded tail, and soft brown, pink, or gray-blue feathers.

Pigeons and doves are **birds** that eat **seeds** or **fruit**. Many make soft cooing sounds. Pigeons are larger than doves. The crowned pigeon is bigger than a chicken, but the diamond dove is almost as small as a lark.

Tame pigeons are all descended from rock doves, which nest on cliffs. Pigeons and doves have become domesticated. Some are pets, while others are used for racing. Homing pigeons will fly great distances to return home—one even flew 806 mi. (1,300km) in one day.

Pilgrim

△ The **Pilgrims** sailed on the *Mayflower*, a galleon weighing 180 tons that was probably only about 115 ft. (35m) long. The journey took 66 days. One passenger died during the voyage, but two were born.

A pilgrim is a person who makes a journey to a place, often holy, as an act of religious faith. The journey is known as a pilgrimage. Among Christians pilgrimages were highly organized in the **Middle Ages** and included trips to the Holy Land, **Rome**, and shrines to the Virgin Mary such as the one at Lourdes in southern **France**.

Some groups of people who settle in foreign lands are also described as pilgrims. In 1620 a group of English Puritans seeking religious freedom sailed from **England** across the **Atlantic** Ocean. They landed on the coast of what is now Massachusetts and founded a colony there. The 102 men, women, and children are known as the "Pilgrim Forefathers."

There are still many pilgrimages today. The birthplace of the prophet **Muhammad** is **Mecca** in **Saudi Arabia**. It is a holy city and a place of pilgrimage for more than two million Muslims every year. Muslim men and women are expected to make at least one pilgrimage there in a lifetime.

Pine *see* Conifer

Plague

The word "plague" comes from the Latin *plaga*, meaning "disaster" or "pestilence." Since ancient times terrible diseases have swept through **Europe**, **Asia**, and **Africa** from time to time. Bubonic plagues, such as the **Black Death**, have wiped out hundreds of thousands of people over the centuries.

The word "plague" is also used to describe an overwhelming invasion by something that is not welcome, for example "a plague of tourists" or "a plague of locusts."

△ **A plague** of locusts so big that it blocked the sun devastated Africa in the summer of 1988. As many as 50 billion hungry insects ate thousands of tons of crops, and the people faced famine.

Planet

The word "planet" comes from the Greek word *planetes*, meaning "wanderer." Long ago skywatchers gave this name to stars that appeared to move. We now know that planets are not **stars** but are bodies that travel around stars.

Earth and other planets of our **solar system** travel around the star we call the **Sun**. Each planet travels in its own **orbit**, but they all move in the same direction and, except for Pluto and Mercury, lie in the same plane.

Astronomers think the planets originated from a band of **gas** and dust that once whirled around the Sun. They think that **gravity** pulled parts of this band together as masses that became planets. The nine planets in our solar system are **Mercury**, **Venus**, **Earth**, **Mars**, **Jupiter**, **Saturn**, **Uranus**, **Neptune**, and **Pluto**. Mercury is closest to the Sun, and Pluto is usually farthest away. Viewed from Earth, the other planets shine because of reflected sunlight.

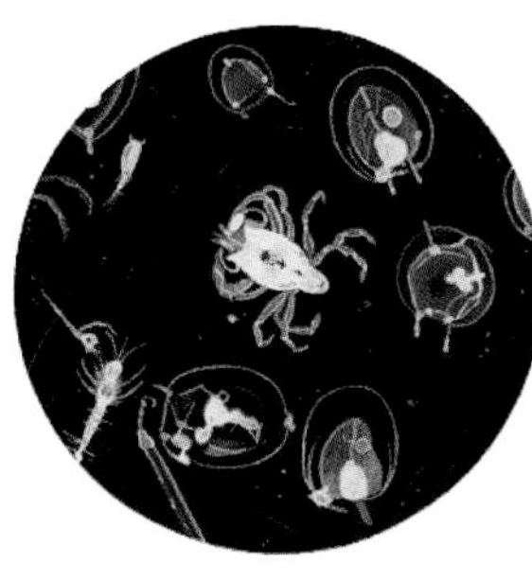

△ **Plankton** often have beautiful and complex structures despite their tiny size. These diatoms have shells that are made of silica, a protective, hard, colorless solid.

Plankton

Plankton is the mass of tiny **plants** and **animals** that drifts around in the sea and inland **waters**. Most plankton are so small they can be seen only with a **microscope**.

Planktonic plants are called phytoplankton. They live near the surface of the water where they find the **light** they need. Some tiny plants swim by lashing the water with little whiplike organs. Others have spiky shells that look like glass.

Planktonic animals are called zooplankton. Some live deep underwater and rise at night to feed. Zooplankton includes tiny one-celled creatures and baby **crabs** and **fish**.

Plankton forms the base for the ocean **food chain**. All sea creatures either depend directly on plankton for food or on animals that feed on plankton.

PLANTS

△ *The violet is an example of a very versatile plant. It is used in the production of perfumes. It can be eaten in salads, fried in oil, and candied. It is also used to treat skin complaints and in poultices for ulcers.*

Plants are living organisms that harness the energy of the sun to feed themselves and build up living matter. They take in carbon dioxide from the air and release oxygen. Without plants our planet would be a lifeless world. Plants release all the oxygen that animals need to breathe. They also provide food for animals and form the basis for the habitats in which they live.

There are more than 375,000 different kinds of plants ranging in size from tiny mosses only a few inches long to giant redwood trees, which grow to over 328 ft. (100m) tall. Plants live in nearly all the regions of the world, although half the known plant species grow in tropical forests—this large mass of plants produces so much oxygen that the forests are often described as the "lungs" of the planet. Each plant has adapted to its own habitat, sometimes in extreme conditions. Desert plants, such as cactuses and succulents, have long, widely spreading roots to collect water, which they store in their fleshy stems and leaves. Plants in cold places grow in low, thick clumps, which protect them from the cold and wind.

PLANT GROUPS

There are several different plant groups. Liverworts and mosses grow in moist places with no roots, flowers, or seeds, just simple leaves. Horsetails are an ancient group of plants that are found in damp, shady areas and have small leaves and hollow stems. Ferns have curled stems and feathery leaves known as fronds. They reproduce by spreading spores from packets on their leaves.

Conifers (gymnosperms), such as pines and firs, are cone-bearing plants. They produce bare seeds that are contained in cones, and they were the earliest seed-bearing plants to evolve. Many conifers grow in relatively dry, cold places.

Flowering plants (angiosperms) produce covered seeds. This group includes a large range of plants that live in most habitats and conditions throughout the world. They are divided into two classes: monocotyledons and dicotyledons. Monocotyledons grow from seeds that contain only one seed leaf, or cotyledon. They have long, narrow leaves and include grasses, bamboos, palms, lilies, and bluebells. Dicotyledons grow from seeds that contain two seed leaves. They are the largest group of plants with over 200,000 species, including oak, apple, beech, cactuses, daisies, and potatoes.

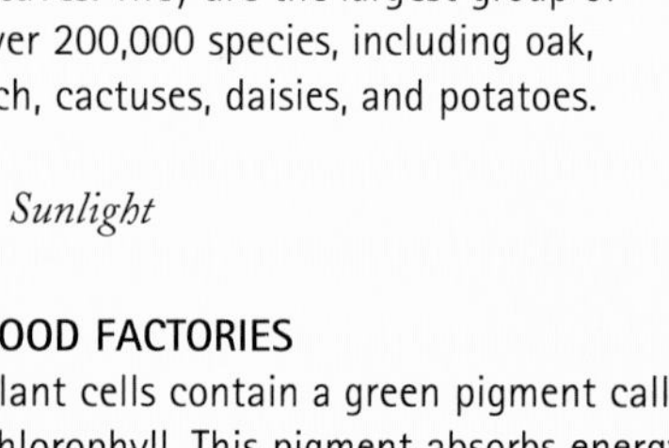

△ *Leaves are the plant's food-making factories. In the leaves, cells are arranged so they absorb as much sunlight as possible.*

FOOD FACTORIES

Plant cells contain a green pigment called chlorophyll. This pigment absorbs energy from sunlight to make glucose—a type of sugar—from carbon dioxide in the air and water in the soil. This process, unique to plants, is called photosynthesis. The glucose molecules made in photosynthesis are joined together to form other substances. One of these is cellulose, which is used for growth and to build new cells, and the other is starch, which is used as a reserve food source.

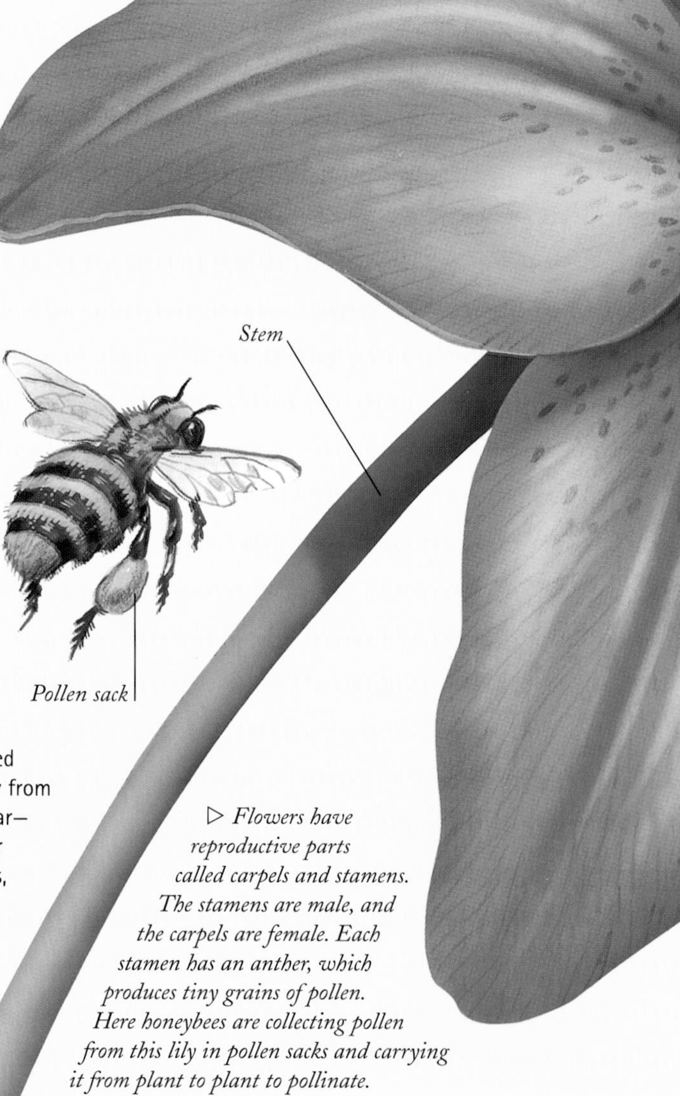

▷ *Flowers have reproductive parts called carpels and stamens. The stamens are male, and the carpels are female. Each stamen has an anther, which produces tiny grains of pollen. Here honeybees are collecting pollen from this lily in pollen sacks and carrying it from plant to plant to pollinate.*

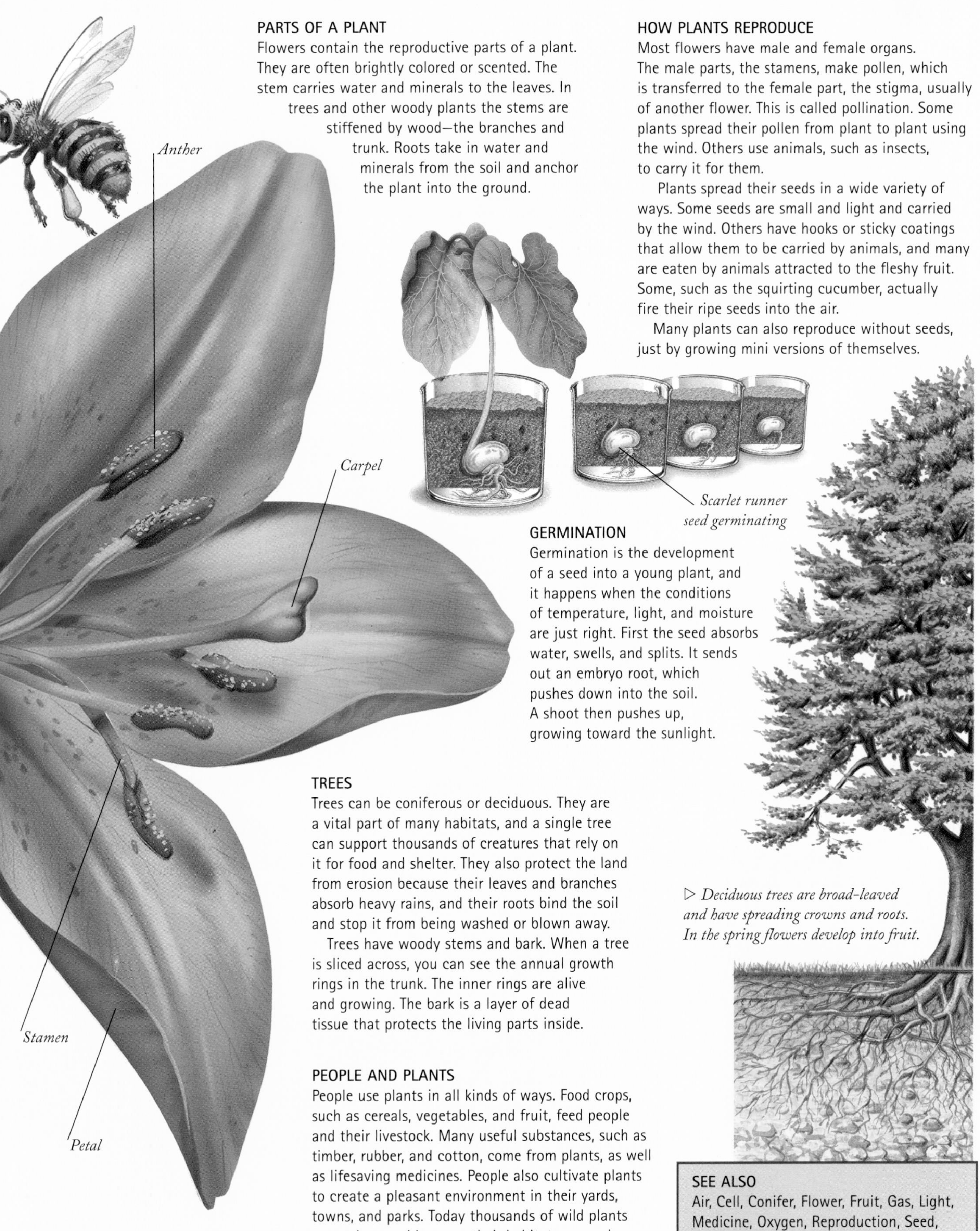

PARTS OF A PLANT

Flowers contain the reproductive parts of a plant. They are often brightly colored or scented. The stem carries water and minerals to the leaves. In trees and other woody plants the stems are stiffened by wood—the branches and trunk. Roots take in water and minerals from the soil and anchor the plant into the ground.

HOW PLANTS REPRODUCE

Most flowers have male and female organs. The male parts, the stamens, make pollen, which is transferred to the female part, the stigma, usually of another flower. This is called pollination. Some plants spread their pollen from plant to plant using the wind. Others use animals, such as insects, to carry it for them.

Plants spread their seeds in a wide variety of ways. Some seeds are small and light and carried by the wind. Others have hooks or sticky coatings that allow them to be carried by animals, and many are eaten by animals attracted to the fleshy fruit. Some, such as the squirting cucumber, actually fire their ripe seeds into the air.

Many plants can also reproduce without seeds, just by growing mini versions of themselves.

Scarlet runner seed germinating

GERMINATION

Germination is the development of a seed into a young plant, and it happens when the conditions of temperature, light, and moisture are just right. First the seed absorbs water, swells, and splits. It sends out an embryo root, which pushes down into the soil. A shoot then pushes up, growing toward the sunlight.

TREES

Trees can be coniferous or deciduous. They are a vital part of many habitats, and a single tree can support thousands of creatures that rely on it for food and shelter. They also protect the land from erosion because their leaves and branches absorb heavy rains, and their roots bind the soil and stop it from being washed or blown away.

Trees have woody stems and bark. When a tree is sliced across, you can see the annual growth rings in the trunk. The inner rings are alive and growing. The bark is a layer of dead tissue that protects the living parts inside.

▷ *Deciduous trees are broad-leaved and have spreading crowns and roots. In the spring flowers develop into fruit.*

PEOPLE AND PLANTS

People use plants in all kinds of ways. Food crops, such as cereals, vegetables, and fruit, feed people and their livestock. Many useful substances, such as timber, rubber, and cotton, come from plants, as well as lifesaving medicines. People also cultivate plants to create a pleasant environment in their yards, towns, and parks. Today thousands of wild plants are endangered because their habitats are under threat so it is important to protect them.

SEE ALSO
Air, Cell, Conifer, Flower, Fruit, Gas, Light, Medicine, Oxygen, Reproduction, Seed, Temperature, Tree, Vegetable, Water

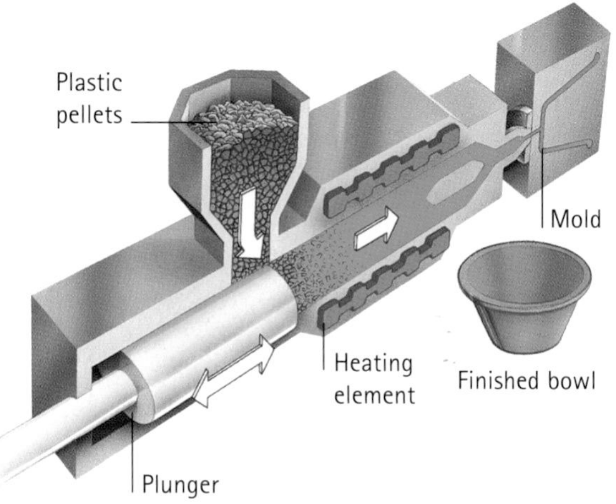

◁ **Plastic** objects can be made by a process called injection molding. Plastic pellets are heated and then injected into a mold. There is another common method for molding plastic. This is used to make rods or sheets of plastic. It is called hot extrusion, and the plastic is forced through openings.

Plastic

Plastics are manufactured substances and can be molded into different shapes. They are used to make anything from furniture and car seats to shoes and bags and cups and plates.

Most plastics are largely made from chemicals obtained from petroleum **oil**. **Coal**, limestone, **salt**, and **water** are also used. Plastics can be hard, soft, or **liquid**. They can be made to look like **glass**, **metal**, **wood**, or other substances.

Hard plastics are used in **radio** and **camera** cases. But fine threads from hard plastic nylon make soft stockings. Some bags and bottles are made of soft plastics like polyethylene. The first plastic was celluloid, which was discovered in the 1800s.

Plato

Plato (c. 427–347 B.C.) was a great Greek thinker whose ideas were very important in the establishment of the field of **philosophy**. Plato believed that the things we see around us are only poor copies of the perfect things in an ideal world. He developed ideas such as the notion of justice, and in his book *The Republic* he described his idea of a perfect nation, or utopia, ruled by philosopher kings. Plato traveled widely before settling in Athens, where he founded his own academy with **Aristotle** as one of his students.

△ As a **plow** travels up and down the field it turns up the soil, leaving ridges and furrows.

▽ The duck-billed **platypus** is just one of a number of very unusual animals found only in Australia and New Zealand. These landmasses were cut off millions of years ago when the continents drifted apart. The animals there evolved in isolation from those elsewhere.

Platypus

The platypus is an Australian **mammal** that lays eggs. Its name means "flat- footed." The platypus uses its webbed feet to swim in **rivers** and its ducklike beak to hunt for **worms** and **insects** underwater. It lives in a burrow in riverbanks. The female lays her soft-shelled eggs in a nest. They are as small as marbles.

Plow

This farm **machine** has blades that turn over the surface of the soil. It is used to bury weeds, stubble, and other **plants** on the surface in preparation for the cultivation of a new crop.

Pluto

The **planet** Pluto is named after the Greek **god** who ruled the dreary world of the dead. Pluto must be bitterly cold because it is farther away from the **Sun** than any of the other planets. It is almost 40 times farther from the Sun than **Earth** is.

Pluto spins and moves around the Sun much more slowly than Earth. A day on Pluto may equal nearly a week on Earth. One year on Pluto lasts almost 248 Earth years. Pluto is only half as big as Earth and weighs one sixth as much.

Pocahontas

Native American Pocahontas (c. 1595–1617) was the daughter of Chief Powhatan. According to John Smith, one of the English founders of the Jamestown settlement of Virginia, Pocahontas saved his life twice when he was at the mercy of her tribe. In 1613 Pocahontas was taken captive by the Jamestown colonists and while a prisoner became a Christian and took the name Rebecca. The following year she married James Rolfe, a tobacco planter. She traveled to **England** with her husband in 1616, where she was received by royalty. She became sick and died of smallpox just as she set out on a ship to return to North America.

Poetry

Poetry is the oldest form of literature. Before people developed a system of writing they found that the best way to remember a story was to sing it or put it in a rhyming pattern. Poets choose words carefully, for their **sound** as well as their meaning. Poetry can be compared to music because it creates beautiful sounds with words.

Much poetry is written in rhyme. This means that the words at the ends of lines have the same final sound. However, rhyme is not necessary in poetry. Poets use rhyme in some poems and not in others.

Poems are usually divided into parts, or verses. The lines of a verse have a rhythm that is built up by strong and weak sounds.

There are three main types of poetry. They are narrative, lyric, and dramatic. Narrative poetry tells a story. Lyric poetry describes the poet's own feelings. Dramatic poetry has characters who tell a story, just as a play does. **Shakespeare** wrote many of his plays in verse.

△ Many **poisons** are so dangerous that they have to have a clear warning label when they are being shipped from one place to another or when they are stored. The international symbol for poisonous substances is a skull and crossbones. The other symbol shows that the contents of the barrel are radioactive.

Poisons

Poisons are chemical substances that kill or damage living things. Some poisons get into the body through the **skin**, while some are swallowed. Poisonous **gases** are harmful if someone breathes them in with **air**. Different poisons work in different ways. Strong **acids** or alkalis burn. **Nerve** poisons can stop the **heart**. Some other poisons can make the body bleed inside. If they are administered in time, **drugs** called antidotes can cure people who have ingested certain poisons.

▽ **Pluto** has one moon, Charon (left), which is about half as large as the planet it orbits. Many astronomers think that they are twin planets rather than a planet with a moon.

PLUTO FACTS

Average distance from Sun: 3.66 billion mi.
Nearest distance from Earth: 3.6 billion mi.
Average temperature: –382°F
Diameter across the equator: 1,860 mi.
Number of moons: 1 known
Length of day: 6 days and 9 hours
Length of year: 247.7 Earth years

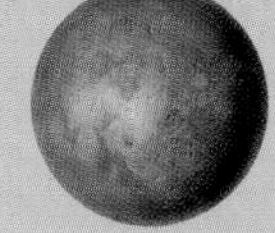

Poland

Poland lies in Eastern **Europe** south of the Baltic Sea and is the seventh largest country in Europe. Most of Poland is low farmland, although **forests** sprawl across the Carpathian **Mountains** in the south. Poland's largest **river** is the Vistula. It rises in the mountains and flows into the Baltic Sea. Rivers often freeze in Poland's cold, snowy winters.

There are more than 38 million Poles. Most of them speak Polish, and most are Roman Catholics.

In 1989 Poland had its first free **elections** in 40 years. The independent trade union Solidarity swept into power, and Poland became the first non-communist country in the former Eastern Bloc. In 1999 Poland joined **NATO,** and it seems likely that it will move closer to countries in the West.

POLAND
Government: Democratic state
Capital: Warsaw
Area: 3117,400 sq. mi.
Population: 38,633,912
Language: Polish
Currency: Zloty

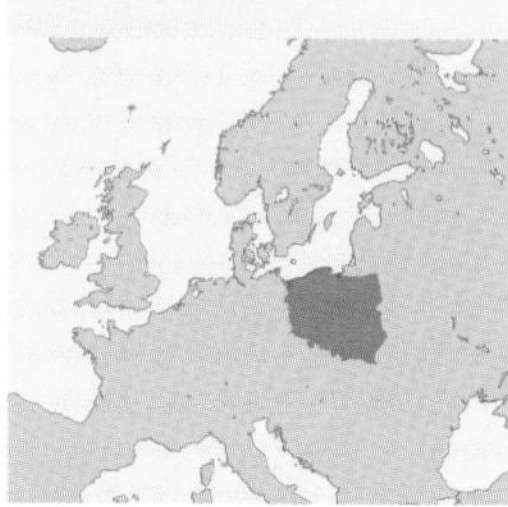

Police

Police are employed by a **government** to enforce the **laws** of a country and maintain order. Part of this job involves protecting people's lives and property. Police officers patrol streets, direct traffic, control crowds, find missing persons, and help people who have been hurt in accidents. Police officers try to prevent crime, and track down and capture criminals. This can be dangerous, and sometimes officers are killed. Most police forces today are armed with weapons of some kind, and many carry **guns.**

Other branches of police work include forensics (the scientific investigation of a crime that includes fingerprinting and the analysis of clues) and criminology (the study of criminals, their crimes, and the way that their minds work).

△ The modern **police** rely heavily on contacts with members of the public. When officers patrol, it can be on horseback (like this officer in New York), on foot, or in a car.

◁ **Pollution**, such as this oil spill at sea, can harm wildlife and permanently damage the ecology of an area. These seabirds stand little chance of survival.

Pollution

Pollution occurs when harmful substances are released into the environment in such large quantities that they cause damage to people, wildlife, or **habitats**. Before the **Industrial Revolution** in **Europe** most of the wastes produced by living things had been used by other living things. Today people produce more waste matter than can be coped with naturally, and more and more pressure is being put on **governments** to control industry and combat pollution.

Cars and factories pour smoke and fumes into the air. Chemical **fertilizers** and pesticides can kill wild **plants** and **animals**. Poor sewage disposal and **oil** spills devastate seas and **rivers**. International agreements have been drawn up to reduce such pollution and stop countries dumping waste at sea.

Polo, Marco

Marco Polo (1254–1324) was an Italian who traveled to **China** at a time when the people of **Europe** knew little about the East. His father and his uncle were merchants in **Venice**, and they decided to take the young Marco with them on their second journey to the East in 1271. They crossed Persia (modern-day **Iran**) and the vast Gobi Desert. In 1275 the

Polos reached Peking in China (today's **Beijing**) and were welcomed at the court of **Kublai Khan**, a great **Mongol** conqueror. The Polos stayed for many years during which Marco traveled all over China as an envoy in the service of the Khan. They left China in 1292 and arrived home in Venice in 1295. Later, Marco Polo wrote down his adventures in a book, *Travels of Marco Polo*.

Pompeii

Two thousand years ago Pompeii was a small Roman city in southern **Italy**. A sudden disaster killed many of its citizens and drove out the rest. However, the same disaster preserved the streets and buildings. Today visitors to Pompeii can learn a great deal about what life was like inside a Roman city.

In A.D. 79 the nearby **volcano** of **Vesuvius** erupted and showered the town of Pompeii with volcanic ash and cinders. Poisonous **gases** swirled through the streets. About one citizen in every ten was poisoned by fumes contained in the clouds of hot ash that swept down the volcano's slopes. Their remains were buried by ash and pumice stone, which also covered their homes. In time people forgot that Pompeii had ever existed.

For centuries Pompeii's thick coat of ash, which was 20–23 ft. (6–7m) deep, hardened and protected it from the **weather**. Finally in the 1700s people began to dig out the city. The excavation continues today. Archaeologists have discovered whole buildings, streets, tools, and statues. They have even found hollows in the ash left by the decayed bodies of people and dogs killed by the eruption. The archaeologists poured plaster into these hollows, allowing it to harden. Then they cleared away the ash to reveal life-size plaster models of the dead bodies. Part of the city still remains buried, and the modern town lies to the east.

△ Archaeologists have uncovered almost half the city of **Pompeii**. Bodies of the people trapped in the ash while fleeing have been recreated by making plaster casts of their imprints in the ash.

Pope

"Pope" is the title of the head of the Roman Catholic Church. (The word "pope" comes from the Italian word *papa*, which means "father.") The Pope is also the Bishop of Rome. He lives in **Vatican City** inside **Rome**.

Roman Catholics believe that **Jesus** made St. Peter the first pope. Since then there have been many popes. Each time one dies church leaders choose another. The Pope makes Church laws, chooses bishops, and can declare people saints.

△ As the current **pope** John Paul II is recognized by Roman Catholics as the representative of Jesus Christ on earth. He is also head of Vatican City, the smallest state in the world.

Pop music

Pop music is short for "popular music." Modern pop music has strong, lively rhythms and simple, frequently catchy, tunes. Most pop tunes are songs. A pop group usually has one or more singers with session musicians who play electric guitars, bass, drums, and keyboards. Many people start pop groups when they are still in high school, and a few have achieved success by being "discovered" at a young age and given recording contracts.

Elvis Presley was one of the first rock 'n' roll stars to become a cult hero. Famous pop groups and stars like Ricky Martin, Madonna, Michael Jackson, and Britney Spears, have attracted huge audiences to their concerts all over the world.

Population

All the people living in a place make up its population. That place may be a village, a city, a country, or the world. In the **Stone Age** the whole world held only a few million people. Their numbers were kept low by injuries, **diseases**, and lack of **food**. As people have solved these problems the **population** of the world has increased.

Between A.D. 1 and 1650 the world's population doubled. It doubled again in only 150 years after 1650. Since then it has risen even faster. In 1930 the world had two billion people. It passed the six billion mark on the eve of the 21st century, and it is still increasing fast.

Porcupine

Porcupines are named from the Latin words for "spiny pig." A porcupine is really a **rodent** with many **hairs** shaped as long, sharp spines, or quills. If a porcupine is attacked, it backs toward its enemy and lashes its tail. Some of the spines stick into the attacker and cause painful wounds or even death.

Ground-living, or terrestrial, porcupines are found in southern **Asia**, **Africa**, southern **Europe**, and the East Indies. A tree-living, or arboreal, species is found in both **North America** and **South America**.

▽ The North American **porcupine** is not hurt by losing some of its quills. They are part of its defense system and soon grow back.

Porpoise *see* Dolphin

Portugal

PORTUGAL
Government: Parliamentary democracy
Capital: Lisbon
Area: 35,300 sq. mi.
Population: 10,066,253
Language: Portuguese
Currency: Euro

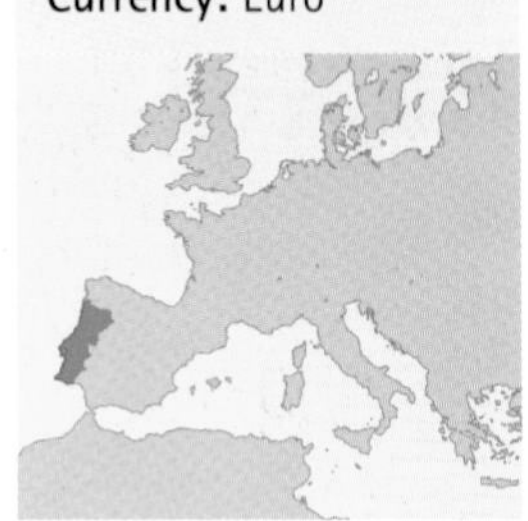

This is a long, narrow country in southwest **Europe**. It is sandwiched between the **Atlantic Ocean** and **Spain**, a country four times the size of Portugal. Much of Portugal is mountainous. **Rivers** flow from the **mountains** through valleys and across plains to the sea. Portugal's mild winters and warm summers help its people grow olives, oranges, and **rice**. Its grapes produce port, a **wine** named after the Portuguese city of Oporto. Portugal's **forests** yield more cork than those of any other nation. Its fishermen catch sardines and other sea **fish**. Portugal also has mines that produce **minerals** such as **copper** and **tin** and factories for products such as textiles, leather, and electrical machinery.

There are over 10 million people in Portugal. They speak Portuguese, which is also the official language of Brazil. The capital of Portugal is Lisbon.

Potato

△ The **potato** is a root crop. The tubers—the part that we eat—vary greatly in size, shape, color, and flavor depending on the variety of potato. Potatoes can be cooked and eaten as a vegetable or processed to make french fries or chips.

Potatoes are valuable **foods**. They are rich in **starches** and contain **proteins** and different **vitamins**. Potatoes must be cooked to give us nutrients that our bodies can use. Potato **plants** are related to tomatoes. Each plant is low and bushy with a soft stem. Each potato grows on a root as a kind of swelling called a tuber. When its tubers have grown, the plant dies, but new plants spring up from the tubers.

Potatoes were first grown by South

American Indians. Spanish **explorers** brought potatoes back to **Europe**. After **wheat**, **rice**, and corn they are the world's most important crop.

In 1845 and 1846 the Irish potato crops failed because of a plant **disease**. As a result, thousands of Irish people died of starvation, and many more emigrated to the **United States**.

Pottery

All kinds of objects made of baked **clay** are called pottery. Many cups, saucers, plates, bowls, pots, vases, and other objects and ornaments are made of this very useful substance.

People have been making pottery for thousands of years. Early pots were thick and gritty. They leaked, and they cracked if heated. In time people learned to make pottery that was more useful and more beautiful. Today the two main kinds of pottery are porcelain and stoneware. Porcelain is fine pottery made of white China clay. It is so thin that it lets the light shine through. Stoneware is usually much thicker.

To make a pot a potter puts a lump of moist clay on a spinning disk called a **wheel**. Potters use their thumbs and fingers to shape the clay into a pot and then leave it to dry. Next they may coat it with a wet mixture called a glaze. Then they fire (heat) the pot with others in an oven called a kiln. Firing makes the pots rock-hard and turns their glaze into a smooth, hard, shiny coat. Different glazes produce different **colors**. Some glazes even produce a metallic sheen on a pot.

Most pottery today is mass-produced in factories because it can be shaped, fired, and decorated quickly and cheaply on an assembly line.

Poultry

All birds kept for meat or eggs are known as poultry. To most people poultry means chickens, **ducks**, **geese**, and turkeys, but **ostriches**, partridges, guinea fowl, **peacocks**, pheasants, and pigeons are kept as poultry too.

Chickens outnumber other kinds of poultry. There are probably more chickens than people in the world, and they lay enough **eggs** to give everyone on earth several hundred eggs each year. The meat from chickens is produced more cheaply than **sheep** or **cattle**.

△ On farms **poultry** like these chickens can roam free—called free-range—or be raised intensively in tightly packed units.

△ **Pottery** objects like these jugs can be made by pouring "slip," or liquid clay, into a mold. They can also be shaped on a potter's wheel. The jug on the right has been fired and glazed.

Power plant

Power plants are places where the **energy** in **heat** or in running **water** is changed into electrical energy for use in homes and factories. Most power plants obtain their energy from a **fuel** that makes steam that powers a **generator** or a group of generators.

The generators produce **electric currents** that often travel overland through power lines slung between tall **metal** towers. First the current passes through a transformer. This raises the voltage (pressure) of the current and reduces the amount that leaks away as the current flows. The voltage is reduced again before it reaches homes and factories.

▽ A coal-fired **power plant** transforms the energy locked in coal into electricity. Coal, oil, and natural gas are fossil fuels, and these fuels are used in the majority of power plants around the world. Most power plants burn huge quantities of fossil fuels to produce steam from water.

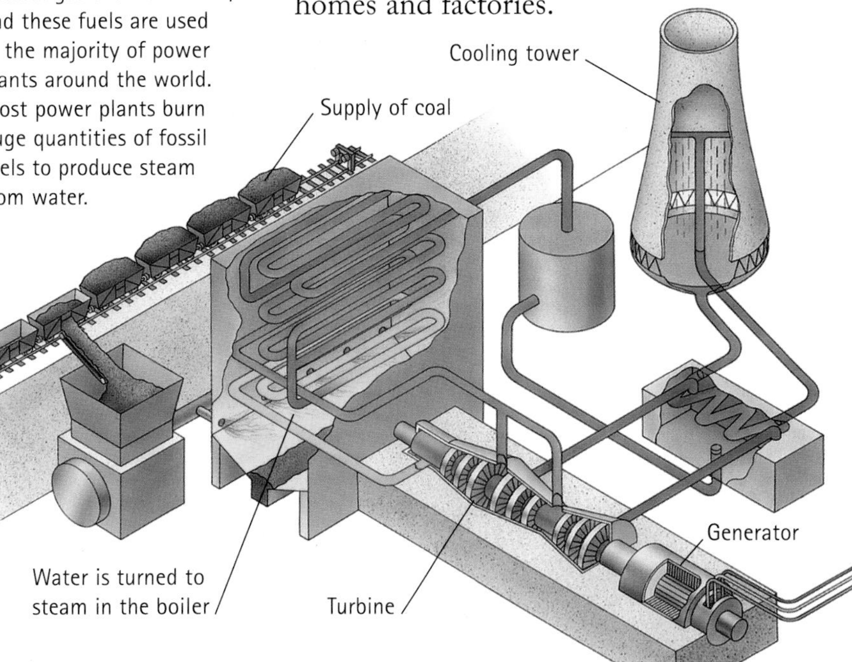

◁ *Ornithocheirus was a coastal pterosaur with a 39 ft. (12m) wingspan—almost five times bigger than the largest living bird. Behind it, the pterosaur* Tapejara *and some early birds crowd the cliffs.*

▽ Meganeura, *one of the first flying insects, had a wingspan of up to 27 in. (70cm). It lived in warm forests at the same time as the early reptiles around 300 million years ago.*

PREHISTORIC ANIMALS

Prehistoric animals are those that lived more than 5,000 years ago. The fossils (preserved remains) of many animals have been found all over the world. Some are hundreds of millions of years old.

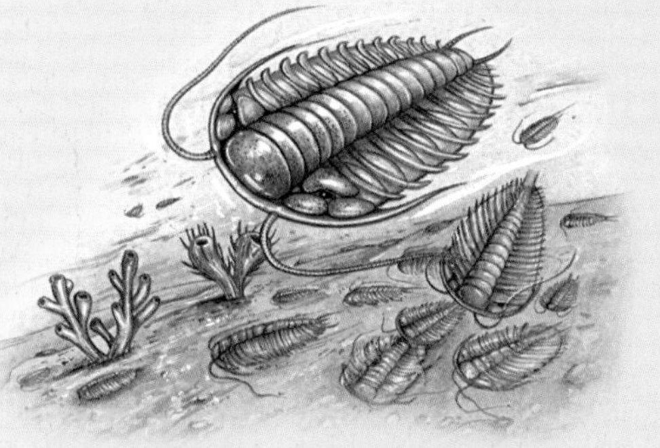

△ *Trilobites were among the first animals to develop a tough protective shell.*

SIGNS OF LIFE

The earliest animals appeared in seas and oceans about 3.5 billion years ago. Most of them were single-celled organisms that drifted in the water. Around 550 million years ago the first complex animals evolved—soft-bodied invertebrates (animals without a backbone) such as jellyfish and worms.

ARMORED ANIMALS

Some of the early, soft-bodied sea creatures developed shells or hard, jointed limbs. These included shellfish, corals, and ammonites. Shelled trilobites were once the most common sea animals on earth between 570 and 245 million years ago. The hard parts of their bodies were often preserved as fossils.

THE FIRST FISH

The earliest fish evolved around 500 million years ago. They were the first vertebrates, or animals with a backbone. At first they had no jaws and could only draw in specks of food through their suckerlike mouths. Then some fish developed bony armor and strong, movable jaws equipped with sharp teeth. These adaptations allowed fish to take over from giant, 6.6-ft. (2-m) -long water scorpions as masters of the oceans.

FROM WATER TO LAND

Around 380 million years ago some fish began to crawl onto dry land to find new sources of food. They had primitive lungs and muscular fins that were strong enough to pull their bodies out of the water. At first these adventurous fish may have been able to stay on land for only a few hours before struggling back to the water, but gradually they evolved into the first amphibians—animals that can live in both water and on land. Some of them may have looked like large newts or salamanders.

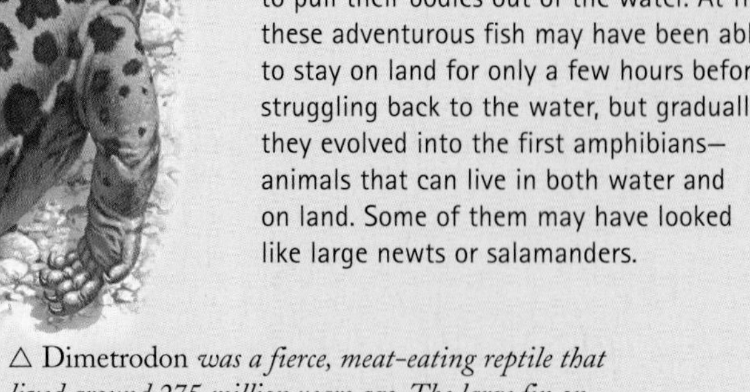

△ Dimetrodon *was a fierce, meat-eating reptile that lived around 275 million years ago. The large fin on its back helped this animal control its body temperature.*

EARLY REPTILES

Reptiles evolved from amphibians. They had thicker skins and laid eggs with thick shells, which allowed them to live far from water. Some reptiles, called pterosaurs, developed leathery wings and learned to fly. Others, such as the ichthyosaurs, returned to the sea. During the Triassic, Jurassic, and Cretaceous periods—between 230 and 65 million years ago—the dominant land reptiles were the dinosaurs.

INSECTS AND BIRDS

Insects were the first animals to take to the air about 300 million years ago—long before the pterosaurs. The largest flying insect was *Meganeura*, which looked like a giant dragonfly. The first bird, *Archaeopteryx*, is believed to have evolved from a dinosaur about 150 million years ago.

SMALL MAMMALS

The first mammals evolved from reptiles around 230 million years ago. During the reign of the dinosaurs they remained small and ratlike, living on worms, insects, and dinosaur eggs. Once the dinosaurs had become extinct some mammals began to grow larger and take on different shapes. Before long they had taken over as rulers of earth.

▽ *This scene from South America one million years ago shows just how varied mammals became after the demise of the dinosaurs.* Toxodon, *for example, was a thick-skinned plant eater about the size of a rhinoceros.*

△ Archaeopteryx *was the size of a magpie. It had birdlike feathers but also the teeth and long, bony tail found in many reptiles.*

THE WORLD OF MAMMALS

Prehistoric mammals were all shapes and sizes. An early horse, *Hyracotherium*, stood just 7.8 in. (20cm) tall at the shoulders. One group of large mammals, the brontotheres, each had a huge forked horn on their snouts. *Baluchitherium* was probably the largest mammal ever to live on land. This giant, giraffe-shaped rhinoceros carried its head about 26 ft. (8m) above the ground.

SABER-TOOTHED CATS

Saber-toothed cats lived in many parts of the world during the last 25 million years. Their huge canine teeth measured up to 6 in. (15 cm) long—ideal for piercing the thick hides of large plant-eating mammals. The last saber-tooths died out a few tens of thousands of years ago.

SEE ALSO
Amphibians and Reptiles, Birds, Dinosaurs, Elephant, Evolution, Fish, Forest, Horse, Insects, Mammals, Rhinoceros, Teeth

PREHISTORIC ELEPHANTS

Elephants were among the most common and varied of prehistoric mammals. Pig-sized elephants lived in the Mediterranean region, while the wooly mammoths of Europe and Asia and the mastodonts of the Americas stood up to 10 ft. (3m) tall. The mammoths and mastodonts adapted to the severe cold of the ice ages by developing a coat of long, thick fur. These animals were among the last prehistoric species to die out around 10,000 years ago. They were probably wiped out by early human hunters.

▷ Megatherium, *a 16.4-ft. (5-m) -tall sloth, died out 11,000 years ago.*

▽ Glyptodon *was a slow-moving, armored mammal that was probably hunted by saber-toothed cats.*

△ About 20,000 years ago **prehistoric people** lived in caves or crude huts built of wood or hides. They used tools of stone and bone for hunting and preparing food, as well as for making clothing and shelters. During the Stone Age it has been estimated that only a few thousand people lived in the whole of Africa and another few thousand in Asia.

Prehistoric people

Prehistoric people lived long ago before there were any written records of **history**. We know about them from their remains. Prehistory is divided into the **Stone Age**, the **Bronze Age**, and the Iron Age. The ages are named after the materials that people used to make their tools and weapons.

The Stone Age lasted for a long time. It began around 2.5 to 3 million years ago when humanlike creatures began to appear on earth. They were different from the apelike animals that lived at the same time. They had larger **brains**, used stone tools, and could walk upright.

Around 1.5 million years ago a more humanlike creature appeared. Scientists call this early human *Homo erectus*, meaning "upright man." *Homo erectus* is probably the ancestor of more advanced types of humans called *Homo sapiens*, meaning "intelligent man." One kind of *Homo sapiens* were the Neanderthals, who appeared about 100,000 years ago. Modern humans, *Homo sapiens*, first appeared in Europe and Asia around 35,000 years ago.

Toward the end of the Stone Age prehistoric people began to use **metals**, the first of which was **copper**. They made copper tools about 10,000 years ago. About 5,000 years ago people invented **bronze**, a hard **alloy** of copper and tin. This development signaled the start of the Bronze Age when the earliest civilizations began. The Bronze Age ended about 3,300 years ago in southeastern **Europe** when people learned how to make tools from iron. Iron is much harder than bronze, and with it people were able to develop farming and building methods.

△ Of all the **prehistoric peoples** *Homo habilis* was probably the first human being to make and use tools such as flint knives.

President

A president is the elected head of a state or **republic**, and in some countries they are also the head of the government. In the **United States** the president—the most powerful elected person in the world—is head of the government. In **France**, on the other hand, the president is the head of state and appoints a prime minister to lead the government. The title of president is also given to heads of clubs, business organizations, and societies.

Printing

Printing is a way of copying words and pictures by mechanical means. It is used to produce **books**, **newspapers**, magazines, and other items such as **food** labels and printed shopping bags. It can also be used to print on fabrics.

The earliest printing, using carved wooden blocks, was in China, probably as early as the A.D. 700s. Around 1455 Johannes **Gutenberg** of **Germany** invented the first printing press using movable type, which has raised **metal** letters that can be used again and again. The process is known as relief printing, and ink is put onto the raised letters, which are then pressed against **paper**.

The most common relief method today is letterpress printing, but there are many other kinds of printing.

In intaglio or gravure printing, often used by artists, the image is not raised. Instead it is etched or cut away.

In other kinds of printing the ink is put onto a flat surface. Offset lithography uses printing plates that are made photographically. The plates are treated with chemicals so that the greasy ink sticks only to the images to be printed. This method, invented in the early 1900s, made mass-production **color** printing possible.

Today most publications are printed from **computer**-generated pages. **Laser** printers work by spraying ink onto a page, while dot matrix printers form images from tiny dots.

Protein

Proteins are substances in **food** that are vital to life. They contain **carbon**, **hydrogen**, **oxygen**, and nitrogen. They build up body tissue, especially **muscle**, and repair damaged **cells**. They also give **heat** and **energy**, help us grow, and protect us from **disease**. Our bodies do not store extra protein so we have to eat a regular supply.

△ Most of the **protein** we need is found in foods that come from animals—meat, fish, eggs, and cheese are all good sources of protein. But some plant foods, such as peanuts, peas, and beans, are also rich in protein.

Proverb

A proverb is a short sentence containing a piece of wisdom. The **Bible** contains a **book** called Proverbs. All the peoples of the world have proverbs, and many are international. "A bird in the hand is worth two in the bush" is first found in English in a manuscript from about 1470. The Spanish version is "A sparrow in the hand is worth a vulture flying," and the German is "A sparrow in the hand is better than a stork on the roof."

Psychology

Psychology is the scientific study of the mind and behavior of **animals** and **humans**. Psychologists are interested in how the mind and **senses** work and can measure some things, such as **intelligence**, by using special tests.

There are several branches of psychology. Child psychology is the study of how children behave and what they do at different ages. Psychiatry is a similar science, but psychiatrists are doctors who cure mental illness and abnormal kinds of behavior such as drug addiction and depression.

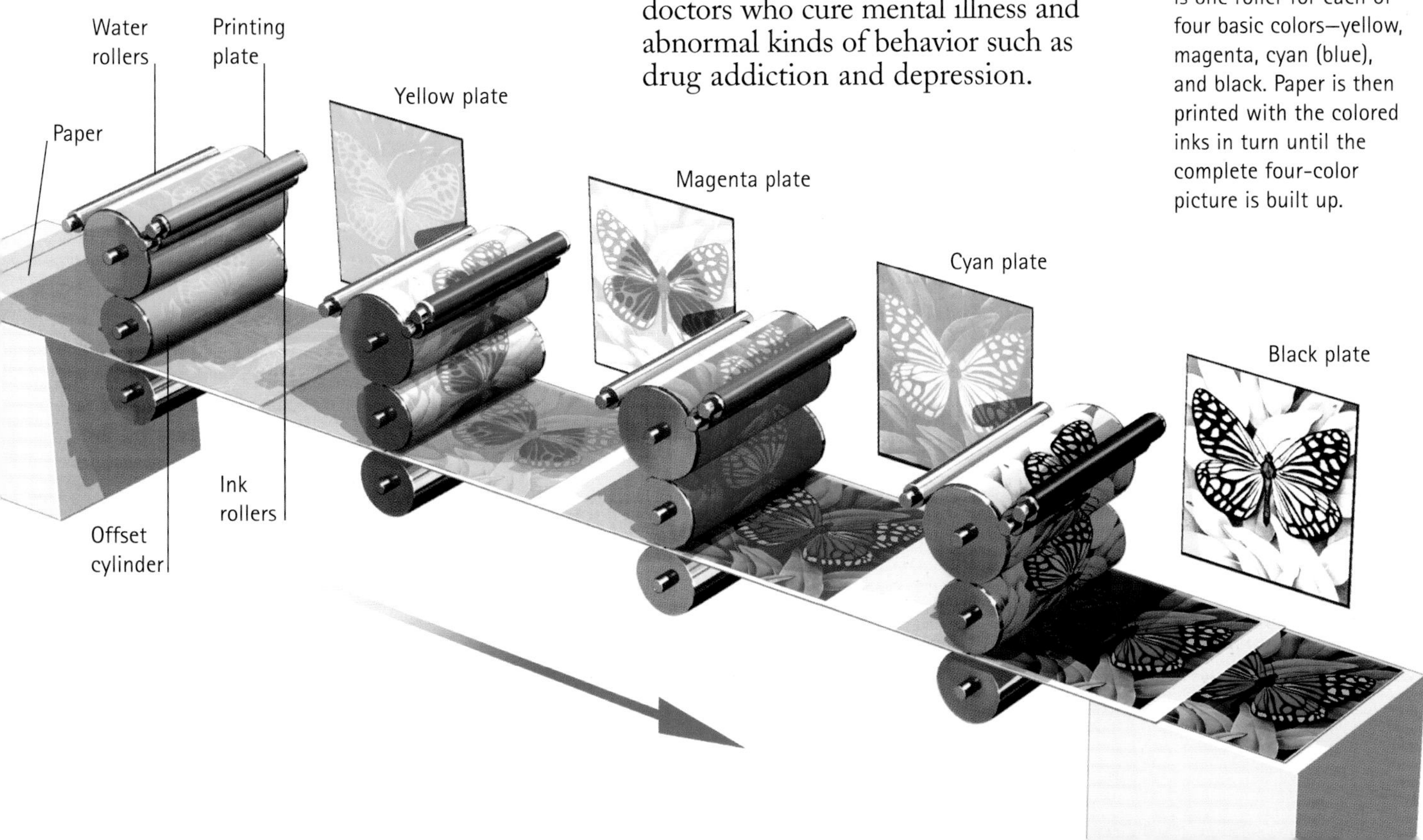

▽ In **printing** that uses offset lithography rubber rollers are offset (stamped) with a printing image, for example a butterfly. There is one roller for each of four basic colors—yellow, magenta, cyan (blue), and black. Paper is then printed with the colored inks in turn until the complete four-color picture is built up.

PUERTO RICO
Government: Self-governing commonwealth of the U.S.
Capital: San Juan
Area: 3,470 sq. mi.
Population: 3,890,000
Languages: English, Spanish
Currency: U.S. Dollar

Puerto Rico

Puerto Rico is a tropical **island** in the **Caribbean**. It is a **commonwealth** that governs itself, but it benefits from the military protection of the **United States**. Puerto Ricans are U.S. citizens, but they cannot vote in American **elections**. Puerto Rico is densely populated, and many people have emigrated to the United States. One of the main industries is tourism.

Pulley

A pulley is a simple **machine** consisting of a **wheel** on a motionless axle. A rope or belt passed over the wheel is tied to a load. When the rope is pulled, the load is raised into the air.

A movable pulley runs along a rope that has one end fixed to a support. The load hangs from the pulley itself. When the other end of the rope is pulled, the pulley moves the load along the rope. Pulleys are used in machines such as cranes.

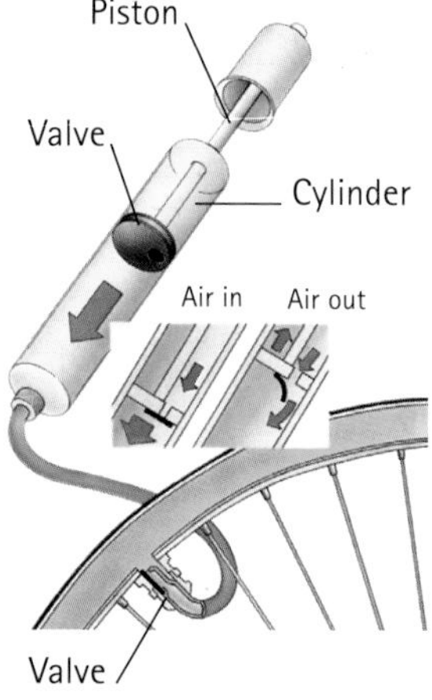

△ **Pumps** like this one, which is used to inflate a bicycle tire, are simple mechanisms. Air is pushed into the tire by a piston, which is pumped up and down in a cylinder. A valve inside the cylinder allows the air to flow only one way. There is a second valve on the tire so it will remain inflated when the pump is taken away.

Pulsar

Sometimes a huge star several times larger than **Earth**'s **Sun** becomes so hot that it explodes. For a few days it sends out as much **energy** as a whole **galaxy** of stars. It has become a supernova. After such an explosion all that is left is a very hot ball of **matter** a few miles across. This spins at a fast rate and sends out a beam of **light** and **radio** waves like a revolving searchlight. The beam seems to pulse on and off so it is called a pulsar. Most pulsars are too faint to be seen except with a very large **telescope**, but they send out powerful radio waves.

Pulse

The pulse is a rhythmic beat or throb in the body's **arteries**. These blood vessels carry blood away from the **heart**. A pulse beat occurs as the heart contracts (becomes smaller) and **pumps** blood into the arteries.

Doctors measure pulse rates to find out if the heart is beating normally. They usually feel the radial artery in the wrist. But the pulse can be felt wherever an artery passes over a **bone**. The normal pulse rate for men is 72 beats per minute. For women it is 76 to 80 beats. However, pulse rates between 50 and 85 are considered normal. Children have faster pulses.

Pump

Most pumps are used to move **liquids**, but some move **gases**. There are several kinds of pumps. For example, a **bicycle** pump is a simple reciprocating pump—it has a piston that moves up and down inside a cylinder. A similar pump is the lift pump, which can raise water about 30 ft. (9m) from the bottom of a well. It has an upright barrel with a close-fitting piston controlled by a handle. Force pumps are used to raise water from greater depths.

Pyramid

Pyramids are huge, four-sided buildings with square bases. The sides are triangles that meet in a point at the top.

The Egyptians built pyramids as

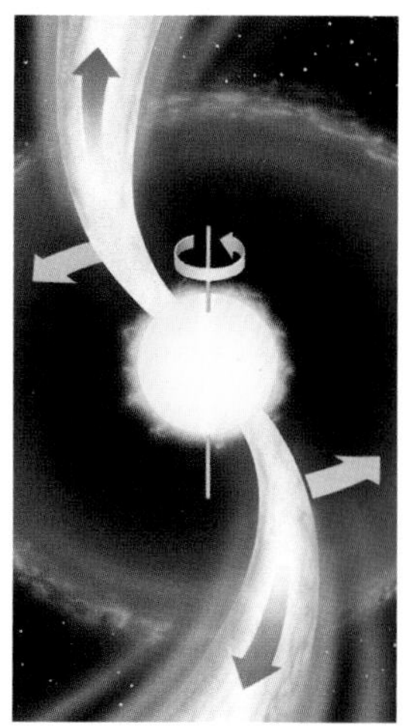

◁ As a **pulsar**, or neutron star, spins its signal sweeps through space like the beam of light from a lighthouse. The signal reaches earth once in every rotation and can be photographed or picked up by radio. Over millions of years pulsars slow down.

royal tombs. The first, which was built in about 2650 B.C. at Sakkara, is 203 ft. (62m) high. The three most famous pyramids are near Giza. The Great Pyramid, built in the 2600s B.C. by the **pharaoh** Khufu, is 449 ft. (137m) high. Khafre, who ruled soon after Khufu, built the second at 446 ft. (136m) high. The third, built by Khafre's successor, Menakaure, is 239 ft. (73m) high. About 80 pyramids still stand in Egypt.

Central and South American Indians also built pyramids as temples during A.D. 1–500. One huge example is at Cholula near Mexico City, which is about 177 ft. (54m) high.

△ The huge **pyramids** built thousands of years ago in Egypt are great feats of engineering, but it took countless numbers of slaves to move the great blocks of stone.

Pyrenees

The Pyrenees are a chain of **mountains** that lie between **France** and **Spain**. They stretch about 270 mi. (435km) from the Bay of Biscay to the **Mediterranean Sea**. They form a natural barrier between France and Spain so most of the trade between the two countries has been by sea. **Iron**, **lead**, **silver**, and cobalt are mined in the mountains, and the beautiful scenery attracts many tourists.

The peaks of the Pyrenees rise to over 9,840 ft. (3,000m), though most average about 3,608 ft. (1,100m). The highest peak is Pico de Aneto at 11,165 ft. (3,404m). On the southern slope of the eastern Pyrenees lies the tiny republic of **Andorra**.

Python

Pythons are large **snakes** that are egg-laying members of the boa family. They live in **Africa** and Southeast **Asia**, and a few species are found in **Australia**. Some grow as long as 30 ft. (9m). They are constrictors. This means that they squeeze their prey, such as **hares**, **rats**, and **antelopes**, to death before swallowing it whole.

▷ The African rock **python** lives on or near the forest or savanna floor in sub-Saharan Africa, where it preys on birds and relatively large mammals. It may also hunt by staying submerged near riverbanks. Its pattern and coloring are well-matched to its surroundings so it is difficult for prey to avoid it. It is the longest snake in the world—one has been measured at 33 ft. (10m).

△ The **Quaker** Society was founded in England in the 1600s. They were Puritans and disliked priestly control of the church. Quakers, including women, were encouraged to preach and speak out.

Quakers

The Quakers are a religious movement also known as the Society of Friends. They are a Protestant group that was begun by George Fox (1624–1691) in **England** during the 1650s.

They were called Quakers because some of them shook with emotion at their meetings. Early Quakers were often badly treated because of their belief that **religion** and **government** should not be mixed. Quakers have simple religious meetings and they appoint elders, not priests.

Quantum

We think of **light** and other forms of **energy**, such as **radio** waves and **X rays,** as traveling in waves. Light can also be thought of as a stream of tiny quanta (the plural of quantum) or photons. The energy of each photon depends on the wavelength and therefore the **color** of the light. A photon of white light has more energy than a photon of red light. Scientists combine the two ways of thinking about light. They think of light streaming out in packets of waves, with each packet representing a quantum or photon. They also think that tiny particles of **matter**, such as electrons, behave like waves as well as behaving like solid particles.

When you look at the light from a lightbulb, it seems to be steady. Actually light is not as steady as it seems. It is given off in a large number of tiny packages of energy, like the pulsing of a strobe light. Each package is a quantum.

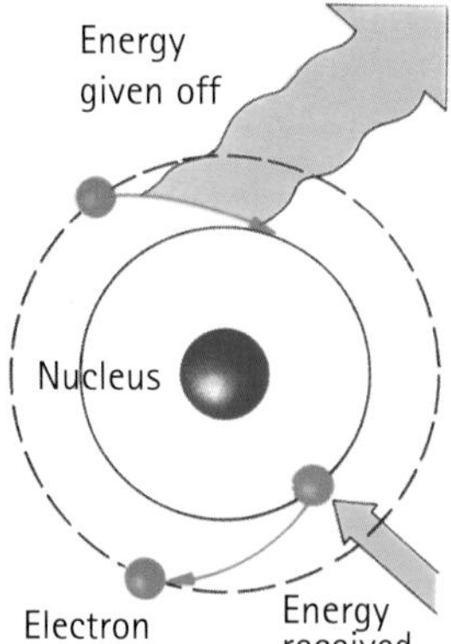

△In **quantum** theory the electrons orbiting the nucleus of an atom can absorb energy and move from a normal orbit to a high one. If they move back again, they give off energy. The amount of energy given off is measured in quanta.

Quarrying

Quarries are huge pits where **rocks** are cut or blasted out of the ground. Since prehistoric times people had quarries where they dug up **flint** to make into tools and weapons.

Today rock is quarried in enormous quantities. **Explosives** blast loose thousands of tons at a time. This is scooped up by bulldozers and diggers and carried to crushers. The rock is ground into stones for use in **roads**, **railroads**, **concrete**, and cement.

Not all rock is removed in this way. Stone that is used in building and paving is cut out of the ground rather than blasted. Electric cutters, wire saws, and drills are used to cut the rock.

Quartz

Quartz is one of the most common **minerals** in the world and is found everywhere. **Sand** is mostly made of quartz, and many **rocks** contain quartz.

Quartz forms six-sided crystals. It is a very hard substance, harder even than **steel**. In its pure form it is called rock crystal and has no color and is as clear as glass. Most quartz is smoky white or tinted with various **colors**. Many semiprecious **gems**, such as agate, amethyst, opal, and onyx, are examples of quartz.

Quartz is an important mineral. It is used in many things, including abrasives such as sandpaper, cement, **lenses**, **clocks**, and **electronics**.

Quasar

Quasars are very distant, powerful objects farther out in space than the most remote **galaxies**. Quasars were not discovered by astronomers until the 1960s. They may be galaxies with some extra-powerful **energy** source at their center. Quasars send out strong **radio** waves, **X rays**, **infrared rays**, and light. All quasars are millions of light-years away, and we see them now as they were that long ago. From **Earth** they look like very faint **stars**.

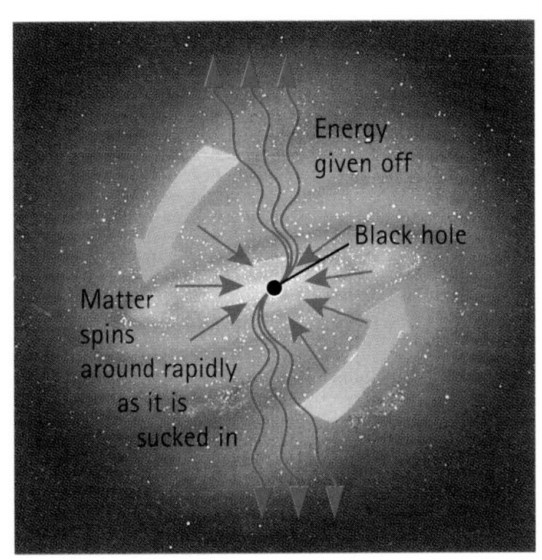

△ **Quasars** are among the most powerful objects in the universe. It is believed that a huge black hole lies at the center. As the gas and possibly complete stars are sucked into the black hole huge amounts of energy in the form of radio waves, infrared light, and X rays are sent into space.

Quebec

Quebec is the largest province in **Canada**. It stretches from the St. Lawrence River in the south to the Hudson Strait in the north. Much of northern Quebec is a forested wilderness so most people live in the south in cities such as Montreal and Quebec City. The province is the center for French culture in Canada.Jacques Cartier claimed the Quebec region for France in 1534, and Quebec joined the Canadian confederation in 1867. In 1980 the people of Quebec voted against a plan to make their province politically independent. Quebec's industries include the manufacture of **cars**, machinery, **aircraft**, and chemical and petroleum products. The lumber business and tourism are other important industries.

△ Pure **quartz** crystals are colorless, but when they are mixed with other substances, they take on many different shades.

◁ **Quarrying** is usually carried out by using dynamite or other explosives to break up the rock. Diggers load it into trucks for carrying to the crushing plant. There the rock is broken down even further for use on railroad lines, roadbeds, and as cement for concrete buildings. The world's largest quarry is Bingham Canyon copper mine in Utah. It is about 2,526 ft. (770m) deep.

All breeds of **rabbits** are related to the **Mediterranean** wild rabbit (left), although today rabbits are all different **colors**, shapes, and sizes. The tiny dwarf lop-eared rabbit has ears that droop. The Himalayan rabbit is not really from the Himalayas. Its name refers to a certain type of coat marking with a darker face, ears, legs, and tail.

Rabbit

Rabbits were originally found only in southern **Europe**. Humans have now introduced them throughout the world. They are small **mammals** with short tails and long, pointed ears. Rabbits live in burrows in the ground. Each burrow is the home of a single rabbit family. A group of burrows is known as a warren.

Raccoon

Raccoons live in **North America.** They have long fur, a short, pointed nose, a black mask across the **eyes,** and a bushy tail with black rings.

▽ **Raccoons** are often thought of as pests in the **United States** and are sometimes hunted. Davy Crockett's famous hat was made of raccoon fur with the striped tail left hanging down at the back.

Raccoons may grow to as long as 35 in. (90cm) from nose to tail.

Raccoons live in **forests.** They make their homes in holes in **trees** and are good climbers. At night they leave their hollows to hunt for **food.** They will eat almost anything—**fruits** and **plants**, **eggs**, **insects**, **fish**, **birds**, and small **mammals**—but their main food comes from **rivers** so their tree holes are usually found close by. Raccoons also scavenge for food in towns and can sometimes be heard scampering across rooftops at night.

Race

All the people on earth belong to the **human** race. But "race"also means any group of people who look alike in particular ways. It is not known when and how the different races came into being, but there are three main races—Mongoloid, Caucasian, and Negroid.

The Mongoloid race is known for its straight, dark **hair**, yellow-brown **skin,** and almond-shaped **eyes**. Caucasians have hair **colors** that range from blond and red to black, are fair-skinned or dark-skinned, and have round eyes. The Negroid race has dark, tightly

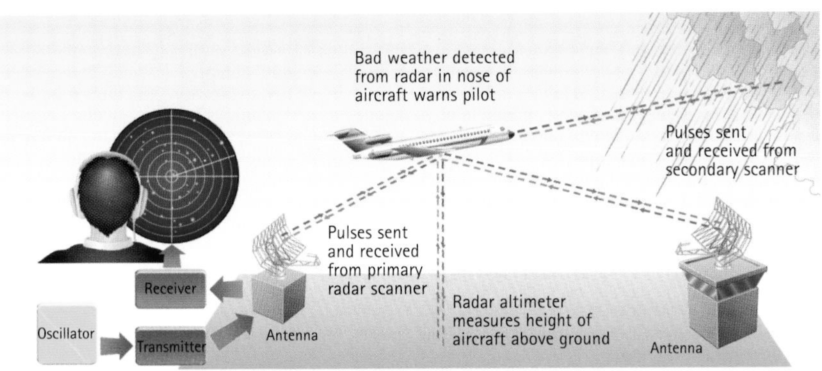

◁ **Radar** is used by air traffic controllers at airports. They need to know the height and position of aircraft to prevent collisions. They have small screens to relay this information. Large aircraft have onboard radar to detect other planes and bad weather.

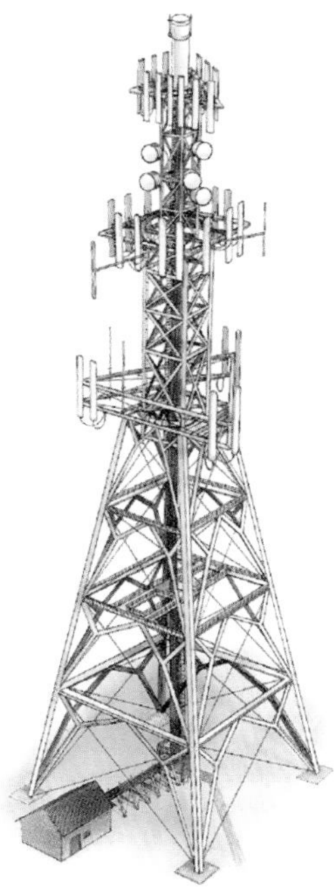

△ A **radio** broadcast is turned into a vibrating electric current, which is sent through the air to a transmitter (above). The transmitter mixes the vibrating current with another faster current, turning them into a radio wave that is then beamed out through the air.

curling hair and a dark skin color.

In addition to the three main races there are also a number of smaller groups. Because thousands of years of migration, conquest, and marriage have mixed all the races, pure racial types probably do not exist anymore.

Racism

Racism is a form of discrimination against people because of their **race**. It is practiced by people who believe that their race is superior to that of another group. For centuries in many parts of the **United States** white people discriminated against black people. In **World War II** Adolf **Hitler** practiced racism against minority groups in **Germany**. South African **apartheid** was also a form of racism.

Radar

The name radar comes from the phrase "*ra*dio *d*etecting *a*nd *r*anging." Radar is a system for tracking objects through the use of **radio** beams. It is a very useful **invention** because it works in the dark and in fog and can detect objects thousands of miles away.

Radar works by sending out a narrow, high-powered beam about 500 times per second. It travels at a steady 984 ft. (300m) every millionth of a second. When the beam strikes an object, a faint **echo** bounces back. The echo is picked up and turned into a "blip" of **light** on a screen. A radar operator can tell by studying the blip how far away the object is, in what direction it is moving, and at what speed. Radar is used by the military to track **missiles** and planes and by **weather** stations to find and follow the path of storms. **Satellites** fitted with radar can map **Earth** from space.

Radio

The common household object we call a radio is only the receiving end of a large system of radio **communications**. A radio program begins in a studio. There voices and music are turned into **electronic** signals. These are amplified (made stronger) and then sent out from tall masts as radio waves. The waves are picked up by a radio in the home and changed back into **sounds**. Radio waves travel at the speed of **light**—so fast that a signal can circle the world 7.5 times in one second.

The first person to generate radio waves was Heinrich Hertz (1857–1894) in 1887. Guglielmo **Marconi** sent the first messages in 1894.

Radioactivity

The atoms of some substances shoot off tiny particles and rays that we cannot see or feel. This radioactivity was discovered in 1896 by Marie and Pierre **Curie**, who found that in time these radioactive substances changed into other substances and that they did this at a steady rate.

▽ The three forms of **radioactivity** are alpha, beta, and gamma radiation. Their different abilities to penetrate substances are illustrated here.

continued on page 272

RAILROADS

Railroads are networks of smooth metal tracks on which trains run. This system of transportation expanded rapidly during the 1800s. It enabled goods and people to travel long distances at relatively high speeds. Today railroads are used to carry people and goods in nearly every country in the world.

△ *The Native Americans called the train the "iron horse," and it crossed the continent of North America for the first time in the 1860s. A typical engine was powerful enough to haul 40 tons of train. Behind the engine the tender carried wood for the fire, and a large metal "cowcatcher" was fitted at the front of the train. This nudged stray cattle off the tracks and cleared snowdrifts or loose rocks.*

△ *In 1829 George Stephenson and his son designed and built the* Rocket *for use on the Liverpool and Manchester Railroad. It reached a speed of 25 mph (40 km/h).*

△ *Railroads operated by electricity run underground in many cities. There is usually an interchange system so that people can continue their journey by road, subway, bus, or taxi.*

THE FIRST RAILROADS

The first passenger railroad, the Stockton and Darlington in northeast England, was designed in 1825 by British engineer George Stephenson (1781–1848). The Liverpool to Manchester railroad opened soon after in 1829. By 1900 most of the developed countries of the world had extensive railroad networks, and millions of people were traveling by train.

POWERING UP

The first trains were powered by steam engines. In 1804 mine owner Richard Trevithick (1771–1833) developed a steam engine to carry heavy loads. George Stephenson urged the owners of the first railroads to use steam engines, and they were a great success. Today's trains can travel at high speeds, and most are powered by electricity from wires overhead or by diesel engines. Maglev trains are powered by magnets that lift the train above the tracks. These "floating" trains are able to travel very fast and create little noise.

SIGNALS AND TRACKS

Trains run on steel tracks, switching from one track to another at a point—moving rails where tracks divide or join to make a train change direction. Railroad lines are divided into sections with a signal at the beginning of each section. The signals and points are controlled from signal boxes with the aid of computers, and the computers ensure that only one train is traveling on a section of track at a time. Signals work like traffic lights.

SUBWAYS

Many cities around the world have railroads that run in tunnels under the streets. These railroads are called subways in the U.S. and are extremely useful for avoiding congestion on the roads above. The first subway was the Metropolitan line, which opened in London, England, in 1863. Soon after other cities began to build underground railroads—Boston in 1895, Budapest in 1896, Paris in 1898, and New York in 1904.

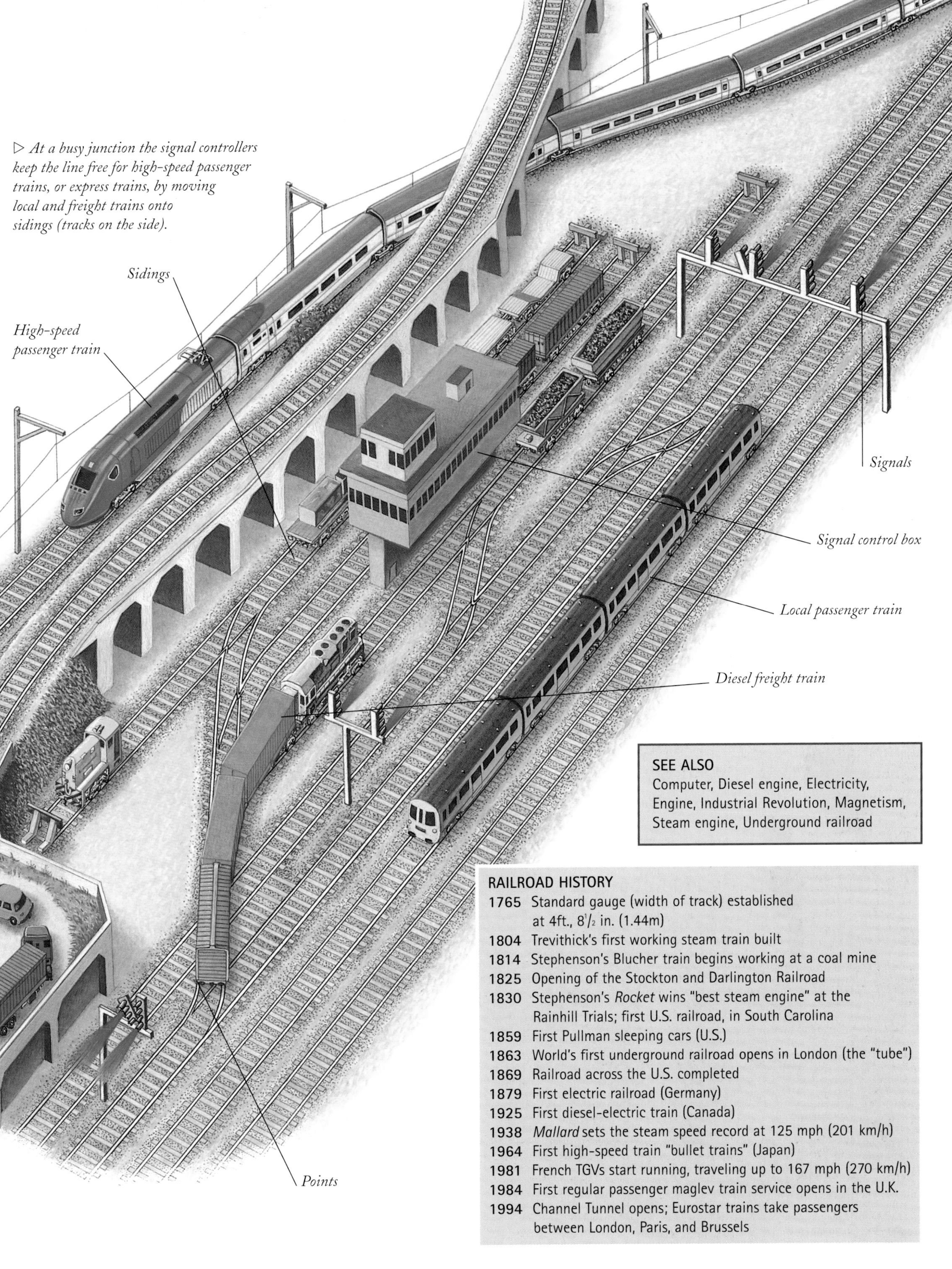

▷ *At a busy junction the signal controllers keep the line free for high-speed passenger trains, or express trains, by moving local and freight trains onto sidings (tracks on the side).*

SEE ALSO
Computer, Diesel engine, Electricity, Engine, Industrial Revolution, Magnetism, Steam engine, Underground railroad

RAILROAD HISTORY

1765 Standard gauge (width of track) established at 4ft., $8\frac{1}{2}$ in. (1.44m)
1804 Trevithick's first working steam train built
1814 Stephenson's Blucher train begins working at a coal mine
1825 Opening of the Stockton and Darlington Railroad
1830 Stephenson's *Rocket* wins "best steam engine" at the Rainhill Trials; first U.S. railroad, in South Carolina
1859 First Pullman sleeping cars (U.S.)
1863 World's first underground railroad opens in London (the "tube")
1869 Railroad across the U.S. completed
1879 First electric railroad (Germany)
1925 First diesel-electric train (Canada)
1938 *Mallard* sets the steam speed record at 125 mph (201 km/h)
1964 First high-speed train "bullet trains" (Japan)
1981 French TGVs start running, traveling up to 167 mph (270 km/h)
1984 First regular passenger maglev train service opens in the U.K.
1994 Channel Tunnel opens; Eurostar trains take passengers between London, Paris, and Brussels

continued from page 269

For example, if a piece of radioactive **uranium** was left for millions of years, it would decay and turn into a piece of **lead**. Scientists measure the rate of decay in radioactive **carbon** in **animal** and **plant** remains to find out how long ago the animals and plants lived.

Radioactive materials can be highly dangerous. A nuclear explosion causes life-threatening levels of radioactivity.

Radium

Radium is an **element**. It is found only in **uranium** ore and was first discovered by Marie **Curie** in 1898. She was examining uranium and realized that it had much more **radioactivity** than was expected. Radium is very radioactive and dangerous to handle.

In its pure form radium is a whitish **metal**. Around five tons of uranium ore have to be mined (see **mining**) to produce just 0.035 oz (1g) of radium. Each year less than 2.6 oz (75g) of uranium are produced in the entire world, mostly from **Zaire** and **Canada**.

Radium is used in **medicine** to treat **cancer**. **Compounds** of it are used to make luminous dials glow in the dark.

Railroad *see* pages 270–271

Rain forest *see* pages 274–275

Rainbow

The wonderful **colors** of a rainbow are formed by sunlight shining on drops of rain. The best time to see a rainbow is immediately after a rain shower when the clouds break up, and the sunlight streams through.

Rainbows can be seen only when the **sun** is behind you and low over the horizon. When the sun's rays strike the raindrops, each drop acts as a prism and splits the **light** into a **spectrum** of **colors** ranging from red to violet. The lower the sun, the higher the rainbow and the fuller its curved arch.

△ Toward the end of **Ramadan**, the ninth and most holy month in the Muslim year, people search the night skies with small telescopes or binoculars. They are trying to see the crescent of the new **moon** because this will signal the end of the **festival**.

△ It is said that there is a pot of gold at the end of a **rainbow**. Nobody has ever found the treasure because a rainbow really has no end—it is a full circle. The bottom half of the circle lies below the horizon and out of sight.

Ramadan

In **Islam**, Ramadan is the ninth month of the Muslim year, during which Muslims fast (go without **food**) between sunrise and sunset. The fast is one of the five pillars, or basic duties, of Islam and ends with **Eid**-ul-Fitr, the Festival of the Breaking of the Fast.

Rat

Rats are **rodents**. They are found all over the world in enormous numbers and can live equally successfully in cities and in the country. Both the black and more common brown rat will eat almost anything. They are harmful to people because they cause **food** to go bad, and they spread **diseases**. Some rats carry a type of **flea** that can cause bubonic **plague** in **human beings**.

Like all rodents rats have a set of four sharp front **teeth** called incisors. These work like chisels and are used to gnaw food, chop up nesting material, and move through anything that obstructs their way. Female brown rats can breed when they are only two months old and will produce as many as 12 babies a time and up to five litters per year.

△ In the country most **rats** live outside and do not represent much of a health risk. But rats in cities steal food intended for humans and are a major health hazard.

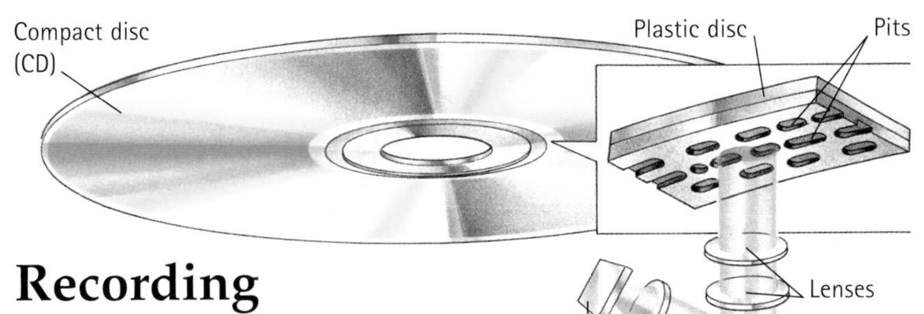

Recording

Sound can be recorded in a number of ways—on magnetic tape, tape cassettes, CDs, and DVDs.

A CD is a disc on which sound information is recorded using a **laser** beam. The digital signals are represented by a series of depressions on the surface of the disc, which can be played back using another laser. This technology is also used to create DVDs.

A tape recorder works by changing sound waves into **magnetism**. The sound is recorded as a magnetic pattern along the recording tape. When the tape is played, the magnetic pattern is turned back into sound.

You use a videotape to record a **television** program on a VCR. The videotape contains tape just like a sound cassette. It records the electric signal coming from the television aerial. Sound recording was pioneered by Thomas **Edison**.

△ To make a CD a **recording** is fed onto a disc. Each track on the CD contains a sequence of pits that store **sounds** in digital form. As the disc spins in a **laser** beam inside the CD player the pits reflect pulses of **light** onto a light-sensitive detector. This detector converts the code signals into electrical pulses. These are then changed back into reproductions of the original sounds.

Red Sea

The Red Sea is a narrow strip of **water** that is part of the **Indian Ocean**. It stretches for 1,178 mi. (1,900km), dividing Arabia from northeast **Africa**. It has an area of about 171,717 sq. mi. (440,300 sq km). At its northern end it is linked to the **Mediterranean Sea** by the **Suez Canal**. Its southern end is guarded by the narrow straits of Bab el Mandeb. The Red Sea is a very shallow body of water. Because there are no major currents that flow through it, it is also very warm and salty.

Reformation

The Reformation is the name given to the period of great religious upheaval that began in **Europe** in the 1500s.

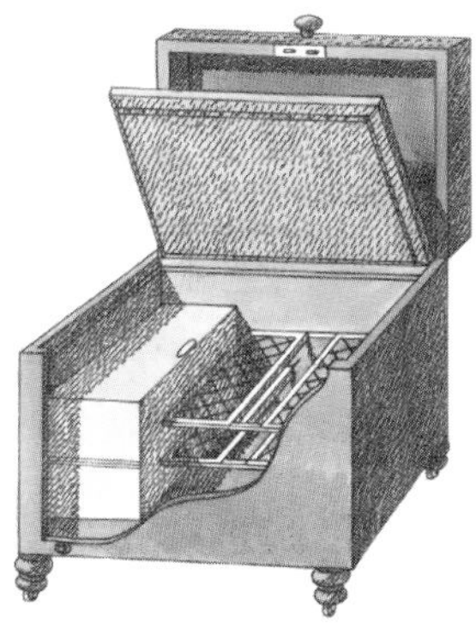

△ Most people think that the **refrigerator** is a recent invention. However, the one above was invented by Ferdinand Carré in France in 1858.

In the **U.S.** ice-making machines were slipped through the Union blockade of the South during the **Civil War** in the 1860s.

At that time a revolt occurred in the Roman Catholic Church. In protest at what they saw as bad practice and errors in the Church some groups of the protesting people broke away to set up their own churches. They became known as Protestants.

What many Protestants wanted was a simpler, more basic form of **Christianity**, allowing them more freedom to worship as they chose. As the number of Protestants grew many rulers saw the new movement as a chance to broaden their power at the expense of the Church. They were happy to support the Protestant cause because the religious protests helped them gain more influence. The Reformation led to wars between Protestant and Roman Catholic rulers.

Refrigerator

Refrigerators are used to keep **food** cold. The simplest ones are boxes with an electric **motor** running a cooling system. Refrigerators are made from insulating material that keeps the inside of the box cold for some time, even when the motor is not running. The average **temperature** inside a fridge is between 36–45°F (2–7°C).

The cooling system has a special **gas** in it. This gas is first compressed (squeezed) to turn it into a **liquid**. The liquid flows through hollow tubes inside the fridge into an evaporator, which turns it back into gas. The gas is then pumped throughout the system. As it moves around it draws out any **heat** from within the refrigerator.

When it is pumped outside the fridge, the gas is compressed again. This turns it back into a liquid, and it gives off the heat it picked up on the inside. The liquid is pumped around and around, turning from liquid to gas and back again. The **air** inside the fridge becomes colder, and the heat is carried to the outside. The process works like a type of heat sponge.

RAIN FORESTS

Tropical rain forests are found in an area called the tropics around the equator where the weather is hot and rainy. These forests are home to over half of the world's 10 million species of animals and plants, and they are some of the oldest places on earth. There are tropical rain forests in South and Central America, Africa, and parts of Southeast Asia and Australia. Each rain forest is different. Some animals and plants can only be found in rain forests in one area. Lemurs, for example, which are related to monkeys, are only found in the rain forests on the island of Madagascar.

▷ *All types of animals live in the canopy of a rain forest—birds, monkeys, snakes, butterflies, and tree frogs find plenty to eat and places to shelter. Giant woody plants, called lianas, loop from one tree to another, and hummingbirds feed on the nectar and pollen in orchid flowers.*

Emerald tree boa

Bromeliad

Tamandua

LAYERS OF A RAIN FOREST

Rain forests are made up of millions of trees. It rains nearly every day, and many plants and trees grow quickly, becoming very tall. The tallest trees in a forest are known as the emergents. Below them the canopy is made up of the tops of the smaller trees. The canopy is home to insects, birds, reptiles, amphibians, and more than half of the mammals of the rain forest.

The area between the canopy and the forest floor is called the understory. This is a darker, cooler environment below the branches and leaves of the trees. Because of all the foliage, it can take up to 10 minutes for rain to reach the forest floor. All types of animals live here, including anteaters, lemurs, and tree kangaroos. The forest floor is full of small forms of life, especially insects, as well as large animals such as forest elephants. Many of the animals are nocturnal—they only come out to hunt for food at night.

RAIN FOREST FOOD AND MEDICINE

The rain forest is a treasure chest of millions of plants. At least 80 percent of the developed world's diet originated in a rain forest environment. These foods include coffee, cacao beans for chocolate, bananas, pineapples, vanilla, peanuts, potatoes, pepper, and sugar. There are at least 3,000 types of fruits in the Amazon rain forest. In the West we grow and eat only 200 of them, while the local people use 2,000.

Many of the plants have medicinal properties that have not yet been fully researched. An extraordinary one fourth of the world's medicines are derived from rain forest ingredients, and yet only one percent of the tree and plant species have been tested by scientists. Many rain forest plants are disappearing. For example, the rosy periwinkle, originally from the island of Madagascar off the coast of Africa, is used to make a medicine to treat a type of cancer called leukemia. Unfortunately it is now extinct in the wild.

▷ *The high branches of the trees are covered with plants and flowers called epiphytes. Some have spongy roots that hang from the branches and absorb moisture from the air. Bromeliads collect water in overlapped leaves at their bases. More than 28,000 different types of epiphytes grow on rain forest trees.*

IN DANGER

Rain forests are very important. Without them weather patterns change—there is less rain, fewer plants, and when it does rain, there can be more flooding because there are fewer trees to soak up the water. Rain forests also remove carbon dioxide from the atmosphere and help prevent global warming—the greenhouse effect.

But rain forests are under threat. In 1950 they covered 14 percent of the world's land surface, but now they cover just 6 percent. They are being cut down for wood and to clear land for farming and grazing animals, especially in poor countries. Scientists estimate that we lose over 137 species of rain forest plants, animals, and insects every day. This amounts to 50,000 species per year. Rain forests are disappearing at such a fast rate that they may vanish completely by 2040.

There are many groups of people living in tropical rain forests around the world. Some of them, such as the Yanomamo tribe of the Amazon forests of Brazil and southern Venezuela, have lived in villages there for hundreds, sometimes even thousands, of years. The populations are declining either because of diseases caught from people outside the rain forest or because of government land seizure. If indigenous people die out, a whole way of life and a huge amount of plant and animal knowledge will die with them.

SEE ALSO
Amazon River, Amphibians and Reptiles, Birds, Global warming, Insects, Madagascar, Mammals, Medicine, Plants, Trees, Weather

△ One result of hostility between the Arabs and the Jews in 1948 was the migration of nearly one million Arabs from Palestine. They left their homes and became **refugees** because they were afraid of the action **Israel** might take after the war with the Arab League.

△ **Rembrandt** excelled as a portrait painter, and many of his portraits were of himself. This one was painted late in his life in 1661–1662.

Refugee

A refugee is a person who seeks shelter or protection from danger or trouble in another country. They may be trying to escape religious or political persecution, **famine**, or **flood**. There are many refugee organizations today that provide international assistance to people who have had to leave their own countries. The main one is the **United Nations** High Commissioner for Refugees (UNHCR), which gives protection and assistance to more than 22 million refugees and displaced people around the world, the majority of whom are women and children.

Relativity

If you are traveling in a **car** at 60 mph and are passed by another car traveling at 80 mph, the second car pulls away from you at 20 mph. Its true speed relative to the ground is 80 mph, but its speed relative to you is 20 mph. This is the basic idea of relativity. Assuming you are not moving, relativity describes the speed of something that is moving in relation to you.

At the end of the last century scientists discovered that the speed of **light** is always the same no matter how fast the source of the light is moving. In 1905 Albert **Einstein** put forward his special theory of relativity to explain this strange fact. One aspect of his theory concerns the effect of motion on **time**, length, and mass. For example, the theory predicts that in a spaceship hurtling across the **universe** at the speed of light time would pass more slowly, the spaceship's length would become smaller, and its mass would become greater than on a similar stationary spaceship on **Earth**. Later in 1915 Einstein produced his general theory of relativity. This theory has helped scientists understand more about space, **gravity**, and the nature of the universe.

Religion

The five great religions today are **Buddhism** (based on the teachings of **Buddha**), **Christianity** (based on the teachings of **Jesus**), **Hinduism** (followed by Hindus), **Islam** (followed by Muslims), and **Judaism** (followed by Jews). All are very ancient. The most recent is Islam, which was founded about 1,300 years ago by **Muhammad**. The largest religion, Christianity, has about two billion followers.

There are also some people who follow ancient religions based on the worship of many **gods** and spirits. Frequently these gods are seen as part of the natural world as rocks, trees, and lakes.

Buildings that are devoted to religious worship include magnificent shrines, temples, and **churches**. Statues and works of art are used to convey religious messages or to tell stories. Trained priests and holy people say prayers and lead religious ceremonies. They also study the **laws** and teachings of the religion. These are often written down in holy **books**, for example, the **Bible** and the **Koran**.

Rembrandt

Rembrandt van Rijn (1606–1669) is one of the most famous of all Dutch painters. Helped by assistants in his large studio, he produced an amazing 650 oil **paintings**, 2,000 drawings and studies, and 300 etchings.

Rembrandt is best known for his portraits of the wealthy townspeople of the **Netherlands**, particularly in Amsterdam, where he lived most of his life. Unlike many other painters, he became very successful while he was still alive. However, later in his career many of the wealthy people no longer bought his pictures because they did not like the way his style of painting had changed. At the end of his life he lived in poverty, but it was at this time that he painted some of his best works.

Renaissance

The Renaissance is the name given to a period of about 200 years in the **history** of **Europe**. The word means "rebirth" in French, and the Renaissance was the time when people again became interested in every aspect of **art**, **science**, **architecture**, and literature.

Since the times of the ancient Greeks and Romans there had been little interest in new ideas. Then during the 1300s Italian scholars began to take a fresh interest in the past. They also looked for new scientific explanations of the mysteries of the world and the **universe**. During the Renaissance a large number of painters, sculptors, and architects began working in **Italy**. The works of art of Leonardo **da Vinci** and **Michelangelo** are among the most famous achievements of this time. From Italy the ideas of the Renaissance quickly spread to the rest of Europe.

There was a great growth in **trade** at the same time as all of these artistic and scientific ideas. Later there were voyages to explore **Africa** and **India**, and in 1492 **North America** was discovered by Christopher **Columbus**.

△ During the **Renaissance**, Florence was the cultural and intellectual center of **Italy**. Revived interest in classic **art** and **architecture** began there, and the first academy of art was founded in Florence in 1563.

Reproduction

Reproduction is the process by which **plants** and **animals** make new plants and animals like themselves. Some plants and animals can reproduce on their own by simply splitting in half. Many plants reproduce asexually by producing buds that drop off and plant themselves. Others produce spores that may be carried away by **wind**, **water**, or on an animal's fur.

In sexual reproduction a male **cell** (a sperm) joins with, or fertilizes, a female cell (an ovum, or **egg**) to form a new fertilized cell. This cell divides over and over again until a whole new organism has been created.

Most female **fish** lay their eggs in the water. The male swims over the eggs and releases his sperm on them. The developing fish, or embryo, grows while using the supply of food inside the egg.

In many animals fertilization takes place inside the female's body. After fertilization a female **bird** or **reptile** lays her eggs. The embryo develops inside the egg until it is ready to hatch. In **mammals** fertilization also occurs inside the female, but the embryo develops inside its mother, receiving **food** from her bloodstream until it is ready to be born. After birth the mother feeds it with her **milk**.

The number of offspring a mother gives birth to at one time depends on the number of eggs fertilized. In humans usually only one egg is fertilized. If more than one egg is fertilized, there may be twins or triplets.

▽ For **reproduction** the parts of the body are very different in men and women. The woman produces eggs in her ovaries. These eggs travel down the oviducts and if fertilized by sperm provided by a man during sexual intercourse may develop into a baby in the woman's uterus, or womb (below). Men produce millions of sperm in their testicles. The sperm and the egg each contain half of what is needed to make another human being.

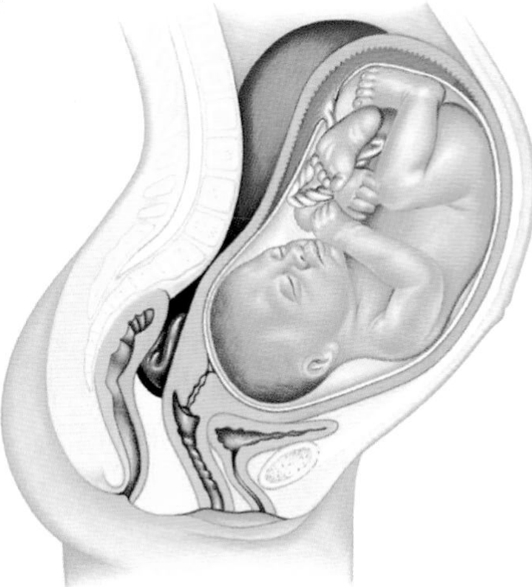

Reptiles *see* Amphibians and Reptiles

Republic

A republic is a form of **government** in which the people are supposed to rule themselves. Usually they hold **elections** to choose their leaders. Many republics have been formed to take over powers from rulers who are considered to be reigning unfairly. The first republics were in ancient **Greece** and Rome (see **Roman Empire**), but many of the people in these countries were slaves. Today some republics are run by people who have not been elected by the people. There are both communist (see **communism**) and democratic (see **democracy**) republics.

Revolution

A revolution is the usually violent overthrowing of a **government** or political system by those who are governed such as the **Revolutionary War**. Sometimes revolutions are peaceful but effective rejections of a system. For example, there can be a revolution in ideas—a complete change in a way of thinking about a particular subject.

Revolutionary War

The Revolutionary War was fought between Great Britain and its 13 U.S. colonies from 1775 to 1783. The colonies won their independence from Great Britain and became a new nation, the **United States of America**.

For many years before the war Great Britain and the U.S. colonies had disagreed about a number of things, in particular **taxes**. The British tried to force the colonies to pay but would not allow them any representation in the British **parliament**. The colonies responded by insisting on "no taxation without representation."

△ British grenadier c. 1775

△ American revolutionary soldier c. 1775

The first shot in the war was fired in Lexington, Massachusetts, on April 19, 1775. In July 1775 George **Washington** was made commander of the U.S. forces. On July 4, 1776 the colonies declared their independence.

At first the war went badly for the Americans, but in October 1777 the British were defeated at the Battle of Saratoga in New York. This was the turning point. On October 19, 1781 a British army under Charles Cornwallis (1738–1805) surrendered to Washington. The final peace treaty, the Treaty of Paris, was signed in 1783.

Rhinoceros

Sometimes described as a "tank on legs," the rhinoceros is one of the largest and strongest of all land **animals**. A fully grown male can weigh as much as 3.5 tons. This massive beast has tough, leathery skin and sprouts one or two **horns** (actually made of hair) on its snout. These may grow as long as 50 in. (127cm).

The rhinoceros lives in **Africa** and **Southeast Asia** where it feeds on leafy twigs, shrubs, and **grasses**. Although an adult rhino has no natural enemies it is so widely hunted for its horns that it has become an endangered species. When ground into a powder, rhino horn is believed, wrongly, to be a powerful **medicine**. The rhino's ability to charge swiftly over short distances makes it a dangerous animal to hunt.

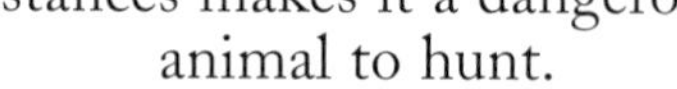

▽ **Rhinoceroses** have poor eyesight. This would make them an easy target for hunters, except that they have heightened senses of hearing and smell.

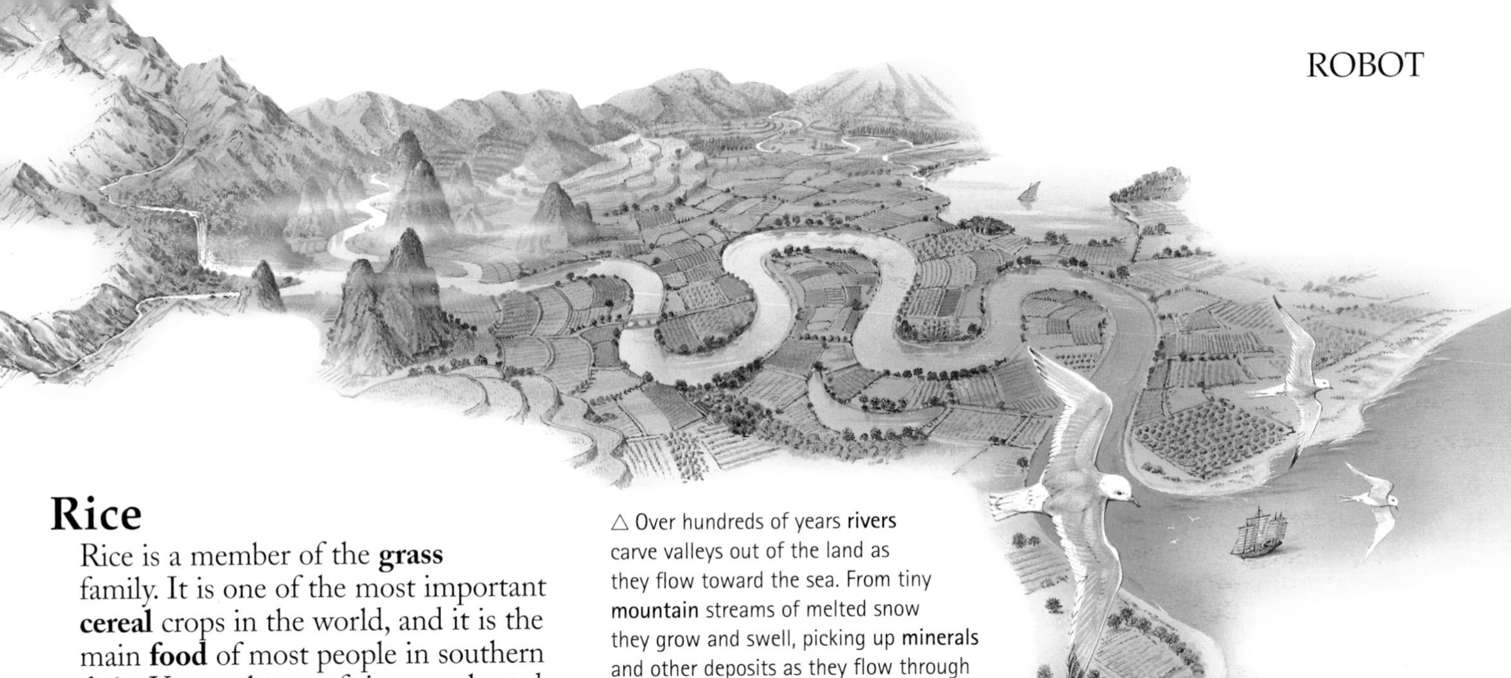

△ Over hundreds of years **rivers** carve valleys out of the land as they flow toward the sea. From tiny **mountain** streams of melted snow they grow and swell, picking up **minerals** and other deposits as they flow through the landscape. These deposits sink to the bottom when the **rivers** slow down as they near the sea, forming great deltas.

Rice

Rice is a member of the **grass** family. It is one of the most important **cereal** crops in the world, and it is the main **food** of most people in southern **Asia**. Young shoots of rice are planted in flooded areas called rice paddies where they grow in 2–4 in. (5–10cm) of **water** until they are ready to be harvested. Young rice has long, narrow leaves and clusters of **flowers** that turn into the grains we eat.

River

Rivers are one of the most important geographical features in the world. They range in size from small streams to waterways that flow for thousands of miles. The largest rivers in the world are the **Amazon**, the **Mississippi**, and the **Nile**. They all drain huge areas of land. The basin of the Amazon River stretches over an area larger than all of Western **Europe**. Some rivers serve as transportation links that allow ocean-going **ships** to sail far inland. In tropical **rain forests** they are often the only way to travel. Rivers with **dams** supply power to produce **electricity**. **Water** from rivers is also used to irrigate farmland in **desert** lands and other dry parts of the world (see **irrigation**).

Road

The Romans were the first great road builders, and some of their long, straight roads survive today. They made their roads with gravel and stones. The surface paving stones were arched so the rain would run off into ditches.

Modern road building began during the **Industrial Revolution**. In the early 1800s Scottish engineer John McAdam (1756–1836) became the pioneer of modern road making, but the stony surfaces of his roads were not good for vehicles with rubber tires. Later "macadamized" roads were built. They are covered with tar or asphalt to make them smooth. Many roads, especially highways, are now made of concrete.

▽ Modern **roads** are made of a smooth layer of concrete or of asphalt and small stones over a base course of 1.6 in. (4cm) stones and a subbase of stones to even the ground.

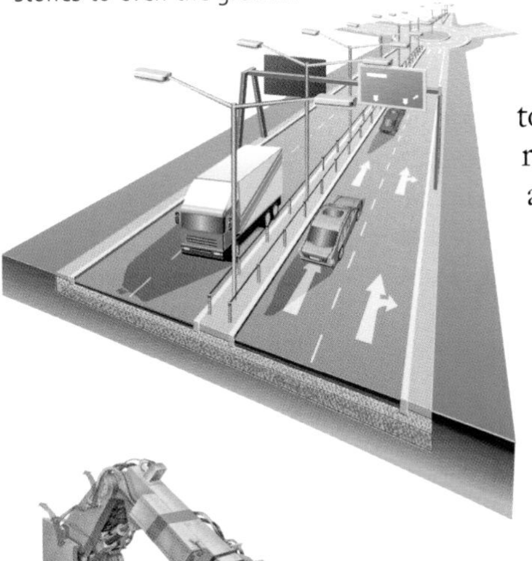

Robot

In movies and books set in the future robots often look like **metal** people, and they can walk, talk, and even think. Real robots are very different. They are **machines** with limbs that can move in several directions and are made in various shapes—some like people and others like **insects**. They are programmable. This means that they can be taught to perform different tasks. The instructions, or programs, are stored in the robot's **computer** brain. Most robots work in factories and do jobs such as paint spraying, welding, and heavy lifting. Some robots work in places that are dangerous for humans such as nuclear **power plants** and in space.

△ This Japanese industrial **robot** can do a variety of jobs depending on how it is controlled. The automated arm can weld metal, use spray paint, or move objects from place to place.

Rock

Rocks consist of grains of **minerals**. Igneous rocks form when magma (molten rock) hardens. Some harden on the surface to form rocks like basalt and obsidian, while others harden underground to form rocks like **granite**. Sedimentary rocks are composed of sediments like **sand**. For example, conglomerates are rocks made up of pebbles and sand, and many limestones are made of sediments formed mainly from the remains of dead **plants** and **animals**. Metamorphic rocks are igneous or sedimentary rocks that have been changed by great **heat** and pressure—limestones may be metamorphosed (changed) into **marble**.

Rocket

A **firework** rocket and the rockets that took astronauts to the **Moon** (see **space exploration**) work in much the same way. Both burn **fuel** to produce hot **gases**. The gases shoot out backward, and this creates a force that thrusts the rocket forward. Rockets do not need **air** for their **engines**, unlike **jets**, so they are ideal for moving in space where there is no air.

The Chinese used rockets as weapons as early as the 1200s. Rockets used to launch **satellites** and spacecraft were developed after **World War II**.

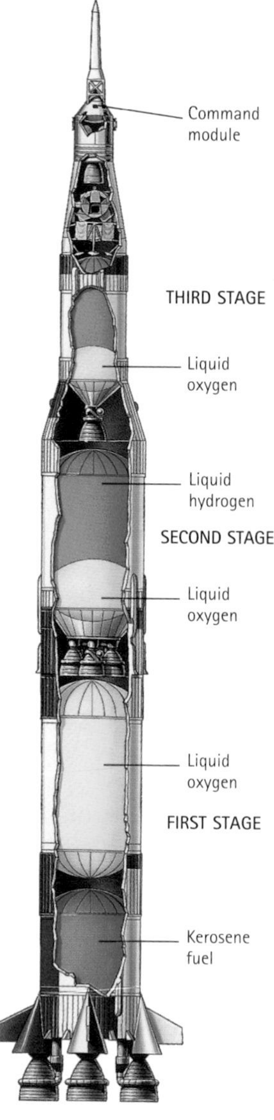

△ The **rocket** *Saturn V* took the U.S. *Apollo 11* crew to the Moon in 1969. It had three separate sections, or stages. After the powerful first stage ran out of fuel it fell away, and the second-stage engines ignited. When the fuel in this stage was used up, the third-stage engines helped it complete its journey to the Moon.

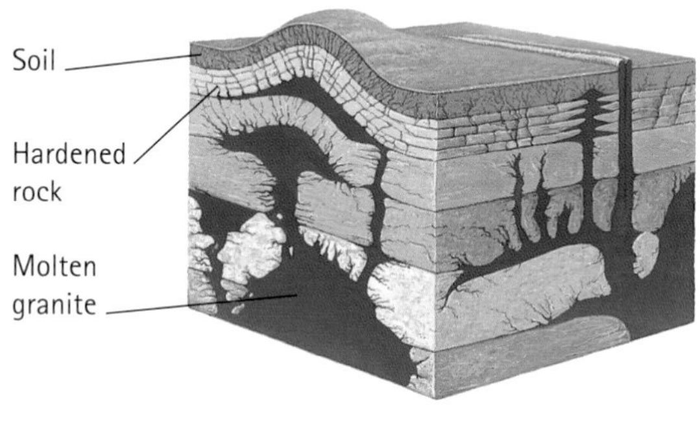

◁ This section shows an igneous **rock** (granite) in its molten form rising toward the surface. As it moves it pushes the layers of already hardened rock and soil above it into a dome shape.

They are multistage rockets—several rockets joined together. Each stage fires one after the other.

Fuel for early rockets, such as **Germany**'s V2 in **World War II**, was a mixture of kerosene and **oxygen**. Today's space rockets use **liquid** fuels—usually a liquid called hydrazine or liquid **hydrogen**. In a liquid-fuel rocket the fuel needs oxygen before it will burn. The fuel and the oxidizer are stored in separate tanks. When they are both pumped into a combustion chamber, they burn explosively and produce the gases that rush out of a nozzle and give lift to the spacecraft.

Rocky Mountains

The Rocky Mountains are a huge range of **mountains** (3,000 mi./4,800km long) in **North America**. They stretch from **Alaska** through western **Canada** and the **U.S.** as far south as New Mexico. The highest peak, Mount Elbert, is in the U.S. at 14,429 ft. (4,399m) above sea level. In Canada the highest point is Mount Robson at 12,969 ft. (3,954m). The Rockies include several national parks, such as Yellowstone, Banff, and Glacier, where many wild **animals** live.

Rodent

Rodents are a group of gnawing **animals**. They have large, sharp front **teeth** that grow all the time. They wear down these teeth by gnawing their **food**. They also use their teeth to dig burrows in the ground for their homes and **nests**. **Beavers** are able to cut down large trees for their **dams** with their gnawing teeth.

The 2,000 or so rodents include mice, **rats**, **porcupines**, and **squirrels**. The South American capybara is the largest rodent. It looks like a giant **guinea pig**, grows to a length of 4 ft. (1.25m), and weighs over 100 lbs (45kg). The smallest rodent is the European harvest **mouse**. It grows to around 3 in. (7cm) long.

Rodeo

Rodeos are exciting displays where U.S. **cowboys** show off their skills. In bareback riding a cowboy rides a bronco (a half-wild or bad-tempered **horse**). In saddle bronco riding the cowboy rides one-handed using one rein, a saddle, and a halter. Bull riding and calf roping are other events. In steer wrestling the cowboy chases a young bull, or steer, on horseback, grabs its head, and pulls the steer down. The first recorded rodeo was held in 1869.

△ A **rodeo** gives the cowboy a chance to show off riding and roping skills. However, many cowboys are thrown out of their saddles in the bucking bronco contests.

Roman Empire

see **pages 282–283**

Romania

Romania is a small country in southeast **Europe**. It has beautiful **mountains** and many **forests**. Most of its people farm, but there is also **mining** and **oil** production. In 1989 the Romanians overthrew the corrupt Communist **government** (see **communism**). A new democratic constitution (see **democracy**) was introduced in 1991, and free **elections** were held in the 1990s.

ROMANIA
Government: Republic
Capital: Bucharest
Area: 88,800 sq. mi.
Population: 22,364,022
Languages: Romanian, Hungarian, German
Currency: Leu

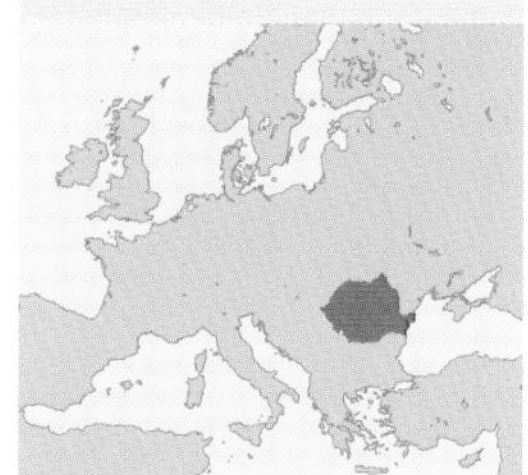

Rome

Rome is the capital of **Italy**. With a population of 2,645,000, it is also Italy's largest city. Rome stands on the Tiber **River** about 17 mi. (27km) from the **Mediterranean Sea**. Many tourists visit Rome to see the great ruins of ancient Rome (see **Roman Empire**) and the beautiful **churches**, fountains, palaces, and art galleries.

Roosevelt, Franklin D.

Franklin Delano Roosevelt (1882–1945) was the 32nd **president** of the **U.S.** Born in **New York** into a wealthy family, he became a lawyer. By 1923 he had become paralyzed, but this did not stop him from becoming governor of New York in 1928. He was elected president in 1932 and was immediately faced with the economic crisis known as the Great Depression. Roosevelt responded with the New Deal program, which was so successful that he was reelected by a landslide victory in 1936 and secured a third term in 1940 and a fourth in 1944. He took his country into **World War II** on the side of the Allies and met with Winston **Churchill** and Joseph **Stalin** at Tehran in 1943 and Yalta in 1945.

Roses, Wars of the

The Wars of the Roses was the name given to a struggle between Lancaster and York for control of the English throne in the 1400s. The wars were named after emblems, a red rose for Lancaster and a white rose for York.

For many years York was the winning side. Not until Lancastrian Henry Tudor defeated Richard III at Bosworth Field in 1485 and married Elizabeth of York did the two houses unite. The crown passed to the Tudors.

◁ *This map shows the extent of the Roman empire c. A.D. 100. The Romans—citizens of Rome—became so powerful that they began to conquer lands around them. By A.D. 100 they ruled a huge empire and were one of the mightiest peoples in the ancient world.*

▷ *Most Roman soldiers had to stay in the army for 25 years. Those who were Roman citizens were luckier—they could leave after just 20. They were far from home and had to put up with danger, tough training, and harsh punishments.*

ROMAN EMPIRE

The Roman Empire (c. 449 B.C.–A.D. 476) was one of the most powerful ancient civilizations ever to have existed. At the height of its power it controlled all of the land from the Mediterranean Sea in the south to Germany in the north and from England in the west to central Asia in the east. At its center was the capital, Rome, the largest city in the world with an estimated one million inhabitants.

RULED BY THE SENATE

Rome was ruled by a Senate, an assembly that was governed mainly by the rich aristocracy in Rome. The highest office in the Senate was that of consul. Two consuls ruled together for one year, ensuring that no one person could achieve total control over the state. The rights of the poor were protected by two other offices in the Senate called the tribunes.

THE EMPIRE IS BORN

In 45 B.C. Julius Caesar (c. 100–44 B.C.) received the title "Father of his Country." He was also made consul for ten years and granted the office of Perpetual Dictator by the Senate. It was the greatest honor that could be bestowed on an individual, and it allowed him to act without approval from the Senate. The fact that Caesar was made dictator in perpetuity effectively meant the end of the Roman republic and the start of the empire. In 44 B.C. Caesar was assassinated by his rivals.

Caesar was followed by his adopted son Octavian (63 B.C.–A.D. 14), who successfully pursued his father's killers. Octavian then changed his name to Augustus and became the second emperor of Rome.

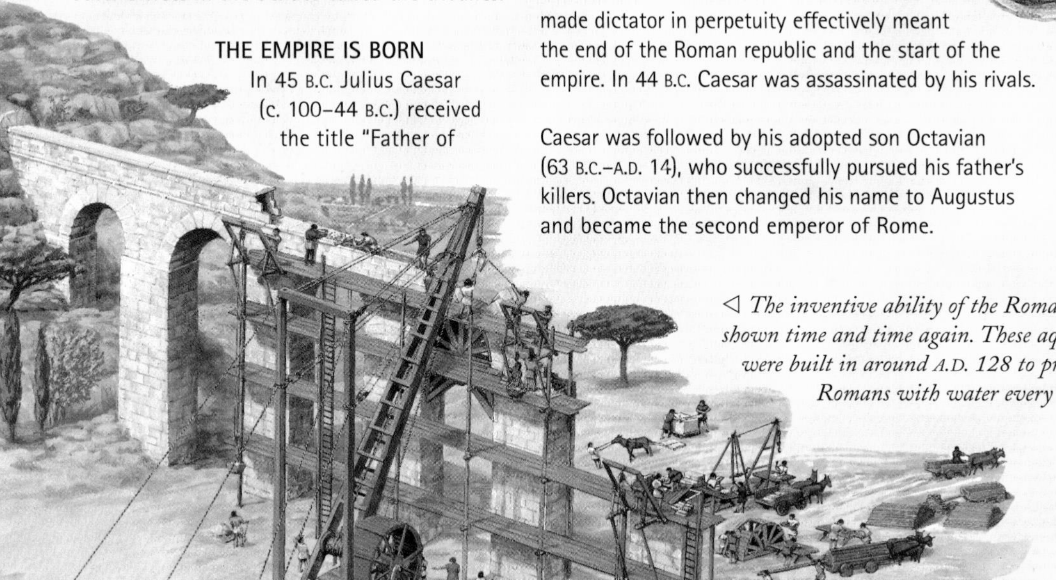

◁ *The inventive ability of the Romans was shown time and time again. These aqueducts were built in around A.D. 128 to provide Romans with water every day.*

TIME OF CHANGE

It was in Augustus' reign that a huge project to improve the city began in Rome. Augustus believed that Rome should be an example to the empire of the power and might of the Romans. He famously claimed that he had found Rome a city of wood and left it a city of marble.

The Caesars continued to rule Rome in a dynasty that lasted many generations. During this time the living conditions in the empire changed dramatically. Many of the nations that were conquered by the Romans were, to use the Roman word, extremely "barbaric." The Romans introduced many things that changed life in the provinces forever. Central heating, baths, wine, and paved roads are all Roman inventions.

GLADIATORS AND AMPHITHEATERS

Another famous Roman creation was the Games. The Romans celebrated the lives of famous citizens by holding gladiatorial contests in amphitheaters—notably the Colosseum in Rome. In these contests slave gladiators would fight to the death for the pleasure of the Roman people. There would also be public executions of prisoners and the matching of men against terrifying foreign beasts such as the tiger and hippopotamus. Another popular form of public entertainment was the staging of historical battles on a lifelike scale with real combatants. Famously this included the staging of sea battles on a huge flooded plain.

A NATION OF SLAVES

In many ways the Roman Empire only survived because of its huge slave population. The Romans forced most of their conquered opponents into slavery, and the slaves did most of the manual labor in the Empire, working on the farms and in the highly dangerous mines as well as in the houses of the rich Romans.

THE FALL OF THE ROMAN EMPIRE

Over time the Roman Empire changed a great deal. The Emperor Constantine (ruled A.D. 324–337) was the first emperor to tolerate Christianity. Gradually the whole Empire also became Christian. The seat of the Empire also moved from Rome to Byzantium, which later was called Constantinople (modern-day Istanbul). This became the eastern Roman Empire.

It became harder and harder to defend the borders of the Empire until, in A.D. 455, the Vandals from Germany finally managed to sack the city of Rome. The last Roman emperor, Romulus Augustus, was deposed in A.D. 476, and his throne was taken by a German chief, Odoacer (d. 493). This event marked the end of the Roman Empire and the beginning of the Dark Ages. Some of the Roman colonies, such as Great Britain, returned to pre-Roman ways, losing the technological advantages that they had gained under Roman rule.

△ *On special days of the Roman calendar people flocked to see spectacular shows at the amphitheater. Christians, criminals, and slaves were thrown into a ring with lions and other animals and were chased, wounded, and killed.*

▽ *Rome's spiritual heart was the forum, or marketplace, where Romans met to conduct business.*

SEE ALSO

Caesar (Julius), Calendar, Christianity, Colosseum, Dark Ages, Dictator, Invention, Italy, Republic, Road, Rome, Wine

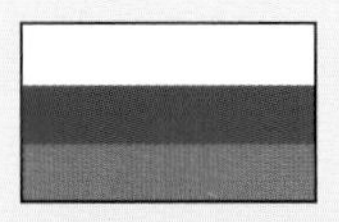

RUSSIA
Government: Republic
Capital: Moscow
Area: 6,585,000 sq. mi.
Population: 145,470,197
Language: Russian
Currency: Ruble

RWANDA
Government: Republic
Capital: Kigali
Area: 9,600 sq. mi.
Population: 7,312,756
Languages: French, English, Kinyarwandu
Currency: Rwanda franc

Rubber

Rubber is an important material with many uses in industries and homes. Most natural rubber comes from the rubber **tree**. When the bark of the tree is cut, a white juice, called latex, oozes out. The juice is collected and made into rubber. Today most natural rubber comes from **Malaysia** and **Indonesia**.

Scientists found ways of making synthetic rubber during **World War I**. Synthetic rubber is made from **oil** and **coal**. About two thirds of the rubber used today is synthetic.

Rugby *see* Sports

Russia

Russia is by far the largest of the countries that formed from the former **Soviet Union**. It contains more people than the other states put together and has most of the great cities, including **Moscow** and St. Petersburg. It is rich in **mineral** resources and is industrially powerful. **Farming**, including **cereal** crops and **cattle**, is also important.

Russian Revolution

The Russian Revolution was in fact two revolutions in one year. In 1917 Russia was ruled by Czar Nicholas II (1868–1918), the peasants were repressed, and the urban poor had no civil rights. After mass demonstrations by workers and soldiers in Petrograd the czar was forced to abdicate in February, and a short period of democratic rule by the middle classes followed (see **democracy**). However, there were still many social problems and **Lenin**, leader of the Communist Party (see **communism**), took advantage of this to start an uprising in many major cities. In November 1917 Lenin seized power and established the first Soviet **government**. The czar and his entire family were shot in 1918.

Rust

Rust is a brownish-red crust that forms on ordinary **iron** and **steel** when they are left in damp air. As rust forms the surface of the **metal** is eaten away. Grease, **oil**, and paint protect the **metal**.

Rwanda

Rwanda is a small country in central **Africa**. Much of the country is mountainous, and the **climate** is cool and pleasant. The Rwandan people farm, producing **coffee**, **tea**, corn, and beans. They also raise **cattle**. The country is one of the most densely populated in Africa. Rwanda became independent in 1962. In 1994 it was torn apart by **civil war**.

▷ During the **Russian Revolution** armed workers were supported by soldiers and sailors. On November 6, 1917 they attacked the Winter Palace in Petrograd (today's St. Petersburg). Although it was the headquarters of the czar's government, it was weakly defended and soon fell into their hands.

S

Sahara Desert

The Sahara is the world's largest hot **desert** covering about 3.5 million sq. mi. (9.1 million sq km) of northern **Africa**. It extends from the **Atlantic Ocean** in the west to the **Red Sea** in the east. In the north it stretches to the **Mediterranean** coast of **Libya** and **Egypt**. Recently very little **rain** has fallen on the land south of the Sahara. As a result, the desert is spreading south.

About one third of the Sahara is covered by **sand**. Other parts are covered by gravel and stones or by bare **rock**. The Sahara is the hottest place on **earth**—the world's highest air **temperature** in the shade, 135.8°F/57.7°C, was recorded there.

△ Strangely eroded rocks, sand, and salts shimmer in the heat of the Libyan Desert. This harsh, dry landscape is part of the enormous **Sahara Desert** in northern Africa.

Sailing

At one time almost all types of **ships** used sails. But by the mid-1800s sailing ships had been largely replaced by steamships. Today people sail mostly for pleasure or as a **sport**.

Sailboats vary in size from small dinghies to large yachts. The hull, or body, of the boat is made of fiberglass or molded plywood. The sails are usually made of a synthetic material such as nylon. They can be moved to catch the **wind** by pulling on ropes called rigging. Sailboats can sail in any direction except straight into the wind.

One of the most famous sailing races is for the America's Cup, which began in 1870. Sailing has been an **Olympic** sport since 1908.

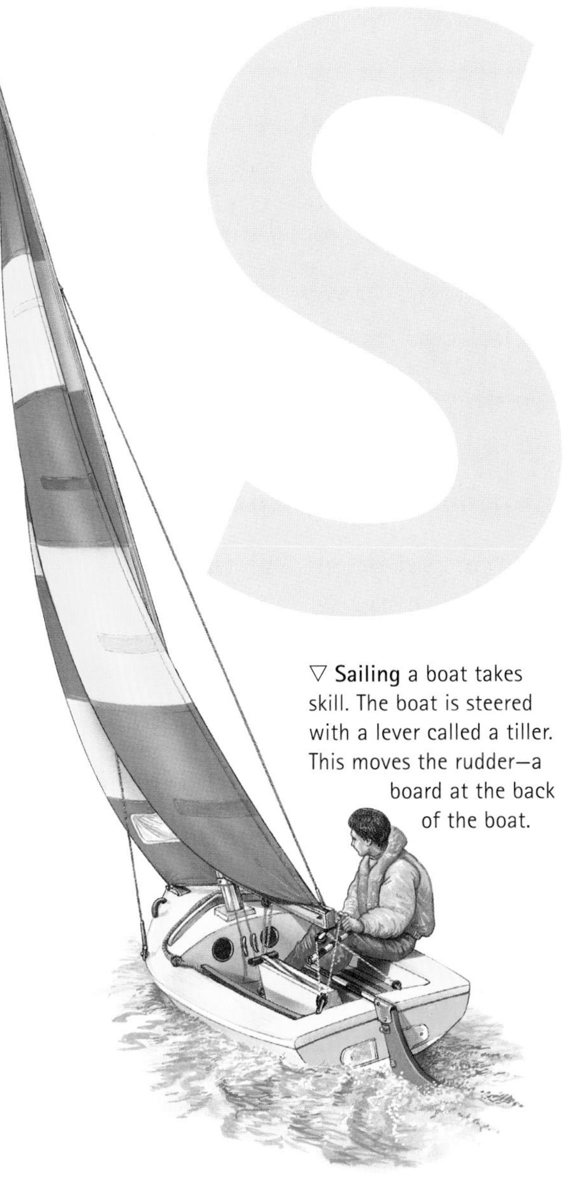

▽ **Sailing** a boat takes skill. The boat is steered with a lever called a tiller. This moves the rudder—a board at the back of the boat.

Salamander and Newt

Salamanders are **amphibians** with short legs and long tails. As adults some salamanders live in damp woods, while others spend their lives in ponds and streams. Most salamanders feed on **worms** and **insects** and have smooth, shiny **skin**.

Salamanders in **Europe** and **North America** that spend long periods in **water** are called newts. Many adult newts have webbed tails, and some males grow a crest down their backs at breeding time. Most male newts perform a complicated dance to attract females.

△ Most **salamanders** produce poison from glands in their skin. This fire salamander's bright colors are a warning to predators to stay away.

Salmon

Salmon are **fish** that breed in shallow **rivers**. After the **eggs** hatch the young fish swim down the river to the sea. The salmon spend their adult lives in the sea before returning to their birthplaces to breed.

▽ Two **salmon** leap up a waterfall on their way to their breeding grounds. Salmon use so much energy during the journey that they can lose half their body weight.

This may mean a journey of hundreds or even thousands of miles. Most salmon die after laying their eggs.

△ Pure **salt** crystals are cube shaped. We need to eat some salt every day because the body loses it all the time—for example, in sweat.

Salt

The chemical name for the salt we eat is sodium chloride. We need some salt to stay healthy but not too much. Salt is also used to preserve **foods** and to make **dyes**, **paper**, **pottery**, **leather**, and many **medicines**. Much of our salt comes from seawater, but some is mined from deposits in the ground.

San Francisco

△ In 1906 the San Andreas fault moved 21 ft. (6.5m), causing an earthquake that devastated San Francisco. Much of the city burned down as the gas mains broke and caught fire.

San Francisco, in California, is a hilly city that lies on the **Pacific** coast of the **United States**. It is a major port and financial center and has a **population** of around 732,000. The most famous of the five **bridges** that cross San Francisco Bay is the Golden Gate Bridge, a suspension bridge built in 1937.

San Francisco has suffered several strong **earthquakes** because it is built across the San Andreas fault. In 1906 most of the city was destroyed by severe tremors and raging fires. The most recent strong quake was in 1989.

▽ Weather **satellites** take photographs of weather conditions from space. The information they send back to earth allows accurate weather forecasts to be made several days in advance.

Sand

Sand is a loose material made up of small grains of **rock**. Sand grains are smaller than those in gravel but larger than those in silt or mud. On **seashores** sand piles up to form sandy beaches. Inland in dry places it forms hills called dunes. Sand is also an important ingredient in **soil**. Layers of sand in the ground may be pressed together to form a hard rock called sandstone—the second most common rock in the world. The main **mineral** in sand is **quartz**.

Satellite

A body that moves in **orbit** around another body is called a satellite. **Earth** and the other **planets** in the **solar system** are satellites of the **Sun**. The **Moon** is just one of Earth's many satellites. The others are artificial satellites launched by **rockets** into fixed orbits. **Weather** satellites have **cameras** that send back pictures of cloud and storm formations. **Communications** satellites relay **television** and **telephone** signals around the world. They have **radios** and other equipment powered by **batteries** charged by the Sun's rays. The satellites receive a signal from a transmitting station on Earth, amplify it, and beam it down to another Earth station, which may be thousands of miles away.

The first artificial satellite was *Sputnik 1*, launched by the former **Soviet Union** in 1957.

Saturn

Saturn is the second largest **planet** in the **solar system** after **Jupiter**. It measures about 74,400 mi. (120,000km) across. Saturn is famous for the rings that circle it. These are very thin and are made of billions of icy particles. The particles in the rings

SATURN FACTS
Average distance from Sun: 773 million mi.
Closest distance to Earth: 793 million mi.
Average temperature (clouds): –310°F
Diameter across equator: 74,524 mi.
Diameter of ring system: 168,640 mi.
Atmosphere: Hydrogen, helium
Number of moons: 23 known
Length of day: 10 hours and 14 minutes
Length of year: 29.5 Earth years

may be the remains of a **moon** that drifted too close to Saturn and broke up.

To the naked eye Saturn looks like a bright **star**. The planet is actually mostly made up of light **gases**, and it is less dense than **water**, but scientists think that it may have a solid core. Saturn has at least 23 **satellites**. The largest, Titan, measures about 3,224 mi. (5,200km) across—larger than **Mercury**. Titan is the only known moon to have an atmosphere—a layer of gases surrounding it.

△ Saturn's rings are less than 98 ft. (30m) thick and are made up of pieces of ice, rock, and dust. They form a band that, measured across, is more than 20 times the diameter of Earth.

Saudi Arabia

Saudi Arabia is a large country that occupies most of the Arabian peninsula in southwest **Asia**. It is named after the Saudi family that has ruled the country since it was founded in 1932. In 1933 **oil** was discovered along the Persian Gulf coast. Today it is estimated that Saudi Arabia has about one fourth of the world's oil reserves. The money from oil has been used to modernize the country. During the **Gulf War** (1991) Saudi Arabia was the base for the Allied forces' liberation of Kuwait.

Savanna

A savanna is a large area of tropical grassland. The land is flat or gently rolling and covered by **grasses**. **Trees** and bushes are scattered among the grasses or clustered along streams and **rivers**.

Savannas are found in southern **Brazil** and **Australia** but mainly in **Africa**. These regions have wet and dry **seasons**. The grasses grow quickly, flower, and produce **seeds** in the short wet season. They die or do not grow in the longer dry season.

On the African savanna the **temperature** is hot all year round. Herds of grazing **animals**, such as **zebras**, wildebeests, and **elephants**, wander across the savanna in search of **food** and **water**. These animals are hunted by predators such as **lions**, cheetahs, and **hyenas**.

SAUDI ARABIA
Government: Monarchy
Capital: Riyadh
Area: 829,000 sq. mi.
Population: 22,757,092
Language: Arabic
Currency: Saudi riyal

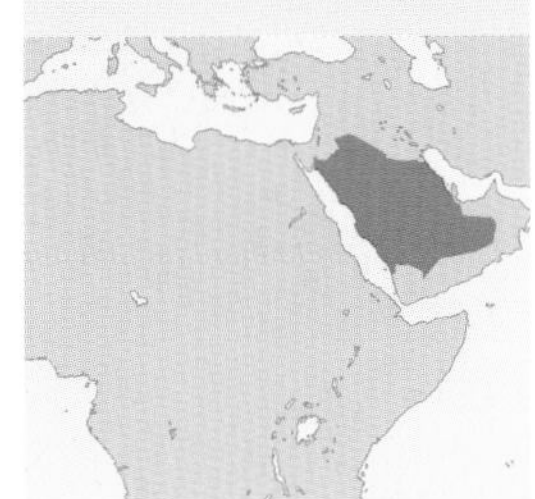

School

Almost all countries try to provide enough schools to give their children some education. In many countries there is a **law** that children have to go to school between certain ages such as between 5 and 16. But some poorer countries do not have enough schools or teachers. They try to make sure that children go to school for long enough to learn to read, write, and use **numbers**. However, nearly one third of the world's people over 15 cannot read or write.

Science

The main divisions of science are **astronomy**, **biology**, **chemistry**, **geology**, **mathematics**, **medicine**, and **physics**, which deals with the different types of **energy**.

Modern scientists use the scientific method. First they observe, or look at, something carefully to find out everything they can about it. Then they create a theory that explains what the thing is made of or how it works. Then they test the theory with experiments. If the experiments agree with the theory, it becomes a **law** of science. Sometimes a law is changed when scientists discover new facts about something. Science is always changing.

Scientific studies began in early times. Great advances were made during the first civilizations, especially in ancient **Greece** and **China**. Science almost died out in **Europe** in the **Middle Ages**, but during the **Renaissance** scientists began making discoveries that changed the way people thought and lived. This process accelerated during the **Industrial Revolution**, and scientific research has been speeding up ever since.

△ The French author Jules Verne wrote some of the first **science fiction** stories. This illustration is from *20,000 Leagues Under the Sea*, published in 1870.

▽ Baby **scorpions** hatch inside their mother's body and then cling to her back for the first week or two of their lives. Once they climb down they live on their own.

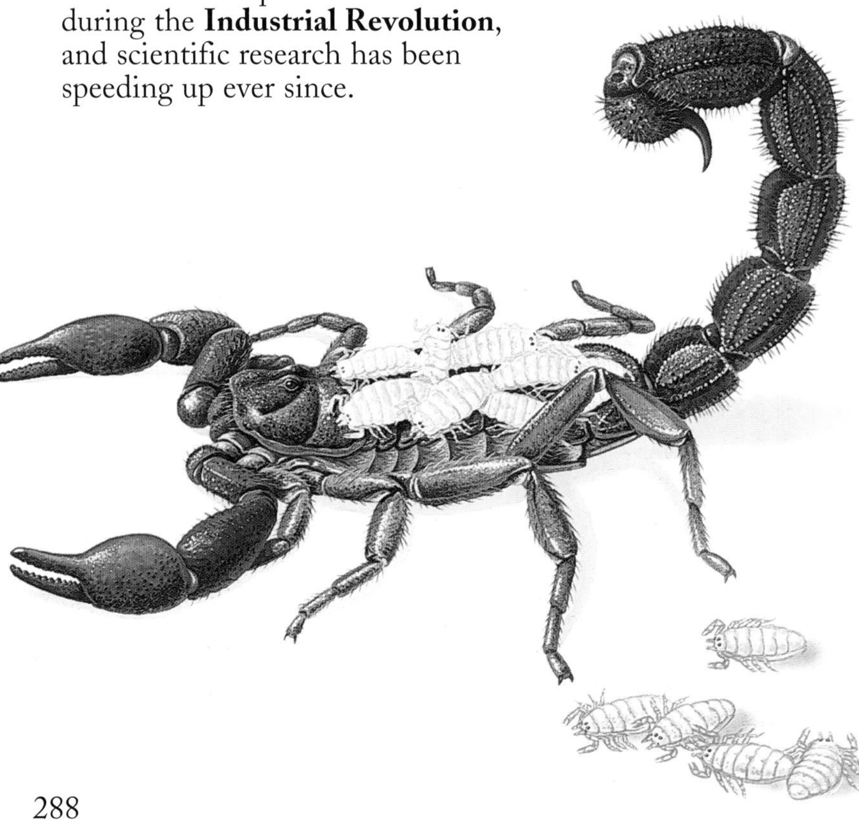

Science fiction

Stories that are set in the future or on other **planets** are called science fiction. The authors often use new scientific discoveries in their stories. They imagine how these discoveries might change the world in the future.

Many science-fiction stories are about space travel and **time** travel and meetings with or between creatures from other planets.

Jules Verne (1828–1905) and H. G. Wells (1866–1946) were two of the first great science fiction writers. Recent writers include Isaac Asimov, Ray Bradbury, and Arthur C. Clarke.

Scorpion

Scorpions are related to **spiders** and mostly live in warm, dry places. They have four pairs of legs, a pair of large claws, and a poisonous stinger in their tails. Scorpions use the stinger to stun or kill their prey. The **poison** can make people sick, but it very rarely kills them.

Scotland

Scotland is part of the **United Kingdom**. Most Scots live in the south of the country in Glasgow, Scotland's largest city, and Edinburgh, the capital. Most of Scotland's industry is also found in the south. The Highlands have very few people and many beautiful **mountains** and lochs. Ben Nevis, at 4,405 ft. (1,343m), is the highest mountain in the U.K. There are many **islands** off the Scottish coast such as the Hebrides, Orkneys, and Shetlands.

Scotland joined with **England** and **Wales** in 1707, but in 1997 the Scots voted in favor of having their own **parliament**. In 1999 the people elected the parliament, which has powers to vary its **taxes** and run its own **health** and education services. Scotland has its own executive (cabinet), which is headed by the First Minister.

Scott, Robert Falcon

Captain Robert Falcon Scott (1868–1912) was an English naval officer and an **explorer** of the **Antarctic**. His first expedition was in 1901–1904. In 1911 he began a march to the **South Pole** with four companions. After a great struggle he reached the South Pole on January 17, 1912, but he was disappointed to find that Roald **Amundsen** of **Norway** had been there a month earlier. Scott and his companions died in a snowstorm during their journey.

Scott, Walter

Sir Walter Scott (1771–1832) was one of the most popular writers in the English **language**. He was born in **Scotland**. He became a lawyer but was more interested in Scottish **history** and folklore. He wrote **poetry** and many novels of historical adventures, including *Rob Roy* and *Ivanhoe*.

Scouting

Scouting is an international movement for boys and girls. It was founded in **England** in 1907 by Robert Baden-Powell (1857–1941) for boys only. The Boy Scouts were bought to the **U.S.** in 1910 by an American businessman who was impressed with a British Boy Scout who helped him find his way in a London fog. The movement rapidly spread to other countries.

In 1910 the Girl Guides were started in the **U.K.**, making their way to **Canada** at the same time and then in 1912 to the U.S., where their name was changed to Girl Scouts.

One aim of scouting is to build character and self-reliance. Another is to teach helpfulness to others.

Screw

A screw is a simple **machine**. There are many types of screws, but the best known are the **metal** ones used to join things. The spiral part of a screw is called the thread. When a screw is turned around in a piece of **wood** by a screwdriver, the thread pulls the screw into the wood.

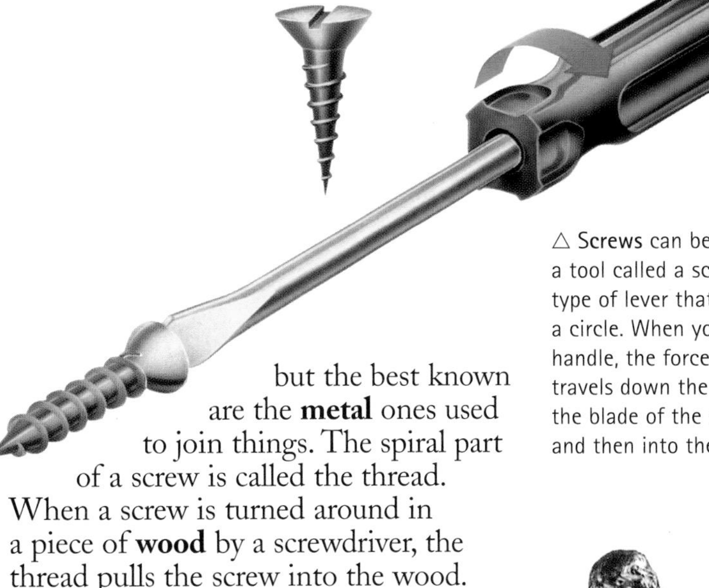

△ **Screws** can be twisted by a tool called a screwdriver—a type of lever that moves in a circle. When you turn the handle, the force of the turn travels down the shaft to the blade of the screwdriver and then into the screw.

Sculpture

Sculpture is a way of making attractive models, statues, and objects as works of **art**. They may be carved from stone or **wood**, or they may be made by casting. To make a cast the sculptor first makes a model in **clay** or wax. This model is used to make a mold. Hot, molten **metal**, such as **bronze**, is then poured into the mold. When the metal has cooled and hardened, it is taken out of the mold. The metal cast is a perfect copy of the original model.

Early Greek statues were models for **Renaissance** sculptors such as **Michelangelo**, who was possibly the finest sculptor ever. Many modern sculptors have moved away from lifelike figures. Great artists, such as Henry Moore (1898–1986), have made **abstract** figures and groups.

△ *The Thinker* (1880) is one of the best-known **sculptures** by the French artist Auguste Rodin (1840–1917).

Sea anemone

Sea anemones are soft-bodied, tubelike **animals**. They are closely related to **corals**, but they do not build a hard layer around themselves as corals do. Sea anemones cling to **rocks**. Many live on or near the **seashore**. They have one or more rings of petallike tentacles around their mouths.

△ A **sea anemone** attaches itself to rocks with a suckerlike disk. When the anemone is covered by the tide, its tentacles float in the water. When the tide goes out, the anemone pulls in its tentacles to stop them from drying out.

△ **Sea horses** swim upright. To feed they hold onto seaweed with their tails and eat food from the water as it floats past.

The tentacles have stinging **cells** and trap small **fish** and other tiny, floating animals. The sea anemone then pulls the **food** into its **stomach** through its mouth and digests it.

Sea horse

Sea horses are unusual, delicate **fish** with bony bodies. They are called sea horses because of their horse-shaped heads. Most grow to between 6–10 in. (15–25cm) long.

Sea horses swim by waving the fin on their backs. They often cling to **seaweed** with their tails. The males take care of the **eggs**, keeping them in a pouch on their bellies until they hatch. Sea horses are found all around the world in tropical and warm seas.

△ **Seals** are excellent swimmers, but on land they move slowly. They spend most of their time at sea but come ashore to breed.

Seal and Sea lion

Seals and sea lions are large sea **mammals**. Many of them live in icy waters. They spend most of their time in the sea but sometimes come ashore to lie in the sun. They also give birth to their young, called pups, on land. Seals can swim fast because they have streamlined bodies and strong flippers. They also have a thick layer of **fat**, or blubber, under their **skin** to protect them from the cold. Seals and sea lions eat **fish** and other sea creatures. Sea lions have small **ears** outside their heads and fur all over their bodies. The males often have a shaggy mane. The California sea lion is the smallest and can often be seen in **zoos**.

Seashore

The shores surrounding **earth**'s seas and **oceans** are shaped by **water**. Along some shores fierce **waves** hammer at **rocks** and carry away stones and soil. Along others the waves and **tides** bring in pebbles and **sand** and dump them.

There are several types of seashores. They can be made of rocks, sand, mud, pebbles, or a mixture. All shores are home to many living things.

Limpets, winkles, whelks, barnacles, **sea anemones**, and **sponges** are some of the creatures found on rocky shores. All of these animals cling to rocks and eat tiny pieces of **food** that float by in the water. Others, such as cockles, razor shells, mussels, and **crabs**, live on sandy and muddy beaches.

Seashores have their own **plants**, many of which are **seaweeds**, but other plants also grow in these wet, salty places. Most shore plants and animals are able to live both in and out of water. When the tide is in, they are often underwater, but when

▽ Some of the many animals found along the **seashore** include: (1) Oystercatcher (2) Common shore crab (3) Limpet (4) Edible lobster (5) Shrimp (6) Hermit crab (7) Goby (8) Mussel (9) Masked crab (10) Tellin (11) Razor shell (12) Lugworm (13) Starfish (14) Black-headed gull (15) Curlew (16) Jellyfish

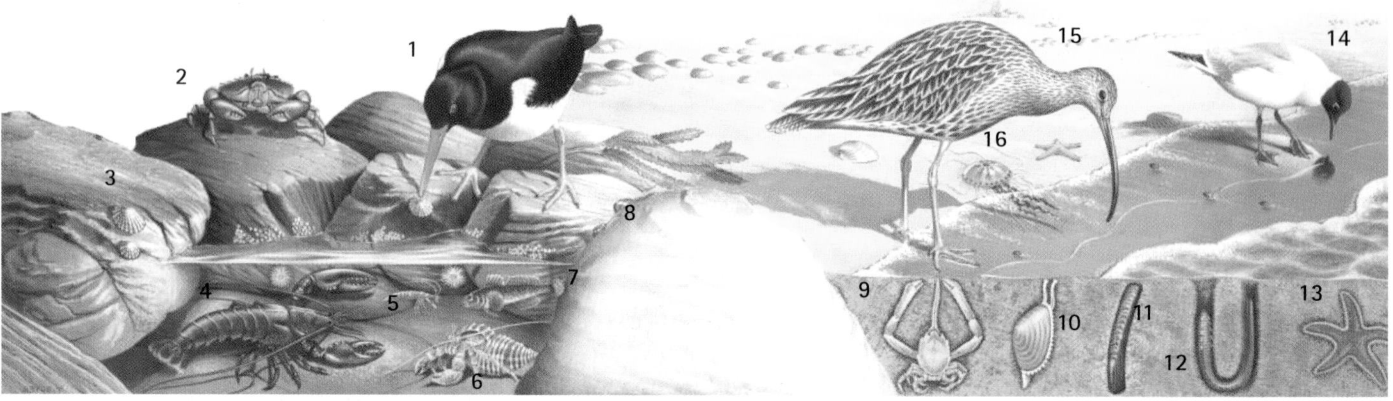

the tide is out, they are left on land.
Many **birds** live along the seashore. Some shore birds use their long beaks to dig for **worms** and **insects** in the mud. Others catch **fish** in the sea.

Season

The **year** is divided into four seasons. They are spring, summer, fall, and winter. Each season has its own type of **weather**.

In the spring, for example, the **days** become warmer, **plants** begin to grow again after the winter cold, and most **animals** have their young. In the fall the days are cooler, **leaves** fall from the **trees**, and many **birds** fly to warmer places for the winter.

Seasons happen because **Earth** is tilted on its axis (an imaginary line through the center of the planet between the North and South poles). As Earth travels around the **Sun** first one pole and then the other leans toward the Sun. When the **North Pole** tips toward the Sun, it is summer in the northern half of the world and winter in the southern half. Six months later, it is the **South Pole**'s turn to lean toward the Sun, making it summer in southern lands and winter in northern ones. Spring and fall, the halfway seasons between summer and winter, happen when Earth is between its summer and winter positions.

At the poles there are only two seasons—summer and winter. During the winter the Sun never rises, and days are dark. In the summer the Sun shines all the time, and there are no real nights.

Farthest from the poles, at the **equator**, Earth's tilt has no effect. There are no clear differences between the seasons in this part of the world.

△ In the northern half, or hemisphere, of Earth summer officially begins on June 21. The other **seasons** begin on September 23 (fall), December 21 (winter), and March 21 (spring). In the southern hemisphere the seasons are reversed.

Seaweed

Seaweeds are a group of **plants** that live in the sea. They grow on **rocks** or on the seabed. Seaweeds do not have **leaves** or **flowers**. Instead they have tough, leathery fronds. Like most plants, seaweeds need sunlight to make **food**. Because the **sun**'s rays do not reach very far down into the sea, there are no seaweeds in deep **water**.

In some countries, such as **China** and **Japan**, people eat different types of seaweeds as **vegetables**.

▷ **Seaweeds** all belong to the class of simple plants called algae. They live in shallow water where they give off oxygen. Seaweeds provide food and shelter for many animals such as crabs, snails, and shrimp.

Seed

Seeds are the most important part of a **plant**; each one is able to grow into a new plant under the right conditions. A seed forms when pollen reaches the female part of a **flower**. The new seed grows inside a **fruit**, which protects it.

Seeds have to be scattered to find new ground to grow on. Some fruits have wings and are carried by the **wind**. Others are prickly and stick to the fur of passing **animals**. Many seeds contain the baby plant and a small supply of **food**. When the seed begins to grow, the baby plant takes in this food until it has roots and **leaves** and can make its own food.

Semiconductor

Some materials, called conductors, allow **electricity** to pass through them easily. Most of these materials are **metals**. Other materials do not allow electricity to pass—they are insulators. Semiconductors are materials, such as silicon and germanium, that are neither conductors nor insulators. When small amounts of other **elements** are added to semiconductors, important **electronic** devices can be made. These devices, such as the **silicon chip**, can be made to pass different amounts of electric current, to block it completely, or to allow it to pass only in one direction. **Transistors** are made from semiconductors.

Senegal

The country of Senegal lies on the west coast of **Africa**. Neighboring **Gambia** is surrounded on three sides by Senegal. Peanuts, **rice**, and millet are Senegal's main crops, and **fishing** is an important industry.

Senegal was the first French colony in Africa. Independence came in 1960.

SENEGAL
Government: Republic
Capital: Dakar
Area: 74,000 sq. mi.
Population: 10,284,929
Language: French
Currency: CFA franc

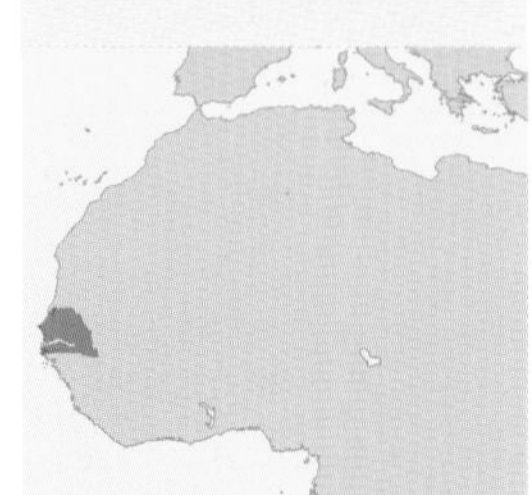

UNION OF SERBIA AND MONTENEGRO
Government: Federal republic
Capital: Belgrade
Area: 39,400 sq. mi.
Population: 10,616,000
Languages: Serbo-Croatian and Albanian
Currency: Dinar

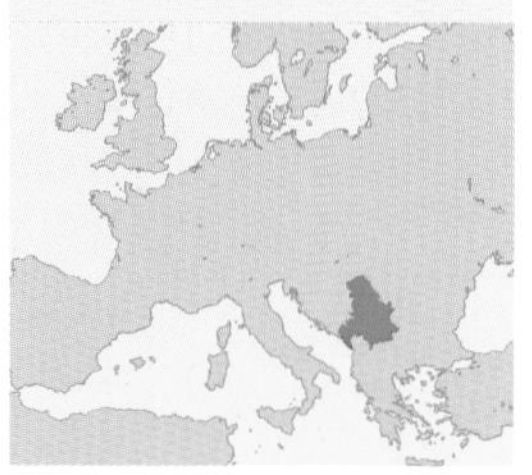

Senses *see* Hearing, Sight, Smell, Taste, Touch

Serbia and Montenegro, Union of

Serbia and Montenegro were formerly the last two **republics** of Yugoslavia. In 2002 the Yugoslav **parliament** voted to form a new country, the Union of Serbia and Montenegro.

In the early 1990s Serbia fought **wars** against **Slovenia**, **Croatia**, and **Bosnia-Herzegovina**. A peace agreement was signed in 1995, but in Kosovo, a region in the south of Serbia, the Albanian-speaking people called for independence. Serbian troops attacked the Albanians. As a result, a **NATO** force bombed the Serbs, who withdrew from Kosovo in 1999.

Seven Wonders of the World

The Seven Wonders of the World were seven outstanding objects that were built in ancient times. They got their name because people marveled at their size and beauty. Only one of these wonders, the **pyramids**, exists today. The others have all been destroyed.

The Hanging Gardens of **Babylon** were built high on the walls of temples. They were probably a gift from Nebuchadnezzar II (c. 630–562 B.C.) to one of his wives.

▽ The Hanging Gardens of Babylon were one of the **Seven Wonders of the World**. Babylon stood on the banks of the Euphrates River (now in Iraq).

The Temple of Artemis at Ephesus (now in **Turkey**) was one of the largest temples in the ancient world. Some of its **marble** columns are in the British Museum in **London**.

The Statue of Zeus at Olympia, **Greece**, showed the king of the **gods** on his throne. It was made of **gold** and **ivory**.

The tomb at Halicarnassus (now in Turkey) was built for Mausolus (d. 353 B.C.), a ruler in Persia. It was so huge and became so famous that all large tombs are now called mausoleums.

The Colossus of Rhodes, in Greece, was a huge, bronze statue of the **sun** god, Helios. It stood towering high over the harbor entrance.

The Pharos of Alexandria, in **Egypt**, was the first modern lighthouse. It was built in 270 B.C. on the **island** of Pharos outside Alexandria harbor. It had a wood **fire** burning on top.

Seychelles

The **islands** of the Seychelles make up a small country about 990 mi. (1,600km) off the east coast of **Africa** in the **Indian Ocean**. The country has volcanic **mountains**, sandy beaches, and coconut **palm** plantations.

The islands were ruled by Great Britain until they gained independence in 1976. The inhabitants are of mixed African and European ancestry. Tourism is an important business.

SEYCHELLES
Government: Republic
Capital: Victoria
Area: 176 sq. mi.
Population: 79,715
Languages: English, French, Creole
Currency: Seychelles rupee

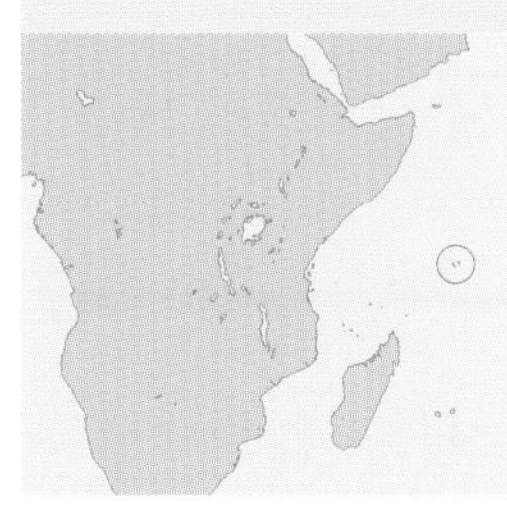

Shakespeare, William

William Shakespeare (1564–1616) is thought by most people to be **England**'s greatest writer. He is most famous for his plays—about 40 altogether—which include *A Midsummer Night's Dream*, *Hamlet*, *Macbeth*, and *Romeo and Juliet*.

Very little is known about Shakespeare's life. He was born in Stratford-upon-Avon and was the son of a glovemaker. When he was 18, he married Anne Hathaway, a farmer's daughter, and they had three children. At the age of 20 he left Stratford and went to **London**, where he became an actor and playwright. Toward the end of his life he returned to Stratford.

Shakespeare's plays are acted and studied all over the world. Many of the words and phrases we use today were first used by Shakespeare.

Shark

The shark family includes the world's largest and fiercest **fish**. Many sharks have a wedge-shaped head, a long body, and a triangular back fin that frequently sticks out of the **water**. Their **skeletons** are made of rubbery cartilage, not **bone**. Most sharks live in warm seas. They vary greatly in size. The dogfish, one of the smallest sharks, is only 23 in. (60cm) long. The largest fish in the **oceans**, the whale shark, measures over 49 ft. (15m)—longer than a bus.

The whale shark and the basking shark are harmless because they live on **plankton**. But many sharks are killers with rows of razor-sharp **teeth** and in certain circumstances may attack humans. The great white shark even swallows its prey whole. The remains of large animals, such as **dolphins**, **seals**, and other sharks, have been found in its **stomach**.

Other sharks include the blue shark, the tiger shark and the leopard shark, which has leopardlike spots. Today up to 80 percent of shark species are endangered mainly owing to humans who eat them, catch them for their oil, or accidentally catch them in fishing nets.

▽ The great white **shark** grows up to 26 ft. (8m) long. Like most sharks it can pick up the electrical signals given off by the twitching muscles of other animals in the sea.

Sheep

Sheep have been kept as domestic **animals** for thousands of years. At first they were kept for their **milk** and **skins**. The milk could be made into **cheese**, and the skins were used for **clothing**. Then people discovered that the animals' thick coats could be sheared (shaved off) and the **wool** woven into cloth. Today sheep are kept mostly for wool and for meat (mutton or lamb).

△ Modern **sheep** have been specifically bred to give the best combination of wool and meat.

Shells and Shellfish

Many **animals** live inside shells. This is because they have soft bodies that need protection. Shells are usually hard and are all sizes and **colors**. The shells of some sea **snails** are no larger than a grain of **sand**, but the giant clam of the **Pacific Ocean** has a shell 47 in. (120cm) across.

Some land animals, such as snails, have shells, but most creatures with shells live in the sea. These include **mollusks** and **crustaceans**. Some of these, such as **oysters**, scallops, and **lobsters**, can be eaten. They are often called shellfish, although they are not really **fish** at all. Shellfish have been an important **food** for thousands of years. In some places the remains of **prehistoric peoples'** meals has been found to contain enormous amounts of shells—equaling the height of a two-story **house**.

Shinto

Shinto is a Japanese **religion**. The word "Shinto" means "the way of the **gods**." Unlike other religions, Shinto does not teach that there is one supreme being. It says that there is an eternal truth called *kami*. *Kami* is found in every form of nature and in **rivers**, **mountains**, and **lakes**. All over **Japan** there are shrines dedicated to different *kami*.

Ship and Boat

Today most ships are cargo vessels. They are usually built to carry a certain type of cargo. Tankers carry **liquids** such as **oil** and **wine**. Some oil tankers are so long that the crew can ride **bicycles** around the deck. Bulk carriers take dry cargo, like **coal** and **wheat**, that can be loaded loose. Container ships carry all kinds of goods packed into large boxes called containers. **Refrigerator** ships are for carrying fresh **food** such as **fruit** and meat.

Planes have replaced most passenger ships for long journeys, but ferries still carry people, **cars**, and trucks across smaller stretches of **water**. There are also luxury cruise liners. Various types of warships are used by the navy.

▷ The largest passenger **ship** in the world, a cruise liner called the *Grand Princess*, carries 2,600 people on 12 decks. The facilities on board include a library offering CD-ROM and Internet access, a virtual reality game area, a swimming pool that is protected by a moving roof, and a casino decorated with holograms.

Shrew

Shrews are furry **animals** about the size of a mouse. They have pointed snouts and are seldom seen because they only come out at night. Shrews are very active animals and have to eat **insects** and **worms** almost continually to stay alive. They often fall prey to larger night hunters such as **owls** and **cats**.

△ **Shrews**, such as this pygmy shrew, are very fierce mammals. They often use their sharp teeth to attack mice and other shrews.

Siberia

Siberia is a vast region that covers most of Russian **Asia** east of the Ural **Mountains**. It is a very cold land. Along Siberia's northern coast lies the **tundra**, a cold semi**desert**. **Forests** cover about one third of the 5.9 million sq. mi. (15 million sq km) that make up the area. Toward the Mongolian border lies Lake Baikal, the largest freshwater **lake** in Asia or **Europe**.

During the period when **Russia** was part of the **Soviet Union** the Communist **government** encouraged people to settle in and develop Siberia.

Sierra Leone

Sierra Leone is a country on the west coast of **Africa**. It is about the size of North Carolina with a **climate** that is hot and damp. Around Freetown, the capital, about 148 in. (380cm) of **rain** falls per year. Most people are farmers, producing **rice**, **palm** kernels, ginger, **coffee**, and cocoa. **Iron** ore, bauxite, and **diamonds** are mined.

Sierra Leone was a British colony. It became an independent state in 1961 and a **republic** in 1971, but **civil war** broke out in the 1990s. A peace agreement was reached in 1999.

Sight

Sight is the sense that allows people and **animals** to see things. The sense organ that makes this possible is the **eye**. Sight is the most important sense for most animals because it allows them to look for **food** and mates and to watch for danger.

Most **invertebrates** (animals without backbones) have simple eyes that give only a rough picture of what is around them. Animals with backbones (**vertebrates**) are able to see clearly. Only humans and a few types of animals can see in full **color**.

Sikhism

Sikhism is a **religion** that began in the Punjab region of northern **India**. Followers of Sikhism are called Sikhs. The first Sikh guru (teacher) was **Nanak** (1469–1539). The teachings of the gurus were written in the Sikh sacred book, the *Granth*.

Sikhs follow three important beliefs: first they should remember God by saying God's name often; second they should work hard to earn an honest living; and third they should share their earnings and help others.

△ The Golden Temple in Amritsar, India, is sacred to the followers of **Sikhism**. It was built to house the Sikh sacred book, the *Granth*.

SIERRA LEONE
Government: Republic
Capital: Freetown
Area: 27,600 sq. mi.
Population: 5,426,618
Language: English
Currency: Leone

Silicon chip

Silicon chips are tiny pieces of the **element** silicon. (Silicon is a **semiconductor**.) The chips can be made to carry very small electrical circuits called microcircuits. These are used in **radios**, digital watches, **calculators**, and **computers**. Because the chips are so small, the **electronic** devices in which they are used can be small too.

Silk

Silk is a natural fiber made from the cocoon of one type of **moth**. Silkworms, which are really **caterpillars**, are kept in special containers and fed on mulberry **leaves** for about four weeks. At the end of this time they spin their cocoons and start to turn into moths. Then they are killed, and each cocoon is unwound as a long thread between 2,000—3,000 ft. (600–900m) long.

Silk was first used in **Asia** centuries ago, especially in **China** and **Japan**. Silk **weaving** in **Europe** began in the 1400s. Silk makes a very fine, soft material. It was used for stockings before nylon was invented. Silk can be made into other fabrics, such as satin and chiffon, and can be dyed many beautiful **colors**.

Silver

Silver is a precious **metal**. It has been used by people all over the world for thousands of years. Although many countries have silver deposits the **mining** process is very expensive.

Silver bends very easily and can be beaten into many shapes and patterns. Like **gold** it can be hammered out into thin sheets. It is used to make handy and decorative things such as spoons and forks, bowls, and **jewelry**. Sometimes it is used as a coating on cheaper metals, such as **copper** or nickel, to make them look like silver.

Silver is used by industries because it carries **electricity** well. Some chemicals made from silver react to **light** and are used in **photography**.

SINGAPORE
Government: Republic
Capital: Singapore
Area: 250 sq. mi.
Population: 4,300,419
Languages: Chinese, Malay, Tamil, English
Currency: Singaporean dollar

Singapore

Singapore is a small country in **Southeast Asia** off the southern end of the Malay peninsula. Three fourths of the **population** are Chinese, but people from all over the world live there.

The capital city is also called Singapore. It has one of the busiest ports in the world and trades with many countries. For a short time Singapore was part of **Malaysia**, but now it has its own **government**. It is a member of the **Commonwealth**.

Skating

Roller-skating and ice-skating are both popular **sports**. In the past roller skates had four **wheels** made of **steel** and **rubber**. Most people today use in-line skates, which have wheels instead of a thin steel blade like ice skates.

There are two main types of ice-skating. Figure skating and ice dancing to **music** are **Olympic** sports. Speed skaters race against each other.

The first ice skates had runners, or blades, of **bone**. Today figure skates have jagged teeth at the front to help grip the ice when starting and stopping. Speed skates have longer blades. Skates are also worn by hockey players.

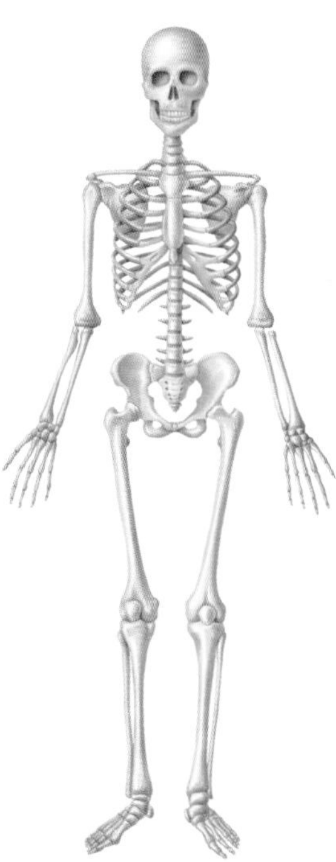

△ The **skeleton** of an adult human has around 206 bones. Babies are born with around 350 bones, but as a child grows some of these bones become connected.

Skeleton

Our skeleton is made up of **bones**. Without a skeleton our bodies would be shapeless blobs. The skeleton protects our vital organs such as the **heart**, **liver**, and **lungs**. It is also an anchor for the **muscles**.

In humans and other **vertebrates** (animals with backbones), the skeleton is inside the body covered by flesh and **skin**. In other animals, such as **insects** and **spiders**, the skeleton is like a hard crust on the outside of the body. It is called an exoskeleton. Some animals, such as **jellyfish** and **octopuses**, lack skeletons. Their bodies are supported by the **water** in which they live.

There are more than 200 bones in the human skeleton. These include the bones of the spine, skull (which protects the **brain**), breastbone, ribs, pelvis, and limbs. Joints are places where bones meet. Some joints, such as those in the skull, do not move. Others, like those in the shoulders and hips, help us move around. Muscles across the joints tighten, or contract, to move the bones.

Skiing

Skiing is a way of moving across **snow** on long runners, or skis. It probably started around 3000 B.C. The oldest skis ever found date back to 2500 B.C., and we know that the **Vikings** used skis. Today skiing is a popular **sport** and is part of the Winter **Olympic Games**.

There are four main types of skiing: downhill, cross-country, slalom (a type of obstacle course), and ski jumping. Downhill skiing, in which the skier glides down a steep **mountain** run at high speed, is especially popular. There are special ski resorts in the mountains of **Australia**, **Europe**, and **North America** where people can enjoy skiing vacations.

Skin

Skin is a waterproof, stretchy covering on the outside of the body. It protects the body from dirt and **germs** and can even repair itself. Skin is sensitive to **heat**, cold, and **pain**. Human skin can be thick and hard on places that get a lot of wear such as the soles of the feet. In other places, such as the eyelids, it can be very thin.

Human skin is made up of two layers. The outer layer, the epidermis, is made up of dead skin **cells** and has a chemical called melanin that gives skin its **color**. The inner layer, the dermis, contains **nerves**, **blood** vessels, sweat **glands**, and the roots of **hairs**. The skin of an adult human covers an area of about 2 sq. ft. (1.7 sq m).

Skunk

Skunks are **mammals** and members of the same family as weasels and **badgers**. There are three types: the hog-nosed, the spotted, and the striped. They all live in **North America**. The best known is the striped skunk, which is black with white markings on its back. All skunks are able to drive away enemies by squirting a foul-smelling **liquid** from a **gland** under their tails. If another **animal** is hit by this liquid, the smell will cling to its fur for days.

Skunks eat most types of **food**, including **insects**, **rats**, **mice**, **birds**, **eggs**, and **plants**. They feed at night and sleep in burrows during the **day**.

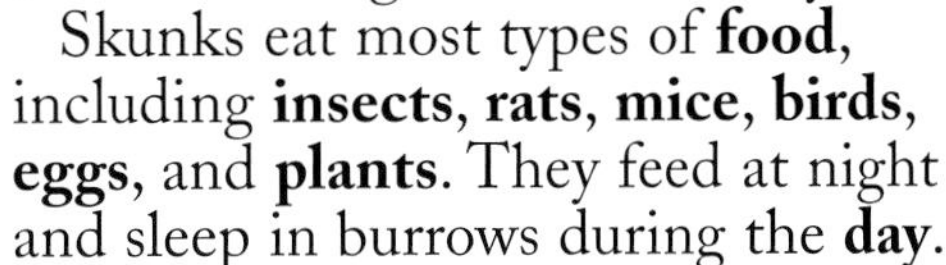

△ **Skunks** are harmless if left alone, but if they feel threatened, the foul-smelling liquid they squirt drives off any attacker. Before a skunk sprays it gives a warning by stamping its front feet and hissing.

▷ Downhill **skiing** is a popular sport. The skiers wear protective helmets and smooth, tight-fitting costumes to reduce resistance from the wind.

△ The Empire State Building (left), in **New York** City, was the world's tallest **skyscraper** when it was completed in 1930. It stands 1,250 ft. (381m) high. The Sears Tower (right), in Chicago, was built in 1970–1973 and is 1,453 ft. (443m) high.

Skyscraper

"Skyscraper" is a name for a very tall building. The first one was built in 1884 in Chicago. It was designed by William Le Baron Jenney and had an **iron** frame. All of the early skyscrapers were built in **New York** City and Chicago. Now they are built all over the world.

For many years the tallest skyscraper was the Empire State Building in New York at 102 stories high. Today the world's tallest skyscrapers are the Petronas Twin Towers in Kuala Lumpur, **Malaysia**. Completed in 1996, the buildings stand 1,482 ft. (451.9m) high.

Slavery

Slavery is when one person becomes the property, or slave, of another. Slaves can be bought and sold. In ancient civilizations prisoners captured in **war** were often forced to become slaves, and poor people sometimes sold their children as slaves.

From the 1500s the Spanish took people from **Africa** as slaves for their colonies in the Americas. By the 1770s the British were also carrying slaves to the Americas. They were packed tightly into **ships** in terrible conditions, and many of them died on the way.

Great Britain abolished the slave trade in 1833. In the **United States** slavery was ended in 1865 after the **Civil War**. But racial discrimination continued even after **civil rights** laws were passed to guarantee equal rights for black people.

▽ African people captured for **slavery** suffered terrible treatment. They were rounded up in gangs and marched to the coast. As they boarded ships the slaves were held in leg irons with their hands tied behind their backs.

Sleep

Sleep is a time when we are unconscious and resting. People and some **animals** need sleep to stay healthy. Without some sleep people become bad-tempered, and after a long period without sleep they may start having hallucinations—seeing things that are not there.

There are four different stages of sleep. At each stage the electrical **waves** given off by the **brain** change. When we are deeply asleep, these waves are slow and large. When we are only lightly asleep, the waves are faster. This is the time when we—and all **mammals**—have **dreams**.

Sloth

Sloths are a group of **mammals** that live in **South America**. They move very slowly, usually at night. Sloths spend most of their lives hanging upside down in **trees**. They eat **leaves**, buds, and twigs. Their fur is often covered with a mass of tiny green **plants** called algae. There are two main types of sloths—those with two toes on their front feet and those with three.

Slovakia

This country in Eastern **Europe** was once part of the country known as Czechoslovakia. The territory was ruled for many centuries by the Hungarians, but in 1918 the Slovak and Czech regions were joined into Czechoslovakia. The country came under Communist rule in 1948.

A democratic **government** took over after the Communists fell in 1989. However, the Slovak people soon felt that they were being treated unfairly and called for independence. The country split into Slovakia and the **Czech Republic** in 1993.

SLOVAKIA
Government: Republic
Capital: Bratislava
Area: 18,800 sq. mi.
Population: 5,414,937
Languages: Slovak and Hungarian
Currency: Koruna

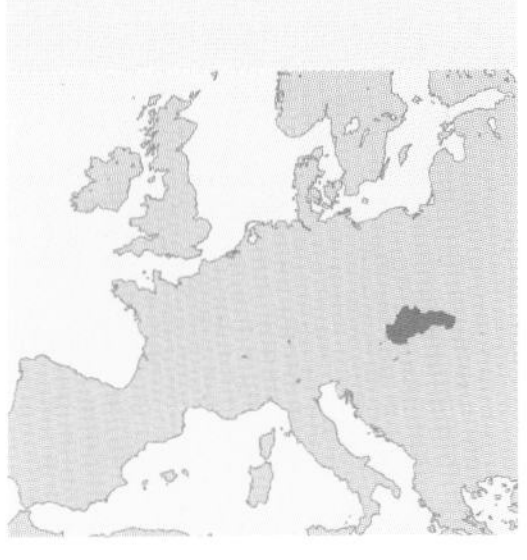

Slovenia

Slovenia was the most westerly **republic** of the former country of Yugoslavia. It declared its independence in 1991. Until 1918 Slovenia was ruled by **Austria**. It is the most Westernized of the former Yugoslav republics, and its people are mainly Roman Catholic. Ljubljana, the capital of Slovenia, is also an important industrial center.

SLOVENIA
Government: Republic
Capital: Ljubljana
Area: 7,800 sq. mi.
Population: 1,930,132
Languages: Slovenian and Serbo-Croatian
Currency: Tolar

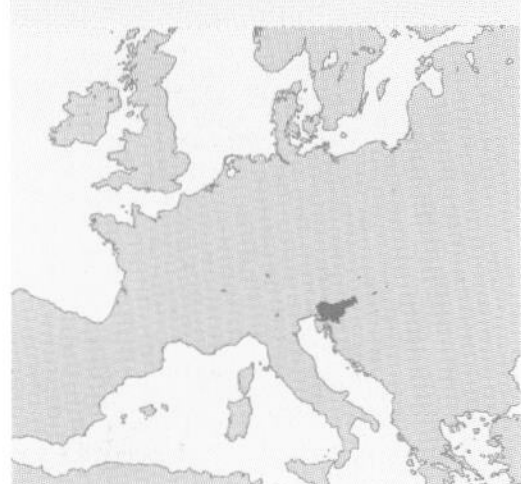

Smell

Smell is an important sense like **sight** and **hearing**. **Humans beings**, like other **mammals**, smell through the nose. We sniff the **air**, and the scents given off by things around us are picked up by special **cells** in the nose. These cells send messages to the **brain**.

Our sense of smell is useful when we are eating. It helps us **taste** things. It can also let us know when **food** is bad. Most other **animals** have a much better sense of smell than humans. **Dogs** can use their sense of smell to track down and follow prey. **Moths** do not have noses, but they can still smell things. Some male moths can smell a female moth many miles away.

Snail and Slug

Snails are **mollusks** with a coiled **shell** on their backs. There are more than 80,000 types in the world. They live on land, in freshwater, and in the sea. Most snails are less than 1 in. (3cm) long, but one of the largest, the giant land snail, is about 8 in. (20cm) long.

Unlike a snail a slug does not have a large shell on its back. Some slugs have a small, flat shell under their **skin**. Both slugs and snails glide along on a muscular part of their body called the foot, and they both have one or two pairs of tentacles.

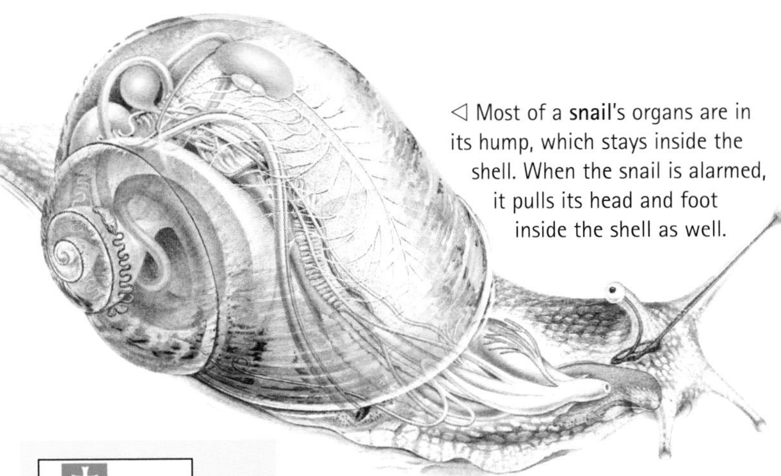

◁ Most of a **snail**'s organs are in its hump, which stays inside the shell. When the snail is alarmed, it pulls its head and foot inside the shell as well.

Snake

Snakes are **reptiles**. They are long and thin and have no legs. They move by wriggling their bodies.

Snakes have dry, smooth **skin**. Most live in warm places. Those that live in colder **climates** spend the winter in **hibernation**.

A few snakes give birth to live young, but most hatch from **eggs**. A female snake lays up to 10 eggs at a time.

Some snakes can inject **poison** into their prey through large **teeth** called fangs. The rattlesnake and the cobra are both poisonous snakes.

The largest snakes are pythons and anacondas, which can grow up to 33 ft. (10m) long. Both of these snakes suffocate their prey. They coil their massive bodies around their victims and squeeze.

Soap

Soap is used for cleaning things. It is made by mixing **fat** or vegetable **oil** with a chemical such as lye. It loosens dirt in clothes and then

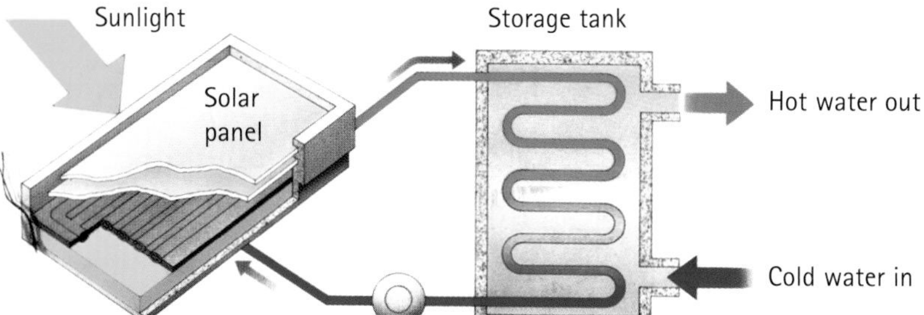

△ Solar panels use **solar energy** to heat water for houses and other buildings.

carries it away. Today chemical cleaners called **detergents** are often used instead. Detergents clean better than soap in hard water.

Soil

Soil is a layer of small **mineral** particles on the surface of **earth**. It covers the **rocks** that earth is made of and is sometimes very thick. Soil is made up of small pieces of rock, the rotted remains of **plants** (humus), **fungi**, **bacteria**, and many tiny **animals**.

Good soil is a mixture of **clay**, silt, and **sand** with plenty of humus. People often add animal manure or chemical **fertilizers** to poor soil, making it richer in certain minerals.

Solar energy

Solar energy is **energy** from the **sun**. It reaches **earth** as **light** and **heat**. Without these things there could be no life on earth.

Only about 15 percent of the sun's energy that reaches earth is absorbed by earth's surface. Much of it bounces back into space. Solar energy can be collected by special panels and **mirrors** and is used to make **electricity**.

Solar system

see **pages 302–303**

Somalia

Somalia is a country in the east of **Africa** on the coast of the **Indian Ocean**. It is a poor country, and most of the people are **nomads**. Low rainfall means that farming is possible only around the Shebelle and Juba **Rivers**. The chief crops are **sugar**, bananas, sorghum, and incense. Since the early 1990s the country has suffered from drought and **civil war**.

SOMALIA
Government: Republic
Capital: Mogadishu
Area: 241,900 sq. mi.
Population: 7,488,773
Languages: Somali, Arabic, Italian, English
Currency: Somali shilling

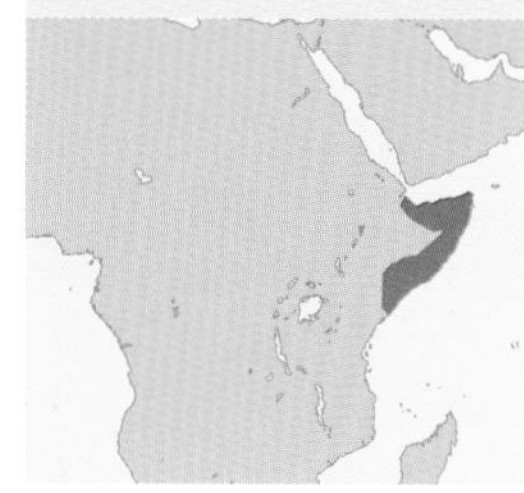

Sonar

Sonar stands for "*so*und *na*vigation and *r*anging." It is used in **ships** to find the depth of anything beneath them. It can measure the depth of the seabed as well as locate **submarines** and schools of **fish**. It works like **radar** except that sonar uses **sound** signals instead of **radio** signals.

The sonar device on a ship turns electric signals into pulses of sound. These travel down through the **water**. Any object in the water struck by the sound pulses sends back an **echo**. The sonar equipment turns the echoes back into electric signals (see **electricity**) and measures the time delay. This indicates where the object is in the water. The depth is shown on a screen.

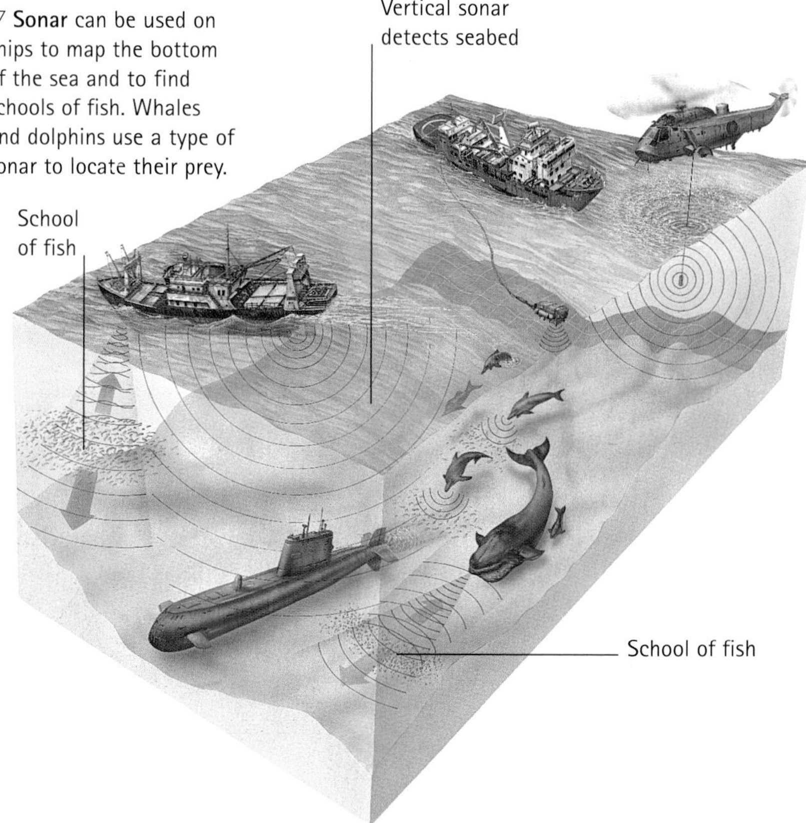

▽ **Sonar** can be used on ships to map the bottom of the sea and to find schools of fish. Whales and dolphins use a type of sonar to locate their prey.

Sound

Sound is made by vibrating objects that send sound **waves** through the **air**. When these vibrations reach our **ears**, we hear them as sounds.

Sound travels through air at about 1,096 ft. per second (334 m/second). This is slow enough for us to see a far-off explosion, for example, before we hear it. The sound takes time to reach us.

The speed of the vibrations makes a difference to the type of sound we hear. If the vibrations are very fast, they are said to be high frequency, and the sound we hear is high-pitched. If they are slow, the sound is said to be low frequency, and the sound we hear is low-pitched.

South Africa

South Africa is a country in southern **Africa**. Most of the country is tableland, a high region of flat-topped hills. Around the coast is a narrow plain. The **climate** is warm and dry.

South Africa is a rich country with factories making a wide range of goods. Mines produce **gold**, **diamonds**, **uranium**, **copper**, **iron**, and other **minerals**. Farms grow large crops of corn, **wheat**, and **fruit**.

Over 43 million people live in South Africa. Almost three fourths are black Africans. There are fewer than five million whites. The whites, who are descended mainly from Dutch and British settlers, used to control the country's **government** and **money**. From the 1940s South Africa had a policy of **apartheid**, or "apartness." This meant that whites and nonwhites lived separately. In 1991 the government ended apartheid, and in 1994 the majority black African National Congress (ANC) won South Africa's first nonracial **elections**. Its leader, **Nelson Mandela**, became **president**. Mandela retired in 1999 and was succeeded by Thabo Mbeki.

South America

see **pages 306–307**

Southeast Asia

Southeast Asia is a large area that lies to the south of **China** and to the east of **India**. It is made up of many countries. Joined to the Asian mainland are **Myanmar** (Burma), **Thailand**, **Malaysia**, **Singapore**, **Cambodia**, **Vietnam**, and **Laos**. Farther east and south lie chains of **islands** that are divided into the countries of the **Philippines**, **Indonesia**, and Brunei.

Southeast Asia is mainly mountainous. It has a tropical **climate** with heavy rainfall in the wet **season**. Most of the people are farmers. They grow **rice**, **tea**, corn, **rubber**, and sugarcane. **Mineral** resources include **oil**, **tin**, and bauxite (**aluminum** ore). Although many Southeast Asian people live in small villages there are also large cities such as Bangkok in Thailand, Kuala Lumpur in Malaysia, Ho Chi Minh City in Vietnam, and Singapore, one of the world's greatest ports.

Southeast Asia is densely populated. Its people belong to a variety of ethnic groups and speak many **languages**. Their lifestyles also vary greatly.

SOUTH AFRICA
Government: Republic
Capitals: Cape Town (legislative); Pretoria (administrative); Bloemfontein (judicial)
Area: 470,900 sq. mi.
Population: 43,586,097
Languages: Afrikaans, English, and nine others
Currency: South African rand

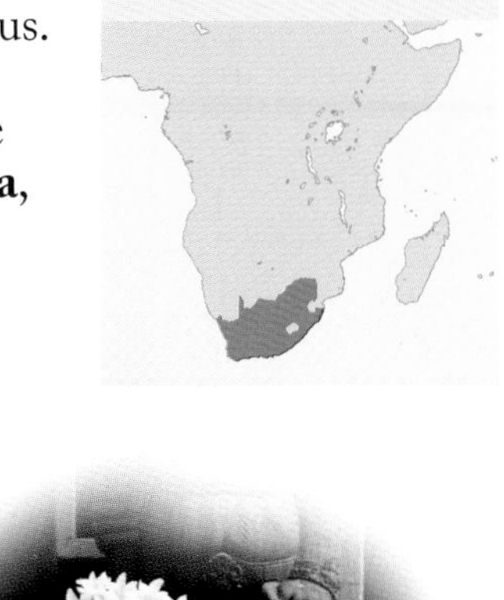

▷ This dancer is from the small Indonesian island of Bali in **Southeast Asia**. Dancers perform in villages across the island. Some dances are religious, while others are for the entertainment of friends, family, and tourists.

SOLAR SYSTEM

The solar system is the Sun and the family of objects that orbit it. They stay together because of the Sun's strong gravity.

THE POWERFUL SUN

The Sun, our local star, is the largest object in the solar system. It is made up of over 95 percent of all the material in the system. The rest is used up in the objects that orbit the Sun. These are nine planets, more than 80 moons, and billions of asteroids and comets. Because of the Sun's great size, it has a powerful gravitational pull. This pull keeps the solar system together and controls the movements of the planets.

BIRTH OF THE SOLAR SYSTEM

About five billion years ago the solar system was born from a great cloud of gas and dust called the solar nebula. This material was left over from the formation of the Milky Way galaxy. The nebula began to condense into a nursery of protostars. One of these protostars started to develop into the young Sun. Gas and dust collected around the sun in a disk. The disk cooled, and grains of solid matter began to freeze and stick together. Over thousands of years these lumps of matter merged to form the planets.

A STABLE SYSTEM

Little has changed in the solar system over the past four billion years. The Sun has brightened slightly and a few comets and asteroids have crashed, but the nine planets have remained in stable orbits. Only Earth has changed significantly as life developed on its surface.

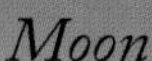

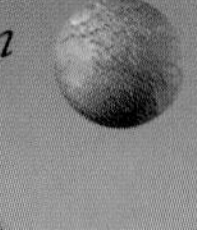

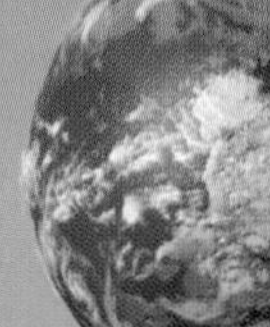

Mercury

Venus

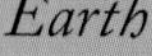

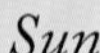

Mars

Asteroids

ROCKY WORLDS AND GAS GIANTS

Most of the matter from which the planets formed consisted of hydrogen and helium. The planets closest to the Sun—Mercury, Venus, Earth, and Mars—were too warm to hold onto these plentiful light gases. Instead they became small worlds of rock and metal. Farther from the Sun where temperatures were very low the planets attracted huge amounts of hydrogen and helium. They became the gas giants Jupiter, Saturn, Uranus, and Neptune. Pluto is the smallest planet and is the farthest from the Sun. It is more like a moon than a major planet. Some astronomers believe that there is a tenth planet, known as Planet X, that is yet to be discovered.

THE PLANETS OF THE SOLAR SYSTEM

Name	Av. distance from sun (million mi.)	Diameter (mi.)	Length of day	Length of year	Moons
Mercury	36	3,024	59 days	88 days	0
Venus	67	7,504	243 days	225 days	0
Earth	93.8	7,883	23 hrs., 56 mins.	365.26 days	1
Mars	141	4,212	24 hrs., 37 mins.	687 days	2
Jupiter	482	88,164	9 hrs., 50 mins.	11.9 years	28
Saturn	885	74,524	10 hrs., 14 mins.	29.5 years	23
Uranus	1,780	31,693	17 hrs. 14 mins.	84 years	21
Neptune	2,788	30,008	18 hrs.	164.8 years	8
Pluto	3,658	1,860	6 days, 9 hrs.	247.7 years	1

DISTANT SOLAR SYSTEMS

There are many more stars like the Sun in the universe. Astronomers have always thought it was possible that one of these had a system of planets orbiting around it. But the stars are so distant and so bright that detecting a dull planet close to a star was impossible for a long time.

During the 1980s astronomers discovered the first stars surrounded by disks of gas and dust. A decade later the first solar systems other than our own were discovered. The first was in 1995 around a star called 51 Pegasi. The planet is at least 150 times larger than Earth and 20 times closer to its star than Earth is to the Sun. It orbits every 4.2 days.

Around 15 other stars with planets have now been found. Astronomers cannot see the planets directly, but they can detect a small wobble in the stars. This is produced by the pull of the planet's gravity as it orbits around the star.

ASTEROIDS AND COMETS

Between the orbits of Mars and Jupiter is a gigantic belt made up of more than 4,000 lumps of rock. These are called asteroids. They range in size from a few feet across to the biggest, called Ceres, which is about 620 mi. (1,000km) across. The outer edge of our solar system is marked by a huge cloud of billions of frozen comets called the Oort Cloud. Scientists think the cloud may be leftover debris from when the solar system formed.

SEE ALSO
Asteroid, Astronomy, Comet, Earth, Eclipse, Galaxy, Gravity, Jupiter, Mars, Mercury, Meteor, Milky Way, Moon, Neptune, Planet, Pluto, Saturn, Solar energy, Universe, Uranus, Venus

△ Supply planes land at the **South Pole** almost every day. No people live permanently in Antarctica, but research bases are visited by teams of scientists.

South Pole

The South Pole is the point on a **map** that marks the southern end of **earth**'s axis. The **North Pole** marks the northern end. The South Pole lies among frozen **mountains** in the middle of the **Antarctic**. The first person to journey to the pole was the Norwegian **explorer** Roald **Amundsen** (1872–1928) in December 1911.

In 1956 the **United States** set up a scientific base at the South Pole. They called it the Amundsen-Scott Station.

Soviet Union (former)

The huge area that was the Soviet Union in 1990 is now a complex of independent states. The three **Baltic States**—Latvia, Lithuania, and Estonia—declared their independence from the Soviet Union in 1991.

By 1992, 11 of the remaining **republics** that had formerly made up the Soviet Union had become members of the Commonwealth of Independent States (CIS). They were: Armenia, Azerbaijan, Belarus, Kazakhstan, Kyrgyzstan, Moldova, **Russia**, Tajikistan, Turkmenistan, **Ukraine,** and Uzbekistan. Georgia, the final former Soviet republic, joined later. However, each country is now fully independent with its own **government**, military, and **economic** system. The CIS has been dominated economically and militarily by Russia under the leadership of Boris Yeltsin (b. 1931) and, from 2000, Vladimir Putin (born 1952).

Before 1922 the Soviet Union was called Russia. It was ruled by czars, or emperors. After a **revolution** in 1917 a Communist government took over (see **communism**) led by Vladimir **Lenin**. Russia was nearly destroyed by a **civil war** between the Communists and their enemies. The Communists won and began to turn the Soviet Union into a great industrial nation.

During **World War II** the Soviets occupied **Hungary**, **Bulgaria**, **Romania**, **Czechoslovakia**, **Poland**, and part of **Germany**. Communist governments closely tied to the Soviet Union were set up in these countries after the war.

From the 1950s the **United States** and the Soviet Union grew to distrust each other, and the Cold War developed. Under its last leader, Mikhail **Gorbachev** (b. 1931), the Soviet Union entered a period of change and unrest. When the country began to break apart in 1991, the Communist Party was disbanded. **Food** shortages became widespread as the economy worsened.

The former Soviet states are rich in **minerals**. They have large deposits of **coal**, **oil**, natural **gas**, **iron**, **lead**, chromium, and manganese. Farmers grow a variety of crops, including **wheat**, rye, and barley. They also grow **vegetables**, **fruit**, **tea**, and **cotton**. **Fishing** and forestry are also important.

Space exploration

see **pages 310–311**

SPAIN
Government: Constitutional monarchy
Capital: Madrid
Area: 192,600 sq. mi.
Population: 40,037,995
Language: Spanish
Currency: Euro

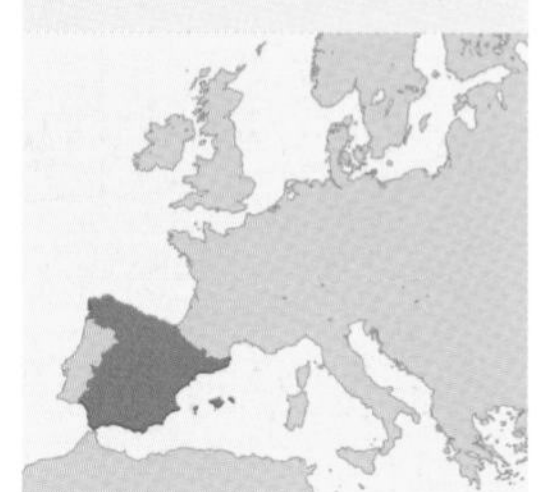

Spain

Spain lies in southwest **Europe** beyond the **Pyrenees**. Most of the country is covered by high plains and **mountains** with a low plain around the coast. The highlands have hot summers, cold winters, and little **rain**. The coast is milder and wetter, especially in the north.

Many people work on farms, growing potatoes, **wheat**, grapes, olives, and **fruits**. **Wine**, olive **oil**, and oranges are exported. Many Spaniards who live on the coast are fishermen. Others work in the tourist trade. Each year millions of tourists visit Spain to enjoy its sunny beaches. The two main industrial areas are around Bilbao in the north and Barcelona in the northeast.

Spectrum

Where do the **colors** in a **rainbow** come from? The answer was found in 1666 when Sir Isaac **Newton** put a triangle-shaped block of glass, called a prism, in front of a beam of sunlight. The prism bent the **light** and separated it into the different colors of the rainbow. Newton showed that sunlight is made up of different colors—a spectrum of colors. Sunlight is white because it contains all of the colors of the rainbow mixed together.

The spectrum of light is only one small part of the whole electromagnetic spectrum. This is arranged according to the wavelength (distance between **waves**) and frequency (number of waves per second) of the waves. **Radio** waves have the lowest frequency and the longest wavelength. Gamma rays have the highest frequency and shortest wavelength. In between these come **ultraviolet** rays and **X rays**.

Speech

Once the only sounds people could make were grunts and yells. Then over tens of thousands of years people learned to form words. **Languages** slowly developed.

Speech sounds are made by **air** from the **lungs** passing around two membranes called vocal cords. We change the pitch of the sound by altering the tension of the vocal cords just as the pitch of a **guitar** can be altered by tightening or loosening the strings. By changing the shape of the passages in our throat, mouth, and nose and by using our **tongue**, we can alter the sounds produced. This allows us to make the words of speech.

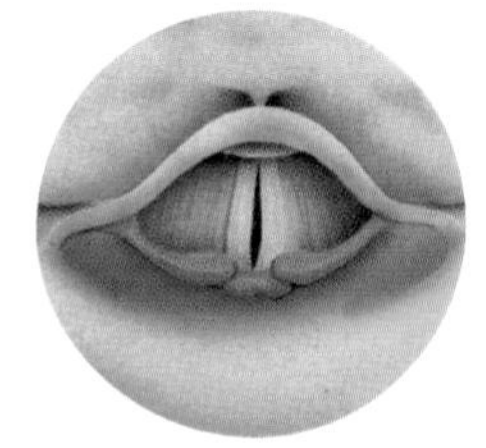

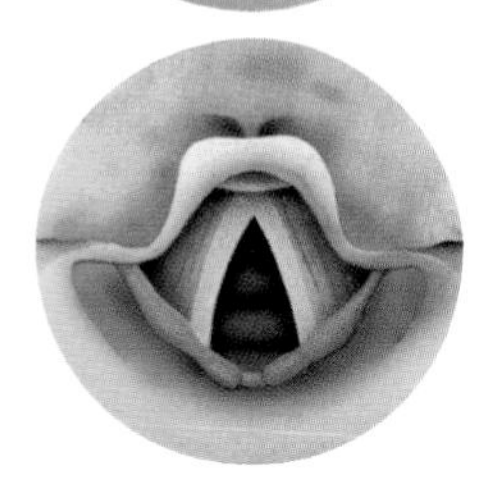

△ In **speech** the vocal cords are tightened and loosened. When the vocal cords are relaxed (top), they produce low notes. When they are taut (bottom), the vocal cords produce high notes.

Spice

Pepper, ginger, cloves, cinnamon, and nutmeg are common spices. Spices have a strong **taste** and **smell** and are used to flavor **foods** and drinks. They are the dried parts of **plants**, usually ground into a powder. Most spice plants grow in hot places such as **Africa**, **India**, and **Southeast Asia**.

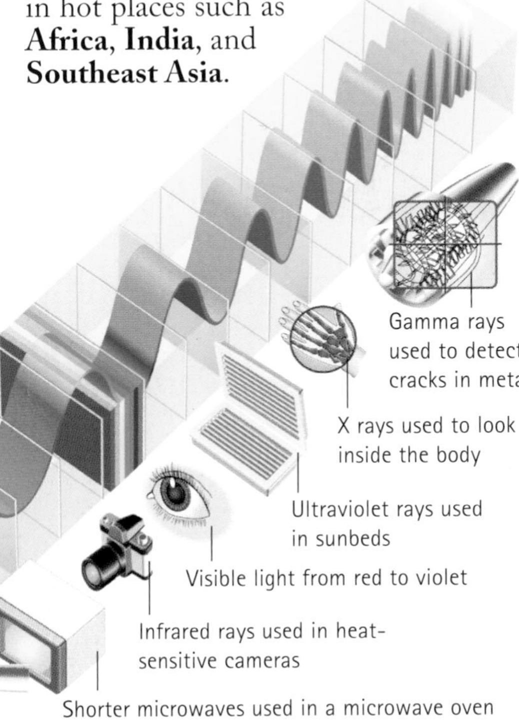

▽ The electromagnetic **spectrum** covers a huge range of energy waves. The only waves that humans can see are light waves, but unseen waves are around us all the time. Different wavelengths of the electromagnetic spectrum are used for different things and have many different effects.

SOUTH AMERICA

South America is the world's fourth largest continent. It stretches from Colombia in the north to the southernmost tip of Chile. It contains the world's longest mountain range and its largest area of rain forest.

▷ *Skilled cowboys, called gauchos, herd their cattle on the vast grasslands of Argentina.*

MOUNTAINS AND RAIN FOREST

South America has an amazing variety of landscapes. The Andes mountain range runs along the Pacific coast for over 5,000 mi. (8,000km). It includes the continent's highest peak, Mount Aconcagua in Argentina, which is 22,829 ft. (6,960m) above sea level. High in the Andes is the starting point of the Amazon River, one of the world's greatest waterways, which travels for 4,055 mi. (6,540km) across the continent before emptying into the Atlantic Ocean in Brazil. The Amazon Basin is an area that includes a huge region of tropical rain forest, which is home to an enormous variety of plant and animal life. This important natural habitat is being reduced in size every day as a result of deforestation.

GRASSLANDS AND COLD DESERTS

Although much of the east of the continent is made up of lush jungle there are immense regions of grassland farther south. On the grasslands of Argentina and Venezuela there are huge cattle ranches and fertile arable land. South America also has cold desert areas—the Atacama desert in northern Chile is one of the world's driest places. In the far south of the continent lies the Patagonian desert in Argentina and Chile, a desolate and inhospitable region.

△ *Fishermen on coasts of the Pacific Ocean fish for anchovies. Sardines and tuna are also canned for export worldwide.*

PEOPLE THROUGH THE AGES

The earliest settlers in South America were the Native Americans. There is evidence that they came across the Bering Straits from Asia and migrated through North America into South America by c. 9000 B.C. These people formed some of the most extraordinary ancient civilizations in the world, including those of the Aztecs and Incas. These two civilizations were destroyed by invading Europeans in the 1500s.

△ *La Boca, with its colorful houses, is the artists' quarter of Buenos Aires, Argentina. The area was settled by Italians from Genoa in the 1800s.*

CONQUEST AND PLUNDER

In the late 1500s Europeans conquered much of South America. They were attracted by the gold and other precious minerals they found there. European adventurers plundered much of the continent's riches. They also transmitted many European diseases to the native people, many of whom died after contact with the invaders.

TODAY'S PEOPLES

There are 12 independent countries in South America. The largest of these, Brazil, takes up half the continent, including most of the Amazon Basin. Most of the peoples of South America speak Spanish, reflecting their Spanish colonial past. However, in Brazil, Portuguese (the language of its conquerors) is the national language, and in Guyana, English is spoken. In Andean countries, such as Bolivia and Peru, native peoples still make up a large part of the population. Argentina's population is largely white, while Brazil's population includes many descendants of African slaves.

NATURAL RESOURCES

The continent is rich in a variety of natural resources. The Andes mountains are full of minerals such as silver in Peru, tin in Bolivia, and copper in Chile. Venezuela is a source of large amounts of oil. Brazil produces one third of all the world's coffee, and the grasslands of Argentina, Uruguay, and Paraguay support the sheep and cattle that feed much of the continent. Many life-saving medicines have been developed from rain forest plants.

CULTURE AND SPORT

South America is home to some of the world's most vibrant and exciting peoples and cultures. South Americans adore soccer, and two of the world's greatest national teams, the Brazilians and the Argentinians, are South American. Pelé, one of the greatest soccer players of all time, played for Brazil.

Brazil is also the venue for the world's biggest carnival in Rio de Janeiro. During the carnival celebrations in February or March millions of people take to the streets to celebrate and watch the amazing processions as they move through the city. It is by far the largest single party in the world.

◁ *Many native peoples in remote areas follow ancient ways of life. This Amazonian boy is hunting by shooting a poison arrow.*

△ *An imposing statue of Christ stands high above Rio de Janeiro in Brazil.*

SOUTH AMERICA FACT FILE
Area: 6,942,000 sq. mi.
Highest mountain: Aconcagua (22,834 ft.)
Lowest point: Peninsula Valdes, Argentina (131 ft. below sea level)
Largest lake: Maracaibo (16,300 sq. mi.)
Longest river: Amazon (3,991 mi.)
Largest desert: Atacama
Number of countries: 12
Largest country: Brazil
Smallest country: Uruguay
Largest city: Sáo Paulo, Brazil (17 million)
Total population: 350 million

SEE ALSO
Amazon River, Andes, Argentina, Aztecs, Bolivia, Brazil, Chile, Ecuador, Equator, Inca, Medicine, Minerals, Paraguay, Peru, Rain forest, Sports, Uruguay, Venezuela

△ Bird-eating **spiders** are among the largest spiders in the world with a leg span of up to 10 in. (25cm). All spiders have two body parts—an abdomen (back end) and a cephalothorax (head and chest). The brain and stomach are in the cephalothorax. The heart and silk spinners are in the abdomen.

Spider

Spiders are small **animals**. They are not **insects**, although many people think they are. An insect has six legs and a body made up of three parts. A spider has eight legs and a body with two parts.

All spiders spin **silk** threads. Many of them use the threads to make a sticky web for catching insects. Others are hunters and chase their prey; some lie in wait and then pounce. When a spider catches something, it stuns or kills it with a poisonous bite. All spiders can inject **poison**, but in most cases it does not hurt **human beings**.

There are about 30,000 types of spiders. The comb-footed spider is no larger than a pinhead, but some **bird**-eating spiders can grow up to 10 in. (25cm) across. Some spiders live for only one year, while others live for 20 years. Some mate in winter, and others mate in spring. Tiny spiders lay a few **eggs**, sometimes only one, but the largest lay up to 2,000.

△ Prairie dogs are ground **squirrels** that live in large groups in huge burrow systems. Members of the group take turns to do jobs that benefit the whole group. This prairie dog is standing guard at the entrance to its burrow.

Sponge

A sponge is a simple **water animal.** Most sponges live in warm seas and **oceans**, but some are found in cold seas. A few are freshwater creatures.

A sponge's body is a mass of jellylike flesh full of tiny tubes, which lead to small surface holes. Water, carrying **oxygen** and pieces of **food**, flows in through the holes and travels along the tubes. This is how the animal breathes and feeds. Waste products are taken away through other tubes.

When a sponge dies, the flesh rots, and the **skeleton** is left behind. Some skeletons are soft and are used in homes as bath or kitchen sponges. Today most sponges used at home are made from **rubber** or **plastic**.

Sports *see* pages 314–315

Squid

Squid are **mollusks** related to the **octopus**. Many live in the deep sea by day but rise to feed at night. A squid uses its 10 tentacles to catch **fish** and feed them into its beaklike mouth. Some are the size of a thumb, but the giant squid grows up to 40 ft. (12m) in length.

Squirrel

Squirrels are **rodents** that are active during the day unlike most small **mammals**. The most common squirrel in the **U.S.** is the red squirrel.

Tree squirrels have sharp claws for climbing and a long, bushy tail for balance. They can leap 10 ft. (3m) from tree to tree. Flying squirrels jump up to 98 ft. (30m). They have flaps of **skin** between their front and back legs. When a flying squirrel jumps and spreads its limbs, the flaps form a parachute. Both tree squirrels and flying squirrels feed on **leaves**, twigs, and **seeds**.

Ground squirrels live in underground burrows. They include prairie dogs, chipmunks, and woodchucks, which all live in **North America**.

Sri Lanka

Sri Lanka is an **island** country off the southern tip of **India**. Until 1972

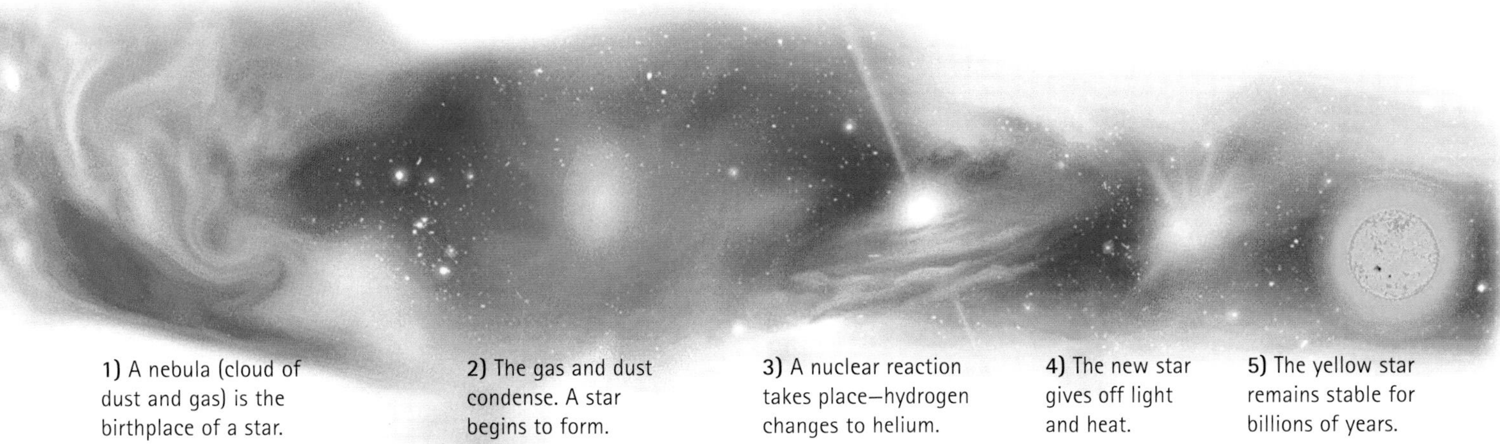

Sri Lanka was called Ceylon. The island is near the **equator** so the **climate** is tropical. Most of the **trees** and shrubs have been cleared away to make room for crops, but there are still bamboo and **palm** trees. **Elephants**, **leopards**, **monkeys**, **snakes**, and colorful **birds** live in the wilder areas. Sri Lanka's crops include **tea**, **rubber**, and coconuts.

There is continuing unrest between the ruling Sinhalese, who are mainly Buddhist (see **Buddhism**), and the Tamils, who are mainly Hindu (see **Hinduism**).

Stalin, Joseph

Joseph Stalin (1879–1953) ruled the **Soviet Union** from 1929 to 1953. After Vladamir **Lenin** died in 1924 Stalin made the Soviet Union one of the two most powerful nations in the world. He was a **dictator** who killed or imprisoned millions who disliked him or disagreed with his form of **communism**.

Stamp

A stamp can be a special mark or a piece of printed **paper** with a sticky back. A passport must bear the correct **government** stamp. Postage stamps are stuck on letters and packages to be mailed by the post office. Each nation has its own postage stamps.

Star

The stars we can see from **Earth** are just a few of the many billions scattered through space. Stars look small because they are so far away, but most are huge, fiery balls of **gas** like the **Sun**.

Stars begin as clouds of gas. **Gravity** pulls the gas particles in toward the middle of each cloud. There the particles collide and heat up. More and more particles press in until a star forms. **Hydrogen** atoms inside the star change into helium **atoms** by a process called nuclear fusion. This gives off **nuclear energy**, which makes the star glow brightly.

When all of the hydrogen at the center of a star is used up, the outer layers swell until the star is much larger than before. Astronomers (see **astronomy**) call these stars red giants. Red giants later shrink into tiny, white-hot stars called white dwarfs. In time these cool and fade into the darkness of space.

Starch

Starch is a substance found in **plants**. **Cereals** are particularly rich in starch. Other plants that contain starch are peas, beans, and potatoes. Starch is a carbohydrate, which means that it is made up of **carbon**, **oxygen**, and **hydrogen**, the same ingredients found in **sugar**. It is important to have starch in our diet because it gives us **energy**.

Pure starch is a white powder used in the making of many **food** products. It is also used to give some types of **paper** a shiny coating and to stiffen **cottons**, linens, and other materials.

△ A **star** forms from a cloud of gas and dust and then shines steadily for billions of years.

SRI LANKA
Government: Republic
Capital: Colombo
Area: 25,000 sq. mi.
Population: 19,408,635
Languages: Sinhala, Tamil, English
Currency: Sri Lankan rupee

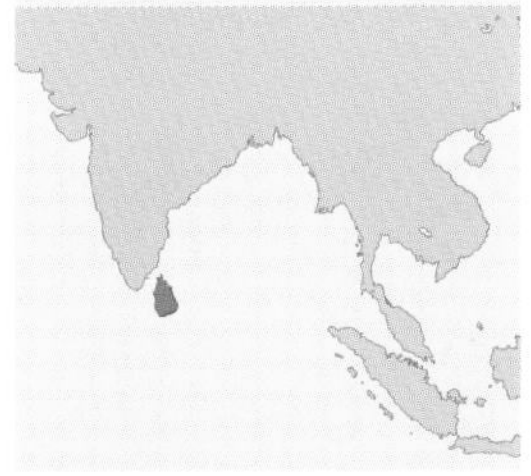

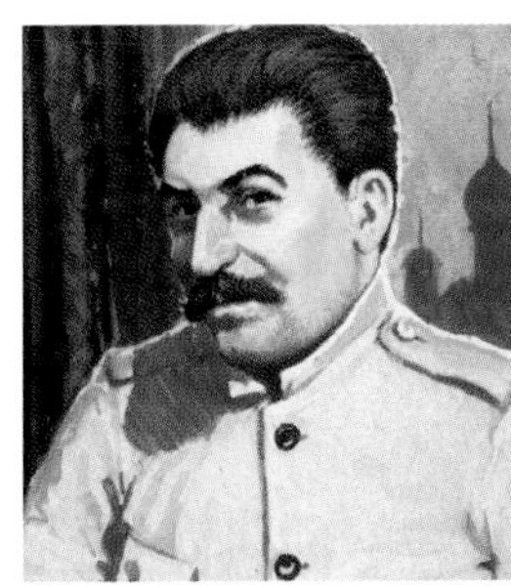

△ Joseph **Stalin** ruled the Soviet Union as a dictator. The name Stalin means "man of steel."

SPACE EXPLORATION

Space exploration began in 1957 with the launch of the first artificial satellite. The U.S. put the first man on the Moon in 1969. Today probes search ever farther throughout the universe, and the first tourist space flights have taken place.

△ *After intense competition between the Americans and Soviets, U.S. astronaut Neil Armstrong walked on the Moon in 1969.*

WARLIKE BEGINNINGS

The technology that fueled early space exploration originated in World War II with the development of an unpiloted rocket engine, the German V2 rocket. After the war many of Germany's best scientists emigrated to the **United States**. As the Cold War between the United States and the Soviet Union escalated both superpowers wanted to develop the capability to launch a decisive strike from space.

The United States and the Soviet Union raced to become the first to launch a satellite into space. They built on the technology of the V2 rocket but on a greater scale.

On October 4, 1957 the Soviets successfully sent a satellite, *Sputnik*, into orbit. The radio messages it relayed back to Earth were proof of the Soviet Union's achievement.

FIRST MAN IN SPACE

In the U.S., NASA (the National Aeronautics and Space Administration) started to recruit pilots to train as astronauts. Seven men were chosen who were excited to be the first humans in space. But on April 12, 1961 the Soviet Union strengthened their lead when they launched the cosmonaut (Soviet astronaut) Yuri Gagarin into orbit around Earth. The first words uttered by a human in space were, "I see Earth. It's so beautiful."

The United States was not far behind and on May 5, 1961 launched astronaut Alan Shepard into orbit in the *Mercury* space capsule. On May 25, 1961 U.S. President John F. Kennedy, worried at the lack of progress made by the Americans, promised that the U.S. would put a man on the Moon by the end of the decade.

▷ *Space rockets are made of three parts, or stages, each with its own fuel tank. The first stage falls away as the rocket leaves Earth's atmosphere, and the second is dropped at 118 mi. (190km).*

TARGETING THE MOON

The fact that the U.S. had lost the race to put the first human in space made them all the more determined to be the first to the Moon. By the late 1960s the U.S. was ready to attempt a moon landing.

ONE GIANT LEAP

Following numerous setbacks the U.S. scientists and engineers finally succeeded with *Apollo 11.* On July 20, 1969 astronaut Neil Armstrong became the first human to step on the surface of the Moon. His words have become legendary, "One small step for man, one giant leap for mankind." His steps were watched on TV by millions around the world.

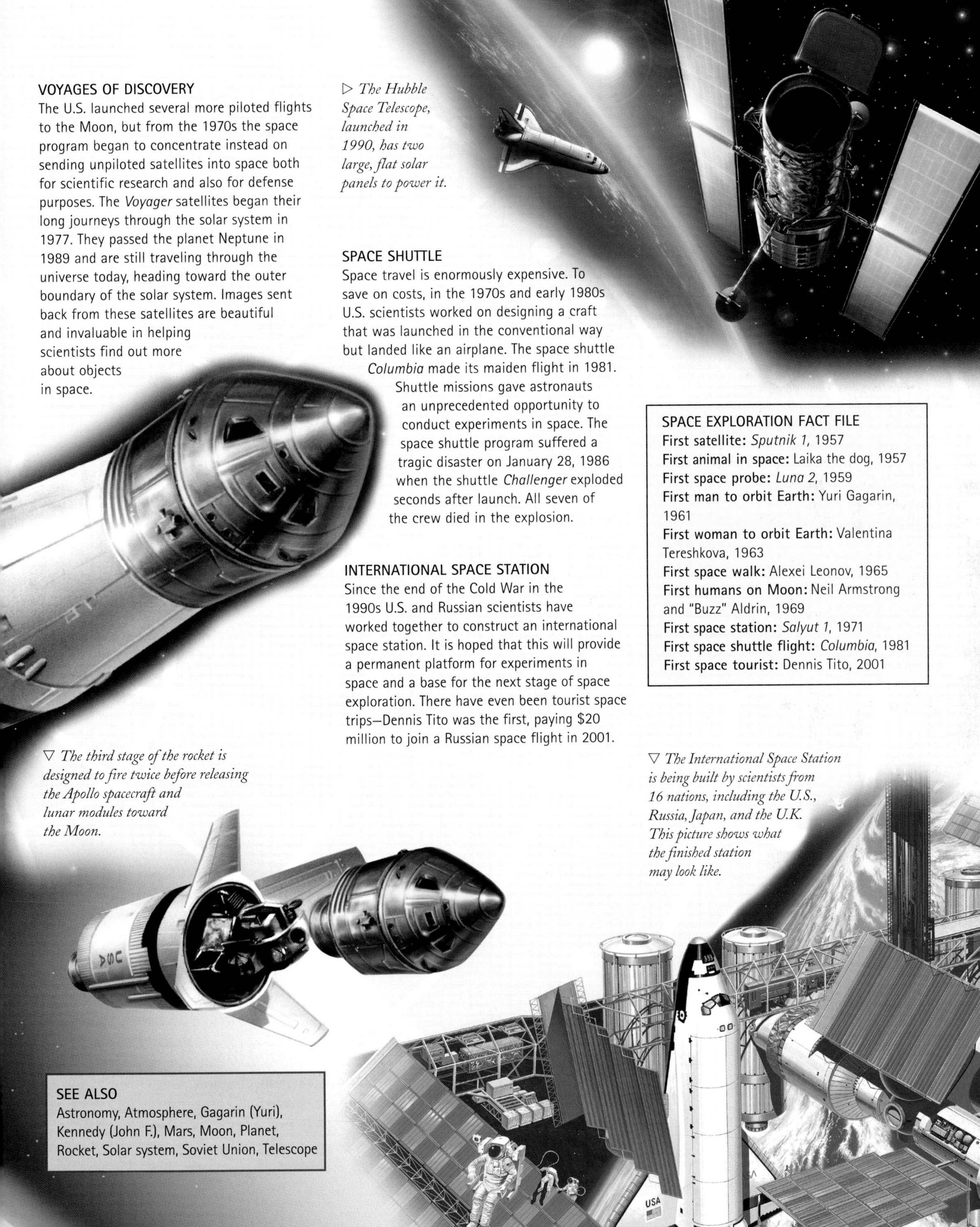

VOYAGES OF DISCOVERY

The U.S. launched several more piloted flights to the Moon, but from the 1970s the space program began to concentrate instead on sending unpiloted satellites into space both for scientific research and also for defense purposes. The *Voyager* satellites began their long journeys through the solar system in 1977. They passed the planet Neptune in 1989 and are still traveling through the universe today, heading toward the outer boundary of the solar system. Images sent back from these satellites are beautiful and invaluable in helping scientists find out more about objects in space.

▷ *The Hubble Space Telescope, launched in 1990, has two large, flat solar panels to power it.*

SPACE SHUTTLE

Space travel is enormously expensive. To save on costs, in the 1970s and early 1980s U.S. scientists worked on designing a craft that was launched in the conventional way but landed like an airplane. The space shuttle *Columbia* made its maiden flight in 1981. Shuttle missions gave astronauts an unprecedented opportunity to conduct experiments in space. The space shuttle program suffered a tragic disaster on January 28, 1986 when the shuttle *Challenger* exploded seconds after launch. All seven of the crew died in the explosion.

INTERNATIONAL SPACE STATION

Since the end of the Cold War in the 1990s U.S. and Russian scientists have worked together to construct an international space station. It is hoped that this will provide a permanent platform for experiments in space and a base for the next stage of space exploration. There have even been tourist space trips—Dennis Tito was the first, paying $20 million to join a Russian space flight in 2001.

SPACE EXPLORATION FACT FILE

First satellite: *Sputnik 1*, 1957
First animal in space: Laika the dog, 1957
First space probe: *Luna 2*, 1959
First man to orbit Earth: Yuri Gagarin, 1961
First woman to orbit Earth: Valentina Tereshkova, 1963
First space walk: Alexei Leonov, 1965
First humans on Moon: Neil Armstrong and "Buzz" Aldrin, 1969
First space station: *Salyut 1*, 1971
First space shuttle flight: *Columbia*, 1981
First space tourist: Dennis Tito, 2001

▽ *The third stage of the rocket is designed to fire twice before releasing the Apollo spacecraft and lunar modules toward the Moon.*

▽ *The International Space Station is being built by scientists from 16 nations, including the U.S., Russia, Japan, and the U.K. This picture shows what the finished station may look like.*

SEE ALSO

Astronomy, Atmosphere, Gagarin (Yuri), Kennedy (John F.), Mars, Moon, Planet, Rocket, Solar system, Soviet Union, Telescope

△ Common **starfish** have five arms, which can regrow if they are cut off. A starfish has no head or brain although it has a network of nerves in its body. The mouth is on the underside.

Starfish

Starfish are **animals** that live on the seabed. Most have five arms that stick out like the spokes of a wheel. Starfish do not have backbones, but they do have **skeletons** made up of bony plates. They move slowly on tiny tube feet arranged along the undersides of their arms.

A starfish can open and eat a mollusk. It grips both halves of the mollusk's **shell** with its tube feet and then pulls the shell open. The starfish pushes part of its **stomach** out of its mouth, which is under the middle of its body. The stomach slips inside the cockle shell and digests the mollusk's soft body.

Steam engine

Boiling **water** turns into steam. Steam will fill 1,700 times more space than the water that it came from. So if steam is squashed into a small container, it presses hard against the sides. If one side is free to move, the steam pressure will push it out.

In the 1700s British inventors, such as Thomas Newcomen (1663–1729), used this fact to build **engines** powered by steam. In Newcomen's engine a furnace heated water in a boiler. The water gave off steam that pushed a piston up inside a cylinder. When the steam cooled and turned back to water, **air** pressed the piston down again. The engine was used to pump water from flooded mines.

James **Watt** built a more powerful engine where steam pushed the piston first one way and then the other. Rods from the piston spun a **wheel**. By the early 1800s such engines were moving heavy loads faster than **horses** could.

Steam engines powered factory machines that made the **Industrial Revolution** possible. They also powered locomotives and steamships.

The internal combustion engine has largely taken the place of steam engines. But many **ships'** propellers and power plant **generators** are powered by steam that spins wheels called **turbines**.

▽ Until the 1950s most trains were hauled by locomotives powered by **steam engines**. This picture shows the world's fastest steam engine, the *Mallard*. In 1938 this streamlined locomotive reached a record speed of 124.6 mph (201 km/h).

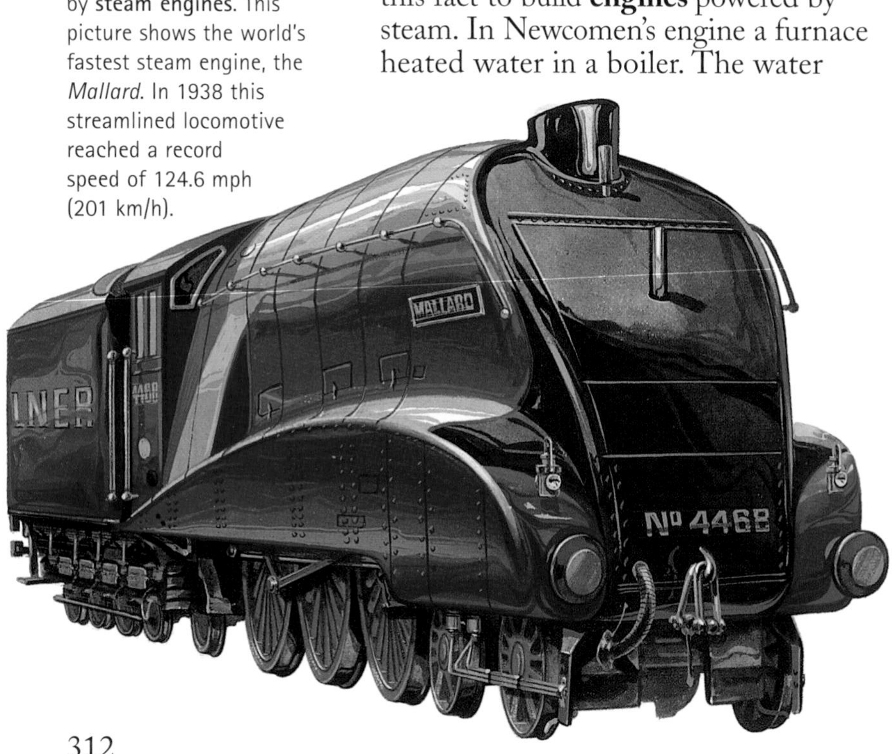

Steel *see* Iron and Steel

Stevenson, Robert Louis

Robert Louis Stevenson (1850–1894) was a Scottish author of adventure stories such as *Treasure Island*, an exciting tale about a hunt for pirate treasures, and *Kidnapped*, an adventure story set in the wilds of **Scotland** in the 1700s. Stevenson also wrote *A Child's Garden of Verses*, a collection of poems especially for children.

Stock exchange

A stock exchange is a place where people called stockbrokers buy and sell stocks and shares—pieces of paper that show that someone owns a share in a **company**. A company's stock tends to cost more if the company does well and gets cheaper if it does badly. People buy stock hoping to sell it at a higher price later. Millions of stocks change hands each day in the exchanges of **London**, **New York**, and **Tokyo**.

Stomach

The human stomach is a muscular bag that is open at both ends and shaped like a fat letter "J." It plays an important part in the **digestion** of **food**.

When you eat a meal, food travels down the throat to the stomach. Juices produced in the stomach kill **germs** in the food. They also moisten and start to break down the food. Stomach **muscles** churn the mixture and then force it into tubes called the small intestine.

Stone Age

The Stone Age was the long period of time before people learned how to make **metal** tools. Stone Age people used stone, **wood**, and **bone** instead of metal. The Stone Age probably began more than three million years ago. It ended when the **Bronze Age** began in **Iraq** and **Egypt** around 5,000 years ago.

The Stone Age had three parts: Old, Middle, and New. In the **Middle East** the Old Stone Age lasted until 10,000 years ago. When it began, hunters could barely chip a stone to sharpen it. When the Old Stone Age ended, people had learned to chip **flint** into knives, spearheads, and scrapers.

In the Middle Stone Age hunters used tiny flakes of flint in arrows and harpoons.

The New Stone Age began in the Middle East around 9,000 years ago. New Stone Age people made smooth ax heads of ground stone. During this period **farming** took over from hunting as the main way of collecting **food**.

Stonehenge

Stonehenge is a huge prehistoric temple on Salisbury Plain in southern **England**. The main part is a huge circle of standing stones. Each is more than twice as tall as an average person and weighs nearly 30 tons. Flat stones were laid across the tops of the standing stones to form a ring. Inside the ring stood smaller stones and a large block that may have been an altar. The large stones were raised 3,500 years ago, but some parts are older.

Stork

These large **birds** have long beaks and legs. They wade into swamps to catch **fish** and **frogs**. Some storks prefer to feed on dead **animals**. More than a dozen types of storks live in the warm parts of the world.

The white stork is the best-known species. In the summer white storks nest in **Europe** and central **Asia**. In the fall they fly south. Storks soon become tired of flapping their wings so they prefer to soar and glide.

△ In northern and Eastern **Europe** pairs of white **storks** often build their **nests** on rooftops. The female usually lays four **eggs**, which take about five weeks to hatch.

▷ Archaeologists can tell that some of the huge stones that form **Stonehenge** were dragged from a site over 250 mi. (400km) away. This task must have taken our prehistoric ancestors years to complete.

SPORTS

A sport is a game or activity involving physical skill, usually in competition. Sports are enjoyed by millions of people around the world and provide big-business entertainment.

△ *A discus thrower spins around before releasing the discus from his hand.*

COMPETITION

Hundreds of different sports are played throughout the world, pitting individuals or teams against each other and challenging participants to perform at their physical best. Sports offer fun and exercise for the non-competitive athlete or at an amateur level, while professional sports are a multi-million-dollar business. The stars of many sports, such as basketball's Michael Jordan, golf's Tiger Woods, or soccer's David Beckham, are worldwide celebrities.

In ancient times sporting contests were tests of strength, bravery, or proficiency at the skills needed to hunt, fight, and flee. The ancient Egyptians played forms of handball, hockey, fencing, tug-of-war, and long-distance running. The greatest sporting event of ancient times was the Olympiad held every four years at Olympia in Greece. Today's Olympic Games, featuring dozens of sports and thousands of athletes, is a modern version of this ancient event.

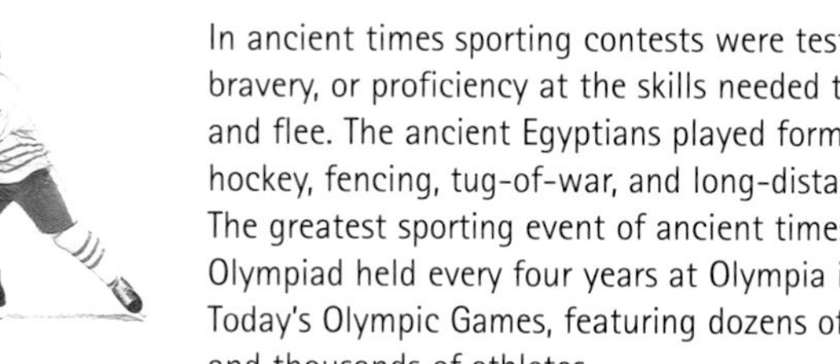

△ *Hockey players speed across the ice and shoot a hard, disk-shaped puck into the goal to score.*

TRACK AND FIELD

Track and field events are held on and around a 1,312-ft. (400-m) -long oval track. Many of the events date from ancient times and involve being the fastest or the strongest—the winner of the 100m sprint is known as the fastest person on earth. Track events include sprints over 100m, 200m, or 400m, races over hurdles, and middle- and long-distance running events. Field events include four throwing events (the discus, the javelin, the shot put, and the hammer throw) and three jumping events (the high jump, long jump, and pole vault).

◁ *Baseball, played in the United States since the 1800s, is one of the world's most popular games. Thousands of people watch the World Series, supporting teams such as the New York Yankees and the Seattle Mariners.*

SOCCER

Soccer is simple to understand and is the most played sport in the world. The full game is played by two 11-per-side teams for two halves of 45 minutes each. Players can use any part of their bodies except their hands and arms to get the ball into the opponent's goal. The one exception is the goalie, who can handle the ball to prevent it from going into the goal. Soccer has been an organized sport since the late 1800s, and by the 1930s over 100 countries had their own soccer competitions. The best soccer players are picked to play for their countries in international competitions such as the European Championships, the African Nations Cup, and the biggest soccer event of all, the World Cup.

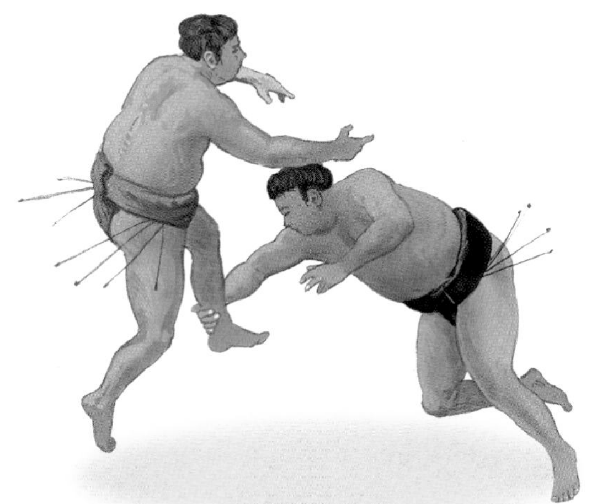

◁ *Influenced by wrestling in both China and Korea, sumo wrestling developed in Japan between 300 and 200 B.C. Amid much ceremony and ritual, the two competitors try to wrestle each other out of the circle.*

◁ *Heading the ball is a useful skill in soccer. Players use their foreheads to direct the ball out of danger, if they are defending, or into the goal if they are on the attack.*

▽ *Basketball is the most popular indoor team sport in the world. The best players, such as Michael Jordan and Magic Johnson, earn huge salaries and are national heroes in the U.S.*

FOOTBALL

Football is a tough contact sport that developed from rugby and soccer. Two teams compete to get the oval-shaped ball over the opponent's end line and score a touchdown. Each team consists of up to 45 players divided into three units—one for offense when their team has possession of the ball, one for defense, and a special team for taking kicks. Players move the ball up the field by running with it or throwing it to a teammate. In the United States professional teams compete during each season to reach the two-team final, the Superbowl.

SEE ALSO
Baseball, Basketball, Boxing, Danger sports, Golf, Gymnastics, Horseback riding, Ice hockey, Marathon, Martial arts, Olympic Games, Rowing, Sailing, Skating, Skiing, Swimming, Table tennis, Tennis, Weightlifting

△ A **submarine**'s smooth shape helps it slip through the water with the least resistance. The submarine is steered by rudders, while its depth is controlled by winglike hydroplanes at the front and back.

Stowe, Harriet Beecher

Harriet Beecher Stowe (1811–1896) was an American author whose most famous **book**, *Uncle Tom's Cabin*, described the suffering of slaves in the south of the **United States**. The novel became a bestseller and played an important part in the struggle to bring an end to **slavery** in the U.S.

Submarine

Submarines are **boats** that can travel under**water**. A submarine floats on the surface when its large ballast tanks are full of **air**. If water is pumped into the tanks, the submarine begins to sink. To come back to the surface compressed air is pumped back into the ballast tanks, forcing the water out.

Early submarines were hand-powered and slow. A steam-powered submarine was invented in the 1870s, but each time it dived the crew had to pull down its chimney and put out the **fire** that heated water to produce steam.

By 1900 the American inventor John P. Holland had built the first truly successful submarine. Gasoline **engines** drove it on the surface. Because gas needs **air** to burn, the boat ran on **battery**-driven **motors** underwater.

In 1955 the first nuclear-powered submarine was invented (see **nuclear energy**). These can travel around the world without having to surface. In 1958 the nuclear submarine *Nautilus* the **United States** Navy made the first submerged crossing under the **North Pole**. The largest modern nuclear submarines weigh more than 20,000 tons and have room for around 150 crew members and 16 nuclear **missiles**.

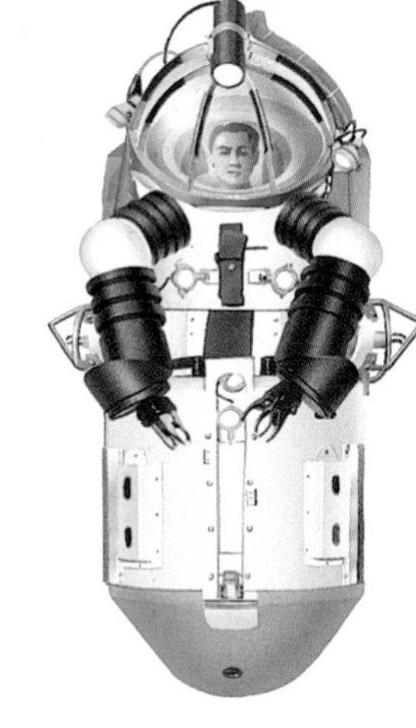

△ This one-person **submarine** can withstand the crushing effect of water pressure. It allows divers to work at a depth of up to 984 ft. (300m).

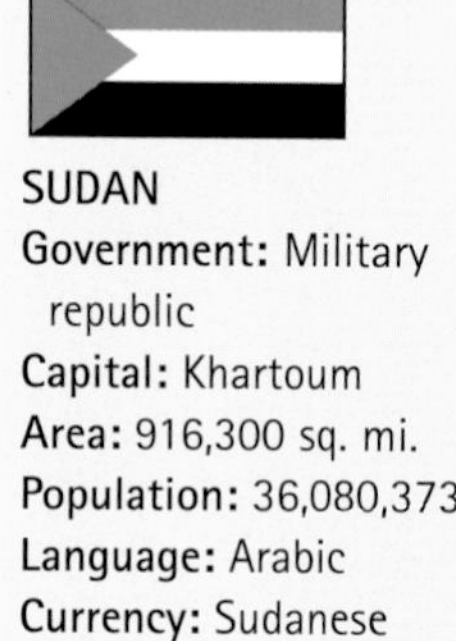

SUDAN
Government: Military republic
Capital: Khartoum
Area: 916,300 sq. mi.
Population: 36,080,373
Language: Arabic
Currency: Sudanese dinar

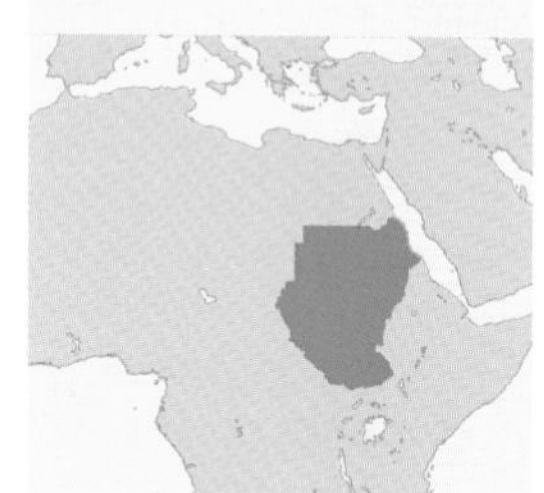

Sudan

Sudan, the largest African nation, is over three times the size of Texas. It is a hot country in northeast **Africa**. **Desert** sprawls across the north, and there are flat grasslands in the center. The south has **forests** and huge swamps.

Most Sudanese people live near the **Nile River**, which flows north across the country. Khartoum is the capital. A **civil war** has been fought between the north and south of the country since 1988. The war, together with severe droughts, is threatening the traditional way of life of many tribes.

Suez Canal

The Suez **Canal** crosses **Egypt** between Port Said on the **Mediterranean Sea** and Suez on the **Red Sea**. It is the world's longest canal that can be used by large **ships**. It measures 99 mi. (160km) from end to end and 197 ft. (60m) across its bed. Ships use it as a shortcut on voyages between **Europe** and **Asia**. This saves them from sailing 5,580 mi. (9,000km) around southern **Africa**.

The canal was begun in 1859 by French engineer Ferdinand de Lesseps (1805–1894). More than 8,000 men, using hundreds of **camels**, worked on it for ten years. **France** and the **United Kingdom** operated the canal until

Egypt took it over in 1956. Sunken ships blocked the canal for eight years after Egypt's **war** with **Israel** in 1967.

Sugar

Sugar is a sweet-tasting **food**. It is an ingredient in ice cream, candy, and soda. We use sugar crystals to sweeten **cereal**, **coffee**, and **tea**. Sugar gives the body **energy** more quickly than any other food, but eating too many sugary foods can cause tooth decay.

Sugar contains **carbon**, **hydrogen**, and **oxygen**. Different groupings of these **atoms** produce different types of sugars. The type we eat most often is known as sucrose.

Every green **plant** produces sugar. Most of the sugar that we use comes from two plants—sugarcane, a type of giant **grass**, and sugar beet, a plant with a thick root that is rich in sugar.

Sulfur

Sulfur is an **element** frequently found as yellow crystals lying at the mouths of **volcanoes** and hot springs. Cabbages, **eggs**, and other **foods** contain some sulfur. **Plants** and **animals** need a little sulfur in order to grow well.

Sulfur is used to make **fertilizer**, **drugs**, gunpowder, and many other useful chemicals.

Sun

The Sun is just one of many millions of **stars** in the **Milky Way**. It is also the center of the **solar system**—the **planets** and their **moons** all whirl around it. The **heat** and **light** given off by the Sun make it possible for **plants** and **animals** to live on **Earth**.

The Sun seems small because it is far from Earth. A spacecraft that took one hour to fly around Earth would need five months to reach the Sun. In fact the Sun is so big that you could fit one million Earths inside it with room to spare. A bucketful of the material that makes up the Sun would weigh much less than a bucketful of **rock** from Earth. But the whole Sun would weigh over 750 times more than all of the planets put together.

The Sun is a huge glowing ball of **gases**. In the middle of the Sun a process called nuclear fusion turns **hydrogen** gas into helium gas. The change releases huge amounts of **nuclear energy**. The Sun beams out this energy in all directions as electromagnetic **waves**. Some of these waves give us heat and light. But there are also **radio** waves, **ultraviolet** rays, **X rays**, and others.

The Sun was formed from a mass of gas and dust five billion years ago. It contains enough **fuel** to keep it glowing for another five billion years.

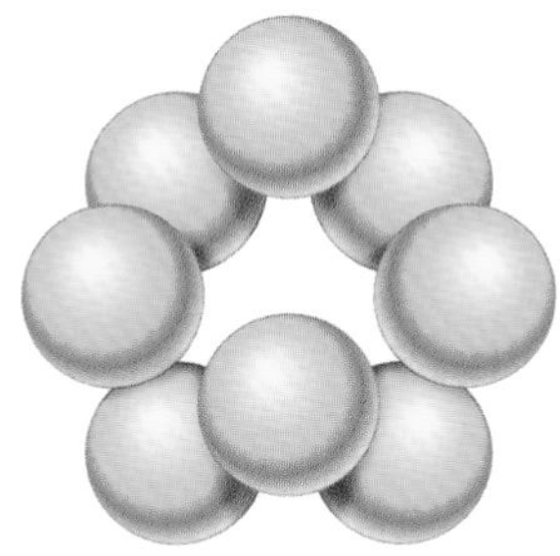

△ **Sulfur** is a bright yellow element. A molecule of sulfur contains eight atoms in a ring.

▽ The shining surface of the **Sun** is called the photosphere. The dark patch is a cooler area called a sunspot.

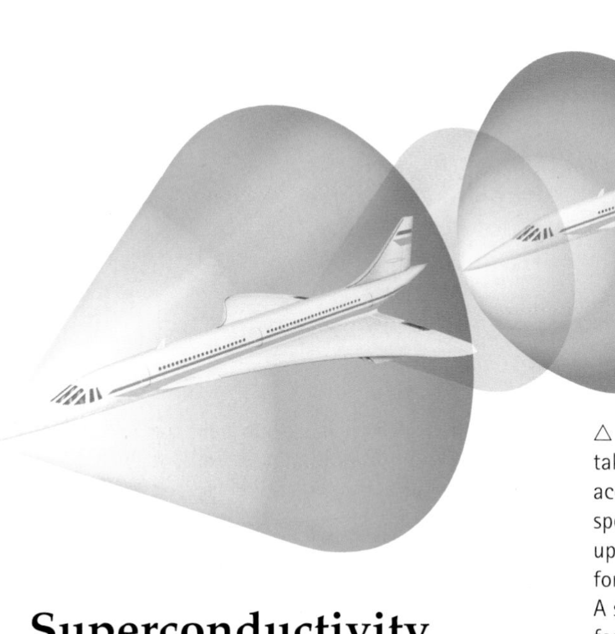

△ **A supersonic flight** takes place when a jet accelerates through the speed of sound. Air piles up in front of the jet, forming a shock wave. A second shock wave forms at the tail. The shock waves reach the ground, making a double bang, or sonic boom, as they pass over.

Superconductivity

Some materials allow **electricity** to flow through them more easily than others. These conductors, such as **copper** and **silver**, have little resistance to electric currents, but they do have some, so the electricity struggling to pass through them makes them warm. In 1911 it was discovered that a **metal** called **mercury** loses all of its electrical resistance when it is cooled to -459.4°F (-273°C)—the coldest possible **temperature**. Mercury became a superconductor, but it was very expensive and difficult to produce such a low temperature.

Today scientists have created ceramic (**clay**-based) materials that superconduct at higher temperatures. They use dry ice (solid **carbon** dioxide) to cool the ceramics to -109.3°F (-78.5°C). Now the race is on to find materials that are superconductors at room temperature. If this is achieved, the whole **electronics** industry will change. **Computers** will become smaller and faster, and **machines** will be much cheaper to produce and run.

Supersonic flight

Supersonic flight means flying faster than the speed at which **sound** travels through the **air**—about 760 mph (1,225 km/h) at sea level. Higher up, sound travels at a slower speed.

When a plane flies slower than the speed of sound, the air ahead has time to divide smoothly and flow around the plane. But with supersonic flight the air ahead has no time to prepare for the arrival of the plane. Instead the air is disturbed so much that it forms a shock **wave** that makes a loud bang and may badly buffet the plane.

Aircraft builders prevented buffeting by building planes, such as the Concorde, with long, sharp noses and thin, swept-back wings. One supersonic plane has flown six times faster than sound.

Surgery

Surgery involves cutting into a person's body to remove or fix a damaged part. Surgery is performed in a **hospital** by a specifically trained doctor called a surgeon. **X rays** and other tests help show the surgeon how best to operate. Before an operation patients are given an anesthetic so that they feel no **pain**.

The surgeon cuts the patient open with a sharp knife, called a scalpel, or with a delicate **laser**. Other tools help prevent bleeding and hold back flaps

▽ During **surgery** the surgeon and the surgical team wear sterile gowns, gloves, and masks. This makes sure that they do not pick up or transmit germs.

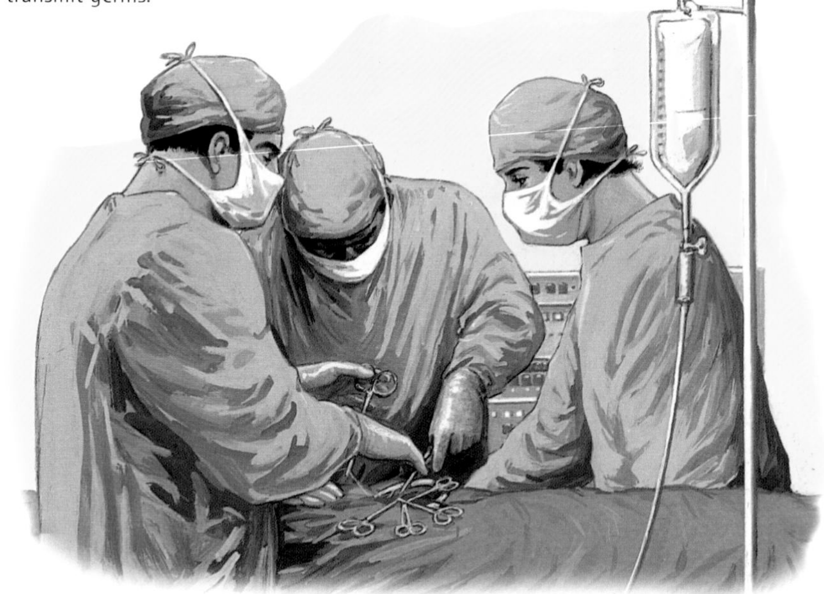

of **skin**. After operating the surgeon closes the wound with a special tape or sews its edges together.

Suriname

Suriname is a small country on the northeast coast of **South America**. People of many races live there. They grow **rice**, bananas, cocoa, **sugar**, and **fruits** on the coastal plains. Suriname's most important product is bauxite, from which **aluminum** is made.

Suriname became a Dutch possession in 1667 when Great Britain handed it over in exchange for the Dutch colony of New Amsterdam (now **Manhattan**). Suriname became independent in 1975.

SURINAME
Government: Republic
Capital: Paramaribo
Area: 62,300 sq. mi.
Population: 433,998
Languages: Dutch, Sranang Tongo, English
Currency: Guilder

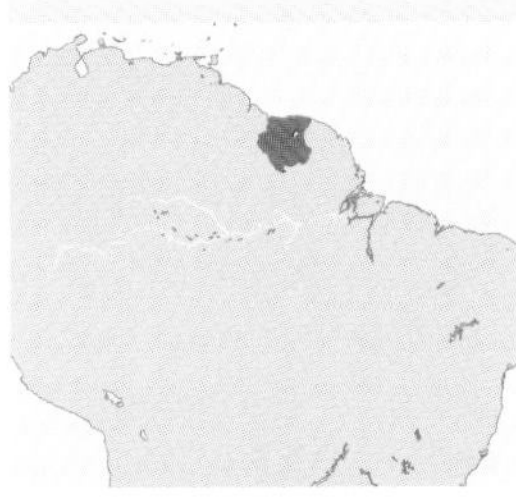

Surveying

Surveying involves using measuring instruments and figuring out certain equations to find out the exact positions of places on **Earth**'s surface. This type of information makes it possible for people to make **maps** and charts and to build **bridges**, **roads**, and buildings.

Swan

These large, graceful waterbirds are among the heaviest **birds** that are able to fly. To take off they need a long, clear stretch of **water**. Some species of swans fly south in V-shaped flocks in the spring and the fall.

Swans swim with webbed feet and lower their necks to feed on underwater **plants**. They build bulky **nests** by pools or **rivers**. Young swans are known as cygnets.

△ Mute **swans** are heavy birds, but their long, wide wings and powerful breast muscles allow them to fly well. They need a long running start on land or water to take off.

Sweden

Sweden is the fifth largest nation in **Europe**, lying between **Norway** and the Baltic Sea. **Mountains** rise in most of the west, and **forests** cover more than half of the land. Their **conifer** trees yield much of the world's softwood.

Most of Sweden's **electricity** comes from fast-flowing mountain **rivers**. Farmers produce **milk**, meat, **cereals**, and **sugar** beets on farmland near the coast. The north is too cold for farming, but it has rich **iron** mines. **Fishing** is also an important part of the Swedish economy.

Most of the 8.9 million Swedes live in the south of the country. The capital is Stockholm.

SWEDEN
Government: Constitutional monarchy
Capital: Stockholm
Area: 158,700 sq. mi.
Population: 8,875,053
Language: Swedish
Currency: Swedish krona

Swift, Jonathan

Jonathan Swift (1667–1745) was an English writer who is well known for **books** that made fun of the silly, cruel behavior of people and **governments**. Swift's most famous book is *Gulliver's Travels*, which tells of voyages to very strange lands. On his first voyage Gulliver reaches the land of Lilliput, where the people are only 0.78 in. (2cm) tall. Then he travels to a land of giants.

Swimming

Swimming is the skill or **sport** involving moving through **water**. Many **animals** know how to swim from birth, but people have to learn, usually with the help of a trained teacher.

Swimmers usually use one or more of four main strokes. These are called the breaststroke, butterfly stroke, backstroke, and crawl, or freestyle. Swimming is one of the best forms of **exercise**.

SWITZERLAND
Government: Federal state
Capital: Bern
Area: 15,300 sq. mi.
Population: 7,283,274
Languages: German, French, and Italian
Currency: Swiss franc

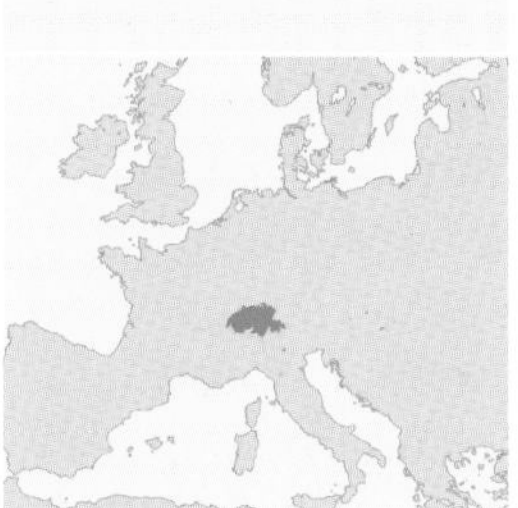

SYRIA
Government: Republic
Capital: Damascus
Area: 71,000 sq. mi.
Population: 16,728,808
Language: Arabic
Currency: Syrian pound

Switzerland

This small, mountainous country lies in central **Europe**. The snowy peaks of the **Alps** and their steep-sided valleys fill most of southern Switzerland. Tourism is an important industry—many people visit the **mountains** for **skiing** and hiking vacations.

Most of the country's crops are grown where the mountains meet the lower land of the Swiss plateau. Here, too, are most of Switzerland's cities, including Bern, the capital. Swiss factories make chemicals, machinery, and watches. **Chocolate** and **cheese** are made from the **milk** of **cattle** that graze in the Alpine meadows.

The seven million Swiss speak mainly German, French, or Italian. The Swiss people are among the wealthiest in the world.

Sydney

Sydney is the largest city in **Australia** and the capital of New South Wales. More than three million people live in Sydney. It stands on a natural harbor (Port Jackson) crossed by a famous **steel**-arch **bridge**. Sydney makes chemicals, machinery, and **ships** and is an important port. It was founded in 1788 as a settlement for convicts sent there from **England**.

Synagogue

The building where Jews (the followers of **Judaism**) gather to study and pray is called a synagogue. The main prayer services take place on the Jewish Sabbath—from sunset on Friday to sunset on Saturday. They are often led by a rabbi (teacher). Children come to the synagogue to learn the Hebrew **language** and study the Torah, the **book** of Jewish teachings.

Syria

This Arab country lies just east of the **Mediterranean Sea**. Much of Syria is covered by dry plains that are hot in the summer and cold in the winter. **Nomads** drive flocks of **sheep** and **goats** over the dry lands. Farmers grow **cereals**, grapes, and apricots in areas where **rivers** or **rain** provide **water**.

Most Syrian towns developed along the routes used long ago to bring goods from the East. From 1516 Syria was was ruled by **Turkey** for 400 years. After **World War I** the French ruled the country on behalf of the League of Nations. Syria became fully independent in 1946. In 1967 Syria lost an area, called the Golan Heights, to **Israel**. Unsuccessful negotiations for the return of this disputed area took place in the late 1990s.

▷ The battle of Yarmuk was fought in **Syria** in A.D. 636. Muslim forces defeated a Byzantine army twice their size. The Muslims captured Syria and Palestine, the most prosperous part of the Byzantine empire. They took Jerusalem and established the beginnings of a large empire.

△ The **Taj Mahal** is built of white marble. Its four sides are identical, with a minaret, or tower, at each corner.

Table tennis

Table **tennis** is a fast-moving indoor game played by hitting a small, light **plastic** ball back and forth across a table. Each player has a **rubber**-covered paddle. The ball has to be hit so that it clears the net across the middle of the table, bouncing once on the other side of the net. If a player fails to return the ball, the other player scores a point.

The game was invented in **England** in the early 1900s as an after-dinner game. It is now a popular **sport** around the world and an **Olympic** event.

Taiwan

TAIWAN
Government: Democracy
Capital: Taipei
Area: 12,400 sq. mi.
Population: 22,370,461
Languages: Mandarin Chinese, Taiwanese
Currency: Taiwanese dollar

Taiwan, once called Formosa, is an **island** country 89 mi. (140km) off the coast of **China**. **Rice** is the main crop. Most Taiwanese are Chinese whose ancestors emigrated to the island in the 1700s. Others are Chinese who fled from the mainland after the Communist (see **communism**) takeover of China in 1949. Taiwan held the Chinese seat in the **United Nations** until 1971 when China was admitted and Taiwan was expelled. China regards Taiwan as part of China, but many Taiwanese prefer to keep their island separate from the mainland.

Taj Mahal

This is the world's most beautiful tomb. It stands on the Jumna **River** in Agra in northern **India**. The emperor Shah Jahan (1592–1666) built it for his favorite wife, Mumtaz Mahal (1598–1631). The graves of both the emperor and Mumtaz Mahal are inside the tomb.

The building of the Taj Mahal began in 1632. More than 20,000 people worked daily on the tomb, and the building was completed in 1648.

Tanzania

TANZANIA
Government: Republic
Capital: Dodoma
Area: 341,700 sq. mi.
Population: 36,232,074
Languages: Swahili, English
Currency: Tanzanian shilling

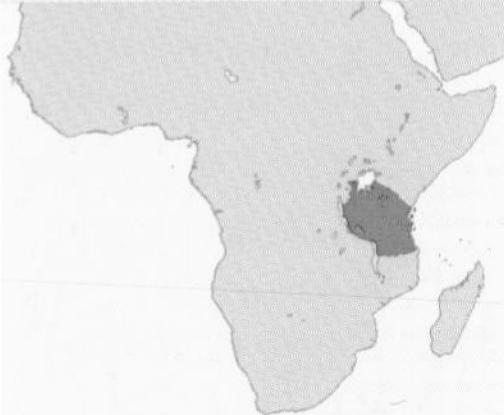

Tanzania consists of two parts—Tanganyika on the east African mainland and the **islands** of Zanzibar and Pemba off the coast. They joined to form one country in 1964. Tanzania contains part of **Africa**'s largest **lake**, Lake Victoria, and Africa's highest **mountain**, Mount Kilimanjaro (19,336 ft./5,895m). The country has diverse wildlife and beautiful scenery. **Diamonds** are the country's most valuable **mineral**. **Gold** is also mined (see **mining**). Tanzania's former capital and largest city is Dar es Salaam.

Tape recorder

A tape recorder (see **recording**) turns **sound** waves into a magnetic (see **magnetism**) pattern on tape. When played, the pattern changes back into sound.

A **microphone** inside or connected to the recorder changes sound into an electrical signal (see **electricity**). This is amplified (made stronger) and fed to the recording head. The recording head produces a magnetic field, which magnetizes the tape as it passes the head.

When playing back the tape, the magnetic field produces an electrical signal, which goes to an amplifier and **loudspeaker**.

Tapestry

Tapestries are designs or pictures woven in cloth. Making tapestries is a very old craft. The Egyptians made tapestries about 1,700 years ago.

Tapestries are made by **weaving** colored **silk** thread across rows of strong linen or **wool** threads held in a frame.

The tapestry design is drawn onto the linen threads with ink. The weaver works from the back of the tapestry.

△ In the Middle Ages colorful **tapestries** decorated the walls of wealthy people's homes.

Taste

We can taste **food** because we have taste buds on our **tongues**. The tongue is covered in tiny bumps called papillae, and the taste buds are buried in the sides of these bumps. There are 10,000 microscopic taste buds, which are scattered in clusters on the back, tip, and sides of the tongue. Each taste bud is a tiny pit containing a ball-shaped cluster of 20 to 30 gustatory (taste) **cells**. As the flavor of the food being eaten dissolves in the mouth the cells in the taste buds trigger signals along **nerves** running from the buds to the **brain**. This tells you whether the food you are eating is sweet, sour, bitter, or salty.

Flavor is a mixture of the taste and the **smell** of food. If you have a bad cold and your nose is blocked, food hardly tastes of anything because you cannot smell it. The easiest way to take bad-tasting **medicine** is to hold your nose while you swallow it.

Bitter
Sour
Salty
Sweet

△ **Taste** has only four main types of flavors—sweet, salty, sour, and bitter. Each patch of taste buds on the tongue picks up one kind of flavor, with the tip of the tongue most sensitive to sweetness. The middle of the tongue has hardly any taste buds.

Tax

The **government** of a country must have money in order to function. It gets most of this money by taxing people. Direct taxes on income, called income tax, are those that people pay directly to the government. How much income tax a person pays depends on several things. The higher a person's income, the more they pay in tax, and a married person may pay less than a single person with the same income.

Indirect taxes are those charged on some products bought in shops or elsewhere. This tax is called value-added tax (VAT) in **Europe** and sales tax in the **United States**. Some countries impose these taxes on luxury goods such as **alcohol** and cigarettes, which makes them expensive to buy.

The taxes that people pay are used to keep essential services running so that they are available to everyone. These services may include emergency services (ambulance, police, and fire services), **schools**, **hospitals**, **road** building, and defense (**army**, navy, and air force). The spending of money raised by taxes differs from country to country.

Tchaikovsky, Pyotr Ilich

Pyotr Tchaikovsky (1840–1893) was one of the most famous and popular musical composers. He was born in Votkinsk, **Russia**, and studied **music** at the conservatory in St. Petersburg. Tchaikovsky lived in great poverty until a wealthy lady, Nadezhda von Meck, offered to pay him a yearly allowance. Tchaikovsky never met Madame von Meck, but they wrote many letters to each other.

Tchaikovsky was a lonely man and was very unhappy, but his music was full of warmth. He toured abroad, but he preferred to be at home in the country. Among his best-known works are the **ballets** *Swan Lake*, *The Nutcracker Suite*, and *Sleeping Beauty*, his first piano concerto, *the Violin Concerto in D Major*, and his *Symphony No. 6*, the "Pathétique."

△ In Japan there is an ancient **tea** ceremony called *chanoyu*. The tea is made slowly and sipped so carefully that it can take all afternoon to drink a cup.

Tea

Tea is a refreshing drink that is made by pouring boiling **water** over the dried, chopped leaves of a tea **plant**.

Tea was first grown in **China**. It was brought to **Europe** by Dutch traders in the 1660s. Today most tea is grown in northern **India**, China, and **Sri Lanka**.

A tea plant at full height can reach 33 ft. (10m). As a crop the plant is kept small and bushy by regular pruning so that all of its **energy** goes into making new leaves for use in tea production.

Teeth

Teeth are designed to cut, tear, or crush **food** so that it can be swallowed (see **digestion**). Cutting teeth are called incisors; tearing teeth are called canines; and crushing teeth are called molars. Meat-eating **animals**, or **carnivores**, have large canines for tearing flesh. Plant-eating animals, or **herbivores**, have sharp incisors and large molars for snapping off and grinding stringy stalks. **Human beings** have all three kinds of teeth because we are omnivores—we eat all types of food.

There are two parts to a tooth. The root, which has either one, two, or three prongs, is attached to the jaw bone. The crown is the part you can see. Tooth decay happens when **bacteria** mixes with **sugar**. This mixture dissolves the tooth enamel, making holes that let germs get inside the tooth.

A human being's first set of teeth are called baby teeth. There are 10 on top and 10 on the bottom. As you grow these teeth become loose and fall out. They are replaced by a permanent set of teeth—32 in all.

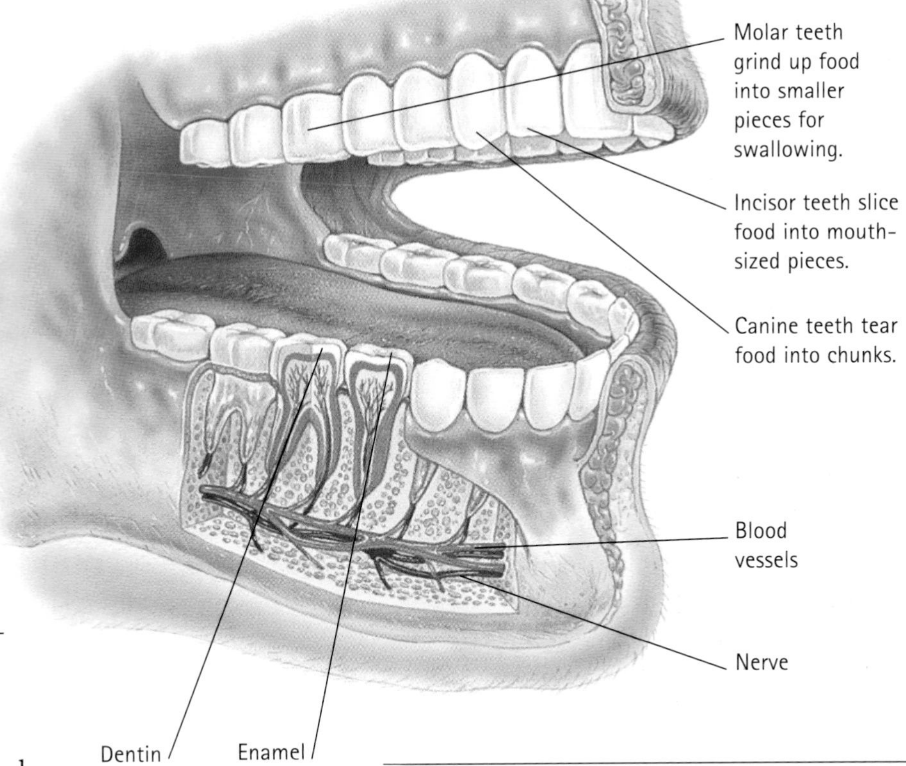

△ People have three types of **teeth**—molars, canines, and incisors. Each tooth has three layers. At the center is a space full of nerves and blood vessels, and around that is a bony wall of dentin. On top is a layer of hard, shiny enamel.

Telecommunication

The Greek word *tele* means "far off." Telecommunication refers to long-distance **communication** by **radio**, telegraph, **telephone**, and **television**. Most of today's long-distance communication is **electronic**.

Telecommunication is very fast because the **sound** and picture signals travel as electric currents along **wires**, radio waves through the **air** and space, or **light** waves along **glass** fibers. Radio and light waves travel at 186,000 mi. (300,000km) per second. Electric signals travel almost as fast. Cable, telephone, and radio networks use communication **satellites** orbiting in space high above **earth**.

The rapid growth of the **Internet** has revolutionized the telecommunication industry. An electronic mail (E-mail) sent from one country to another can travel by several routes. For example, an E-mail sent by **computer** travels by **fiber-optic** cable and then is transmitted via microwaves to a satellite before arriving at the receiver by cable.

Telex and facsimile (fax) **machines** also play a part in communications. A fax machine is equipped with a telephone. When sending a message, the scanner inside the fax machine reads the page and converts it into electronic signals that can be sent through the phone line. The machine at the receiving end then translates the signals and prints out a copy.

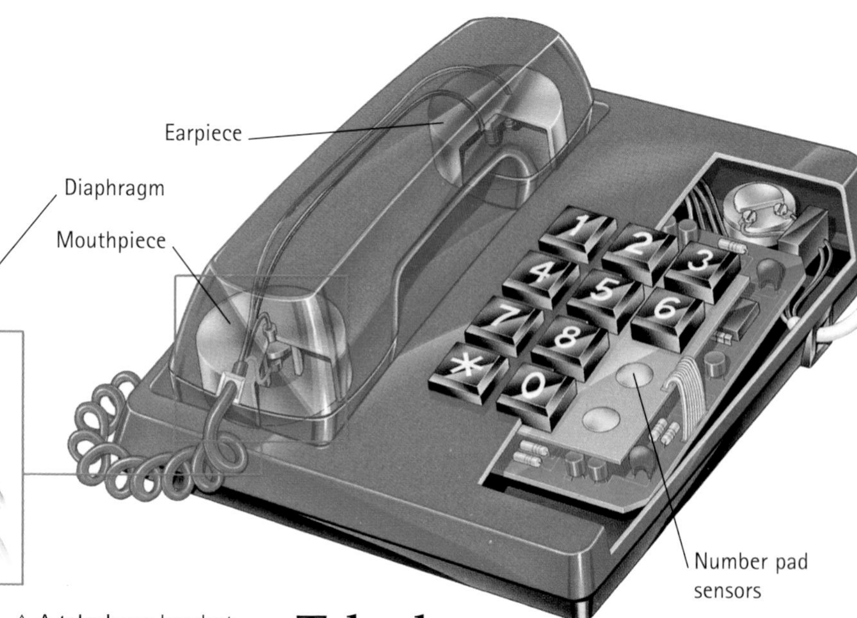

△ A **telephone** handset has a mouthpiece that you speak into and an earpiece that you hold to your ear to listen.

▽ People use many **telecommunication** systems in their homes. Computers use telephone networks to send and receive electronic mail (E-mail) and to connect to the Internet. Most homes have a radio, television, and telephone.

Telephone

Telephones let you speak to someone who is faraway. When you pick up a telephone receiver, a weak electric current is switched on. When you speak into the mouthpiece, you are actually speaking into a **microphone**.

Sound waves from your voice hit a **metal** disk, the diaphragm, inside the microphone and make it vibrate. These vibrations travel along the telephone **wires** as electrical waves. When they reach the other end, they hit another diaphragm in the earpiece. This changes the vibrations back into sound waves, which the person you are calling hears as your voice.

The first electric telephone, made by Alexander **Bell** (1847–1922) in 1876, produced only a very weak sound over a long distance. Today telephone networks use a worldwide system of cables and communication **satellites**.

One of the most popular ways to contact people is by cellular phone. These handy, pocket-sized phones use **radio** waves to put people in touch with one another from almost anywhere around the world. Cell phones also use radio waves to send text messages from one phone to another. Some cell phones can even connect to the **Internet**.

Telescope

Telescopes make things that are faraway appear closer. They work by gathering the **light** from an object and bending it to make a tiny image. The image is then made larger so we can see it.

There are two types of telescopes. The **lens,** or refractor, telescope uses two lenses fixed in a tube to keep out unwanted light. A large lens—the object lens—at one end of the tube collects the light. A smaller lens—the eyepiece—makes the image larger. The image seen through this type of telescope is upside down. To turn the image the right way around a third lens is needed.

The other type of telescope is called a reflecting telescope. Instead of a lens it has a curved **mirror** to collect light. The mirror is shaped so that the light rays bouncing off of it are directed at a second mirror that reflects the ray toward the eyepiece.

Television

Television is a way of sending **sounds** and pictures through the **air**. Scientist John Logie Baird (1888–1946) demonstrated the first television in 1926.

Cathode ray tube

Electron guns

Phosphor strips

Television screen

▷ The main part of a **television** set is the cathode ray tube. The large end is the television screen. The narrow end contains three electron guns that fire electrons onto the phosphor strips on the screen. As each electron hits the screen it lights up a dot. These tiny flashes of color build up the picture on the screen. All the colors on a color television screen are made up from three colors—red, blue, and green. Each of the colors is supplied by one of the guns.

The first television service began in 1936 in the **United Kingdom**. To begin with all television was black and white. **Color** television was introduced in the **United States** in 1956.

Television works by changing **light** waves into electric signals (see **electricity**). This happens inside a television **camera**. A picture of what is happening in front of the camera forms on a screen behind the **lens**. Behind the screen is an electron gun. This scans the screen. It moves from left to right to cover each part of the picture. Each part is turned into an electric signal that is

▽ The Keck **telescopes** on top of Mount Kea, Hawaii, each have 36 six-sided mirrors joined together to make one large mirror that is 33 ft. (10m) wide.

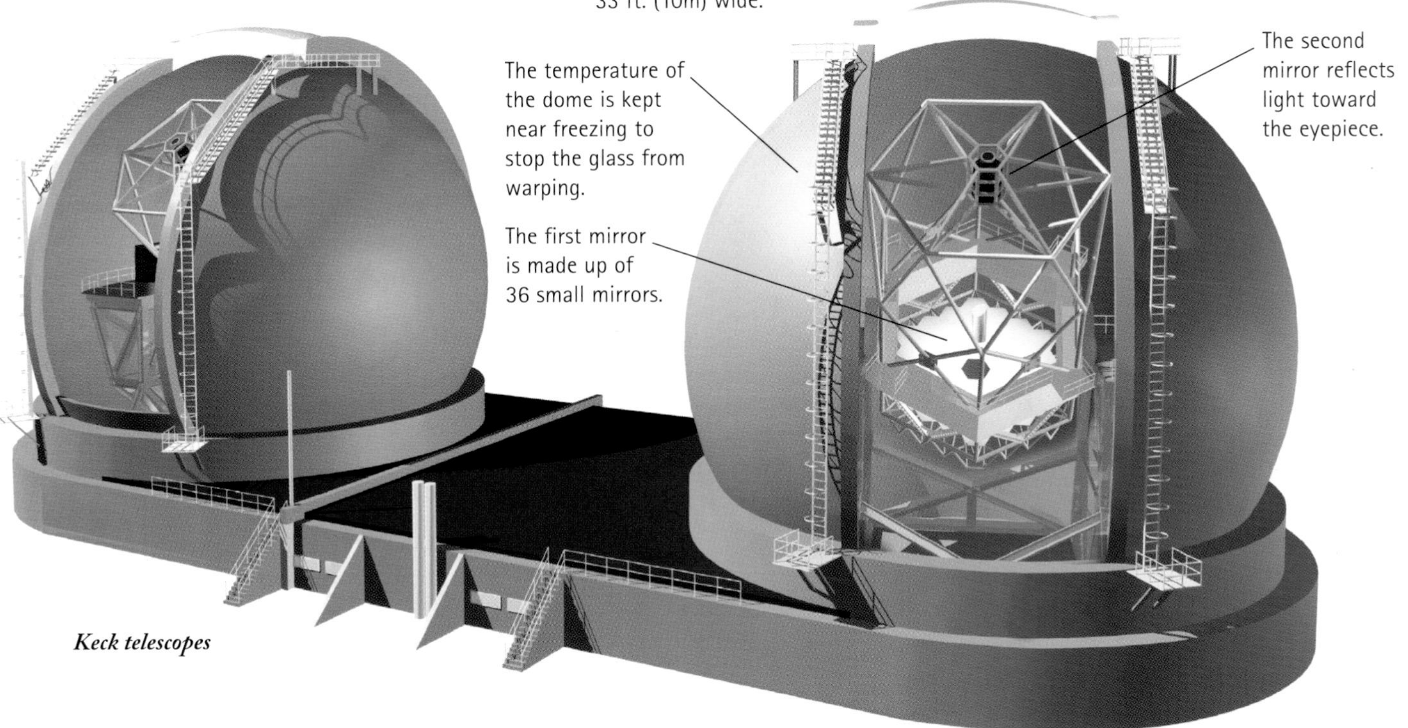

Keck telescopes

made stronger and then sent to a transmitter. All the signals are broadcast by the transmitter as **radio** waves. They are beamed via **satellite** or sent along cable networks and changed back into electric signals, which are sent directly into television sets in homes.

Live television programs show you what is happening in real time. Most programs are recorded on **film** or videotape and are broadcast later.

Recently the quality of television sound and vision has improved greatly with the introduction of digital technology, which produces a clearer sound and image.

Temperature

Temperature is the measurement of **heat**. It is measured on a scale marked on a **thermometer**. Most people in the world use the Celsius scale. The Fahrenheit scale is most often used in the **United States**.

Some **animals**, including **mammals** such as **human beings**, are warm-blooded—their temperature stays almost constant. A healthy person's normal body temperature is 98.6°F (37°C). When people get sick, their temperature might go up to 105.8°F (41°C) or more.

Other animals, such as **snakes** and **frogs**, are cold-blooded—their body temperature goes up and down with the temperature of their surroundings.

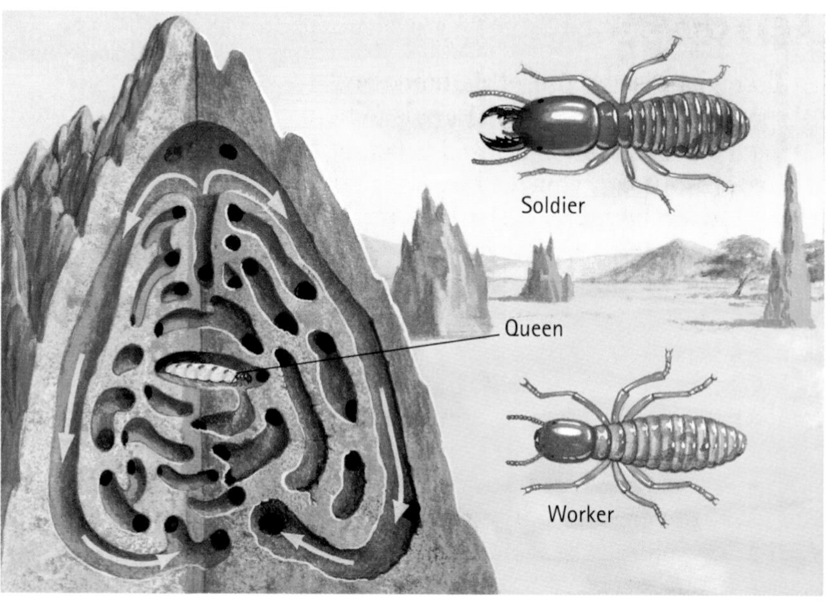

△ Many **termites** build their nests inside huge mounds of soil. Inside the nest is a maze of tunnels and chambers where the workers take care of the young. The queen is at the center of the nest. Soldier termites defend the nest against attacks.

△ Many cold-blooded animals, such as lizards, can survive when their body **temperature** drops almost to the freezing point. A lizard's temperature in the desert is hot during the baking heat of the day and cold during the chilly night.

Tennis

Tennis is a **sport** played by two or four people on a specially marked court, which is divided in half by a net that is 35 in. (91cm) high. If two people play, it is called a singles match. If four people play, it is called a doubles match.

Tennis balls are about 3 in. (63 mm) in diameter and weigh about 2 oz (56.7g). Most rackets are 26.5 in. (68cm) long.

A tennis match is divided into sets. Usually women play the best of three sets and men the best of five. Each set has at least six games. To win a game a player, or pair of players, must score at least four points. The object of tennis is to hit the ball into the opponent's court so that it cannot be returned. Modern tennis is a version of an old French game called "real" tennis or royal tennis.

Termite

Termites are **insects** that eat **wood**. They have soft, pale bodies and thick waists and live in the warmer parts of the world. Some termites burrow underground or tunnel into house timbers, causing a lot of damage. Others live in huge mounds of soil.

All termites live in large groups called colonies. Each colony has a queen, her king, soldiers, and workers. Most termites are workers and are small, blind, and wingless. They dig tunnels or build the mound and find food for the rest of the colony.

Soldiers have large, strong heads and are also blind and wingless. They defend the colony. The queen is much larger than the other termites, and her role is to lay **eggs**. She is kept in a chamber in the middle of the colony with her king. The workers feed her and take care of the eggs until they hatch.

Terrorism

Terrorism is the use of violence and terror to achieve political goals. There has been a marked increase in terrorism throughout the world since the end of **World War II**. Terrorists murder by bombing and shooting; they hijack **aircraft**; they kidnap people and hold them as hostages; they rob **banks** and often take part in **drug** trafficking.

Terrorism is a worldwide problem. On September 11, 2001 four U.S. planes hijacked by terrorists crashed in **New York**, **Washington, D.C.**, and Pennsylvania, killing more than 3,000 people in a matter of hours. Since then the U.S. has declared a **war** on terrorism, and countries around the world are working together against terrorist groups.

Textile

A textile is any cloth made by **weaving.** Before the **Industrial Revolution** all cloth was made by hand from natural fibers of **wool**, **silk**, **cotton**, or linen. Since this time scientists have developed many types of manufactured fibers. Rayon is made from **wood**. Nylon comes from **oil**. There are even some fibers made from **glass**. Manufactured fibers are cheaper to produce and are often easier to wash and take care of. Sometimes they are mixed with natural fibers to get the best qualities of both materials. Some fabrics are treated to keep them from creasing or fading.

THAILAND
Government: Constitutional monarchy
Capital: Bangkok
Area: 197,400 sq. mi.
Population: 61,797,351
Language: Thai
Currency: Baht

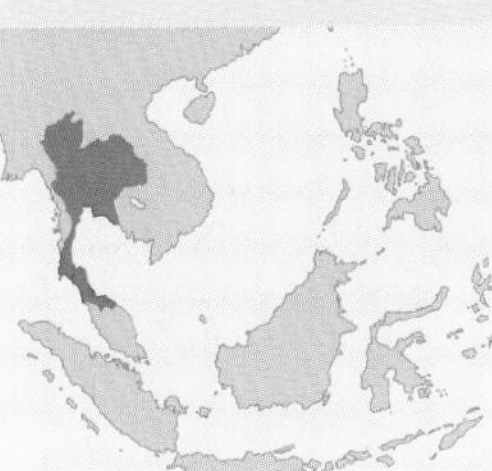

Thailand

Thailand is a country in **Southeast Asia**. It is surrounded by **Myanmar** (Burma), **Laos**, and **Cambodia**. The south coast opens onto the Gulf of Thailand, which is the westernmost part of the South China Sea.

Thailand is a tropical landscape of **mountains** and **rain forests** with plains at the center of the country, where most of the **population** live. Many **rivers** flow through this area, making it very fertile. Most people are farmers, and **rice** is the main crop. They also grow **cotton**, **tobacco**, corn, coconuts, and bananas. In the north there are large **forests** of teak (see **wood**), which is a major export. The peninsula in the southwest of Thailand is very rich in **minerals**, especially **tin**.

Most Thais are Buddhists (see **Buddhism**). Many Thai men live for several years as monks in one of the many Buddhist temples. They wear distinctive bright-orange robes.

Thailand was called Siam before 1939. Thai means "free," so Thailand means the "land of the free." There is a king, but the country is ruled by an elected **government**.

◁ Airports and planes are targets for **terrorism**. In the past planes have been hijacked or bombed. Airports now have increased security and detect bombs and weapons with metal detection equipment and X-ray machines.

Thanksgiving

Thanksgiving is a national holiday celebrated on the fourth Thursday of November in the **United States**. The **festival** originated in the fall of 1621, and President Abraham **Lincoln** declared it a national holiday in 1863. People gather to give thanks for the harvest and share a traditional meal. This meal is usually a feast of turkey and pumpkin pie. **Canada** adopted Thanksgiving as a national holiday in November 1879, and it is now celebrated on the second Monday in October.

△ The first **Thanksgiving** was celebrated in 1621 by the Pilgrims of Plymouth Colony in Massachusetts. A number of Native Americans joined the feast.

Theater

A theater is a place where plays are performed by actors and watched by an audience. The theater may be just a patch of ground or a large building.

The earliest theaters were in Greece (see ancient **Greece**). The Greeks cut a half-moon shape in the hillside and lined it with rows of stone seats that looked down on a round, flat stage.

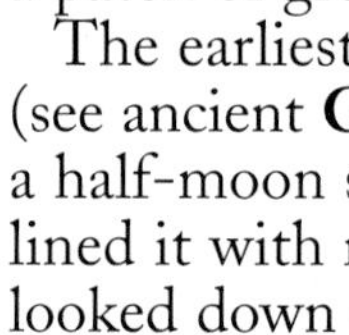

The Romans (see **Roman Empire**) copied the Greek pattern, but they built most of their theaters on flat ground. The rows of seats were held up by a wall.

In **Europe** before the 1500s troupes of traveling actors used their carts as stages. Later they performed in wealthy people's houses and in courtyards. The first theaters were made of **wood**. The stage jutted out into a large yard, and rows of seats ran all around the sides. There were seats on the stage but only for rich people. These theaters had no roofs. When it rained, the groundlings—people who stood around the edge of the stage—got wet. **Shakespeare**'s plays were performed in theaters like this. In the 1800s music halls became popular. They staged shows featuring actors, singers, and comedians. Lavish **opera** and **ballet** productions also became increasingly popular at this time.

Toward the end of the 1800s electric lighting (see **electricity**), revolving stages, and special effects with **water** and smoke were used to add excitement to some shows.

Today theaters range from huge professional theaters offering the latest **electronic** effects, lighting, and **sound** systems to simple productions by amateurs in small church halls and **schools**. Modern theater productions cover a huge range of entertainment, including **opera**, ballet, historical and modern drama, and comedy.

▽ The Metropolitan Opera House, known as the Met, is a **theater** in **New York** City that stages both operas and ballets. Each time a performance is put on the Met employs a team of about 1,000 people.

Thermometer

A thermometer is an instrument that measures **temperature**. It is usually a **glass** tube marked with a scale. Inside is another, thinner glass tube, which ends in a bulb containing **mercury** or **alcohol**. When the temperature rises, the mercury or alcohol gets warm and expands (grows bigger). It travels up the tube. When it stops, the temperature can be read on the marked scale. When it gets cold, the mercury contracts (grows smaller) and sinks down the tube. If alcohol is used in a thermometer, it is usually colored red. Most thermometers measure temperatures between the boiling and freezing points of **water**. This is between 0°C and 100°C on the Celsius scale. Most countries use the Celsius scale, but some, such as the **United States of America**, also use the Fahrenheit scale, in which the freezing point of water is 32°F and the boiling point is 212°F.

Medical thermometers are small enough to go in your mouth and measure your body's temperature.

Thermostat

A thermostat is an instrument that keeps a **temperature** steady. It is usually part of a central heating system (see **heat**). It switches the boiler on or off when the temperature gets too low or high. Thermostats are also found in **cars**, spacecraft, ovens, hot **water** heaters, and other **machines**.

Until recently thermostats were made with **metal** strips inside. When the strips got hot, they expanded. They had to bend to fit into their space. When they bent, they broke off their electrical contacts. This switched off the boiler or heater. Modern thermostats are **electronic** and can work in temperatures that would melt most metals.

△ **Thunderstorms** are most frequent in the tropics. In some areas they may occur as many as 200 days per year.

△ Household **thermometers** measure how warm or cold the air is inside or outside buildings. Most of these thermometers contain alcohol because it is cheaper and safer than mercury.

Thunderstorm

Thunderstorms are caused by **electricity** in the **air**. Different electrical charges build up inside large **rain** clouds. When the charges are strong enough, a spark leaps from one charged part of the cloud to another. Sometimes the spark jumps from the cloud to the ground, and we see the spark as **lightning**. Lightning heats up the air. The air expands so quickly thatit explodes, making the crashing noise we call thunder.

Since **sound** travels much slower than **light** you always hear thunder after you see lightning. It takes the noise of thunder about three seconds to travel 0.62 mi. (1km). To find out how many miles away a storm is, count the seconds between seeing the lightning and hearing the thunder and divide the number by three.

△ Lhasa in **Tibet** is the world's highest city at 11,808 ft. (3,600m) above sea level. It was the home of the **Dalai Lama**, the head of the Tibetan Buddhists, until he sought exile in India in 1959.

Tibet

Tibet is a region in central **Asia**. It is the highest nation in the world at 16,072 ft. (4,900m) above sea level—as high as the peaks of the **Alps**. Enormous **mountain** ranges surround the flat plain in the country's center. In the south lie the **Himalayas**—the home of Mount **Everest**. In the west lie the Karakoram mountains in Kashmir, and in the north lie the Kunlun mountains.

Tibet used to be ruled by Buddhist monks (see **Buddhism**) called lamas. In 1959 the country was taken over by **China**.

Spring tide

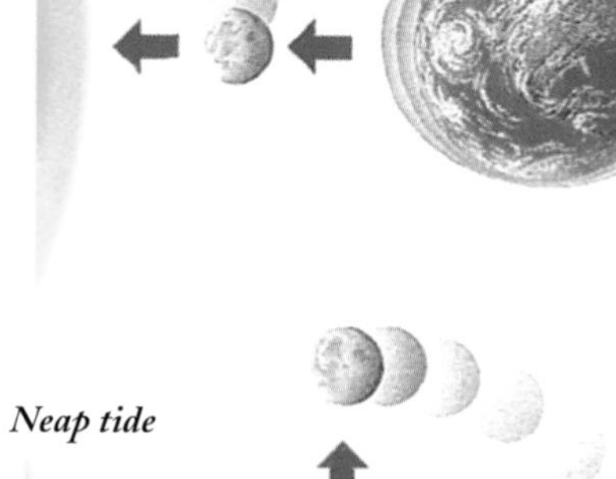

Neap tide

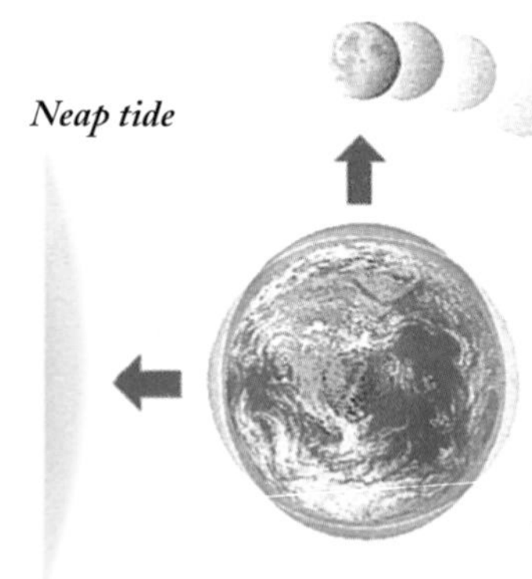

△ Spring **tides** are caused by the combined pull of the Sun and the Moon. Neap tides occur when the Sun and the Moon are at right angles to each other. The red arrows show the pull of gravity.

Tide

Tides are regular movements of the **oceans**. They are mainly caused by the **Moon**. The Moon's **gravity** is like a giant magnet (see **magnetism**). It tugs the oceans toward it as it loops around **Earth**. Earth is spinning at the same time, so most places get two high tides and two low tides about every 24 hours.

A high tide happens when the **water** flows as far inland as it can. A low tide happens when the water flows out as far as it can.

When the Sun's gravity and the Moon's gravity pull in the same direction, their combined force causes a very high, or spring, tide. These tides occur when there is a full or new moon. Twice a month, when the Sun and the Moon pull against each other at right angles, a very low, or neap, tide occurs.

Tiger

Tigers are the largest members of the **cat** family. Siberian tigers, from a remote region of southeastern **Russia**, can be up to 13 ft. (4m) long from nose to tail and weigh over 663 lbs (300kg).

Tigers live in the **forests, mountains**, and plains of **Asia** and **Indonesia** in both tropical and very cold regions. They hunt **deer, fish, turtles**, and **cattle**. They usually lie still during the day and hunt alone during the night. These powerful hunters stalk their prey near trails and waterholes and then drag their kill to a quiet spot to eat it. One tiger can pull a dead buffalo that is too heavy for a group of people to move.

Until the 1800s thousands of tigers roamed through the forests of Asia. Then hunters began to shoot them both for sport and for their skins. Today tigers are hunted for their body parts, which are highly prized ingredients in some traditional Chinese **medicines**. Also the forest **habitats** in which they live are slowly being destroyed. As a result, all types of tigers are now endangered.

Time

Nobody has ever really explained what time is, but people have invented many ways of measuring it. First they divided up the **years** and months by natural things that happen regularly such as the **seasons** and the change in the size and shape of the **Moon**. The position of the **Sun** in the sky told them the time of day.

The very first **clock**—a sundial—was probably invented by the Egyptians (see **Egypt, ancient**). As the sun moved across the sky an upright rod in the middle of the dial cast a shadow onto a scale of hours drawn around it. However, this was no use at night.

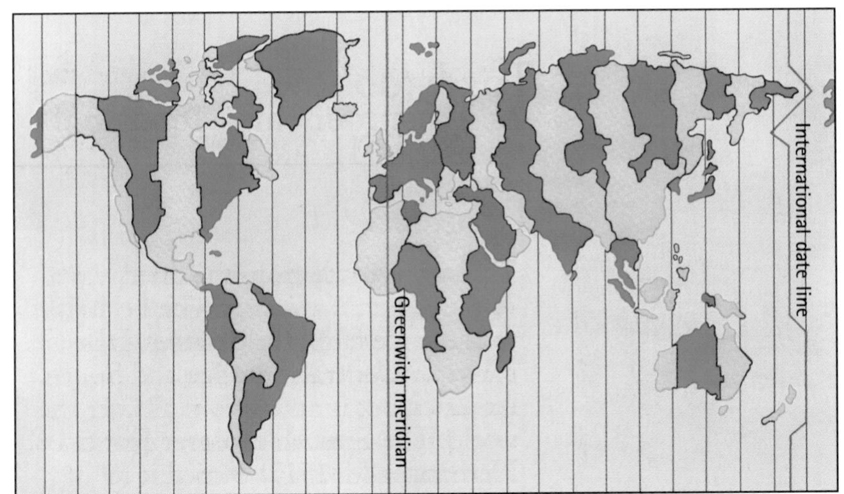

△ The world is divided into 24 **time** zones, starting at the prime meridian at Greenwich in the U.K. Each zone west of the meridian is an hour earlier than the last. Each zone to the east is one hour ahead.

Other ways of telling the time without the Sun's help were invented, for example, the hourglass. This was two **glass** bulbs joined together. **Sand** in one bulb took exactly one hour to trickle through a hole into the other bulb. Mechanical clocks driven by weights were not made until the 1200s. Clocks powered by springs were made in the 1500s, and in the early 1600s the **pendulum** was used to make clocks more accurate. Modern clocks are very precise. They work by **electronics**. Scientists need even more accurate timekeeping. They use atomic (see **atom**) clocks that are accurate to 10 millionths of a second.

We think of time as being something that is the same in all situations, but this is not necessarily so. Albert **Einstein** showed that the rate at which time passes varies according to the speed at which we are traveling. On a **supersonic** jet clocks and watches move very slightly slower than they do on the ground. The difference would only be noticeable, however, in a spacecraft traveling at close to the speed of **light**.

Because of the rotation of **Earth**, sunrise in the eastern **United States** occurs three hours earlier than in the western part. For this reason the world has been divided into 24 time zones. At the International Date Line the date changes.

▽ The Siberian **tiger** is the largest and rarest type of tiger, with less than 400 left in the wild.

△ **Tokyo** is Japan's center of culture as well as being the largest built-up area in the country. More than 10 percent of Japan's population lives in this bustling city.

Tin

Tin is a soft, white **metal** and is one of the oldest known to us. People were **mining** tin before **iron** was discovered. Tin was mixed with **copper** to make **bronze**.

Tin was mined in **Europe** long before the birth of Christ. An ancient people called the Phoenicians sailed to **England** from the **Mediterranean** Sea to trade cloth and precious stones for tin.

Tin is not a common metal. The main tin mines are in **Bolivia**, **Southeast Asia**, and western **Africa**.

Tin is useful for packaging because it does not **rust**. It can also be used for plating other metals to give a bright, shiny surface. Tin cans are made from sheets of steel that have been coated with tin. Mixed with antimony and **copper**, tin makes pewter—a soft **alloy** once used for most tableware.

△ In the 1600s European settlers in America grew **tobacco** as well as other crops such as wheat and cotton.

Toad *see* Frog and Toad

Toadstool
see Mushroom and Toadstool

Tobacco

Tobacco is made from the dried leaves of the **plant** *Nicotiana*, which belongs to the same family as potatoes. It is native to **Central America** and **South America** but is now grown all over the world. The Spanish **explorer** Francisco Hernandez (d. 1517) carried it to **Europe** in 1599.

Tobacco leaves are picked, dried, and can be rolled together to make cigars or shredded to be smoked in pipes or cigarettes. Tobacco is also chewed and is made into snuff—a powder that can be sniffed. All of these forms of tobacco are harmful to people's **health**, especially to the **lungs**, **heart**, and blood vessels.

Tokyo

Tokyo is the capital of **Japan** and is situated on the southeastern coast of Honshu—Japan's main **island**. It is one of the largest cities in the world. The population of Tokyo and the surrounding area is 26 million. Its houses, buildings, and factories sprawl over the western side of Tokyo Bay.

Tokyo is Japan's leading center for business, finance, and manufacturing, producing a large variety of products, including electrical and **electronic** goods, **cameras**, and **cars**. Its location near the sea makes it a busy shipping port. There are also huge shipyards and **oil** refineries along the coast.

Tolstoy, Leo

Leo Tolstoy (1828–1910) was a Russian author who is known particularly for his novels *War and Peace* and *Anna Karenina*. He was born into a noble family and fought in the Crimean War (1854–1856). Tolstoy hated the greed and selfishness he found in people he met on his travels. He turned away from the Russian Orthodox Church and followed a way of life that was based on **Christianity** and the teachings of **Jesus Christ**. He felt that all violence, as well as having wealth, was wrong—only love and pity would bring happiness.

Leo Tolstoy had very advanced ideas for his time. He made sure the people who worked for him had homes and were educated.

Tolstoy died at the age of 82. He was refused burial by the Church, but people thronged to his funeral, seeing him as a man who had done his best to improve their situation.

Tomato

Tomatoes are round, red, fleshy **fruits**. They contain a very good supply of some of the **vitamins** people need, especially vitamins A and C.

Tomatoes were first grown thousands of years ago in **South America**. In 1596 the Spanish carried them to **Europe**, but at first no one would eat them because they thought they were poisonous. So they were kept as ornamental **plants**. For a long time tomatoes were called "love apples" or "golden apples."

Although tomatoes are fruits they are almost always eaten as **vegetables**. In the 1900s they became a popular **food**. Now they are grown all over the world.

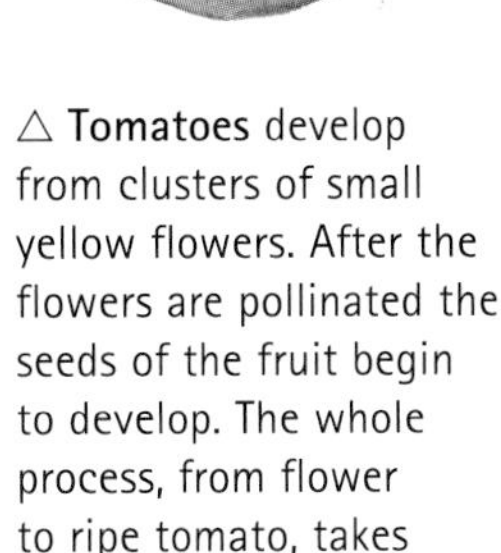

△ **Tomatoes** develop from clusters of small yellow flowers. After the flowers are pollinated the seeds of the fruit begin to develop. The whole process, from flower to ripe tomato, takes 40 to 75 days.

Tongue

The tongue is a muscular, flexible flap fixed inside the mouth. Only **vertebrates** have tongues. Our own tongues help us to **taste** and eat food and to talk. The letters "T" and "D," for example, cannot be said without using the tongue in a certain way.

In toads the tongue is attached to the front of the mouth. **Cats**' rough tongues are covered in tiny hooks of flesh called papillae. They help the cat lap up **liquids** and keep its fur clean.

Many **reptiles**, such as **snakes,** have split, or forked, tongues, which flick in and out of their mouths to "smell" the **air**. Some **amphibians** and **lizards** have long, sticky tongues that shoot out of their mouths to catch **insects**.

▽ This grass snake has a forked, or split, **tongue** that can "smell" the air.

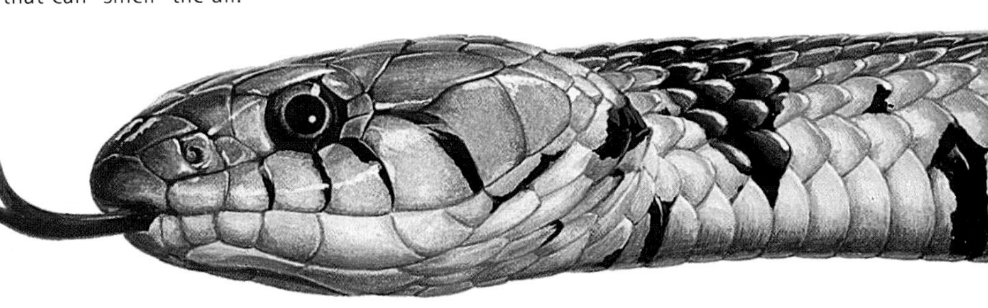

Tonsils

Tonsils are two small lumps at the back of the throat, one on each side. They help protect the body from **germs** coming in through the mouth.

Children have very large tonsils. These gradually shrink as they grow older. Sometimes tonsils can become infected. They swell up and are very painful. This illness is called tonsillitis. The tonsils may have to be taken out by doctors in a **hospital**. Having tonsils taken out does not seem to harm our bodies in any way.

Tornado

Tornadoes are violent, whirling windstorms (see **wind**). Most of them happen in **North America**, but they can occur anywhere in the world.

Hurricanes are strong winds that build up over the sea, while tornadoes build up over land. Tornadoes happen when large masses of clouds meet. The clouds begin to whirl around each other and gradually join to make a gigantic, twisting funnel. When this touches the ground, it sucks up anything in its path—**trees**, houses, or people.

At the tornado's center, wind speeds can reach almost 403 mph (650 km/h).

Tortoise

Tortoises are slow-moving **reptiles**. They can walk only about 16 ft. (5m) per minute. When frightened, they pull their heads and legs inside of their domed shells. There are about 40 types of tortoises, and they live on land, mostly in warm parts of the world. They are similar to **turtles** and terrapins, but those reptiles live in **water**.

Giant tortoises live in the Galápagos Islands and **islands** in the **Indian Ocean**. They can weigh up to 497 lbs (225kg) and can be 6 ft. (1.8m) long. Some tortoises can live for 150 years.

Touch

There are different **nerve cells** in **skin** called receptors that respond to five main types of sensations—light touch, heavy touch (pressure), pain, **heat**, and cold. Receptors transmit sensations along nerves to the **brain**.

Pain receptors are the most numerous, and cold receptors are the least numerous. Some parts of the body, such as the **tongue** and fingertips, have more receptors than others.

There are also receptors inside the **human body**. Usually we do not realize that these are working except when they produce sensations such as hunger or fatigue.

△ This drawing shows which areas of our body are most sensitive to **touch**. The enlarged body parts—mouth, feet, and hands—are the most sensitive.

△ The most visible **trade** is carried out by ships on waterways. They carry goods that are cheaply packed in large containers.

▽ Desert **tortoises** are up to 14 in. (35cm) long and live in North American deserts. As long as they have juicy **cactuses** to eat they do not need to drink.

Trade

The buying and selling of goods and services is called trade. Trade also includes bartering, which is the exchange of one type of good for a different type. Domestic trade is trade that takes place within one country. **Companies** that buy goods in large quantities and then sell them to middlemen are called wholesalers. Companies that sell the goods to stores are called retailers.

International trade is trade between countries. Imports are things that a country buys. Exports are things that a country sells. Some imports and exports are said to be "visible." These include raw materials, such as **iron** ore, and farm products such as **wheat**. They also include factory-made goods, ranging from pencils to jets. Other imports and exports are "invisible." These include banking (see **bank**), **insurance**, transportation services, and money spent by tourists.

The chief trading nations are those with the most industries. But almost every country now depends on trade.

Transistor

Transistors are small **electronic** devices. They are usually made to amplify (strengthen) electric currents in electronic equipment such as **radios**, **televisions**, **computers**, and **satellites**. They can also switch electric currents on and off. Transistors have largely replaced valves, which were once used for the same purpose.

Today complicated circuits containing thousands of transistors can be put into **silicon chips** that are less than a square inch in size. The first practical transistors were developed in the 1940s by the

American scientists Walter Brattain (1902–1987), John Bardeen (1908–1991), and William Shockley (1910–1989). The invention of transistors completely revolutionized electronics, and millions of these devices are now made every year.

Transistors

Electric circuit

△ **Transistors** can act as switches or amplifiers in an electric circuit. These circuits contain many electronic components through which an electric current flows to make an electrical device, such as a toaster or computer, work.

Tree

Trees are beautiful to look at and are also very useful **plants**. Some trees give us **fruits** and nuts. Many trees, especially **conifers**, are grown for timber. **Wood** is not only a valuable building material, but it is also used to make **paper**, and in some countries it is burned for **fuel**. Trees are vital to the environment because they enrich the **atmosphere** with **oxygen** and help protect the **soil** from erosion by **wind** and **rain**.

Trees are the largest and oldest living things on **earth**. The largest tree is a type of sequoia. These giants can grow to more than 328 ft. (100m) high. One bristlecone pine in Nevada is thought to be at least 4,900 years old.

There are two main types of trees—conifers, or softwood trees, and deciduous trees, or hardwoods. Conifers, such as pines, firs, larches, hemlocks, and spruces, have needlelike leaves. They are also called evergreens because they keep their leaves throughout the year. Conifers produce **seeds** on the woody scales that make up their cones.

Deciduous trees, such as oak, ash, maple, elm, beech, and horse chestnut, are broad-leaved, flowering trees that shed their leaves in the fall. Deciduous trees have **flowers** that develop into fruits. The seeds of the trees are within the fruits.

The outer layer of wood on the trunk and branches of a tree is the bark. Bark is dead wood. It is tough and waterproof and protects the living wood underneath. In this way it has the same purpose as the outer layers of **skin** on our bodies.

As trees grow they form layers, or rings, of new wood and become thicker. When this new wood is formed inside a tree, it pushes against the dead bark and makes it crack and peel off.

▽ Different **tree** species can be identified through their characteristics. Each type of tree has a certain combination of bark color and pattern, seed and leaf shape, and color. At a distance some trees can also be identified by their distinctive shapes.

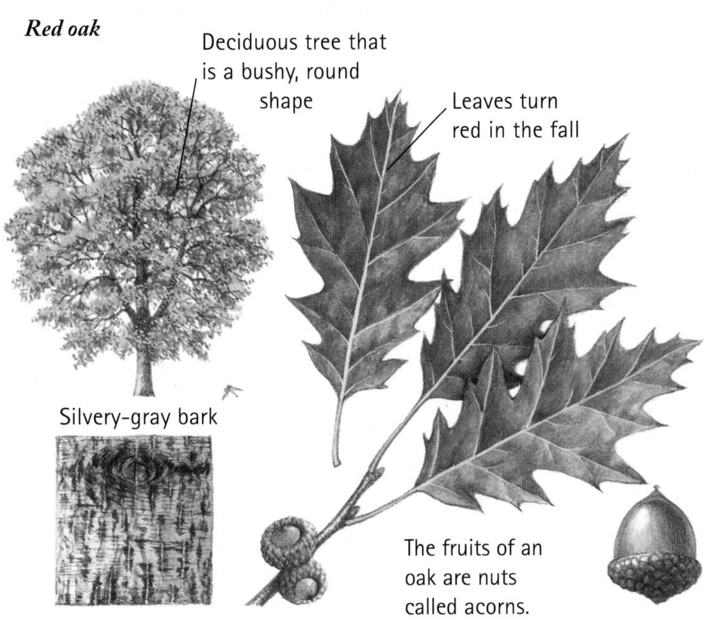

Red oak

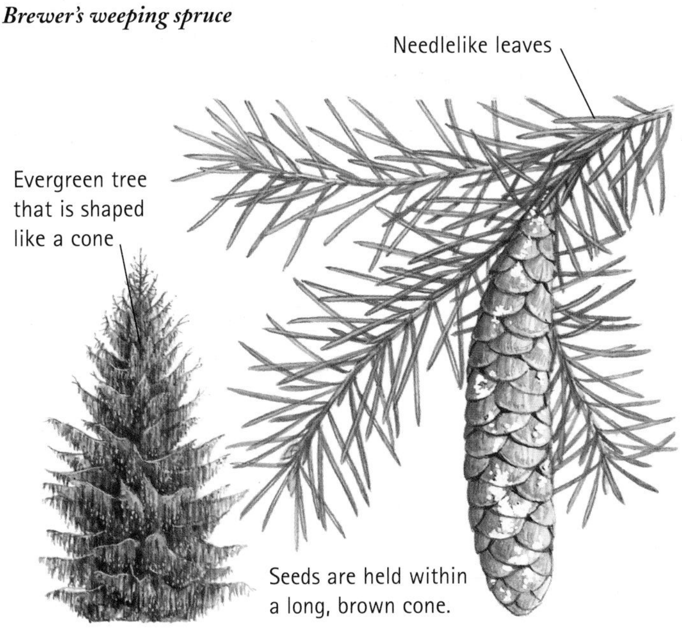

Brewer's weeping spruce

Trinidad and Tobago

Trinidad and Tobago is a country made up of two **islands** in the **Caribbean**. The islands lie near the coast of **Venezuela**. The **climate** is warm and damp, and the main occupation is **farming**. Trinidad is a large producer of **oil**, and this brings in most of the island's wealth. An annual carnival attracts many tourists, who come to hear the steel bands and calypsos for which Trinidad is famous.

TRINIDAD AND TOBAGO
Government: Parliamentary democracy
Capital: Port-of-Spain
Area: 2,000 sq. mi.
Population: 1,169,682
Languages: English, Hindi, French, Spanish
Currency: Trinidad dollar

Trojan War

The Trojan War was fought in around 1200 B.C. between the Trojans of Troy, a city in what is now **Turkey**, and the Greeks. It lasted for 10 years. The poet **Homer**, in his poem the *Iliad*, tells the story of a few days during the war. We know about the rest from other writings.

Paris was a prince of Troy. He fell in love with **Helen**, the wife of King Menelaus of Sparta, **Greece**. Paris took Helen to Troy, and Menelaus, along with other Greek kings and soldiers, went to get her back. They besieged Troy for years. In the end they won by tricking the Trojans with a huge wooden **horse** filled with Greek soldiers, which they left standing outside the city. The Trojans, believing the horse to be a gift, took it inside the city walls. The Greek soldiers then opened the gates, and Troy was destroyed.

No one knows if the story is true. But in the late 1900s archaeologists in Turkey discovered the remains of a walled town that had suffered a siege, violence, and fire around the time the Greeks destroyed Troy.

△ According to **Homer's** poem, during the **Trojan War** the hero Odysseus and other men from the Greek army hid inside a wooden **horse**.

Tropical fish

Tropical **fish** are among the most colorful fish in the world. They live in the warm seas of tropical regions, frequently along the edges of **coral** reefs. The bright **colors** warn predators not to attack the fish.

Many small, brightly colored freshwater tropical fish are popular aquarium pets. Marine fish can also be kept, but they are more expensive and difficult to take care of. They have to have saltwater containing just the right amount of salt in which to live.

Most tropical fishtanks have a heater to keep the **water** at around 75°F (24°C). A cover on the tank holds in the **heat** and stops the water from evaporating. Electric lightbulbs in the cover illuminate the tank and also heat the water. Most aquariums have air **pumps** that add **oxygen** to the water and filter it to keep it clear. Water **plants** also provide oxygen. Special **food** for tropical fish can be bought at pet stores.

The most common species of tropical freshwater fish is the guppy. Others are angelfish, barbels, and neon tetras.

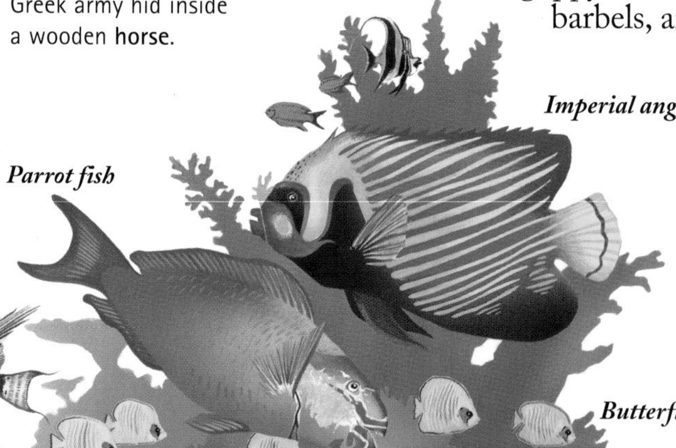

◁ Angelfish, clownfish, and parrot fish are just some of the thousands of **tropical fish** that live on **coral** reefs. Fish such as these often have dazzling colors and bold patterns.

Tuna

The tuna, also called tunny, is a large **fish** whose firm flesh is rich in **proteins** and **vitamins**. Most tuna live in warm seas, but they may swim into northern waters in the summer. Different types of tuna include the bluefin, which may be 10 ft. (3m) long, and the albacore. Tuna are the only fish whose body **temperature** is higher than that of the **water** around them.

Tundra

Tundra is the word used in **geography** to describe the huge, treeless plains of northern **North America**, **Europe**, and **Russia** where it is too cold for **trees** to grow. Tundra regions lie just south of the ice-capped polar regions.

Winters are long on the tundra, where the **sun** may not rise for several weeks or months. Snow covers the land at this time, and the ground is frozen solid. The average **temperature** in the summer is around 50°F (10°C).

Despite the harsh **climate**, strong **plants**, including **mosses**, dwarf shrubs, and **lichens,** manage to grow. The land is also home to a large variety of **insects**, which provide a rich source of food for **birds** such as **swans**, geese, and **ducks**. In the summer the tundra attracts migrating **animals**, such as musk oxen and caribou (reindeer), escaping from the winter. Other animals that live on the tundra include Arctic **foxes**, **bears**, **hares**, wolves, and lemmings.

Only a few people, including the **Inuit**, live on the tundra. The tundra is a source of **minerals** such as **oil** and natural **gas**.

△ Temperatures on the **tundra** rise above the freezing point for only two to four months each year. Despite this, the land supports a variety of plants.

△ **Tuna** is one of the most important types of fish that is eaten. It has been a key food for people of the **Mediterranean** since the time of the ancient Greeks.

TUNISIA
Government: Republic
Capital: Tunis
Area: 59,900 sq. mi.
Population: 9,705,102
Languages: Arabic and French
Currency: Tunisian dinar

Tunisia

Tunisia is a warm country in North **Africa**. Its beaches attract many tourists. The north is rugged and gets the most **rain**. The south is part of the dry **Sahara**. **Farming** and tourism are the main industries in Tunisia, but **oil** and phosphates are important exports.

Over nine million people live in Tunisia, most of whom are Muslims (see **Islam**). Near the capital, Tunis, are the ruins of Carthage. Carthage was a great **Mediterranean** power until it was destroyed by the **Roman Empire** in 146 B.C.

Tunnel

Tunneling is important in **mining**, transportation, and the supplying of **water**. The Romans (see **Roman Empire**) built tunnels to carry water called aqueducts. Today a tunnel that brings water to **New York** City is the world's longest at 105 mi. (169km).

Different methods are used to build tunnels. In hard **rock** the tunnel is blasted out with **explosives**. Cutting **machines**, such as those used to drill **oil** wells, are used in softer rock. In the softest rocks tunnel shields are used. These are giant **steel** tubes, which are the same size as the intended tunnel. The front edge of the shield is sharp and is pushed into the ground. The soil is dug out, and the tunnel behind the shield is lined to stop it from caving in.

Some tunnels under **rivers** are built by lowering sections of tunnel into the river. Divers join them together. When the tunnel is complete, the water is pumped out. Subway tunnels can be built in deep trenches. When completed, the tunnel is covered. The largest current tunneling operation is the digging of the world's longest rail tunnel under the Gotthard **mountain** range—part of the **Alps**—in **Switzerland**. It is due to be finished in 2006 and will be 36 mi. (58km) long. The tunnel will allow express trains to travel at high speeds from Milan, in northern **Italy**, to Zurich, Switzerland.

◁ The automatic **tunnel** digging **machines** used today are called moles. They have rotating cutters at the front, and the soil or rock they dig out is carried away by a conveyor belt. Hydraulic jacks act like springs to force the mole forward. The mole is powered by **electricity** and hydraulic motors.

Turbine

A turbine is a **machine** in which a **wheel**, drum, or **screw** is turned around by fast, flowing **water** or by steam, **wind**, or **gas** to produce **energy**. Waterwheels and **windmills** are simple turbines.

Water turbines are used at hydroelectric **power plants**. These plants are next to **dams** or **waterfalls**. The force of falling water carried through a pipe from the dam turns the turbine. The turbine does not produce **electricity** itself, but as it spins it drives a **generator**, which produces the electricity. Some turbines are wheels or drums with blades or cup-shaped buckets around their edges. Others are shaped like screws or propellers.

Steam turbines are operated by jets of steam. They have many uses. They are used to produce electricity in power plants, to propel **ships**, and to operate **pumps**.

Gas turbines are turned by fast-moving jets of gas. The gases are produced by burning **fuels** such as **oil**. The force of the expanding hot **air** escaping from the combustion chamber within the gas-turbine system is used to make the turbine rotate. Gas turbines are used to turn the propellers of **aircraft**.

Tiny air turbines driven by compressed air are used for dentists' drills. These turbines drive the drill at more than 250,000 revolutions per minute so the drilling of a tooth is done quickly.

Wind turbines are a good source of renewable **energy** because they generate electricity through wind power so they do not need **fuel** to generate power.

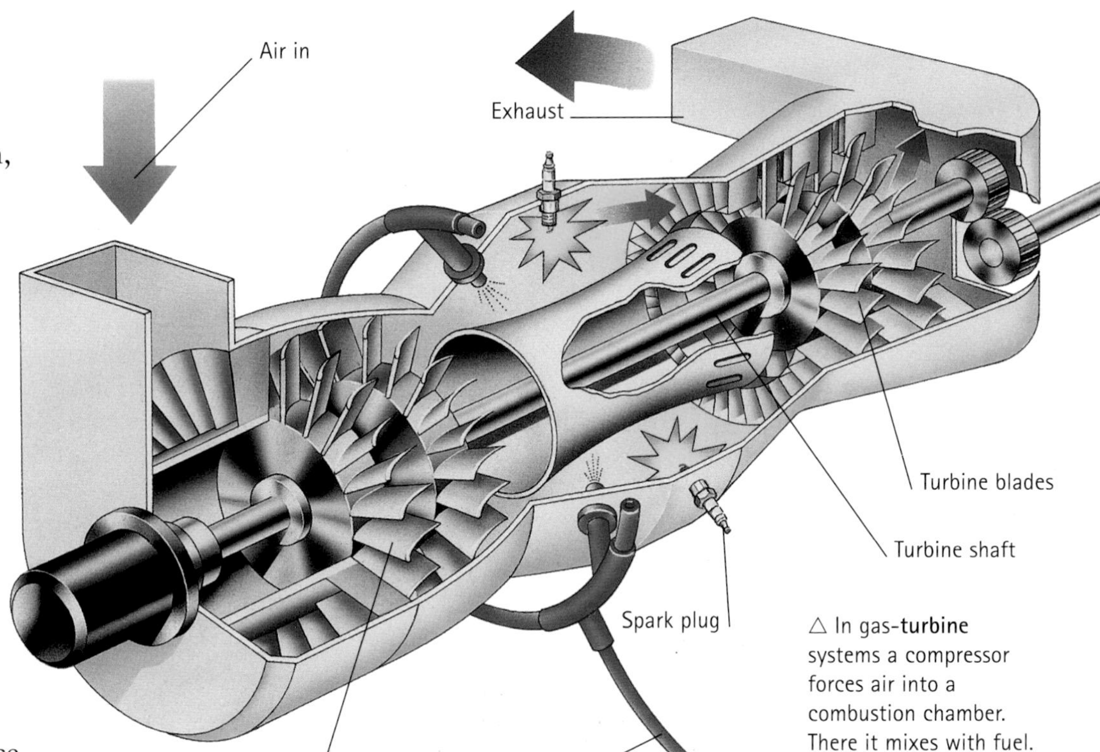

△ In gas-**turbine** systems a compressor forces air into a combustion chamber. There it mixes with fuel. The mixture is ignited by a spark. Hot gases are produced when the fuel burns. They expand and drive a series of fan blades—the turbine. The rotation of the turbine can be used to drive a generator.

Turkey

Turkey is a country that is partly in **Europe** and partly in **Asia**. The small European part covers three percent of the land. It lies west of the waterway that links the Black Sea to the **Mediterranean Sea**. This part includes the largest city, Istanbul, which was once called **Constantinople**. The Asian part, which is sometimes called Anatolia or Asia Minor, includes the capital, Ankara.

Most of Turkey's people follow the religion of **Islam**. Much of the land is mountainous, and large areas are covered by dry plateaus (tablelands). However, the coastal plains are fertile, and **farming** is the main industry. Turkey also produces chromium—a **metal** used to strengthen **iron** and **steel**.

Turkey was once part of the **Byzantine empire**, which was the eastern part of the **Roman Empire**. After Constantinople fell in A.D. 1453

TURKEY
Government: Republic
Capital: Ankara
Area: 297,200 sq. mi.
Population: 66,493,970
Language: Turkish
Currency: Turkish lira

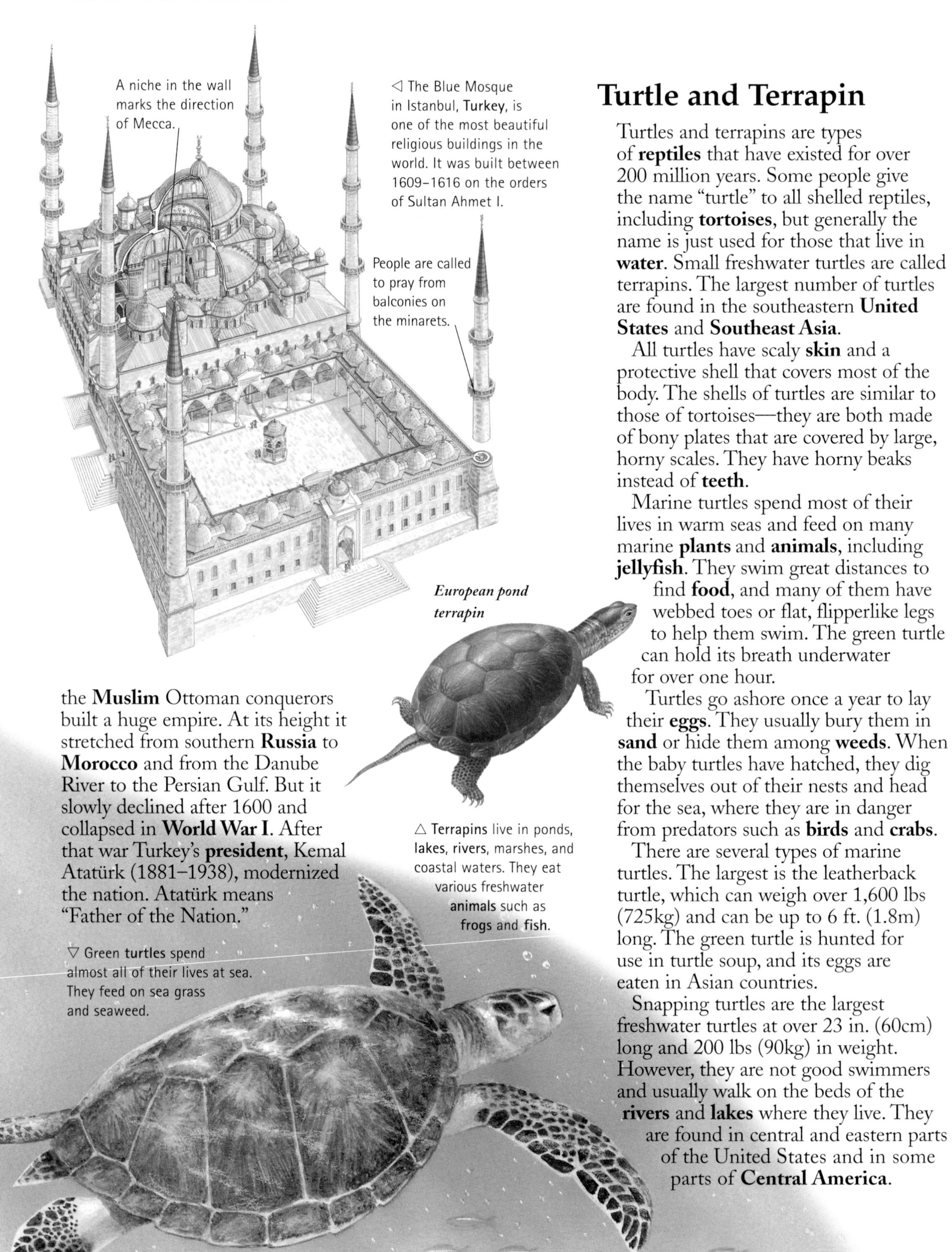

◁ The Blue Mosque in Istanbul, **Turkey**, is one of the most beautiful religious buildings in the world. It was built between 1609–1616 on the orders of Sultan Ahmet I.

the **Muslim** Ottoman conquerors built a huge empire. At its height it stretched from southern **Russia** to **Morocco** and from the Danube River to the Persian Gulf. But it slowly declined after 1600 and collapsed in **World War I**. After that war Turkey's **president**, Kemal Atatürk (1881–1938), modernized the nation. Atatürk means "Father of the Nation."

▽ Green **turtles** spend almost all of their lives at sea. They feed on sea grass and seaweed.

△ **Terrapins** live in ponds, **lakes**, **rivers**, marshes, and coastal waters. They eat various freshwater **animals** such as **frogs** and **fish**.

Turtle and Terrapin

Turtles and terrapins are types of **reptiles** that have existed for over 200 million years. Some people give the name "turtle" to all shelled reptiles, including **tortoises**, but generally the name is just used for those that live in **water**. Small freshwater turtles are called terrapins. The largest number of turtles are found in the southeastern **United States** and **Southeast Asia**.

All turtles have scaly **skin** and a protective shell that covers most of the body. The shells of turtles are similar to those of tortoises—they are both made of bony plates that are covered by large, horny scales. They have horny beaks instead of **teeth**.

Marine turtles spend most of their lives in warm seas and feed on many marine **plants** and **animals**, including **jellyfish**. They swim great distances to find **food**, and many of them have webbed toes or flat, flipperlike legs to help them swim. The green turtle can hold its breath underwater for over one hour.

Turtles go ashore once a year to lay their **eggs**. They usually bury them in **sand** or hide them among **weeds**. When the baby turtles have hatched, they dig themselves out of their nests and head for the sea, where they are in danger from predators such as **birds** and **crabs**.

There are several types of marine turtles. The largest is the leatherback turtle, which can weigh over 1,600 lbs (725kg) and can be up to 6 ft. (1.8m) long. The green turtle is hunted for use in turtle soup, and its eggs are eaten in Asian countries.

Snapping turtles are the largest freshwater turtles at over 23 in. (60cm) long and 200 lbs (90kg) in weight. However, they are not good swimmers and usually walk on the beds of the **rivers** and **lakes** where they live. They are found in central and eastern parts of the United States and in some parts of **Central America**.

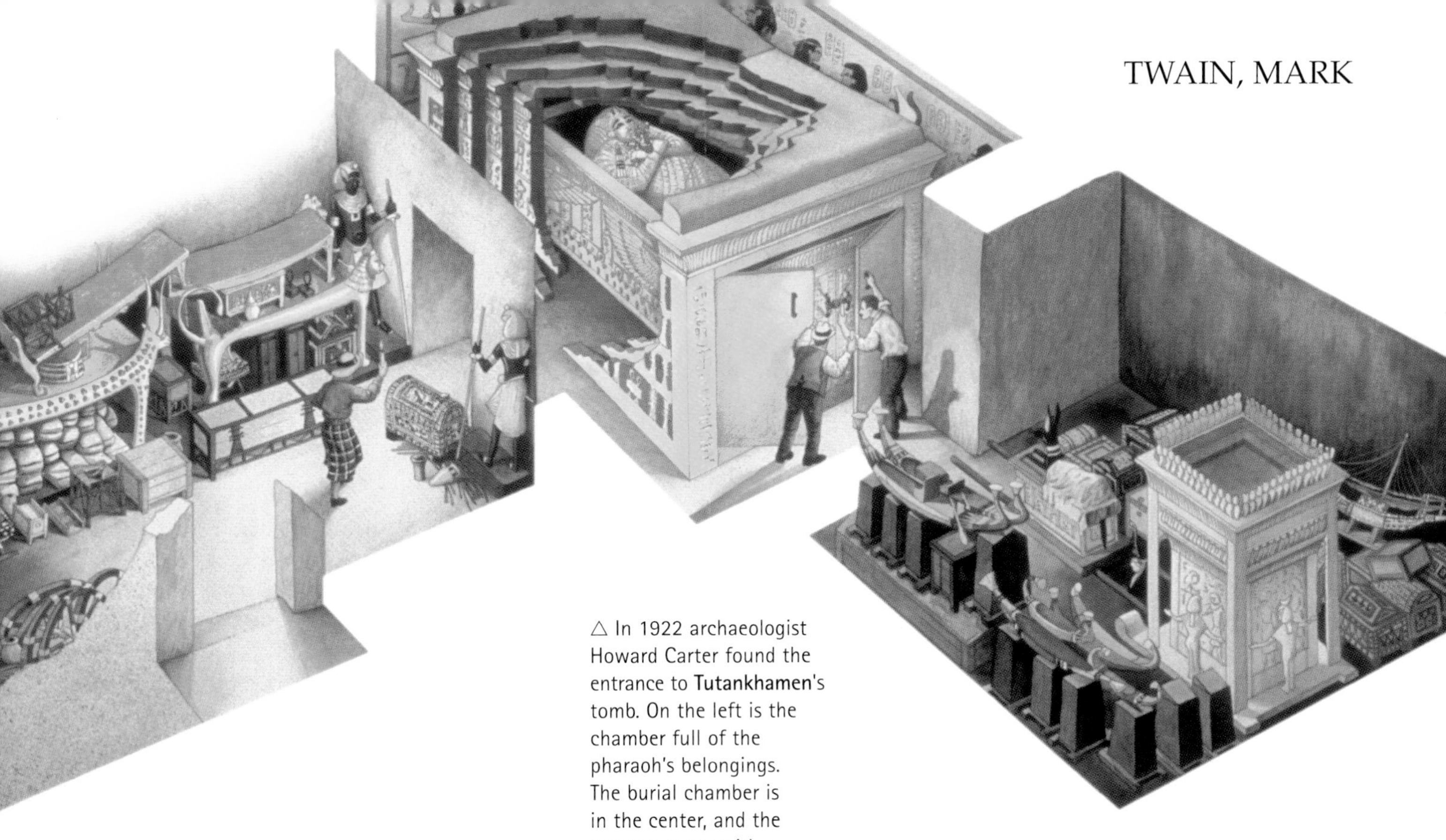

△ In 1922 archaeologist Howard Carter found the entrance to **Tutankhamen**'s tomb. On the left is the chamber full of the pharaoh's belongings. The burial chamber is in the center, and the treasure room with a shrine is on the right.

Tutankhamen

Tutankhamen was a **pharaoh** in ancient **Egypt**. His tomb was discovered in 1922 by British archaeologist Howard Carter (1873–1939). Carter and the Earl of Carnarvon (1866–1923) were digging in the Valley of the Kings in Egypt. The discovery was an exciting one because they had found the only tomb of a pharaoh that had not already been robbed of its treasures. In the tomb were a golden throne, caskets, statues, precious stones, and furniture. There were four **gold** shrines, one inside another, in the burial chamber.

Tutankhamen became a pharaoh when he was around 11 years old. He probably became the ruler because, as a child, he had married the daughter of the pharaoh Akhenaton. Akhenaton was a worshiper of the **sun** god Aton and had set up a new capital in Amarna. Tutankhamen brought back the old **religion** and returned the capital to Thebes. He died in 1352 B.C., having ruled for about eight years.

◁ The body of **Tutankhamen** was protected by a nest of human-shaped mummy cases. The cases were put inside a big stone coffin called a sarcophagus. Each mummy case was decorated with gold and jewels. The mummy itself was wearing a beautiful mask made of solid gold. The coffins provided a home for Tutankhamen's spirit, or *ka*.

Twain, Mark

Mark Twain was the pseudonym used by author Samuel Langhorne Clemens (1835–1910). His most famous books are *The Adventures of Tom Sawyer* and *The Adventures of Huckleberry Finn*.

Twain grew up in Hannibal, Missouri, on the **Mississippi River**. He had various jobs, including steamboat worker. It was from this experience that he took his pen name. The steamboat expression "mark twain" means "two fathoms" (a fathom is a nautical measure equal to 6 ft./1.8m). Twain lectured all over the world and wrote about his travels and life on the Mississippi.

Uganda

Uganda is a small **republic** in East **Africa**. It was ruled by the **United Kingdom** until 1962 when it became independent. General Idi Amin (born c. 1925) seized power in 1971, but in 1979 Ugandan and Tanzanian troops (see **Tanzania**) took over Uganda, and Amin fled to **Saudi Arabia**. Most Ugandans are farmers. They grow **coffee**, **tea,** and **cotton**. Coffee is their main export.

UGANDA
Government: Republic
Capital: Kampala
Area: 77,000 sq. mi.
Population: 23,985,712
Languages: Luganda, Swahili, English
Currency: Ugandan shilling

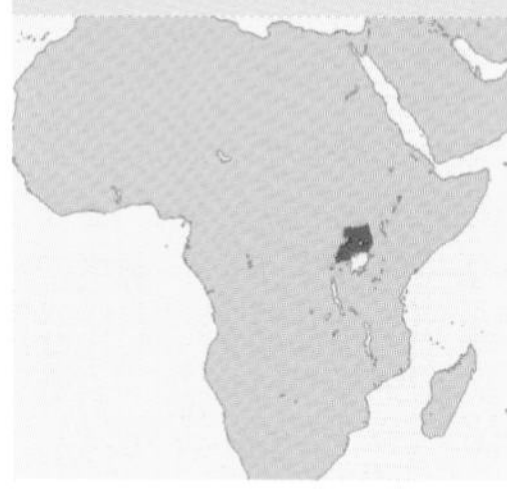

Ukraine

Ukraine became independent in 1991 following the break up of the **Soviet Union**. The land varies from fertile plains to forested **mountains**. Ukraine has great **mineral** wealth. Its factories produce **steel**, chemicals, and cement.

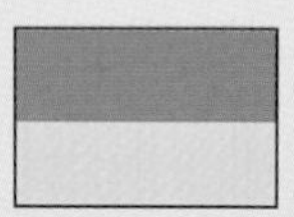

UKRAINE
Government: Republic
Capital: Kiev
Area: 232,800 sq. mi.
Population: 48,760,474
Languages: Ukrainian and Russian
Currency: Hryvnya

Ultrasound

Ultrasound is the use of high-frequency **sound** (ultrasonic) waves, which can produce pictures of parts within the **human body**. Ultrasonic waves are too high-pitched to be heard by **human beings**. They are produced by sending a high-frequency electric current (see **electricity**) through a crystal of **quartz**, causing the quartz to vibrate.

Ultrasound pictures can help doctors detect tumors and **blood** clots. They can also help ensure that a baby is developing normally.

Ultrasound is also used in **sonar** to detect underwater objects, such as **submarines**, and to map the seabed.

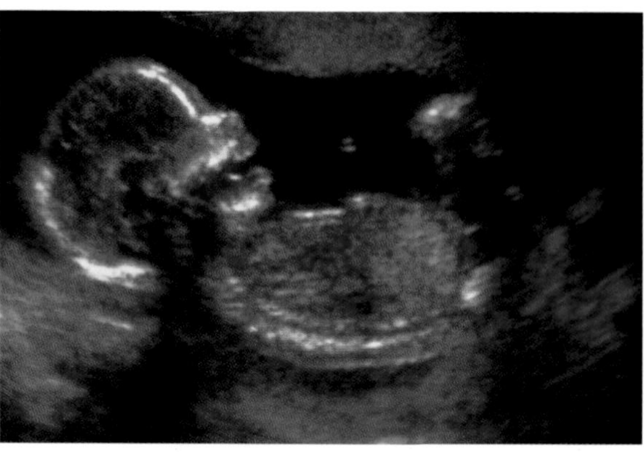

◁ **Ultrasound** is most commonly used to monitor a baby's development within the mother's womb.

Ultraviolet light

If **light** from the **sun** shines through a prism, it splits up into a rainbow of **colors** called a **spectrum**. Red is at one end of the spectrum, and violet is at the other. Ultraviolet (UV) light lies just beyond the violet end of the spectrum. **Human beings** cannot see it, but it blackens photographic film (see **photography**) and makes some chemicals glow. Most ultraviolet light from the sun is lost in the **atmosphere**, but enough rays reach **earth** to give people suntans. If more ultraviolet rays reached us, they would be very harmful.

Ultraviolet light has many uses. It is a powerful **germ** killer and can be used to sterilize **food** and medical equipment. Forged documents can be detected by shining ultraviolet light on them—the different types of ink on a document give off a certain glow.

Uluru

Uluru is the aboriginal name for the world's largest isolated **rock** formation. Sometimes known as Ayers Rock, it is 273 mi. (440km) southwest of Alice Springs in **Australia**. The rock is 1,100 ft. (335m) high and 6 ft. (10km) around its base.

▽ **Underground railroad** stations, or subways, have a network of tunnels, stairs, and escalators so that passengers can get up to the surface or move from one train line to another.

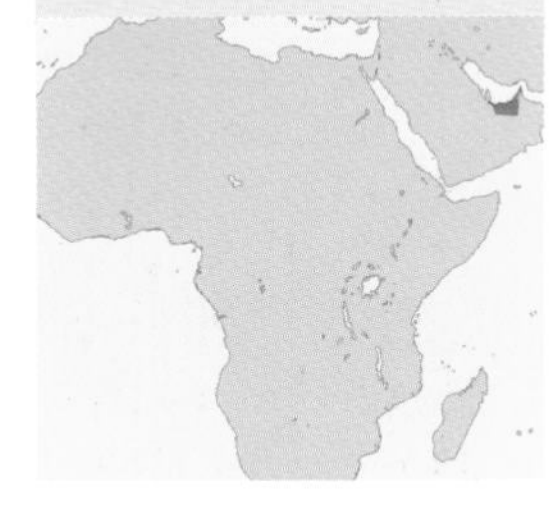

UNITED ARAB EMIRATES
Government: Federation
Capital: Abu Dhabi
Area: 32,000 sq. mi.
Population: 2,407,460
Language: Arabic
Currency: Dirham

Underground railroad, or subway

Every day millions of people use underground **railroads**, or subways. Underground electric trains (see **electricity**) carry passengers across cities much faster than **cars** and buses driving slowly through the busy streets above. Most subways run through **tunnels** excavated out of the **rock** beneath a city.

The best-known subways are in **London**, **New York**, **Moscow**, and **Paris** because they were the first cities to have an underground railroad system. The world's first subway opened in London in 1863. Today there are over 60 subway systems in the world. The London and New York subways are the longest networks, each having around 250 mi. (400km) of track. New York has the busiest subway—one billion people travel on it every year. The largest and most beautifully decorated subway stations are in Moscow.

The subway system in London is called the "tube." It is called the "métro" in Paris.

United Arab Emirates

The United Arab Emirates is made up of seven small states—Abu Dhabi, Ajman, Dubai, Al Fujayrah, Ash Shariqah, Umm al Qaywayn, and Ras al Khaymah. Most of the country is hot, dry **desert**, but **oil** in Abu Dhabi and Dubai make the area one of the richest in the world. Each state is led by a sheikh (ruler), and each sheikh sits on a governing council for the whole country, with one sheikh as **president**.

United Kingdom

The United Kingdom of Great Britain and **Northern Ireland** is the eleventh largest nation in **Europe**. **England**, **Wales**, and **Scotland** make up Great Britain. Northern Ireland, Scotland, and Wales are mountainous—the highest **mountain** is Ben Nevis in Scotland. Plains and valleys cover much of England. The longest **river** is the Severn, which flows through parts of England and Wales, and the **climate** is mild.

UNITED KINGDOM
Government: Constitutional monarchy
Capital: London
Area: 93,200 sq. mi.
Population: 59,647,790
Languages: English, Welsh, Scottish, Gaelic
Currency: Pound sterling

▽ During the 1800s thousands of Europeans emigrated to the **United States of America** with large shipping companies such as Cunard. Most people on board experienced cramped, overcrowded conditions.

Over 59 million people live in the United Kingdom. Few other countries are so crowded. Four out of five people live in cities such as Belfast, Glasgow, and the capital, **London**. The United Kingdom manufactures a wide range of goods, including **aircraft** components and **electronics**. Service industries, such as tourism, which provide services rather than producing goods, are increasing. Traditional industries, such as coal **mining**, are declining.

United Nations

Most of the world's countries belong to the United Nations. This organization was founded in 1945 after **World War II** to discuss problems, negotiate solutions, and help people worldwide. Each member country sends delegates to regular meetings of the United Nations' General Assembly in **New York**. The General Assembly suggests how countries should behave. It cannot make them take its advice, but the United Nations' Security Council can ask member countries for peacekeeping troops to help stop nations from fighting and to protect innocent people caught in the crossfire.

The United Nations works largely through 14 agencies to promote **health**, education, and cultural understanding. The Food and Agriculture Organization helps countries grow more **food**. The World Health Organization fights **disease**. The International Monetary Fund gives financial support to countries.

United States of America

The United States of America is the world's fourth largest nation. **Russia**, **Canada**, and **China** are larger in area, and more people live in China and **India**. There are 50 states in the United States. Forty-eight are in the same part of **North America**. The other two are Alaska in the north and the **Pacific** islands of Hawaii.

Mainland United States stretches from the Pacific Ocean to the **Atlantic Ocean**. Long **mountain** ranges run down the Pacific coast. Inland are flat-topped mountains and valleys, including Death Valley, the lowest place in the Americas, and the **Grand Canyon**, a huge gorge cut by the Colorado **River**. Farther east lie the tall peaks of the **Rocky Mountains**, which run from Canada to **Mexico**. Beyond these stretch the Great Plains, where the mighty **Mississippi River** flows. Another mountain range, the Appalachians, runs down the eastern side of the U.S.

The United States is a young country—in 2001 it was just 225 years old. The original 13 colonies declared their independence from Great Britain in 1776, and George **Washington** was elected the first **president** in 1789. By the mid-1800s the U.S. had grown to much the same size as it is today. **Explorers** had added new land to the original colonies, and the country stretched as far west as the Pacific Ocean. From 1861 to 1865 a **civil war** was fought between the South, which supported **slavery**, and the North, which wanted every person to be free. The North won, and slavery was abolished.

Between 1870 and 1900 thousands of Europeans (see **Europe**) came to seek land and new lives in the U.S. By 1900 the country's **population** had doubled. The 278 million citizens of the U.S. include **Native Americans**, **Inuit**, Polynesians, and people whose ancestors came from Europe, **Africa**, or **Asia**. Out of every 100 Americans 76 live in cities and large towns. **Washington, D.C.** is the capital, but **New York** is the largest city. Other large cities include **Los Angeles** and Chicago.

◁ Immigrants who sailed into the **United States of America** through New York harbor were greeted with the sight of the Statue of Liberty. The statue was a gift from France in 1884 to commemorate 100 years of U.S. independence.

The United States is one of the world's richest countries. Its huge farms produce **wheat** and more oranges, meat, **eggs**, and **cheese** than any other country. American miners extract the most **coal**, **copper**, **lead**, and **uranium** (see **mining**) in the world. The United States is the world's largest manufacturer of **cars** and chemicals.

UNITED STATES OF AMERICA
Government: Federal republic
Capital: Washington, D.C.
Area: 3,535,000 sq. mi.
Population: 278,058,881
Languages: English, Spanish
Currency: U.S. dollar

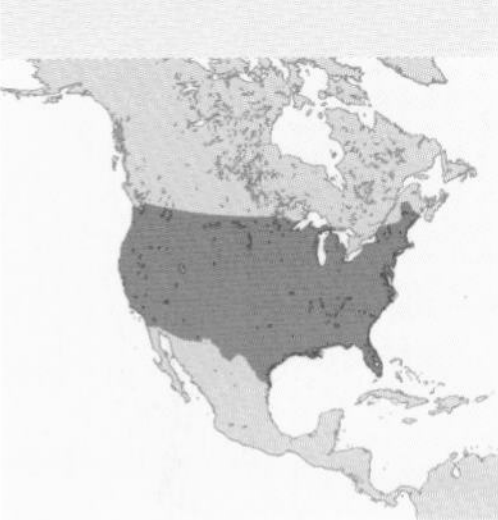

Universe

The universe is made up of **stars**, **planets**, **moons**, and other **matter** scattered through space. **Earth** is just a tiny part of the **solar system** in a **galaxy**—a large group of stars—known as the **Milky Way**. Beyond our galaxy lie possibly one billion other galaxies. Some are so far away that the light from them takes billions of years to reach us.

Scientists think that all matter in the universe was once squashed together as a fireball that exploded, shooting the matter out in all directions. As the matter spread it cooled, and clouds of **gas** and dust came together to form the stars, planets, and moons. This idea is called the Big Bang Theory.

Scientists are trying to figure out the future of the universe. In the Neverending Universe Theory galaxies will continue to break apart until space is almost all black emptiness. In the Big Crunch Theory the galaxies will stop moving apart. Their **gravity** will then pull them in again until they collide and explode.

▽ Scientists think that the **universe** was created by a huge explosion, called the Big Bang, 15 billion years ago. It generated a huge amount of heat and sent gases and other matter into space.

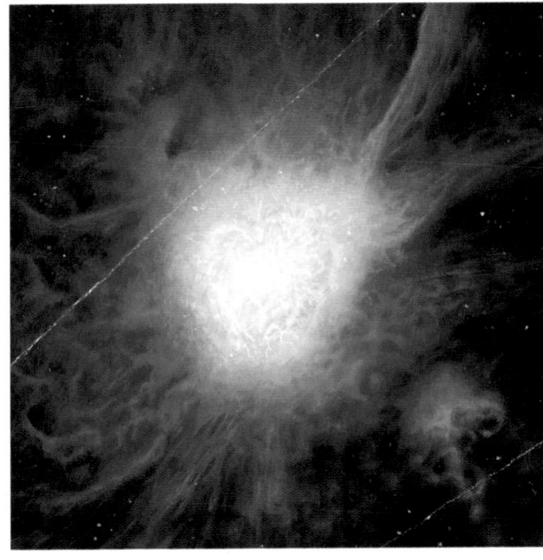

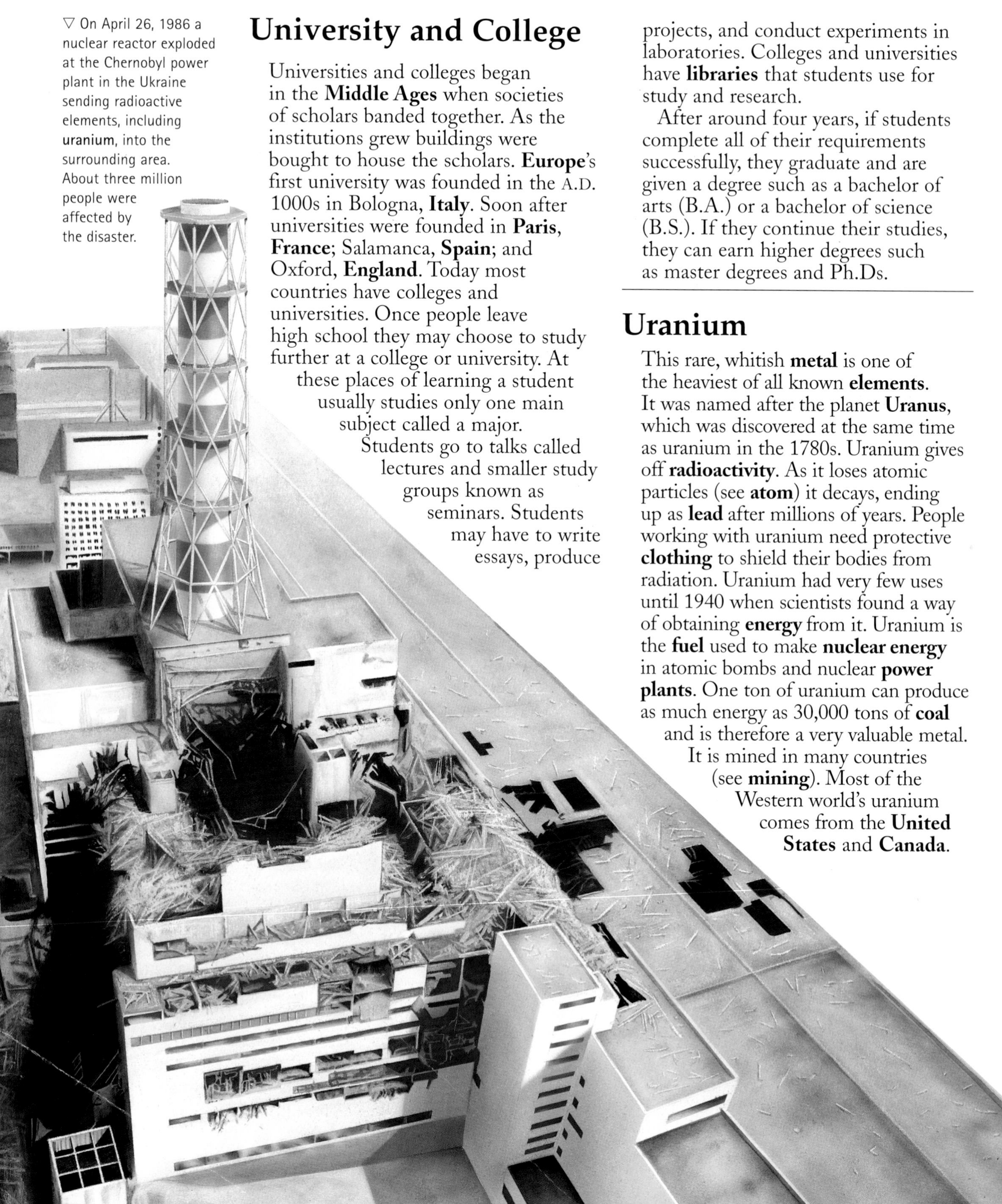

▽ On April 26, 1986 a nuclear reactor exploded at the Chernobyl power plant in the Ukraine sending radioactive elements, including **uranium**, into the surrounding area. About three million people were affected by the disaster.

University and College

Universities and colleges began in the **Middle Ages** when societies of scholars banded together. As the institutions grew buildings were bought to house the scholars. **Europe**'s first university was founded in the A.D. 1000s in Bologna, **Italy**. Soon after universities were founded in **Paris, France**; Salamanca, **Spain**; and Oxford, **England**. Today most countries have colleges and universities. Once people leave high school they may choose to study further at a college or university. At these places of learning a student usually studies only one main subject called a major. Students go to talks called lectures and smaller study groups known as seminars. Students may have to write essays, produce projects, and conduct experiments in laboratories. Colleges and universities have **libraries** that students use for study and research.

After around four years, if students complete all of their requirements successfully, they graduate and are given a degree such as a bachelor of arts (B.A.) or a bachelor of science (B.S.). If they continue their studies, they can earn higher degrees such as master degrees and Ph.Ds.

Uranium

This rare, whitish **metal** is one of the heaviest of all known **elements**. It was named after the planet **Uranus**, which was discovered at the same time as uranium in the 1780s. Uranium gives off **radioactivity**. As it loses atomic particles (see **atom**) it decays, ending up as **lead** after millions of years. People working with uranium need protective **clothing** to shield their bodies from radiation. Uranium had very few uses until 1940 when scientists found a way of obtaining **energy** from it. Uranium is the **fuel** used to make **nuclear energy** in atomic bombs and nuclear **power plants**. One ton of uranium can produce as much energy as 30,000 tons of **coal** and is therefore a very valuable metal. It is mined in many countries (see **mining**). Most of the Western world's uranium comes from the **United States** and **Canada**.

Uranus

The **planet** Uranus is 19 times farther away from the **Sun** than **Earth**. It was the first planet discovered with the help of a **telescope**. Although it is four times the size of Earth, Uranus looks like a tiny, greenish-blue disk when seen through a telescope.

Unlike our planet, Uranus is mainly made up of **gases**. It has a rocky core surrounded by **water**, and its dense atmosphere is made up of the gases helium, **hydrogen**, and methane. The methane gas gives the planet its distinctive blue-green **color**.

Uranus spins at a speed that makes one of its days about the length of 17 Earth hours, and one of its years lasts 84 Earth years. It is the only planet in our **solar system** to rotate at right angles to its **orbit** around the Sun. This gives Uranus strange **seasons**—the poles are the warmest places on the planet, with a summer lasting 42 years on the south pole, where the Sun never sets. At the same time the north pole is plunged into 42 years of darkness.

No one knew what the surface of Uranus looked like until 1986 when *Voyager II* flew close to it and took pictures. The pictures *Voyager* sent back showed that there are clouds on the surface, with **winds** blowing at up to 186 mph (300 km/h). The planet is circled by 11 rings of very dark, boulder-sized fragments. The planet also has at least 21 **moons**, one of which—Miranda—has **mountains** 16 mi. (26km) high.

△ **Uranus** viewed from Miranda, its smallest moon. Miranda's surface is covered with craters, mountains, and ice cliffs.

URANUS FACTS
Average distance from Sun: 1.78 billion mi.
Closest distance to Earth: 1.64 billion mi.
Average temperature (clouds): -328°F
Diameter across the equator: 31,693 mi.
Atmosphere: Hydrogen, helium, methane
Number of moons: 21 known
Length of day: 17 hours and 14 minutes
Length of year: 84 Earth years

Uruguay

Uruguay is one of the smallest countries in **South America** and is only 310 mi. (500km) long from north to south. It lies in the southeast between the **Atlantic Ocean** and its two large neighbors, **Argentina** and **Brazil**. Uruguay was a province of Brazil, but it became independent in 1825.

URUGUAY
Government: Republic
Capital: Montevideo
Area: 67,000 sq. mi.
Population: 3,360,105
Language: Spanish
Currency: Uruguayan peso

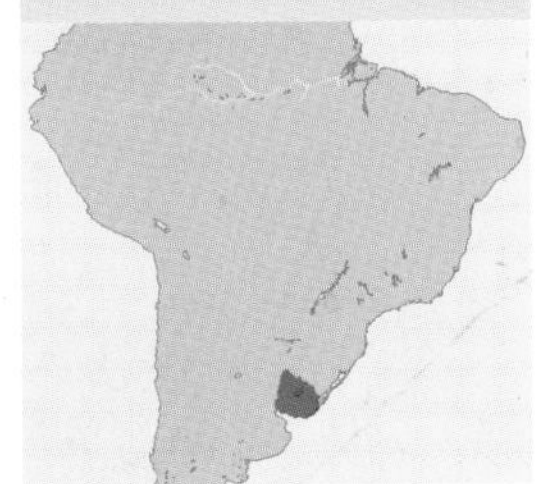

Low, grassy hills and lowlands cover most of Uruguay. Many streams and **rivers** flow into the large Uruguay River or into the river mouth, called the Río de la Plata. Uruguay has mild winters and warm summers.

Most of Uruguay's inhabitants are descended from Spanish or Italian settlers. More than one in three of them live in the capital, Montevideo. Its factories make **clothing**, furniture, and other goods. But most Uruguayans work in meatpacking plants, **wool** warehouses, or on country ranches. Cowboys, called gauchos, herd the millions of **sheep** and **cattle** that graze on these ranches. Sheep and cattle rearing is one of the most important industries, and wool is Uruguay's most valuable export.

◁ **Van Gogh** painted around 30 self-portraits in the short space of five years, from 1885 to the year he died, 1890. He painted this self-portrait in 1889.

Vaccination *see* Immunity

Vacuum

A vacuum is a space with nothing in it. It gets its name from *vacuus*, the Latin word for "empty." In fact there are no complete vacuums. When you try to empty a container by pumping out the **air**, a small amount of air always stays behind. This partly empty space is called a partial vacuum, and new air always rushes in to fill the space. This is how your **lungs** work. When you breathe out, you make a partial vacuum in your lungs. Air rushes to fill the space, making you breathe in. However, the space does not always fill up with air. When you suck in air from a straw dipped in lemonade, it is the lemonade that rushes to fill the vacuum and so reaches your mouth. It is a partial vacuum that helps keep **aircraft** in the air. An airplane's wings are shaped like they are to make a partial vacuum just above them. Air underneath the wings pushes them up to fill the space.

▽ Suction pulls dirty air into a **vacuum** cleaner. A swirling vortex of **air** spins the dirt out. The dirt is trapped in the machine while the air is pushed out. The red arrows show the direction taken by the dirty air.

Dirty air is sucked in

Clean air is pushed out of the machine

van Gogh, Vincent

Vincent van Gogh (1853–1890) was a Dutch painter who worked mostly in the south of **France**. Van Gogh lived a troubled life. Only his brother Theo (1857–1891) believed in his genius while he was alive. But now van Gogh's **paintings** are famous all over the world.

Van Gogh failed in every career he attempted. He turned to **art** to express his strong religious feelings, but it was not until 1880 that he decided to become a painter. In 1886 he went to **Paris** to visit his brother, who was a director of an art gallery, and was immediately attracted to the work of the Impressionists (see **Impressionism**). Influenced by this work, he began painting with vibrant **colors** and distinctive brushwork. In 1888 van Gogh moved to Arles, in the south of France, where he did most of his best-known paintings. During his last years he suffered from depression. He sold his first painting in 1890, but he committed suicide in July of that year.

During his short life van Gogh produced around 750 paintings and 1,600 **drawings**. Much is known about his life because of 700 letters he wrote to Theo and others.

Vatican City

St. Peter's Basilica

Sistine Chapel

Papal Palace

△ **Vatican City**'s buildings include St. Peter's Basilica, which was built between 1506–1614. Next to it stands the Papal Palace and the Sistine Chapel, which is decorated with frescoes by the painter Michelangelo.

Vatican City is the world's smallest country—only the size of a small farm—and about 870 people, mainly priests and nuns, live there. Located on Vatican Hill in northwest **Rome**, **Italy**, it is the **pope**'s home and the headquarters of the Roman Catholic Church (see **Christianity**). Despite its small size, the city has its own **flag**, **radio** station, banking system, and **railroad**. It also issues its own **stamps**.

Vatican City is surrounded by walls and contains many famous buildings. These include the Vatican Palace, which has more than 1,000 rooms; the Sistine Chapel, decorated by **Michelangelo**; and St. Peter's Basilica—the world's largest Christian **church**.

Vegetables

Vegetables are **plants** with parts that we can eat. They taste less sweet than the plant **foods** we call **fruits**. Vegetables, such as lettuce and spinach, are eaten for their leaves. Other vegetables are eaten for their roots or stems. Carrots and parsnips are roots. Celery and asparagus are stems. Peas, beans, and corn are **seeds**. **Tomatoes** and squash are really fruits but are sometimes described as vegetables.

Seeds supply body-building **proteins**. Leafy and root vegetables provide **vitamins**, **minerals**, and fiber to help keep our digestive systems working properly. Potatoes contain **starches**, which the body can burn up to make **energy**.

Canned vegetables often lose their valuable vitamins and minerals, but frozen and dried vegetables keep them. Vegetables can lose their vitamins and minerals and their flavor if they are overcooked. The best way of eating many vegetables is raw or in salads, by baking or steaming, or in a quick stir-fry. Some vegetables, including potatoes, cannot be eaten raw and have to be cooked first.

Many people are vegetarians—they do not eat the flesh of **animals**, including red meat, **poultry**, and **fish**. Vegetarians eat a diet of vegetables, **cereals**, nuts, seeds, and fruits. People who eat well-balanced vegetarian diets generally have lower **blood** pressure and less excess **fat** than those who eat meat. Vegetarians must be careful, however, to consume enough protein, such as soybeans, and vitamins to keep themselves healthy.

▽ There are many different **vegetables** that can be eaten as part of our daily diet. Most are grown from seeds, bulbs, or tubers and are then harvested within one year. A few grow on long-life plants.

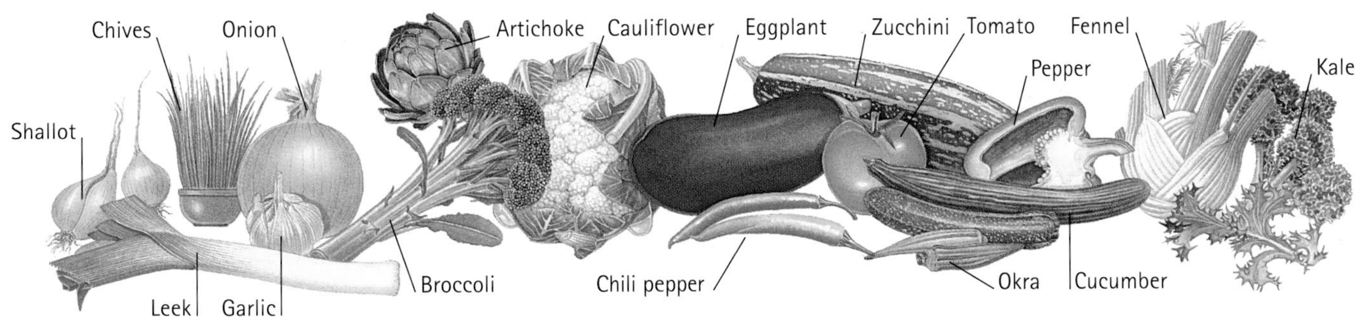

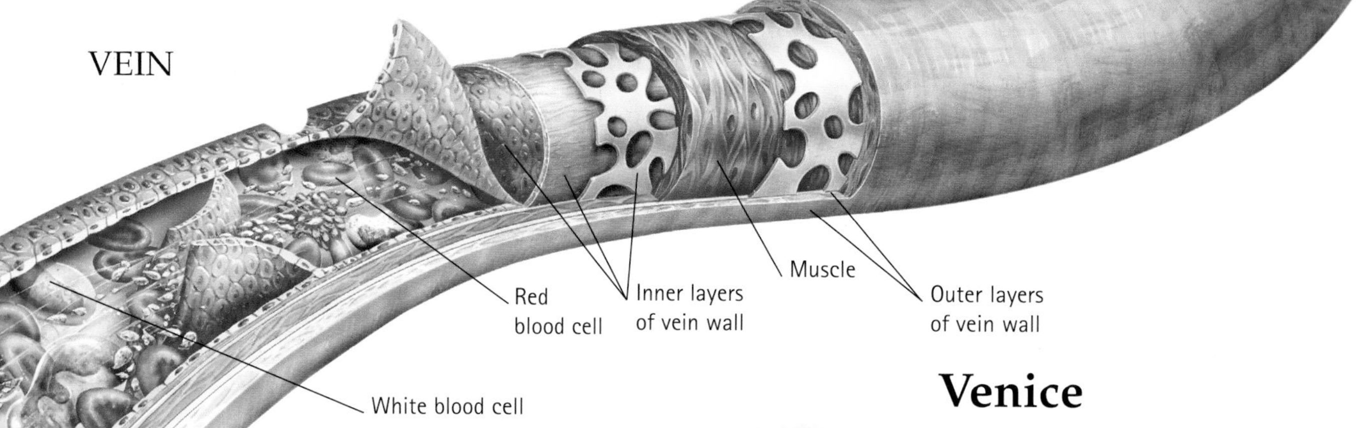

△ **Veins** carry blood toward the heart so it can be pumped to the lungs and then to the rest of the body.

Vein

Veins are narrow tubes that carry used **blood** from all parts of your body back to the **heart**. Blood flowing through the **arteries** is pushed along by the pumping of the heart. Blood in the veins has nothing to push it along, so many veins have flaps, or valves, inside them that close the tube if the blood begins to flow backward.

Venezuela

Venezuela is a large country on the north coast of **South America**. Its name means "little Venice" in Spanish because its many rivers reminded the **explorer** who named the country of the **canals** of Venice, Italy. In the northeast Venezuela is covered by high, flat-topped **mountains**—part of the **Andes** range. The Guiana Highlands in the southeast are covered with dense **rain forests**. Here the Angel Falls—the highest **waterfall** in the world—plunges down 3,211 ft. (979m). Grassy plains, called llanos, stretch across the middle of the country on either side of the Orinoco **River**. Thousands of **cattle** are raised on the plains.

Most Venezuelans live in towns and cities along the coast. Venezuela grows **coffee**, **cotton**, and cocoa. Its resources, especially **oil**, make it the richest country in the continent.

△ Beautiful masks, gowns, and cloaks are worn by people during the annual carnival in **Venice**. Many of the costumes are based on designs from the 1700s, when the **festival** was at its most grand.

VENEZUELA
Government: Federal republic
Capital: Caracas
Area: 340,200 sq. mi.
Population: 23,926,810
Language: Spanish
Currency: Bolívar

Venice

Venice is a beautiful city in **Italy** on the Adriatic Sea. It is built on a cluster of about 120 low, mud **islands**. The houses are built on wooden posts driven into the mud. A highway of just over 2 mi. (4km) connects the city with the mainland and carries a **road** and **railroad**. Within the city there is a network of over 180 **canals** instead of roads. Ferry boats take people into the center of the city. There are also elegant, black, flat-bottomed gondola boats for rent, which are propelled by an oarsman called a gondolier. These boats are very popular with the many tourists who travel to the city.

For hundreds of years Venice was the most important center for sea **trade** between **Europe** and the empires of the East. The city became very rich and is still full of palaces and beautiful houses built by merchants.

Venus

The **planet** Venus is named after the Roman **goddess** of beauty and love. Venus is the brightest planet in the **solar system**. We see it as the morning **star** or the evening star depending on where it is on its journey around the **Sun**. If you look at Venus through binoculars, you may see it looking like a small **moon**, showing just the part that is lit by the Sun.

Venus takes only 225 days to go around the Sun so more than three years pass on Venus for every two on **Earth**. But Venus spins so slowly that one day there lasts 243 Earth days. It is the only planet in our solar system to spin in the opposite way to the direction of its **orbit**.

Venus is about the same size as Earth and is made up of volcanic **rock**. But this planet has one of the most hostile environments in the solar system. The surface of Venus is hidden under a dazzling white cloak of clouds, which may be made up of tiny drops of sulfuric **acid**. Because it is the second planet from the Sun, its surface is much hotter than Earth. The **atmosphere** on Venus consists mainly of the **gas** carbon dioxide, which acts like a greenhouse, trapping the Sun's **heat** (see **global warming**). The average **temperature** on Venus is 896°F (480°C)—many times hotter than boiling **water**. Fierce **winds** above the surface blow at more than 102 mph (320 km/h), and chemical reactions in the atmosphere create electrical storms.

◁ In 1982 the Russian space probe *Venera 13* landed on **Venus** and sent back pictures and information to Earth. Soon after landing the probes were destroyed owing to the terrible climate on the planet.

VENUS FACTS
Average distance from Sun: 67 million mi.
Closest distance to Earth: 26 million mi.
Average temperature: 896°F
Diameter across the equator: 7,448 mi.
Atmosphere: Carbon dioxide, nitrogen
Number of moons: 0
Length of day: 243 Earth days
Length of year: 225 Earth days

Verb

Verbs are action words such as "go," "hit," "choose," "have," and "be." They describe what people or things are doing or what is happening to them.

Here are three examples of verbs in sentences: "It *is* a cold night. Tom *ate* the hamburger. Jill *was drinking* a milkshake." In the first two examples the verb is one word—"is" and "ate." In the third example it is two words—"was drinking."

In the first sentence the verb is describing something happening in the present. We call this the use of the present tense. If the action happened in the past, the verb changes—"It *was* a cold night." Similarly if the action is to happen in the future, the verb changes again—"It *will be* a cold night."

Verbs can also be active or passive. In the sentence "Tom *ate* the hamburger" the verb "ate" is active. If we said "The hamburger *was eaten* by Tom," the verb "was eaten" is passive.

Versailles

Versailles is a famous palace in **France**. It stands in a town, also called Versailles, just outside of **Paris**.

The palace at Versailles was begun by **Louis XIV** (1638–1715) in 1661 as a sort of vacation home for the king and his court. The most famous architects, sculptors, and gardeners of the time worked on the palace and its gardens to enable the king to live in greater luxury than any other **monarch** at the time.

The palace is built of pink and cream stone and is more than 2,624 ft. (800m) long. Inside are hundreds of beautiful rooms. The most famous is the Hall of Mirrors, which is lined with 483 enormous mirrors. Louis XIV spent enormous sums of **money** on the palace. The great expense and luxury of the palace at Versailles was one of the causes of the **French Revolution**.

Today the palace is a museum and attracts tourists from all over the world.

▽ Louis XIV wanted **Versailles** to be the most splendid palace in France. He spent about $87 million on the building—an enormous sum at that time.

VIKINGS

From about A.D. 800 people called Vikings began to leave their homes in Norway, Denmark, and Sweden in search of new farmland. Their strength and seamanship became legendary in Europe.

△ *Viking chieftains, or jarls, had weapons of high quality with carved gold or silver hilts.*

SHIPS

The Vikings were amazing seamen. For long sea journeys they sailed longships, which were extremely fast and had bows that were carved into fierce figureheads. They were known as "dragon ships" by the people who saw them. Longships were sleek and built of thin, overlapping planks that bent in rough seas. The boats were light and had low sides so the Vikings could sail up rivers as well as over seas. The Vikings were the first Europeans to build ships with sails, which meant their ships sailed very fast. Longships could also be rowed when there was no wind or when the ships sailed close to the coast in preparation for landing. They also built wider, deeper ships for trade and small rowing boats for coastal sailing.

EXPLORERS AND SETTLERS

The Vikings were a farming community, and the need to find more suitable farmland drove them to travel and explore. They used their skills as sailors to travel over much of the North Atlantic—an ocean known for its rough and treacherous waters. The Vikings discovered and then settled in Iceland and Greenland.

According to legend, the Viking Eric the Red (c. 950–1003) named the lush, green island "Iceland" in order to deter any potential raiders. Within 60 years of settling in Iceland (c. 874) the Vikings had already set up a national assembly, the Althing, which is now the oldest parliament in the world. Many of England's great northern cities, such as York, were founded by the Vikings. It is now also believed that the Viking explorer Leif Eriksson landed in North America in A.D. 1003, around 500 years before it was settled by Christopher Columbus (1451–1506) in 1492.

△ *Here is a picture of the Viking Althing in Iceland. This assembly made laws and discussed important issues.*

TRADE

Vikings were very successful traders. They founded many great trading posts, such as Dublin, in Ireland, and York, in England, from which goods flowed back into the Viking homelands. These trading routes also expanded east into Kiev and Novgorod, both in Russia, and as far south as Iraq and Syria. This allowed the Vikings access to goods that could never be produced in their own lands such as silk, honey, and spices.

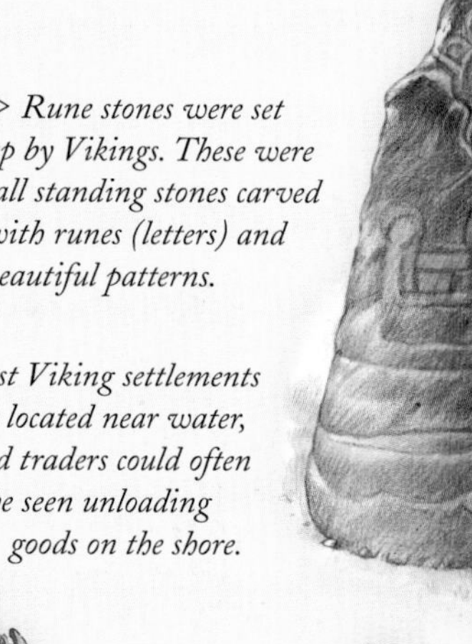

▷ *Rune stones were set up by Vikings. These were tall standing stones carved with runes (letters) and beautiful patterns.*

◁ *Most Viking settlements were located near water, and traders could often be seen unloading goods on the shore.*

VIKING SOCIETY

Viking homelands were divided into several kingdoms with a king at the head of each. However, people were more loyal to their local chieftains, or jarls, than to their king. The jarls therefore were the most wealthy and powerful people in society. They ruled over an area of land and had their own band of warriors who they could call on for raids. The largest group of people in Viking society were the *karls*—free men and women who were farmers or craftspeople. The poorest people were the *thralls*—slaves who were captured in raids or karls who had committed crimes. The thralls worked as servants of farmhands.

RELIGION

Vikings worshiped many gods and goddesses in the open air beside natural landmarks such as waterfalls or large rocks. Different gods controlled different aspects of their lives, and Odin, the king of the gods, ruled over all things. Vikings believed that the gods also controlled what happened to them after they died. By the 1100s many Vikings had converted to Christianity.

▷ *When a jarl died, he had a spectacular burial. His body was placed in a boat, which was then set on fire.*

LONGHOUSES

Most Viking families lived in large, low rectangular buildings called longhouses. Each house had one main room where the family lived and slept. In the middle of the room was a huge fireplace, which provided heat and light and was used for cooking food. Smoke from the fire escaped through a small hole in the roof. Family life centered around the fire. Women and girls did most of the household chores such as cooking. They also spun wool and flax, which was then woven on a loom to make cloth.

Inside a longhouse

ENTERTAINMENT

In the evenings Viking households settled down for entertainment. Vikings were excellent storytellers and loved to recite poems and stories called sagas. These were memorized because Vikings had no pens or paper with which to write them down. The tales told of the great deeds of gods and famous warriors. Vikings also enjoyed playing board games similar to chess or checkers and enjoyed competitive sports such as wrestling and skiing.

WARRIORS

The Vikings earned a reputation for being bloodthirsty warriors and were feared throughout Europe. Every able-bodied Viking man was trained to fight. Warriors were led by their chieftains and went raiding or trading in the summer. The warriors did not fear dying because death in battle meant that they would be taken to Valhalla (the god Odin's great hall) and feast and drink forever. So they fought ferociously and bravely with their weapons, which included swords, axes, spears, and wooden shields. Rich warriors wore protective chain-mail shirts and metal helmets.

END OF THE VIKING AGE

The power of the Vikings started to come to an end around A.D. 1066 when the king of Norway, Harald Hardrada (1015–1066), was killed at the Battle of Stamford Bridge, in England, by the Anglo-Saxon King Harold of England (1020–1066). When King Harold himself was killed later in the same year during the Battle of Hastings against William the Conqueror of Normandy (1028–1087), it signaled the end of the Viking age and the beginning of Norman power in Europe.

▷ *Viking raids involved up to 60 longships filled with warriors. They targeted treasure-filled churches and plundered coastal towns.*

SEE ALSO

Anglo-Saxons, Christianity, Dark Ages, God and Goddess, Myths and Legends, Ship and Boat, Slavery, Weaving, William the Conqueror

△ Around 520 million years ago Pikaia (center) was the first fish and the first **vertebrate**, or **animal** with a backbone.

△ Queen **Victoria's** character and long reign, from 1837 to 1901, restored strength and popularity to the British monarchy.

△ This picture shows the first eruption of **Vesuvius** in A.D. 79.

Vertebrate

Vertebrates are **animals** with a backbone or spine. The backbone is made up of short **bones** called vertebrae. This word comes from a Latin word that means "to turn." Most vertebrates can bend and straighten their backbones by turning their vertebrae slightly.

Many things make vertebrates different from other animals. Most have a bony case to protect their **brain**, ribs to protect their **heart**, **lungs**, and other delicate parts, and one or two pairs of limbs. And most vertebrates have a **skeleton** made of bone.

There are seven main groups of vertebrates. The simplest group includes the lampreys. Lampreys are eellike **fish** with no jaws. They have a spine but no skeleton. Next come **sharks** and skates, which have a skeleton of a light, bendable material called cartilage. All other vertebrates have bones. They are the bony **fish**, **amphibians**, **reptiles**, **birds**, and **mammals**.

Vesuvius

Vesuvius is one of the world's most famous **volcanoes** and the only active volcano on the mainland of **Europe**. The **mountain** rises over the Bay of Naples in southern **Italy**. It is about 4,000 ft. (1,200m) high but gets smaller every time it erupts.

The first eruption happened in A.D. 79. Nobody realized that Vesuvius was an active volcano, so people had built towns close by and farmed the slopes of the **mountain**. For three days Vesuvius threw out ash and lava that buried the Roman cities of **Pompeii** and Herculaneum. There have been nine destructive eruptions in the last 200 years. The worst in recent years happened in 1944 during **World War II**. One village was destroyed, and Allied troops helped people escape from the flowing lava.

Victoria, Queen

Queen Victoria (1819–1901) ruled the **United Kingdom** and British empire for 64 years—longer than any other British **monarch**. During her reign the nation grew richer and its empire larger than ever before. She was the queen of many countries, including **Australia**, **New Zealand**, **Canada**, and **South Africa** and was the empress of **India**.

Victoria was the daughter of Edward, Duke of Kent (1767–1820). George III (1738–1820) was her grandfather. She was just 18 when she inherited the throne from her uncle, William IV (1789–1837), in 1837. Two years later she married her German cousin, Prince Albert (1819–1861). They had four sons and five daughters. Prince Albert died of typhoid fever in 1861. His death left the queen deeply unhappy. For many years she wore only black clothes to show her grief. She also stopped going to public ceremonies.

Victoria was very popular with her people. In 1887 she had been queen for 50 years. All over the British empire there were huge parades and parties to celebrate this Golden Jubilee. In 1897 there were more celebrations for her Diamond Jubilee. Her reign is known as the Victorian Age.

Video

A video is a **recording** of moving pictures and **sound**. Most of the programs you see on **television** are video recordings.

Videotape was invented in 1956. A videotape is played in a video recorder (VCR) that is connected to a television, and the video appears on the television screen. A VCR can record television programs on videotape in much the same way as a tape recorder records sound (see **recording**). Old recorded programs can be erased, and new ones can be recorded on the same tape.

Many people record their own home videos using camcorders, or video **cameras**, which are handheld devices. Electric signals (see **electricity**) from the camera or from a television program are recorded on magnetic tape (see **magnetism**). The main difference from a tape recorder is that the "record" and "replay" heads in a video recorder spin around as the tape passes through it. This allows the heads to move very quickly over the surface of the tape, giving the high recording speed needed to record picture signals. Recorded camcorder images can be played back on a television.

Video images and sounds can also be stored on digital versatile discs (DVDs), which are similar to compact discs (CDs). However, DVDs can hold seven times more data, and so a whole movie can be recorded onto one DVD. The signals are stored in small pits and bumps on the surface of the DVD and can be played back by a **laser** in a DVD player. DVDs have a much clearer sound and picture quality than videotapes. There are also DVD recorders that can record video onto DVDs. However, each disc can be recorded on only once.

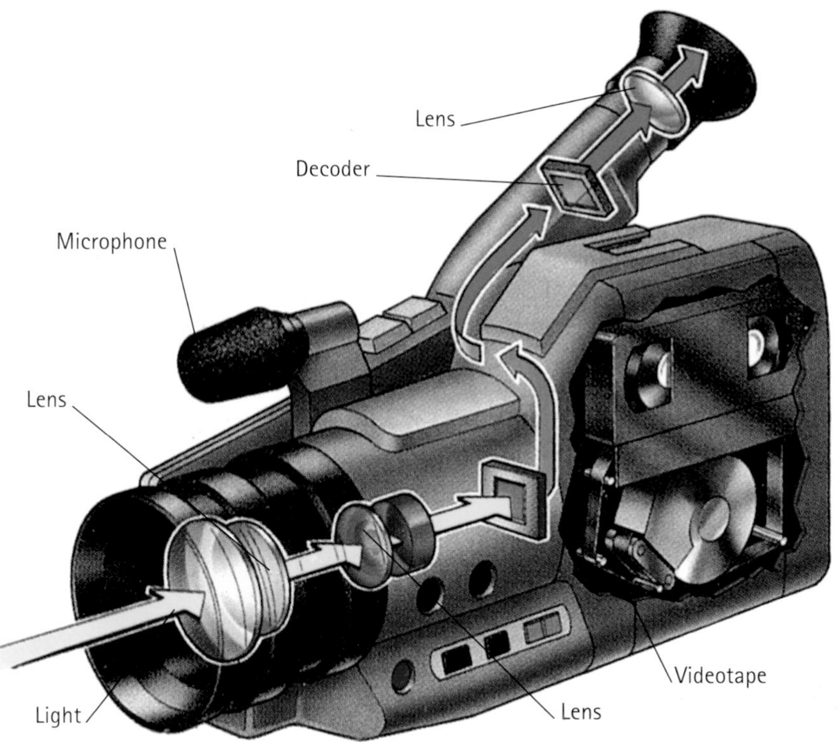

△ **Videos** can be recorded onto videotape using a handheld device called a camcorder. Many people use them on vacations or to record events such as weddings or birthdays.

Vienna

Vienna is the capital of **Austria** and stands in the east of the country on the Danube River. It is a very ancient place. **Celts** settled there more than 2,000 years ago. Then the Romans (see **Roman Empire**) built a city called Vindobona. Many buildings from the **Middle Ages** still stand in Vienna. The most famous is St. Stephen's Cathedral. Until the end of **World War I** it was the home of the powerful **Hapsburg** family.

Vienna has always been popular with artists and musicians. **Beethoven** (1770–1827) and **Mozart** (1756–1791), among many other famous musicians, lived there. Great people of **science** and **medicine**, such as Sigmund **Freud**, also lived there. Today more than 1.5 million people live in Vienna.

Vienna is an important center for industries, **trade**, and **communications**. Its main products are electrical goods, **paper**, and **clothing**. Tourism is one of the most important industries.

▽ The Austrian city of **Vienna** is known for its beautiful architecture as well as its music. In the 1800s, when **Beethoven** lived in Vienna, opera houses and other magnificent buildings were built.

Vietnam

Vietnam is a small country in **Southeast Asia**. It has a hot and damp **climate**.

Vietnam was once ruled by **France** as part of Indochina. After **World War II** it was divided into two countries—North Vietnam and South Vietnam. Hanoi was the main city in the north, and Saigon (now called Ho Chi Minh City) was the capital of the south. From the 1950s Communist North Vietnam (see **communism**) was at **war** with the South, which was supported by the **United States**. The war ended in 1975, with more than one million Vietnamese civilian casualties and the deaths of around 58,000 U.S. soldiers. North and South Vietman were then united under a Communist **government**.

VIETNAM
Government: Communist
Capital: Hanoi
Area: 125,500 sq. mi.
Population: 79,939,014
Language: Vietnamese
Currency: Dong

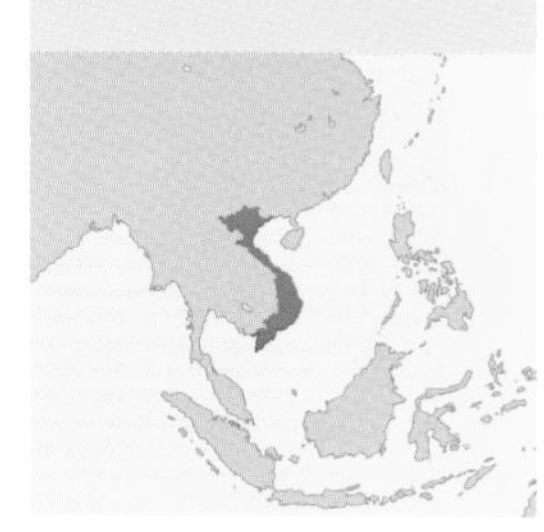

Vikings *see* pages 352–353

Violin

The violin is a **musical instrument**. It belongs to the string family and is usually the smallest string instrument in an **orchestra**.

A violin is a curved wooden box shaped like a figure eight. A long neck is attached to one end of the box. Four strings made of cat-gut or nylon are stretched from the top of the neck to the bottom end of the box.

The violin is played with a bow that has a flat ribbon made up of about 150 horsehairs. When this is drawn across the strings, they vibrate to make musical **sounds**. The strings can also be plucked.

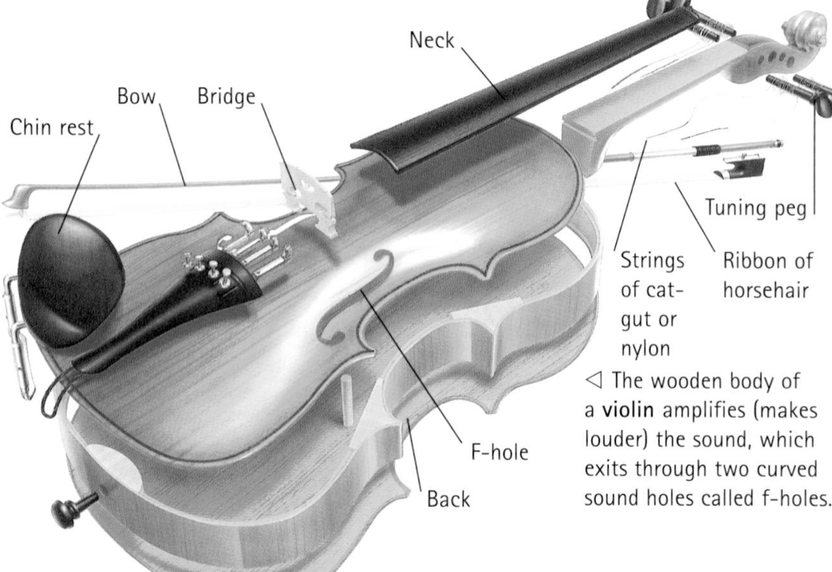

◁ The wooden body of a **violin** amplifies (makes louder) the sound, which exits through two curved sound holes called f-holes.

Virus

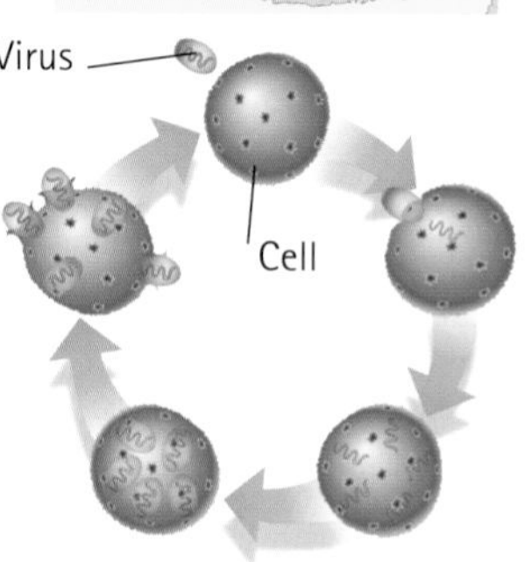

△ A **virus** spreads in the body by using the body's cells to make copies of itself. As the replicas form they destroy the cell, and each virus starts again.

Viruses are very small living things that cause **diseases** in **plants** and **animals**. They are smaller than **bacteria** and can be seen only with very powerful electron **microscopes**.

You can be infected with viruses by swallowing them or breathing them in. Some **insects** carry viruses, which they pass on when they bite you. Once inside the body a virus travels through the bloodstream (see **blood**). It gets inside a living **cell**, where it produces more viruses. Sometimes the cell is entirely destroyed by the viruses.

Diseases caused by viruses include measles, chicken pox, mumps, **AIDS**, influenza, and colds. Viruses are very hard to kill. Vaccination helps prevent some of these diseases.

When a virus enters the body, the blood produces substances called antibodies. After a while there are usually enough antibodies to kill all of the viruses, and the patient recovers.

Vitamins and Minerals

Vitamins are chemicals that **human beings** need to stay healthy. They are found in different types of **food**. The six kinds of vitamins are A, B, C, D, E, and K. Vitamin B is a group of vitamins.

The first people to realize that certain types of food were important to **health** were sailors. On long voyages they got a **disease** called scurvy, caused by a lack of vitamin C, if they could not eat fresh **fruits** and **vegetables**. From the 1700s English sailors were given limes to eat to prevent scurvy and were nicknamed "limeys" by the Americans.

No single food has all the vitamins a person needs. That is why it is important to eat a mixture of foods. Some people get their vitamins from pills, but no one really needs pills if they eat a varied, healthy diet. The elderly, babies, and pregnant women all need to take more vitamins than usual. However, too much of some vitamins, such as vitamin A, can be harmful.

Human beings also need **minerals** in small amounts. Calcium, found in **milk** and **cheese,** builds healthy **bones** and **teeth**. Iron is needed for hemoglobin—the part of red **blood cells** that carries **oxygen** from your **lungs** to the tissues. Other minerals needed are iodine, phosphorus, sodium, and potassium.

△ Limes are a valuable source of **vitamin** C.

Volcano

A volcano is an opening in the surface of **earth**. Burning **gas**, molten **rocks**, and ash escape from this opening. Sometimes they trickle out, and sometimes they explode. An explosion is called an eruption.

Some volcanoes are gently sloping **mountains** with cracks, or fissures, in them. Hot, **liquid** rock, called lava, flows out through the fissures. Other volcanoes are steep-sided mountains with large holes at the top. These are called cone volcanoes and explode when they erupt.

Erupting volcanoes can do a lot of damage. The Roman city of **Pompeii** was destroyed by **Vesuvius** in A.D. 79. In 1883 Krakatoa, a volcano in **Indonesia**, erupted, causing a tsunami (tidal wave) that killed 36,000 people. Volcanoes can also make new land. An **island** called Surtsey, south of **Iceland**, was made by a volcano erupting under the sea in 1963.

Volcanoes appear in long mountainous chains. These chains mark the edges of the huge plates that form earth's surface. They are the most unstable parts of earth's crust. One chain, called "the ring of fire," circles the **Pacific Ocean**. **Earthquakes**, **geysers**, and hot springs are all found in the same areas as volcanoes.

▽ Far below the surface of a cone **volcano** is a chamber containing magma (molten rock) and hot, bubbling gases. During an eruption the magma shoots up through a chimneylike vent, and lava and ash explode out of the volcanic cone.

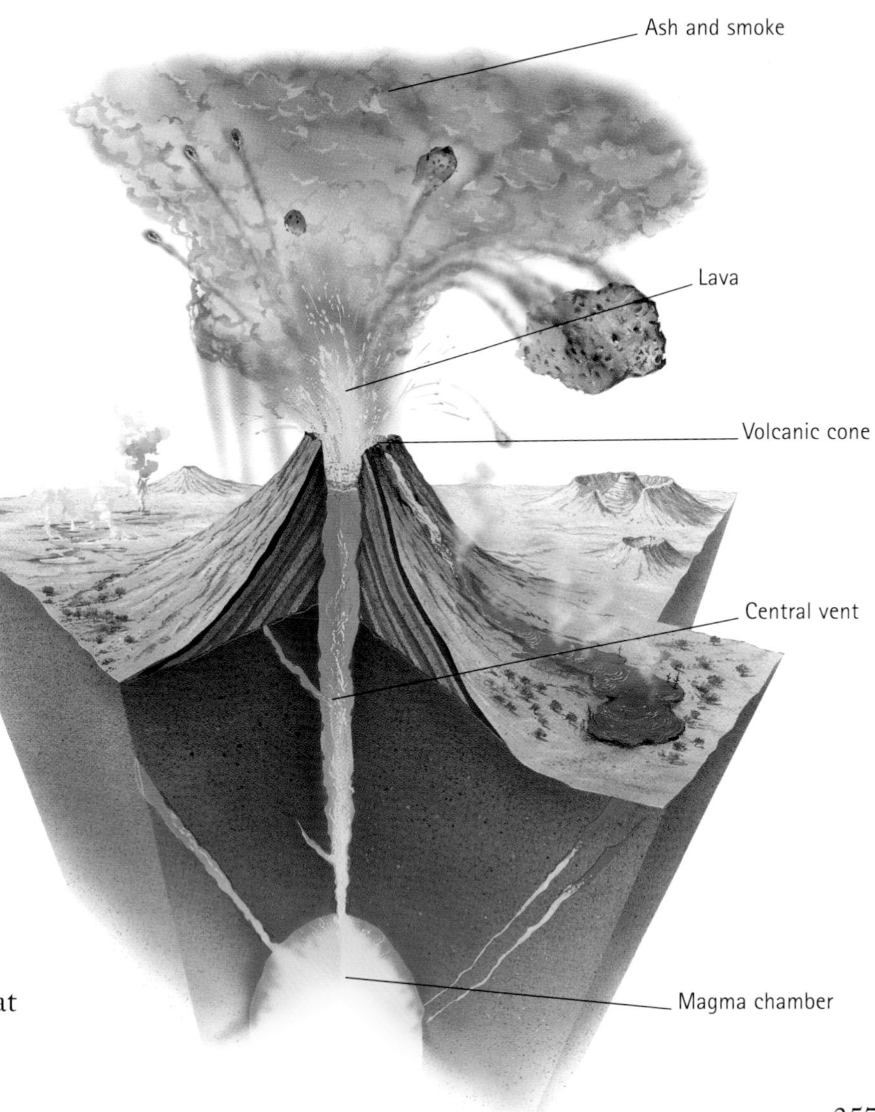

Volume

The volume of an object is the amount of space it takes up. You can find out the volume of a solid by measuring its height, width, and depth and then multiplying the figures together. So a block with equal sides, each 10 in. long, has a volume of 1,000 cubic in.—10 in. x 10 in. x 10 in.

It is easy to find out the volume of boxes or bricks or anything with straight edges. Measuring the volume of something with an irregular shape is more difficult. A very simple method was discovered by Archimedes (c. A.D. 290–211), a Greek scientist. A story told about him says that he was getting into a bathtub, which was full to the brim, and **water** spilled over the side. He suddenly realized that the volume of water that had spilled must be exactly the same as the volume of his body. This means that any irregular object can be measured by plunging it into **water** and measuring the rise in the water level.

Vowel

Vowels are the letters A, E, I, O, and U. Sometimes the letters Y and W are used as vowels. Vowels are pronounced with the mouth open. What they sound like depends on the position of your **tongue** in your mouth. The shape your lips make is also important. If they are pushed forward, as if you are whistling, you make an "oo" **sound**. If your lips are pulled back, you make an "ee" sound.The tongue and the lips c an shape themselves in hundreds of different ways so there are hundreds of different vowel sounds. Sometimes two or three vowel sounds are run together to make a new sound. The vowel sounds in one **language** are often very difficult for speakers of another language to say.

The pronunciation of vowel sounds changes over the years. The author Geoffrey Chaucer (c. 1342–1400), pronounced "do" with the vowel sound we use for "go." He pronounced "bee" with the vowel sound we use for "bay," "by" the way we say "bee," and "cow" as we pronounce "coo."

Vulture

Vultures are large **birds** of prey. They live in the warm areas and **mountains** of **Asia**, **Africa**, **North America**, **South America**, and southern **Europe**. The largest land bird in **North America** is a type of vulture—the California condor. When its wings are spread out, they measure up to 10 ft. (3m) from tip to tip.

Vultures do not hunt for their **food**. They live on carrion—the rotting bodies of dead **animals**. Sometimes vultures have to wait for their meal until a large hunter, such as a **lion**, has made a kill and eaten its fill. Vultures may spend hours soaring high on their long wings, waiting for an opportunity to eat. When one vulture swoops down, others follow it and join in the feast.

Most vultures have bald heads and necks. This stops their **feathers** from getting messy when they plunge their heads into large carcasses. Most vultures have strong beaks to tear into meat. They have very good eyesight and can spot dead or dying animals from far away. They also have a superb sense of **smell**.

Vultures nest in groups on cliffs, in trees, or on the ground. They lay only one or two **eggs** at a time.

▽ **Vultures**, such as these African white-backed vultures, do a vital job because they clean up the carcasses left behind by predators. Once they spot a carcass they glide down to feed. Some vultures have adapted to living in towns and scavenge in garbage dumps.

Wagner, Richard

Richard Wagner (1813–1883) was a German composer whose **music** changed **opera**. He believed that the music and plot of an opera should be closely bound together in the same way as the dialogue and plot of a play are. Unlike many other composers, Wagner wrote his own librettos (scripts).

In 1848 Wagner took part in a political **revolution** in **Germany** and had to escape to **Switzerland**. There he began his greatest work, *The Ring of the Nibelung*. This long piece consists of four music dramas based on old German legends. When Wagner returned to Germany, he designed a **festival theater** in Bayreuth especially for his operas. Today people from all countries still go to Bayreuth to hear them.

Richard Wagner spent the last part of his life in debt. He died one year after his final opera, *Parsifal*, was performed.

Wales

Wales is part of the **United Kingdom** of Great Britain and **Northern Ireland**. It lies to the west of **England** and is a country of low **mountains** and green valleys. The highest mountain is Snowdon (3,559 ft./1,085m above sea level), and Cardiff is the capital.

English is the main **language**, but more than one fifth of the people still speak Welsh as well.

△ The **walrus** lives in the shallow Arctic seas. It has flippers but no tail. Although clumsy on land the walrus can swim at speeds of about 15 mph (24 km/h).

The Atlantic and the Pacific walruses are big animals. The male Atlantic walrus can be up to 50 ft. (4m) long and can weigh as much as 4,000 lbs (1,800kg).

△ German composer Richard **Wagner**'s operas include *The Flying Dutchman, Tannhauser, Tristan and Isolde, Lohengrin, The Master Singers of Nuremberg,* and *Parsifal.*

Wallaby

Wallabies are small members of the **kangaroo** family. They live in **Australia**, **New Zealand**, and parts of **New Guinea**. There are many different types of wallabies. Most are about the size of **hares**, although the biggest is about 3.28 ft. (1m) long with a 23 in. (60cm) tail.

Wallabies feed mostly on **grass**. They also make good **food** for other animals. Two of their natural enemies are the dingo—the Australian wild **dog**—and the **eagle**. Some breeds of wallabies are hunted for their valuable fur.

Walrus

Walruses belong to the **seal** family and live in the cold waters of the **Arctic** and northern **Atlantic Ocean**. Their enormous canine **teeth** look like two tusks and can be up to 3.29 ft. (1m) long. Walruses use them to scrape up clams and **shellfish** to eat. They also use their tusks to fight, and even polar **bears** stay away from fully grown walruses.

WARFARE

Warfare is armed conflict between two countries or states or between groups within a country or state. This type of conflict is common throughout the history of humankind, as nations and sometimes religions struggle for power.

△ *The Parthians (nomadic people from between 250 B.C. to A.D. 350) tricked their enemies by pretending to retreat but then turned in their saddles and fired arrows at their pursuers.*

△ *The Battle of Agincourt in 1415 was a notable English victory. The French had at least three times as many heavily armed troops, but they were badly led and organized.*

WHY GO TO WAR?

A war can start for many reasons. Frequently a group may wish to gain something by conflict, such as food, land, or natural resources. Ancient civilizations, such as the Romans, declared war on other nations to build up their empires. Some wars, such as the Crusades and the Thirty Years' War, were fought for religious reasons.

▽ *Galleons were important weapons of war in the 1600s. Here an English galleon brings down the masts of a Dutch ship during a broadside attack in the Anglo-Dutch War.*

WEAPONS

A war is usually won by the nation with the most powerful weapons. Early battles were fought with simple, handheld weapons such as spears and stone axes. Around 1000 B.C. iron swords were developed. Huge siege weapons, such as battering rams and catapults, were used by the Romans from 200 B.C. to A.D. 400 to batter down enemy defenses. During medieval times crossbows and handheld weapons, such as maces, were popular. Then came the invention of gunpowder, which brought with it a new range of destructive weapons. Cannons were first used in European warfare in the 1300s, and a handheld firearm that could be used by one person was first developed in 1500. However, it was not until the development of steel and machine tools in the late 1800s that firearms became really powerful and accurate.

MECHANIZED WARFARE

During the Civil War (1861–1865) machine guns that reloaded automatically were used. Much improved machine guns in World War I (1914–1918) were able to fire explosive shells over 3,488 yds. (3,200m). World War I also saw the first use of aircraft, submarines, and tanks in warfare. During World War II the first long-range rocket weapons—the German VI flying bomb and V2 rocket—were fired from aircraft. Weapons became much more destructive with the invention of the atomic bomb. World War II was finally brought to an end when the U.S. dropped atomic bombs on Hiroshima and Nagasaki, in Japan, devastating both cities. About 200,000 people died, and thousands more were wounded or suffered radiation sickness.

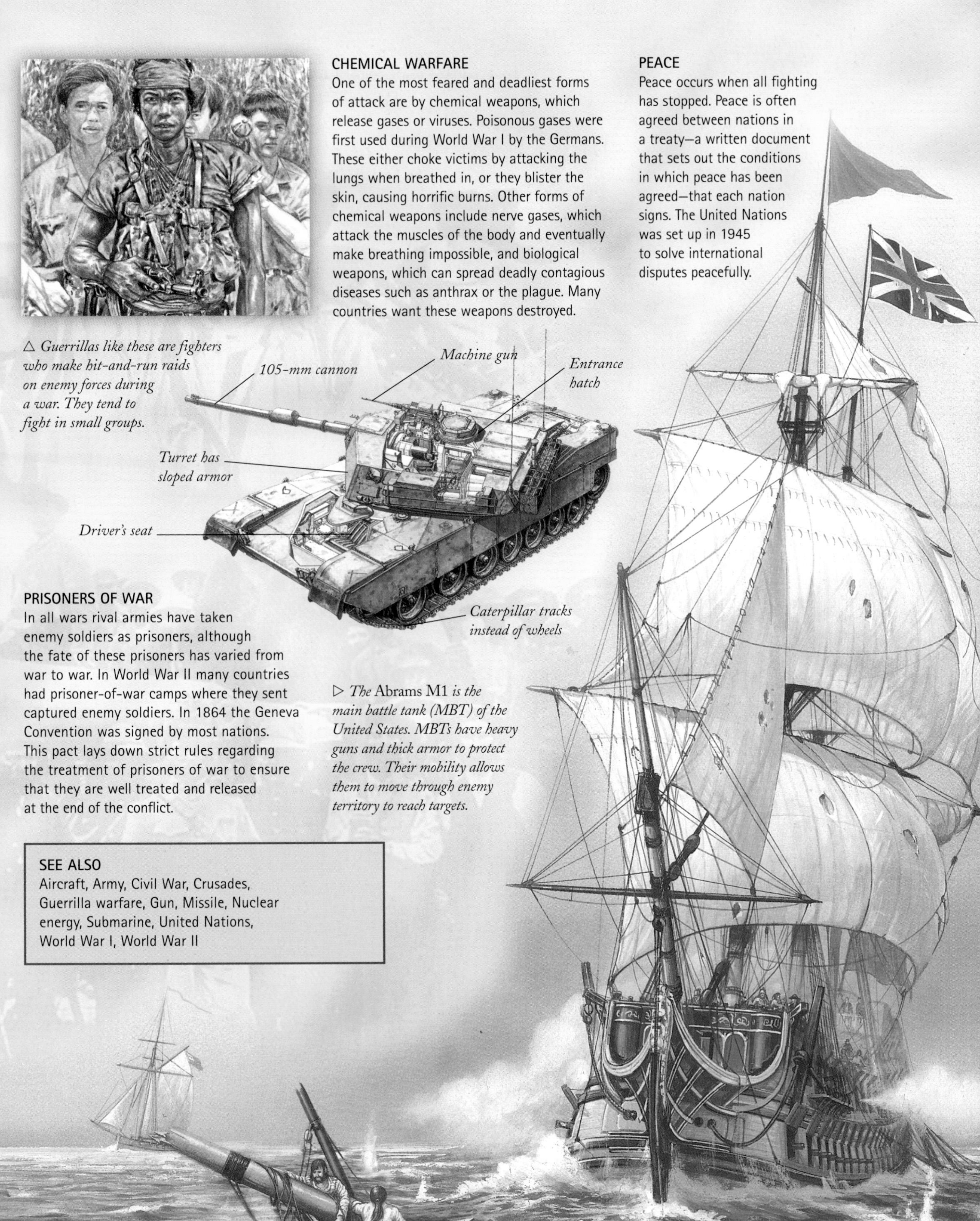

△ *Guerrillas like these are fighters who make hit-and-run raids on enemy forces during a war. They tend to fight in small groups.*

▷ *The* Abrams M1 *is the main battle tank (MBT) of the United States. MBTs have heavy guns and thick armor to protect the crew. Their mobility allows them to move through enemy territory to reach targets.*

CHEMICAL WARFARE

One of the most feared and deadliest forms of attack are by chemical weapons, which release gases or viruses. Poisonous gases were first used during World War I by the Germans. These either choke victims by attacking the lungs when breathed in, or they blister the skin, causing horrific burns. Other forms of chemical weapons include nerve gases, which attack the muscles of the body and eventually make breathing impossible, and biological weapons, which can spread deadly contagious diseases such as anthrax or the plague. Many countries want these weapons destroyed.

PEACE

Peace occurs when all fighting has stopped. Peace is often agreed between nations in a treaty—a written document that sets out the conditions in which peace has been agreed—that each nation signs. The United Nations was set up in 1945 to solve international disputes peacefully.

PRISONERS OF WAR

In all wars rival armies have taken enemy soldiers as prisoners, although the fate of these prisoners has varied from war to war. In World War II many countries had prisoner-of-war camps where they sent captured enemy soldiers. In 1864 the Geneva Convention was signed by most nations. This pact lays down strict rules regarding the treatment of prisoners of war to ensure that they are well treated and released at the end of the conflict.

SEE ALSO
Aircraft, Army, Civil War, Crusades, Guerrilla warfare, Gun, Missile, Nuclear energy, Submarine, United Nations, World War I, World War II

Washington, D.C.

Washington, D.C. is the capital of the **United States**. It is named after the first **president**, George **Washington**, who chose its site on the Potomac River between Maryland and Virginia on a piece of land called the District of Columbia, which is why it is always called Washington, D.C. It is not the largest city in the U.S., but it is important because it houses many of the federal **government** buildings, the **White House**, and the headquarters of the United States' armed forces. One third of Washington's workers are employed by the government. The city also has the embassies and consulates of around 140 nations.

△ In 1781, after a six-year war, the British finally surrendered to the U.S. army in Yorktown, Virginia. George **Washington**, who had been commander-in-chief, went home to Mount Vernon. But he soon returned to public life and became the first president of the new nation in 1789.

Washington, George

George Washington (1732–1799) was the first **president** of the **United States of America**. He commanded the victorious colonial troops in the **Revolutionary War** against the British. One of his officers said this about him in a speech to Congress: "He was first in war, first in peace, and first in the hearts of his countrymen."

George Washington was born on a farm in Westmoreland County, Virginia. In 1752 he inherited an estate called Mount Vernon, and for a while he farmed his land. Then in 1775 the Revolutionary War broke out, and Washington was chosen to be commander-in-chief of the U.S. troops. Despite many problems, the U.S. colonies won their independence from Great Britain.

Washington tried to return to **farming**, but in 1787 he was asked to help draw up the Constitution. In the first **election** he became president. Altogether he held office for 10 years (1789–1797). When he finally resigned from public life, he retired to his beloved Mount Vernon, where he died two years later.

Water

The world's surface is made up of 71 percent water—the majority is saltwater in the sea with the remaining freshwater in **rivers**, **lakes**, and **glaciers**. Without water life would be impossible. Life first began in water, and the bodies of all living things are mostly made of water.

Water contains **minerals**, which are picked up from the surrounding soil

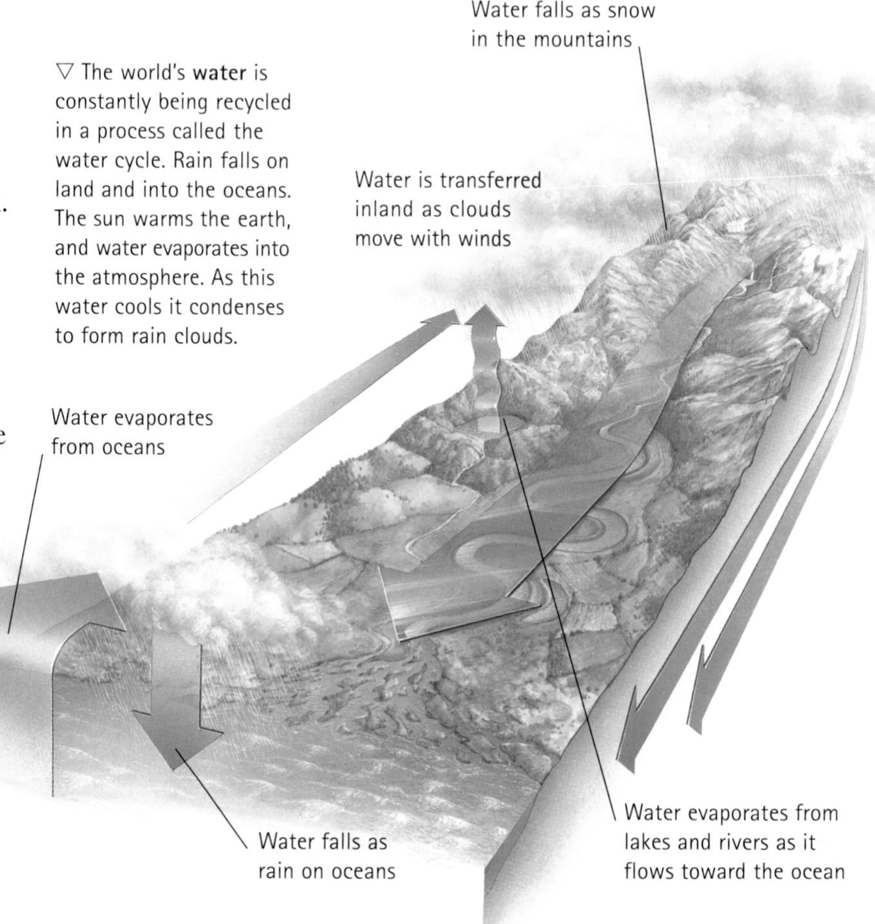

▽ The world's **water** is constantly being recycled in a process called the water cycle. Rain falls on land and into the oceans. The sun warms the earth, and water evaporates into the atmosphere. As this water cools it condenses to form rain clouds.

and **rocks** and exists as ice, **liquid**, or steam. At 32°F (0°C) it freezes into solid ice. At 212°F (100°C) it boils into steam.

Clouds (see also **weather**) are huge collections of water particles. Clouds contain millions of tons of water, which fall back to earth as rain. Some of this water stays in the soil or underground for years, but most of it returns to the **oceans** by rivers or streams.

The chemical formula for water is H_2O. This means that each molecule of water is made up of two **atoms** of **hydrogen** and one atom of **oxygen**. By using two electrodes to pass **electricity** through water, it can be separated into hydrogen and oxygen **gas**. This process is known as electrolysis.

△ The most famous **waterfalls** are Niagara Falls between the **U.S.** and **Canada** and Victoria Falls in the Zambezi River in Africa.

Waterfall

Any sudden drop or fall in a **river** is categorized geographically as a waterfall. These drops are made by the **water** slowly eroding (wearing away) the **rock** of the riverbed over which it flows. Some types of rocks are more permeable (softer) than others and get worn away faster. When permeable rock is worn away, it leaves a cliff of nonpermeable (hard) rock over which the river's water pours.

There are waterfalls all over the world. The highest is Angel Falls in **Venezuela**. It is 3,211 ft. (979m) high. The Iguaçu Falls lie on the border of **Argentina** and **Brazil**. The falls plunge over 270-ft. (82-m) -high cliffs in separate cascades totaling over 1.86 mi. (3km) in width. The great Victoria Falls on the Zambezi River are more than 350 ft. (107m) high and about 1 mi. (1.6 km) wide. Almost 26 million gallons of water plunge over this waterfall every minute. If all of this power was used, there would be enough energy to supply all of the **electricity** for a city of five million people.

Watt, James

James Watt (1736–1819) was a Scottish engineer who spent most of his life developing **steam engines**. In early steam engines steam was heated and cooled inside a cylinder, but Watt designed a model in which steam cooled outside the cylinder. This made the engine much more powerful.

Watt made many other improvements to steam engines so that they could work all types of **machines**. His steam engine was more efficient than other steam engines of his time. One of the improvements Watt made was to add a "steam governor," using two heavy balls mounted on swinging arms. This steadied the speed of the engine by regulating the amount of steam admitted from the boiler.

Other than the steam engine James Watt also invented the screw propeller for use in **ships**.

▽ Pressure, produced by steam, drove the various parts of James **Watt's steam engine**. His engines were first used to pump **water** from **tin** and **copper** mines in Cornwall, **England**. Later they were used in **cotton** mills.

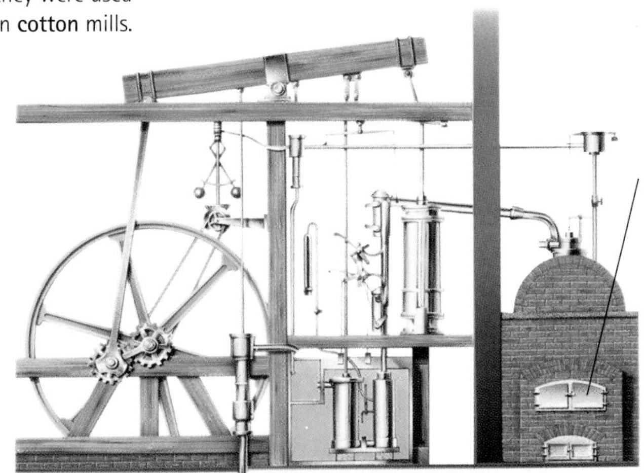

Burning wood or coal generated heat that was used to boil water, which created steam.

WEATHER

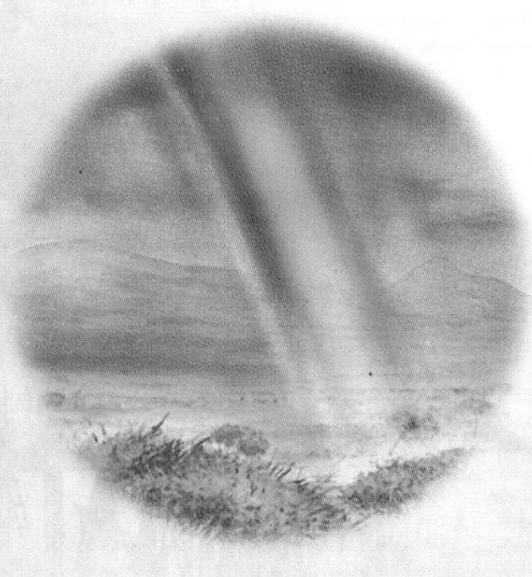

△ *Rainbows appear when the sun comes out from behind a cloud when it is still raining. The colors never change—red at the top and then orange, yellow, green, blue, indigo, and violet.*

In most regions of the world weather conditions,such as rain, wind, and sunshine, are constantly changing. This is because the air in the lowest layer of earth's atmosphere is always on the move.

THE TROPOSPHERE

The lowest 7 mi. (11km) of the atmosphere, called the troposphere, contains all the weather that we experience. The sun heats different areas of the troposphere to different degrees. For example, air over the oceans heats up and cools down more slowly than air over the land, while air at the equator is heated more strongly than air at the poles. These differences in temperature drive the world's weather.

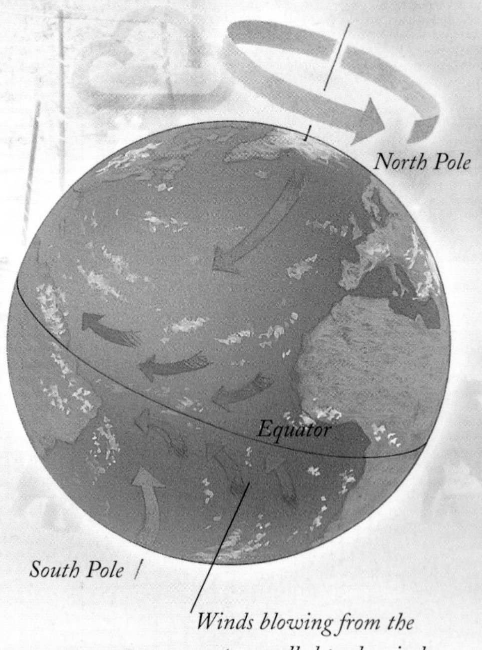

Winds blowing from the east are called trade winds.

AIR MASSES AND FRONTS

The boundary between two air masses of different temperatures is called a front. Most changes in the weather occur at the front. A cold front forms when cold air catches up with a mass of warm air and rapidly pushes the warm air up. Then the weather is often rainy. A warm front is created when warm air catches up with cold air and rises slowly above the cold air. This brings clouds and long periods of gentle rain. An occluded front is where cold and warm air masses mix. As this happens the front weakens and disappears.

CLOUD COVER

Clouds are formed by rising and cooling air. When air cools, invisible water vapor begins to condense (turn to liquid). If it is cold enough, the water droplets freeze into ice crystals. Clouds are formed from these droplets and crystals.

△ *Earth spins on its axis like a top, so the air that moves across the planet flows in a curve. This is called the Coriolis effect. Air moving from the poles to the equator curves to the west. Air moving from the equator to the poles curves to the east.*

▽ *Different types of clouds form when air rises and cools under different conditions.*

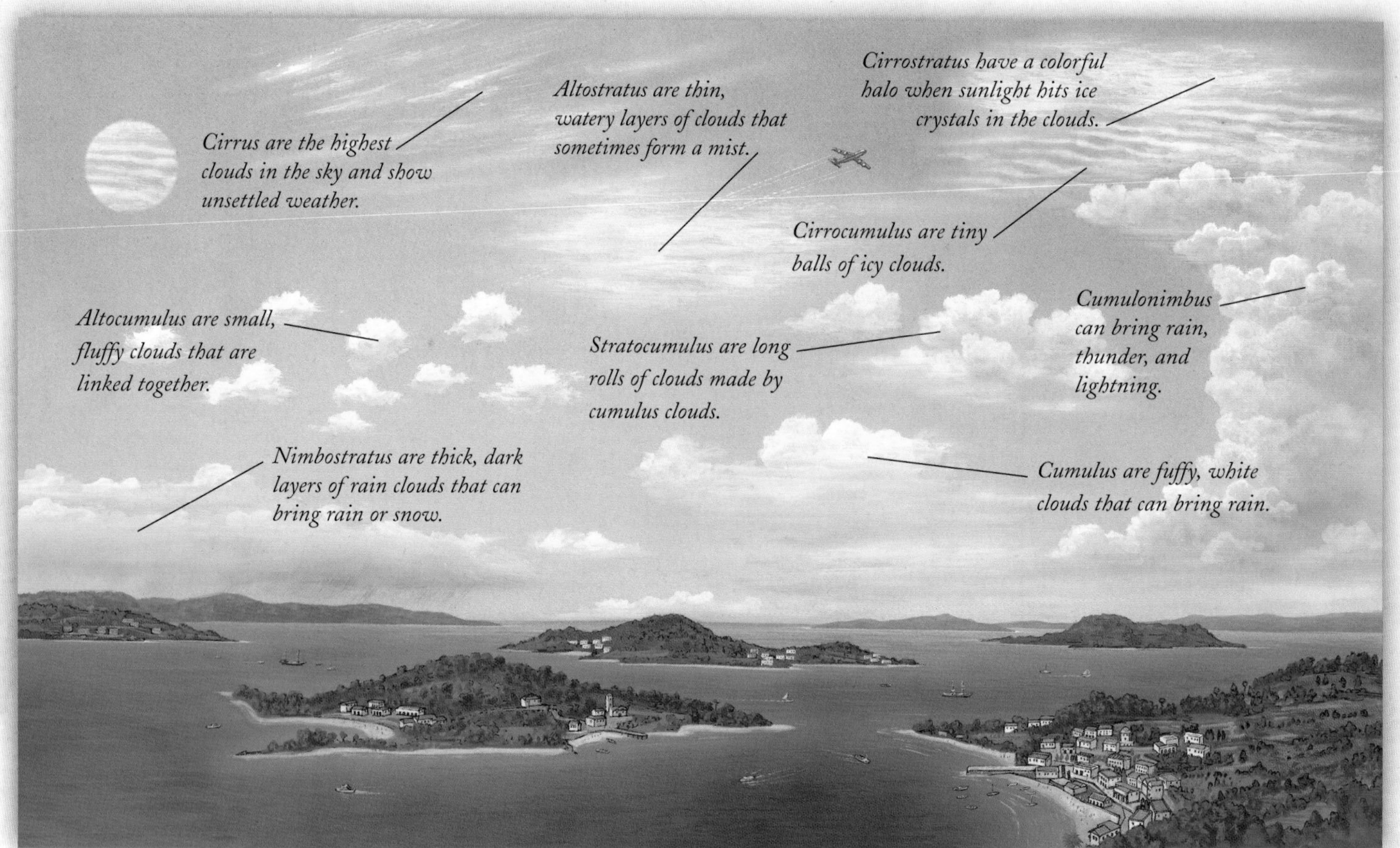

Cirrus are the highest clouds in the sky and show unsettled weather.

Altostratus are thin, watery layers of clouds that sometimes form a mist.

Cirrostratus have a colorful halo when sunlight hits ice crystals in the clouds.

Cirrocumulus are tiny balls of icy clouds.

Altocumulus are small, fluffy clouds that are linked together.

Stratocumulus are long rolls of clouds made by cumulus clouds.

Cumulonimbus can bring rain, thunder, and lightning.

Nimbostratus are thick, dark layers of rain clouds that can bring rain or snow.

Cumulus are fuffy, white clouds that can bring rain.

△ *Weather forecasters use data from weather stations, high-altitude balloons, planes, and satellites to track the movement of fronts and areas of high and low pressure across the globe. This allows them to make fairly accurate predictions of weather patterns for up to one week ahead.*

PRECIPITATION

Water that falls from clouds as rain, snow, sleet, or hail is called precipitation. In the tropics raindrops form when air currents cause the water droplets that make up a cloud to bump into each other and join. Eventually the droplets grow heavy enough to fall as rain. Outside the tropics rain begins as ice crystals in very cold clouds. The crystals grow as water droplets freeze onto them until they form snowflakes and start to fall. If the ground level temperature is below 32°F (0°C), the ice crystals reach the ground as snow. If the temperature is a few degrees above freezing, the crystals partially melt and fall as sleet. At higher temperatures they melt completely and fall as rain. Hail forms when strong air currents carry ice crystals up and down between the two layers of a thundercloud. The crystals become larger until they fall to earth as hailstones.

△ *Tornadoes (or twisters) are the most violent of all storms and consist of winds that swirl in the shape of a funnel at speeds of up to 280 mph (450 km/h). They form during a thunderstorm.*

▽ *Hurricanes are large tropical storms that form over oceans. Winds swirl around a calm center, the eye of the storm, at speeds of up to 124 mph (200 km/h). They bring very heavy rain and huge waves and often cause severe flooding.*

FUTURE WEATHER PATTERNS

Scientists predict that the average temperature of earth's surface could rise by between 34–41°F (1–5°C) by 2100. This global warming is believed to be the result of the greenhouse effect—the buildup of gases that trap more of the sun's energy in earth's atmosphere. This temperature change could cause sea levels to rise and more violent weather patterns to appear.

SEE ALSO
Acid rain, Air, Antarctic and Arctic, Atmosphere, Barometer, Climate, Earth, Gas, Global warming, Hurricane, Temperature, Thermometer, Wind

Wave

When the **wind** blows over the sea, it creates waves. The size and speed of a wave depends upon the wind's strength and fetch (how far across the sea it blows). A light breeze causes gentle ripples, but a storm can whip up waves higher than a **house**.

Although ripples and waves move across the sea the **water** itself does not travel with them. Instead each passing wave just lifts the water particles that support floating objects (such as sea**birds** and bottles) up, forward, down, and back again. This explains why these floating objects bob up and down but do not travel with the waves.

The biggest waves are seismic sea waves, or tsunamis. These are set off by underwater **earthquakes**, landslides, or **volcanoes**. Tsunamis sometimes flood coasts and can cause a large number of human fatalities as a result.

Sea waves carry **energy** from the wind. This energy can be used to make **electricity**. One experimental machine for harnessing wave energy is called the nodding boom, or "duck." The ducks have small generators inside of them. As waves make the "beak" of each duck move up and down electricity is produced by the **generators**.

△ For thousands of years **weaving** was slow work. First the fibers were drawn out and twisted into a long thread (spinning). Then rows of threads (the warp) were stretched lengthwise side by side on a frame called a loom. A crosswise thread (the weft) was then passed through from one side of the loom to the other, going over and under the warp. A large needle, the shuttle, was used to feed the weft through the warp.

◁ Surfers travel the world looking for the "perfect **wave**." The Polynesians (from Hawaii in the Pacific Ocean) invented surfing many centuries ago. They called it *he'e nalu* ("wave sliding").

Weaving

Curtains and sheets, shirts and carpets, and towels and suits are just some of the many useful articles made by a process known as weaving, where threads are joined together in a crisscross pattern to make cloth.

People have been weaving cloth to make **clothing** since the **Stone Age**. The oldest fabric we know of was woven almost 8,000 years ago in what is now **Turkey**. These weavers learned to make linen from flax (fibers from the linum **plant**). By 2000 B.C. the Chinese were weaving cloth from **silk**. In **India** people learned to use fibers from the **cotton** plant. Meanwhile **nomads** (travelers) from the **deserts** and **mountains** of **Asia** discovered how to weave **wool**.

Spinning **wheels** and looms were worked by hand until the 1700s. Then **machines** were invented for spinning and weaving. These machines worked much faster than hand looms, and cloth became cheap and plentiful.

Today most woven fabrics are made by machine, and fully automatic looms are now common in most countries, although hand looms are still used for very special woolen or silk fabrics. One person can easily operate 20 of today's fully automatic looms.

Website *see* Internet

Weed

A weed is any **plant** that grows where it is not wanted. On farms and in **gardens** weeds damage crops and **flowers** by taking a large share of **water**, **minerals**, and sunlight. In places where weeds grow thickly, cultivated plants do not develop properly—they may produce only a few flowers, small **seeds**, unhealthy leaves, or weak roots.

There are several ways of controlling weeds. In gardens people break up the **soil** with a hoe. This disturbs the weed roots and stops growth. They also pull the weeds out of the ground; this is called weeding. On farms the soil is broken up by plowing and harrowing. Some farmers spray their fields with weedkillers, which are **chemicals** that destroy weeds. Most weedkillers are selective. This means the chemicals only affect certain plants, so they destroy weeds without harming crops.

Weeds grow in a variety of places. Black bindweed grows on cultivated land; dandelions grow in fields and meadows; greater plantain grows on paths; and purple loosestrife grows in damp places. Some weeds are edible and used in salads.

△ **Weeds** are only a nuisance when they interfere with cultivated plants. In woods and fields away from gardens and farms weeds are useful plants and food for many animals.

Weightlifting

Weightlifting is one of the **sports** included in the **Olympic Games**. In a weightlifting contest the competitors lift very heavy **weights** from the floor to above their heads. Weightlifters, like **boxers**, are divided into classes according to their own body weight. Champion weightlifters can lift over 552 lbs (250kg).

Many other athletes, such as swimmers and football players, do weightlifting as an exercise to strengthen their **muscles** and improve their **breathing**.

Weights and Measures

Weights and measures are used to figure out how heavy something is or its length, width, and height. Length multiplied by width gives the area (for example, the amount of floor space in a room), while length multiplied by width and height gives the **volume** (the amount of space within something).

People first needed units of measurement when they began to build towns and **trade** goods. In **ancient Egypt** people based their measurements on the proportions of the body. Four digits equaled one palm. Seven palms, or two spans (pinkie to thumbtip), equaled one cubit (the distance from a person's fingertips to the elbow).

Most countries now use the metric system for measuring distances. The metric system is a decimal system based on the number "10" and was first used in **France** in the late 1700s. Another system, the imperial system, was originally used in Great Britain and the **United States**.

Welding

Welding is a way of joining metals by heating them. The edges of two pieces of **metal** are heated (by **gas** or **electricity**) until they melt together. When they cool, they form one piece of metal. A join made by welding is extremely strong.

△ **Welders** have to protect their eyes from the heat by wearing masks.

△ **Wheat** grows best in dry, mild **climates.** Farmers sow the seed in the winter or the spring. They harvest it when the grain is dry and hard.

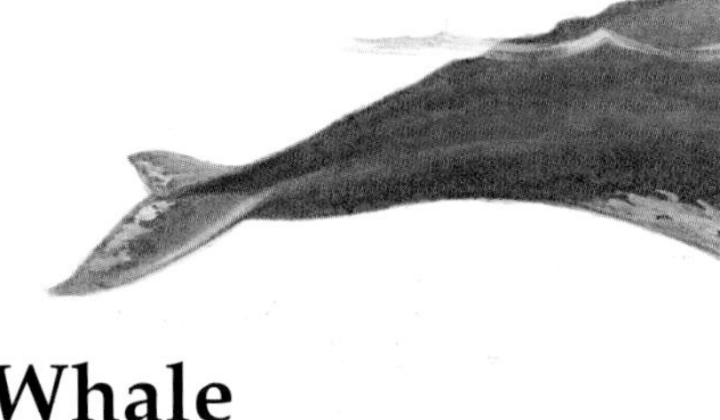
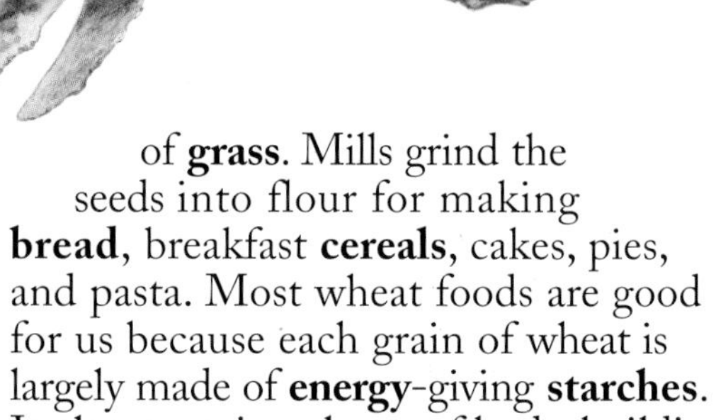

◁ The blubber under the skin of large **whales** can be up to 1.6 ft. (0.5m) thick. For hundreds of years whales have been killed for this blubber. Oil was taken from it and used to make soap.

Whale

Whales are large sea **mammals** that are physically adapted for living in the water. A thick layer of blubber (fat) keeps out the cold. A whale's body is shaped for easy **swimming**. Its front limbs are flippers. It also has a broad tail flattened from top to bottom, not from side to side like a **fish**.

Unlike fish, whales must swim to the surface to breathe. Before **breathing** in they blow out stale **air** through a blowhole (two slits on top of the head). Baby whales are born in water and must immediately swim to the surface to take a breath of air.

The blue whale is the largest mammal in the world. It can grow as long as 100 ft. (30m). The orca, or killer whale, is a **carnivore**. It feeds on other whales, **seals, penguins**, and **fish**. Bottle-nosed whales have beaks like some **dolphins**. They move around in schools of up to 50 animals. Humpback whales feed on fish, krill, and **plankton**.

Wheat

Wheat is a valuable **food** crop. Grains of wheat are **seeds** produced by a certain type of **grass**. Mills grind the seeds into flour for making **bread**, breakfast **cereals**, cakes, pies, and pasta. Most wheat foods are good for us because each grain of wheat is largely made of **energy**-giving **starches**. It also contains plenty of body-building **protein** as well as **fats, minerals**, and bran.

Most wheat is produced from **China, India**, the **United States, France**, and **Russia**. The world produces more wheat than any other type of grain.

Wheel

The wheel is one of the most useful **inventions**. This is because a wheel turning on an axle is a very good way to move loads. It is easier to move a heavy load with wheels than it is to lift the load or drag it on the ground.

People first invented the wheel about 5,000 years ago in the **Bronze Age**. The oldest known wheels looked like slices cut across a log. But each solid disk was made up of three parts.

At first the wheels were attached to the axle, and it was the axle that turned in holes in the cart frame. Later the axle did not move, and the wheels revolved on its ends.

Then people learned that a wheel with spokes was just as strong as a solid wheel but much lighter in weight. Today the wheels of **cars** and planes have hollow **rubber** tires filled with air to make them springy.

▽ Modern **wheels** are different from the wheels invented 5,000 years ago. This illustration shows some of the wheels that have been used throughout history.

Ball bearings keep wheel hubs turning easily on their axles. Wheels with notched edges turn one another within the gears that help to work all types of machinery.

Although the wheel was used throughout a large part of the East by 1500 B.C. it is interesting that the wheel was unknown anywhere on the North American continent until it was introduced by **Europeans** in the A.D. 1500s.

White House

The White House is the official residence of the **president** of the **United States** and is located in **Washington, D.C**. This is where the president lives and works. Theodore **Roosevelt** was the first president to use the name—before it was simply called the President's House. In 1814 the **British** burned down the White House so today's building is the second White House.

△ The name "**White House**" comes from the fact that it is white. The first White House was built in 1792.

Whitman, Walt

Walt Whitman (1819–1892) was the greatest American **poet** of the 1700s. He is best known for *Leaves of Grass*, a collection of poems that he wrote and edited for a period of 40 years.

William the Conqueror

William the Conqueror is another name for William I of **England** (1027–1087). He was England's first Norman king. William was born in **France**, where his father, Robert, was the Duke of Normandy.

When William visited England in 1050, his relative Edward the Confessor allegedly promised him the throne of England. In 1064 William forced Edward's brother-in-law, Harold, to agree to help make him king, but when Edward died in 1066, Harold had himself crowned king of England.

William then invaded England to seize it for himself. His Norman army defeated Harold's **Anglo-Saxon** army at the Battle of Hastings. He was crowned William I of England in Westminster Abbey on **Christmas** Day in 1066.

William and his nobles brought over their own language, Norman French, and the English ruling classes began to speak French as a result. Modern English contains many words that came from Norman French.

▽ People in many parts of **England** rebelled against **William**'s rule. He built strong castles from which his knights rode out to defeat their Anglo- Saxon enemies. He also ordered a huge survey (the Domesday Book) of all of the land and people in his new English kingdom.

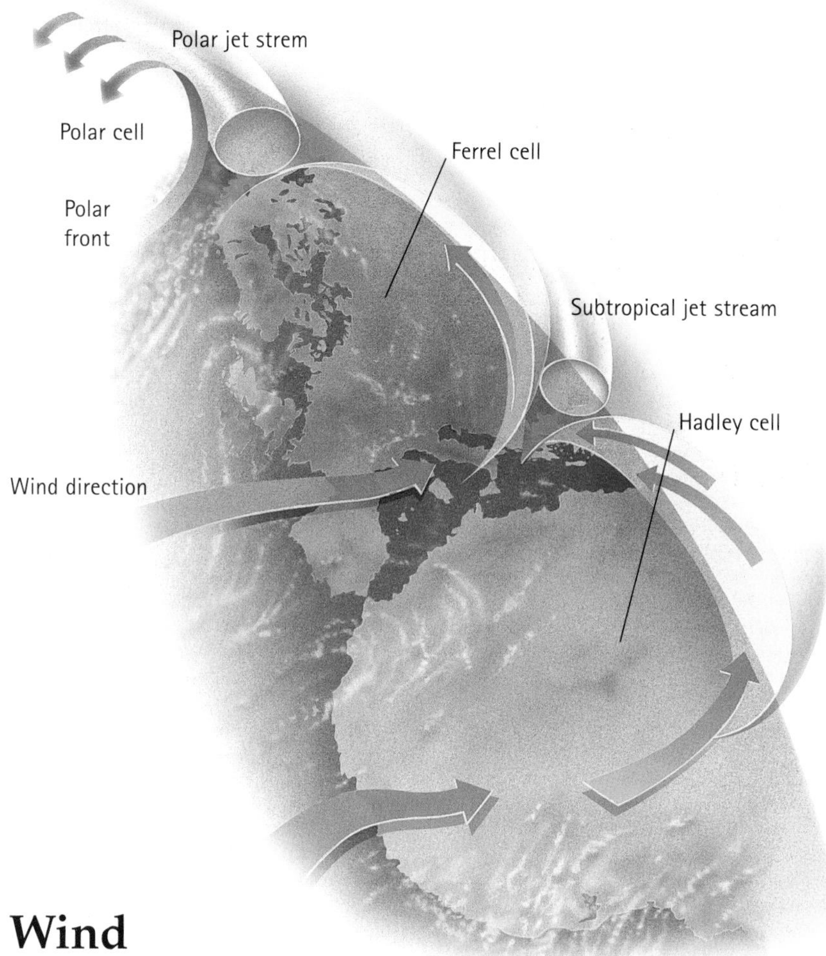

Wind

Wind is moving **air**. Slow winds are gentle breezes. Fast winds are gales. You can see the speed of the wind by its effect on **trees** and buildings.

Wind blows because some air masses become warmer than others. In warm air the tiny particles of air spread out. A mass of warm air is lighter than a mass of cold air that fills the same amount of space, because warm air is so light it rises. As the warm air rises cool air flows in to take its place. This causes the steady trade winds that blow over tropical **oceans**. **Climate** and **weather** are determined by the wind.

A scale of wind speeds was created in 1805 by Admiral Sir Francis Beaufort. It is called the Beaufort Scale. In it the force of the wind is shown by numbers from 0 to 12. The number 0 indicates calm weather (no wind). By the time it reaches 4 there is a breeze in which small branches are moving and **flags** flap. At force 7 whole trees are moving, and it is difficult to walk against the wind. Force 12 is something few of us will ever see. It is a full **hurricane** with terrible damage to **ships** at sea and **houses** on land.

Weather vanes show the direction of wind. The arrow points in the direction of north, east, south, or west.

△ At each pole cold air sinks and spills out to be replaced by warmer air from above. This is a polar cell. Ferrel cells form between 86–140°F (30–60°C). The cold air moving away from the poles meets warm **wind** from the subtropics and pushes the warm air back to the equator.

◁ This **windmill** was used to grind corn. As the wind blew, the axle turned the millstones that ground the corn.

Windmill

Windmills are **machines** that use the wind's **energy** to generate power. They were used in **Asia** as early as the A.D. 600s and came to **Europe** in the 1100s.

In early windmills a **wheel** with long sails was attached to a tower. The whole tower could frequently turn to face the **wind**. As the wind turned the **sails** the turning wheel moved machinery inside the mill. This machinery was used to do useful work such as turning heavy stone wheels to grind corn or pumping **water** from wells.

Today people use windmills as a way of generating **electricity**. These windmills, called wind **turbines**, are usually on a tower made of **steel** girders. Some have blades like airplane propellers (see **aircraft**), which turn at a high speed when the wind blows. The propellers power a **generator** that produces electricity.

Wine

Wine is a drink made from **plant** juice, and it contains **alcohol** produced by a process called **fermentation**.

Most wine is made from grapes. But you can make wine from other **fruits** as well. First the fruit is crushed. Then the juice is fermented in containers called vats. The wine is stored in casks until it is ready to drink. Sweet wines are rich in **sugar**. In dry wines most of the sugar has become alcohol.

Grapes go through many processes

before they become bottled wine. After fermentation some wines are stored in cellars to mature into fine wines. Cheaper wines are not allowed to mature. They are filtered, pasteurized, (see **Pasteur, Louis**) and then bottled as soon as they are taken out of the casks.

Wire

Wire is **metal** that has been melted into a long, thin rod that is easy to bend. Wire has many uses. Barbwire fences keep **sheep** and cows in fields. Wires twisted together form cables that are strong enough to hold up some of the world's largest **bridges**. Wires carry electric currents. **Telephone** lines also use wires.

Metals used for making wire include **copper**, **iron**, **aluminum**, and **silver**. Heavy blocks of metal are heated and then passed through rollers that squeeze the part-melted metal into long, narrow holes to make longer and thinner strips. Then the wire is wound around a turning drum. Finally the wire is heated in a furnace to make it less brittle.

For centuries wire was made by hand. The piece of metal to be drawn was beaten to a point and pushed through a small hole in a fixed metal block. The wiredrawer grasped it and pulled it through the hole to make wire. The fineness of the wire was therefore limited by the strength of the wiredrawer.

Witch

Many people once believed in witches (people with **magic** powers). It was claimed that witches worshiped the devil and that they cast spells that "bewitched" people, sometimes causing death or **diseases**. Witches supposedly rode through the **air** at night on broomsticks, and they met at secret meetings called sabbaths.

Long ago many innocent women were burned to death because they were accused of being witches. Today some societies still believe in witches, including the Hopi and Navajo Native Americans, the Maori of New Zealand, and many southern African peoples. There are some people who still claim to practice magic, offering herbal cures and mixing things such as "love potions."

△ The image of a **witch** as an ugly, old woman who casts evil spells is still with us today, mainly through children's fairy tales.

Wolf

These **carnivores** include the gray wolf that lives in Eastern **Europe** and parts of **North America**. Gray wolves used to be found in most of the Northern Hemisphere. But they are now only found in remote areas and dense **forests** because humans hunted them almost to the point of extinction. Gray wolves have thick fur, long legs, and powerful jaws. They can be up to 6 ft. (1.8m) in length. A pack of wolves can chase and kill a sick or injured **deer** that is much larger than themselves. They share their kill, but wolves have an order of seniority within each pack—young wolves must submit to larger, older animals. When gray wolves are hunting, they howl to signal to each other where they are.

A pack consists of a pair of adults with many generations of their young. Each spring the female wolf has four to six pups.

▽ Like many other **mammals**, **wolves** live in family groups. They hunt together in packs led by a dominant male.

Women's rights

"Women's rights" is the term used when discussing the increased social, economic, and political involvement of women. Traditionally women have had fewer rights and lower social status than men. Even today some countries do not grant women equal citizenship with men. In 1848 Lucretia Mott (1793–1880) and Elizabeth Cady Stanton (1815–1902) organized the first women's rights convention in the **U.S.** in Seneca Falls, New York. There they adopted a Declaration of Sentiments, which called for women to receive "all the rights and privileges which belong to them as citizens of the United States." Stanton joined women's rights leader Susan B. Anthony (1820–1906), and in 1890 an association was formed to fight for suffrage (the right to vote) in the U.S. In 1920 the 19th Amendment to the U.S. Constitution gave women the right to vote.

During the 1960s and 1970s women's rights groups focused on equal pay and job opportunites, child care, and other social programs. These efforts resulted in many reforms, including the Equal Pay Act of 1963; Title VII of the Civil Rights Act of 1964, prohibiting job discrimination on the basis of sex as well as color, race, national origin, and religion; and the Equal Credit Opportunity Act of 1975. Despite these gains, women's struggle for equality is not yet done.

◁ The gilded flicker is a species of **woodpecker** that lives in the deserts of the southwestern United States. It nests in tall saguaro **cactuses**.

△ Dendrochronology is the dating and study of rings in trees. If a tree is felled (chopped down) and the trunk cut is in half, we can tell the age of the tree by counting the rings in the **wood**. Variation in the rings tells us about the changes in environmental conditions as the tree grew.

Wood

Wood is one of the most valuable materials that people use. It can be sawed, carved, and worked into almost any shape.

Thick timber is used for buildings and boats, while roughly cut logs and boughs are used as **fuel** for **fires**. Planks of wood are made into furniture, barrels, and boxes. "Seasoned" pieces can be shaped into **musical instruments** and delicate ornaments.

The wood we use is the tough inner material of **trees** and shrubs and is protected by a thin layer of bark. It is very strong, supporting many times its own weight. The wood of a tree is made up of thick fibers that give it that strength.

Softwood, from **pines** and firs, is used mostly as pulp to make **paper**. Some is used for building. Hardwood, such as oak and mahogany, is used to make furniture.

Wood and wood products are made into sheets for building. Plywood is made up of thin sheets of timber glued together. Most modern furniture is made from plywood. Blockboard is used for making doors. Although it looks like plywood, it has blocks of softwood within it. Hardboard and chipboard, used in building and furniture making, are made from wood chips. The chips are heated and rolled out into sheets.

Woodpecker

There are about 200 different types of woodpeckers. They are found in many parts of the world, but most live in **North America, South America**, and **Asia.**

Woodpeckers have sharp, powerful bills with which they drill holes through the bark of **trees**. They reach in with their long tongues to fish out **insects**. Some woodpeckers also nest in holes in trees.

Most woodpeckers have bright **colors** and markings, especially on their heads.

Wool

Wool comes from the fleece of **sheep** and some other **animals**. It is long, thick hair that can be turned into yarn easily. The yarn may be woven into blankets, carpets, and **clothing** or it can be knitted. Woolen cloth is heavy and warm.

Wool has been spun and woven since the **Stone Age**. Modern wool, however, comes from specifically bred sheep that have good, fine wool. The best wool comes from Merino sheep. These are white sheep that originally came from **Spain**. Most wool is produced in **Australia**, **New Zealand**, **Argentina**, and **Russia**.

△ The **wool** we wear comes from the fleece of sheep. Sheep were once clipped by hand, but the invention of electric shears makes it possible for farmers to clip over 200 sheep per day.

Worm

There are hundreds of different **animals** with soft, flat bodies that are commonly called worms. Some, such as roundworms or flatworms, are very simple creatures. Others, such as earthworms, leeches, and the larvae of some **insects**, are more complicated. Their bodies are divided into several segments.

Most of the simple worms are small. They usually live as **parasites** inside the bodies of animals or **plants**. Liver flukes and tapeworms are two such creatures.

△ The common earth**worm** has both male and female organs. Ragworms and lugworms live in muddy and sandy shores.

Wren, Christopher

Christopher Wren (1632–1723) was a highly regarded English architect (see **architecture**). He was responsible for many beautiful buildings in **England**, including the Royal Exchange, Kensington Palace, and an addition to Hampton Court in **London**, as well as worldwide.

In 1666 the Great Fire of London destroyed St. Paul's Cathedral, a famous landmark. Christopher Wren designed its replacement, which still stands today.

Wren also designed the College of William and Mary in Virginia. This is the oldest academic structure in the **United States** that is in continuous use.

▷ As well as building the famous St. Paul's Cathedral, Christopher **Wren** built more than 50 other churches in his lifetime.

WORLD WAR I

World War I took place between 1914 and 1918 and involved 22 countries. More than 17 million people were killed.

△ *A British recruiting poster at the start of World War I featured the war minister, Lord Kitchener.*

ALLIANCES

At the beginning of the 1900s the relationships between the countries in Europe were strained. Germany was becoming increasingly powerful, and France and Great Britain felt threatened. Austria-Hungary and Russia were rivals in the Balkans, which resented their outside interference. Based on these hostilities alliances developed with Austria-Hungary and Germany, known as the Central Powers, on one side and France, Russia, and Great Britain, known as the Allies, on the other.

△ *The British* Vickers FB 5 Gunbus *was produced to stop the German* Fokker E. III.

△ *The German* Fokker E.III *carried a machine gun rigged to fire forward.*

WAR BREAKS OUT

War broke out in 1914 after Archduke Franz Ferdinand, the heir to the Austro-Hungarian emperor, was assassinated by a Serbian in Sarajevo in Bosnia (part of the Balkan States). Austria threatened Serbia with war unless it submitted to Austrian rule. Serbia refused, and in July 1914 Austria declared war. Other countries soon became involved. Russia supported Serbia, and in August 1914 Germany, Austria's ally, declared war on Russia and its ally, France. Intent on invading France, Germany marched through Belgium, a neutral country since 1839. On August 4 Great Britain declared war in defense of Belgium. Turkey joined the Central Powers in 1914, followed by Bulgaria in 1915. Italy joined the Allies in 1915, followed by Romania and Portugal in 1916 and the U.S. in 1917.

THE TREATY OF VERSAILLES

Russia withdrew from the war in 1917, and Germany then concentrated fully on the Western Front. The U.S. joined the Allies when Russia surrendered. In the spring of 1918 the Germans marched through Paris but were halted by the Allies and gradually pushed back. By November 1918 the German army was defeated. In 1919 Germany signed the Treaty of Versailles, admitting guilt for the war and promising to pay compensation to the Allies for their losses.

◁ *The war was fought from a system of ditches called trenches, which were protected by barbwire and machine guns, on the Western Front. However, until tanks were introduced in 1918 by the Allies it was very difficult for either side to attack successfully without huge losses of life.*

▷ *Horses, such as the Australian Waler, were used as officers' mounts and for hauling artillery and ambulances.*

WORLD WAR II

Twenty-one years after the Germans surrendered to the Allies in November 1918 a world war broke out in Europe once again. However, this time technology was more advanced, and everybody, civilians and military alike, in all the countries, was directly affected by the mass destruction.

ADOLF HITLER

After World War I Germany suffered humiliation and huge economic problems, and many Germans were enthusiastic when military strength and national pride were championed by a party called the National Socialists, or Nazis, led by Adolf Hitler.

GERMANY MAKES A MOVE

In 1938 Hitler marched into part of the Czech Republic. At a meeting in Munich, Great Britain and France (the Allies), wanting to avoid another major war, allowed Hitler to keep the area that he had annexed. Hitler then annexed the rest of the country and threatened Poland. Great Britain and France agreed to declare war if Poland was invaded. On September 1, 1939 Hitler marched into Poland, and the Allies declared war two days later. Germany, allied with Italy and Japan in 1940 and 1941, were called the Axis Powers. The U.S. joined the Allies in 1941 after Japanese aircraft bombed the U.S. Pacific Fleet in Pearl Harbor on December 7.

▷ *Japanese kamikaze pilots—kamikaze means "divine wind"—died for their emperor by diving their aircraft, laden with bombs, straight into Allied ships.*

THE ARMISTICE

On June 6, 1944—D day—the Allies landed in Normandy, in northern France, and forced the Germans to retreat. On March 24, 1945 they crossed the Rhine River and met the Russians coming from the east. Hitler committed suicide on April 30, 1945, and the war in Europe ended on May 8, 1945.

It continued in the Pacific until August 14 when the Japanese were devastated by U.S. atomic bombs dropped on the Japanese cities of Hiroshima and Nagasaki. The armistice, which ended the war, was signed on September 2, 1945.

THE HOLOCAUST

The word "holocaust" means the wholesale slaughter or destruction of life. It is also used as an historical term to refer to the mass murder of between 5.2 and 5.8 million Jews and 5 million other people, including the mentally ill, gypsies, and political adversaries, who were killed by the Nazi Party.

△ *Between July and October 1940 the German air force (Luftwaffe) bombed British cities and attacked the British air force (RAF). Technology had moved on from World War I, and fighters' top speeds rose from 360 mph (580 km/h) to 540 mph (870 km/h). Almost all of the new warplanes were monoplanes such as this* Hawker Hurricane.

▽ *This photograph shows Adolf Hitler triumphantly entering the town of Wildenan in the Sudetenland, a region in the west of the former Czechoslovakia. Hitler's armies went on to conquer the rest of the country.*

SEE ALSO
Aircraft, Army, Balloon and Airship, Bosnia-Herzegovina, D day, Europe, Fascism, Germany, Gun, Hitler (Adolf), Nuclear energy, Submarine, Warfare

△ It is said that Wilbur **Wright** was twisting a cardboard carton containing a bicycle inner tube when he noticed the shape of the carton changed but not its size. This inspired the inventor to make the wing-warping mechanism that steered his 1903 aircraft.

▽ The earliest **writings** were on stone or clay, and only a few people could read them.

Wright brothers

Wilbur and Orville Wright were two American **bicycle** engineers who built and flew the first powered **aircraft**. Their successful **machine** was made after years of testing models and gliders.

The first actual flight took place at Kitty Hawk, North Carolina, in December 1903. Their simple, gasoline-engined craft flew for 12 seconds. Five years later the brothers flew an improved machine for almost 75 minutes.

The original Wright *Flyer I* is in the National Air and Space Museum in **Washington, D.C**.

Writing

The earliest forms of writing were simple picture messages. Gradually pictures that were used again and again became simplified as symbols such "man" or "house." Egyptian **hieroglyphics** were used in this way.

In time the symbols came to stand for **sounds** and could be combined to form words. Later on **alphabets** of these sounds were developed. **Vowels** appeared in the **languages** spoken by the ancient Greeks and Romans. From their alphabets developed the one used today in English.

The Chinese invented **paper** in A.D. 105. In 1824 Frenchman Louis Braille (1809–1852) designed an alphabet of raised dots (braille) on paper enabling blind people to feel words. Nowadays we can buy E-books (electronic books). These are on disks and are read on a **computer** screen or a handheld computer designed for the E-book market.

Words are powerful, and many authors use satire (a form of humor) to attack people or ideas. *Gulliver's Travels* by Jonathan Swift (1667–1745) pokes fun at **human beings**.

X ray

X rays are waves of **energy** that are similar to **radio** or **light** waves. They can pass through or into most living things. They can also leave an image on a photographic plate, taking a picture of whatever they have passed through. Doctors use X rays to take photographs of the insides of people. This helps them find out what is wrong.

Computerized tomography (CT) scanners also help with diagnosis. A patient is moved slowly through the scanner as X rays are beamed through their body. A powerful **computer** processes this information, displaying slices of the patient's body on its screens.

High doses of X rays can damage body **cells**, but the harmful effects are frequently used to help cure **cancers**. Radiographers target X rays at cells in tumors, killing them.

X rays are produced inside a **glass** tube that has no **air** or other **gases** in it. At opposite ends of the tube are a cathode, which gives off electrons, and an anode, or target. When the cathode is heated, electrons fly off it and strike the anode, producing X rays.

German scientist Wilhelm Röntgen (1845–1923) discovered X rays by accident in 1895 when he passed **electricity** through a gas.

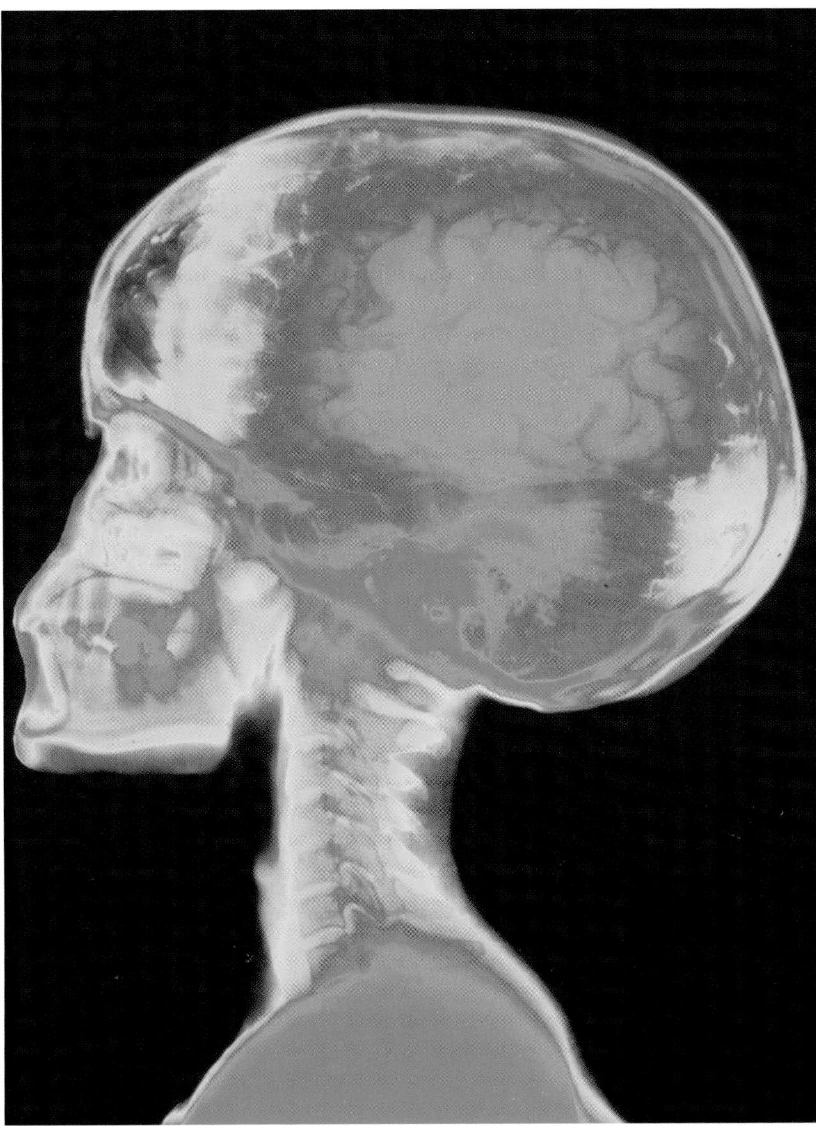

△ A radiographer has taken this **X ray** of a human head. The resulting photograph has been colored to show the skull and brain more clearly.

△ The **xylophone** is a type of percussion instrument that has a clear, distinctive sound.

Xylophone

The xylophone is an odd-looking **musical instrument** that produces a crisp, bell-like **sound** when played. It consists of graded rows of solid wooden or **metal** bars that are attached to a frame. Each bar is a different length and produces a different sound when struck with a hammer. The sound is produced by the **wood** or metal from which the xylophone is made. An electric version of the xylophone—the vibraphone—also exists.

The xylophone is used in **orchestras** and bands across the world. Resonators (metal tubes below each bar) help to amplify (increase) the sound.

Yak

The yak is a large, shaggy type of ox with a pair of long, thick **horns**. Yaks live in mountainous areas of **Tibet**, **China**, and northern **Asia**. Wild yaks may be as tall as a man, but domestic yaks are about the size of a cow (see **cattle**).

Yangtze River (Chang Jiang)

The Yangtze River, or Chang Jiang, is the longest, most important **river** in **China** and the third longest river in the world. From its beginnings high in the **mountains** of **Tibet** it flows 4,000 mi. (6,380km) across the center of China, emptying into the Yellow Sea near Shanghai.

The river takes its name from the ancient kingdom of Yang, which developed along its banks 3,000 years ago. Today the Yangtze is still one of the main **trade** routes in China, and the port of Shanghai, China's largest city, lies at its mouth.

The Three Gorges Dam is a controversial project in which the world's largest **hydroelectric** plant will stretch nearly 1 mi. (1.6km) across and 575 ft. (175m) above the Yangtze. The completion is expected in 2009, with 1.4 million people requiring relocation from their homes along the banks of the river.

Year

A year is the length of **time** it takes **Earth** to **orbit** (travel around) the **Sun**. This journey takes 365 days and six hours (see **day and night**). A **calendar** year is only 365 days long so every four years the leftover quarter days are added together to make an extra day. These longer years of 366 days are called leap years.

The first people to measure the length of a year were the ancient Egyptians. They noticed that the **Nile River** always overflowed its banks when Sirius—the brightest **star** in the sky—rose just before sunrise. They counted the days that went by until this happened again—365 days had passed, one year.

Yeast

Yeast is a **plant** that is also a type of **fungus**. The whole plant consists of just one **cell**, which is so tiny that you cannot see it without a **microscope**. Yeast is useful because it turns **sugar** into **alcohol** and carbon dioxide **gas**. This process is called **fermentation**. Yeast plants ferment because they do not produce their own **food**. They live on sugar instead. Today yeast is grown in huge vats. It is then pressed into cakes or small pellets, ready to be sold.

In **wine** and beer making, yeast turns the sugar in grapes or malted barley into alcohol, while most of the gas it produces bubbles away. In **bread** making, the carbon dioxide gas yeast creates forms bubbles, which make the bread dough rise.

Yemen, Republic of

The Republic of Yemen is a country on the coasts of the **Red Sea** and the Gulf of Aden. The **republic** was formed when North and South Yemen united in 1990 after years of political upheaval. Before then North Yemen had been under Ottoman–Turkish rule for years until its independence in 1918. South Yemen was made up of the former British colony of Aden and the former British protectorate of South Arabia. It became independent in 1967.

Yemeni land is among the most fertile of the Arabian Peninsula owing to the **monsoon** rains that fall on its **mountains** each spring. Many Yemenis are farmers (see **farming**), growing **cotton**, **wheat**, **coffee**, millet, and **fruit**. The port of Aden on the south coast has been a trading post between the East and the West for 2,000 years. In 1994 **civil war** broke out between the north and the south but ended when **government** forces took control of Aden. Despite this, kidnappings, bombings, and other acts of terrorism continued to disrupt the country into the late 1990s.

△ This is a photograph of what some people believe to be a footprint of a **yeti**. It was taken by **mountain** climbers in 1951, and it is as long as the head of the ice pick.

Yeti

The yeti, or abominable snowman, is a large, apelike **animal** that is believed to live in the **Himalayas**—the highest **mountains** on **earth**. Several sightings have been reported since the late 1800s, and photographs (see **photography**) of yeti footprints over 18 in. (30cm) long have been published. Although the yeti is believed by many to exist, expeditions have failed to uncover evidence of this.

Yom Kippur

Yom Kippur (the Day of Atonement) is the most important **festival** in the Jewish **calendar** (see **Judaism**). It comes at the end of a 10-day period of reflection. Yom Kippur is a festival of prayer and fasting (going without food or drink) that lasts for 25 hours. Jews spend the majority of the day in the **synagogue** attending special services. Services begin early in the morning and continue until sunset. Jews pray to confess their sins of the past year and ask for God's forgiveness. The end of the prayers is signaled by the blowing of a special **horn** called a shofar (ram's horn).

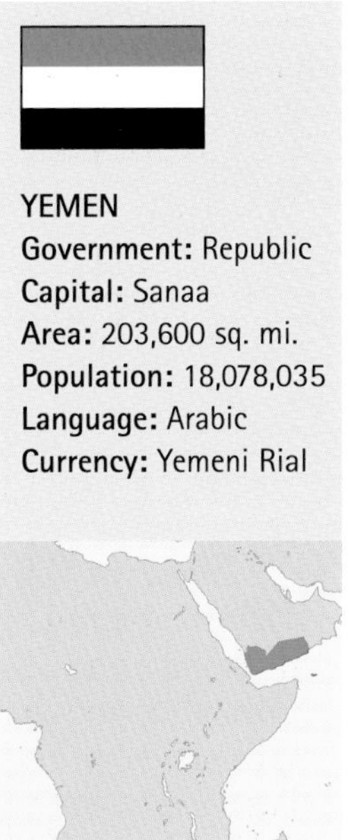

YEMEN
Government: Republic
Capital: Sanaa
Area: 203,600 sq. mi.
Population: 18,078,035
Language: Arabic
Currency: Yemeni Rial

Zambia

Zambia is a landlocked country in southern **Africa** that shares borders with the **Democratic Republic of Congo**, **Tanzania**, Malawi, **Mozambique**, **Botswana**, **Zimbabwe**, **Namibia**, and **Angola**.

Zambia is named after the Zambezi River, which runs across the western part of the country and along the border with Zimbabwe.

The majority of Zambians are farmers, but it is usually the women who cultivate the crops because most of the men work in the **mining** industry. The majority of the country's wealth comes from its **copper** mines.

Zambia was the British protectorate of Northern Rhodesia until it became an independent **republic** in 1964. It then became a one-party state in 1972, and democratic **elections** were first held in 1991.

Like many African countries Zambia has a low life expectancy for its population—37 years old for both men and women. This is because **AIDS** (acquired immune deficiency syndrome) ravages the continent of Africa—with 7,000 people dying every day.

△ Burchell's **zebra** is the most common type of zebra found in eastern Africa. This picture shows a newborn zebra foal, still covered with the afterbirth, suckling from its mother.

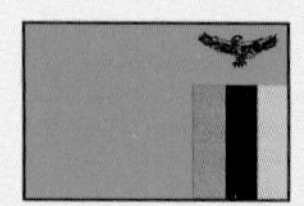

ZAMBIA
Government: Democracy
Capital: Lusaka
Area: 285,700 sq. mi.
Population: 9,770,199
Languages: English and indigenous languages
Currency: Kwacha

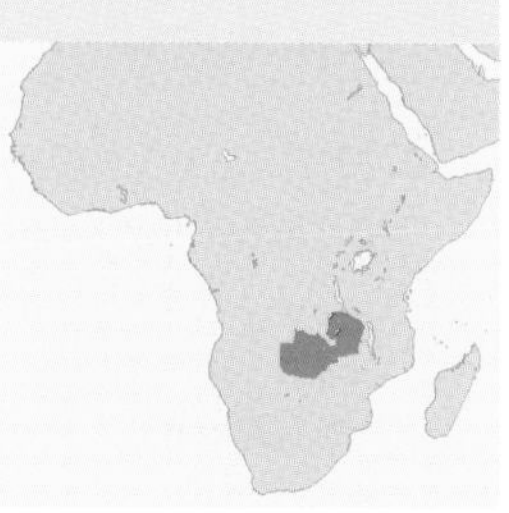

Zebra

Zebras belong to the **horse** family. They live on the open grasslands of **Africa** to the south of the **Sahara**. Zebras have creamy-white coats covered with black or dark brown stripes. Each **animal** has a different pattern of stripes.

Zebras live in herds. They feed on **grass** and are often found roaming the grasslands with herds of **antelope**. Although zebras can run very fast, they are often hunted by **lions**, **leopards**, and **hyenas**. Like other wild horses the zebra depends on speed for survival. It can run up to 25 mph (40 km/h).

People also used to hunt zebras for their attractive **skins** and tasty meat, but this is now illegal in most countries.

Zimbabwe

Zimbabwe is a small country in southern **Africa**. It lies inland about 150 mi. (240km) from the **Indian Ocean**. Almost 98 percent of the population are black Africans. In the north, Zimbabwe is bordered by the Zambezi River, famous for the Victoria Falls (see **waterfall**) and the Kariba Dam. The **dam** is part of a great **hydroelectric** operation that supplies power to both Zimbabwe and its neighbor, **Zambia**.

A wealthy empire first developed in what is now called Zimbabwe from around the A.D. 900s through the **Middle Ages**. The large Zimbabwe stone ruins are an impressive reminder of this early civilization. It became known to the rest of the world in 1868 when it was discovered accidently by a hunting party.

Until 1965 Zimbabwe was the British colony of Southern Rhodesia. But white settlers seized power in Zimbabwe in that year and declared their independence from Great Britain. The settlers fought a bitter **civil war** with black African rebels. Rebel leader Robert Mugabe (b. 1924) eventually took power, but violence flared again in the late 1990s when Mugabe began to confiscate land owned by white farmers, arguing that this land had been taken illegally from black Africans.

ZIMBABWE
Government: Republic
Capital: Harare
Area: 149,100 sq. mi.
Population: 11,365,366
Languages: English, Shona, Sindebele
Currency: Zimbabwean dollar

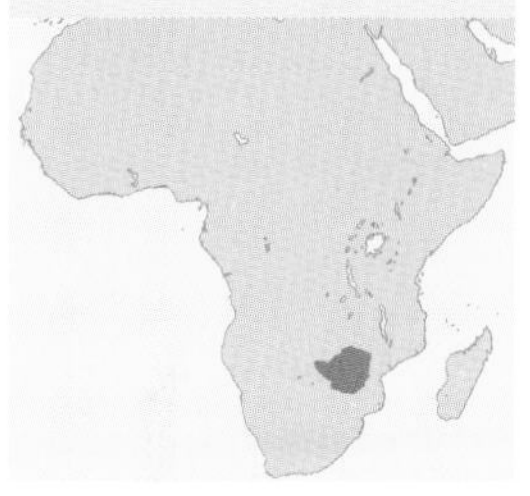

Zinc

Zinc is a hard, blue-white **metal**. It has been used to make brass for over 2,000 years. Brass is an **alloy** of zinc and **copper**.

A large share of the world's zinc comes from **Canada**, **Australia**, and the **United States**. Zinc mines usually contain other metals such as copper, **gold**, **lead**, and **silver**. Most zinc is used to galvanize steel; this means putting a thin coat of zinc on steel to protect it. Zinc is also used to make cells in batteries (see **electricity**). As well as brass, zinc forms part of many other alloys, including nickel and **bronze**. Zinc is always found combined with other substances.

We all need a small quantity of zinc in our diets. People who do not get enough zinc are anaemic (they do not have enough red **blood cells**), and their growth is slowed down. A normal diet gives us all the zinc we need to grow and remain healthy.

Zoo

Zoos are places where wild **animals** are kept, frequently in a different country to the one from which they originated. The animals are cared for, bred, studied, and sometimes saved from extinction (dying out).

There are now more than 330 zoos in the world. The first were in ancient **Egypt**. It is known that Queen Hatshepsut (c. 1540–1481 B.C.) had a zoo as long ago as 1500 B.C. More than 3,000 years ago the emperors of **China** kept animals, **birds**, and **fish** in natural **gardens** where they would feel at home. In the **Middle Ages** in **Europe** kings gave each other gifts of **apes**, **peacocks**, and **lions**. Private collections of animals are called menageries. In the 1800s traveling menageries were very popular and toured through the towns of Europe.

Scientists have been interested in the study of animals since the 1700s. At that time they began to sort animals into groups and give them Latin names so that a particular animal would be recognized by the same name all over the world. Their work led directly to the building of the first public zoos. These were called zoological gardens—shortened to "zoo" later. One of the first was **London** Zoo, which was built in 1829.

▽ **Zoos** have done a great deal to save **animals**, like this golden lion tamarin, from extinction. These monkeys live in a heavily populated coastal region of Brazil where less than 2 percent of the **forest** remains. There are only around 1,000 golden lion tamarins left in the wild. About 500 live in family groups in zoos worldwide.

COUNTRIES OF THE WORLD

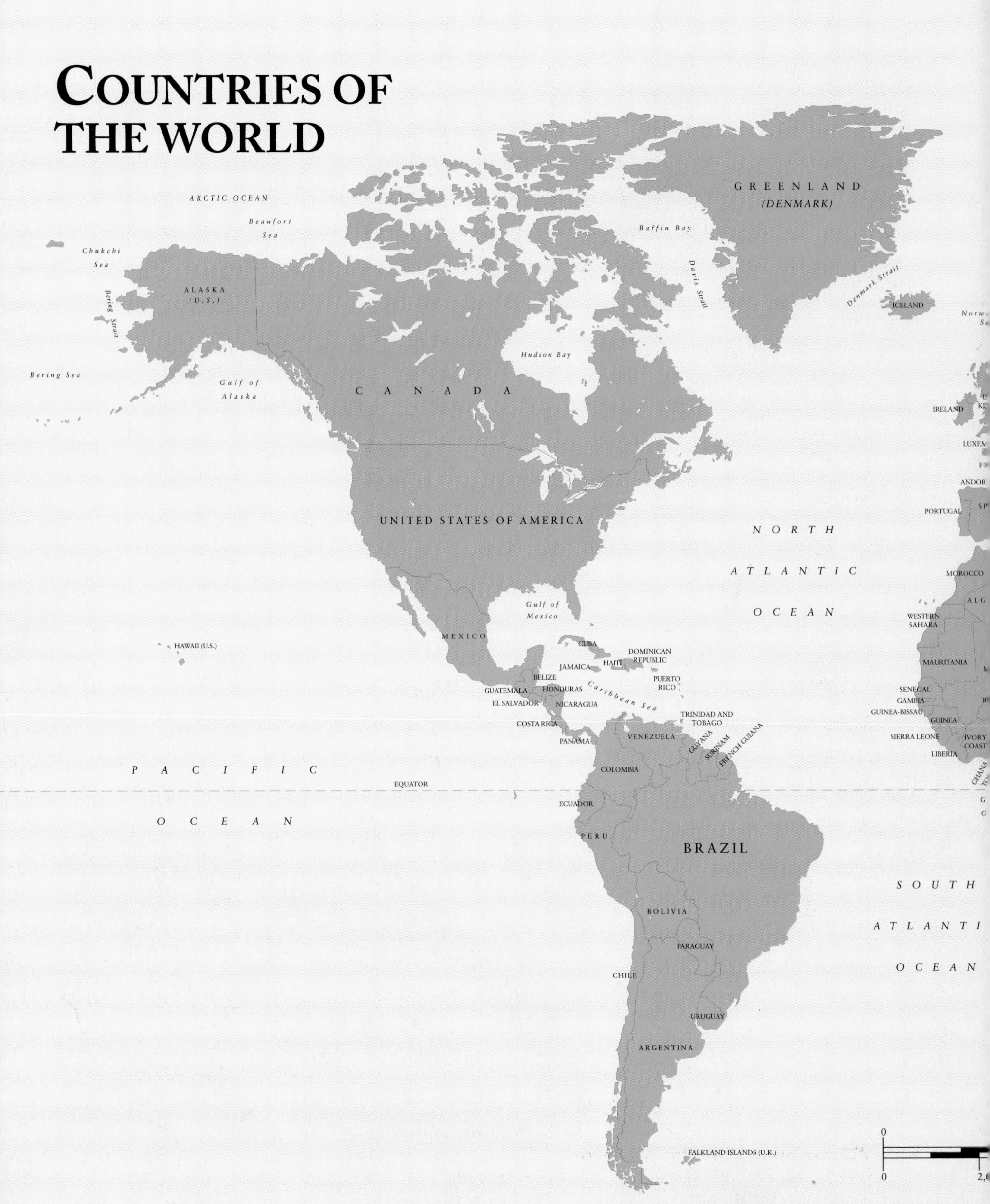

ARCTIC OCEAN
Barents Sea
Kara Sea
Laptev Sea
ARCTIC OCEAN
East Siberian Sea
Chukchi Sea
Bering Strait
SWEDEN
FINLAND
RUSSIA
ESTONIA
LATVIA
Baltic Sea
LITHUANIA
RUSSIAN FEDERATION
BELARUS
POLAND
UKRAINE
CZECH REP.
SLOVAKIA
AUSTRIA
HUNGARY
MOLDOVA
ROMANIA
CROATIA
UNION OF SERBIA AND MONTENEGRO
BULGARIA
Black Sea
GEORGIA
ITALY
MACEDONIA
ALBANIA
ARMENIA
GREECE
TURKEY
AZERBAIJAN
KAZAKHSTAN
Caspian Sea
Aral Sea
UZBEKISTAN
TURKMENISTAN
KYRGYZSTAN
TAJIKISTAN
MONGOLIA
CHINA
Sea of Okhotsk
Bering Sea
NORTH KOREA
SOUTH KOREA
Sea of Japan
JAPAN
Yellow Sea
East China Sea
TUNISIA
CYPRUS
LEBANON
ISRAEL
SYRIA
IRAQ
IRAN
AFGHANISTAN
JORDAN
KUWAIT
LIBYA
EGYPT
SAUDI ARABIA
BAHRAIN
QATAR
PAKISTAN
NEPAL
BHUTAN
Red Sea
UNITED ARAB EMIRATES
BANGLADESH
INDIA
MYANMAR
TAIWAN
PACIFIC OCEAN
OMAN
LAOS
CHAD
SUDAN
ERITREA
YEMEN
VIETNAM
THAILAND
Bay of Bengal
South China Sea
Philippine Sea
Gulf of Aden
DJIBOUTI
CAMBODIA
PHILIPPINES
CENTRAL AFRICAN REPUBLIC
ETHIOPIA
SRI LANKA
BRUNEI
SOMALIA
MALAYSIA
Celebes Sea
EQUATORIAL GUINEA
CONGO
UGANDA
KENYA
DEMOCRATIC REPUBLIC OF CONGO
RWANDA
BURUNDI
TANZANIA
INDIAN OCEAN
INDONESIA
PAPUA NEW GUINEA
SOLOMON ISLANDS
ANGOLA
MALAWI
ZAMBIA
Mozambique Channel
MOZAMBIQUE
MADAGASCAR
Coral Sea
VANUATU
FIJI
NAMIBIA
ZIMBABWE
MAURITIUS
RÉUNION
BOTSWANA
NEW CALEDONIA
AUSTRALIA
SWAZILAND
SOUTH AFRICA
LESOTHO
N
Tasman Sea
NEW ZEALAND
4,000
6,000
8,000 miles (at equator)
4,000
6,000
8,000
10,000
12,000 kilometers (at equator)

WEB ADDRESSES

There are hundreds of thousands of websites on the World Wide Web—so many, in fact, that finding the one you want can be a challenge. This is a guide to some of the most useful websites. All of the websites listed here include links to other sites of interest.

The history of the Internet and how it works is explained in a special feature on pages 168–169 of this encyclopedia.

SEARCH ENGINES

www.yahooligans.com
Yahoo's Internet guide for children has links to thousands of websites, organized into categories to make searching easier.

directory.google.com/Top/Kids_and_Teens
This search engine from Google is specifically designed for children and is easy to use.

GENERAL REFERENCE

www.thinkquest.org/library/IC_index.html
The Thinkquest Library is a collection of over 5,000 websites designed by participants in the Thinkquest competitions.

www.EnchantedLearning.com/Home.html
Enchanted Learning is a valuable research tool that provides information on most subject areas.

www.bbc.co.uk/learning
Produced by the British Broadcasting Company (BBC), this site offers a wealth of educational material.

about.com/homework
This homework guide produced by About.com has a list of links covering a wide range of subjects.

www.encyclopedia.com
The 14,000 articles contained in this easy-to-use website provide simple definitions and explanations.

www.infoplease.com/encyclopedia.html
The Infoplease online encyclopedia includes thousands of useful articles.

www.museumnetwork.com
This site is a directory to more than 30,000 museums across the world. There are also links to the museums' own websites.

GEOGRAPHY

www.altapedia.com
Altapedia is an online atlas that features world maps and detailed information about the countries of the world.

www.cyberschoolbus.un.org/infonation/index.asp
Infonation, the official children's site of the United Nations (UN), has maps, facts, and figures for all of the UN's members.

PHYSICAL EARTH

kids.earth.nasa.gov/site.htm
This NASA site explores our own planet. It covers topics such as climate, volcanoes, and movements of earth's crust.

www.geography4kids.com
This educational website is packed with information about the physical geography of our planet.

NATURAL WORLD

www.kidsplanet.org/factsheets/map.html
Online fact sheets about many animals from all over the world.

www.EnchantedLearning.com/science/dictionary
This illustrated scientific dictionary has features on a wide variety of animals, plants, and natural habitats.

www.worldwildlife.org/fun/kids.cfm
Produced by the World Wildlife Fund, this is an educational and fun website about wildlife and conservation issues.

www.bbc.co.uk/dinosaurs
This BBC site is full of useful information about dinosaurs.

HUMAN BODY

kidshealth.org/kid
This is a fun site that covers many aspects about the human body.

www.bbc.co.uk/health/kids/index.shtml
Visitors to this BBC website can do an online "body tour."

SCIENCE

www.physics4kids.com
www.biology4kids.com
www.chem4kids.com
These websites cover almost every aspect of science and are full of interactive features that help explain difficult topics.

MATHEMATICS

mathforum.org/library/drmath/drmath.elem.html
"Dr. Math" is a helpful site that explains topics such as arithmetic, geometry, measurement, and special numbers.

INVENTIONS AND TECHNOLOGY

www.enchantedlearning.com/inventors
An A-Z of inventions from adhesive tape to the zipper.

howstuffworks.lycoszone.com
This Lycos site is packed with interesting articles that show how machines, gadgets, and other useful objects work.

library.thinkquest.org/22522
Computer Chronicle describes the history of computing from the abacus to the invention of the silicon chip and powerful PCs.

www.aviation-history.com/right_index.htm
This site offers lots of information about the history of flight plus data panels about different types of aircraft throughout history.

FOOD AND AGRICULTURE

museum.agropolis.fr/english/default.htm
The online Agropolis Museum describes the history of farming from prehistoric times to present-day intensive agriculture.

HISTORY

www.historyforkids.org
This website covers many periods of history from ancient civilizations to the 21st century.

www.bbc.co.uk/history/bytopic/index.shtml
This site has information about almost every aspect of history.

www.thebritishmuseum.ac.uk/childrenscompass
Visitors to this site can see a varied selection of the British Museum's huge collection of artifacts, both ancient and modern.

library.thinkquest.org/C001692
"Voyage of Exploration" has details about explorers and expeditions throughout the world since ancient times.

RELIGION AND BELIEFS

www.bbc.co.uk/religion/religions/index.shtml
This BBC site offers an independent look at the world's major religions—Buddhism, Christianity, Hinduism, Islam, Judaism, Mormonism, and Sikhism. It also explores other human beliefs.

www.windows.ucar.edu/tour/link=/mythology/mythology.html
This site is full of information about the myths, legends, folktales, gods, and goddesses of many different cultures around the world.

LANGUAGE AND LITERATURE

library.thinkquest.org/26451
The history of communication is explored in this site, including the development of languages, writing, alphabets, and computers.

uk.dir.yahoo.com/arts/humanities/literature/authors/children_s
Produced by Yahoo and regularly updated, this is a directory to websites about writers and books suitable for children.

ART AND ARCHITECTURE

www.tate.org.uk/home/default.htm
This site features a vast online database that allows you to learn about 50,000 works of art from the collections of the four Tate galleries in England.

www.louvre.fr/anglais/fr_g.htm
This is the English website of the Louvre, in Paris, France, one of the world's greatest museums. Visitors can do an online tour to see a selection of paintings, drawings, and sculptures.

www.greatbuildings.com
Key facts, photographs, and 3-D models of 750 of the world's most important buildings are included in this site.

PERFORMING ARTS

www.empire.k12.ca.us/capistrano/Mike/capmusic/music_room/themusic.htm
The Music Room is an educational website produced by a music school. It has features about musical instruments, famous composers, and musical styles through the ages.

library.thinkquest.org/J002266F
"And They Kept On Dancing" provides all kinds of information about folk dance, ballet, tap, jazz, and modern dance.

www.learner.org/exhibits/cinema
Discover how movies are made at this fun interactive website.

SPORT

library.thinkquest.org/10480
Sports Central explains the rules of most major sports and describes how different sports have changed over the years.

www.top-education.com/sports
SportsWorld has information about many sports and sporting events (including the Olympic Games and Superbowl), plus biographies of famous athletes.

SPACE

kids.msfc.nasa.gov
This is a NASA site that introduces the wonders of space and space travel. Visitors can play games and take part in projects.

www.bbc.co.uk/science/space
This site offers information about space and space exploration.

INDEX

Page numbers in **bold** refer to main entries

INDEX

G

H

I

J

N

O

P

Q

R

S

T

W

ACKNOWLEDGMENTS

The publishers wish to thank the following for supplying photographs for this book:

ABBREVIATIONS
(*t* = top; *b* = bottom; *c* = center; *l* = left; *r* = right)

Illustrators

Susanna Addario, Anderson Geographics, Marion Appleton, Mike Atkinson, Julian Baker, Julie Banyard, Russell Barnett, Julian Baum, Richard Berridge, Mark Bergin, Simone Boni, Trevor Boyer, Peter Bull, John Butler, Robin Carter, Harry Clow, M. Coates, Dan Cole, Tom Connell, David Cook, Peter Dennis, Sandra Doyle, Richard Draper, Les Edwards, Bridget Ellison, Gill Elsbury, Dean Entwistle, Andy Farmer, James Field, Michael Fisher, Chris Forsey, Terry Gabbey, Luigi Galante, Lee Gibbons, Peter Goodfellow, Jeremy Gower, Craig Greenwood, Ray Grinaway, Alan Hancocks, David Hardy, Donald Harley, Keith Harmer, Gary Hinks, Adam Hook, Christian Hook, Richard Hook, Andre Hrydziusko, Ian Jackson, John James, Lovell Johns, Kevin Jones, Peter Kesterton, Martin Knowldon, Eddy Krahenbuhl, Mike Lacey, Ruth Lindsay, Bernard Long, Steiner Lund, Chris Lyon, Kevin Maddison, Shirley Mallinson, Janos Marffy, Shane Marsh, David Marshall, Joannah May, Jamie Medlin, Simon Mendez, Justin Moat, Chris Molan, Patrick Mulrey, Steve Noon, Nicki Palin, Alex Pang, Darren Patenden, Robert Payne, Andie Peck, John Porter, Sebastian Quigley, John Ridyard, Steve Roberts, Bernard Robinson, Susan Rowe, David Salariya, Claudia Saraceni, Mike Saunders, Chris Shields, Rob Shone, Nick Shewring, Guy Smith, Clive Spon, Roger Stewart, John Storey, Mike Taylor, Ian Thompson, Mike Trim, Bob Watton, Joanne Williams, David Wright

Picture libraries

Pages: **6**: *(tr)* Powerstock/Zefa/Christie's Images; **27**: *(tr)* The Bridgeman Art Library/Christie's Images, *(bl)* The Bridgeman Art Library/Galleria degli Uffizi, Florence, Italy; **30**: *(tl)* Corbis; **66**: *(tl)* ILN; **81**: *(tc)* The Bridgeman Art Library/Christie's Images; **87**: *(c)* ILN; **90**: *(tc)* ILN; **104**: *(tc)* ILN; **113**: *(tl)* ILN; **152**: *(bl)* ILN; **153**: *(tc)* ILN; **155**: *(tc)* Corbis; **225**: *(tr)* Corbis/David Zimmerman; **250**: *(tl)* ILN; **276**: *(cl)* The Bridgeman Art Library/Kenwood House, London; **314–315**: *(bc)* Corbis/Dmitri Lundt; **332**: *(tl)* Corbis; **342**: *(br)* Science Photo Library; **348**: *(tc)* The Art Archive/Musée d'Orsay, Paris; **354**: *(cl)* ILN; **375**: *(cr)* ILN; **379**: *(tr)* Science Photo Library, *(tr)* Corbis/Hulton-Deutsch; **383**: *(br)* Corbis/Kevin Schaeffer

The publishers would also like to thank the following for their help in supplying information used as visual reference:

Pages: **14–15**: Boeing Aircraft Corporation (Boeing 747 cutaway); **294–295**: Princess Cruises (ship cutaway)